DLA Piper UK LLP Leeds

HALSBURY'S
Laws of England

FIFTH EDITION
2017

Volume 1A

This is volume 1A of the Fifth Edition of Halsbury's Laws of England, containing the title AGRICULTURAL PRODUCTION AND MARKETING.

The title AGRICULTURAL PRODUCTION AND MARKETING replaces the title of the same name contained in volume 1 (2008). The remaining titles of volume 1 (2008), AGENCY and AGRICULTURAL LAND, are replaced by the titles AGENCY and AGRICULTURAL LAND AND ALLOTMENTS contained in volume 1 (2017). Upon receipt of volume 1 (2017) and volume 1A (2017), volume 1 (2008) may be archived.

For a full list of volumes comprised in a current set of Halsbury's Laws of England please see overleaf.

Fifth Edition volumes:

1 (2017), 1A (2017), 2 (2017), 3 (2011), 4 (2011), 5 (2013), 6 (2011), 7 (2015), 8 (2015), 9 (2017), 10 (2017), 11 (2015), 12 (2015), 12A (2015), 13 (2017), 14 (2016), 15 (2016), 15A (2016), 16 (2017), 17 (2017), 18 (2009), 19 (2011), 20 (2014), 21 (2016), 22 (2012), 23 (2016), 24 (2010), 25 (2016), 26 (2016), 27 (2015), 28 (2015), 29 (2014), 30 (2012), 31 (2012), 32 (2012), 33 (2017), 34 (2011), 35 (2015), 36 (2015), 37 (2013), 38 (2013), 38A (2013), 39 (2014), 40 (2014), 41 (2014), 41A (2014), 42 (2011), 43 (2011), 44 (2011), 45 (2010), 46 (2010), 47 (2014), 47A (2014), 48 (2015), 49 (2015), 50 (2016), 50A (2016), 51 (2013), 52 (2014), 53 (2014), 54 (2017), 54A (2017), 55 (2012), 56 (2017), 57 (2012), 58 (2014), 58A (2014), 59 (2014), 59A (2014), 60 (2011), 61 (2010), 62 (2016), 63 (2016), 64 (2016), 65 (2015), 66 (2015), 67 (2016), 68 (2016), 69 (2009), 70 (2012), 71 (2013), 72 (2015), 73 (2015), 74 (2011), 75 (2013), 76 (2013), 77 (2016), 78 (2010), 79 (2014), 80 (2013), 81 (2010), 82 (2010), 83 (2010), 84 (2013), 84A (2013), 85 (2012), 86 (2017), 87 (2017), 88 (2012), 88A (2013), 89 (2011), 90 (2011), 91 (2012), 92 (2015), 93 (2017), 94 (2017), 95 (2017), 96 (2012), 97 (2015), 97A (2014), 98 (2013), 99 (2012), 100 (2009), 101 (2009), 102 (2016), 103 (2016), 104 (2014)

Consolidated Index and Tables:

2017 Consolidated Index (A–E), 2017 Consolidated Index (F–O), 2017 Consolidated Index (P–Z), 2018 Consolidated Table of Statutes, 2018 Consolidated Table of Statutory Instruments, 2018 Consolidated Table of Cases (A–G), 2018 Consolidated Table of Cases (H–Q), 2018 Consolidated Table of Cases (R–Z, ECJ Cases)

Updating and ancillary materials:

2017 annual Cumulative Supplement; monthly Noter-up; annual Abridgments 1974–2016

December 2017

HALSBURY'S
Laws of England

Volume 1A

2017

Members of the LexisNexis Group worldwide

United Kingdom	RELX (UK) Ltd, trading as LexisNexis, 1–3 Strand, London WC2N 5JR and 9–10 St Andrew Square, Edinburgh EH2 2AF
Australia	Reed International Books Australia Pty Ltd trading as LexisNexis, Chatswood, New South Wales
Austria	LexisNexis Verlag ARD Orac GmbH & Co KG, Vienna
Benelux	LexisNexis Benelux, Amsterdam
Canada	LexisNexis Canada, Markham, Ontario
China	LexisNexis China, Beijing and Shanghai
France	LexisNexis SA, Paris
Germany	LexisNexis GmbH, Dusseldorf
Hong Kong	LexisNexis Hong Kong, Hong Kong
India	LexisNexis India, New Delhi
Italy	Giuffrè Editore, Milan
Japan	LexisNexis Japan, Tokyo
Malaysia	Malayan Law Journal Sdn Bhd, Kuala Lumpur
New Zealand	LexisNexis New Zealand Ltd, Wellington
Singapore	LexisNexis Singapore, Singapore
South Africa	LexisNexis, Durban
USA	LexisNexis, Dayton, Ohio

FIRST EDITION	*Published in 31 volumes between 1907 and 1917*
SECOND EDITION	*Published in 37 volumes between 1931 and 1942*
THIRD EDITION	*Published in 43 volumes between 1952 and 1964*
FOURTH EDITION	*Published in 56 volumes between 1973 and 1987, with reissues between 1988 and 2008*
FIFTH EDITION	*Published between 2008 and 2014, with reissues from 2014*

© 2017 RELX (UK) Ltd

ISBN 978-1-4743-0947-9

9 781474 309479

ISBN for the set: 9781405734394
ISBN for this volume: 9781474309479
Typeset by LexisNexis
Printed and bound by CPI Group (UK) Ltd, Croydon, CR0 4YY

Visit LexisNexis at www.lexisnexis.co.uk

AGRICULTURAL PRODUCTION AND MARKETING

Consultant Editor

SIAN EDMUNDS, LLB (Hons),
Partner, Burges Salmon

The law stated in this volume is in general that in force on 1 November 2017, although subsequent changes have been included wherever possible.

Any future updating material will be found in the Noter-up and annual Cumulative Supplement to Halsbury's Laws of England.

TABLE OF CONTENTS

HOW TO USE HALSBURY'S LAWS OF ENGLAND

Volumes

Each text volume of Halsbury's Laws of England contains the law on the titles contained in it as at a date stated at the front of the volume (the operative date).

Information contained in Halsbury's Laws of England may be accessed in several ways.

First, by using the tables of contents.

Each volume contains both a general Table of Contents, and a specific Table of Contents for each title contained in it. From these tables you will be directed to the relevant part of the work.

Readers should note that the current arrangement of titles can be found in the Noter-up.

Secondly, by using tables of statutes, statutory instruments, cases or other materials.

If you know the name of the Act, statutory instrument or case with which your research is concerned, you should consult the Consolidated Tables of statutes, cases and so on (published as separate volumes) which will direct you to the relevant volume and paragraph.

(Each individual text volume also includes tables of those materials used as authority in that volume.)

Thirdly, by using the indexes.

If you are uncertain of the general subject area of your research, you should go to the Consolidated Index (published as separate volumes) for reference to the relevant volume(s) and paragraph(s).

(Each individual text volume also includes an index to the material contained therein.)

Updating publications

The text volumes of Halsbury's Laws should be used in conjunction with the annual Cumulative Supplement and the monthly Noter-up.

The annual Cumulative Supplement

The Supplement gives details of all changes between the operative date of the text volume and the operative date of the Supplement. It is arranged in the same volume, title and paragraph order as the text volumes. Developments affecting particular points of law are noted to the relevant paragraph(s) of the text volumes.

For narrative treatment of material noted in the Cumulative Supplement, go to the annual Abridgment volume for the relevant year.

Destination Tables

In certain titles in the annual *Cumulative Supplement*, reference is made to Destination Tables showing the destination of consolidated legislation. Those Destination Tables are to be found either at the end of the titles within the annual *Cumulative Supplement*, or in a separate *Destination Tables* booklet provided from time to time with the *Cumulative Supplement*.

The Noter-up

The Noter-up is issued monthly and notes changes since the publication of the annual Cumulative Supplement. Also arranged in the same volume, title and paragraph order as the text volumes, the Noter-up follows the style of the Cumulative Supplement.

For narrative treatment of material noted in the Noter-up, go to the annual Abridgment volume for the relevant year.

REFERENCES AND ABBREVIATIONS

ACT	Australian Capital Territory
A-G	Attorney General
Admin	Administrative Court
Admlty	Admiralty Court
Adv-Gen	Advocate General
affd	affirmed
affg	affirming
Alta	Alberta
App	Appendix
art	article
Aust	Australia
B	Baron
BC	British Columbia
C	Command Paper (of a series published before 1900)
c	chapter number of an Act
CA	Court of Appeal
CAC	Central Arbitration Committee
CA in Ch	Court of Appeal in Chancery
CB	Chief Baron
CCA	Court of Criminal Appeal
CCR	County Court Rules 1981 (as subsequently amended)
CCR	Court for Crown Cases Reserved
CJEU	Court of Justice of the European Union
C-MAC	Courts-Martial Appeal Court
CO	Crown Office
COD	Crown Office Digest
CPR	Civil Procedure Rules
Can	Canada
Cd	Command Paper (of the series published 1900–18)
Cf	compare
Ch	Chancery Division
ch	chapter
cl	clause
Cm	Command Paper (of the series published 1986 to date)
Cmd	Command Paper (of the series published 1919–56)
Cmnd	Command Paper (of the series published 1956–86)
Comm	Commercial Court

Comr	Commissioner
Court Forms (2nd Edn)	Atkin's Encyclopaedia of Court Forms in Civil Proceedings, 2nd Edn. See note 2 post.
CrimPR	Criminal Procedure Rules
DC............................	Divisional Court
DPP...........................	Director of Public Prosecutions
EAT...........................	Employment Appeal Tribunal
EC	European Community
ECJ	Court of Justice of the European Community (before the Treaty of Lisbon (OJ C306, 17.12.2007, p 1) came into force on 1 December 2009); European Court of Justice (after the Treaty of Lisbon (OJ C306, 17.12.2007, p 1) came into force on 1 December 2009)
EComHR	European Commission of Human Rights
ECSC..........................	European Coal and Steel Community
ECtHR Rules of Court	Rules of Court of the European Court of Human Rights
EEC...........................	European Economic Community
EFTA	European Free Trade Association
EGC	European General Court
EWCA Civ	Official neutral citation for judgments of the Court of Appeal (Civil Division)
EWCA Crim	Official neutral citation for judgments of the Court of Appeal (Criminal Division)
EWHC	Official neutral citation for judgments of the High Court
Edn	Edition
Euratom......................	European Atomic Energy Community
EU	European Union
Ex Ch	Court of Exchequer Chamber
ex p...........................	ex parte
Fam...........................	Family Division
Fed...........................	Federal
Forms & Precedents (5th Edn)	Encyclopaedia of Forms and Precedents other than Court Forms, 5th Edn. See note 2 post
GLC	Greater London Council
HC............................	High Court
HC............................	House of Commons
HK............................	Hong Kong
HL	House of Lords
HMRC........................	Her Majesty's Revenue and Customs
IAT	Immigration Appeal Tribunal
ILM............................	International Legal Materials

INLR	Immigration and Nationality Law Reports
IRC	Inland Revenue Commissioners
Ind	India
Int Rels	International Relations
Ir	Ireland
J	Justice
JA	Judge of Appeal
Kan	Kansas
LA	Lord Advocate
LC	Lord Chancellor
LCC	London County Council
LCJ	Lord Chief Justice
LJ	Lord Justice of Appeal
LoN	League of Nations
MR	Master of the Rolls
Man	Manitoba
n.	note
NB	New Brunswick
NI	Northern Ireland
NS	Nova Scotia
NSW	New South Wales
NY	New York
NZ	New Zealand
OHIM	Office for Harmonisation in the Internal Market
OJ	The Official Journal of the European Union published by the Publications Office of the European Union
Ont	Ontario
P.	President
PC	Judicial Committee of the Privy Council
PEI	Prince Edward Island
Pat	Patents Court
q.	question
QB	Queen's Bench Division
QBD	Queen's Bench Division of the High Court
Qld	Queensland
Que	Quebec
r	rule
RDC	Rural District Council
RPC	Restrictive Practices Court
RSC	Rules of the Supreme Court 1965 (as subsequently amended)
reg	regulation
Res	Resolution

revsd	reversed
Rly	Railway
s	section
SA	South Africa
S Aust	South Australia
SC	Supreme Court
SI	Statutory Instruments published by authority
SR & O	Statutory Rules and Orders published by authority
SR & O Rev 1904	Revised Edition comprising all Public and General Statutory Rules and Orders in force on 31 December 1903
SR & O Rev 1948	Revised Edition comprising all Public and General Statutory Rules and Orders and Statutory Instruments in force on 31 December 1948
SRNI	Statutory Rules of Northern Ireland
STI	Simon's Tax Intelligence (1973–1995); Simon's Weekly Tax Intelligence (1996-current)
Sask	Saskatchewan
Sch	Schedule
Sess	Session
Sing	Singapore
TCC	Technology and Construction Court
TS	Treaty Series
Tanz	Tanzania
Tas	Tasmania
UDC	Urban District Council
UKHL	Official neutral citation for judgments of the House of Lords
UKPC	Official neutral citation for judgments of the Privy Council
UN	United Nations
V-C	Vice-Chancellor
Vict	Victoria
W Aust	Western Australia
Zimb	Zimbabwe

NOTE 1. A general list of the abbreviations of law reports and other sources used in this work can be found at the beginning of the Consolidated Table of Cases.

NOTE 2. Where references are made to other publications, the volume number precedes and the page number follows the name of the publication; eg the reference '12 Forms & Precedents (5th Edn) 44' refers to volume 12 of the Encyclopaedia of Forms and Precedents, page 44.

NOTE 3. An English statute is cited by short title or, where there is no short title, by regnal year and chapter number together with the name by which it is commonly known or a description of its subject matter and date. In the case of a foreign statute, the mode of citation generally follows the style of citation in use in the country concerned with the addition, where necessary, of the name of the country in parentheses.

NOTE 4. A statutory instrument is cited by short title, if any, followed by the year and number, or, if unnumbered, the date.

TABLE OF STATUTES

TABLE OF STATUTORY INSTRUMENTS

PARA

C

D

PARA

E

TABLE OF EUROPEAN UNION LEGISLATION

Secondary Legislation

Directives

Regulations

TABLE OF CASES

Decisions of the European Court of Justice are listed below numerically. These decisions are also included in the preceding alphabetical list.

AGRICULTURAL PRODUCTION AND MARKETING

1. COMMON AGRICULTURAL POLICY

1. Common Agricultural Policy.

The regulation of agriculture in the United Kingdom is subject to the law of the European Union (EU)[1]. In particular, it is subject to the measures required to achieve the objectives of the Common Agricultural Policy ('the CAP')[2].

Pillar 1 of the CAP provides for direct payments to be made to farmers[3] and is made up of a basic payment[4], a payment for greening[5] and a payment for young farmers[6] and is financed by the European Agricultural Guarantee Fund ('EAGF')[7].

Pillar 2 of the CAP promotes rural development and is financed by the European Agricultural Fund for Rural Development ('EAFRD')[8].

The Secretary of State and the Welsh Ministers have functions in relation to the administration and enforcement of the CAP[9].

1   See EUROPEAN UNION vol 47A (2014) PARA 109. 'United Kingdom' means Great Britain and Northern Ireland: Interpretation Act 1978 s 5, Sch 1. 'Great Britain' means England, Scotland and Wales: Union with Scotland Act 1706, preamble art I; Interpretation Act 1978 s 22(1), Sch 2 para 5(a). Neither the Isle of Man nor the Channel Islands are within the United Kingdom. Provision for schemes relevant to agriculture are usually made under the European Communities Act 1972 and have included:

    (1)   the Agricultural Products Processing and Marketing (Improvement Grant) Regulations 1977, SI 1977/2112;

    (2)   the Agriculture and Horticulture Development Regulations 1980, SI 1980/1298;

    (3)   the Farm and Horticulture Development Regulations 1981, SI 1981/1707;

    (4)   the Suckler Cow Premium Regulations 1982, SI 1982/1683;

    (5)   the Butter Subsidy (Protection of Community Arrangements) Regulations 1984, SI 1984/1739;

    (6)   the Agriculture Improvement Regulations 1985, SI 1985/1266;

    (7)   the Farm and Conservation Grant Regulations 1989, SI 1989/219;

    (8)   the Farm and Conservation Grant Regulations 1991, SI 1991/1630;

    (9)   the Suckler Cow Premium Regulations 1991, SI 1991/2632;

    (10)   the Moorland (Livestock Extensification) (Wales) Regulations 1995, SI 1995/1159;

    (11)   the Apple and Pear Orchard Grubbing Up Regulations 1998, SI 1998/1131.

2   The objectives of the Common Agricultural Policy are:

    (1)   to increase agricultural productivity by promoting technical progress and by ensuring the rational development of agricultural production1 and the optimum utilisation of the factors of production, in particular labour;

    (2)   thus to ensure a fair standard of living for the agricultural community, in particular by increasing the individual earnings of persons engaged in agriculture;

    (3)   to stabilise markets;

    (4)   to assure the availability of supplies;

    (5)   to ensure that supplies reach consumers at reasonable prices: see Treaty on the Functioning of the European Union (Rome, 25 March 1957; TS 1 (1973); Cmnd 5179) ('TFEU') art 39(1).

   Provision is made for appeals in relation to Pillar 1 and 2 decisions: see the Common Agricultural Policy (Control and Enforcement, Cross-Compliance, Scrutiny of Transactions and Appeals) Regulations 2014, SI 2014/3263, Pt 5 (regs 30–32). In relation to Wales, the Welsh Ministers have established a national reserve under which payments can be made: see the Common Agricultural Policy Basic Payment and Support Schemes (Wales) Regulations 2015, SI 2015/1252, reg 18 (added by SI 2016/217). The Welsh Ministers may also grant payments for agricultural practices beneficial for the climate and the environment: see the Common Agricultural Policy Basic Payment and Support Schemes (Wales) Regulations 2015, SI 2015/1252, reg 19 (added by SI 2016/217).

3   The direct payment scheme replaced the single farm payment scheme. See PARA 2.

4   The basic payment scheme allows payment to be made at regional level to defined regions (see European Parliament and Council Regulation (EU) 1307/2013 (OJ L347, 20.12.2013, p 608–670), art 23) and, in relation to England and Wales, three payment regions have been defined (see the Common Agricultural Policy Basic Payment Scheme (Provisional Payment Region Classification) (Wales) Regulations 2014, SI 2014/1835 (amended by SI 2014/2367); and the Common Agricultural Policy Basic Payment and Support Schemes (England) Regulations 2014,

SI 2014/3259, reg 3). The production of short rotation coppice trees is eligible for support under the basic payment scheme and these have been defined by statutory instrument along with their maximum harvest cycle: see reg 4; and the Common Agricultural Policy Basic Payment and Support Schemes (Wales) Regulations 2015, SI 2015/1252, reg 7.

5   See the European Parliament and Council Regulation (EU) 1307/2013 (OJ L347, 20.12.2013, p 608–670) establishing rules for direct payments to farmers under support schemes within the framework of the common agricultural policy, arts 43–47 (payment for agricultural practices beneficial for the climate and the environment). See also the Common Agricultural Policy Basic Payment and Support Schemes (England) Regulations 2014, SI 2014/3259, regs 11 (crop diversification), 12 (permanent grassland), 13, Schedule (ecological focus area) and the Common Agricultural Policy Basic Payment and Support Schemes (Wales) Regulations 2015, SI 2015/1252, regs 14 (crop diversification), 15 (permanent grassland), 16 (ecological focus area); and PARA 4.

6   See PARA 5.

7   See the European Parliament and Council Regulation (EU) 1306/2013 (OJ L347, 20.12.2013, p 549) on the financing, management and monitoring of the common agricultural policy (the 'Horizontal Regulation'), art 4(1)(b). Provision is made for the scrutiny of commercial documents and transactions financed by EAGF (ie the implementation of the Horizontal Regulation arts 79–88), excluding certain payments made directly to farmers: see the Common Agricultural Policy (Control and Enforcement, Cross-Compliance, Scrutiny of Transactions and Appeals) Regulations 2014, SI 2014/3263, Pt 4 (regs 20–29).

8   See PARA 9.

9   See the Common Agricultural Policy (Competent Authority and Coordinating Body) Regulations 2014, SI 2014/3260, regs 2, 3; and the Common Agricultural Policy (Control and Enforcement, Cross-Compliance, Scrutiny of Transactions and Appeals) Regulations 2014, SI 2014/3263, Pt 2 (regs 3–17). See also the Paying Agency (National Assembly for Wales) Regulations 1999, SI 1999/2223.

2.   Basic payment scheme.

To be eligible to apply for the basic payment scheme (BPS) an applicant must:

(1)   have the required payment entitlements[1];

(2)   be an active farmer through the calendar year[2];

(3)   claim against at least five eligible hectares[3].

1   No direct payments may be granted to a farmer where the eligible area of the holding for the payments claimed or due is less than 5 hectares: see the Common Agricultural Policy Basic Payment and Support Schemes (England) Regulations 2014 SI 2014/3259, reg 5; and the Common Agricultural Policy Basic Payment and Support Schemes (Wales) Regulations 2015 SI 2015/1252, reg 3 (both implementing European Parliament and Council Regulation (EU) 1307/2013 (OJ L347, 20.12.2013, p 608–670) establishing rules for direct payments to farmers under support schemes within the framework of the common agricultural policy, art 10).

The SPS (single payment scheme) entitlements held by farmers in England on 31 December 2014 became BPS entitlements on 1 January 2015: see the introduction to the Rural Payments Agency's *The Basic Payment Scheme in England 2015, Guidance for Farmers about the Basic Payment Scheme in 2015*. In Wales, SPS entitlements were extinguished at the end of 2014 and new BPS entitlements were allocated to eligible farmers in 2015.

Support under the basic payment scheme is granted to farmers, by means of declaration in accordance with European Parliament and Council Regulation (EU) 1307/2013, art 33(1), upon activation of a payment entitlement per eligible hectare in the member state where it has been allocated: art 32(1). In relation to any year in which the farmer makes a declaration in respect of parcels pursuant to art 33(1), the date on which those parcels must be at the farmer's disposal is 15 May or, in relation to England only, if that day is not a working day, the next working day: Common Agricultural Policy Basic Payment and Support Schemes (England) Regulations 2014, SI 2014/3259, reg 6; Common Agricultural Policy Basis Payment and Support Schemes (Wales) Regulations 2015, SI 2015/1252, reg 4.

2   See European Parliament and Council Regulation (EU) 1307/2013 (OJ L347, 20.12.2013, p 608–670), art 9. No direct payments may be granted to natural or legal persons, or to groups of natural or legal persons, who operate airports, railway services, waterworks, real estate services, permanent sport and recreational grounds and, where appropriate, member states may, on the basis of objective and non-discriminatory criteria, decide to add any other similar non-agricultural businesses or activities: see art 9(2). As to additional criteria see the Common Agricultural Policy Basic Payment and Support Schemes (England) Regulations 2014, SI 2014/3259, reg 10(1), (2) (substituted by SI 2015/1997); and the Common Agricultural Policy Basic Payment and Support

Schemes (Wales) Regulations 2015 SI 2015/1252, reg 9(1), (2). Persons falling outside of the active farmer test may qualify for BPS if they meet one of the 3 readmission criteria set out in European Parliament and Council Regulation (EU) 1307/2013 (OJ L347, 20.12.2013, p 608–670), art 9(2)(a)–(c).

3   Support under the BPS must be granted to famers by means of declaration upon activation of a payment entitlement per eligible hectare in the member state where it has been allocated: see the European Parliament and Council Regulation (EU) 1307/2013 (OJ L347, 20.12.2013, p 608–670 establishing rules for direct payments to farmer under support schemes within the framework of the common agricultural policy, art 32(1). The definition of 'eligible hectares' for the purposes of art 32 includes any agricultural area of a holding used or predominantly used for agricultural activities: see art 32(2)(a). 'Agricultural area' means any area taken up by arable land, permanent grassland and permanent pasture, or permanent crops: art 4(1)(e)). 'Agricultural activity' means:

(1)   production, rearing or growing of agricultural products, including harvesting, milking, breeding animals, and keeping animals for farming purposes;

(2)   maintaining an agricultural area in a state which makes it suitable for grazing or cultivation without preparatory action going beyond usual agricultural methods and machineries, based on criteria established by member states on the basis of a framework established by the Commission; or

(3)   carrying out a minimum activity, defined by member states, on agricultural areas naturally kept in a state suitable for grazing or cultivation: art 4(1)(c).

As to maintaining agricultural areas in a state suitable for grazing or cultivation and carrying out minimum agricultural activity on land naturally kept in a state suitable for grazing or cultivation as applied in Wales, see the Common Agricultural Policy Basic Payment and Support Schemes (Wales) Regulations 2015, SI 2015/1252, regs 5, 6.

3. Cross-compliance.

Farmers receiving direct payments ('beneficiaries')[1] must observe the 'cross compliance' conditions established in the relevant Council Regulation, and minimum standards for good agricultural and environment condition[2], along with permitted derogations[3], are set out in domestic legislation.

Requirements include establishing buffer strips along watercourses and limits on timings for trimming hedges and trees, applying manures with high nitrogen content and burning heather and rough grass[4].

The Secretary of State and the Welsh Ministers[5] have been designated as competent control authorities with responsibilities for carrying out controls and checks in respect of the requirements and standards in question[6] but he or they may require a relevant authority to carry out certain controls and checks[7].

1   Ie payments under European Parliament and Council Regulation (EU) 1307/2013 (OJ L347, 20.12.2013, p 608) establishing rules for direct payments to farmers under support schemes within the framework of the common agricultural policy (the 'Direct Payments Regulation'), under European Parliament and Council Regulation (EU) 1308/2013 (OJ L347, 20.12.2013, p 671) establishing a common organisation of the markets in agricultural products, arts 46, 47 and the annual premia under European Parliament and Council Regulations (EU) 1305/2013 (OJ L347, 20.12.2013, p 487) on support for rural development by the European Agricultural Fund for Rural Development (EAFRD), arts 21(1) points (a), (b), 28–31, 33, 34: European Parliament and Council Regulation (EU) 1306/2013 (OJ L347, 20.12.2013, p 549) on the financing, management and monitoring of the common agricultural policy (the 'Horizontal Regulation') arts 91, 92; Common Agricultural Policy (Control and Enforcement, Cross-Compliance, Scrutiny of Transactions and Appeals) Regulations 2014, SI 2014/3263, Sch 2 para 1; Common Agricultural Policy (Integrated Administration and Control System and Enforcement and Cross Compliance) (Wales) Regulations 2014, SI 2014/3223, reg 2(1).

2   See the Common Agricultural Policy (Control and Enforcement, Cross-Compliance, Scrutiny of Transactions and Appeals) Regulations 2014, SI 2014/3263, 18(1); and the Common Agricultural Policy (Integrated Administration and Control System and Enforcement and Cross Compliance) (Wales) Regulations 2014, SI 2014/3223, reg 13(1). The minimum standards are set out, in relation to England, in the Common Agricultural Policy (Control and Enforcement, Cross-Compliance, Scrutiny of Transactions and Appeals) Regulations 2014, SI 2014/3263, Sch 2 and, in relation to Wales, in the Common Agricultural Policy (Integrated Administration and Control System and Enforcement and Cross Compliance) (Wales) Regulations 2014, SI 2014/3223, Sch 1.

3   As to circumstances in which a breach of the minimum standards for good agricultural and environmental condition does not constitute a breach see the Common Agricultural Policy (Control and Enforcement, Cross-Compliance, Scrutiny of Transactions and Appeals) Regulations 2014, SI 2014/3263, Sch 3 and the Common Agricultural Policy (Integrated Administration and Control System and Enforcement and Cross Compliance) (Wales) Regulations 2014, SI 2014/3223, Sch 2: Common Agricultural Policy (Control and Enforcement, Cross-Compliance, Scrutiny of Transactions and Appeals) Regulations 2014, SI 2014/3263, reg 18(2); Common Agricultural Policy (Integrated Administration and Control System and Enforcement and Cross Compliance) (Wales) Regulations 2014, SI 2014/3223, reg 13(2).

4   See the Common Agricultural Policy (Control and Enforcement, Cross-Compliance, Scrutiny of Transactions and Appeals) Regulations 2014, SI 2014/3263, Sch 2 paras 2, 5, and the Common Agricultural Policy (Integrated Administration and Control System and Enforcement and Cross Compliance) (Wales) Regulations 2014, SI 2014/3223, Sch 1 paras 1, 9, 14.

5   As to the Secretary of State and the Welsh Ministers see PARA 390.

6   Ie the competent control authority for the purposes of Commission Implementing Regulation (EU) 809/2014 (OJ L227, 31.7.2014, p 69) laying down rules for the application of Regulation 1306/2013 with regard to the integrated administration and control system, rural development measures and cross compliance, art 67: see the Common Agricultural Policy (Control and Enforcement, Cross-Compliance, Scrutiny of Transactions and Appeals) Regulations 2014, SI 2014/3263, reg 19(1); and the Common Agricultural Policy (Integrated Administration and Control System and Enforcement and Cross Compliance) (Wales) Regulations 2014, SI 2014/3223, reg 14(1), (2).

7   See the Common Agricultural Policy (Control and Enforcement, Cross-Compliance, Scrutiny of Transactions and Appeals) Regulations 2014, SI 2014/3263, reg 19(2)–(4); and the Common Agricultural Policy (Integrated Administration and Control System and Enforcement and Cross Compliance) (Wales) Regulations 2014, SI 2014/3223, reg 14(3)–(6).

4. Greening.

Farmers entitled to a payment under the basic payment scheme (BPS) must observe, on all their eligible hectares[1], the following agricultural practices beneficial for the climate and the environment[2]:

(1)   crop diversification[3];
(2)   maintenance for permanent grassland[4];
(3)   ecological focus areas[5].

1   As to the meaning of 'eligible hectares' see the European Parliament and Council Regulation (EU) 1307/2013 (OJ L347, 20.12.2013, p 608–670) establishing rules for direct payments to farmers under support schemes within the framework of the common agricultural policy, art 32(2)–(5); and PARA 2 note 3.

2   Note that European Parliament and Council Regulation (EU) 1307/2013 (OJ L347, 20.12.2013, p 608–670) art 43(3) provides for equivalent practices.

3   Where the arable land of the farmer covers between 10 and 30 hectares and is not entirely cultivated with crops under water for a significant part of the year or for a significant part of the crop cycle, there must be at least two different crops on that arable land; the main crop must not cover more than 75 per cent of that arable land: European Parliament and Council Regulation (EU) 1307/2013 (OJ L347, 20.12.2013, p 608–670), art 44(1). Where the arable land of the farmer covers more than 30 hectares and is not entirely cultivated with crops under water for a significant part of the year or for a significant part of the crop cycle, there must be at least three different crops on that arable land; the main crop must not cover more than 75 per cent of that arable land and the two main crops together must not cover more than 95 per cent of that arable land: art 44(1). As to exemptions to the crop diversification rules see art 44(3).

4   See European Parliament and Council Regulation (EU) 1307/2013 (OJ L347, 20.12.2013, p 608–670), art 45. 'Permanent grassland and permanent pasture' (together referred to as 'permanent grassland') means land used to grow grasses or other herbaceous forage naturally (self seeded) or through cultivation (sown) and that has not been included in the crop rotation of the holding for five years or more; it may include other species such as shrubs and/or trees which can be grazed provided that the grasses and other herbaceous forage remain predominant as well as, where member states so decide, land which can be grazed and which forms part of established local practices where grasses and other herbaceous forage are traditionally not predominant in grazing areas; and 'grasses or other herbaceous forage' means all herbaceous plants traditionally found in

natural pastures or normally included in mixtures of seeds for pastures or meadows in the member state, whether or not used for grazing animals: art 4(h), (i).

5   Where the arable land of a holding covers more than 15 hectares, the farmer must ensure that an area corresponding to at least 5 per cent of the arable land of the holding that the farmer declared for direct payments in accordance with European Parliament and Council Regulation (EU) 1306/2013 (OJ L347, 20.12.2013, p 549) on the financing, management and monitoring of the common agricultural policy (the 'Horizontal Regulation'), art 72(1) point (a) and, if they are considered to be ecological focus area by the member state in accordance with European Parliament and Council Regulation (EU) 1307/2013 (OJ L347, 20.12.2013, p 608–670), art 46(2), including the areas mentioned in art 46(2)(c), (d), (g) and (h), is ecological focus area: see art 46. As to ecological focus areas see the Common Agricultural Policy Basic Payment and Support Schemes (England) Regulation 2014, SI 2014/3259, reg 13; and the Common Agricultural Policy Basic Payment and Support Scheme (Wales) Regulations 2015, SI 2015/1252, reg 16.

5.   Young farmers.

Member states must grant an annual payment to young farmers who are entitled to a payment under the basic payment scheme (BPS)[1]. The payment for young farmers must be granted annually upon activation of payment entitlements by the farmer[2]. A young farmer is a natural person:

(1)   who is setting up for the first time an agricultural holding as head of the holding, or who has already set up such a holding during the five years preceding the first submission of an application under the basic payment scheme; and

(2)   who is no more than 40 years of age in the year of submission of the application[3].

1   European Parliament and Council Regulation (EU) 1307/2013 (OJ L347, 20.12.2013, p 608–670) establishing rules for direct payments to farmers under support schemes within the framework of the common agricultural policy, art 50(1). As to young farmer payments see further the Common Agricultural Policy Basic Payment and Support Schemes (England) Regulation 2014, SI 2014/3259, reg 9; and the Common Agricultural Policy Basic Payment and Support Scheme (Wales) Regulations 2015, SI 2015/1252, reg 8.

2   See European Parliament and Council Regulation (EU) 1307/2013 (OJ L347, 20.12.2013, p 608–670), art 50(4).

3   See European Parliament and Council Regulation (EU) 1307/2013 (OJ L347, 20.12.2013, p 608–670), art 50(2).

6.   Milk and sugar quotas.

Milk quotas were introduced on 2 April 1984[1] and implemented in England and Wales by statutory instrument[2]. Although abolished 31 March 2015, UK legislation continues to make provision for the payment to certain agricultural tenants on the termination of their tenancies of compensation in respect of the milk quota[3].

The sugar quota system was initially introduced in 1968[4] undergoing significant reform from 2006 to 2010[5]. The quota was abolished in September 2017 and as from 1 October 2017 sugar beet growers and sugar undertakings are to conclude written agreements within the trade[6].

1   See Council Regulation (EC) 804/68 (OJ L148, 28.6.68, p 13) on the common organisation of the market in milk and milk products, art 5(c) (added by Council Regulation (EC) 856/84 (OJ L90, 1.4.84, p 10) art 1) (now repealed).

2   See the Dairy Produce Quotas Regulations 2005, SI 2005/465 and the Dairy Produce Quotas (Wales) Regulations 2005, SI 2005/537. These instruments implemented Council Regulation (EC) 1788/2003 (OJ L279, 21.10.2003, p 123) establishing a levy in the milk and milk products sector. This directive has been repealed and, as EU legislation no longer provides for milk quotas, the statutory instruments are considered spent. See also the Reporting of Prices of Milk Products (England) Regulations 2008, SI 2008/1428 and the Reporting of Prices of Milk Products (Wales) Regulations 2011, SI 2011/1009 (which require milk processors to provide the Secretary of State or the Welsh Ministers with such information relating to the prices of certain milk products, as

they may require by notice for the purposes of Commission Regulation (EU) 479/2010 (OJ L 135, 2.6.2010, pp 26–35) laying down rules for the implementation of Council Regulation (EC) 1234/2007 as regards member states' notifications to the Commission in the milk and milk products sector, arts 2, 3).

3 See the Agriculture Act 1986 s 13, Sch 1.

4 See Council Regulation (EEC) 1009/67 (OJ L308 18.12.67, p 304) on the common organisation of the market in sugar (repealed).

5 Ie Council Regulation (EC) 1234/2007 (OJ L299, 16.11.2007, p 1) establishing a common organisation of agricultural markets and on specific provisions for certain agricultural products ('the Single Common Market Organisation Regulation') (repealed). For the sugar regime as implemented prior to the single common market organisation regulation see Council Regulation (EC) 318/2006 (OJ L58, 28.2.2006, p 1) on the common organisation of the markets in the sugar sector (repealed).

6 See European Parliament and Council Regulation (EU) 1308/2013 (OJ L347, 20.12.2013, p 671–854) establishing a common organisation of the markets in agricultural products, art 125, Annex X (which sets out the purchase terms which sugar trade agreements must conform to as from 1 October 2017).

7. Aid schemes.

EU legislation provides for emergency payments to be made to milk producers and has been implemented by statutory instrument in the UK[1].

1 See:
    (1)   the Single Common Market Organisation (Emergency Aid) (England and Northern Ireland) Regulations 2017, SI 2017/599 (which provided for payments to milk producers who submitted an application by 31 May 2017 and implemented Commission Delegated Regulation (EU) 2016/1613 (OJ L 242, 9.9.2016, p 10) providing for exceptional adjustments aid to milk producers and farmers in other livestock sectors);

    (2)   the Single Common Market Organisation (Emergency Aid for Milk Producers) Regulations 2015, SI 2015/1896 (which required the Secretary of State to make payments to milk producers based on the amount of milk and milk equivalents they produced in the 2014 to 2015 milk quota year and implemented Commission Delegated Regulation (EU) 2015/1853 (OJ L271, 16.10.2015, p 25) providing for temporary exceptional aid to farmers in the livestock sectors);

    (3)   the Dairy (Specific Market Support Measure) Regulations 2010, SI 2010/1085 (revoked in relation to England by SI 2015/639) (which provided for the distribution of monies as an emergency support measure for the dairy sector).

8. Environmentally sensitive areas and environmental stewardship in England.

Provision is made for the designation of an area as an environmentally sensitive area[1]. This scheme closed to new entrants following the introduction of the environmental stewardship scheme in England[2].

Under the terms of the Environmental Stewardship Scheme for England the Secretary of State[3] had power to make grants for the management of land under one of three optional elements: Entry Level Stewardship ('ELS'), Organic Entry Level Stewardship ('OELS') and Higher Level Stewardship ('HLS')[4]. Following introduction of the Countryside Stewardship, this scheme is now closed[5].

1 See the Agriculture Act 1986 s 18. For these purposes 22 environmentally sensitive areas were designated as follows:
    (1)   Stage I environmentally sensitive areas: the Broads; the Pennine Dales; the Somerset Levels and Moors; the South Downs; and West Penwith (see the Environmentally Sensitive Areas (Stage I) Designation Order 2000, SI 2000/3049);

    (2)   Stage II environmentally sensitive areas: Breckland; Clun; North Peak; the Suffolk River Valleys; and the Test Valley (see the Environmentally Sensitive Areas (Stage II) Designation Order 2000, SI 2000/3050);

    (3)   Stage III environmentally sensitive areas: the Avon Valley; Exmoor; the Lake District; the North Kent Marshes; the South Wessex Downs; and the South West Peak (see the Environmentally Sensitive Areas (Stage III) Designation Order 2000, SI 2000/3051);

(4)   Stage IV environmentally sensitive areas: the Blackdown Hills; the Cotswold Hills; Dartmoor; the Essex Coast; the Shropshire Hills; and the Upper Thames Tributaries (see the Environmentally Sensitive Areas (Stage IV) Designation Order 2000, SI 2000/3052).

2   See notes 3, 4.

3   As to the Secretary of State see PARA **390**.

4   See the Environmental Stewardship (England) Regulations 2005, SI 2005/621 (made under the European Communities Act 1972 s 2(2); and the Environment Act 1995 s 98).

5   As to the new scheme see PARA **9**.

9.   Rural development programme.

Pillar 2 of the CAP promotes rural development[1] and is financed by the European Agricultural Fund for Rural Development (EAFRD)[2]. It is now implemented as Countryside Stewardship[3].

1   As to the main legal framework for the rural development programme of each region or member state of the EU see European Parliament and Council Regulation (EU) 1305/2013 (OJ L347, 20.12.2013) on support for rural development by the European Agricultural Fund for Rural Development ('EAFRD') (the 'Rural Development Regulation'). The Rural Development Regulation sets out three rural development objects:
    (1)   fostering the competitiveness of agriculture;
    (2)   ensuring the sustainable management of natural resources, and climate action; and
    (3)   achieving a balance territorial development of rural economies and communities including the creation and maintenance of employment: art 4.
It also sets out 6 rural development priorities and a number of measures for member states to choose from to meet them: see art 5.
    In relation to the implementation of EU requirements relating to support for rural development, see:
    (a)   the Rural Development (Enforcement) (England) Regulations 2007, SI 2007/75, regs 1–13 (which continue to apply despite their revocation (see the Common Agricultural Policy (Control and Enforcement, Cross-Compliance, Scrutiny of Transactions and Appeals) Regulations 2014, SI 2014/3253, reg 35(4)) and implemented Council Regulation (EC) 1698/2005 (OJ L277, 21.10.2005, p 1) the predecessor to (EU) 1305/2013 (OJ L347, 20.12.2013);
    (b)   the Rural Development Grants (Agriculture and Forestry) Regulations 2000, SI 2000/2907; and
    (c)   the Rural Development Programmes (Wales) Regulations 2014, SI 2014/3222.
Provision was previously made by statutory instrument for an uplands transitional payment in relation to severely disadvantaged land: see the Uplands Transitional Payment Regulations 2014, SI 2014/112, the Uplands Transitional Payment Regulations 2013, SI 2013/109, the Uplands Transitional Payment Regulations 2012, SI 2012/114 and the Uplands Transitional Payment Regulations 2011, SI 2011/135. The uplands transitional payment was a support scheme introduced following the abolition of the hill farm allowance. Although the statutory instruments providing for the uplands transitional payment have not been revoked they are considered lapsed.

2   See European Parliament and Council Regulation (EU) 1306/2013 (OJ L347, 20.12.2013, p 549) on the financing, management and monitoring of the common agricultural policy, art 5.

3   In relation to England, Countryside Stewardship (also known as NELMS: New Environmental Land Management Scheme) is the current Environmental Land Management Scheme under the Rural Development Programme for England. Countryside Stewardship has three main elements:
    (1)   Mid Tier: multi-year agreements for environmental improvements in the wider countryside, that include multi-year options and capital items (see further Natural England, *Countryside Stewardship: Mid Tier Manual which applies to all Mid Tier multi-year (including Water Capital Items) agreements commencing on 1 January 2018* (10 March 2017));
    (2)   Higher Tier: multi-year agreements for environmentally significant sites, commons and woodlands where more complex management requires support for Natural England or the Forestry Commission, that include multi-year options and capital items (see further Natural England, *Countryside Stewardship: Higher Tier Manual which applies to all Higher Tier multi-year agreements commencing on 1 January 2018* (10 March 2017));
    (3)   Capital Grants: a range of 2 year grants specific to outcomes for hedgerows and boundaries, developing implementation plans, feasibility studies, woodland management plans, woodland creation (establishment), and tree health (see further

Natural England, *Countryside Stewardship: Hedgerows and Boundaries Grant Manual which applies to all Hedgerows and Boundaries Grant agreements commencing in 2017* (1 February 2017)).

Further information can be found on the Government website.

In relation to Wales, the Wales Rural Development Programme 2014-2020 is the current environmental land management scheme under the Rural Development Programme for Wales. There are a number of schemes under the programme, all with differing qualification criteria, details of which are provided on the Government of Wales website.

2. MANAGEMENT OF LAND USED IN AGRICULTURE

10. **'Agriculture', 'agricultural', 'agricultural land' and 'farming'.**

For the purposes of all of the principal legislation relating to agricultural production and marketing[1], 'agriculture' is defined as including horticulture, fruit growing, seed growing, dairy farming and livestock[2] breeding and keeping, the use of land as grazing land[3], meadow land, osier land, market gardens and nursery grounds[4], and the use of land for woodlands where that use is ancillary to the farming of the land for other agricultural purposes, and 'agricultural' is construed accordingly[5]. References to the 'farming' of land include references to the carrying on in relation to the land of any agricultural activity[6].

For the purposes of the Agriculture Act 1947 and the Agriculture Act 1967 'agricultural land' means land used for agriculture[7] which is so used for the purposes of a trade or business[8], or which is designated[9] by the Secretary of State or the Welsh Ministers[10], and it includes any land so designated as land which in the opinion of the Secretary of State or the Welsh Ministers ought to be brought into use for agriculture[11].

1   Ie for the purposes of the Agriculture Act 1947, the Agriculture Act 1967, the Agriculture Act 1970, the Agricultural Statistics Act 1979 and the Farm Land and Rural Development Act 1988. This definition is also applied for the purposes of the Food and Environment Protection Act 1985, the Agriculture Act 1986 ss 1, 17, the Environmental Protection Act 1990 s 152 and the Agriculture Act 1993 ss 50, 58, and qualified versions are applied for the purposes of the legislation governing employment in agriculture, the establishment of agricultural boards and the making of agricultural loans (see note 5).

2   'Livestock' includes any creature kept for the production of food, wool, skins or fur or for the purpose of its use in the farming of land, and in the Agricultural Holdings Act 1986 also includes any creature kept for the purpose of its use in the carrying on in relation to land of any agricultural activity: Agriculture Act 1947 s 109(3); Agriculture Act 1970 s 37(4); Agricultural Holdings Act 1986 s 96(1). Hence it will normally exclude horses; and land used for keeping horses rather than grazing by horses is not land used for agriculture: see *Belmont Farm Ltd v Minister of Housing and Local Government* (1962) 60 LGR 319, 13 P & CR 417, DC; *Sykes v Secretary of State for the Environment* (1980) 42 P & CR 19, [1981] 1 EGLR 137, DC; *McClinton v McFall* (1974) 232 Estates Gazette 707. Fish farming is agriculture (*Minister of Agriculture, Fisheries and Food v Appleton* [1970] 1 QB 221, [1969] 3 All ER 1051, DC), as is keeping bees for the production of honey, but keeping pheasants for shooting is not (*Earl of Normanton v Giles* [1980] 1 All ER 106, [1980] 1 WLR 28, HL; *Reeve v Atterby* [1978] CLY 73; *Lord Glendyne v Rapley* [1978] 2 All ER 110, [1978] 1 WLR 601, CA). The definition of 'livestock' does not apply for the purposes of the Agricultural Statistics Act 1979: see s 6(2).

3   The grazing need not be by 'livestock' as defined in note 2: see *Rutherford v Maurer* [1962] 1 QB 16, [1961] 2 All ER 775, CA (decided in relation to the identical definition in the Agricultural Holdings Act 1948 s 94(1) (repealed)).

4   There is no definition of 'market gardening' in any of the principal legislation relating to agricultural production and marketing. An experimental bulb farm is not a market garden (*Watters v Hunter* 1927 SC 310 at 317, Ct of Sess), but land used for growing raspberries for jam-making has been held to be (*Grewar v Moncur's Curator Bonis* 1916 SC 764, Ct of Sess) and so has land used as an orchard with rhubarb and other crops grown underneath the trees, the fruit and crops being sold (*Lowther v Clifford* [1927] 1 KB 130, CA). In *Bickerdike v Lucy* [1920] 1 KB 707 (decided under the Corn Production Act 1917 (repealed)) a person employed in a private garden, some of the produce of which was sold, was held not to be employed in a market garden; see also *Re Wallis, ex p Sully* (1885) 14 QBD 950; and cf *Roberts v Wynn* [1950] WN 300, DC (garden run as business within definition). Land covered with glass-houses for the purpose of growing fruit and vegetables for sale was held to be a market garden or nursery ground for the purposes of assessment under the Public Health Act 1875 s 211(1)(b) (repealed): *Purser v Worthing Local Board of Health* (1887) 18 QBD 818, CA; but cf *Smith v Richmond* [1899] AC 448, HL.

5   Agriculture Act 1947 s 109(3); Agriculture Act 1967 s 75(2); Agricultural Statistics Act 1979 s 6(2); Agriculture Act 1970 s 28(1) (amended by the Agriculture Act 1986 s 22(1)); Food and Environment Protection Act 1985 s 24(1); Agriculture Act 1986 ss 1(6), 17(2); Farm Land and

Rural Development Act 1988 s 1(5); Environmental Protection Act 1990 s 152(5); Agriculture Act 1993 ss 50(9), 58(3). This definition is also applied, without the reference to the ancillary use of land for woodlands, for the purposes of the Natural Environment and Rural Communities Act 2006 Pt 8 Ch 2 (ss 87–97), which makes provision for the establishment of agricultural boards (see PARAS 397–400): s 88(4). The qualified definition of 'agriculture' for the purposes of the legislation governing the making of agricultural loans (ie the Agricultural Credits Act 1928) provides that 'agriculture' and 'cultivation' are deemed to include horticulture and the use of land for any purpose of husbandry, inclusive of the keeping or breeding of livestock, poultry, or bees, and the growth of fruit, vegetables, and the like (s 5(7)), and the definition applicable to the legislation governing employment in agriculture (ie the Agricultural Wages Act 1948 and the Gangmasters (Licensing) Act 2004) is that 'agriculture' includes dairy farming, the production of any consumable produce which is grown for sale or for consumption or other use for the purposes of a trade or business or of any other undertaking (whether carried on for profit or not), and the use of land as grazing, meadow or pasture land or orchard or osier land or woodland or for market gardens or nursery grounds (Agricultural Wages Act 1948 s 17(1); Gangmasters (Licensing) Act 2004 s 3(3); Agricultural Sector (Wales) Act 2014 s 18). This latter definition is not exhaustive and also includes poultry farming: *Walters v Wright* [1938] 4 All ER 116. 'Consumable produce' means produce grown for consumption or other use after severance from the land on which it is grown: Agricultural Wages Act 1948 s 17(1); Gangmasters (Licensing) Act 2004 s 3(3); Agricultural Sector (Wales) Act 2014 s 18.

6   Agriculture Act 1947 s 109(5); Agriculture Act 1967 s 75(2); Agriculture Act 1970 s 37(4).

7   References in the Agriculture Act 1947, the Agriculture Act 1967 and the Farm Land and Rural Development Act 1988 to 'the use of land for agriculture' include, in relation to land forming part of an agricultural unit, references to any use of the land in connection with the farming of the unit: Agriculture Act 1947 s 109(6); Agriculture Act 1967 s 75(2); Farm Land and Rural Development Act 1988 s 2(6). A dwelling house may be land 'used for agriculture'; it is a question of fact and degree whether it is so used in any particular case: *Blackmore v Butler* [1954] 2 QB 171, [1954] 2 All ER 403, CA (where a cottage occupied by an agricultural worker, without land other than its site and a garden, was held in the particular circumstances of that case to be 'agricultural land').

     An 'agricultural unit' is land which is occupied as a unit for agricultural purposes, including any dwelling house or other building occupied by the same person for the purpose of farming the land and any other land falling within the definition of 'agricultural land' which is in the occupation of the same person, being land as to which the Secretary of State is or the Welsh Ministers are satisfied that, having regard to its character and situation and other relevant circumstances (which, in relation to an owner or occupier, include all circumstances affecting management or farming other than the personal circumstances of the owner or occupier (Agriculture Act 1947 s 109(3))), it ought in the interests of full and efficient production to be farmed in conjunction with the agricultural unit, and he directs or they direct accordingly (s 109(2); Agriculture Act 1967 s 75(2); Agricultural Statistics Act 1979 s 6(2)). The Secretary of State and the Welsh Ministers must not give such a direction as respects any land unless it is for the time being not in use for any purpose which appears to him or them to be substantial, having regard to the use to which it might be put for agriculture: Agriculture Act 1947 s 109(2) proviso. 'Owner' was defined by s 21 (repealed) and meant, subject to certain exceptions, the person in whom the legal estate in fee simple was vested. In relation to any agricultural activity, the person having the right to carry it on is deemed to be the 'occupier' of the land: s 109(5); Agriculture Act 1970 s 37(4); Agricultural Statistics Act 1979 s 6(2).

8   'Trade or business' is not confined to agricultural trades or businesses: *Rutherford v Maurer* [1962] 1 QB 16, [1961] 2 All ER 775, CA (tenancy of a field let for grazing horses for a riding school is an agricultural holding, whereas an identical letting for the tenant's personal hunting horses will not be). The use of the land, however, must be agricultural: see *Blackmore v Butler* [1954] 2 QB 171, [1954] 2 All ER 403, CA (see note 7); *Iredell v Brocklehurst* (1950) 155 Estates Gazette 268, CA. See also *Dow Agrochemicals Ltd v EA Lane (North Lynn) Ltd* (1965) 115 LJo 76, 192 Estates Gazette 737, CCA.

9   Ie designated for the purposes of the Agriculture Act 1947 s 109(1).

10   As to the Secretary of State and the Welsh Ministers see PARA 390.

11   Agriculture Act 1947 s 109(1); Agriculture Act 1967 s 75(2). This definition is also applied for the purposes of the Environmental Protection Act 1990 s 152 (see s 152(5)). Such designations are not to extend to land used as pleasure grounds, private gardens or allotment gardens, or to land kept or preserved mainly or exclusively for the purposes of sport or recreation, except where the Secretary of State or the Welsh Ministers are satisfied that its use for agriculture would not be

inconsistent with its use for those purposes and it is so stated in the designation: Agriculture Act 1947 s 109(1) proviso. As to allotment gardens see AGRICULTURAL LAND AND ALLOTMENTS vol 1 (2017) PARA 424 note 11.

11. Rules of good estate management.

An owner[1] of agricultural land[2] is deemed to fulfil his responsibilities to manage it in accordance with the rules of good estate management in so far as his management of the land, and, so far as it affects the management of that land, of other land managed by him, is such as to be reasonably adequate to enable an occupier[3] of the land who is reasonably skilled in husbandry[4] to maintain efficient production as respects both the kind of produce and the quantity and quality of the produce[5]. For this purpose, the character and situation of the land, and other relevant circumstances[6], in particular, the extent to which the owner is providing, improving, maintaining and repairing fixed equipment[7] on the land, must be taken into account[8].

1   As to the meaning of 'owner' see PARA 10 note 7.
2   As to the meaning of 'agricultural land' see PARA 10.
3   As to the meaning of 'occupier' of land see PARA 10 note 7.
4   As to the rules of good husbandry see PARA 12.
5   Agriculture Act 1947 s 10(1). 'Produce' includes anything (whether live or dead) produced in the course of agriculture: s 109(3).
6   As to the meaning of 'relevant circumstances' see PARA 10 note 7.
7   'Fixed equipment' includes any building or structure affixed to land and any works on, in, over or under land; it also includes anything grown on land for a purpose other than use after severance from the land, consumption of the thing grown or of produce thereof, or amenity: Agriculture Act 1947 s 109(3). References to 'fixed equipment on land' are to be construed accordingly: s 109(3). Where land is in the occupation of a person other than the owner, the owner's responsibilities do not include a duty to maintain and repair fixed equipment if the obligation for this falls on the occupier by virtue of any agreement: s 10(3).
8   Agriculture Act 1947 s 10(1), (2).

12. Rules of good husbandry.

The occupier[1] of an agricultural unit[2] is deemed to fulfil his responsibilities to farm it in accordance with the rules of good husbandry in so far as the extent to which and the manner in which the unit is being farmed (as respects both the kind of operations carried out and the way in which they are carried out) is such that the occupier is maintaining a reasonable standard of efficient production, as respects both the kind of produce[3] and the quality and quantity of the produce, while keeping the unit in a condition to enable such a standard to be maintained in the future[4]. For this purpose the character and situation of the unit, and the standard of management by the owner and other relevant circumstances must be taken into account[5]. In particular, in determining whether the manner in which a unit is being farmed is such as to maintain that standard, regard must be had to the extent to which:

(1)   permanent pasture[6] is being properly mown or grazed and maintained in a good state of cultivation and fertility and in good condition[7];

(2)   the manner in which arable land is being cropped is such as to maintain that land clean and in a good state of cultivation and fertility and in good condition[8];

(3)   the unit is properly stocked where the system of farming practised requires the keeping of livestock[9], and an efficient standard of management of livestock is maintained where livestock is kept and of breeding where the breeding of livestock is carried out[10];

(4)   the necessary steps are being taken to secure and maintain crops and livestock free from disease and from infestation by insects and other pests[11];

(5)   the necessary steps are being taken for the protection and preservation of crops harvested or lifted, or in course of being harvested or lifted[12]; and

(6)   the necessary work of maintenance and repair is being carried out[13].

1 As to the meaning of 'occupier' of land see PARA 10 note 7.
2 As to the meaning of 'agricultural unit' see PARA 10 note 7.
3 As to the meaning of 'produce' see PARA 11 note 5.
4 Agriculture Act 1947 s 11(1). As to the corresponding rules of good estate management see PARA 11.
5 Agriculture Act 1947 s 11(1).
6 'Pasture' includes meadow: Agriculture Act 1947 s 109(3).
7 Agriculture Act 1947 s 11(2)(a).
8 Agriculture Act 1947 s 11(2)(b).
9 As to the meaning of 'livestock' see PARA 10 note 2.
10 Agriculture Act 1947 s 11(2)(c).
11 Agriculture Act 1947 s 11(2)(d).
12 Agriculture Act 1947 s 11(2)(e).
13 Agriculture Act 1947 s 11(2)(f). Where an agricultural unit is occupied by a person other than the owner, there is no obligation on that person to carry out any work of maintenance or repair which it is the duty of the owner of the unit (or part of it) to carry out in order to fulfil his responsibilities to manage in accordance with the rules of good estate management: s 11(3).

13. Enforcement of rules of good estate management and good husbandry.
When introduced in 1947[1], the statutory standards of good husbandry and good estate management reflected the post-war policy emphasis on producing food as efficiently and cheaply as possible, having particular relevance to the need to maintain optimum levels of agricultural production on tenanted holdings[2]. The original sanctions for breach of the rules[3] were repealed in 1958[4]; the rules continue, however, to have considerable importance in the following respects, principally in relation to agricultural holdings governed by the Agricultural Holdings Act 1986[5]:

(1)   Although the rules of good estate management are not enforceable by an agricultural tenant unless incorporated into the tenancy agreement as a term of the farm tenancy, the landlord may rely on the standards embodied by these rules, whether or not they have been incorporated into the tenancy agreement, to seek the consent of an agricultural land tribunal[6] to the operation of a notice to quit[7].

(2)   The rules of good husbandry are enforceable by an agricultural landlord in that breach of the rules will give the landlord a right to apply for a certificate of bad husbandry from the agricultural land tribunal[8]: if the tribunal issues a certificate of bad husbandry, the landlord may serve a notice to quit the holding[9]. Additionally, even in a case where a certificate of bad husbandry has not been applied for or issued, the Tribunal can consent to the operation of a notice to quit if it considers that the termination of the tenancy is in the interests of good husbandry[10].

(3)   Many agricultural tenancy agreements will incorporate the rules of good husbandry, making compliance with the rules a term of the tenancy. In this case, breach of the rules will also give rise to potential

liabilities for breach of tenancy, and in appropriate cases forfeiture proceedings under the general law or the Agricultural Holdings Act 1986 will be applicable[11].

(4)   The rules of good husbandry also have indirect relevance in that many of the statutory rights and duties of the landlord and the tenant are qualified by reference to them; so, for instance, in possession proceedings under the Agricultural Holdings Act 1986, the breach of tenancy complained of must be one that is not inconsistent with the tenant's responsibilities to farm in accordance with the rules of good husbandry[12]. Similarly, in order to compel the provision of fixed equipment by the landlord, a tenant must satisfy the Tribunal that this is reasonable 'having regard to the tenant's responsibilities to farm the holding in accordance with the rules of good husbandry'[13].

1   Ie under the Agriculture Act 1947 ss 10, 11 (see PARAS **11, 12**).
2   See PARAS **11, 12**.
3   See the Agriculture Act 1947 ss 12–15 (repealed by the Agriculture Act 1958 Sch 2 Pt I), which provided for the making of supervision orders and the giving of directions by the Secretary of State in cases of bad husbandry or bad estate management, and the Agriculture Act 1947 ss 16–19 (also so repealed), which provided for dispossession and compulsory acquisition in such cases.
4   See note 3.
5   As to these see AGRICULTURAL LAND AND ALLOTMENTS vol 1 (2017) PARA 421 et seq.
6   Ie in England, the First-tier Tribunal (see AGRICULTURAL LAND AND ALLOTMENTS vol 1 (2017) PARA 768) and in Wales, the Agricultural Land Tribunal for Wales (see AGRICULTURAL LAND AND ALLOTMENTS vol 1 (2017) PARA 767).
7   See the Agricultural Holdings Act 1986 s 27(3)(b); and AGRICULTURAL LAND AND ALLOTMENTS vol 1 (2017) PARA 472.
8   See the Agricultural Holdings Act 1986 Sch 3 Pt II para 9(1); and AGRICULTURAL LAND AND ALLOTMENTS vol 1 (2017) PARA 476.
9   See the Agricultural Holdings Act 1986 Sch 3 Pt I Case C; and AGRICULTURAL LAND AND ALLOTMENTS vol 1 (2017) PARA 476. The notice to quit must be given not more than six months from the date of the certificate of bad husbandry: Sch 3 Pt I Case C. This procedure is available even where the tenant's alleged bad husbandry is attributable to his participating in a publicly funded agri-environment scheme: see *Davies v Agricultural Land Tribunal* [2007] EWHC 1395 (Admin), in which it was held that a certificate of bad husbandry was valid when issued in circumstances where the tenant was burying waste on farmland (a clear breach of the rules of good husbandry) and had also left semi-natural grazing land unmanaged, allegedly under the terms of an agreement under the Tir Cynnal agri-environment scheme in Wales.
10 See the Agricultural Holdings Act 1986 s 27(3)(a); and AGRICULTURAL LAND AND ALLOTMENTS vol 1 (2017) PARA 472.
11 See the Agricultural Holdings Act 1986 Sch 3 Pt I Case D (remediable breach of tenancy) or Case E (irremediable breach); and AGRICULTURAL LAND AND ALLOTMENTS vol 1 (2017) PARAS 477, 478.
12 See the Agricultural Holdings Act 1986 Sch 3 Pt I Case D(b) and Case E; and AGRICULTURAL LAND AND ALLOTMENTS vol 1 (2017) PARAS 477–478.
13 See the Agricultural Holdings Act 1986 s 11(1); and AGRICULTURAL LAND AND ALLOTMENTS vol 1 (2017) PARA 437.

14.   Restriction on removal of surface soil.

The removal of surface soil from agricultural land[1] with a view to the sale of the soil is an offence[2] if the removal constitutes development[3] and is carried out without planning permission[4] and if the amount of soil so removed in any period of three months exceeds five cubic yards[5]. This does not apply to the cutting of peat or to the removal of so much surface soil as is reasonably necessary in the course of cutting turf[6]. It is a defence to show that before the carrying out of the operations in respect of which proceedings were brought a certificate was issued[7] that the operations would be lawful[8].

1　This includes land the use of which as agricultural land has been discontinued in consequence of the intention to remove the surface soil: Agricultural Land (Removal of Surface Soil) Act 1953 s 1(3). As to the meanings of 'agriculture' and 'agricultural' for these purposes see the Town and Country Planning Act 1990 s 336(1); and PLANNING vol 81 (2010) PARA 23 (definition applied by the Agricultural Land (Removal of Surface Soil) Act 1953 s 5(2) (amended by the Planning (Consequential Provisions) Act 1990 s 4, Sch 2 para 3(4))).

2　Agricultural Land (Removal of Surface Soil) Act 1953 s 1(1)(a). Until a day to be appointed a person convicted of this offence is liable on summary conviction to a fine not exceeding level 3 on the standard scale or, where it is shown that the offence was substantially a repetition or continuation of an earlier offence, to imprisonment for a term not exceeding three months or to a fine not exceeding £50 for every day on which the earlier offence has been so repeated or continued by him, or £200, whichever is the greater (s 2(1) (amended by virtue of the Criminal Justice Act 1982 ss 38, 46)); as from that day, the option of imprisonment (either as an additional or alternative punishment) is removed (Agricultural Land (Removal of Surface Soil) Act 1953 s 2(1) (as so amended; prospectively amended by the Criminal Justice Act 2003 Sch 37 Pt 9)). At the date at which this volume states the law no such day had been appointed. As to the standard scale and the powers of magistrates' courts to issue fines on summary conviction see SENTENCING vol 92 (2015) PARA 176.

　　Where the offence has been committed by a body corporate and is proved to have been committed with the consent or connivance of, or to be attributable to any neglect on the part of, any director (ie, in relation to any body corporate established by or under any enactment for the purpose of carrying on under national ownership any industry or part of an industry or undertaking, being a body corporate whose affairs are managed by members thereof, a member of that body), manager, secretary or other similar officer of the body, or any person purporting to act in any such capacity, he as well as the body is guilty of that offence and liable to be proceeded against and punished accordingly: Agricultural Land (Removal of Surface Soil) Act 1953 s 2(2). The consent of the Attorney General or the Director of Public Prosecutions is required to bring any prosecution under the Act: s 3.

3　Ie within the meaning of the Town and Country Planning Act 1990 s 55 (see PLANNING vol 81 (2010) PARAS 292–298): see the Agricultural Land (Removal of Surface Soil) Act 1953 s 1(1)(b) (amended by the Planning (Consequential Provisions) Act 1990 Sch 2 para 3(1)).

4　Ie the grant of permission required for the purposes of the Town and Country Planning Act 1990 Pt III (ss 55–106B) (see PLANNING vol 81 (2010) PARA 292 et seq): see the Agricultural Land (Removal of Surface Soil) Act 1953 s 1(1)(b) (as amended: see note 3).

5　Agricultural Land (Removal of Surface Soil) Act 1953 s 1(1)(c).

6　Agricultural Land (Removal of Surface Soil) Act 1953 s 1(2).

7　Ie under the Town and Country Planning Act 1990 s 192 (see PLANNING vol 82 (2010) PARA 778).

8　Agricultural Land (Removal of Surface Soil) Act 1953 s 2(3) (amended by the Planning (Consequential Provisions) Act 1990 Sch 2 para 3(2)).

3. SEEDS AND OTHER PROPAGATING MATERIAL

(1) SEEDS

(i) Regulation of Sale and Marketing of Seeds

15. Seeds regulations.

The Secretary of State and the Welsh Ministers[1], after consultation with representatives of interests concerned, may make regulations, to be known as seeds regulations[2], for the purpose of:

(1)   ensuring that reliable and adequate information is afforded as to the nature, condition and quality of seeds[3] which are sold or are for sale[4];

(2)   preventing the sale of seeds which are deleterious and preventing the sale of seeds which have not been tested for purity and germination, or which are of a variety the performance of which has not been subjected to trials[5];

(3)   preventing the spread of plant disease by means of seeds[6];

(4)   regulating the descriptions under which seeds are sold[7]; and

(5)   regulating the marketing, or the importation or exportation, of seeds or any related activities (whether by reference to officially published lists of permitted varieties or otherwise)[8].

Seeds regulations may include provision as to the packets, bags, trays or other containers in which seeds may be sold or delivered and requirements as to the marking of such containers[9], may make provision with regard to the manner in which samples of seeds are taken[10], may exempt, or authorise the Secretary of State and the Welsh Ministers to exempt, any person or class of persons, or persons generally, from compliance with any of their provisions[11], and may make provision as to the collection of information and the regulation of testing[12]. Seeds regulations concerned with the marketing, importation or exportation of seeds may also include provision for the registration or licensing of persons engaged in the seeds industry or related activities[13] and other measures[14].

Regulations have been made covering the marketing of a variety of seeds and the activities involving seeds that require a person to have a licence[15]. Regulations have also been made for fees[16]. The Secretary of State and the Welsh Ministers are required to prepare and publish National Lists of Varieties of specified kinds of agricultural and vegetable crops[17].

Provision is also made in connection with the marketing of forest reproductive material, although such provision is not made under the Plant Varieties and Seeds Act 1964[18].

1   As to the Secretary of State and the Welsh Ministers see PARA 390. As to modifications in relation to the Isle of Man see the Plant Varieties and Seeds (Isle of Man) Order 2016, SI 2016/758, Sch 1 Pt 1 para 1.

2   In addition to the matters set out in the text, seeds regulations may also prescribe anything which, under the Plant Varieties and Seeds Act 1964 Pt II (ss 16–31), is authorised or required to be prescribed: s 16(1)(e). Regulations under the Plant Varieties and Seeds Act 1964 generally may make different provision for different types or classes of plant varieties, for different seasons of the year and for other different circumstances and may contain such supplemental, incidental and transitional provisions as may appear to the Secretary of State to be expedient (s 36).

    Any statutory statement made as respects seeds which are in distinct portions is to be presumed to be made both as respects the seeds as a whole and also as respects each portion: s 19. It is an offence to contravene seeds regulations (any reference to an offence under Pt II includes, unless the context otherwise requires, a reference to a contravention of any provision contained in seeds regulations (s 30(3))), but such a contravention does not affect the validity of a contract for the sale of seeds, or the right to enforce such a contract (s 17(5)). As to the institution of proceedings see PARA 24.

3   'Seeds' means seeds for sowing (Plant Varieties and Seeds Act 1964 s 38(2)); it includes agricultural and horticultural seeds, vegetable seeds, flower seeds, seeds of grasses, whether used for agricultural purposes or other purposes, and seeds of trees (s 30(1)). Moreover, Pt II applies to seed potatoes, other vegetative propagating material and silviculture planting material as it applies to seeds; and references to seeds are to be construed accordingly: s 29(1) (amended by the European Communities Act 1972 Sch 4 para 5).

4   Plant Varieties and Seeds Act 1964 s 16(1)(a).

5   Plant Varieties and Seeds Act 1964 s 16(1)(b).

6   Plant Varieties and Seeds Act 1964 s 16(1)(c) (s 16(1)(c) amended, and s 16(1A) added, by the European Communities Act 1972 Sch 4 para 5).

7   Plant Varieties and Seeds Act 1964 s 16(1)(d). A description or mark applied in pursuance of the Plant Varieties and Seeds Act 1964 is not a 'trade description' for the purposes of the Trade Descriptions Act 1968: see s 2(4)(c); and CONSUMER PROTECTION vol 21 (2016) PARA 443.

8   Plant Varieties and Seeds Act 1964 s 16(1A) (as added: see note 6).

9   Plant Varieties and Seeds Act 1964 s 16(2). See note 7.

10 Plant Varieties and Seeds Act 1964 s 16(4)(a)–(c). See further PARA 19.

11 Plant Varieties and Seeds Act 1964 s 16(5)(a).

12 Seeds regulations may:
    (1)   require information to be given as regards seeds which are sold or offered or exposed for sale and, in particular, require the seller to deliver a statement containing prescribed particulars to the purchaser (Plant Varieties and Seeds Act 1964 s 16(3)(a));
    (2)   require any of those particulars to be particulars ascertained on a test of the seeds (s 16(3)(b));
    (3)   prohibit the selling, or the offering or exposing for sale, of seeds containing more than a prescribed proportion of weed seeds (s 16(3)(c));
    (4)   prohibit the sale or offer or exposure for sale of seeds under a prescribed name, designation or description except where the seeds have been grown or selected under prescribed conditions (s 16(3)(d));
    (5)   require dealers to supply information as to, and keep records of, transactions in seeds and statutory statements (see PARA 16) and other statements given or received by them, processes or treatments applied to seeds and the results of tests of seeds (s 16(3)(e));
    (6)   require dealers who also grow seeds to supply information as to, and keep records of, areas sown and yields of crops and authorise officers and other persons to call for production of those records (s 16(3)(f) (amended by SI 1977/1112));
    (7)   regulate the procedure at, and the conduct of, official seed testing stations (as to which see PARA 21) and other establishments at which tests may be carried out (Plant Varieties and Seeds Act 1964 s 16(3)(g));
    (8)   regulate the manner in which tests are to be made (s 16(3)(h)); and
    (9)   provide for the licensing of establishments for the testing of seeds, other than official testing stations, and provide for the attachment of conditions to, and the charging of a fee for, such a licence (s 16(3)(i)).
    'Official testing station' means an official seed testing station maintained under Pt II: s 30(1) (amended by the European Communities Act 1972 Sch 4 para 5). See further PARA 21.
    Provision for the licensing of seed testing stations is made for England by the Seed Marketing Regulations 2011, SI 2011/463, regs 20–22 (amended by SI 2012/3035) and for Wales by the Seed Marketing (Wales) Regulations 2012, SI 2012/245, regs 20–22 (amended by SI 2013/889).

13 Plant Varieties and Seeds Act 1964 s 16(1A)(a) (as added: see note 6).

14 Such regulations may include provision for:
    (1)   ensuring that seeds on any official list remain true to variety (s 16(1A)(b));
    (2)   the keeping and inspection of records and the giving of information (s 16(1A)(c));
    (3)   conferring rights of appeal to the Plant Varieties and Seeds Tribunal (as to which see PARAS 285–291) (s 16(1A)(d)); and
    (4)   excluding, extending or modifying, in relation to or in connection with any provision of the regulations, the operation of any provision made by ss 17–19 or of Pt IV (ss 34–41), and for the charging of fees (s 16(1A)(e)).

15 In relation to seed potatoes see the Seed Potatoes (England) Regulations 2015, SI 2015/1953; and the Seed Potatoes (Wales) Regulations 2016, SI 2016/106 (see PARA 35) and in relation to beets, cereals, fodder plants, small and large seeded legumes, crucifers, oil and fibre plants and vegetables

see the Seed Marketing Regulations 2011, SI 2011/463 and the Seed Marketing (Wales) Regulations 2012, SI 2012/245 (the seeds to which those provisions apply are set out in the Sch 1 to those provisions).

16 In relation to England fees are prescribed by the Plant Health (Fees) (England) Regulations 2014, SI 2014/601; and relation to Wales fees are prescribed by the Seed Potatoes (Fees) (Wales) Regulations 2014, SI 2014/1792.

In determining fees to be charged under seeds regulations, the Secretary of State and the Welsh Ministers may have regard to costs incurred in enforcing regulations: Plant Varieties and Seeds Act 1964 s 16(5A) (added by the Agriculture Act 1986 s 2).

17 See the Seeds (National Lists of Varieties) Regulations 2001, SI 2001/3510. As to fees payable under these regulations see the Seeds (National Lists of Varieties) (Fees) Regulations 1994, SI 1994/676.

18 See FORESTRY vol 52 (2014) PARAS 108–109.

16. Statutory statements.

A 'statutory statement' is a statement given in pursuance of seeds regulations[1]. It may be in the form of a notice or other document, in the form of particulars given on any label or container or package, or in any other form[2]. Such statements, when received by the purchaser, have effect as a written warranty by the seller that the particulars in them are correct[3]. Moreover, the particulars in a statutory statement are deemed to be true for the purposes of any legal proceedings on a contract for the sale of seeds[4] to which the statement relates[5], except in so far as there is a misstatement in the particulars which exceeds the limits of variation prescribed in the relevant seeds regulations[6] and unless it appears on an official test[7] that the particulars were untrue[8].

Subject to a number of specified statutory defences[9], a person who includes in a statutory statement anything which is false in a material particular, or who contravenes any provision contained in seeds regulations[10] commits an offence[11].

1   As to seeds regulations see PARA 15. Note that these provisions apply also to the marketing of seed potatoes (see PARAS 15 note 3, 35). Statutory statements will have only the legal effects described in the text and notes 2–11 to the extent that seeds regulations provide for them so to do: see the Plant Varieties and Seeds Act 1964 s 17(1)–(3).

2   Plant Varieties and Seeds Act 1964 s 30(1). A statutory statement includes a statement delivered under s 25(6) (powers of entry) (see PARA 18): ss 25(7), 30(1).

3   Plant Varieties and Seeds Act 1964 s 17(1). This applies only if and so far as seeds regulations provide that a statutory statement constitutes a statutory warranty for the purposes of s 17, and where it does apply, it applies notwithstanding any contract or notice to the contrary: s 17(1). As to the remedies of a buyer for a breach of warranty see the Sale of Goods Act 1979 s 53; and SALE OF GOODS AND SUPPLY OF SERVICES vol 91 (2012) PARAS 305–308.

4   As to the meaning of 'seeds' see PARA 15 note 3.

5   Plant Varieties and Seeds Act 1964 s 17(2), (3). This applies if and so far as seeds regulations apply s 17(2), (3) to a statutory statement and prescribe limits of variation in relation to the particulars in such statements: s 17(2), (3).

6   Plant Varieties and Seeds Act 1964 s 17(2). See also the text and note 9.

7   Ie a test carried out at an official testing station on a sample taken in the manner and within the period prescribed by seeds regulations: Plant Varieties and Seeds Act 1964 s 17(3). As to the meaning of 'official testing station' see PARA 15 note 12; and as to official testing stations see PARA 21. As to the admissibility in evidence and the evidential weight of the results of such a test see PARA 23. Where a purchaser intends to obtain a test for these purposes, the seller is to be given written notice of the purchaser's intention not more than the prescribed period after delivery to the purchaser of the seeds under the sale, and seeds regulations are required to prescribe a procedure for taking a sample to be tested for these purposes which will afford the seller or his agent an opportunity of being present when the sample is taken and of obtaining part of the sample: s 17(4). As to the certification of results see s 24(6); and PARA 23.

8   Plant Varieties and Seeds Act 1964 s 17(3).

9   If and so far as seeds regulations prescribe for these purposes limits of variation in relation to the particulars in a statutory statement, it is a defence to proceedings for including in a statutory statement any false particulars to prove that the misstatements alleged to be false do not exceed

those limits of variation: Plant Varieties and Seeds Act 1964 s 18(1). Subject to this, it is also a defence to proceedings for including false particulars in a statutory statement and to proceedings for any other offence against seeds regulations to prove:

(1)   that the accused took all reasonable precautions against committing an offence of the kind alleged, and had not at the time of the alleged offence any reason to suspect that an offence was being committed by him (s 18(2)(a), (b), (i)); and

(2)   where the accused obtained the seeds to which the alleged offence relates from some other person, that on demand by or on behalf of the prosecutor the accused gave all the information in his power with respect to the name and address of that other person, and with respect to any statutory statement or other document in his possession or power relating to the seeds, and the contract of sale (s 18(2)(a), (b), (ii)).

If, however, in any proceedings for including false particulars in a statutory statement any of the particulars alleged to be false are particulars which by seeds regulations are to be ascertained by means of a test, the defence described above is not available unless it is proved:

(a)   that those particulars were so ascertained and that the test was not earlier than the date, if any, prescribed by seeds regulations for the purpose (s 18(3)(a)); or

(b)   that the accused purchased the seeds from another person who duly delivered to the accused a statutory statement giving particulars of the seeds which were the same as the particulars alleged to be false and the accused had no reason to believe the particulars were not ascertained by means of a test made after the prescribed date, if any, in accordance with seeds regulations (s 18(3)(b)).

10 References to a contravention of seeds regulations include references to a failure to comply therewith, to anything which, by the regulations, is expressed to be an offence, and to any failure to comply with a condition subject to which an exemption is granted by or under the regulations: Plant Varieties and Seeds Act 1964 s 30(2).

11 Plant Varieties and Seeds Act 1964 s 16(7). A person who commits the offence is liable on summary conviction to a fine not exceeding level 5 on the standard scale: s 16(7) (amended by the European Communities Act 1972 s 4(1), Sch 4 para 5(1), (2); and by virtue of the Criminal Justice Act 1982 ss 38, 46)). As to the standard scale and the powers of magistrates' courts to issue fines on summary conviction see SENTENCING vol 92 (2015) PARA 176. Contravention of seeds regulations does not, however, affect the validity of a contract for the sale of seeds, or the right to enforce such a contract: see s 17(5); and PARA 15 note 2.

Where an offence punishable under the Plant Varieties and Seeds Act 1964 committed by a body corporate is proved to have been committed with the consent or connivance of, or to be attributable to any neglect on the part of, any director, manager, secretary or other similar officer of the body corporate, or any person who was purporting to act in any such capacity, he, as well as the body corporate, is guilty of that offence and is liable to be proceeded against and punished accordingly: s 35(1). As to the institution of proceedings see PARA 24.

17. Publication of notices.

Notice of matters to be published under the provisions of the Plant Varieties and Seeds Act 1964 governing transactions in seeds and other propagating material[1] or the provisions of the Plant Varieties Act 1997 concerned with the registration, protection and licensing of plant breeders' rights[2] is to be published in the gazette[3].

1 Ie the Plant Varieties and Seeds Act 1964 Pt II (ss 16–31): see PARA 15 et seq.
2 Ie the Plant Varieties Act 1997 Pt I (ss 1–41): see PARA 239 et seq.
3 Plant Varieties and Seeds Act 1964 s 34(1) (amended by the Plant Varieties Act 1997 s 51(1)(a)).

(ii) Enforcement, Tests and Samples

18. Powers of entry.

Any person duly authorised by the Secretary of State or the Welsh Ministers[1] may, on production if so required of his authority, at all reasonable hours enter any premises[2]:

(1)   which he has reasonable cause to believe to be used for any purpose of a business in the course of which seeds[3] are sold[4]; or

(2)   on which he has reasonable cause to believe that there are seed potatoes which have been sold and which are to be delivered, or are in the course of delivery, to the purchaser[5].

These powers of entry are conferred for the purpose of:

(a)   examining and taking samples of seeds[6];

(b)   requiring an owner of seeds for the purposes of sale to deliver to the authorised person a statutory statement[7];

(c)   any powers of calling for, inspecting or taking copies of records or other documents conferred by seeds regulations[8]; and

(d)   ascertaining whether there is, or has been, on or in connection with the premises (including any vehicle or vessel) any contravention of an applicable statutory provision[9].

A person who obstructs or impedes any person acting in the exercise of these powers commits an offence[10].

1   As to the Secretary of State and the Welsh Ministers see PARA 390.
2   These provisions do not authorise entry into premises used exclusively as a private dwelling: Plant Varieties and Seeds Act 1964 s 25(2).
3   As to the meaning of 'seeds' see PARA 15 note 3. These provisions apply as respects all kinds of seeds in respect of which an offence may under any circumstances be committed under seeds regulations: Plant Varieties and Seeds Act 1964 s 25(8) (amended by the European Communities Act 1972 Sch 3 Pt III). As to seeds regulations see PARA 15. Note that these provisions apply also in connection with the marketing of seed potatoes (see PARAS 15 note 3, 35).
4   Plant Varieties and Seeds Act 1964 s 25(3). This power is conferred whether the sales conducted in the business are wholesale or retail, and whether the person conducting it acts as principal or agent: s 25(3).
5   Plant Varieties and Seeds Act 1964 s 25(4). This power of entry may be exercised when the seed potatoes are in transit in the course of delivery to the purchaser and in particular when they are in any vehicle or vessel: s 25(4).
6   Plant Varieties and Seeds Act 1964 s 25(1)(a). These powers are conferred by s 25(5), which provides that a person may, on any premises (including any vehicle or vessel) which he has power to enter, examine any seeds which he finds there and may without payment take samples of them. As to the taking of samples for the purposes of criminal proceedings see further PARA 19.
7   Plant Varieties and Seeds Act 1964 s 25(1)(a). These powers are conferred by s 25(6), which provides that the owner of any seeds which are offered or exposed for sale, or are stored for purposes of sale, or any person authorised to sell those seeds, may be required by a person duly authorised to deliver such a statement, if any, as the person selling them would by seeds regulations be obliged to deliver to a purchaser of those seeds and to deliver it within the time prescribed for such a statement. As to statutory statements (ie, in this context, statements such as seeds regulations would require to be delivered to a purchaser (s 25(7)) see PARA 16. Subject to a number of specified statutory defences (see PARA 16 note 9), a person who includes in a statutory statement anything which is false in a material particular, commits an offence: see s 16(7); and PARA 16 note 11. Failure to comply with any requirement under s 25(6) is punishable on summary conviction by a fine not exceeding level 3 on the standard scale: s 25(7) (amended by the European Communities Act 1972 Sch 4 para 5(1), (2); and by virtue of the Criminal Justice Act 1982 ss 37, 38, 46). As to the standard scale and the powers of magistrates' courts to issue fines on summary conviction see SENTENCING vol 92 (2015) PARA 176. As to offences by bodies corporate see PARA 16 note 11. As to the institution of proceedings see PARA 24.
8   Plant Varieties and Seeds Act 1964 s 25(1)(b).
9   Plant Varieties and Seeds Act 1964 s 25(1). The applicable statutory provisions for these purposes are Pt II (ss 16–31) or seeds regulations: s 25(1).
10   Plant Varieties and Seeds Act 1964 s 25(9). A person who commits such an offence is liable on summary conviction to a fine not exceeding level 3 on the standard scale: s 25(9) (amended by virtue of the Criminal Justice Act 1982 ss 39, 46, Sch 3).

19.   Taking and use of samples.

Seeds regulations[1] may:

(1)   impose conditions as to the persons authorised to take samples and the places where samples may be taken[2];

(2)   require part of a sample to be given to the owner of the seeds[3] or some other person[4];

(3)   prescribe the manner of division of samples[5];

(4)   impose duties as to the marking, labelling and preservation of parts of samples[6]; and

(5)   provide for the identification, by the labelling or marking of their container or by some other method, of seeds from which a sample has been taken[7].

Where a sample is being taken for the purpose of adducing it in evidence in criminal proceedings[8], seeds regulations must provide for it to be divided into at least two parts, for one of the parts to be given to the owner of the seeds or to such other person as may be prescribed, and for a third part to be retained for production in all cases where use of it may be made by the court[9]. Evidence may not be adduced in such proceedings unless the sample was taken in the manner so prescribed[10].

1   As to seeds regulations see PARA 15. Note that these provisions apply also in connection with the marketing of seed potatoes (see PARAS 906 note 3, 939).
2   Plant Varieties and Seeds Act 1964 s 16(4)(a).
3   As to the meaning of 'seeds' see PARA 15 note 3.
4   Plant Varieties and Seeds Act 1964 s 16(4)(b).
5   Plant Varieties and Seeds Act 1964 s 16(4)(b).
6   Plant Varieties and Seeds Act 1964 s 16(4)(b).
7   Plant Varieties and Seeds Act 1964 s 16(4)(c).
8   Ie criminal proceedings for an offence under the Plant Varieties and Seeds Act 1964 Pt II (ss 16–31). As to admissibility in evidence see PARA 23.
9   Plant Varieties and Seeds Act 1964 s 26(2). Where part of a sample taken by an authorised officer is sent to the chief officer of an official testing station, it must be sent as soon as practicable after the sample is taken and the person to whom any other part is given must be informed before the first-mentioned part is sent: s 26(4). In proceedings for including in a statutory statement false particulars concerning matters which under seeds regulations must be ascertained by a test (see PARA 16), if any sample has been taken by an authorised officer the third part of that sample required by seeds regulations to be retained must be produced at the hearing: s 26(7). The court may on the request of either party cause the part so produced to be sent to the chief officer of an official testing station, who must transmit to the court a certificate of the result of a test of that part: s 26(8). If, in a case where an appeal is brought, no such action has been taken, s 26(8) applies also to the court by which the appeal is heard: s 26(9). An 'authorised officer' is an officer of, or a person authorised by, the Secretary of State or the Welsh Ministers to execute Pt II: s 30(1). This includes an officer of the Forestry Commissioners: s 29(2)(a) (s 29(2) added by the European Communities Act 1972 Sch 4 para 5(1), (4)). As to the Secretary of State and the Welsh Ministers see PARA 390. As to the Forestry Commissioners see FORESTRY vol 52 (2014) PARA 37 et seq. As to the meaning of 'official testing station' see PARA 15 note 12; and as to official testing stations see PARA 21.
10   Plant Varieties and Seeds Act 1964 s 26(1). The regulations provide that the sample must be divided into three parts, of which one must be delivered to the owner of the seeds and the other two delivered to an official testing station, one for testing (which must be retained for 2 years) and the other for retention pending production to the court if required: see the Seed Marketing Regulations 2011, SI 2011/463, reg 24 (amended by SI 2016/613); and the Seed Marketing (Wales) Regulations 2012, SI 2012/245, reg 24 (amended by SI 2016/1242). A certificate in the form prescribed by seeds regulations purporting to be issued by an authorised officer and stating that a sample was taken in the prescribed manner is sufficient evidence of the facts stated in the certificate: Plant Varieties and Seeds Act 1964 s 26(3). As to the prescribed certificate see the Seed Marketing Regulations 2011, SI 2011/463, reg 25; and the Seed Marketing (Wales) Regulations 2012, SI 2012/245, reg 25.

20.　Tampering with samples.

A person commits an offence[1] if he:

(1)　tampers with any seeds[2] so as to procure that a sample taken in the manner prescribed by seeds regulations[3] does not correctly represent the bulk of the seeds[4];

(2)　tampers with any sample so taken[5]; or

(3)　with intent to deceive sends, or causes or allows to be sent, to any official testing station[6] or licensed testing establishment[7], to be tested for any purpose, a sample of seeds which to his knowledge does not correctly represent the bulk of the seeds[8].

1　Until a day to be appointed the offence is punishable on summary conviction by a fine not exceeding level 5 on the standard scale or imprisonment for a term not exceeding three months or both (Plant Varieties and Seeds Act 1964 s 27(1) (amended by virtue of the Criminal Justice Act 1982 ss 38, 46)); as from that day the maximum term of imprisonment is increased to a term not exceeding 51 weeks (Plant Varieties and Seeds Act 1964 s 27(1) (as so amended; prospectively amended by the Criminal Justice Act 2003 s 280(2), (3), Sch 26 para 22(1), (11))). At the date at which this volume states the law no such day had been appointed. As to the standard scale and the powers of magistrates' courts to issue fines on summary conviction see SENTENCING vol 92 (2015) PARA 176. As to the institution of proceedings see PARA 24.

2　As to the meaning of 'seeds' see PARA 15 note 3.

3　As to seeds regulations see PARA 15. Note that these provisions apply also in connection with the marketing of seed potatoes (see PARAS 906 note 3, 939). As to the manner of taking samples prescribed by seeds regulations see PARA 19.

4　Plant Varieties and Seeds Act 1964 s 27(1)(a).

5　Plant Varieties and Seeds Act 1964 s 27(1)(b).

6　As to the meaning of 'official testing station' see PARA 15 note 12; and as to official testing stations see PARA 21.

7　Ie an establishment licensed under seeds regulations for the testing of seeds: Plant Varieties and Seeds Act 1964 s 27(2). As to the licensing of such establishments see PARA 21 note 3.

8　Plant Varieties and Seeds Act 1964 s 27(1)(c).

21.　Testing of samples.

Where seed samples are required by seeds regulations[1] to be tested, they must be sent either to official testing stations[2] or to other establishments licensed for the testing of seeds[3]. The Secretary of State and the Welsh Ministers are required to maintain the official seed testing stations originally established for England and Wales under former legislation[4]. The Secretary of State and the Welsh Ministers may also unite with the Scottish Ministers in establishing and maintaining, on such terms as may be agreed between them, a common official seed testing station for the whole of Great Britain[5]. The arrangements for official seed testing stations may be altered, and testing stations may be established in conjunction with other bodies[6]. With Treasury approval, fees may be charged for services given[7].

The Forestry Commissioners[8], or in relation to Wales, the Welsh Ministers, may establish and maintain an official seed testing station for silvicultural propagating and planting material[9].

1　As to seeds regulations see PARA 15. Note that these provisions apply also in connection with the marketing of seed potatoes (see PARAS 906 note 3, 939).

2　As to the meaning of 'official testing station' see PARA 15 note 12.

3　Seeds regulations may provide for the licensing by the Secretary of State and the Welsh Ministers of establishments for the testing of seeds, other than official testing stations, and may authorise the attachment of conditions and the charging of a fee in respect of such a licence and the licensing of crop inspectors and seed samplers: see the Plant Varieties and Seeds Act 1964 s 16(3)(i); and PARA 15. As to the meaning of 'seeds' see PARA 15 note 3. As to the licensing of such establishments see the Seed Marketing Regulations 2011, SI 2011/463, reg 21; and the Seed Marketing (Wales) Regulations 2012, SI 2012/245, reg 21. As to the Secretary of State and the Welsh Ministers see PARA 390.

4   Plant Varieties and Seeds Act 1964 s 24(1). The former legislation establishing official seed testing stations for England and Wales is the Seeds Act 1920 (repealed).

5   Plant Varieties and Seeds Act 1964 s 24(2). As to Great Britain see PARA 1 note 1.

6   Plant Varieties and Seeds Act 1964 s 24(3).

7   Plant Varieties and Seeds Act 1964 s 24(4). As to the Treasury see CONSTITUTIONAL AND ADMINISTRATIVE LAW vol 20 (2014) PARA 263 et seq.

8   As to the Forestry Commissioners see FORESTRY vol 52 (2014) PARA 37 et seq.

9   Plant Varieties and Seeds Act 1964 s 29(2), (4) (added by the European Communities Act 1972 Sch 4 para 5(1), (4); and the Plant Varieties and Seeds Act 1964 s 29(2) amended and s 29(4) added by SI 2013/755). Seeds regulations may confer on the Commissioners any functions which they may confer on the Secretary of State and the Welsh Ministers: Plant Varieties and Seeds Act 1964 s 29(2) (as so added). The Commissioners may also charge or authorise the charging of fees for services given at any such station: s 29(2) (as so added).

22. Certification of test results.

A certificate of the result of a test at an official seed testing station[1] of a sample taken by an authorised officer[2] is to be in the form prescribed by seeds regulations[3]. A copy of a certificate issued by an official testing station stating the result of a test of part of a sample taken by an authorised officer must be sent to the person to whom any other part of the sample is given[4]. A certificate of the result of a test at an official seed testing station may be used in evidence in proceedings for an offence concerning seeds[5].

1   As to the meaning of 'official testing station' see PARA 15 note 12; and as to official testing stations see PARA 21.

2   As to the meaning of 'authorised officer' see PARA 19 note 9.

3   Plant Varieties and Seeds Act 1964 s 24(5). As to seeds regulations see PARA 15. Note that these provisions apply also in connection with the marketing of seed potatoes (see PARAS 15 note 3, 35).

4   Plant Varieties and Seeds Act 1964 s 26(5).

5   See PARA 23. As to the meaning of 'seeds' see PARA 15 note 3.

23. Evidential value of test certificates.

A certificate of the result of a test of a sample[1] carried out at an official seed testing station[2] which purports to be issued by an officer of such a testing station may be given in evidence in proceedings[3]. Where such a certificate is admitted for the purposes of proceedings on a contract for the sale of seeds[4], it is sufficient evidence of the facts stated in it for the purposes of those proceedings[5]. Where such a certificate is admitted as evidence in proceedings for an offence, it will be sufficient evidence provided the sample to which it relates was taken by an authorised officer[6] and a copy has been served on the accused with the summons[7]. The certificate will not, however, be sufficient evidence if either party to the proceedings requires that the person under whose direction the test was made be called as a witness[8].

1   Ie a sample taken for the purposes of the Plant Varieties and Seeds Act 1964 Pt II (ss 16–31) (see PARA 19).

2   As to the meaning of 'official testing station' see PARA 15 note 12; and as to official testing stations see PARA 21.

3   Ie proceedings under the Plant Varieties and Seeds Act 1964 Pt II.

4   Ie if the sample was taken by a person other than an authorised officer in order to obtain the test for the purposes of the Plant Varieties and Seeds Act 1964 s 17(3) (see PARA 16). As to the meaning of 'seeds' see PARA 15 note 3.

5   Plant Varieties and Seeds Act 1964 s 24(6)(b).

6   As to the meaning of 'authorised officer' see PARA 19 note 9.

7   Plant Varieties and Seeds Act 1964 s 24(6)(a). In any proceedings for an offence in respect of seeds which have been sampled by an authorised officer, the summons must not be made returnable less than 14 days from the day on which the summons is served, and a copy of any certificate of an official testing station which the prosecutor intends to adduce as evidence must be served with the summons: s 26(6).

8   Plant Varieties and Seeds Act 1964 s 24(6). In any proceedings for an offence in which a copy of a certificate of the result of a test has been served with the summons (see PARA 24), the accused, unless the court otherwise directs, is not to be entitled to require that the person under whose direction the test was made be called as a witness unless he has, at least three clear days before the day on which the summons is returnable, given notice to the prosecutor that he intends to do so: s 24(7).

24. Instituting proceedings.

Proceedings for contravening a provision contained in seeds regulations[1] may be brought at any time not more than one year from the time when the contravention occurred[2].

Where a part of a sample of seeds[3] has been tested at an official testing station[4], proceedings for including in a statutory statement[5] false particulars concerning the matters which under seeds regulations must be ascertained for the purposes of the statement by a test of the seeds[6] may be brought at any time not more than six months from the time when the sample was taken[7]. Moreover, if at any time before a test is begun at an official testing station to ascertain whether a part of a sample of seeds is of a specified variety or type, and not more than six months after the sample was taken, the person to whom any other part of the sample was given, or any other person, is notified[8] in writing by an authorised officer[9] that it is intended so to test the seeds and that, after the test, proceedings may be brought against that person for including in a statutory statement a false statement that seeds were of a specified variety or type, then any such proceedings relating to the seeds from which the sample was taken may be brought against the person so notified at any time not more than two years from the time when the sample was taken[10].

Proceedings for an offence relating to a statutory statement which has been delivered to a purchaser of seeds, or relating to seeds which have been sold and delivered to the purchaser, may be brought before a court having jurisdiction at the place of delivery of the statement or seeds[11].

1   As to seeds regulations see PARA 15. Note that these provisions apply also in connection with the marketing of seed potatoes (see PARAS 15 note 3, 35).

2   Plant Varieties and Seeds Act 1964 s 28(2A) (added by the Plant Varieties Act 1997 s 47). The Plant Varieties and Seeds Act 1964 s 28(1), (2), (2A) have effect notwithstanding the general time limit for proceedings laid down by the Magistrates' Courts Act 1980 s 127 (see MAGISTRATES vol 71 (2013) PARA 526): Plant Varieties and Seeds Act 1964 s 28(1), (2) (amended by the Magistrates' Courts Act 1980 Sch 7 para 44); Plant Varieties and Seeds Act 1964 s 28(2A) (as so added). As to the taking of samples see PARA 19.

3   As to the meaning of 'seeds' see PARA 15 note 3.

4   As to the meaning of 'official testing station' see PARA 15 note 12; and as to official testing stations see PARA 21.

5   As to statutory statements see PARA 16.

6   See PARA 16.

7   Plant Varieties and Seeds Act 1964 s 28(1) (as amended: see note 2). Section 28(1) has effect notwithstanding the Magistrates' Courts Act 1980 s 127: see note 2.

8   A certificate issued by an authorised officer stating that a person was so notified is sufficient evidence of that fact: Plant Varieties and Seeds Act 1964 s 28(2).

9   As to the meaning of 'authorised officer' see PARA 19 note 9.

10   Plant Varieties and Seeds Act 1964 s 28(2) (as amended: see note 2). Section 28(2) has effect notwithstanding the Magistrates' Courts Act 1980 s 127: see note 2.

11 Plant Varieties and Seeds Act 1964 s 28(3). Without prejudice to the jurisdiction in relation to such offences, proceedings for any offence punishable under the Plant Varieties and Seeds Act 1964 may be taken against a person before the appropriate court in Great Britain having jurisdiction in the place where that person is for the time being: s 35(2). As to Great Britain see PARA 1 note 1.

(2) PLANT PROPAGATING MATERIAL

(i) Vegetable and Fruit Plant Material

25. Regulations controlling sale and marketing of vegetable and fruit plant material.

The sale and marketing[1] of vegetable plant material[2] and fruit plant material[3] is controlled by regulations, which apply to all plant material of specified genera and species and their hybrids[4], and to rootstocks and other parts of plants of other genera or species and their hybrids if plant material of such a specified genus or species or of a hybrid of such a genus or species is (or is to be) grafted on to them[5].

Inspectors[6] are provided with certain powers to enforce provisions regulating the marketing of vegetable and fruit plant propagating material[7].

1 'Marketing' means the delivery, offer for sale, exposure for sale, sale and possession with a view to sale of plant material; and 'market' and 'marketed' are to be construed accordingly: Marketing of Vegetable Plant Material Regulations 1995, SI 1995/2652, reg 2(1).
2 For these purposes 'vegetable plant material' means parts of plants and all vegetative material, including rootstocks, or entire plants (including the grafted components of grafted plants), intended for the production of vegetables, other than seeds: Marketing of Vegetable Plant Material Regulations 1995, SI 1995/2652, reg 2(1).
3 'Fruit plant' means a plant intended to be planted or replanted, after marketing: Marketing of Fruit Plant and Propagating Material (England) Regulations 2017, SI 2017/595, reg 2; Marketing of Fruit Plant and Propagating Material (Wales) Regulations 2017, SI 2017/691, reg 2.
4 Marketing of Vegetable Plant Material Regulations 1995, SI 1995/2652, reg 3(1)(a) (amended in relation to England by SI 2014/487 and in relation to Wales by SI 2014/519); Marketing of Fruit Plant and Propagating Material (England) Regulations 2017, SI 2017/595, reg 4(1), (2); Marketing of Fruit Plant and Propagating Material (Wales) Regulations 2017, SI 2017/691, reg 4(1), (2). The genera and species of vegetable plant material to which the Marketing of Vegetable Plant Material Regulations 1995, SI 1995/2652 apply are set out in Council Directive (EC) 2008/72 (OJ L205, 1.8.08, p 28) on the marketing of vegetable propagating and planting material, other than seed, Annex II: Marketing of Vegetable Plant Material Regulations 1995, SI 1995/2652, reg 3(1)(a) (as so amended). The genera and species of fruit plant material to which the Marketing of Fruit Plant and Propagating Material (England) Regulations 2017, SI 2017/595, reg 4(1) and the Marketing of Fruit Plant and Propagating Material (Wales) Regulations 2017, SI 2017/691 apply are set out in Sch 3 of the relevant regulations: Marketing of Fruit Plant and Propagating Material (England) Regulations 2017, SI 2017/595, reg 4(1), (2); Marketing of Fruit Plant and Propagating Material (Wales) Regulations 2017, SI 2017/691, reg 4(1).
5 Marketing of Vegetable Plant Material Regulations 1995, SI 1995/2652, reg 3(1)(b) (as amended: see note 3); Marketing of Fruit Plant and Propagating Material (England) Regulations 2017, SI 2017/595, regs 2(1), 4(1), (2); Marketing of Fruit Plant and Propagating Material (Wales) Regulations 2017, SI 2017/691, reg 2(1), 4(1), (2).
6 For the purposes of the Marketing of Vegetable Plant Material Regulations 1995, SI 1995/2652 and the Marketing of Ornamental Plant Propagating Material Regulations 1999, SI 1999/1801 (as the case may be) an inspector is any person authorised by the Secretary of State or the Welsh Ministers to be an inspector for the purposes of that provision (Marketing of Vegetable Plant Material Regulations 1995, SI 1995/2652, reg 2(1); Marketing of Ornamental Plant Propagating Material Regulations 1999, SI 1999/1801, reg 2(1)); and for the purposes of the Marketing of Fruit Plant and Propagating Material (England) Regulations 2017, SI 2017/595 an inspector is a person appointed under the Marketing of Fruit Plant and Propagating Material (England) Regulations 2017, SI 2017/595, reg 16 or the Marketing of Fruit Plant and Propagating Material (Wales) Regulations 2017, SI 2017/691, reg 16 (as the case may be) (Marketing of Fruit Plant and

Propagating Material (England) Regulations 2017, SI 2017/595, reg 2; Marketing of Fruit Plant and Propagating Material (Wales) Regulations 2017, SI 2017/691, reg 2). As to the Secretary of State and the Welsh Ministers see PARA 390.

7   See the Marketing of Vegetable Plant Material Regulations 1995, SI 1995/2652, reg 11; the Marketing of Fruit Plant and Propagating Material (England) Regulations 2017, SI 2017/595, regs 16–21; and the Marketing of Fruit Plant and Propagating Material (Wales) Regulations 2017, SI 2017/691, regs 16–21. A person who contravenes or fails to comply with any of the Marketing of Vegetable Plant Material Regulations 1995, SI 1995/2652.commits an offence unless he can prove that he had reasonable excuse for the contravention: 13(1). The offence is punishable on summary conviction by a fine not exceeding level 3 on the standard scale: 13(2). As to the standard scale and the powers of magistrates' courts to issue fines on summary conviction see SENTENCING vol 92 (2015) PARA 176. As to offences under the Marketing of Fruit Plant and Propagating Material (England) Regulations 2017, SI 2017/595, and the Marketing of Fruit Plant and Propagating Material (Wales) Regulations 2017, SI 2017/691: see the Marketing of Fruit Plant and Propagating Material (England) Regulations 2017, SI 2017/595, regs 24, 25; and the Marketing of Fruit Plant and Propagating Material (Wales) Regulations 2017, SI 2017/691, regs 24, 25.

(ii) Ornamental Plant Material

A. REGULATION OF SALE AND MARKETING OF ORNAMENTAL PLANT MATERIAL

26. Regulations controlling sale and marketing of plant material for propagation or production of ornamental plants.
The marketing[1] of plant material intended for the propagation[2] or production of ornamental plants[3] is controlled by regulations with which all suppliers[4] are required to comply[5]. The regulations provide for the registration of suppliers[6], make provision for the marketing of propagating material by reference to its variety[7], require such material to be marketed in lots[8], prohibit the marketing of unhealthy or inferior material[9], require suppliers to maintain the standards of material[10], control the importation of propagating material from third countries[11], and make provision as to the information accompanying marketed material[12] and record-keeping[13]. The regulations do not, however, apply to material intended for export to third countries[14], for trials or scientific purposes[15], for selection work[16], or for use in the conservation of genetic diversity[17].

A person who contravenes or fails to comply with provisions regulating the marketing of ornamental plant propagating material commits an offence unless he can prove that he had reasonable excuse for the contravention[18].

Inspectors[19] are provided with certain powers to enforce provisions regulating the marketing of ornamental plant propagating material[20].

1   For these purposes 'marketing' means holding available or in stock, displaying with a view to sale, offering for sale, sale or delivery by a supplier to another person: see the Marketing of Ornamental Plant Propagating Material Regulations 1999, SI 1999/1801, reg 2(1).
2   Ie reproduction by vegetative or other means: Marketing of Ornamental Plant Propagating Material Regulations 1999, SI 1999/1801, reg 2(1).
3   Ie 'propagating material'. In the case of production from complete plants, the material used is considered to be propagating material for these purposes only if the resulting ornamental plant is intended for further marketing: Marketing of Ornamental Plant Propagating Material Regulations 1999, SI 1999/1801, reg 2(1).
4   'Supplier' means any person professionally engaged in the marketing or in the importation from third countries of propagating material: Marketing of Ornamental Plant Propagating Material Regulations 1999, SI 1999/1801, reg 2(1). 'Third country' means a country other than a member state: reg 2(1).
5   Marketing of Ornamental Plant Propagating Material Regulations 1999, SI 1999/1801, reg 3(1).
6   See PARA 27.
7   See PARA 28.
8   See PARA 29.

9 See PARA 30.
10 See PARA 31.
11 See PARA 32.
12 See PARA 33.
13 See PARA 34.
14 Marketing of Ornamental Plant Propagating Material Regulations 1999, SI 1999/1801, reg 3(2)(a). To qualify for this exemption material must be identified as intended for export to a third country and must be kept sufficiently isolated from plant material not intended for such export: reg 3(2)(a).
15 Marketing of Ornamental Plant Propagating Material Regulations 1999, SI 1999/1801, reg 3(2)(b).
16 Marketing of Ornamental Plant Propagating Material Regulations 1999, SI 1999/1801, reg 3(2)(c).
17 Marketing of Ornamental Plant Propagating Material Regulations 1999, SI 1999/1801, reg 3(2)(d).
18 See the Marketing of Ornamental Plant Propagating Material Regulations 1999, SI 1999/1801, reg 15.
19 As to the meaning of 'inspector' see PARA 47 note 6.
20 See the Marketing of Ornamental Plant Propagating Material Regulations 1999, SI 1999/1801, reg 13.

27. Registration of suppliers.

Other than in the case of a supplier[1] marketing[2] ornamental plants or propagating material[3] only to persons who are not professionally engaged in the production or sale of such material[4], it is prohibited, and is an offence[5], for any person to carry on business as a supplier of ornamental plant material unless he is registered as such by the Secretary of State or the Welsh Ministers[6]. Suppliers may register under the provisions governing the marketing of ornamental plant propagating material[7], although registration under the legislation controlling the introduction and spreading of pests[8] is also deemed to constitute registration for these purposes[9].

1 As to the meaning of 'supplier' see PARA 26 note 4.
2 As to the meaning of 'marketing' see PARA 26 note 1.
3 As to the meaning of 'propagating material' see PARA 26 note 3; and as to the scope of the Marketing of Ornamental Plant Propagating Material Regulations 1999, SI 1999/1801, see PARA 26.
4 Marketing of Ornamental Plant Propagating Material Regulations 1999, SI 1999/1801, reg 7(2).
5 See the Marketing of Ornamental Plant Propagating Material Regulations 1999, SI 1999/1801, reg 15(1); and PARA 26.
6 Marketing of Ornamental Plant Propagating Material Regulations 1999, SI 1999/1801, reg 7(1). As to the Secretary of State and the Welsh Ministers see PARA 390.
7 Ie under the Marketing of Ornamental Plant Propagating Material Regulations 1999, SI 1999/1801. Applications for registration must be made in writing and be accompanied by the name of the applicant (reg 7(3)(a)), the address of the main premises at which the applicant carries on or intends to carry on business as a supplier (reg 7(3)(b)), and the activities which the applicant carries on or intends to carry on which are or will be covered by the Marketing of Ornamental Plant Propagating Material Regulations 1999, SI 1999/1801 (reg 7(3)(c)).
8 Ie the Plant Health (England) Order 2015, SI 2015/610 and the Plant Health (Wales) Order 2006, SI 2006/1643 (see PARAS 112–113).
9 Marketing of Ornamental Plant Propagating Material Regulations 1999, SI 1999/1801, reg 7(4).

B. DUTIES OF SUPPLIERS

28. Marketing of propagating material.

It is prohibited, and is an offence[1], for any supplier[2] to market[3] propagating material[4] with reference to a variety[5] unless the material is the subject of Community or national plant variety rights[6], or the existence of that variety is a matter of common knowledge[7], or the variety is entered on a list kept by a supplier[8]. Where a supplier markets propagating material with reference to the group of plants to which it belongs, the supplier must indicate the group of plants in such a way as to avoid confusion with any varietal denomination[9], and commits an offence if he fails so to do[10].

1   See the Marketing of Ornamental Plant Propagating Material Regulations 1999, SI 1999/1801, reg 15(1); and PARA 26.
2   As to the meaning of 'supplier' see PARA 26 note 4.
3   As to the meaning of 'market' see PARA 26 note 1.
4   As to the meaning of 'propagating material' see PARA 26 note 3; and as to the scope of the Marketing of Ornamental Plant Propagating Material Regulations 1999, SI 1999/1801, see PARA 26.
5   Where propagating material is marketed with reference to a variety it must have satisfactory varietal identity and purity: see the Marketing of Ornamental Plant Propagating Material Regulations 1999, SI 1999/1801, reg 4(e); and PARA 30.
6   Marketing of Ornamental Plant Propagating Material Regulations 1999, SI 1999/1801, reg 11(1)(a). The reference in the text to Community plant variety rights is a reference to Community plant variety rights pursuant to Council Regulation (EC) 2100/94 (OJ L227, 1.9.99, p 1) on Community plant variety rights, and the reference to national plant variety rights is a reference to plant variety rights under any jurisdiction: Marketing of Ornamental Plant Propagating Material Regulations 1999, SI 1999/1801, reg 11(1)(a). As to Council Regulation (EC) 2100/94 (OJ L227, 1.9.99, p 1), plant breeders' rights and plant variety rights generally see PARAS 239–264.
7   Marketing of Ornamental Plant Propagating Material Regulations 1999, SI 1999/1801, reg 11(1)(b). As to the meaning of 'common knowledge' see the Plant Varieties Act 1997 s 38(3), (4); and PARA 239 note 21.
8   Marketing of Ornamental Plant Propagating Material Regulations 1999, SI 1999/1801, reg 11(1)(c). Such a list must be made available to the Secretary of State or the Welsh Ministers on request (reg 11(3)), and must include:
    (1)   the name of the variety together with its commonly known synonyms, where appropriate (reg 11(1)(c)(i));
    (2)   a description of the variety (which must include, where appropriate, the characteristics of the variety which would be relevant for the purpose of an application for a Community plant variety right in respect of the variety under Council Regulation (EC) 2100/94 (OJ L227, 1.9.99, p 1)) (Marketing of Ornamental Plant Propagating Material Regulations 1999, SI 1999/1801, reg 11(1)(c)(iii)); and
    (3)   except where the supplier is engaged only in the marketing of plant material, information as to how the varietal identity and purity of the variety is being maintained and as to the propagation system used and an explanation of how the variety differs from other varieties most closely resembling it (reg 11(1)(c)(ii), (iv), (2)).
    As to the Secretary of State and the Welsh Ministers see PARA 390.
9   Marketing of Ornamental Plant Propagating Material Regulations 1999, SI 1999/1801, reg 11(4).
10   See the Marketing of Ornamental Plant Propagating Material Regulations 1999, SI 1999/1801, reg 15(1); and PARA 26.

29.   Propagating material to be marketed in lots.

Other than in the case of a supplier[1] marketing[2] propagating material[3] only to persons who are not professionally engaged in the production or sale of ornamental plants or propagating material[4], it is prohibited, and is an offence[5], for any supplier to market propagating material other than in lots[6], although the sale of different lots in a single consignment is permitted provided the supplier keeps appropriate records[7].

1   As to the meaning of 'supplier' see PARA 26 note 4.
2   As to the meaning of 'marketing' see PARA 26 note 1.
3   As to the meaning of 'propagating material' see PARA 26 note 3; and as to the scope of the Marketing of Ornamental Plant Propagating Material Regulations 1999, SI 1999/1801, see PARA 26.
4   Marketing of Ornamental Plant Propagating Material Regulations 1999, SI 1999/1801, reg 10(2)(b).

5   See the Marketing of Ornamental Plant Propagating Material Regulations 1999, SI 1999/1801, reg 15(1); and PARA **26**.
6   Marketing of Ornamental Plant Propagating Material Regulations 1999, SI 1999/1801, reg 10(1). 'Lot' means a number of units of a single commodity, identifiable by its homogeneity of composition and origin: reg 2(1).
7   Marketing of Ornamental Plant Propagating Material Regulations 1999, SI 1999/1801, reg 10(2)(a). Such records must record the composition and origin of the different lots: reg 10(2)(a). As to the keeping of records generally see PARA **34**.

30. Duty not to market unhealthy or inferior material.

When marketed[1], propagating material[2] must:

(1)   be substantially free from any defects likely to impair its quality as propagating material and in particular, at least on visual inspection, be substantially free from any harmful organisms impairing quality, or any signs or symptoms of such organisms, which reduce its usefulness[3];

(2)   have satisfactory vigour and dimensions in respect of its usefulness as propagating material[4];

(3)   in the case of seeds, have a satisfactory germination capacity[5];

(4)   have satisfactory identity and purity relative to the genus or species or group of plants to which it belongs[6]; and

(5)   if marketed with reference to a variety[7], have satisfactory varietal identity and purity[8].

Failure to comply with any of these requirements is an offence[9].

1   As to the meaning of 'marketed' see PARA **26** note 1.
2   As to the meaning of 'propagating material' see PARA **26** note 3; and as to the scope of the Marketing of Ornamental Plant Propagating Material Regulations 1999, SI 1999/1801, see PARA **26**.
3   Marketing of Ornamental Plant Propagating Material Regulations 1999, SI 1999/1801, reg 4(a). Additional requirements are imposed in connection with the marketing of flower bulbs and citrus propagating material: flower bulbs are required to have been derived directly from material which, at the time the crop of bulbs concerned was growing, was checked and found to be substantially free from any harmful organisms and diseases or any signs or symptoms of such organisms and diseases (reg 6); and citrus propagating material must have been derived from initial source material which has been checked and found to show no symptoms of any viruses, virus-like organisms or diseases (reg 5(a)), must have been checked and found to be substantially free of such viruses, organisms and diseases since the beginning of the last cycle of vegetative growth (reg 5(b)) and, where grafting has taken place, must have been grafted on to rootstocks of a kind which are not susceptible to viroids (reg 5(c)). Suppliers are required to treat or, where appropriate, remove any propagating material which, on the basis of visible signs or symptoms, is not substantially free of harmful organisms impairing quality: see reg 8(2); and PARA **31**.
4   Marketing of Ornamental Plant Propagating Material Regulations 1999, SI 1999/1801, reg 4(b).
5   Marketing of Ornamental Plant Propagating Material Regulations 1999, SI 1999/1801, reg 4(c).
6   Marketing of Ornamental Plant Propagating Material Regulations 1999, SI 1999/1801, reg 4(d).
7   Ie pursuant to the Marketing of Ornamental Plant Propagating Material Regulations 1999, SI 1999/1801, reg 11 (see PARA **28**).
8   Marketing of Ornamental Plant Propagating Material Regulations 1999, SI 1999/1801, reg 4(e).
9   See the Marketing of Ornamental Plant Propagating Material Regulations 1999, SI 1999/1801, reg 15(1); and PARA **26**.

31. Maintenance of standards of material.

Suppliers[1] engaged in the production of propagating material[2] must identify and monitor critical points in their production process which influence the quality of the material[3], take samples where necessary and send them to be analysed in a laboratory with suitable facilities and expertise[4], and ensure that lots[5] of propagating material remain separately identifiable during production[6]. If a supplier engaged in the production of propagating material finds a notifiable plant pest[7] on his premises he must, if he would not otherwise be required to notify it[8], report it to the Secretary of State and the Welsh Ministers[9] and carry out any measures laid down by him or them[10]. Without prejudice to this, suppliers are generally required to treat or, where appropriate, remove any propagating material which, on the basis of visible signs or symptoms, is not substantially free of harmful organisms impairing quality[11]. Failure to comply with any of these requirements is an offence[12].

1   As to the meaning of 'supplier' see PARA 26 note 4.
2   As to the meaning of 'propagating material' see PARA 26 note 3; and as to the scope of the Marketing of Ornamental Plant Propagating Material Regulations 1999, SI 1999/1801, see PARA 26.
3   Marketing of Ornamental Plant Propagating Material Regulations 1999, SI 1999/1801, reg 8(1)(a). Such monitoring must be recorded: see reg 8(1)(b); and PARA 34.
4   Marketing of Ornamental Plant Propagating Material Regulations 1999, SI 1999/1801, reg 8(1)(b).
5   As to the meaning of 'lot' see PARA 29 note 6. Subject to specified exemptions, propagating material be marketed only in lots: see the Marketing of Ornamental Plant Propagating Material Regulations 1999, SI 1999/1801, reg 10; and PARA 29.
6   Marketing of Ornamental Plant Propagating Material Regulations 1999, SI 1999/1801, reg 8(1)(c).
7   See the Plant Health (England) Order 2015, SI 2015/610, art 42; and the Plant Health (Wales) Order 2006, SI 2006/1643, art 42. See further PARAS 112–113.
8   Ie under the provisions referred to in note 7.
9   As to the Secretary of State and the Welsh Ministers see PARA 390.
10   Marketing of Ornamental Plant Propagating Material Regulations 1999, SI 1999/1801, reg 8(3).
11   Marketing of Ornamental Plant Propagating Material Regulations 1999, SI 1999/1801, reg 8(2). Suppliers are required not to market such material: see PARA 30.
12   See the Marketing of Ornamental Plant Propagating Material Regulations 1999, SI 1999/1801, reg 15(1); and PARA 26.

32. Importation of propagating material.

It is prohibited, and is an offence[1], for any supplier[2] to import propagating material[3] from a third country[4] unless he has ensured prior to its import that the material to be imported is of an equivalent standard to propagating material produced in accordance with the regulatory provisions applicable to member states[5]. Suppliers who import a consignment of propagating material from a third country must give the Secretary of State or the Welsh Ministers[6] written notification of the importation within one month of it[7], and keep the necessary records[8].

1   See the Marketing of Ornamental Plant Propagating Material Regulations 1999, SI 1999/1801, reg 15(1); and PARA 26.
2   As to the meaning of 'supplier' see PARA 26 note 4.
3   As to the meaning of 'propagating material' see PARA 26 note 3; and as to the scope of the Marketing of Ornamental Plant Propagating Material Regulations 1999, SI 1999/1801, see PARA 26.
4   As to the meaning of 'third country' see PARA 26 note 4.
5   Marketing of Ornamental Plant Propagating Material Regulations 1999, SI 1999/1801, reg 12(1). The reference in the text to propagating material produced in accordance with the regulatory provisions applicable to member states is a reference to material produced in accordance with Council Directive (EC) 1998/56 (OJ L226, 13.8.98, p 16) on the marketing of propagating material of ornamental plants: Marketing of Ornamental Plant Propagating Material Regulations 1999, SI 1999/1801, reg 12(1).
6   As to the Secretary of State and the Welsh Ministers see PARA 390.
7   Marketing of Ornamental Plant Propagating Material Regulations 1999, SI 1999/1801, reg 12(2). A supplier is deemed to have complied with these requirements if he delivers a phytosanitary certificate or reforwarding phytosanitary certificate in respect of the consignment in accordance

with the Plant Health (England) Order 2015, SI 2015/610, art 15 or the Plant Health (Wales) Order 2006, SI 2006/1643, art 15: Marketing of Ornamental Plant Propagating Material Regulations 1999, SI 1999/1801, reg 12(3).

8 Marketing of Ornamental Plant Propagating Material Regulations 1999, SI 1999/1801, reg 12(4). As to the records required to be kept see PARA 34.

33. Information to accompany marketed material.

Other than in the case of propagating material[1] which is marketed[2] to persons who are not professionally engaged in the production or sale of ornamental plants or propagating material[3], no supplier[4] may market any propagating material unless it is accompanied by a label or other document made out by him on which specified information appears[5]. Where propagating material is accompanied by a plant passport[6], the plant passport may constitute the label or other document for these purposes provided it contains the specified information[7]. Failure to comply with these requirements, and the marketing of plant material in contravention thereof, is an offence[8].

1 As to the meaning of 'propagating material' see PARA 26 note 3; and as to the scope of the Marketing of Ornamental Plant Propagating Material Regulations 1999, SI 1999/1801, see PARA 26.
2 As to the meaning of 'marketed' see PARA 26 note 1.
3 Marketing of Ornamental Plant Propagating Material Regulations 1999, SI 1999/1801, reg 9(3).
4 As to the meaning of 'supplier' see PARA 26 note 4.
5 Marketing of Ornamental Plant Propagating Material Regulations 1999, SI 1999/1801, reg 9(1). The following information must appear on the supplier's document: indication that the material is 'EC quality'; indication of EC member state code; indication of responsible official body (ie the Secretary of State or the Welsh Ministers) or its distinguishing code; supplier's registration number; individual serial, week or batch number; botanical name; denomination of the variety or, in the case of rootstock, denomination of the variety or its designation (where appropriate); denomination of the group of plants (where appropriate); quantity; and, in the case of propagating material imported from a third country (see PARA 32), the name of the country of production: reg 9(1), Schedule.
6 The Marketing of Ornamental Plant Propagating Material Regulations 1999, SI 1999/1801, reg 9(2) defines a 'plant passport' for this purpose as a plant passport issued in accordance with Council Directive (EC) 1977/93 (OJ L026, 31.10.77, p 20) on protective measures against the introduction into the member states of harmful organisms of plants or plant products: however, that Directive has been revoked and replaced by Council Directive (EC) 2000/29 (OJ L169, 10.7.2000, p 1) on protective measures against the introduction into the member states of harmful organisms of plants or plant products, and it is accordingly submitted that that is the Directive to which reference is made for these purposes. With effect from 14 December 2019 European Parliament and Council Directive (EC) 2000/29 (OJ L169, 10.7.2000, p 1) is revoked and replaced by European Parliament and Council Regulation (EU) 2016/2031 (OJ L317, 23.11.2016, p 4) on protective measures against pests of plants.
7 Marketing of Ornamental Plant Propagating Material Regulations 1999, SI 1999/1801, reg 9(2). As to the specified information see note 5.
8 See the Marketing of Ornamental Plant Propagating Material Regulations 1999, SI 1999/1801, reg 15(1); and PARA 26.

34. Record-keeping.

A registered supplier[1] must keep, and retain for a period of not less than 12 months, records of his sales and purchases of propagating material[2]. Suppliers are also required to keep records of their production process monitoring[3] and, where they sell different lots[4] in a single consignment and thereby benefit from the exemption from the requirement that propagating material may be marketed only in lots[5], to keep records of the composition and origin of the different lots[6]. Suppliers must also retain documentary evidence of every contract relating to the import of propagating material from a third country[7] during the subsistence of the contract and for at least 12 months after its termination[8]. Failure to comply with any of these requirements is an offence[9].

1 Ie a supplier registered in accordance with the Marketing of Ornamental Plant Propagating Material Regulations 1999, SI 1999/1801, reg 7: reg 7(5). As to registration see PARA 27. As to the meaning of 'supplier' see PARA 26 note 4.
2 Marketing of Ornamental Plant Propagating Material Regulations 1999, SI 1999/1801, reg 7(5). As to the meaning of 'propagating material' see PARA 26 note 3; and as to the scope of the Marketing of Ornamental Plant Propagating Material Regulations 1999, SI 1999/1801, see PARA 26.
3 Marketing of Ornamental Plant Propagating Material Regulations 1999, SI 1999/1801, reg 8(1)(b). For a supplier's duty to monitor his production process see PARA 31.
4 As to the meaning of 'lot' see PARA 29 note 6.
5 As to this requirement, and the exemption, see PARA 29.
6 Marketing of Ornamental Plant Propagating Material Regulations 1999, SI 1999/1801, reg 10(2)(a).
7 As to the importation of propagating material from third countries see PARA 32.
8 Marketing of Ornamental Plant Propagating Material Regulations 1999, SI 1999/1801, reg 12(4).
9 See the Marketing of Ornamental Plant Propagating Material Regulations 1999, SI 1999/1801, reg 15(1); and PARA 26.

(3) SEED POTATOES

35. Marketing of seed potatoes.

The only seed potatoes[1] which may be marketed[2] in England and Wales are pre-basic seed potatoes, basic seed potatoes, certified seed potatoes, scientific and selection seed potatoes or test and trial seed potatoes[3]. No person may market any such potatoes which have been treated with a product which is produced primarily as an application for inhibiting germination[4].

There are restrictions on marketing and producing potatoes of a conservation variety[5] with stringent requirements applying to the marketing of seed potatoes in the county of Cumbria (excluding the districts of Barrow-in-Furness and South Lakeland) and the county of Northumberland (excluding the districts of Blyth Valley and Wansbeck)[6]. Seed potatoes cannot be marketed unless they comply with specified size requirements[7].

The Secretary of State and the Welsh Ministers may authorise the marketing of small quantities of seed potatoes for scientific purposes or selection work and seed potatoes for test and trial purposes[8].

Seed potatoes (other than retail sales of small quantities of seed potatoes meeting certain conditions) may only be marketed in properly sealed and labelled packages or containers[9] with specific provision made for the identification of genetically modified seed potatoes[10].

There are requirements for any person marketing more than two kilograms of seed potatoes that have been imported into England or Wales from a country outside the European Union to notify the Secretary of State or the Welsh Ministers, as appropriate[11].

1 'Seed potatoes' means:
   (1) potatoes which bear that description or any description indicating their suitability for planting and propagation and which are capable of being used for planting and propagation; or
   (2) any potatoes that are intended to be used for planting and propagation: Seed Potatoes (England) Regulations 2015, SI 2015/1953, reg 2(1); Seed Potatoes (Wales) Regulations 2016, SI 2016/106, reg 2(1).

'Potato' means any tuber or part thereof or any plant or part thereof of *Solanum tuberosum L* or other tuber-forming species or hybrids of *Solanum*: Seed Potatoes (England) Regulations 2015, SI 2015/1953, reg 2(1); Seed Potatoes (Wales) Regulations 2016, SI 2016/106, reg 2(1).

2 'Marketing' means selling, holding with a view to sale and offering for sale, and any disposal, supply or transfer for the purpose of commercial exploitation of seed potatoes to third parties, whether or not for consideration and for these purposes 'commercial exploitation' is not to be taken to include the supply of seed potatoes to official testing and inspection bodies, or the supply of seed potatoes to any person for the purpose of processing or packaging them provided that person does not acquire title to the seed potatoes supplied, and 'market' and 'marketed' are to be construed accordingly: Seed Potatoes (England) Regulations 2015, SI 2015/1953, reg 2(1); Seed Potatoes (Wales) Regulations 2016, SI 2016/106, reg 2(1)).

3 Seed Potatoes (England) Regulations 2015, SI 2015/1953, reg 4(1)(a)–(e); Seed Potatoes (Wales) Regulations 2016, SI 2016/106, reg 5(1)(a)–(e). As to the meanings of 'pre-basic seed potatoes', 'basic seed potatoes', 'certified seed potatoes' and 'test and trial seed potatoes' see the Seed Potatoes (England) Regulations 2015, SI 2015/1953, reg 2(1); and the Seed Potatoes (Wales) Regulations 2016, SI 2016/106, reg 2(1). As to the meaning of 'scientific and selection seed potatoes' see the Seed Potatoes (England) Regulations 2015, SI 2015/1953, reg 4(3); and the Seed Potatoes (Wales) Regulations 2016, SI 2016/106, reg 5(3)).

4 See the Seed Potatoes (England) Regulations 2015, SI 2015/1953, reg 4(2); and the Seed Potatoes (Wales) Regulations 2016, SI 2016/106, reg 5(2).

5 Seed Potatoes (England) Regulations 2015, SI 2015/1953, reg 5; Seed Potatoes (Wales) Regulations 2016, SI 2016/106, reg 6.

6 See the Seed Potatoes (England) Regulations 2015, SI 2015/1953, reg 6.

7 See the Seed Potatoes (England) Regulations 2015, SI 2015/1953, reg 7; and the Seed Potatoes (Wales) Regulations 2016, SI 2016/106, reg 7.

8 See the Seed Potatoes (England) Regulations 2015, SI 2015/1953, regs 8, 9; and the Seed Potatoes (Wales) Regulations 2016, SI 2016/106, regs 8, 9.

9 See the Seed Potatoes (England) Regulations 2015, SI 2015/1953, regs 12–14; and the Seed Potatoes (Wales) Regulations 2016, SI 2016/106, regs 12–14.

10 See the Seed Potatoes (England) Regulations 2015, SI 2015/1953, reg 15; and the Seed Potatoes (Wales) Regulations 2016, SI 2016/106, reg 15.

11 See the Seed Potatoes (England) Regulations 2015, SI 2015/1953, reg 16; and the Seed Potatoes (Wales) Regulations 2016, SI 2016/106, reg 16.

(4) HEMP

36. Importation of hemp.

Provision is made for controlling the importation from third countries[1] of hemp, that is, one or more of true hemp[2], hemp seeds for sowing[3] and hemp seeds other than for sowing[4]. The importation from third countries of true hemp or hemp seeds for sowing is prohibited where the variety of hemp imported has a THC content[5] exceeding the permitted maximum[6]. Where third country importation of hemp is not so prohibited, it may be undertaken only under authority of a licence[7] and, in the case of hemp seeds other than for sowing, under an authorisation[8]. Consignments of imported hemp must also be accompanied by the relevant consignment documentation[9]. Failure to comply with these requirements (or supplementary requirements as to the provision of information[10], record-keeping[11] and powers of entry and inspection[12]) is an offence punishable by fine[13].

1 'Third country' means a country other than a member state of the European Union: Hemp (Third Country Imports) Regulations 2002, SI 2002/787, reg 2(1) (amended by SI 2011/1043).

2 'True hemp' means harvested plant material of the species *Cannabis sativa L* within the terms of Council Regulation (EC) 1673/2000 (OJ L193, 29.7.2000, p 16) on the common organisation of the markets in flax and hemp grown for fibre, art 5(2) (repealed), whether or not the leaves and seeds have been removed, which is either raw or retted (and 'retted' means a state where the fibres are still attached to the plant but have been loosened): Hemp (Third Country Imports) Regulations 2002, SI 2002/787, reg 2(1).

3 'Hemp seeds for sowing' means seeds of varieties within the terms of Council Regulation (EC) 1673/2000 (OJ L193, 29.7.2000, p 16) art 5(2) (second indent of the first sub-paragraph): Hemp (Third Country Imports) Regulations 2002, SI 2002/787, reg 2(1).

4 'Hemp seeds other than for sowing' means seeds of varieties within the terms of Council Regulation (EC) 1673/2000 (OJ L193, 29.7.2000, p 16) art 5(2) (third indent of the first sub-paragraph): Hemp (Third Country Imports) Regulations 2002, SI 2002/787, reg 2(1).

5 'THC content' means the tetrahydrocannabinol content of hemp, based on quantitative determination by gas chromatography after extraction with a suitable solvent: Hemp (Third Country Imports) Regulations 2002, SI 2002/787, reg 2(1).

6 Hemp (Third Country Imports) Regulations 2002, SI 2002/787, reg 3(c). The permitted maximum THC content is 0.2%: reg 3(c). See further reg 8.

7 Hemp (Third Country Imports) Regulations 2002, SI 2002/787, reg 3(a)(i). 'Licence' means a licence to import hemp from one or more third countries granted by the appropriate authority pursuant to Council Regulation (EC) 1673/2000 (OJ L193, 29.7.2000, p 16) art 5(2): Hemp (Third Country Imports) Regulations 2002, SI 2002/787, reg 2(1). The 'appropriate authority' means the Secretary of State and the Welsh Ministers: reg 2(1). As to the Secretary of State and the Welsh Ministers see PARA 390. As to applications for licences and their issue, use, granting, variation, suspension, revocation and scope see regs 4–7, 15 (reg 15 amended by SI 2002/1924).

8 Hemp (Third Country Imports) Regulations 2002, SI 2002/787, reg 3(a)(ii). 'Authorisation' means an authorisation granted by the appropriate authority pursuant to Council Regulation (EC) 1673/2000 (OJ L193, 29.7.2000, p 16) art 5(2) to import from third countries hemp seeds other than for sowing: Hemp (Third Country Imports) Regulations 2002, SI 2002/787, reg 2(1). As to authorisations, including their suspension and revocation, see further regs 11, 15 (amended by SI 2002/1924).

9 Hemp (Third Country Imports) Regulations 2002, SI 2002/787, reg 3(b). 'Relevant consignment documentation' means a licence permitting the import of the consignment in question by the importer concerned, or a copy of that licence; and, in the case of an import of hemp seeds other than for sowing, the authorisation granted to that importer, or a copy of that authorisation: reg 2(1). 'Import', when used as a noun, means an import into that part of the United Kingdom for which the appropriate authority concerned has responsibility under the Hemp (Third Country Imports) Regulations 2002, SI 2002/787: reg 2(1).

10 See the Hemp (Third Country Imports) Regulations 2002, SI 2002/787, reg 9.

11 See the Hemp (Third Country Imports) Regulations 2002, SI 2002/787, reg 10.

12 See the Hemp (Third Country Imports) Regulations 2002, SI 2002/787, regs 13, 14.

13 Hemp (Third Country Imports) Regulations 2002, SI 2002/787, reg 16. A person guilty of this offence is liable on summary conviction to a fine not exceeding level 3 on the standard scale unless the offence involved knowingly or recklessly making a statement or furnishing any information which is false or misleading in a material particular where the statement was made or the information furnished in purported compliance with any requirement imposed by reg 9 (provision of information) or any request made pursuant to reg 14 (assisting authorised persons), in which case the offence is punishable on summary conviction by a fine not exceeding level 5 on the standard scale: reg 17. As to the standard scale and the powers of magistrates' courts to issue fines on summary conviction see SENTENCING vol 92 (2015) PARA 176. Regulations 18, 19 make provision in connection with time limits for proceedings and the commission of offences by bodies corporate.

4. FERTILISERS AND FEEDING STUFFS

(1) REGULATION OF SALE AND MARKETING OF FERTILISERS AND FEEDING STUFFS

(i) Interpretation

37. 'Fertilisers' and 'feeding stuffs'.

For the purposes of the legislation governing transactions in fertilisers and feeding stuffs[1], 'fertiliser' means a fertiliser used for the cultivation of crops or plants of any description, including trees[2]; and 'feeding stuff' means material for oral feeding to pet animals[3] or farmed creatures[4], whether or not containing additives, which is either:

(1)   a product of vegetable or animal origin in its natural state (whether fresh or preserved)[5];

(2)   a product derived from the industrial processing of such a product[6]; or

(3)   an organic or inorganic substance, used singly or in a mixture[7].

1   Ie the Agriculture Act 1970 Pt IV (ss 66–87) (see PARA 40 et seq). As to the disapplication of Pt IV and the Fertilisers Regulations 1991, SI 1991/2197 to certain fertilisers see PARA 58 note 1. As to the modification of the Agriculture Act 1970 Pt IV with regard to sampling and analysis of feeding stuffs see the Feed (Sampling Analysis and Specified Undesirable Substances) (England) Regulations 2010, SI 2010/2280 and the Feed (Sampling Analysis and Specified Undesirable Substances) (Wales) Regulations 2010, SI 2010/2287.

2   Agriculture Act 1970 s 66(1).

3   'Animal' includes any bird, insect or fish (Agriculture Act 1970 s 66(1)); and 'pet animal' means an animal belonging to a species normally nourished and kept, but not consumed, by man, other than an animal bred for fur (s 66(1) (definition added by SI 1982/980; and substituted by SI 2005/3281 (in relation to England); SI 2006/116 (in relation to Wales)).

4   References in the Agriculture Act 1970 Pt IV to 'feeding stuffs' also apply to all material which is intended for the feeding of animals and with respect to which regulations under s 74A(1) (see PARA 45) apply: s 74A(2) (added by the European Communities Act 1972 Sch 4 para 6).

5   Agriculture Act 1970 s 66(1) (definition substituted by SI 2005/3281 (in relation to England); SI 2006/116 (in relation to Wales)).

6   Agriculture Act 1970 s 66(1) (as amended: see note 5).

7   Agriculture Act 1970 s 66(1) (as amended: see note 5).

38. 'Sale' and 'use'.

For the purposes of the legislation governing transactions in fertilisers and feeding stuffs[1], material is treated as sold for use as a fertiliser or feeding stuff whether it is sold to be so used by itself or as an ingredient in something which is to be so used[2].

The appropriation of any material by one person for use either in the performance for hire or reward of services to another person in pursuance of a contract in that behalf or under arrangements with another person not constituting a sale of the material to that other person, being arrangements which are intended to benefit both the person appropriating the material and that other person but under which the probability or extent of any benefit to that other person may be affected by the quality of the material, is treated as a sale of that material to that other person by the person so appropriating it[3].

1   Ie the Agriculture Act 1970 Pt IV (ss 66–87) (see PARA 40 et seq). As to the meanings of 'fertiliser' and 'feeding stuff' see PARA 37. As to the disapplication of Pt IV and the Fertilisers Regulations 1991, SI 1991/2197 to certain fertilisers see PARA 58 note 1.

2   Agriculture Act 1970 s 66(2) (s 66(2) substituted by SI 2010/2503 and SI 2010/2652).

3   Agriculture Act 1970 s 66(5). References to 'sale or purchase' and cognate expressions are to be construed accordingly: s 66(5).

39. Scope of legislation.

Provisions under the Agriculture Act 1970 that apply to transactions in fertilisers and feeding stuffs[1] apply to all sales[2] except:

(1)   the sale[3] of any material in the exercise of a statutory power to enforce a right or to satisfy a claim or lien[4]; or

(2)   where the sale is made by a sheriff, bailiff or other officer to satisfy a writ of execution or warrant or decree of any court, or a distress for rent or a warrant of distress or a warrant of control[5].

However, provision has been made by statutory instrument[6] for the implementation of EU legislation relating to fertilisers and where an act or omission is an offence under those provisions, it is not an offence under the provisions of the Agriculture Act 1970 or the regulations made under it[7].

Special provision, in many cases modifying the basic statutory provisions[8], is made in connection with the production, distribution and importation of feeding stuffs[9]; the use of genetically modified animal feed[10]; and the prevention of the transmission via animal feeding stuffs of transmissible spongiform encephalopathies[11]. Provision is also made in connection with veterinary residues in animal products[12] and the use in agriculture of sludge from sewage plants[13].

1   Ie the Agriculture Act 1970 Pt IV (ss 66–87) (see PARA 40 et seq). As to the meanings of 'fertiliser' and 'feeding stuff' see PARA 37. See also the Fertilisers Regulations 1991, SI 1991/2197 (see PARA 40 et seq) made under the Agriculture Act 1970 and, as to the disapplication of Pt IV and the Fertilisers Regulations 1991, SI 1991/2197 to certain fertilisers, see PARA 58 note 1.
2   As to what constitutes sale for use as a fertiliser or as a feeding stuff see PARA 38.
3   Ie the sale by a person who is only selling to comply with statutory duties and to protect statutory rights and who has no commercial interest in the sale: see *GC Dobell & Co Ltd v Barber and Garratt* [1931] 1 KB 219, CA.
4   Agriculture Act 1970 s 85(c).
5   Agriculture Act 1970 s 85(d) (amended by the Tribunals, Courts and Enforcement Act 2007 Sch 14 para 30).
6   See the EC Fertilisers (England and Wales) Regulations 2006, SI 2006/2486; and PARA 58 et seq.
7   See the EC Fertilisers (England and Wales) Regulations 2006, SI 2006/2486, reg 21; and PARA 58 note 1.
8   Ie modifying the provisions of the Agriculture Act 1970 set out in PARAS 37–38, 40–57.
9   See PARA 71 et seq.
10 See PARAS 74–75.
11 See ANIMALS vol 2 (2017) PARA 403.
12 See FOOD AND DRINK vol 51 (2013) PARA 719.
13 See PARAS 63–69.

(ii) Duties of Seller

40. Statutory statements.

A person who sells[1] material of a prescribed description[2] for use as a fertiliser[3] or feeding stuff[4] must give to the purchaser a statement in writing (a 'statutory statement')[5] in such form, if any, as may be prescribed, containing such particulars as may be prescribed of the nature, substance or quality of the material[6] and such information or instructions as to the storage, handling or use of the material as may be prescribed[7]. A statutory statement given by a person selling material for use as feeding stuff may also include such additional particulars, information or instructions as may be prescribed[8]. Statutory statements have effect as a warranty by the giver that the particulars contained in the statement are correct[9], and must in general be given not later than the time when the material is to be delivered to the purchaser[10].

It is an offence[11] to:

(1)   fail to give a statutory statement within the time or in the form required, or give a statutory statement which does not contain all or any of the information or instructions required[12];

(2)   give a statutory statement which, as respects a sampled portion[13] of the material, either does not contain all or any of the particulars required to be contained in the statement[14] or contains any such particulars or, in the case of feeding stuffs, any of the additional particulars permitted to be contained in the statutory statement which are false[15] to the prejudice of the purchaser[16]; or

(3)   sell or expose for sale material from a parcel purporting to be labelled in the prescribed manner in a case where the label does not contain all or any of the said particulars or contains any such particulars which are false to the prejudice of the purchaser[17].

1   As to what constitutes sale for use as a fertiliser or as a feeding stuff see PARA 38. As to exempted sales see PARA 39.

2   'Prescribed' means prescribed by regulations: Agriculture Act 1970 s 66(1). For the descriptions of materials prescribed for these purposes see the Fertilisers Regulations 1991, SI 1991/2197, reg 5, Sch 1; the Animal Feed (Composition, Marketing and Use) (England) Regulations 2015, SI 2015/255; and the Animal Feed (Composition, Marketing and Use) (Wales) Regulations 2016, SI 2016/386. The Animal Feed (Composition, Marketing and Use) (England) Regulations 2015, SI 2015/255, and the Animal Feed (Composition, Marketing and Use) (Wales) Regulations 2016, SI 2016/386 (both made under the Agriculture Act 1970 s 68(1)), implement European Parliament and Council Regulation (EC) 1831/2003 (OJ L268, 18.10.2003, p 29) on additives for use in animal nutrition. As to the disapplication of the Agriculture Act 1970 Pt IV (ss 66–87) and the Fertilisers Regulations 1991, SI 1991/2197 to certain fertilisers see PARA 58 note 1.

    Regulations are made by the Secretary of State and the Welsh Ministers after consultation with persons or organisations representing the interests concerned (unless consultation is required by Council Regulation (EC) 178/2002 (OJ L031, 1.1.2002, p 1), art 9): Agriculture Act 1970 ss 66(1), 84(1), (3) (s 84(3) added by SI 2004/3254). As to the Secretary of State and the Welsh Ministers generally see PARA 390.

3   As to the meaning of 'fertiliser' see PARA 37.

4   As to the meaning of 'feeding stuff' see PARA 37.

5   The duty to give a statutory statement does not apply to sales of two or more materials which are mixed at the request of the purchaser before delivery to him (Agriculture Act 1970 s 68(2)(a)) or to sales in quantities of not more than 25 kilograms, or in relation to feeding stuffs, to sales of small quantities (that is to say, sales in quantities of not more than 56 pounds or the prescribed metric substitution) if the material sold is taken in the presence of the purchaser from a parcel bearing a conspicuous label on which are marked in the prescribed manner the matters which would be required to be contained in a statutory statement (s 68(2)(b) (amended by SI 1991/2197; SI 1999/1663; and modified by SI 2010/2280; SI 2010/2287)).

    A statutory statement is not a 'trade description' for the purposes of the Trade Descriptions Act 1968: see s 2(4); and CONSUMER PROTECTION vol 21 (2016) PARA 443.

6   Agriculture Act 1970 s 68(1)(a). The Agriculture Act 1970 s 68(1)–(5) does not apply to anyone to whom the requirements of European Parliament and Council Regulation (EC) 1831/2003 (OJ L268, 18.10.2003, p 29) art 16 (labelling and packaging of feed additives and premixtures) or of European Parliament and Council Regulation (EC) 767/2009 (OJ L229, 1.9.2009, p 1) Ch 4 (arts 11–23) (labelling, presentation and packaging) apply: Agriculture Act 1970 s 68(5A) (s 68(5A), (7) added by SI 2010/2503 (England), SI 2010/2652 (Wales)). Failure to comply with the labelling requirements of European Parliament and Council Regulation (EC) 1831/2003 (OJ L268, 18.10.2003, p 29) art 16 or of European Parliament and Council Regulation (EC) 767/2009 (OJ L229, 1.9.2009, p 1) Ch 4 does not invalidate a contract of sale, but such labelling has effect, regardless of any contract or notice to the contrary, as a warranty by the person who gives it that the particulars contained in it are correct: Agriculture Act 1970 s 68(7).

7   Agriculture Act 1970 s 68(1)(b). See note 6.

8 Agriculture Act 1970 s 68(1A) (added by SI 1982/980). Any seller giving a statutory statement including additional particulars, information or instructions other than those prescribed is liable on summary conviction to a fine not exceeding level 2 on the standard scale: Agriculture Act 1970 s 68(1A) (as so added; and amended by virtue of the Criminal Justice Act 1982 ss 37, 46). As to the standard scale and the powers of magistrates' courts to issue fines on summary conviction see SENTENCING vol 92 (2015) PARA 176.

9 Agriculture Act 1970 s 68(6). This applies notwithstanding any contract or notice to the contrary: s 68(6). No action lies on any warranty for any misstatement as to the nature, substance or quality of any material if the misstatement does not exceed any prescribed limits of variation, although a purchaser's rights under a warranty will not be affected by such prescribed limits if the misstatement exceeds them: s 74(1). As to the remedies of a buyer for a breach of warranty see the Sale of Goods Act 1979 s 53; and SALE OF GOODS AND SUPPLY OF SERVICES vol 91 (2012) PARAS 305–308.

    Failure to comply with the statutory requirements concerning the giving of statutory notices (ie the Agriculture Act 1970 s 68) does not invalidate a contract of sale: s 68(6).

10 Agriculture Act 1970 s 68(3). Regulations may permit the statutory statement to be given later in certain cases: see s 68(3). If given before the prescribed time, the statutory statement is deemed to have been given at that time: s 68(3).

11 Until a day to be appointed the offence is punishable on summary conviction by a fine not exceeding level 5 on the standard scale or imprisonment for a term not exceeding three months, or both (s 68(4) (amended by virtue of the Criminal Justice Act 1982 ss 38, 46)); as from that day the maximum term of imprisonment is increased to a term not exceeding 51 weeks (Agriculture Act 1970 s 68(4) (as so amended; prospectively amended by the Criminal Justice Act 2003 s 280(2), (3), Sch 26 para 22(1), (2))). At the date at which this volume states the law no such day had been appointed. Where an act or omission is an offence under the EC Fertilisers (England and Wales) Regulations 2006, SI 2006/2486 (see PARAS 58–62) it is not an offence under these provisions: reg 21.

12 Agriculture Act 1970 s 68(4)(a).

13 'Sampled portion' means a prescribed amount of any material from which a sample has been taken by an inspector in the prescribed manner, being an amount:

    (1)   consisting either entirely of material packed in one or more containers or entirely of material not so packed; and

    (2)   not exceeding, in the case of an amount consisting of material so packed, the requisite quantity, ie five tonnes or 5,000 litres, except where it consists of material packed in a single container or of material packed in two or more containers each of which holds less than the requisite quantity, in which case the prescribed amount may be the contents of the lowest number of those containers which together hold the requisite quantity: Agriculture Act 1970 s 66(1) (amended by SI 1996/1342; SI 1999/1663).

    The Fertilisers (Sampling and Analysis) Regulations 1996, SI 1996/1342, do not apply to any sampling or analysis of fertilisers carried out pursuant to the EC Fertilisers (England and Wales) Regulations 2006, SI 2006/2486 (see PARAS 58–62): reg 22.

14 Agriculture Act 1970 s 68(4)(b)(i). As to the particulars required to be contained in the statement see note 7. Agriculture Act 1970 s 74(2) does not apply to anyone to whom European Parliament and Council Regulation (EC) 767/2009 (OJ L229, 1.9.2009, p 1–28) art 11(5), Annex IV (permitted tolerances) applies: Agriculture Act 1970 s 74(3) (added by SI 2010/2503 (England), SI 2010/2652 (Wales)).

15 Particulars are not to be treated as false by reason of any misstatement therein as to the nature, substance or quality of the material if the misstatement does not exceed any prescribed limits of variation: Agriculture Act 1970 s 74(2). As to the prescribed limits of variation see note 10.

16 Agriculture Act 1970 s 68(4)(b)(ii) (substituted by SI 1982/980). As to the particulars permitted to be contained in the statement see note 7. In proceedings for this offence the fact that any particulars ought to have been included or are false is proved by evidence of the result of an analysis of the sample taken from the portion in question: Agriculture Act 1970 s 68(5).

17 Agriculture Act 1970 s 68(4)(c). In proceedings for this offence the fact that any particulars ought to have been included or are false is proved by evidence of the result of an analysis of a sample taken by an inspector appointed under s 67 (see PARA 52) in the prescribed manner (see note 14) from the material sold or, where the alleged offence is exposing for sale, from the parcel bearing the label: s 68(5).

41.   Marking of material prepared for sale.

A person who has material of a prescribed[1] description on his premises for the purpose of selling[2] it in the course of trade for use as a fertiliser[3] must mark it in such manner, if any, as may be prescribed[4] with the matters required to be contained in a statutory statement[5] relating to that material[6]; alternatively, the matters required to be marked on any material may be denoted by a mark whose meaning can be ascertained by reference to a register kept in accordance with regulations[7]. Material must be marked as soon as practicable after it is made ready for sale[8] or, if it is ready for sale when it comes on the premises and is not then already marked, as soon as practicable after it comes on the premises[9]; and, except in the case of imported feeding stuffs and specified imported fertilisers, must be marked before it is removed from the premises[10]. In all cases, the person who has the material on his premises must secure that it continues to be marked until it leaves the premises[11].

It is an offence[12] for any person to have on his premises for the purposes of selling it any material to which these provisions are applicable which:

(1)   is not marked in the manner required[13];

(2)   is not marked with all the information or instructions[14] with which it is required to be marked[15]; or

(3)   is marked with a mark which, as respects a sampled portion[16] of the material, does not contain all the particulars with which the material is required to be marked, or contains any such particulars which are false[17] to the prejudice of a purchaser[18].

Except where the time in question is the time of the removal of the material from the premises, it is a defence for the person charged to show that it was not practicable for the material to be marked as required by the time in question[19].

1   For the descriptions of materials prescribed for these purposes see PARA 40 note 2.

2   As to what constitutes sale for use as a fertiliser or as a feeding stuff see PARA 38. As to exempted sales see PARA 39.

3   As to the meaning of 'fertiliser' see PARA 37. As to the disapplication of the Agriculture Act 1970 Pt IV (ss 66–87) and the Fertilisers Regulations 1991, SI 1991/2197 to certain fertilisers see PARA 58 note 1.

4   As to the manner of marking material see the Fertilisers Regulations 1991, SI 1991/2197, reg 8, Sch 2 (Sch 2 amended by SI 1998/2024). As to the making of regulations see PARA 40 note 2.

5   As to statutory statements see PARA 40.

6   Agriculture Act 1970 s 69(1) (amended by SI 2010/2503; SI 2010/2652). As to the status of statements of fact denoted by marks see PARA 47 note 5. A mark applied to material for these purposes is not a 'trade description' for the purposes of the Trade Descriptions Act 1968: see s 2(4); and CONSUMER PROTECTION vol 21 (2016) PARA 443.

7   Agriculture Act 1970 s 69(6). As to the regulations see the Fertilisers Regulations 1991, SI 1991/2197, reg 10 (amended by SI 1998/2024). At the date at which this volume states the law no corresponding provision had effect with regard to feeding stuffs. A person keeping such a register must preserve it for six months commencing with the first day on which none of the material referred to in the register remains on the premises for sale (Agriculture Act 1970 s 69(7); Fertilisers Regulations 1991, SI 1991/2197, reg 10(3)), and must on demand by an inspector appointed under the Agriculture Act 1970 s 67 (see PARA 52) produce it and allow him to take copies (s 69(7)). A person who fails to comply with these requirements is liable on summary conviction to a fine not exceeding level 3 on the standard scale: s 69(7) (amended by virtue of the Criminal Justice Act 1982 ss 38, 46). As to the standard scale and the powers of magistrates' courts to issue fines on summary conviction see SENTENCING vol 92 (2015) PARA 176. As to prosecutions, defences, etc, see PARAS 55–56.

8   Material which is normally packed before being delivered to a purchaser is not to be treated as ready for sale until it is so packed if the packing takes place on the premises where the material is manufactured but, if the packing takes place elsewhere, it is to be treated as ready for sale when it is ready for packing: Agriculture Act 1970 s 69(2).

9   Agriculture Act 1970 s 69(1)(a), (b).
10 Agriculture Act 1970 s 69(1) (modified by s 69(3)); and see the Fertilisers Regulations 1991, SI 1991/2197, reg 9 (amended by SI 1998/2024). At the date at which this volume states the law no corresponding provision had effect with regard to feeding stuffs.
11 Agriculture Act 1970 s 69(1).
12 Until a day to be appointed the offence is punishable on summary conviction by a fine not exceeding level 5 on the standard scale or imprisonment for a term not exceeding three months, or both (Agriculture Act 1970 s 69(4) (amended by virtue of the Criminal Justice Act 1982 ss 38, 46)); as from that day the maximum term of imprisonment is increased to a term not exceeding 51 weeks (Agriculture Act 1970 s 69(4) (as so amended; prospectively amended by the Criminal Justice Act 2003 s 280(2), (3), Sch 26 para 22(1), (3))). At the date at which this volume states the law no such day had been appointed. Where an act or omission is an offence under the EC Fertilisers (England and Wales) Regulations 2006, SI 2006/2486 (see PARAS 58–62) it is not an offence under these provisions: reg 21.
13 Agriculture Act 1970 s 69(4)(a).
14 Ie the information or instructions referred to in the Agriculture Act 1970 s 68(1)(b) (see PARA 40).
15 Agriculture Act 1970 s 69(4)(b).
16 As to the meaning of 'sampled portion' see PARA 40 note 14.
17 As to the meaning of 'false' see PARA 40 note 16.
18 Agriculture Act 1970 s 69(4)(c). In proceedings for an offence under s 69(4)(c) the fact that any particulars ought to have been included or are false must be proved by evidence of the result of an analysis of the sample taken from the portion in question: s 69(5).
19 Agriculture Act 1970 s 69(4). As to other defences see PARA 56.

42. Use of names or expressions with prescribed meanings.

A person who sells for use[1] as a fertiliser[2] or feeding stuff[3] any material which he describes[4] by a name or expression to which a meaning has been assigned by regulations[5], or which is marked[6] with such a name or expression[7], impliedly warrants that the material accords with that meaning[8]. Moreover, a person commits an offence[9] if he either sells for use as a fertiliser or feeding stuff any material which he so describes or which is so marked[10], or has on his premises for the purpose of selling it in the course of trade for such use any material which is ready for sale and is so marked[11], if that material does not accord with the assigned meaning[12].

1   As to what constitutes sale for use as a fertiliser or as a feeding stuff see PARA 38. As to exempted sales see PARA 39.
2   As to the meaning of 'fertiliser' see PARA 37. As to the disapplication of the Agriculture Act 1970 Pt IV (ss 66–87) and the Fertilisers Regulations 1991, SI 1991/2197 to certain fertilisers see PARA 58 note 1.
3   As to the meaning of 'feeding stuff' see PARA 37. As to the modification of the Agriculture Act 1970 s 70(1)(a) in relation to feeding stuffs see the Animal Feed (England) Regulations 2010, SI 2010/2503, reg 14(5)(a); and the Animal Feed (Wales) Regulations 2010, SI 2010/2652, reg 14(5)(a).
4   Ie in a statutory statement or in any document given by him to the purchaser in connection with the sale: Agriculture Act 1970 s 70(1)(a). As to statutory statements see PARA 40.
5   As to the making of regulations see PARA 40 note 2.
6   Material is treated as 'marked' for these purposes whether the mark is on the material itself, on a label attached thereto, on a package or container enclosing it or, in a case within the Agriculture Act 1970 s 70(2)(b) (see the text and note 11), in such a place on the premises that it is likely to be taken as referring to the material: s 70(5).
7   Agriculture Act 1970 s 70(1)(b).
8   Agriculture Act 1970 s 70(1). This applies notwithstanding any contract or notice to the contrary: s 70(1). As to the status of statements of fact which give rise to warranties see PARA 47 note 5. As to warranties see further PARA 44. As to the remedies of a buyer for a breach of warranty see the Sale of Goods Act 1979 s 53; and SALE OF GOODS AND SUPPLY OF SERVICES vol 91 (2012) PARAS 305–308.
    In the case of material which has been imported, s 70(1), (2) may have effect subject to prescribed modifications: s 70(3).

9   Until a day to be appointed the offence is punishable on summary conviction by a fine not exceeding level 5 on the standard scale or imprisonment for a term not exceeding three months, or both (Agriculture Act 1970 s 70(2) (amended by virtue of the Criminal Justice Act 1982 ss 38, 46)); as from that day the maximum term of imprisonment is increased to a term not exceeding 51 weeks (Agriculture Act 1970 s 70(2) (as so amended; prospectively amended by the Criminal Justice Act 2003 s 280(2), (3), Sch 26 para 22(1), (4))). At the date at which this volume states the law no such day had been appointed. As to prosecutions, defences, etc, see PARAS 55–56. As to the standard scale and the powers of magistrates' courts to issue fines on summary conviction see SENTENCING vol 92 (2015) PARA 176. Where an act or omission is an offence under the EC Fertilisers (England and Wales) Regulations 2006, SI 2006/2486 (see PARAS 58–62) it is not an offence under these provisions: reg 21.

10 Agriculture Act 1970 s 70(2)(a). Nothing in s 70(2)–(4) applies to anyone to whom the labelling requirements of European Parliament and Council Regulation (EC) 767/2009 (OJ L229, 1.9.2009, p 1) on the placing on the market and use of feed, apply: Agriculture Act 1970 s 70(6) (added by SI 2010/2503; SI 2010/2652).

11 Agriculture Act 1970 s 70(2)(b).

12 To establish that the offence under the Agriculture Act 1970 s 70(2) has been committed it is necessary for a sampled portion (see PARA 40 note 14) of the material to fail, to the prejudice of a purchaser, to accord with the meaning which has been assigned to the relevant name or expression (s 70(2)); and in proceedings for this offence the fact that a sampled portion fails to accord with the meaning in question is to be proved by evidence of the result of an analysis of the sample taken (s 70(4)).

43. Particulars to be given of certain attributes claimed.

A person who sells for use[1] as a fertiliser[2] or feeding stuff[3] any material which he describes[4] as having any prescribed attribute[5] or which is marked[6] with a statement that it has any such attribute[7], or has on his premises for the purpose of selling it in the course of trade for such use any material which is ready for sale and so marked[8], commits an offence unless the statement or document containing the description, or the mark, also states the prescribed particulars of that attribute[9]; moreover, a seller of any material in relation to which such particulars are or purport to be so stated impliedly warrants that those particulars are correct[10].

1   As to what constitutes sale for use as a fertiliser or as a feeding stuff see PARA 38. As to exempted sales see PARA 39.

2   As to the meaning of 'fertiliser' see PARA 37. As to the disapplication of the Agriculture Act 1970 Pt IV (ss 66–87) and the Fertilisers Regulations 1991, SI 1991/2197 to certain fertilisers see PARA 58 note 1.

3   As to the meaning of 'feeding stuff' see PARA 37.

4   Ie in a statutory statement or in any document given by him to the purchaser in connection with the sale: Agriculture Act 1970 s 71(1)(a). As to statutory statements see PARA 40.

5   Agriculture Act 1970 s 70(1)(a). This excludes any attribute of which particulars are required to be contained in the statutory statement: s 71(1)(a). At the date at which this volume states the law no attributes had been prescribed for these purposes.

6   As to the marking of material see PARA 41. Material is treated as marked whether the mark is on the material itself, on a label attached thereto, on a package or container enclosing it or, in a case falling within the Agriculture Act 1970 s 71(1)(b) (see the text and note 8), in such a place on the premises that it is likely to be taken as referring to the material: s 71(5). The Agriculture Act 1970 s 71(1)–(3) does not apply to anyone to whom European Parliament and Council Regulation (EC) 767/2009 (OJ L229, 1.9.2009, p 1) art 13 (claims) applies: Agriculture Act 1970 s 71(6) (added by SI 2010/2503 (England), SI 2010/2652 (Wales)).

7   Agriculture Act 1970 s 71(1)(a).

8   Agriculture Act 1970 s 71(1)(b).

9   Agriculture Act 1970 s 71(1), (2)(a). It is also an offence to purport to comply with these requirements by describing or marking any material with particulars which, as respects a sampled portion (see PARA 40 note 14) of that material, are false to the prejudice of a purchaser: s 71(2)(b). As to the meaning of 'false' see PARA 40 note 16. In proceedings for an offence under s 71(2)(b) the fact that any particulars are false as respects a sampled portion is to be proved by evidence of

the result of an analysis of the sample taken: s 71(3). Until a day to be appointed an offence under s 71(2)(a) or (b) is punishable on summary conviction by a fine not exceeding level 5 on the standard scale or imprisonment for a term not exceeding three months, or both (s 71(2) (amended by virtue of the Criminal Justice Act 1982 ss 38, 46)); as from that day the maximum term of imprisonment is increased to a term not exceeding 51 weeks (Agriculture Act 1970 s 71(2) (as so amended; prospectively amended by the Criminal Justice Act 2003 s 280(2), (3), Sch 26 para 22(1), (5))). At the date at which this volume states the law no such day had been appointed. As to prosecutions, defences, etc, see PARAS 55–56. As to the standard scale and the powers of magistrates' courts to issue fines on summary conviction see SENTENCING vol 92 (2015) PARA 176. Where an act or omission is an offence under the EC Fertilisers (England and Wales) Regulations 2006, SI 2006/2486 (see PARAS 58–62) it is not an offence under these provisions: reg 21.
10 Agriculture Act 1970 s 71(4). This applies notwithstanding any contract or notice to the contrary: s 71(4). Failure to comply with the requirements of s 71(1) does not invalidate a contract of sale: s 71(4). As to warranties see further PARA 44. As to the remedies of a buyer for a breach of warranty see the Sale of Goods Act 1979 s 53; and SALE OF GOODS AND SUPPLY OF SERVICES vol 91 (2012) PARAS 305–308. As to the modification of the Agriculture Act 1970 s 71(4) as it applies to feeding stuffs see the Animal Feed (England) Regulations 2010, SI 2010/2503, reg 14(6)(a); and the Animal Feed (Wales) Regulations 2010, SI 2010/2652, reg 14(6)(a).

44. Warranty of fitness of feeding stuff.

The seller[1] of any material for use as a feeding stuff[2] impliedly warrants that the material is suitable to be used as such[3]. However, if the material is sold as suitable only for animals[4] of a particular description, no warranty may be implied that the material is suitable for other animals[5]; and if the material is sold to be used as a feeding stuff only after being mixed with something else, no warranty may be implied that the material is suitable to be so used without being so mixed[6].

The seller of any material of a prescribed description[7] for use as a feeding stuff impliedly warrants that the material does not, except as stated in the statutory statement[8], contain any ingredient prescribed for this purpose[9].

1 As to what constitutes sale for use as a feeding stuff see PARA 38. As to exempted sales see PARA 39.
2 As to the meaning of 'feeding stuff' see PARA 37. As to the disapplication of the Agriculture Act 1970 Pt IV (ss 66–87) and the Fertilisers Regulations 1991, SI 1991/2197 to certain fertilisers see PARA 58 note 1.
3 Agriculture Act 1970 s 72(1). The provisions of s 72 apply notwithstanding any contract or notice to the contrary: s 72(3). As to seller's warranties see further PARAS 40, 42–44. As to the remedies of a buyer for a breach of warranty see the Sale of Goods Act 1979 s 53; and SALE OF GOODS AND SUPPLY OF SERVICES vol 91 (2012) PARAS 305–308.
   It appears that the implied warranty arises not only on a sale to the person who uses the feeding stuff as a food for animals but also on a sale to a dealer who intends to resell and that the purchaser may recover from the vendor damages and costs for which he has become liable to sub-purchasers: cf *GC Dobell & Co Ltd v Barber* [1931] 1 KB 219, CA.
4 As to the meaning of 'animal' see PARA 37 note 3.
5 Agriculture Act 1970 s 72(1)(a). Apart from this provision it appears that the warranty might have operated though damage was done only to animals of a different description from that specified: cf *Henry Kendall & Sons v William Lillico & Sons Ltd* [1969] 2 AC 31, [1968] 2 All ER 444, HL (a decision under the Fertilisers and Feeding Stuffs Act 1926 (now repealed and replaced by the Agriculture Act 1970 Pt IV (ss 66–87)).
6 Agriculture Act 1970 s 72(1)(b).
7 to the making of regulations see PARA 40 note 2.
8 As to statutory statements see PARA 40.
9 Agriculture Act 1970 s 72(2). At the date at which this volume states the law no ingredients had been prescribed for these purposes.

(iii) Control of Composition and Content of Fertilisers and Feeding Stuffs

45. Power to make regulations.

The Secretary of State and the Welsh Ministers[1] may make regulations[2] with a view to controlling in the public interest the composition or content of fertilisers[3] and of material intended for the feeding of animals[4]. Such regulations may prohibit or restrict, by reference to its composition or content, the importation and exportation, the sale or possession with a view to sale, or the use, of any prescribed material[5], and may regulate the marking, labelling and packaging of prescribed material and the marks to be applied to any container or vehicle in which any prescribed material is enclosed or conveyed[6]. Moreover, with a view to implementing or supplementing any EU instrument relating to fertilisers or material intended for the feeding of animals, regulations may be made providing for the application, in relation to any material specified in the regulations, of all or any of the applicable statutory provisions[7] subject to any specified modifications[8].

1　As to the Secretary of State and the Welsh Ministers see PARA 390.
2　Ie under the Agriculture Act 1970 Pt IV (ss 66–87). As to the making of regulations see PARA 40 note 2.
3　As to the meaning of 'fertiliser' see PARA 37. As to the disapplication of the Agriculture Act 1970 Pt IV and the Fertilisers Regulations 1991, SI 1991/2197 to certain fertilisers see PARA 58 note 1.
4　Agriculture Act 1970 s 74A(1) (s 74A added by the European Communities Act 1972 Sch 4 para 6). As to the meaning of 'animal' see PARA 37 note 3. The Agriculture Act 1970 s 74A(3) does not apply to regulations concerning feed: Animal Feed (England) Regulations 2010, SI 2010/2503, reg 14(9); Animal Feed (Wales) Regulations 2010, SI 2010/2652, reg 14(9).
5　Agriculture Act 1970 s 74A(1)(a) (as added: see note 4). Regulations under s 74A(1) may include provision excluding or modifying the operation in relation to any material of any other provision of Pt IV but, subject to any such provision, references in Pt IV to feeding stuffs apply to all material which is intended for the feeding of animals and with respect to which such regulations are in force: s 74A(2) (as so added). As to the meaning of 'feeding stuff' see PARA 37. Until a day to be appointed a person who contravenes any prohibition or restriction imposed by such regulations or fails to comply with any other provision thereof is liable on summary conviction to a fine not exceeding level 5 on the standard scale or imprisonment for a term not exceeding three months, or both (s 74A(3) (as so added; and amended by virtue of the Criminal Justice Act 1982 ss 35, 38, 46)); as from that day the maximum term of imprisonment is increased to a term not exceeding 51 weeks (Agriculture Act 1970 s 74A(3) (as so added and amended; prospectively amended by the Criminal Justice Act 2003 s 280(2), (3), Sch 26 para 22(1), (8))). At the date at which this volume states the law no such day had been appointed. As to prosecutions, defences, etc, see PARAS 55–56. As to the standard scale and the powers of magistrates' courts to issue fines on summary conviction see SENTENCING vol 92 (2015) PARA 176.
6　Agriculture Act 1970 s 74A(1)(b) (as added: see note 4). See note 5.
7　Ie applicable provisions of the Agriculture Act 1970 Pt IV.
8　Agriculture Act 1970 s 74A(4) (as added (see note 4); amended by SI 2011/1043).

46. Regulations concerning fertilisers.

Pursuant to the powers conferred on the Secretary of State and the Welsh Ministers[1] to control the composition or content of fertilisers[2], regulations have been made in connection with the sale or possession for sale, packaging, designation and content of fertilisers marked as or indicated to be EC fertilisers or EEC fertilisers[3]. These prohibit the sale or possession with a view to sale of any solid or fluid material which, not being designated as an EC fertiliser or an EEC fertiliser, does not comply with the statutory requirements[4].

1　As to the Secretary of State and the Welsh Ministers see PARA 390.
2　As to the meaning of 'fertiliser' see PARA 37. As to the making, enforcement, etc, of regulations pursuant to these powers see the Agriculture Act 1970 s 74A; and PARA 45. As to the

disapplication of the Agriculture Act 1970 Pt IV (ss 66–87) and the Fertilisers Regulations 1991, SI 1991/2197 to certain fertilisers see PARA 58 note 1.

3   See the Fertilisers Regulations 1991, SI 1991/2197, regs 1A, 2, 3A, Sch 1 (reg 1A added, and reg 2 amended, by SI 1998/2024; Fertilisers Regulations 1991, SI 1991/2197, reg 3A added by SI 1995/16; Fertilisers Regulations 1991, SI 1991/2197, Sch 1 amended by SI 1995/16; SI 1998/2024).

4   See the Fertilisers Regulations 1991, SI 1991/2197, reg 3 (amended by SI 1998/2024). See PARAS 40–41, 52.

(iv) Sampling and Analysis

47.   Purchaser's right to have sample taken and analysed.

The purchaser of any material which was sold[1] to him for use as a fertiliser[2] or feeding stuff[3], and in respect of which a warranty was given or is to be treated as having been given[4], is entitled to have a sample of the material taken in the prescribed manner[5] by an inspector[6] and analysed by the agricultural analyst[7] for the inspector's area[8]. If the warranty is contained in or arises from a statutory statement or document, no sample may be taken after six months from the delivery of the material to the purchaser or the receipt by him of the statutory statement or document, whichever is the later[9]; in any other case, no sample may be taken after six months from the delivery of the material to the purchaser[10].

1   As to what constitutes sale for use as a fertiliser or as a feeding stuff see PARA 38. As to exempted sales see PARA 39.

2   As to the meaning of 'fertiliser' see PARA 37. As to the disapplication of the Agriculture Act 1970 Pt IV (ss 66–87) and the Fertilisers Regulations 1991, SI 1991/2197 to certain fertilisers see PARA 58 note 1.

3   As to the meaning of 'feeding stuff' see PARA 37.

4   For the circumstances in which a warranty is treated as having been given see PARAS 40, 42–44.

5   The manner of taking samples is prescribed by regulations: Agriculture Act 1970 s 66(1). The regulations with respect to the taking of samples under Pt IV (ss 66–87) may also include provision as to the state of the material to be sampled, the handling and storage of samples and the period within which analyses are to be carried out: s 79(1), (2). For the prescribed manner for taking, marking, sealing and fastening up of samples see the Fertilisers (Sampling and Analysis) Regulations 1996, SI 1996/1342, reg 3, Sch 1. The Fertilisers (Sampling and Analysis) Regulations 1996, SI 1996/1342, do not apply to any sampling or analysis of fertilisers carried out pursuant to the EC Fertilisers (England and Wales) Regulations 2006, SI 2006/2486 (see PARAS 58–62): reg 22. As to the making of regulations see PARA 40 note 2.
      Where the method of analysis for determining any fact as to the nature, substance or quality of any material is prescribed by regulations, any statement of that fact in a statutory statement (see PARA 40) or mark (see PARA 41), or in a document or mark which is not a statutory statement but which gives rise to a warranty (see PARA 42), is to be taken to be a statement of that fact as determined by analysis in accordance with the method prescribed: Agriculture Act 1970 s 79(3).

6   Ie an inspector appointed under the Agriculture Act 1970 s 67: s 66(1). As to the appointment of inspectors see PARA 52.

7   Ie an agricultural analyst appointed under the Agriculture Act 1970 s 67, including a deputy agricultural analyst appointed for the same area: s 66(1). As to the appointment of agricultural analysts see PARA 52.

8   Agriculture Act 1970 s 75(1). A purchaser who requests a sample to be taken must, if so required by the inspector, tell him the name and address of the seller (s 75(2)(a)) and furnish him with, or with a copy of, any statutory statement or document containing or giving rise to the warranty relating to the material (s 75(2)(b)). In the case of a warranty which by virtue of s 70(1) (see PARA 42) or s 71(4) (see PARA 43) is implied by reason of the material being marked as mentioned in those provisions, a copy of the matters stated by the mark may also be required by the inspector: s 75(2). Any request for a sample to be taken and analysed is to be accompanied by such fee as may be fixed by the enforcement authority (see PARA 52) whose inspector is to take the sample, and different fees may be fixed for different materials and for different analyses of the same material: s 75(4).

It is an offence to tamper or interfere with a sample taken and submitted for analysis: see PARA 53.

9   Agriculture Act 1970 s 75(3)(a).
10 Agriculture Act 1970 s 75(3)(b).

48. Powers of inspection and taking samples.

An inspector[1] may require a person who has purchased any fertiliser[2] or feeding stuff[3] to tell him the name and address of the seller[4] and to produce, and allow him to take copies of, any statutory statement[5] received from the seller[6] and any relevant[7] document or mark[8]. Failure to comply with any such requirement is an offence[9].

An inspector may at all reasonable times enter[10] any premises on which he has reasonable cause to believe that there is any fertiliser or feeding stuff which is kept there for the purpose of being sold[11] in the course of trade and is ready for sale[12], and any premises (not being premises used only as a dwelling) on which he has reasonable cause to believe that there is any fertiliser or feeding stuff which the occupier of the premises has purchased[13]. Having entered, the inspector may take, in the prescribed manner[14], a sample of any material on the premises (including any material in a vehicle) which he has reasonable cause to believe to be such a fertiliser or feeding stuff[15]. In addition to these powers, an inspector may take, in any manner, a sample of any material which has been sold for use as a fertiliser or feeding stuff or which he has reasonable cause to believe to be intended for sale as such[16].

1   As to the meaning of 'inspector' see PARA 47 note 6. As to the appointment of inspectors see PARA 52.
2   As to the meaning of 'fertiliser' see PARA 37. As to the disapplication of the Agriculture Act 1970 Pt IV (ss 66–87) and the Fertilisers Regulations 1991, SI 1991/2197 to certain fertilisers see PARA 58 note 1.
3   As to the meaning of 'feeding stuff' see PARA 37.
4   Agriculture Act 1970 s 76(2)(a).
5   As to statutory statements see PARA 40.
6   Agriculture Act 1970 s 76(2)(b)(i).
7   Ie where the fertiliser or feeding stuff was described or marked as mentioned in Agriculture Act 1970 s 70(1) (see PARA 42) or s 71(1) (see PARA 43).
8   Agriculture Act 1970 s 76(2)(b)(ii).
9   Agriculture Act 1970 s 76(2). The offence is punishable on summary conviction by a fine not exceeding level 3 on the standard scale: s 76(2) (amended by virtue of the Criminal Justice Act 1982 ss 38, 46). As to the standard scale and the powers of magistrates' courts to issue fines on summary conviction see SENTENCING vol 92 (2015) PARA 176. Where an act or omission is an offence under the EC Fertilisers (England and Wales) Regulations 2006, SI 2006/2486 (see PARAS 58–62) it is not an offence under these provisions: reg 21.
10 An inspector entering premises may take with him such other persons and equipment as appear necessary: Agriculture Act 1970 s 76(3).
11 As to what constitutes sale for use as a fertiliser or as a feeding stuff see PARA 38. As to exempted sales see PARA 39.
12 Agriculture Act 1970 s 76(1)(a).
13 Agriculture Act 1970 s 76(1)(b).
14 As to the prescribed manner for taking, marking, sealing and fastening up of samples see PARA 47 note 5.
15 Agriculture Act 1970 s 76(1). Where an inspector takes some of a sample from each of one or more parcels of any material which are exposed for sale by retail and none of which weighs more than six kilograms, the owner of the parcel or parcels may require him to purchase the parcel or parcels on behalf of the authority for which he acts: s 76(5) (amended by SI 1991/2197; SI 1999/1663).
    It is an offence to tamper or interfere with a sample taken and submitted for analysis: see PARA 53.
16 Agriculture Act 1970 s 76(4). Disclosure of information concerning the place from where and the person from whom such a sample was taken is not an offence: see PARA 53 note 6.

49. Division of samples and sending for analysis.

Where a sample has been taken by an inspector[1] in the prescribed manner[2], the inspector must divide it into three or, if the manufacturer of the material is not a person to whom a part of the sample is required to be sent[3], four parts[4]. The inspector must then send[5] one part to the agricultural analyst for the inspector's area[6]. If the sample was taken pursuant to the request of a purchaser[7], or in any case where the person on whose premises the sample was taken purchased the material for use and not for resale, the inspector must send one of the parts to the seller or his agent[8]; in any other case, the inspector must send one of the parts to the person on whose premises the sample was taken[9]. If there is a fourth part, the inspector must send it to the manufacturer[10]. The inspector must retain the remaining part for nine months[11].

1   As to the meaning of 'inspector' see PARA 47 note 6. As to the appointment of inspectors see PARA 52.

2   As to the prescribed manner for taking, marking, sealing and fastening up of samples see PARA 47 note 5. A sample may be so taken under the Agriculture Act 1970 s 75(1) (see PARA 47) or s 76(1) (see PARA 48).

3   Ie under the Agriculture Act 1970 s 77(1): see the text and notes 4–9.

4   Agriculture Act 1970 s 77(1), (2). The parts must be of as near as may be equal size and each part must be marked, sealed and fastened up in the prescribed manner: s 77(1).

5   Any part of a sample, notice, certificate or other document, required to be sent or served under the Agriculture Act 1970 s 77, s 78 or s 79 is to be sent or served in such a manner, if any, as may be prescribed: s 79(9). Pursuant to this requirement it is provided that any part of a sample required to be sent to any person (other than the agricultural analyst) in pursuance of these provisions must be sent by registered post or by recorded delivery or may be delivered or given by hand: Fertilisers (Sampling and Analysis) Regulations 1996, SI 1996/1342, reg 4. As to the making of regulations see PARA 40 note 2. As to the meaning of 'agricultural analyst' see PARA 47 note 7. The Fertilisers (Sampling and Analysis) Regulations 1996, SI 1996/1342, do not apply to any sampling or analysis of fertilisers carried out pursuant to the EC Fertilisers (England and Wales) Regulations 2006, SI 2006/2486 (see PARAS 58–62): reg 22.

6   Agriculture Act 1970 s 77(1)(a). There is to be sent with the part sent to the agricultural analyst a statement signed by the inspector that the sample was taken in the prescribed manner (s 77(3)(a)), a copy of any statutory statement (see PARA 40) relating to the material sampled, a copy of any matters with which that material had been marked, and, where the material was described or marked as mentioned in s 70(1) (see PARA 42) or s 71(1) (see PARA 43), a copy of the document or the matters stated by the mark (s 77(3)(b)). See further PARA 50.

7   See PARA 47.

8   Agriculture Act 1970 s 77(1)(b)(i).

9   Agriculture Act 1970 s 77(1)(b)(ii).

10   Agriculture Act 1970 s 77(2). An inspector need not comply with this requirement if he does not know the manufacturer's name, or any address of the manufacturer in the United Kingdom, and is unable after making reasonable inquiries to ascertain that name or address before the expiration of 14 days from the date when the sample was taken: s 77(2). As to the meaning of 'United Kingdom' see PARA 1 note 1.

11   Agriculture Act 1970 s 77(1)(c). The retained part may, however, be sent to the Government Chemist: see PARA 51.

50. Analysis of samples by agricultural analyst.

The agricultural analyst[1] must analyse, in such manner, if any, as may be prescribed[2], the part of a sample which is sent to him, and must send a certificate of analysis in the prescribed form[3] to the inspector[4]. The inspector must then send a copy of the certificate to the purchaser, to the seller or his agent (where the sample was taken pursuant to the request of a purchaser)[5], to the person to whom a part of the sample has been sent (in any other case)[6], and to the manufacturer (where he has received a fourth part of the sample)[7].

If the agricultural analyst to whom a sample is sent for analysis determines that for any reason an effective analysis of the sample cannot be made by him or under his direction, he must send it to the agricultural analyst for another area together with any documents received by him with the sample; and thereupon these provisions apply as if that other analyst were the agricultural analyst for the inspector's area and the sample had originally been sent to him[8].

1   As to the meaning of 'agricultural analyst' see PARA 47 note 7.
2   The methods of analysis are laid down in the Fertilisers (Sampling and Analysis) Regulations 1996, SI 1996/1342, reg 6, Sch 2. As to the making of regulations see PARA 40 note 2.
        The Fertilisers (Sampling and Analysis) Regulations 1996, SI 1996/1342, do not apply to any sampling or analysis of fertilisers carried out pursuant to the EC Fertilisers (England and Wales) Regulations 2006, SI 2006/2486 (see PARAS 58–62): reg 22.
3   For the prescribed form see the Fertilisers (Sampling and Analysis) Regulations 1996, SI 1996/1342, reg 7, Sch 3. A certificate of analysis by an analyst appointed under the Agriculture Act 1970 s 67(3)(b) (see PARA 52) must be signed by that analyst or another analyst so appointed for the same area: s 79(5). Any document purporting to be a certificate of analysis is deemed to be such a certificate unless the contrary is proved: s 79(8).
4   Agriculture Act 1970 s 77(4). As to the method of sending see PARA 49 note 5. As to the meaning of 'inspector' see PARA 47 note 6. As to the appointment of inspectors see PARA 52. As to the modification of s 77(4) in relation to feeding stuffs see the Feed (Sampling and Analysis and Specified Undesirable Substances) (England) Regulations 2010, SI 2010/2280, reg 18 and the Feed (Sampling and Analysis and Specified Undesirable Substances) (Wales) Regulations 2010, SI 2010/2287, reg 18.
        Any analysis required to be made by an agricultural analyst may be made by any person acting under his directions: s 79(4).
5   Agriculture Act 1970 s 77(4)(a). As to the taking of samples at the request of the purchaser see PARA 47.
6   Agriculture Act 1970 s 77(4)(b). As to the persons to whom samples must be sent see PARA 49.
7   Agriculture Act 1970 s 77(4). As to the circumstances in which a fourth part of the sample must be sent see PARA 49.
8   Agriculture Act 1970 s 77(5).

51.   Analysis by Government Chemist.

Where a sample of any material has been taken pursuant to the request of a purchaser[1], the inspector[2] may be required to send the part that he has retained[3] to the Government Chemist for analysis[4]. This course of action may be requested by the purchaser, the person who sold the material to him or any other person against whom a claim may lie in respect of the sale of the material in question[5]. When a part is sent to the Government Chemist he must analyse it in such manner, if any, as may be prescribed[6] and send a certificate of analysis[7] to the inspector[8]; and the purchaser, the person who sold the material to him or any other person against whom a claim may lie may require the inspector to supply him with a copy of the certificate, whether the part was sent to the Government Chemist for analysis in pursuance of the request of that person or otherwise[9].

Provision is also made for samples to be sent to the Government Chemist for analysis in anticipation or for the purposes of proceedings for an offence[10].

1   See PARA 47.
2   As to the meaning of 'inspector' see PARA 47 note 6. As to the appointment of inspectors see PARA 52.
3   For the inspector's duty to retain a part of a sample see PARA 49.
4   Agriculture Act 1970 s 78(1)(a). Where a part of a sample is sent for analysis to the Government Chemist there must also be sent a copy of any document which was sent with the part of the sample sent to the agricultural analyst (see PARA 49): s 78(5)(a). As to the method of sending see PARA 49 note 5. As to the meaning of 'agricultural analyst' see PARA 47 note 7. As to the modification of s 78 in relation to feeding stuffs see the Feed (Sampling and Analysis and Specified Undesirable

Substances) (England) Regulations 2010, SI 2010/2280, reg 19 and the Feed (Sampling and Analysis and Specified Undesirable Substances) (Wales) Regulations 2010, SI 2010/2287, reg 19.

5   Agriculture Act 1970 s 78(1). Such a request must be accompanied by the appropriate fee: see s 78(8), (10) (s 78(10) amended by SI 1970/1537).

6   Agriculture Act 1970 s 78(6). As to the prescribed methods of analysis see PARA 50 note 2. Any analysis required to be made by the Government Chemist may be made by any person acting under his directions: s 79(4).

7   As to certificates of analysis see PARA 50 note 3. A certificate of analysis by the Government Chemist must be signed by him or a person authorised by him to sign the certificate: Agriculture Act 1970 s 79(5). Any document purporting to be a certificate of analysis is deemed to be such a certificate unless the contrary is proved: s 79(8).

8   Agriculture Act 1970 s 78(7)(a).

9   Agriculture Act 1970 s 78(1)(b).

10 See PARA 57.

(v) Enforcement and Criminal Proceedings

52. Enforcement authorities, inspectors and analysts.

In England, it is the duty of each county council[1], metropolitan district council and London borough council[2], and the Common Council of the City of London[3], to enforce the legislation relating to fertilisers and feeding stuffs[4] in their areas[5]. The health authority of the Port of London[6] has the same duty as respects the district of the Port of London[7]. In Wales, the duty to enforce the legislation falls on each county and county borough council[8].

Subject to default powers conferred on the Secretary of State and the Welsh Ministers[9], an enforcement authority must appoint such inspectors as may be necessary[10], an agricultural analyst[11] and, if it thinks fit, one or more deputy agricultural analysts[12]. Any such appointment may be made for the areas of two or more authorities by those authorities acting jointly[13].

In the exercise of his powers an inspector is, if so required, to produce written evidence of his authority[14]. Any person who wilfully obstructs an inspector in the exercise of his powers, and any person who, not being an inspector, purports to act as such, commits an offence[15].

1   As to the counties in England and their councils see LOCAL GOVERNMENT vol 69 (2009) PARA 22 et seq.

2   As to the London boroughs and their councils see LONDON GOVERNMENT vol 71 (2013) PARAS 5, 14–15, 20 et seq.

3   As to the Common Council of the City of London see LONDON GOVERNMENT vol 71 (2013) PARA 34 et seq.

4   Ie the Agriculture Act 1970 Pt IV (ss 66–87).

5   Agriculture Act 1970 s 67(1) (amended by the Local Government Act 1972 Sch 30; the Local Government Act 1985 Sch 8 para 15(3); and the Local Government (Wales) Act 1994 Sch 16 para 38(5), Sch 18). The authorities identified in the Agriculture Act 1970 s 67(1) as having the duty to enforce Pt IV within their areas are 'feed authorities' for the purposes of the Animal Feed (Hygiene, Sampling etc and Enforcement) (England) Regulations 2015, SI 2015/454 (see reg 2(1)) and the Official Feed and Food Controls (England) Regulations 2009, SI 2009/3255 (reg 2(1)). As to the duty of each feed authority within its area to execute and enforce the provisions of those regulations (see PARAS 71 et seq, 84 et seq) and Council Regulation (EC) 183/2005 (OJ L38, 8.2.2005, p 1) laying down requirements for feed hygiene (see PARA 71): see the Animal Feed (Hygiene, Sampling etc and Enforcement) (England) Regulations 2015, SI 2015/454, reg 21; and the Official Feed and Food Controls (England) Regulations 2009, SI 2009/3255, reg 23. As to the disapplication of the Agriculture Act 1970 Pt IV (ss 66–87) and the Fertilisers Regulations 1991, SI 1991/2197 to certain fertilisers see PARA 58 note 1.

6   The Common Council of the City of London is the port health authority for the Port of London: see the Public Health (Control of Disease) Act 1984 s 7; and ENVIRONMENTAL QUALITY AND PUBLIC HEALTH vol 45 (2010) PARA 103.

7   Agriculture Act 1970 s 67(1).

8   Agriculture Act 1970 s 67(1A) (added by the Local Government (Wales) Act 1994 Sch 16 para 38(5)). As to local authorities in Wales see LOCAL GOVERNMENT vol 69 (2009) PARAS 22–23, 37 et seq. The authorities identified in the Agriculture Act 1970 s 67(1A) as having the duty to enforce Pt IV within their areas are 'feed authorities' for the purposes of the Animal Feed (Hygiene, Sampling etc and Enforcement) (Wales) Regulations 2016, SI 2016/387 (see reg 2(1)) and the Official Feed and Food Controls (Wales) Regulations 2009, SI 2009/3376 (see reg 2(1)). As to the duty of each feed authority within its area to execute and enforce the provisions of those regulations and Council Regulation (EC) 183/2005 (OJ L38, 8.2.2005, p 1): Animal Feed (Hygiene, Sampling etc and Enforcement) (Wales) Regulations 2016, SI 2016/387, reg 21; Official Feed and Food Controls (Wales) Regulations 2009, SI 2009/3376, reg 23. As to enforcement see PARA 71.

9   As to the Secretary of State and the Welsh Ministers see PARA 390. If the Secretary of State is or the Welsh Ministers are of opinion that the provisions of the Agriculture Act 1970 Pt IV have been insufficiently enforced in any area he or they may appoint one or more inspectors to exercise in that area the powers exercisable by inspectors appointed by the enforcement authority: s 67(8). Any expenses certified by the Secretary of State or the Welsh Ministers as having been incurred pursuant to these requirements are to be repaid by the authority in question: s 67(8). As to the meaning of 'inspector' see PARA 47 note 6.

10   Agriculture Act 1970 s 67(3)(a). An inspector is not to exercise his powers outside the area for which he is appointed except with the consent of the enforcement authority for that other area: s 67(4).

11   As to the meaning of 'agricultural analyst' see PARA 47 note 7.

12   Agriculture Act 1970 s 67(3)(b). A person is not to be appointed as an agricultural analyst or deputy agricultural analyst unless he has the qualifications prescribed in the Fertilisers (Sampling and Analysis) Regulations 1996, SI 1996/1342, reg 5, the Animal Feed (Hygiene, Sampling etc and Enforcement) (England) Regulations 2015, SI 2015/454, reg 14(4) and the Animal Feed (Hygiene, Sampling etc and Enforcement) (Wales) Regulations 2016, SI 2016/387, reg 14(4): Agriculture Act 1970 s 67(5).

13   Agriculture Act 1970 s 67(6).

14   Agriculture Act 1970 s 83(1).

15   Agriculture Act 1970 s 83(2), (3). The offence of wilful obstruction is punishable on summary conviction by a fine not exceeding level 3 on the standard scale: s 83(2) (amended by virtue of the Criminal Justice Act 1982 ss 35, 38, 46). Until a day to be appointed the offence of impersonation is punishable on summary conviction by a fine not exceeding level 4 on the standard scale or imprisonment for a term not exceeding three months, or both (Agriculture Act 1970 s 83(3) (amended by virtue of the Criminal Justice Act 1982 ss 35, 38, 46)); as from that day the maximum term of imprisonment is increased to a term not exceeding 51 weeks (Agriculture Act 1970 s 83(3) (as so amended; prospectively amended by the Criminal Justice Act 2003 s 280(2), (3), Sch 26 para 22(1), (10))). At the date at which this volume states the law no such day had been appointed. As to prosecutions, defences, etc, see PARAS 55–56. As to the standard scale and the powers of magistrates' courts to issue fines on summary conviction see SENTENCING vol 92 (2015) PARA 176. Where an act or omission is an offence under the EC Fertilisers (England and Wales) Regulations 2006, SI 2006/2486 (see PARAS 58–62), it is not an offence under these provisions: reg 21.

53. Tampering with samples and disclosure of information.

It is an offence[1] for a person to tamper with any material so as to procure that any sample taken or submitted for analysis[2] does not correctly represent the material[3] or to tamper or interfere with any sample so taken or submitted[4]. Any person who discloses any information with respect to any manufacturing process or trade secret obtained in premises which he has entered by virtue of the legislation relating to fertilisers and feedings stuffs or any information obtained in pursuance of that legislation also commits an offence[5] unless the disclosure was made in and for the purpose of the performance by him or any other person of functions under the legislation relating to fertilisers and feeding stuffs[6].

1 Until a day to be appointed this offence is punishable on summary conviction by a fine not exceeding level 5 on the standard scale or imprisonment for a term not exceeding three months, or both (Agriculture Act 1970 s 79(10) (amended by virtue of the Criminal Justice Act 1982 ss 35, 38, 46)); as from that day the maximum term of imprisonment is increased to a term not exceeding 51 weeks (Agriculture Act 1970 s 79(10) (as so amended; prospectively amended by the Criminal Justice Act 2003 s 280(2), (3), Sch 26 para 22(1), (9))). At the date at which this volume states the law no such day had been appointed. As to prosecutions, defences, etc, see PARAS 55–56. As to the standard scale and the powers of magistrates' courts to issue fines on summary conviction see SENTENCING vol 92 (2015) PARA 176. Where an act or omission is an offence under the EC Fertilisers (England and Wales) Regulations 2006, SI 2006/2486 (see PARAS 58–62) it is not an offence under these provisions: reg 21.
2 Ie under the Agriculture Act 1970 Pt IV (ss 66–87). As to the disapplication of the Agriculture Act 1970 Pt IV (ss 66–87) and the Fertilisers Regulations 1991, SI 1991/2197 to certain fertilisers see PARA 58 note 1.
3 Agriculture Act 1970 s 79(10)(a).
4 Agriculture Act 1970 s 79(10)(b).
5 The offence is punishable on summary conviction by a fine not exceeding level 5 on the standard scale: Agriculture Act 1970 s 83(4) (amended by virtue of the Criminal Justice Act 1982 ss 38, 46).
6 Agriculture Act 1970 s 83(4). This does not prevent an inspector who has taken a sample under s 76(4) (see PARA 48) from disclosing to the manufacturer or the last seller of the material information as to the place where and the person from whom the sample was taken or from disclosing to that manufacturer or last seller or to any person who had the material on his premises for the purpose of sale information as to the results of any analysis of that sample: s 83(5).

54. Venue for prosecutions.

Proceedings for an offence under the legislation concerning fertilisers and feeding stuffs[1] may be taken in the place where the person charged resides or carries on business[2].

1 Ie under the Agriculture Act 1970 Pt IV (ss 66–87).
2 Agriculture Act 1970 s 80(1). This is without prejudice to any other enactment relating to venue: s 80(1). As to the limits of magistrates' jurisdiction see MAGISTRATES vol 71 (2013) PARA 428. As to the disapplication of the Agriculture Act 1970 Pt IV (ss 66–87) and the Fertilisers Regulations 1991, SI 1991/2197 to certain fertilisers see PARA 58 note 1.

55. Offences due to fault of another person and by bodies corporate.

Where the commission by any person of an offence under the legislation concerning fertilisers and feeding stuffs[1] is due to the act or default[2] of some other person, that other person is to be guilty of the offence, and a person may be charged with and convicted of the offence whether or not proceedings are taken against the first-mentioned person[3]. Provision is also made as to the commission of offences by bodies corporate[4].

1 Ie under the Agriculture Act 1970 Pt IV (ss 66–87). As to the disapplication of the Agriculture Act 1970 Pt IV (ss 66–87) and the Fertilisers Regulations 1991, SI 1991/2197 to certain fertilisers see PARA 58 note 1.
2 'Act or default' means wrongful act or default: see *Noss Farm Products Ltd v Lilico* [1945] 2 All ER 609. Accordingly, the fact that what the other person did became subsequently unlawful is not sufficient to bring the provision into operation: *Noss Farm Products Ltd v Lilico*. Mens rea or negligence need not be proved, but proof of the act or default of the other person is necessary, and it is not sufficient that the contravention may have been due to his act or default and that the original defendant is clearly innocent: *Moore v Ray* [1951] 1 KB 98, [1950] 2 All ER 561.
3 Agriculture Act 1970 s 81. As to offences committed through the act or default of another person see further PARA 56.
4 See the Agriculture Act 1970 s 110; and PARA 427.

56.   Defence of mistake, accident, etc.

In proceedings for certain offences under the legislation concerning fertilisers and feeding stuffs[1] it is a defence for the person charged to prove that the commission of the offence was due to a mistake, or to reliance on information supplied to him, or to the act or default of another person, or to an accident or some other cause beyond his control[2], and that he took all reasonable precautions and exercised all due diligence to avoid the commission of such an offence by himself or any person under his control[3].

The offences in connection with the marketing of fertilisers and feeding stuff to which these defences are available are:

(1)   giving a statutory statement which, as respects a sampled portion[4] of the material, contains insufficient or false particulars[5];

(2)   selling or exposing for sale material in respect of which a statutory statement is not required to be given[6] in a case where the label contains insufficient or false particulars[7];

(3)   having on premises for the purposes of (and ready for) sale material marked with a mark which, as respects a sampled portion of it, contains insufficient or false particulars[8];

(4)   selling, or having on premises ready for sale, material described by or marked with a prescribed name or expression, a sampled portion of which fails to accord to the meaning assigned to that name or expression[9];

(5)   describing or marking any material, in purported compliance with the requirement to give particulars of claimed attributes[10], with particulars which, as respects a sampled portion of the material, are false to the prejudice of the purchaser[11]; and

(6)   contravening or failing to comply with regulations made with a view to controlling the composition or content of fertilisers and feeding stuffs[12].

These defences are also available in connection with the following offences connected with the marketing of feeding stuffs only:

(a)   giving a statutory statement, pursuant to a sale of material for use as a feeding stuff, which contains particulars other than those prescribed[13];

(b)   selling, or having on premises for the purposes of and ready for sale, material a sampled portion of which is shown to contain an ingredient which is deleterious to animals or (through indirect consumption) humans[14]; and

(c)   selling or having on premises for the purposes of and ready for sale material a sampled portion of which is shown to be unwholesome for or dangerous to animals or (through indirect consumption) dangerous to humans[15].

If this defence involves the allegation that the commission of the offence was due to the act or default of another person, or to reliance on information supplied by another person, the person charged is not, without leave of the court, entitled to rely on the defence unless, within a period ending seven clear days before the hearing, he has served on the prosecutor a notice giving such information identifying or assisting in the identification of that other person as was then in his possession[16].

1   Ie under the Agriculture Act 1970 Pt IV (ss 66–87). As to the disapplication of Pt IV to certain fertilisers see PARA 58 note 1.

2   Agriculture Act 1970 s 82(1)(a). As to the meaning of 'act or default of another person' see PARA 55 note 2.

3   Agriculture Act 1970 s 82(1)(b).

4   As to the meaning of 'sampled portion' see PARA 40 note 14.

5   Agriculture Act 1970 s 82(1) (amended by SI 1995/1412). As to this offence see the Agriculture Act 1970 s 68(4)(b); and PARA 40.

6   See the Agriculture Act 1970 s 68(2)(b); and PARA 40.

7   Agriculture Act 1970 s 82(1) (as amended: see note 5). As to this offence see s 68(4)(c); and PARA 40.

8   Agriculture Act 1970 s 82(1). As to this offence see s 69(4)(c); and PARA 41.

9   Agriculture Act 1970 s 82(1). As to this offence see s 70(2); and PARA 42.

10   Ie in purported compliance with the Agriculture Act 1970 s 71(1) (see PARA 43).

11   Agriculture Act 1970 s 82(1). As to this offence see s 71(2)(b); and PARA 43.

12   Agriculture Act 1970 s 82(1) (as amended: see note 5). As to this offence see s 74A(3); and PARA 45.

13   Agriculture Act 1970 s 82(1) (as amended: see note 5). As to this offence see s 68(1A); and PARA 40.

14   Agriculture Act 1970 s 82(1) (as amended: see note 5). As to this offence see s 73 (repealed).

15   Agriculture Act 1970 s 82(1) (as amended: see note 5). As to this offence see s 73A (repealed).

16   Agriculture Act 1970 s 82(2).

57. Analysis by Government Chemist pursuant to proceedings for an offence.

Where a sample of any material has been taken by an inspector[1] in the prescribed manner[2], and it is intended to institute proceedings for an offence[3] and to adduce on behalf of the prosecution evidence of the result of an analysis of the sample, the prosecutor[4] is entitled to require[5] the inspector to send the remaining part of the sample for analysis to the Government Chemist[6] and to supply the prosecutor with a copy of the Government Chemist's certificate of analysis of that remaining part[7]. If the inspector is the prosecutor, he is himself entitled so to send that remaining part[8]. The Government Chemist must analyse the sample in such manner, if any, as may be prescribed[9] and send a certificate of analysis to the inspector[10].

Where proceedings are brought against any person for an offence[11], and evidence is given or sought to be given of the result of an analysis of a sample of any material taken by an inspector in the prescribed manner, but it appears that the sample has not been analysed by the Government Chemist, the court may, of its own motion or on the application of either party, order the remaining part of the sample to be sent for analysis to the Government Chemist[12], who must analyse the sample in such manner, if any, as may be prescribed[13] and send a certificate of analysis to the court[14].

A certificate of analysis by an agricultural analyst or the Government Chemist is, in any legal proceedings, to be received as evidence of the facts stated in it, provided that the party against whom it is to be given in evidence has been served with a copy not less than 21 days before the hearing and has not, before the seventh day preceding the hearing, served on the other party a notice requiring the attendance of the person who made the analysis[15].

1   As to the meaning of 'inspector' see PARA 47 note 6. As to the appointment of inspectors see PARA 52.

2   For the prescribed manner for taking, marking, sealing and fastening up of samples see PARA 47 note 5.

3   Ie an offence under the Agriculture Act 1970 Pt IV (ss 66–87). As to the disapplication of Pt IV and the Fertilisers Regulations 1991, SI 1991/2197 to certain fertilisers see PARA 58 note 1.

4   For these purposes the prosecutor is required to be a person other than the inspector: Agriculture Act 1970 s 78(2)(a).

5   Such a request must be accompanied by the appropriate fee: see the Agriculture Act 1970 s 78(8). 'Appropriate fee' means such fee as may be fixed by the Secretary of State with the approval of the Treasury; and different fees may be fixed for different materials and for different analyses of the same material: s 78(10) (amended by SI 1970/1537).

6   Agriculture Act 1970 s 78(2)(a)(i). Where a prosecutor avails himself of these rights, he must cause to be served with the summons a copy of the agricultural analyst's certificate of analysis (see PARA 50) and a copy of the Government Chemist's certificate of analysis; and where a prosecutor does not avail himself of these rights he must, not less than 14 days before the service of the summons, cause to be served on the person charged a copy of the agricultural analyst's certificate of analysis and a notice of intended prosecution, and if, within the period of 14 days beginning with the service of the notice, that person sends the prosecutor a written request to that effect (accompanied by the fee payable, which is to be refunded if the prosecution is not brought), the prosecutor must exercise his rights and the proceedings are not to be instituted until he has sent that person a copy of the Government Chemist's certificate of analysis: s 78(3). Where a part of a sample is sent for analysis to the Government Chemist under these provisions there must also be sent a copy of any document which was sent with the part of the sample sent to the agricultural analyst (see PARA 49) along with a statement of the particulars on which the proceedings or intended proceedings are based: s 78(5). As to the meaning of 'agricultural analyst' see PARA 47 note 7.

7   Agriculture Act 1970 s 78(2)(a)(ii). This applies whether the remaining part was sent to the Government Chemist for analysis in pursuance of the request of the prosecutor or otherwise: s 78(2)(a)(ii). As to the method of sending see PARA 49 note 5.

8   Agriculture Act 1970 s 78(2)(b). See further note 6.

9   Agriculture Act 1970 s 78(6). As to the prescribed methods of analysis see PARA 50 note 2. Where the part is accompanied by a statement of the particulars on which the proceedings are based (see note 6), the analysis must be made only with respect to the particulars in the statement unless the person or court requesting or ordering the analysis requires it to extend to other matters: s 78(6). Any analysis required to be made by the Government Chemist may be made by any person acting under his directions: s 79(4).

10 Agriculture Act 1970 s 78(7)(a). As to certificates of analysis see PARAS 50 note 3, 51 note 7.

11 Ie an offence under the Agriculture Act 1970 Pt IV.

12 Agriculture Act 1970 s 78(4). Where a part of a sample is sent for analysis to the Government Chemist under these provisions there must also be sent a copy of any document which was sent with the part of the sample sent to the agricultural analyst along with a statement of the particulars on which the proceedings or intended proceedings are based: s 78(5). The appropriate fee (see note 5) for an analysis ordered by the court is to be paid by such party as the court may direct: s 78(8).

13 Agriculture Act 1970 s 78(6). As to the prescribed methods of analysis see PARA 50 note 2. Where the part is accompanied by a statement of the particulars on which the proceedings are based (see note 6), the analysis must be made only with respect to the particulars in the statement unless the person or court requesting or ordering the analysis requires it to extend to other matters: s 78(6).

14 Agriculture Act 1970 s 78(7)(b).

15 Agriculture Act 1970 s 79(6).

(2) REGULATION OF FERTILISERS UNDER EU LAW

58.   Designation and marketing of EC fertilisers.

It is an offence[1] for a manufacturer[2] to place on the market[3] a fertiliser[4] designated as an 'EC fertiliser' unless:

(1)   the manufacturer is established within the EU[5] and the fertiliser is of a type specified for the purpose[6];

(2)   the content of the fertiliser complies with specified tolerances[7] and does not take systematic advantage thereof[8]; or

(3)   the identification markings relating to the fertiliser comply with specified requirements of the relevant EU Regulation[9].

Additional provision is made in connection with the marking and identification of packaged and bulk[10] fertilisers[11], inorganic primary and secondary nutrient fertilisers[12] and inorganic micro-nutrient fertilisers[13]. It is also an offence to fail to comply with the provisions of the EU Regulation concerning traceability[14].

1   A person guilty of an offence under the EC Fertilisers (England and Wales) Regulations 2006, SI 2006/2486, is liable on summary conviction to a fine not exceeding the statutory maximum or to imprisonment for a term not exceeding three months or to both (reg 20(1)(a)), or on conviction

Fertilisers and Feeding Stuffs

on indictment to a fine or to imprisonment for a term not exceeding two years or to both (reg 20(1)(b)). Where a body corporate is guilty of such an offence, and that offence is proved to have been committed with the consent or connivance of, or to have been attributable to any neglect on the part of any director (which, in relation to a body corporate whose affairs are managed by its members, means a member of the body corporate: reg 20(3)), manager, secretary or other similar person of the body corporate (reg 20(2)(a)) or any person who was purporting to act in such a capacity (reg 20(2)(b)), he, as well as the body corporate, is guilty of the offence and liable to be proceeded against and punished accordingly (reg 20(2)). Where an act or omission is an offence under the EC Fertilisers (England and Wales) Regulations 2006, SI 2006/2486, it is not an offence under the Agriculture Act 1970 Pt IV (ss 66–87) (see PARA 37 et seq) or the Fertilisers Regulations 1991, SI 1991/2197 (see PARA 40 et seq): EC Fertilisers (England and Wales) Regulations 2006, SI 2006/2486, reg 21.

    As to the statutory maximum see SENTENCING vol 92 (2015) PARA 176.

    The EC Fertilisers (England and Wales) Regulations 2006, SI 2006/2486, are made under the European Communities Act 1972 s 2(2), and implement Council Regulation (EC) 2003/2003 (OJ L304, 21.11.2003, p 1) relating to fertilisers (the 'EU Regulation').

2 As to the meaning of 'manufacturer' see Council Regulation (EC) 2003/2003 (OJ L304, 21.11.2003, p 1) art 2(x); definition applied by the EC Fertilisers (England and Wales) Regulations 2006, SI 2006/2486, reg 2(2)(b).

3 As to the meaning of 'place on the market' see Council Regulation (EC) 2003/2003 (OJ L304, 21.11.2003, p 1) art 2(w); definition applied by the EC Fertilisers (England and Wales) Regulations 2006, SI 2006/2486, reg 2(2)(b).

4 As to the meaning of 'fertiliser' see Council Regulation (EC) 2003/2003 (OJ L304, 21.11.2003, p 1) art 2(a); definition applied by the EC Fertilisers (England and Wales) Regulations 2006, SI 2006/2486, reg 2(2)(b).

5 EC Fertilisers (England and Wales) Regulations 2006, SI 2006/2486, reg 3(1)(b) (amended by SI 2011/1043). The reference in the text to a manufacturer being 'established within the EU' is a reference to his being established in accordance with Council Regulation (EC) 2003/2003 (OJ L304, 21.11.2003, p 1) art 4: EC Fertilisers (England and Wales) Regulations 2006, SI 2006/2486, reg 3(1)(b) (as so amended).

6 EC Fertilisers (England and Wales) Regulations 2006, SI 2006/2486, reg 3(1)(a). As to the specified types see Council Regulation (EC) 2003/2003 (OJ L304, 21.11.2003, p 1) Annex 1.

7 EC Fertilisers (England and Wales) Regulations 2006, SI 2006/2486, reg 4(a). As to the meaning of 'tolerance' see Council Regulation (EC) 2003/2003 (OJ L304, 21.11.2003, p 1) art 2(s); definition applied by the EC Fertilisers (England and Wales) Regulations 2006, SI 2006/2486, reg 2(2)(b). For the specified tolerances see Council Regulation (EC) 2003/2003 (OJ L304, 21.11.2003, p 1) art 13(1), (3).

    In any proceedings for an offence in relation to which the content of a fertiliser is relevant:

(1)   a court may not conclude that a sample is representative of the fertiliser unless the sample has been taken in accordance with Annex IV (methods of sampling and analysis) (EC Fertilisers (England and Wales) Regulations 2006, SI 2006/2486, reg 17(a)(i)) and it has been subjected to analysis in accordance with Council Regulation (EC) 2003/2003 (OJ L304, 21.11.2003, p 1) Annex IV in a laboratory listed in accordance with Council Regulation (EC) 2003/2003 (OJ L304, 21.11.2003, p 1) art 30(2) or (5) (EC Fertilisers (England and Wales) Regulations 2006, SI 2006/2486, reg 17(a)(ii));

(2)   a certificate given by a person that he is an inspector and took the sample in accordance with Council Regulation (EC) 2003/2003 (OJ L304, 21.11.2003, p 1) Annex IV must, unless the contrary is proved, be taken as evidence of his being one and having done so (EC Fertilisers (England and Wales) Regulations 2006, SI 2006/2486, reg 17(b));

(3)   a certificate given on behalf of a laboratory that it is authorised under Council Regulation (EC) 2003/2003 (OJ L304, 21.11.2003, p 1) art 33 and that it analysed the sample in question in accordance with Annex IV is, unless the contrary is proved, evidence of it being so authorised and having done so (EC Fertilisers (England and Wales) Regulations 2006, SI 2006/2486, reg 17(c)); and

(4)   the combination of those certificates must, unless the contrary is proved, be taken as evidence that the sample is representative of the fertiliser (reg 17(d)).

The Secretary of State and the Welsh Ministers (see PARA 390) are responsible for granting or withdrawing authorisations for the purposes of Council Regulation (EC) 2003/2003 (OJ L304, 21.11.2003, p 1) art 33 (competent laboratories): EC Fertilisers (England and Wales) Regulations 2006, SI 2006/2486, reg 16(1). In deciding whether to grant or withdraw such an authorisation, the Secretary of State and the Welsh Ministers must take into account the actual and expected competence of the laboratory to check compliance of fertilisers designated as EC fertilisers with the requirements of Council Regulation (EC) 2003/2003 (OJ L304, 21.11.2003, p 1): EC Fertilisers (England and Wales) Regulations 2006, SI 2006/2486, reg 16(2). A statement given by the Secretary of State or the Welsh Ministers to the operator of a laboratory in anticipation of the coming into force of the EC Fertilisers (England and Wales) Regulations 2006, SI 2006/2486, reg 16, that the laboratory is authorised for the purposes of Council Regulation (EC) 2003/2003 (OJ L304, 21.11.2003, p 1) art 33 is deemed to be an authorisation under the EC Fertilisers (England and Wales) Regulations 2006, SI 2006/2486, reg 16: reg 16(3).

The Fertilisers (Sampling and Analysis) Regulations 1996, SI 1996/1342 (see PARA 47 et seq) do not apply to any sampling or analysis of fertilisers carried out pursuant to the EC Fertilisers (England and Wales) Regulations 2006, SI 2006/2486: reg 22.

8   EC Fertilisers (England and Wales) Regulations 2006, SI 2006/2486, reg 4(b). See Council Regulation (EC) 2003/2003 (OJ L304, 21.11.2003, p 1) art 13(2); and for the specified tolerances see Annex II, which gives tolerances that are negative values in percentage by mass.

9   EC Fertilisers (England and Wales) Regulations 2006, SI 2006/2486, reg 5(1). For this purpose markings must be borne as specified in Council Regulation (EC) 2003/2003 (OJ L304, 21.11.2003, p 1) art 9(1); comply with art 9(2); include a declaration of contents as specified in art 6(1)(a), (d), (4), (5), (6) (compulsory statements); include the additional instructions called for by art 9(3) if it is a fluid fertiliser; and have been provided as specified in art 7(1) (identification): EC Fertilisers (England and Wales) Regulations 2006, SI 2006/2486, reg 5(1)(a)–(e). As to the meaning of 'fluid fertiliser' see Council Regulation (EC) 2003/2003 (OJ L304, 21.11.2003, p 1) art 2(n); definition applied by the EC Fertilisers (England and Wales) Regulations 2006, SI 2006/2486, reg 2(2)(b).

10 As to the meaning of 'bulk' see Council Regulation (EC) 2003/2003 (OJ L304, 21.11.2003, p 1) art 2(v); definition applied by the EC Fertilisers (England and Wales) Regulations 2006, SI 2006/2486, reg 2(2)(b).

11 A manufacturer must not place on the market a packaged or bulk fertiliser designated as an EC fertiliser unless the identification markings, packaging, labelling and documentation comply with specified requirements of the EU Regulation: EC Fertilisers (England and Wales) Regulations 2006, SI 2006/2486, reg 5(2). The requirements concerning packaged fertilisers are that: the identification markings must appear as specified in the first sentence of Council Regulation (EC) 2003/2003 (OJ L304, 21.11.2003, p 1) art 7(2); the packaging and labelling of the fertiliser must comply with arts 10(1), (2), 12; and the language in which the identification markings appear must comply with art 11: EC Fertilisers (England and Wales) Regulations 2006, SI 2006/2486, reg 5(2)(a)–(d). The requirements concerning bulk fertilisers are that: the identification markings must appear as specified in the second sentence of Council Regulation (EC) 2003/2003 (OJ L304, 21.11.2003, p 1) art 7(2); a copy of the documents containing them must meet the requirements of art 10(3); and the language in which the identification markings appear must comply with art 11: EC Fertilisers (England and Wales) Regulations 2006, SI 2006/2486, reg 5(3)(a)–(c).

12 See the EC Fertilisers (England and Wales) Regulations 2006, SI 2006/2486, regs 6, 7. As to the meanings of 'primary nutrient' and 'secondary nutrient' see Council Regulation (EC) 2003/2003 (OJ L304, 21.11.2003, p 1) art 2(b), (c); definitions applied by the EC Fertilisers (England and Wales) Regulations 2006, SI 2006/2486, reg 2(2)(b).

13 See the EC Fertilisers (England and Wales) Regulations 2006, SI 2006/2486, reg 8. As to the meanings of 'inorganic fertiliser' and 'micro-nutrients' see Council Regulation (EC) 2003/2003 (OJ L304, 21.11.2003, p 1) art 2(d), (e); definitions applied by the EC Fertilisers (England and Wales) Regulations 2006, SI 2006/2486, reg 2(2)(b).

14 EC Fertilisers (England and Wales) Regulations 2006, SI 2006/2486, reg 9. For the provisions concerning traceability see Council Regulation (EC) 2003/2003 (OJ L304, 21.11.2003, p 1) art 8.

59. Enforcement of regulations concerning marketing of fertilisers.

Local authorities[1] are empowered to appoint inspectors for the purpose of enforcing the EU Regulation relating to fertilisers and its implementing legislation[2], and such an inspector may, at all reasonable times and on producing, if requested to do so, some duly authenticated document showing his authority, enter any premises[3] for the purpose of ensuring compliance therewith[4]. If necessary, the authorised officer may secure a warrant to enter premises or to secure entry by force[5]. An inspector entering premises by virtue of these provisions may take with him such other persons and such equipment as may appear to him to be necessary[6] and any representative of the European Commission acting for the purpose of the enforcement of the EU Regulation[7], and on leaving any unoccupied premises must leave them as effectively secured against unauthorised entry as he found them[8].

Inspectors entering premises pursuant to these powers may:

(1)   inspect the premises, and any plant, machinery or equipment[9];

(2)   search the premises[10];

(3)   inspect any material and take samples in the prescribed manner[11];

(4)   examine or seize any documents or records (including financial records)[12];

(5)   seize any computers and associated equipment for the purpose of copying documents[13];

(6)   carry out any inquiries, examinations and tests[14];

(7)   have access to, and inspect and copy, any documents or records[15], or remove such records to enable them to be copied[16]; and

(8)   have access to, inspect and check the operation of any computer and any associated apparatus or material which is or has been in use in connection with the records[17].

The intentional obstruction of any person acting in the execution of these provisions[18] is an offence[19].

1   For this purpose 'local authority' means:
     (1)   where there is a unitary authority for a local government area (ie any authority which is the sole principal council for its local government area), the authority for that area (EC Fertilisers (England and Wales) Regulations 2006, SI 2006/2486, reg 11(3)(a), (4)); and
     (2)   where there is not a unitary authority: (a) in a metropolitan district, the council of that district (reg 11(3)(b)(i)); (b) in a non-metropolitan county, the council of that county (reg 11(3)(b)(ii)); (c) in each London borough, the council of that borough (reg 11(3)(b)(iii)); (d) in the City of London, the Common Council (reg 11(3)(b)(iv)); (e) in the Isles of Scilly, the Council of the Isles of Scilly (reg 11(3)(b)(v)); and (f) in respect of a local government area within Wales, the county council or the county borough council for that area, as the case may be (reg 11(3)(b)(vi)).
    As to local government areas and authorities in England and Wales see LOCAL GOVERNMENT vol 69 (2009) PARA 22 et seq. As to the London boroughs and their councils see LONDON GOVERNMENT vol 71 (2013) PARAS 15, 20–22, 55 et seq. As to the Common Council of the City of London see LONDON GOVERNMENT vol 71 (2013) PARA 34 et seq. As to the Council of the Isles of Scilly see LOCAL GOVERNMENT vol 69 (2009) PARA 36.
2   EC Fertilisers (England and Wales) Regulations 2006, SI 2006/2486, reg 11(1), (2). As to the EU Regulation relating to fertilisers (ie Council Regulation (EC) 2003/2003 (OJ L304, 21.11.2003, p 1) relating to fertilisers) and its implementing legislation (ie the EC Fertilisers (England and Wales) Regulations 2006, SI 2006/2486) see PARA 58.
3   'Premises' includes any place, any vehicle or trailer, any container, any stall or moveable structure, and any ship or aircraft: EC Fertilisers (England and Wales) Regulations 2006, SI 2006/2486, reg 2(1). Admission to any premises used only as a private dwelling house may not be demanded as of right unless 24 hours' notice of the intended entry has been given to the occupier, or the entry is in accordance with a warrant granted under reg 12 (see note 5): reg 12(3).
4   EC Fertilisers (England and Wales) Regulations 2006, SI 2006/2486, reg 12(1).
5   Where a justice of the peace, on sworn information in writing, is satisfied that there are reasonable grounds for entry into any premises for the purposes of the enforcement of the EU Regulation, and: (1) admission to the premises has been refused, or a refusal is expected, and notice of the intention to apply for a warrant has been given to the occupier (EC Fertilisers (England and Wales) Regulations 2006, SI 2006/2486, reg 12(4)(a)); (2) asking for admission, or giving such a notice, would defeat the object of the entry (reg 12(4)(b)); (3) the case is one of urgency (reg 12(4)(c)); or (4) the premises are unoccupied or the occupier is temporarily absent (reg 12(4)(d)), he may by warrant signed by him authorise the inspector to enter the premises, if need be by reasonable force, and to take with him such persons as appear to be necessary (reg 12(4)). Every warrant so granted continues in force for a period of one month: reg 12(5).
6   EC Fertilisers (England and Wales) Regulations 2006, SI 2006/2486, reg 12(2)(a).
7   EC Fertilisers (England and Wales) Regulations 2006, SI 2006/2486, reg 12(2)(b).

8   EC Fertilisers (England and Wales) Regulations 2006, SI 2006/2486, reg 12(6).
9   EC Fertilisers (England and Wales) Regulations 2006, SI 2006/2486, reg 13(1)(a).
10 EC Fertilisers (England and Wales) Regulations 2006, SI 2006/2486, reg 13(1)(b).
11 EC Fertilisers (England and Wales) Regulations 2006, SI 2006/2486, reg 13(1)(c). The prescribed
    manner is that prescribed in Council Regulation (EC) 2003/2003 (OJ L304, 21.11.2003, p 1)
    Annex IV (methods of sampling and analysis).
12 EC Fertilisers (England and Wales) Regulations 2006, SI 2006/2486, reg 13(1)(d).
13 EC Fertilisers (England and Wales) Regulations 2006, SI 2006/2486, reg 13(1)(e). Equipment
    seized pursuant to this power must be returned as soon as practicable: reg 13(1)(e).
14 EC Fertilisers (England and Wales) Regulations 2006, SI 2006/2486, reg 13(1)(f).
15 Ie any documents or records, in whatever form they are held, required to be kept by Council
    Regulation (EC) 2003/2003 (OJ L304, 21.11.2003, p 1): EC Fertilisers (England and Wales)
    Regulations 2006, SI 2006/2486, reg 13(1)(g).
16 EC Fertilisers (England and Wales) Regulations 2006, SI 2006/2486, reg 13(1)(g).
17 EC Fertilisers (England and Wales) Regulations 2006, SI 2006/2486, reg 13(1)(h). For this purpose
    an inspector may require any person having charge of, or otherwise concerned with the operation
    of, the computer, apparatus or material to afford him such assistance as he may reasonably require
    and, where a record is kept by means of a computer, may require the records to be produced in a
    form in which they may be taken away: reg 13(2).
18 Ie the EC Fertilisers (England and Wales) Regulations 2006, SI 2006/2486.
19 EC Fertilisers (England and Wales) Regulations 2006, SI 2006/2486, reg 15(1)(a). As to offences
    see PARA 58 note 1. 'Obstruction' for these purposes includes failure, without reasonable cause,
    to give any person acting in the execution of the regulations any assistance or information which
    that person may reasonably require of him for the performance of his functions under the
    regulations (reg 15(1)(b)) (although this does not require any person to answer any question if to
    do so might incriminate him (reg 15(2))) and furnishing to any person acting in the execution of
    the regulations any information which he knows to be false or misleading (reg 15(1)(c)).

60. Compliance notices.

Where either or both of the Secretary of State and the Welsh Ministers[1] is, or
are, of the opinion that a person is a manufacturer[2] placing on the market[3]
fertiliser[4] that does not comply with the relevant EU Regulation[5], but that person
has not committed an offence under the relevant implementing legislation[6], the
Secretary of State and the Welsh Ministers may each serve a notice in writing on
the person in question giving reasons why he is, or as the case may be, they are of
that opinion and requiring that person to take such steps as are specified in the
notice[7] within such period (being not less than 14 days except in an emergency) as
is so specified[8]. If the Secretary of State considers, or the Welsh Ministers consider,
that a person served with such a notice has failed to comply with its
requirements[9], he or they may appoint a person[10] to ascertain whether such a
failure has occurred[11]. This power is also exercisable where the Secretary of State
or the Welsh Ministers require the local authority to ascertain whether there has
been such a failure[12] and the local authority fails to comply with the
requirement[13]. Failure to comply with a compliance notice is an offence unless the
notice has been withdrawn[14].

1   As to the Secretary of State and the Welsh Ministers see PARA 390.
2   As to the meaning of 'manufacturer' see PARA 58 note 2.
3   As to the meaning of 'placing on the market' see PARA 58 note 3.
4   As to the meaning of 'fertiliser' see PARA 58 note 4.
5   Ie Council Regulation (EC) 2003/2003 (OJ L304, 21.11.2003, p 1) relating to fertilisers: see PARA
    58.
6   Ie under the EC Fertilisers (England and Wales) Regulations 2006, SI 2006/2486, regs 3–9 (see
    PARA 58). The local authority (see PARA 59 note 1) must give the Secretary of State and the Welsh
    Ministers on demand such information as the Secretary of State or the Welsh Ministers require in
    order to exercise any function under reg 10: reg 14(1).
7   The steps to be so specified are steps that the Secretary of State regards or, as the case may be, the
    Welsh Ministers regard as appropriate to cause him or them no longer to be of the opinion referred
    to in the text: EC Fertilisers (England and Wales) Regulations 2006, SI 2006/2486, reg 10(3).

8 EC Fertilisers (England and Wales) Regulations 2006, SI 2006/2486, reg 10(1), (2).
9 EC Fertilisers (England and Wales) Regulations 2006, SI 2006/2486, reg 14(2)(a).
10 A person so appointed is deemed to be an inspector: EC Fertilisers (England and Wales) Regulations 2006, SI 2006/2486, reg 14(3)(b). For the powers of inspectors see PARA 59.
11 EC Fertilisers (England and Wales) Regulations 2006, SI 2006/2486, reg 14(3)(a). The costs incurred by the Secretary of State or the Welsh Ministers in connection with ascertaining whether there has been such a failure are recoverable on demand from the local authority: reg 14(3)(c).
12 EC Fertilisers (England and Wales) Regulations 2006, SI 2006/2486, reg 14(2)(b).
13 EC Fertilisers (England and Wales) Regulations 2006, SI 2006/2486, reg 14(2)(c).
14 EC Fertilisers (England and Wales) Regulations 2006, SI 2006/2486, reg 10(4). As to offences see PARA 58 note 1.

61. Remedial action and seizure.

If an inspector[1] has reasonable grounds to believe that a fertiliser[2] designated as an EC fertiliser[3] is one in relation to which an offence[4] has been committed he may give to the person whom he considers to be in charge of the fertiliser a notice[5] requiring him to take action, specified in the notice[6], to ensure that the fertiliser is removed from the market, and not placed on the market[7] again until it can be so placed without an offence being committed[8]. Any person who fails to comply with such a notice is guilty of an offence[9].

Alternatively, the inspector may seize the fertiliser in order to have it dealt with by a justice of the peace[10]. If he does this he must inform the person whom he considers liable to prosecution of the grounds for his belief[11], and that person may attend before the justice who deals with the fertiliser[12]. If the justice finds that the fertiliser is one in relation to which an offence has been committed he must order that it be destroyed or disposed of in an appropriate manner[13].

1 For the appointment and powers of inspectors see PARA 59.
2 As to the meaning of 'fertiliser' see PARA 58 note 4.
3 See PARA 58.
4 Ie an offence under the EC Fertilisers (England and Wales) Regulations 2006, SI 2006/2486 (see PARAS 58–60). As to offences see PARA 58 note 1.
5 Such a notice must also specify the grounds for the inspector's belief: EC Fertilisers (England and Wales) Regulations 2006, SI 2006/2486, reg 18(3).
6 EC Fertilisers (England and Wales) Regulations 2006, SI 2006/2486, reg 18(1)(a).
7 As to the meaning of 'placing on the market' see PARA 58 note 3.
8 EC Fertilisers (England and Wales) Regulations 2006, SI 2006/2486, reg 18(2).
9 EC Fertilisers (England and Wales) Regulations 2006, SI 2006/2486, reg 18(5).
10 EC Fertilisers (England and Wales) Regulations 2006, SI 2006/2486, reg 18(1)(b).
11 EC Fertilisers (England and Wales) Regulations 2006, SI 2006/2486, reg 18(4)(a).
12 EC Fertilisers (England and Wales) Regulations 2006, SI 2006/2486, reg 18(4)(b). The person is entitled to be heard (reg 18(4)(b)(i)) and may call witnesses (reg 18(4)(b)(ii)).
13 EC Fertilisers (England and Wales) Regulations 2006, SI 2006/2486, reg 18(4)(c)(i). Any expenses reasonably incurred in connection with the destruction or disposal must be defrayed by the person in question: reg 18(4)(c)(ii).

62. Safeguard measures.

Where a risk identified in the relevant EU Regulation[1] applies in relation to a fertiliser[2] covered thereby, the Secretary of State or the Welsh Ministers[3], or both, may direct any person[4] whom he considers or they consider to be in charge of the fertiliser to take such action to mitigate or eliminate the risk as is specified in the direction[5]. Any person who fails to comply with such a direction is guilty of an offence unless the direction has been withdrawn[6].

1 Ie Council Regulation (EC) 2003/2003 (OJ L304, 21.11.2003, p 1) relating to fertilisers, art 15 (safeguard clause). As to the EU Regulation see PARA 58.
2 As to the meaning of 'fertiliser' see PARA 58 note 4.
3 As to the Secretary of State and the Welsh Ministers see PARA 390.

4   A direction must be given by notice served on the person in question: EC Fertilisers (England and
    Wales) Regulations 2006, SI 2006/2486, reg 19(2). If the Secretary of State considers or the Welsh
    Ministers consider that the direction should be given to a number of persons and the most efficient
    way of bringing it quickly to their attention would be publicising it by other means, the direction
    must be given to them by publicising it by those other means: reg 19(3).
5   EC Fertilisers (England and Wales) Regulations 2006, SI 2006/2486, reg 19(1).
6   EC Fertilisers (England and Wales) Regulations 2006, SI 2006/2486, reg 19(4). As to offences see
    PARA 58 note 1. In any proceedings for such an offence it is a defence for the person accused to
    show either that he was not in charge of the fertiliser or that he was not aware of the direction: reg
    19(5).

(3) USE OF SLUDGE ON AGRICULTURAL LAND

63. Restrictions on use of sludge.

No person may cause or knowingly permit sludge[1] to be used[2] on agricultural
land[3] unless:

(1)   the pH value and the content and concentration of specified materials
      are tested at specified regular intervals[4];

(2)   the soil on the land is similarly tested or assessed[5];

(3)   where the land is a dedicated site[6], the average annual rate of addition
      to the land by means of the sludge of any of the specified elements[7] does
      not exceed the specified limit[8];

(4)   where the land is a dedicated site, the concentration in the soil of any of
      the specified elements[9] does not exceed the specified limit[10];

(5)   the pH value of the soil is not less than 5[11];

(6)   no fruit or vegetable crops, other than fruit trees, are growing or being
      harvested in the soil at the time of the use[12]; and

(7)   the sludge is used in such a way that account is taken of the nutrient
      needs of the plants and that the quality of the soil and of the surface and
      ground water is not impaired[13].

1   'Sludge' means residual sludge from sewage plants treating domestic or urban waste waters and
    from other sewage plants treating waste waters of a composition similar to domestic and urban
    waste waters: Sludge (Use in Agriculture) Regulations 1989, SI 1989/1263, reg 2(1).
2   'Use' means spreading on the soil or any other application on or in the soil; and 'used' is to be
    construed accordingly: Sludge (Use in Agriculture) Regulations 1989, SI 1989/1263, reg 2(1).
3   For these purposes 'agriculture' means the growing of all types of commercial food crops,
    including for stock-rearing purposes; and cognate words are to be construed accordingly: Sludge
    (Use in Agriculture) Regulations 1989, SI 1989/1263, reg 2(1).
4   Sludge (Use in Agriculture) Regulations 1989, SI 1989/1263, reg 3(1), (2). Testing is in accordance
    with Sch 1 (see PARA 67): reg 3(2).
5   Sludge (Use in Agriculture) Regulations 1989, SI 1989/1263, reg 3(3). Testing is in accordance
    with Sch 2 (see PARA 68): reg 3(3).
6   As to the meaning of 'dedicated site', and for restrictions in connection with the production of
    crops thereon, see PARA 66.
7   Ie the elements listed in column (1) of the sludge table set out in the Sludge (Use in Agriculture)
    Regulations 1989, SI 1989/1263, Sch 1 para 4 (see PARA 67).
8   Sludge (Use in Agriculture) Regulations 1989, SI 1989/1263, reg 3(4)(a). The 'specified limit' is the
    limit specified in column (2) of the sludge table set out in Sch 1 para 4 (see PARA 67).
9   Ie the elements listed in column (1) of the soil table set out in the Sludge (Use in Agriculture)
    Regulations 1989, SI 1989/1263, Sch 2 para 5 (see PARA 68).
10 Sludge (Use in Agriculture) Regulations 1989, SI 1989/1263, reg 3(4)(b). The 'specified limit' is the
    limit specified in column (2) of the soil table set out in Sch 2 para 5 (see PARA 68). Where the
    specified limit is not exceeded at the time of the use, it must not be exceeded by reason of the use:
    reg 3(4)(b).
11 Sludge (Use in Agriculture) Regulations 1989, SI 1989/1263, reg 3(5).

12   Sludge (Use in Agriculture) Regulations 1989, SI 1989/1263, reg 3(6).

13   Sludge (Use in Agriculture) Regulations 1989, SI 1989/1263, reg 3(7). Any person who contravenes regs 2–8 is guilty of an offence, and liable on summary conviction to a fine not exceeding level 5 on the standard scale: reg 9. As to the power of the Environment Agency to impose civil sanctions in relation to an offence under the Sludge (Use in Agriculture) Regulations 1989, SI 1989/1263, for contravening specified provisions see, in relation to England, reg 10 (added by SI 2010/1159), and, in relation to Wales, Sludge (Use in Agriculture) Regulations 1989, SI 1989/1263, reg 11 (added by SI 2010/1820; and amended by SI 2013/755). As to the standard scale and the powers of magistrates' courts to issue fines on summary conviction see SENTENCING vol 92 (2015) PARA 176.

64.   Precautions to be taken after sludge is used.

Where any sludge[1] or septic tank sludge[2] has been used[3] on agricultural[4] land, no person may cause or knowingly permit the grazing of animals or the harvesting of forage crops to be carried out on that land before the expiry of three weeks commencing on the date of the use, or cause or knowingly permit the harvesting of fruit and vegetable crops which are grown in direct contact with the soil and normally eaten raw to be carried out on that land before the expiry of ten months commencing on that date[5].

Where any untreated sludge[6] has been used on agricultural land without being injected into the soil, the occupier of the land affected must, as soon as reasonably practicable thereafter, cause such sludge to be worked into the soil of the land affected[7].

1   As to the meaning of 'sludge' see PARA 63 note 1.

2   'Septic tank sludge' means residual sludge from septic tanks and other similar installations for the treatment of sewage: Sludge (Use in Agriculture) Regulations 1989, SI 1989/1263, reg 2(1).

3   As to the meaning of 'use' see PARA 63 note 2.

4   As to the meaning of 'agricultural' see PARA 63 note 3.

5   Sludge (Use in Agriculture) Regulations 1989, SI 1989/1263, reg 4(1). Any person who contravenes regs 2–8 is guilty of an offence, and liable on summary conviction to a fine not exceeding level 5 on the standard scale: reg 9. As to the power of the Environment Agency to impose civil sanctions in relation to an offence under the Sludge (Use in Agriculture) Regulations 1989, SI 1989/1263, for contravening specified provisions see, in relation to England, reg 10 (added by SI 2010/1159), and, in relation to Wales, Sludge (Use in Agriculture) Regulations 1989, SI 1989/1263, reg 11 (added by SI 2010/1820; and amended by SI 2013/755). As to the standard scale and the powers of magistrates' courts to issue fines on summary conviction see SENTENCING vol 92 (2015) PARA 176.

6   'Treated sludge' means sludge or septic tank sludge which has undergone biological, chemical or heat treatment, long term storage or any other appropriate process so as significantly to reduce its fermentability and the health hazards resulting from its use; and 'untreated sludge' is to be construed accordingly: Sludge (Use in Agriculture) Regulations 1989, SI 1989/1263, reg 2(1).

7   Sludge (Use in Agriculture) Regulations 1989, SI 1989/1263, reg 4(2) (amended by SI 1990/880).

65.   Restrictions on supply of sludge.

No person may supply sludge[1] for use[2] on agricultural[3] land if he knows or has reason to believe that the requirement that no fruit or vegetable crops, other than fruit trees, may be growing or being harvested in the soil at the time of the use[4], will not be fulfilled when the sludge is so used, or that the precautions required to be taken after the use of sludge[5] will not be observed after such use[6].

1   As to the meaning of 'sludge' see PARA 63 note 1.

2   As to the meaning of 'use' see PARA 63 note 2.

3   As to the meaning of 'agricultural' see PARA 63 note 3.

4   Ie the requirements of the Sludge (Use in Agriculture) Regulations 1989, SI 1989/1263, reg 3(6) (see PARA 63).

5   Ie the precautions set out in the Sludge (Use in Agriculture) Regulations 1989, SI 1989/1263, reg 4 (see PARA 64).

6 Sludge (Use in Agriculture) Regulations 1989, SI 1989/1263, reg 3(1). Any person who contravenes regs 2–8 is guilty of an offence, and liable on summary conviction to a fine not exceeding level 5 on the standard scale: reg 9. As to the power of the Environment Agency to impose civil sanctions in relation to an offence under the Sludge (Use in Agriculture) Regulations 1989, SI 1989/1263, for contravening specified provisions see, in relation to England, reg 10 (added by SI 2010/1159), and, in relation to Wales, Sludge (Use in Agriculture) Regulations 1989, SI 1989/1263, reg 11 (added by SI 2010/1820; and amended by SI 2013/755). As to the standard scale and the powers of magistrates' courts to issue fines on summary conviction see SENTENCING vol 92 (2015) PARA 176.

66. Restrictions on production and sale of crops grown on sludge disposal sites.

A 'dedicated site' is an area of agricultural[1] land which on 17 June 1986 was dedicated to the disposal of sludge[2] but on which commercial food crops were being grown exclusively for animal consumption[3], and if the concentration of zinc, copper, nickel, lead, cadmium or mercury in the soil of an agricultural unit[4] forming part of such a site exceeds the permitted concentration for that substance[5] the occupier of the site may not sell or offer for sale any crop grown on the agricultural unit affected except in accordance with written advice from the Secretary of State, the Welsh Ministers, or the Food Standards Agency[6], and may not grow any commercial food crops on that unit other than crops intended for animal consumption[7].

1 As to the meaning of 'agricultural' see PARA 63 note 3.
2 As to the meaning of 'sludge' see PARA 63 note 1.
3 Sludge (Use in Agriculture) Regulations 1989, SI 1989/1263, reg 2(1). Every sludge producer was required to notify the Environment Agency in writing as soon as may be after 1 September 1989 of the address and area of every dedicated site to which he supplies sludge: reg 8(2) (amended by SI 1996/593). 'Sludge producer' means any person who manages a plant at which sludge is produced for disposal: Sludge (Use in Agriculture) Regulations 1989, SI 1989/1263, reg 2(1). As to the Environment Agency see ENVIRONMENTAL QUALITY AND PUBLIC HEALTH vol 45 (2010) PARA 68 et seq.
4 'Agricultural unit' means an area of agricultural land used for a single agricultural purpose, not exceeding 5 hectares: Sludge (Use in Agriculture) Regulations 1989, SI 1989/1263, reg 2(1).
5 Ie exceeds the concentration in milligrams per kilogram of dry matter specified for that substance in column (2) of the soil table set out in the Sludge (Use in Agriculture) Regulations 1989, SI 1989/1263, Sch 2 para 5 (see PARA 68): reg 8(1) (substituted by SI 1990/880).
6 Sludge (Use in Agriculture) Regulations 1989, SI 1989/1263, reg 8(1), (3)(a), (4)(i), (ii), Sch 2 para 5 (reg 8(1), (3) substituted, and reg 8(4) amended, by SI 1990/880; Sludge (Use in Agriculture) Regulations 1989, SI 1989/1263, reg 8(4) further amended by SI 2000/656). As to the Secretary of State and the Welsh Ministers see PARA 390. As to the Food Standards Agency and its functions see FOOD AND DRINK vol 51 (2013) PARAS 634–653. Any person who contravenes regs 2–8 is guilty of an offence, and liable on summary conviction to a fine not exceeding level 5 on the standard scale: reg 9. As to the power of the Environment Agency to impose civil sanctions in relation to an offence under the Sludge (Use in Agriculture) Regulations 1989, SI 1989/1263, for contravening specified provisions see, in relation to England, reg 10 (added by SI 2010/1159), and, in relation to Wales, Sludge (Use in Agriculture) Regulations 1989, SI 1989/1263, reg 11 (added by SI 2010/1820; and amended by SI 2013/755). As to the standard scale and the powers of magistrates' courts to issue fines on summary conviction see SENTENCING vol 92 (2015) PARA 176.
7 Sludge (Use in Agriculture) Regulations 1989, SI 1989/1263, reg 8(3)(b) (substituted by SI 1990/880).

67. Testing sludge.

Every sludge producer[1] must ensure that sludge produced by him and supplied for the purpose of use in agriculture[2] is tested at intervals of not more than six months, and is also tested where changes occur in the characteristics of the waste water being treated[3]. Representative samples of sludge intended to be used on agricultural land must be taken after processing, but before delivery to the user[4], each of which must be analysed so as to determine the pH value thereof[5], the percentage content of dry matter, organic matter, nitrogen and phosphorous[6], and the concentration in milligrams per kilogram of dry matter of chromium[7], zinc, copper, nickel, cadmium, lead and mercury[8].

As soon as reasonably practicable after testing sludge in accordance with these provisions the sludge producer must provide details of the analysis made thereunder to all persons to whom he supplies sludge[9].

1   As to the meaning of 'sludge producer' see PARA 66 note 3.
2   As to the meaning of 'agriculture' see PARA 63 note 3.
3   Sludge (Use in Agriculture) Regulations 1989, SI 1989/1263, Sch 1 para 1.
4   Sludge (Use in Agriculture) Regulations 1989, SI 1989/1263, Sch 1 para 2.
5   Sludge (Use in Agriculture) Regulations 1989, SI 1989/1263, Sch 1 para 3(a).
6   Sludge (Use in Agriculture) Regulations 1989, SI 1989/1263, Sch 1 para 3(b).
7   Sludge (Use in Agriculture) Regulations 1989, SI 1989/1263, Sch 1 para 3(c)(i). As to analysis for the purposes of Sch 1 para 3(c) see Sch 1 para 5.
8   Sludge (Use in Agriculture) Regulations 1989, SI 1989/1263, Sch 1 paras 3(c)(ii), 4. See note 7.
9   Sludge (Use in Agriculture) Regulations 1989, SI 1989/1263, reg 7(2). Any person who contravenes regs 2–8 is guilty of an offence, and liable on summary conviction to a fine not exceeding level 5 on the standard scale: reg 9. As to the power of the Environment Agency to impose civil sanctions in relation to an offence under the Sludge (Use in Agriculture) Regulations 1989, SI 1989/1263, for contravening specified provisions see, in relation to England, reg 10 (added by SI 2010/1159), and, in relation to Wales, Sludge (Use in Agriculture) Regulations 1989, SI 1989/1263, reg 11 (added by SI 2010/1820; and amended by SI 2013/755). As to the standard scale and the powers of magistrates' courts to issue fines on summary conviction see SENTENCING vol 92 (2015) PARA 176.

68. Testing soil.

The sludge producer[1] must ensure that agricultural[2] soil is tested or assessed[3]:

(1)   where sludge[4] is to be used for the first time[5] on that land[6];

(2)   as soon as may be after the twentieth anniversary of the date when the soil was last tested[7]; or

(3)   where the sludge producer is so requested in writing by the occupier of the land or by the Environment Agency or, in Wales, the Natural Resources Body for Wales[8], and not less than five years have elapsed since the soil was last tested[9].

For each agricultural unit on which sludge is to be used, a representative sample of soil must be obtained[10]. Each such sample must be analysed so as to ascertain its pH value[11] and the concentration in that sample of chromium[12], zinc, copper, nickel, cadmium, lead and mercury[13].

1   As to the meaning of 'sludge producer' see PARA 66 note 3.
2   As to the meaning of 'agricultural' see PARA 63 note 3.
3   Sludge (Use in Agriculture) Regulations 1989, SI 1989/1263, Sch 2 para 1.
4   As to the meaning of 'sludge' see PARA 63 note 1.
5   Ie the first time after 1 September 1989 (the 'operative date'): Sludge (Use in Agriculture) Regulations 1989, SI 1989/1263, reg 3(3), Sch 2 para 2(2)(a).
6   Sludge (Use in Agriculture) Regulations 1989, SI 1989/1263, Sch 2 para 2(2)(a).
7   Sludge (Use in Agriculture) Regulations 1989, SI 1989/1263, Sch 2 para 2(2)(b). The reference in the text to the twentieth anniversary of the date when the soil was last tested is a reference to it last being tested in accordance with Sch 2: Sch 2 para 2(2)(b).
    Where soil was affected by the use of sludge on an agricultural unit before 1 September 1989 and adequate scientific evidence was available, an assessment was to be made as soon as possible after that date and the soil was to be tested not later than 31 December 1991 (see Sch 2 para 2(1)),

and any such testing may accordingly qualify, until 31 December 2011, for the purposes of calculating the date on which a further test is required under Sch 2 para 2(2)(b). As to the meaning of 'agricultural unit' see PARA 66 note 4.

8　As to the Environment Agency see ENVIRONMENTAL QUALITY AND PUBLIC HEALTH vol 45 (2010) PARA 68 et seq.

9　Sludge (Use in Agriculture) Regulations 1989, SI 1989/1263, Sch 2 para 2(2)(c) (amended by SI 2013/755). The reference in the text to the soil having last been tested is a reference to its last being tested in accordance with the Sludge (Use in Agriculture) Regulations 1989, SI 1989/1263, Sch 2: Sch 2 para 2(2)(c).

10　Ie by mixing together 25 separate core samples, each taken to the depth of the soil or 25 centimetres, whichever is the lesser depth: Sludge (Use in Agriculture) Regulations 1989, SI 1989/1263, Sch 2 para 3.

11　Sludge (Use in Agriculture) Regulations 1989, SI 1989/1263, Sch 2 para 4(a).

12　Sludge (Use in Agriculture) Regulations 1989, SI 1989/1263, Sch 2 para 4(b)(i). As to analysis for the purposes of Sch 2 para 4(b) see Sch 2 para 6.

13　Sludge (Use in Agriculture) Regulations 1989, SI 1989/1263, Sch 2 paras 4(b)(ii), 5. See note 12. Any person who contravenes regs 2–8 is guilty of an offence, and liable on summary conviction to a fine not exceeding level 5 on the standard scale: reg 9. As to the power of the Environment Agency to impose civil sanctions in relation to an offence under the Sludge (Use in Agriculture) Regulations 1989, SI 1989/1263, for contravening specified provisions see, in relation to England, reg 10 (added by SI 2010/1159), and, in relation to Wales, Sludge (Use in Agriculture) Regulations 1989, SI 1989/1263, reg 11 (added by SI 2010/1820; and amended by SI 2013/755). As to the standard scale and the powers of magistrates' courts to issue fines on summary conviction see SENTENCING vol 92 (2015) PARA 176.

69.　Records of use and production of sludge.

Where sludge[1] has been used on any agricultural[2] land, other than by or on behalf of the sludge producer[3], the occupier of that land must forthwith provide to the sludge producer:

(1)　the address and area of the agricultural unit[4] concerned[5];

(2)　the date on which the sludge was used[6];

(3)　the quantity of sludge so used[7]; and

(4)　where the occupier has used sludge not supplied by the sludge producer, the name and address of the person who supplied that sludge, and the quantity of sludge so used which was supplied by that person[8].

Every sludge producer must prepare and maintain a register containing, in relation to sludge supplied for the purpose of use in agriculture in any year[9], particulars of:

(a)　the total quantity of sludge supplied[10];

(b)　the composition and properties[11] of that sludge[12];

(c)　the quantities of treated sludge[13] supplied, and the type of treatment[14];

(d)　the names and addresses of the persons to whom the sludge was supplied[15]; and

(e)　the address and area of each agricultural unit on which sludge has been used, the quantity of sludge used thereon, and the amounts of zinc, copper, nickel, cadmium, lead and mercury which have been added thereto[16].

The register must also contain particulars of the total quantity of sludge produced in any year[17], a copy of every analysis or assessment[18] relating to the soil of an agricultural unit on which sludge has been used[19], and a copy of any advice issued in connection with supplies to designated sites[20]. A sludge producer must make this register available for inspection by the Environment Agency or, in Wales, the Natural Resources Body for Wales[21] at all reasonable times and must furnish the Agency with such information or facilities as it may reasonably require relating to (or to verifying the information contained in) the register or otherwise relating to sludge supplied by the sludge producer, including facilities for analysis of representative samples of sludge or soil[22].

1   As to the meaning of 'sludge' see PARA 63 note 1.
2   As to the meaning of 'agricultural' see PARA 63 note 3.
3   As to the meaning of 'sludge producer' see PARA 66 note 3.
4   As to the meaning of 'agricultural unit' see PARA 66 note 4.
5   Sludge (Use in Agriculture) Regulations 1989, SI 1989/1263, reg 5(a) (reg 5 amended by SI 1990/880). Any person who contravenes regs 2–8 is guilty of an offence, and liable on summary conviction to a fine not exceeding level 5 on the standard scale: reg 9. As to the power of the Environment Agency to impose civil sanctions in relation to an offence under the Sludge (Use in Agriculture) Regulations 1989, SI 1989/1263, for contravening specified provisions see, in relation to England, reg 10 (added by SI 2010/1159), and, in relation to Wales, Sludge (Use in Agriculture) Regulations 1989, SI 1989/1263, reg 11 (added by SI 2010/1820; and amended by SI 2013/755). As to the standard scale and the powers of magistrates' courts to issue fines on summary conviction see SENTENCING vol 92 (2015) PARA 176.
6   Sludge (Use in Agriculture) Regulations 1989, SI 1989/1263, reg 5(b). As to the meaning of 'used' see PARA 63 note 2.
7   Sludge (Use in Agriculture) Regulations 1989, SI 1989/1263, reg 5(c).
8   Sludge (Use in Agriculture) Regulations 1989, SI 1989/1263, reg 5(d).
9   'Year' means the period of 12 months commencing on January 1: Sludge (Use in Agriculture) Regulations 1989, SI 1989/1263, reg 6(2).
10   Sludge (Use in Agriculture) Regulations 1989, SI 1989/1263, reg 6(1)(b)(i).
11   Ie as determined in accordance with the Sludge (Use in Agriculture) Regulations 1989, SI 1989/1263, Sch 1 (see PARA 67).
12   Sludge (Use in Agriculture) Regulations 1989, SI 1989/1263, reg 6(1)(b)(ii).
13   As to the meaning of 'treated sludge' see PARA 64 note 6.
14   Sludge (Use in Agriculture) Regulations 1989, SI 1989/1263, reg 6(1)(b)(iii).
15   Sludge (Use in Agriculture) Regulations 1989, SI 1989/1263, reg 6(1)(b)(iv).
16   Sludge (Use in Agriculture) Regulations 1989, SI 1989/1263, reg 6(1)(b)(v), Sch 1 para 4.
17   Sludge (Use in Agriculture) Regulations 1989, SI 1989/1263, reg 6(1)(a).
18   Ie every analysis or assessment made under the Sludge (Use in Agriculture) Regulations 1989, SI 1989/1263, Sch 2 (see PARA 68) or in accordance with advice given for the purposes of reg 8(4) (see PARA 66).
19   Sludge (Use in Agriculture) Regulations 1989, SI 1989/1263, reg 6(1)(c) (amended by SI 1990/880).
20   Sludge (Use in Agriculture) Regulations 1989, SI 1989/1263, reg 6(1)(d) (amended by SI 1990/880). The advice referred to in the text is that issued for the purposes of reg 8(3)(a) (see PARA 66).
21   As to the Environment Agency see ENVIRONMENTAL QUALITY AND PUBLIC HEALTH vol 45 (2010) PARA 68 et seq.
22   Sludge (Use in Agriculture) Regulations 1989, SI 1989/1263, reg 7(1) (amended by SI 1996/593; SI 2013/755).

(4) FEED HYGIENE AND CONTROL

(i) Implementation of EU Provisions Relating to Feed

70. General EU food law requirements.
Provision is made under EU legislation for general principles and requirements for the regulation of food and feed[1]. Statutory instruments have been made that make it an offence to fail to comply with requirements that relate to the following[2]:

    (1)   conditions on export or re-export to third countries in so far as they relate to feed[3];

(2)   the prohibition on the placing on the market or feeding to any animal of unsafe feed[4];

(3)   the prohibition on misleading labelling, advertising or presentation in so far as it relates to feed[5];

(4)   requirements that feed business operators must have traceability information and make such information available to competent authorities[6]; and

(5)   responsibilities of feed business operators regarding feed that does not satisfy feed safety requirements[7].

1   Ie the provisions of Council Regulation (EC) 178/2002 (OJ L031, 1.1.2002, p 1) laying down the general principles and requirements of food law, establishing the European Food Safety Authority and laying down procedures in matters of food safety.

2   See the Animal Feed (Composition, Marketing and Use) (England) Regulations 2015, SI 2015/255, reg 4(1); and the Animal Feed (Composition, Marketing and Use) (Wales) Regulations 2016, SI 2016/386, reg 4(1). A person found guilty of such an offence in England is liable on summary conviction to a term of imprisonment not exceeding 3 months or to a fine not exceeding level 5 on the standard scale, or both and in Wales is liable on summary conviction to a term of imprisonment not exceeding 6 months or to a fine, or both: Animal Feed (Composition, Marketing and Use) (England) Regulations 2015, SI 2015/255, reg 18(1); Animal Feed (Composition, Marketing and Use) (Wales) Regulations 2016, SI 2016/386, regs 18(1). As to the standard scale and the powers of magistrates' courts to issue fines on summary conviction see SENTENCING vol 92 (2015) PARA 176. As to the enforcement of Council Regulation (EC) 178/2202 (OJ L031, 1.1.2002, p 1) in so far as it applies to veterinary medicinal products used in feeding stuffs see the Veterinary Medicines Regulations 2013, SI 2013/2033, Sch 5 para 2; and PARA 86 note 2.

3   Ie Council Regulation (EC) 178/2002 (OJ L031, 1.1.2002, p 1), art 12, in so far as it relates to feed.

4   Ie Council Regulation (EC) 178/2002 (OJ L031, 1.1.2002, p 1), art 15(1).

5   Ie Council Regulation (EC) 178/2002 (OJ L031, 1.1.2002, p 1), art 16 in so far as it relates to feed.

6   Ie Council Regulation (EC) 178/2002 (OJ L031, 1.1.2002, p 1), art 18(2), (3) in so far as they relate to feed business operators.

7   Ie Council Regulation (EC) 178/2002 (OJ L031, 1.1.2002, p 1), art 20: see the Animal Feed (Composition, Marketing and Use) (England) Regulations 2015, SI 2015/255, reg 4(2); and the Animal Feed (Composition, Marketing and Use) (Wales) Regulations 2016, SI 2016/386, reg 4(2).

71.   Feed hygiene.

The EC Feed Hygiene Regulation[1] lays down general rules on feed hygiene[2] as well as conditions and arrangements for ensuring the traceability of feed[3] and for the registration and approval of establishments[4], and has been implemented and supplemented in the United Kingdom by statutory instrument[5]. The legislation applies to the activities of feed business operators at all stages, from and including primary production of feed up to and including the placing of feed on the market[6], the feeding of food-producing animals[7], and imports and exports of feed from and to third countries[8]; it does not, however, apply where the food-producing animals in relation to which the feed is being supplied are being kept for private domestic consumption or are not being kept for food production at all, or to small local supplies or to pet feed[9]. The implementing regulations also provide that the 'feed' and 'feeding stuff' to which they apply does not include coccidiostats, histomonostats, and all other zootechnical additives except digestibility enhancers, gut flora stabilisers, and substances incorporated with the intention of favourably affecting the environment[10].

1   Ie Council Regulation (EC) 183/2005 (OJ L38, 8.2.2005, p 1) laying down requirements for feed hygiene.

2   Council Regulation (EC) 183/2005 (OJ L38, 8.2.2005, p 1) art 1(a). 'Feed hygiene' means the measures and conditions necessary to control hazards and to ensure fitness for animal consumption of a feed, taking into account its intended use: art 3(1)(a).

3   Council Regulation (EC) 183/2005 (OJ L38, 8.2.2005, p 1) art 1(b).

4   Council Regulation (EC) 183/2005 (OJ L38, 8.2.2005, p 1) art 1(c).

5 See the Feed (Hygiene, Sampling etc and Enforcement) (England) Regulations 2015, SI 2015/454, Pt 2 (regs 3–13); the Feed (Hygiene, Sampling etc and Enforcement) (Wales) Regulations 2016, SI 2016/387, Pt 2 (regs 3–13); and PARA 79 et seq.
6 Council Regulation (EC) 183/2005 (OJ L38, 8.2.2005, p 1) art 2(1)(a). As to the meaning of 'feed business operator' see PARA 77 note 1.
7 Council Regulation (EC) 183/2005 (OJ L38, 8.2.2005, p 1) art 2(1)(b).
8 Council Regulation (EC) 183/2005 (OJ L38, 8.2.2005, p 1) art 2(1)(c).
9 See the Council Regulation (EC) 183/2005 (OJ L38, 8.2.2005, p 1) art 2(2); the Feed (Hygiene, Sampling etc and Enforcement) (England) Regulations 2015, SI 2015/454, reg 3(1); and the Feed (Hygiene, Sampling etc and Enforcement) (Wales) Regulations 2016, SI 2016/387, reg 3(1).
10 See the Feed (Hygiene, Sampling etc and Enforcement) (England) Regulations 2015, SI 2015/454, reg 2(4); and the Feed (Hygiene, Sampling etc and Enforcement) (Wales) Regulations 2016, SI 2016/387, reg 2(4).

72. Controlling animal feed additives.

Provision is made by EU legislation, implemented in the UK by statutory instrument, for the authorisation, labelling and control of feed additives[1]. The statutory instruments make it an offence for a person to contravene or fail comply with such EU provisions that regulate additives for use in animal nutitutrion[2] and which concern the following[3]:

(1) the prohibition on placing on the market, processing or using a feed additive unless it is covered by an authorisation and satisfies relevant conditions[4];

(2) the restriction on the persons who may first place on the market certain additives[5];

(3) the requirement that any person using or placing on the market an additive, or a feed into which it has been incorporated, or any other interested party, must ensure that any conditions which have been imposed are respected[6];

(4) the requirement on the holder of an authorisation to observe monitoring obligations where they have been imposed, to inform the Commission of any new information about a product which might affect the evaluation of the safety of its use in feed, or of any prohibition or restriction on the feed imposed by the competent authority in a third country[7];

(5) the prohibition on the placing on the market of feed additives or premixtures unless labelled in the specified manner and with prescribed information[8]; and

(6) the requirement that additives and premixtures must be marketed only in closed packages or containers which must be closed in such a way that the fastener is damaged on opening and cannot be re-used[9].

1 Ie European Parliament and Council Regulations (EC) 1831/2003 (OJ L268, 18.10.2003, p 29) on additives for use in animal nutrition implemented by the Animal Feed (Composition, Marketing and Use) (England) Regulations 2015, SI 2015/255, regs 9, 10 and the Animal Feed (Composition, Marketing and Use) (Wales) Regulations 2016, SI 2016/386, regs 9, 10.
2 As to the enforcement of European Parliament and Council Regulations (EC) 1831/2003 (OJ L268, 18.10.2003, p 29) in so far as it applies to veterinary medicinal products used in feeding stuffs see the Veterinary Medicines Regulations 2013, SI 2013/2033, Sch 5 para 3; and PARA 86 note 2.
3 A person commits an offence if that person contravenes or fails to comply with a provision specified in the Animal Feed (Composition, Marketing and Use) (England) Regulations 2015, SI 2015/255, reg 10(2) or, in relation to Wales, the Animal Feed (Composition, Marketing and Use) (Wales) Regulations 2016, SI 2016/386, reg 10(2) as read, in the case of head (1) or (5) in the text with Commission Regulation (EU) 2015/327 (OJ L58, 3.3.2015, p 46–49) art 2: Animal Feed (Composition, Marketing and Use) (England) Regulations 2015, SI 2015/255, reg 10(1); Animal Feed (Composition, Marketing and Use) (Wales) Regulations 2016, SI 2016/386, reg 10(1). A person found guilty of such an offence in England is liable on summary conviction to a term of

imprisonment not exceeding 3 months or to a fine not exceeding level 5 on the standard scale, or both and in Wales is liable on summary conviction to a term of imprisonment not exceeding 6 months or to a fine, or both: Animal Feed (Composition, Marketing and Use) (England) Regulations 2015, SI 2015/255, reg 18(1); Animal Feed (Composition, Marketing and Use) (Wales) Regulations 2016, SI 2016/386, regs 18(1). As to the standard scale and the powers of magistrates' courts to issue fines on summary conviction see SENTENCING vol 92 (2015) PARA 176.

4   Ie European Parliament and Council Regulations (EC) 1831/2003 (OJ L268, 18.10.2003, p 29) art 3(1). This is to be read with art 3(2) (national authorisation for scientific experimental purposes), art 3(4) (conditions on mixing of additives) and art 10 (status of existing products).

5   Ie European Parliament and Council Regulations (EC) 1831/2003 (OJ L268, 18.10.2003, p 29) art 3(3).

6   Ie European Parliament and Council Regulations (EC) 1831/2003 (OJ L268, 18.10.2003, p 29), art 12(1).

7   Ie European Parliament and Council Regulations (EC) 1831/2003 (OJ L268, 18.10.2003, p 29), art 12(2).

8   Ie European Parliament and Council Regulations (EC) 1831/2003 (OJ L268, 18.10.2003, p 29), art 16(1), (3), (4) as read with art 16(2) (derogation for certain flavouring compounds).

9   Ie European Parliament and Council Regulations (EC) 1831/2003 (OJ L268, 18.10.2003, p 29), art 16(5): Animal Feed (Composition, Marketing and Use) (England) Regulations 2015, SI 2015/255, reg 10(2); Animal Feed (Composition, Marketing and Use) (Wales) Regulations 2016, SI 2016/386, reg 10(2).

73.   Placing on the market and use of feed.

Provision is made by EU legislation for rules on the placing on the market and use of feed for both food-producing and non-food producing animals within the EU, including requirements for labelling, packaging and presentation[1]. Statutory instruments provide for a person to be guilty of an offence if he fails to comply with EU provisions that relate to the following subject matters[2]:

(1)   general safety and other requirements to be met when feed is placed on the market or used[3];

(2)   extension of requirements in relation to feed for food-producing animals in other legislation to apply to feed for non food-producing animals[4];

(3)   obligation on person responsible for labelling to make information available to competent authority[5];

(4)   prohibition or restriction on the marketing or use of certain materials for animal nutritional purposes[6];

(5)   controls on the levels of additives in feeds[7];

(6)   controls on the marketing of feeds for particular nutritional purposes[8];

(7)   rules and principles governing the labelling and presentation of feed[9];

(8)   designation of the person responsible for labelling and the obligations and responsibilities of that person[10];

(9)   general conditions on making a claim about the characteristics or functions of a feed on the labelling or presentation of it[11];

(10)   special conditions applying to claims concerning optimisation of the nutrition and support or protection of the physiological conditions[12];

(11)   requirements for the presentation of the mandatory labelling particulars[13];

(12)   general mandatory labelling requirements for feed materials and compound feeds[14];

(13)   specific labelling requirements for feed materials[15];

(14)   specific labelling requirements for compound feeds[16];

(15)   additional labelling requirements for feed for particular nutritional purposes (dietetic feeds)[17];

(16) additional labelling requirements for pet food[18];

(17) additional requirements for labelling of non-compliant feed, such as that containing contaminated materials[19];

(18) requirements relating to the packaging and sealing of feed materials and compound feeds for placing on the market[20];

(19) requirement that if the name of a feed material listed in the Catalogue of feed materials is used, all relevant provisions of the Catalogue must be complied with[21];

(20) obligation on a person who first places on the market a feed material not listed in the Community Catalogue of feed materials to notify its use[22];

(21) requirement that if use of the EU Codes of good labelling practice is indicated on labelling, all relevant provisions of the codes must be complied with[23].

It is also an offence to place on the market or use a feed that contains or consists of certain restricted or prohibited materials[24].

1 See European Parliament and Council Regulation (EC) 767/2009 (OJ L229, 1.9.2009, p 1) on the placing on the market and use of feed (implemented by the Animal Feed (Composition, Marketing and Use) (England) Regulations 2015, SI 2015/255, regs 11, 12, 13, Sch 1 and the Animal Feed (Composition, Marketing and Use) (Wales) Regulations 2016, SI 2016/386, regs, 11, 12, 13, Sch 1).

2 See the Animal Feed (Composition, Marketing and Use) (England) Regulations 2015, SI 2015/255, reg 12(1)(a); and the Animal Feed (Composition, Marketing and Use) (Wales) Regulations 2016, SI 2016/386, regs 12(1)(a). A person found guilty of such an offence in England is liable on summary conviction to a term of imprisonment not exceeding 3 months or to a fine not exceeding level 5 on the standard scale, or both and in Wales is liable on summary conviction to a term of imprisonment not exceeding 6 months or to a fine, or both: Animal Feed (Composition, Marketing and Use) (England) Regulations 2015, SI 2015/255, reg 18(1); Animal Feed (Composition, Marketing and Use) (Wales) Regulations 2016, SI 2016/386, regs 18(1). As to the standard scale and the powers of magistrates' courts to issue fines on summary conviction see SENTENCING vol 92 (2015) PARA 176.

3 Ie European Parliament and Council Regulation (EC) 767/2009 (OJ L229, 1.9.2009, p 1), art 4(1), (2) as read with art 4(3) and Annex I.

4 Ie European Parliament and Council Regulation (EC) 767/2009 (OJ L229, 1.9.2009, p 1) art 5(1)

5 Ie European Parliament and Council Regulation (EC) 767/2009 (OJ L229, 1.9.2009, p 1) art 5(2) as read with art 12(1)–(3).

6 Ie European Parliament and Council Regulation (EC) 767/2009 (OJ L229, 1.9.2009, p 1) art 6(1) as read with Annex III.

7 Ie European Parliament and Council Regulation (EC) 767/2009 (OJ L229, 1.9.2009, p 1) art 8. As to the enforcement of art 8 in so far as it applies to veterinary medicinal products used in feeding stuffs see the Veterinary Medicines Regulations 2013, SI 2013/2033, Sch 5 para 6; and PARA 86 note 2.

8 Ie European Parliament and Council Regulation (EC) 767/2009 (OJ L229, 1.9.2009, p 1) art 9.

9 Ie European Parliament and Council Regulation (EC) 767/2009 (OJ L229, 1.9.2009, p 1) art 11 as read with art 12(1)–(3), Annexes II and IV and the Community Catalogue of feed materials (see note 21).

10 Ie European Parliament and Council Regulation (EC) 767/2009 (OJ L229, 1.9.2009, p 1) art 12(4) and (5).

11 Ie European Parliament and Council Regulation (EC) 767/2009 (OJ L229, 1.9.2009, p 1) art 13(1) as read with art 12(1)–(3)).

12 Ie European Parliament and Council Regulation (EC) 767/2009 (OJ L229, 1.9.2009, p 1) art 13(2), (3) as read with art 12(1)–(3).

13 Ie European Parliament and Council Regulation (EC) 767/2009 (OJ L229, 1.9.2009, p 1) art 14(1), (2) as read with art 12(1)–(3).

14 Ie European Parliament and Council Regulation (EC) 767/2009 (OJ L229, 1.9.2009, p 1) art 15 as read with arts 12(1)–(3), 21 and Annex VI and VII.

15 Ie European Parliament and Council Regulation (EC) 767/2009 (OJ L229, 1.9.2009, p 1) art 16 as read with arts 12(1)–(3), 21 and Annex II and V and the Catalogue of feed.

16 Ie European Parliament and Council Regulation (EC) 767/2009 (OJ L229, 1.9.2009, p 1) art 17(1), (2) as read with arts 12(1)–(3), 21 and Annex II, VI and VII. See also Animal Feed (Composition, Marketing and Use) (England) Regulations 2015, SI 2015/255, reg 12(2); and the Animal Feed (Composition, Marketing and Use) (Wales) Regulations 2016, SI 2016/386, regs 12(2).
17 Ie European Parliament and Council Regulation (EC) 767/2009 (OJ L229, 1.9.2009, p 1) art 18 as read with art 12(1)–(3).
18 Ie European Parliament and Council Regulation (EC) 767/2009 (OJ L229, 1.9.2009, p 1) art 19 as read with art 12(1)–(3) and Annex VIII.
19 Ie European Parliament and Council Regulation (EC) 767/2009 (OJ L229, 1.9.2009, p 1) art 20(2) as read with art 12(1)–(3) and Annex VIII.
20 Ie European Parliament and Council Regulation (EC) 767/2009 (OJ L229, 1.9.2009, p 1) art 23.
21 Ie European Parliament and Council Regulation (EC) 767/2009 (OJ L229, 1.9.2009, p 1) art 24(5). The Community Catalogue of feed materials referred to in the text is a tool created under art 24(1) to improve the labelling of feed materials and compound food.
22 Ie European Parliament and Council Regulation (EC) 767/2009 (OJ L229, 1.9.2009, p 1) art 24(6).
23 Ie European Parliament and Council Regulation (EC) 767/2009 (OJ L229, 1.9.2009, p 1) art 25(4).
24 Ie that fails to comply with European Parliament and Council Regulation (EC) 767/2009 (OJ L229, 1.9.2009, p 1) art 6(1) or 8: Animal Feed (Composition, Marketing and Use) (England) Regulations 2015, SI 2015/255, reg 12(1)(b); and the Animal Feed (Composition, Marketing and Use) (Wales) Regulations 2016, SI 2016/386, reg 12(1)(b).

74. Control of genetically modified feed.

In addition to the existing statutory regulation of activities involving genetic modification[1], dealing in genetically modified organisms[2], and the use of genetically modified sources in food[3], provision is made for the enforcement of specified EU provisions on genetically modified food and feed[4] in so far as they apply to animal feed[5].

1 As to the statutory regulation of activities involving genetic modification see HEALTH AND SAFETY AT WORK vol 53 (2014) PARA 563 et seq.
2 As to the acquisition, importation, release, marketing and keeping of genetically modified organisms see ENVIRONMENTAL QUALITY AND PUBLIC HEALTH vol 46 (2010) PARAS 794–812. As to the traceability and labelling of genetically modified organisms see ENVIRONMENTAL QUALITY AND PUBLIC HEALTH vol 46 (2010) PARA 792.
3 As to the use of genetically modified sources in food see FOOD AND DRINK vol 51 (2013) PARAS 732–741.
4 Ie Council Regulation (EC) 1829/2003 (OJ L268, 18.10.2003, p 1) on genetically modified food and feed, so far as relating to animal feed.
5 See the Animal Feed (Composition, Marketing and Use) (England) Regulations 2015, SI 2015/255, regs 6, 7, 8; and the Animal Feed (Composition, Marketing and Use) (Wales) Regulations 2016, SI 2016/386, regs 6, 7, 8. The specified EU provisions are:
   (1)   Council Regulation (EC) 1829/2003 (OJ L268, 18.10.2003, p 1) art 16(2) (prohibition on placing on the market, using or processing a product referred to in art 15(1) unless it is covered by an authorisation and satisfies relevant conditions), as read with art 20(6) (requirement that products in relation to which the Commission has adopted a measure under art 20 must be withdrawn from the market);
   (2)   art 21(1) (requirement that the authorisation holder and the parties concerned must comply with conditions imposed on an authorisation for that product, and that the authorisation holder must comply with post-market monitoring requirements);
   (3)   art 21(3) (requirement that an authorisation holder inform the Commission of any new scientific or technical information about a product which might affect the evaluation of the safety of its use in feed, or of any prohibition or restriction on the feed in a third country); and
   (4)   art 25 (requirement for certain labelling indications): Animal Feed (Composition, Marketing and Use) (England) Regulations 2015, SI 2015/255, reg 7(2); Animal Feed (Composition, Marketing and Use) (Wales) Regulations 2016, SI 2016/386, reg 7(2).
It is an offence to fail to comply with the specified EU provisions: Animal Feed (Composition, Marketing and Use) (England) Regulations 2015, SI 2015/255, reg 7(1); Animal Feed

(Composition, Marketing and Use) (Wales) Regulations 2016, SI 2016/386, reg 7(1). A person found guilty of such an offence in England is liable on summary conviction to a term of imprisonment not exceeding 3 months or to a fine not exceeding level 5 on the standard scale, or both and in Wales is liable on summary conviction to a term of imprisonment not exceeding 6 months or to a fine, or both: Animal Feed (Composition, Marketing and Use) (England) Regulations 2015, SI 2015/255, reg 18(1); Animal Feed (Composition, Marketing and Use) (Wales) Regulations 2016, SI 2016/386, regs 18(1). As to the standard scale and the powers of magistrates' courts to issue fines on summary conviction see SENTENCING vol 92 (2015) PARA 176.

75. Undesirable substances.

A person who places on the market any feed that is of a type specified in certain EU provisions relating to the control of undesirable substances in animal feed[1] or who uses any such feed, commits an offence if it contains a specified undesirable substance[2] in excess of the relevant maximum content[3].

A person who places on the market or uses any complementary feed commits an offence if having regard to the quantity of it recommended for use in a daily ration, it contains any undesirable substance[4] in excess of the maximum content specified for it[5] in relation to complete feeds and there is no provision[6] relating to any complementary feed[7].

A person who for the purpose of dilution mixes any feed with any feed that is of a specified type[8] and which contains a specified undesirable substance[9] in excess of the relevant maximum content[10] commits an offence[11].

A person who places on the market or uses any feed which is not sound and genuine and of merchantable quality commits an offence[12].

A person who has, for the purpose of a trade or business, possession or control of any of the following feeds:

(1)   palm kernel expeller;
(2)   feeds obtained from the processing of fish and other marine animals;
(3)   seaweed meal and feed materials derived from seaweed; and
(4)   complete feeds for fish or for fur-producing animals,

must, if required by an inspector, procure and produce to the inspector an analysis in order to demonstrate that the content of inorganic arsenic in the feed is less than two parts per million[13].

1   Ie any feed that is specified in Council Directive (EC) 2002/32 (OJ L140, 30.5.2002, p 10) on undesirable substances in animal feed, Annex I column 2.
2   Ie any undesirable substance listed in Council Directive (EC) 2002/32 (OJ L140, 30.5.2002, p 10), Annex I column 1. For the purposes of the Animal Feed (Composition, Marketing and Use) (England) Regulations 2015, SI 2015/255, reg 15 and the Animal Feed (Composition, Marketing and Use) (Wales) Regulations 2016, SI 2016/386, reg 15 'undesirable substance' means any substance or product, not being a pathogenic agent, which is present in or on a feed and which either constitutes a potential danger to human or animal health or to the environment or could adversely affect livestock production: Animal Feed (Composition, Marketing and Use) (England) Regulations 2015, SI 2015/255, reg 14(2); Animal Feed (Composition, Marketing and Use) (Wales) Regulations 2016, SI 2016/386, reg 14(2).
3   Ie the content specified in Council Directive (EC) 2002/32 (OJ L140, 30.5.2002, p 10), Annex I column 3: Animal Feed (Composition, Marketing and Use) (England) Regulations 2015, SI 2015/255, reg 15(1); Animal Feed (Composition, Marketing and Use) (Wales) Regulations 2016, SI 2016/386, reg 15(1). A person found guilty of an offence under the Animal Feed (Composition, Marketing and Use) (England) Regulations 2015, SI 2015/255, reg 15(1), (2), (3) or (4) is liable on summary conviction to a term of imprisonment not exceeding 3 months or to a fine not exceeding level 5 on the standard scale, or both (reg 18(1)) and person found guilty of an offence under the Animal Feed (Composition, Marketing and Use) (Wales) Regulations 2016, SI 2016/386, reg 15(1), (2), (3) or (4) is liable on summary conviction to a term of imprisonment

not exceeding 6 months or to a fine, or both (reg 18(1)). As to the standard scale and the powers of magistrates' courts to issue fines on summary conviction see SENTENCING vol 92 (2015) PARA 176.

4   Ie any undesirable substance listed in Council Directive (EC) 2002/32 (OJ L140, 30.5.2002, p 10), Annex I column 1.

5   Ie the content specified in Council Directive (EC) 2002/32 (OJ L140, 30.5.2002, p 10), Annex I column 3.

6   Ie in the corresponding entry in Council Directive (EC) 2002/32 (OJ L140, 30.5.2002, p 10) on undesirable substances in animal feed, Annex I column 2.

7   Animal Feed (Composition, Marketing and Use) (England) Regulations 2015, SI 2015/255, reg 15(2); Animal Feed (Composition, Marketing and Use) (Wales) Regulations 2016, SI 2016/386, reg 15(2). As to the penalty for such an offence see note 3.

8   Ie any feed that is specified in Council Directive (EC) 2002/32 (OJ L140, 30.5.2002, p 10) on undesirable substances in animal feed, Annex I column 2.

9   Ie any undesirable substance listed in Council Directive (EC) 2002/32 (OJ L140, 30.5.2002, p 10), Annex I column 1.

10 Ie the content specified in Council Directive (EC) 2002/32 (OJ L140, 30.5.2002, p 10), Annex I column 3.

11 Animal Feed (Composition, Marketing and Use) (England) Regulations 2015, SI 2015/255, reg 15(3); Animal Feed (Composition, Marketing and Use) (Wales) Regulations 2016, SI 2016/386, reg 15(3). As to the penalty for such an offence see note 3.

12 Animal Feed (Composition, Marketing and Use) (England) Regulations 2015, SI 2015/255, reg 15(4); Animal Feed (Composition, Marketing and Use) (Wales) Regulations 2016, SI 2016/386, reg 15(4). As to the penalty for such an offence see note 3. For these purposes a feed listed in Council Directive (EC) 2002/32 (OJ L140, 30.5.2002, p 10) on undesirable substances in animal feed, Annex I column 2.is deemed not to be sound, genuine and of merchantable quality if it contains any undesirable substance specified in column 1 of that Annex in excess of the maximum content specified in relation to it in column 3: Animal Feed (Composition, Marketing and Use) (England) Regulations 2015, SI 2015/255, reg 15(5); Animal Feed (Composition, Marketing and Use) (Wales) Regulations 2016, SI 2016/386, reg 15(5).

13 Animal Feed (Composition, Marketing and Use) (England) Regulations 2015, SI 2015/255, reg 15(6), (7); Animal Feed (Composition, Marketing and Use) (Wales) Regulations 2016, SI 2016/386, reg 15(6), (7). A person who, without reasonable excuse, fails to comply with such a requirement commits an offence for which is liable on summary conviction to a fine not exceeding level 3 on the standard scale: Animal Feed (Composition, Marketing and Use) (England) Regulations 2015, SI 2015/255, regs 15(8), 18(2); Animal Feed (Composition, Marketing and Use) (Wales) Regulations 2016, SI 2016/386, regs 15(8), 18(2).

76.   Feed intended for particular nutritional purposes.

Feed intended for particular nutritional purposes is controlled by EU legislation establishing a list of intended uses of animal feeding stuffs for particular nutritional purposes, and setting out the precise use, the essential nutritional characteristics, the labelling declarations, the recommended length of time of use and, where appropriate, any special labelling requirements[1]. These provisions have been implemented by statutory instruments creating offences for failure to comply with the EU provisions[2].

1   See Commission Direction (EC) 2008/38 (OJ L62, 6.3.2008, p 9) establishing a list of intended uses of animal feeding stuffs for particular nutritional purposes.

2   See the Animal Feed (Composition, Marketing and Use) (England) Regulations 2015, SI 2015/255, regs 16, 17 and the Animal Feed (Composition, Marketing and Use) (Wales) Regulations 2016, SI 2016/386, regs 16, 17 which implement Commission Direction (EC) 2008/38 (OJ L62, 6.3.2008, p 9). As to the offences created see the Animal Feed (Composition, Marketing and Use) (England) Regulations 2015, SI 2015/255, reg 17; and, in relation to Wales, the Animal Feed (Composition, Marketing and Use) (Wales) Regulations 2016, SI 2016/386, reg 17. A person found guilty of such an offence in England is liable on summary conviction to a term of imprisonment not exceeding 3 months or to a fine not exceeding level 5 on the standard scale, or both (Animal Feed (Composition, Marketing and Use) (England) Regulations 2015, SI 2015/255, reg 18(1)) and in Wales is liable on summary conviction to a term of imprisonment not exceeding six months or to a fine, or both (Animal Feed (Composition, Marketing and Use) (Wales)

Regulations 2016, SI 2016/386, reg 18(1)). As to the standard scale and the powers of magistrates' courts to issue fines on summary conviction see SENTENCING vol 92 (2015) PARA 176.

(ii) Regulation of Feed Business Operations

77. The applicable law.

Provision is made for the administration and enforcement of the legislation governing the content and manufacture of animal feeding stuffs by feed business operators[1]. The particular legislation to which such provision applies (referred to as 'specified feed law')[2] is:

(1)   the principal domestic legislation concerning the marketing and sale of animal feeding stuffs[3];

(2)   EU law establishing the European Food Safety Authority and laying down procedures in matters of food and feed safety, in so far as it relates to feed[4];

(3)   EU law on genetically modified food and feed, in so far as it relates to feed[5];

(4)   EU law relating to additives in animal nutrition[6];

(5)   EU law governing compliance with feed law, animal health and animal welfare rules in so far as it relates to feed[7];

(6)   the EC Feed Hygiene Regulation[8];

(7)   EU law as regards the increased level of official controls on imports of certain feed and food of non-animal origin, in so far as it relates to feed[9];

(8)   EU law on the placing on the market and use of feed[10].

1   See the Animal Feed (Hygiene, Sampling and Enforcement etc) (England) Regulations 2015, SI 2015/454, Pt 2 (regs 3–14); and the Animal Feed (Hygiene, Sampling and Enforcement etc) (Wales) Regulations 2016, SI 2016/387, Pt 2 (regs 3–14). These are both made partly under the European Communities Act 1972 s 2(2). See also PARA 78 et seq. 'Feed business operator' means the natural or legal person responsible for ensuring that the requirements of the present EU Regulation are met within the feed business under their control: see Council Regulation (EC) 183/2005 (OJ L38, 8.2.2005, p 1) laying down requirements for feed hygiene, art 3(b); the Animal Feed (Hygiene, Sampling etc and Enforcement) (England) Regulations 2015, SI 2015/454, reg 2(2); and the Animal Feed (Hygiene, Sampling etc and Enforcement) (Wales) Regulations 2016, SI 2016/387, reg 2(2).

2   As to what constitutes 'specified feed law' for these purposes see the Animal Feed (Hygiene, Sampling etc and Enforcement) (England) Regulations 2015, SI 2015/454, Sch 1; and the Animal Feed (Hygiene, Sampling etc and Enforcement) (Wales) Regulations 2016, SI 2016/387, Sch 1.

     Where the commission by any person of an offence under specified feed law is due to the act or default of some other person, that other person is guilty of the offence and may be accused and convicted of the offence whether or not proceedings are taken against the first-mentioned person: Animal Feed (Hygiene, Sampling etc and Enforcement) (England) Regulations 2015, SI 2015/454, reg 35(1); Animal Feed (Hygiene, Sampling etc and Enforcement) (Wales) Regulations 2016, SI 2016/387, reg 35(1). In any proceedings for such an offence it is a defence for a person to prove that the commission of the offence was due to a mistake, or to reliance on information supplied to him, or to the act or default of another person, or to an accident or some other cause beyond his control and that he took all reasonable precautions and exercised all due diligence to avoid the commission of such an offence by himself or any person under his control (Animal Feed (Hygiene, Sampling etc and Enforcement) (England) Regulations 2015, SI 2015/454, reg 35(2); Animal Feed (Hygiene, Sampling etc and Enforcement) (Wales) Regulations 2016, SI 2016/387, reg 35(2)), although if in any case this defence involves the allegation that the commission of the offence was due to the act or default of another person or to reliance on information supplied by another person, the person accused may not, without leave of the court, be entitled to rely on that defence unless at least 7 clear days before the hearing and, where he has previously appeared before a court in connection with the alleged offence, within one month of his first such appearance, he has served on the prosecutor a notice giving such information as he may have to identify or assist in identifying that other person (Animal Feed (Hygiene, Sampling etc and Enforcement) (England)

Regulations 2015, SI 2015/454, reg 35(3); Animal Feed (Hygiene, Sampling etc and Enforcement) (Wales) Regulations 2016, SI 2016/387, reg 35(3)). See also the Animal Feed (Hygiene, Sampling etc and Enforcement) (England) Regulations 2015, SI 2015/454, reg 28(10); and the Animal Feed (Hygiene, Sampling etc and Enforcement) (Wales) Regulations 2016, SI 2016/387, reg 28(10).

Where an offence under specified fee law which has been committed by a body corporate is proved to have been committed with the consent or connivance of, or to be attributable to any neglect on the part of, any director, manager, secretary or other similar officer of the body corporate or any person who was purporting to act in any such capacity, he as well as the body corporate is deemed to be guilty of that offence and liable to be proceeded against and punished accordingly: Animal Feed (Hygiene, Sampling etc and Enforcement) (England) Regulations 2015, SI 2015/454, reg 36(1); Animal Feed (Hygiene, Sampling etc and Enforcement) (Wales) Regulations 2016, SI 2016/387, reg 36(1). For this purpose, 'director' in relation to any body corporate established by or under any enactment for the purpose of carrying on under national ownership any undertaking, being a body corporate whose affairs are managed by its members, means a member of that body corporate: Animal Feed (Hygiene, Sampling etc and Enforcement) (England) Regulations 2015, SI 2015/454, reg 36(2); Animal Feed (Hygiene, Sampling etc and Enforcement) (Wales) Regulations 2016, SI 2016/387, reg 36(2).

Without prejudice to any enactment relating to the place where proceedings may be taken, proceedings for an offence under specified feed law may be taken in the place where the person accused resides or carries on business Animal Feed (Hygiene, Sampling etc and Enforcement) (England) Regulations 2015, SI 2015/454, reg 37(1); Animal Feed (Hygiene, Sampling etc and Enforcement) (Wales) Regulations 2016, SI 2016/387, reg 37(1). No prosecution for an offence under the Animal Feed (Hygiene, Sampling etc and Enforcement) (England) Regulations 2015, SI 2015/454, the Animal Feed (Hygiene, Sampling etc and Enforcement) (Wales) Regulations 2016, SI 2016/387 or under the Animal Feed (Composition, Marketing and Use) (England) Regulations 2015, SI 2015/255, Pt 2 (regs 3–5) or the Animal Feed (Composition, Marketing and Use) (Wales) Regulations 2016, SI 2016/386, Pt 2 (regs 3–5) may be begun after the expiry of three years from the commission of the offence or one year from its discovery by the prosecutor, whichever is the earlier: Animal Feed (Hygiene, Sampling etc and Enforcement) (England) Regulations 2015, SI 2015/454, reg 37(2); Animal Feed (Hygiene, Sampling etc and Enforcement) (Wales) Regulations 2016, SI 2016/387, reg 37(2).

3 Ie the Agriculture Act 1970 Pt IV (ss 66–87) in so far as it relates to animal feeding stuffs; the Official Feed and Food Controls (England) Regulations 2009, SI 2009/3255 and the Official Feed and Food Controls (Wales) Regulations 2009, SI 2009/3376, in so far as they relate to feed; the Animal Feed (Composition, Marketing and Use) Regulations 2015, SI 2015/255 and the Animal Feed (Composition, Marketing and Use) Regulations 2016, SI 2016/386; and the Animal Feed (Hygiene, Sampling etc and Enforcement) (England) Regulations 2015, SI 2015/454 and the Animal Feed (Hygiene, Sampling etc and Enforcement) (Wales) Regulations 2016, SI 2016/387 (as applicable). See PARA 37 et seq.

4 Ie European Parliament and Council Regulation (EC) 178/2002 (OJ L031, 1.1.2002, p 1) laying down the general principles and requirements of food law, establishing the European Food Safety Authority and laying down procedures in matters of food safety (implemented in England by the Animal Feed (Composition, Marketing and Use) (England) Regulations 2015, SI 2015/255, reg 4; and in Wales by the Animal Feed (Composition and Use) (Wales) Regulations 2016, SI 2016/386, reg 4 (see PARA 70)).

5 Ie European Parliament and Council Regulation (EC) 1829/2003 (OJ L268, 18.10.2003, p 1) on genetically modified food and feed (implemented in England by the Animal Feed (Composition, Marketing and Use) (England) Regulations 2015, SI 2015/255, regs 6, 7, 8; and in Wales by the Animal Feed (Composition, Marketing and Use) (Wales) Regulations 2016, SI 2016/386, regs 6, 7, 8 (see PARA 74)).

6 Ie European Parliament and Council Regulation (EC) 1831/2003 (OJ L268, 18.10.2003, p 29) on additives for use in animal nutrition (implemented in England by the Animal Feed (Composition, Marketing and Use) (England) Regulations 2015, SI 2015/255, regs 9, 10 and in Wales by the Animal Feed (Composition, Marketing and Use) (Wales) Regulations 2016, SI 2016/386, regs 9, 10) (see PARA 72).

7 Ie Council Regulation (EC) 882/2004 (OJ L165, 30.4.2004, p 1) on official controls performed to ensure the verification of compliance with feed and food law, animal health and animal welfare rules (implemented in England by the Official Feed and Food Controls (England) Regulations 2009, SI 2009/3255; and in Wales by the Official Feed and Food Controls (Wales) Regulations 2009, SI 2009/3376). Council Regulation (EC) 882/2004 has been repealed and replaced by European Parliament and Council Regulation (EU) 2017/625 (OJ L95, 7.4.2017, p 1) on official

controls and other official activities performed to ensure the application of food and feed law, rules on animal health and welfare, plant health and plant protection products.

8   Ie Council Regulation (EC) 183/2005 (OJ L38, 8.2.2005, p 1) laying down requirements for feed hygiene (see PARA 71) (implemented in England by the Animal Feed (Hygiene, Sampling etc and Enforcement) (England) Regulations 2015, SI 2015/454; and in Wales by the Animal Feed (Hygiene, Sampling etc and Enforcement) (Wales) Regulations 2016, SI 2016/387 (see PARA 78 et seq)).

9   Ie Commission Regulation (EC) 669/2009 (OJ L 194, 25.7.2009, p 11–21) implementing European Parliament and Council Regulation (EC) 882/2004 as regards the increased level of official controls on imports of certain feed and food of non-animal origin, in so far as it relates to feed. See note 7.

10 Ie European Parliament and Council Regulation (EC) 767/2009 (OJ L229, 1.9.2009, p 1) on the placing on the market and use of feed (see PARA 73).

78.   The enforcement authorities.

The enforcement authorities for the purposes of the regulation of feed business operations[1] are the bodies identified as having the duty to execute and enforce the domestic legislation relating to fertilisers and feeding stuffs[2] in their areas[3], and these bodies may authorise officers (whether or not officers of the enforcement authorities), either generally or specially, to act in relation to matters arising under these provisions[4]. An authorised officer is not personally liable in respect of any act done by him, either in the execution or purported execution of his statutory duties or within the scope of his employment, provided he did the act in the honest belief that his statutory duty[5] required or entitled him to do it[6]; and if an action has been brought against an authorised officer in respect of an act done by him in the execution or purported execution of his statutory duty but outside the scope of his employment, the authority may indemnify him against the whole or a part of any damages which he has been ordered to pay or any costs which he may have incurred if it is satisfied that he honestly believed that the act complained of was within the scope of his employment[7].

Any person who wilfully obstructs an authorised officer in the exercise of his powers[8] or fails to comply with any requirement lawfully made by him in the exercise of such powers[9], and any person not being an authorised officer who purports to act as such under these provisions[10], is guilty of an offence[11].

If the Secretary of State considers, or the Welsh Ministers[12] consider, that the applicable provisions[13] have been insufficiently enforced in the area of any enforcement authority, he or they may appoint one or more persons to exercise in that area the powers exercisable by authorised officers appointed by the authority[14].

1   Ie for the purposes of the Animal Feed (Hygiene, Sampling etc and Enforcement) (England) Regulations 2015, SI 2015/454 and the Animal Feed (Hygiene, Sampling etc and Enforcement) (Wales) Regulations 2016, SI 2016/387 (see PARA 79 et seq). See also Council Regulation (EC) 183/2005 (OJ L38, 8.2.2005, p 1) laying down requirements for feed hygiene (see PARA 71); and Council Regulation (EC) 178/2002 (OJ L031, 1.1.2002, p 1) laying down the general principles and requirements of food law, establishing the European Food Safety Authority and laying down procedures in matters of food safety (see PARA 77).

2   Ie the Agriculture Act 1970 Pt IV (ss 66–87) (see PARA 37 et seq). As to these bodies see PARA 52 notes 5, 8.

3   Animal Feed (Hygiene, Sampling etc and Enforcement) (England) Regulations 2015, SI 2015/454, regs 2(1), 14; Animal Feed (Hygiene, Sampling etc and Enforcement) (Wales) Regulations 2016, SI 2016/387, regs 2(1), 14.

4   Animal Feed (Hygiene, Sampling etc and Enforcement) (England) Regulations 2015, SI 2015/454, reg 2(1); Animal Feed (Hygiene, Sampling etc and Enforcement) (Wales) Regulations 2016, SI 2016/387, reg 2(1). An authorised officer may not exercise his powers under these provisions in respect of any premises outside the area for which he is appointed except with the consent of the enforcement authority for the area in which those premises are situated: Animal Feed (Hygiene,

Sampling etc and Enforcement) (England) Regulations 2015, SI 2015/454, reg 22(2); Animal Feed (Hygiene, Sampling etc and Enforcement) (Wales) Regulations 2016, SI 2016/387, reg 22(2). 'Premises' includes any establishment, any place, vehicle, stall or moveable structure and any ship or aircraft: Animal Feed (Hygiene, Sampling etc and Enforcement) (England) Regulations 2015, SI 2015/454, reg 2(1); Animal Feed (Hygiene, Sampling etc and Enforcement) (Wales) Regulations 2016, SI 2016/387, reg 2(1).

5　Ie his duty under the Animal Feed (Hygiene, Sampling etc and Enforcement) (England) Regulations 2015, SI 2015/454 or the Animal Feed (Hygiene, Sampling etc and Enforcement) (Wales) Regulations 2016, SI 2016/387.

6　Animal Feed (Hygiene, Sampling etc and Enforcement) (England) Regulations 2015, SI 2015/454, reg 23(1); Animal Feed (Hygiene, Sampling etc and Enforcement) (Wales) Regulations 2016, SI 2016/387, reg 23(1). Nothing in this provision should be construed as relieving any enforcement authority of any liability in respect of the acts of its officers: Animal Feed (Hygiene, Sampling etc and Enforcement) (England) Regulations 2015, SI 2015/454, reg 23(2); Animal Feed (Hygiene, Sampling etc and Enforcement) (Wales) Regulations 2016, SI 2016/387, reg 23(2). An agricultural analyst (see PARA 83 note 6) is to be treated for the purposes of the Animal Feed (Hygiene, Sampling etc and Enforcement) (England) Regulations 2015, SI 2015/454, reg 23 and the Animal Feed (Hygiene, Sampling etc and Enforcement) (Wales) Regulations 2016, SI 2016/387, reg 23 as being an authorised officer, whether or not his appointment is a whole-time one: Animal Feed (Hygiene, Sampling etc and Enforcement) (England) Regulations 2015, SI 2015/454, reg 23(4); Animal Feed (Hygiene, Sampling etc and Enforcement) (Wales) Regulations 2016, SI 2016/387, reg 23(4).

7　Animal Feed (Hygiene, Sampling etc and Enforcement) (England) Regulations 2015, SI 2015/454, reg 23(3); Animal Feed (Hygiene, Sampling etc and Enforcement) (Wales) Regulations 2016, SI 2016/387, reg 23(3).

8　Ie his powers under Animal Feed (Hygiene, Sampling etc and Enforcement) (England) Regulations 2015, SI 2015/454 or the Animal Feed (Hygiene, Sampling etc and Enforcement) (Wales) Regulations 2016, SI 2016/387.

9　Animal Feed (Hygiene, Sampling etc and Enforcement) (England) Regulations 2015, SI 2015/454, reg 32(1); Animal Feed (Hygiene, Sampling etc and Enforcement) (Wales) Regulations 2016, SI 2016/387, reg 32(1).

10　Animal Feed (Hygiene, Sampling etc and Enforcement) (England) Regulations 2015, SI 2015/454, reg 32(2); Animal Feed (Hygiene, Sampling etc and Enforcement) (Wales) Regulations 2016, SI 2016/387, reg 32(2).

11　The offences of obstruction and impersonation are punishable, in England, on summary conviction to a term of imprisonment not exceeding 3 months or to a fine not exceeding level 5 on the standard scale, or both (Animal Feed (Hygiene, Sampling etc and Enforcement) (England) Regulations 2015, SI 2015/454, reg 34(2)) and in relation to Wales, on summary conviction to a term of imprisonment not exceeding 6 months or to a fine or both (Animal Feed (Hygiene, Sampling etc and Enforcement) (Wales) Regulations 2016, SI 2016/387, reg 34(2)). As to the standard scale see PARA 14 note 2.

12　As to the Secretary of State and the Welsh Ministers see PARA 390.

13　See note 1.

14　Animal Feed (Hygiene, Sampling etc and Enforcement) (England) Regulations 2015, SI 2015/454, reg 22(1); Animal Feed (Hygiene, Sampling etc and Enforcement) (Wales) Regulations 2016, SI 2016/387, reg 22(1). Any expenses certified by the Secretary of State or the Welsh Ministers as having been incurred by him or them under this provision in respect of the area in question must be repaid to the Secretary of State or the Welsh Ministers on demand by the authority in question: Animal Feed (Hygiene, Sampling etc and Enforcement) (England) Regulations 2015, SI 2015/454, reg 22(1); Animal Feed (Hygiene, Sampling etc and Enforcement) (Wales) Regulations 2016, SI 2016/387, reg 22(1).

79.　Feed business improvement notices.

An authorised officer[1] who has reasonable grounds for believing that a feed business operator[2] is failing to comply with specified feed law[3] may serve[4] a 'feed business improvement notice'[5] on that person[6]. Failure to comply with a feed business improvement notice is an offence[7]. Any person who is aggrieved by a decision of an authorised officer to serve a feed business improvement notice may appeal to a magistrates' court[8], and a person who is aggrieved by the decision of a magistrates' court to dismiss such an appeal may appeal to the Crown Court[9].

On an appeal against a feed business improvement notice the court may cancel or affirm the notice and, if it affirms it, may do so either in its original form or with such modifications as the court may in the circumstances think fit[10].

1 As to enforcement authorities and authorised officers see PARA 78.

2 'Feed business operator' means the natural or legal person responsible for ensuring that the requirements of Council Regulation (EC) 183/2005 (OJ L38, 8.2.2005, p 1) laying down requirements for feed hygiene (see PARA 71) are met within the feed business under his or its control: art 3(b); Animal Feed (Hygiene, Sampling etc and Enforcement) (England) Regulations 2015, SI 2015/454, reg 2(2); Animal Feed (Hygiene, Sampling etc and Enforcement) (Wales) Regulations 2016, SI 2016/387, reg 2(2).

3 As to the specified feed law for these purposes see PARA 77. In any proceedings in which it is alleged that a material has contravened or failed to comply with the requirements of specified feed law, it is a defence for the person accused to prove that the material in respect of which the offence was alleged to have been committed was feed to which Council Regulation (EC) 183/2005 (OJ L38, 8.2.2005, p 1) art 25 applies and could lawfully be exported in accordance with the requirements of Council Regulation (EC) 178/2002 (OJ L031, 1.1.2002, p 1) laying down the general principles and requirements of food law, art 12: Animal Feed (Hygiene, Sampling etc and Enforcement) (England) Regulations 2015, SI 2015/454, reg 35(4); Animal Feed (Hygiene, Sampling etc and Enforcement) (Wales) Regulations 2016, SI 2016/387, reg 35(4).

4 Any notice to be given by an enforcement authority under the Animal Feed (Hygiene, Sampling etc and Enforcement) (England) Regulations 2015, SI 2015/454, regs 8, 9, 10, 24, 29 or 31 or under the Animal Feed (Hygiene, Sampling etc and Enforcement) (Wales) Regulations 2016, SI 2016/387, reg 8, 9, 10, 24, 29 or 31 must:

 (1) be in writing and signed by an authorised officer acting on behalf of the enforcement authority (Animal Feed (Hygiene, Sampling etc and Enforcement) (England) Regulations 2015, SI 2015/454, reg 38(1)(a); Animal Feed (Hygiene, Sampling etc and Enforcement) (Wales) Regulations 2016, SI 2016/387, reg 38(1)(a));

 (2) if purporting to bear the signature (which includes a facsimile of a signature by whatever means reproduced) of a person who is expressed to be an authorised officer, must be deemed, unless the contrary is proven, to have been duly issued by such an authorised officer (Animal Feed (Hygiene, Sampling etc and Enforcement) (England) Regulations 2015, SI 2015/454, reg 38(1)(b); Animal Feed (Hygiene, Sampling etc and Enforcement) (Wales) Regulations 2016, SI 2016/387, reg 38(1)(b)); and

 (3) must be given to the feed business operator (or, as the case may be, to the person mentioned in the Animal Feed (Hygiene, Sampling etc and Enforcement) (England) Regulations 2015, SI 2015/454, reg 31(2)(a) or the Animal Feed (Hygiene, Sampling etc and Enforcement) (Wales) Regulations 2016, SI 2016/387, reg 31(2)(a)) by:

  (a) delivering it to that person;

  (b) leaving it, or sending it in a prepaid letter addressed to him at his office;

  (c) in the case of an incorporated company or body, delivering it to the secretary or clerk at the registered or principal office, or sending it in a prepaid letter addressed to him at that office; or

  (d) in the case of any other person, leaving it or sending it in a prepaid letter addressed to him at his usual or last known residence (Animal Feed (Hygiene, Sampling etc and Enforcement) (England) Regulations 2015, SI 2015/454, reg 38(1)(c); Animal Feed (Hygiene, Sampling etc and Enforcement) (Wales) Regulations 2016, SI 2016/387, reg 38(1)(c)).

Where it is not practicable after reasonable inquiry to ascertain the name and address of the person on whom the notice should be served, or where the premises in which a feed business is carried on are unoccupied, the notice may be addressed to the 'owner' or 'occupier' of the premises in which the feed business is carried on, and delivered to some person on those premises, or if there is no person on the premises to whom it can be delivered, by affixing it or a copy of it to some conspicuous part of the premises: Animal Feed (Hygiene, Sampling etc and Enforcement) (England) Regulations 2015, SI 2015/454, reg 38(2); Animal Feed (Hygiene, Sampling etc and Enforcement) (Wales) Regulations 2016, SI 2016/387, reg 38(2). As to the meaning of 'premises' see PARA 78 note 4.

5 A 'feed business improvement notice' is a notice which states the officer's grounds for believing that the feed business operator is failing to comply with specified feed law, specifies the matters which constitute the feed business operator's failure to comply, specifies the measures which, in the officer's opinion, the feed business operator must take in order to secure compliance, and requires the feed business operator to take those measures, or measures which are at least equivalent to

them, within such period (not being less than 14 days) as may be specified in the notice: Animal Feed (Hygiene, Sampling etc and Enforcement) (England) Regulations 2015, SI 2015/454, reg 24(1)(a)–(d); Animal Feed (Hygiene, Sampling etc and Enforcement) (Wales) Regulations 2016, SI 2016/387, reg 24(1)(a)–(d). The notice must also state the right to appeal (as to which see the Animal Feed (Hygiene, Sampling etc and Enforcement) (England) Regulations 2015, SI 2015/454, reg 25; Animal Feed (Hygiene, Sampling etc and Enforcement) (Wales) Regulations 2016, SI 2016/387, reg 25; and the text and note 8) and the appropriate time limit for bringing any such appeal: Animal Feed (Hygiene, Sampling etc and Enforcement) (England) Regulations 2015, SI 2015/454, reg 24(2); Animal Feed (Hygiene, Sampling etc and Enforcement) (Wales) Regulations 2016, SI 2016/387, reg 24(2). Where any such notice would otherwise include any day on which an appeal against that notice is pending, that day must be excluded from that period (Animal Feed (Hygiene, Sampling etc and Enforcement) (England) Regulations 2015, SI 2015/454, reg 27(2); Animal Feed (Hygiene, Sampling etc and Enforcement) (Wales) Regulations 2016, SI 2016/387, reg 27(2)); and any appeal must be regarded as pending for these purposes until it is finally disposed of, is withdrawn or is struck out for want of prosecution (Animal Feed (Hygiene, Sampling etc and Enforcement) (England) Regulations 2015, SI 2015/454, reg 27(3); Animal Feed (Hygiene, Sampling etc and Enforcement) (Wales) Regulations 2016, SI 2016/387, reg 27(3)).

6   Animal Feed (Hygiene, Sampling etc and Enforcement) (England) Regulations 2015, SI 2015/454, reg 24(1); Animal Feed (Hygiene, Sampling etc and Enforcement) (Wales) Regulations 2016, SI 2016/387, reg 24(1).

7   Animal Feed (Hygiene, Sampling etc and Enforcement) (England) Regulations 2015, SI 2015/454, reg 24(3); Animal Feed (Hygiene, Sampling etc and Enforcement) (Wales) Regulations 2016, SI 2016/387, reg 24(3). Anyone guilty of an offence under the Animal Feed (Hygiene, Sampling etc and Enforcement) (England) Regulations 2015, SI 2015/454, reg 24(3), reg 28(5) (see PARA 80) or reg 29(5) or (6) (see PARA 81), or reg 31(2) or under the Animal Feed (Hygiene, Sampling etc and Enforcement) (Wales) Regulations 2016, SI 2016/387, reg 24(3), reg 28(5) (see PARA 80) or reg 29(5) or (6) (see PARA 81) or reg 31(2), is liable on summary conviction to a term of imprisonment not exceeding three months or a fine not exceeding the statutory maximum or both, or on conviction on indictment to a term of imprisonment not exceeding two years or a fine or both: Animal Feed (Hygiene, Sampling etc and Enforcement) (England) Regulations 2015, SI 2015/454, reg 34(1); Animal Feed (Hygiene, Sampling etc and Enforcement) (Wales) Regulations 2016, SI 2016/387, reg 34(1). As to the statutory maximum see PARA 58 note 1. As to offences and penalties generally see PARA 78 note 11.

8   Animal Feed (Hygiene, Sampling etc and Enforcement) (England) Regulations 2015, SI 2015/454, reg 25(1); Animal Feed (Hygiene, Sampling etc and Enforcement) (Wales) Regulations 2016, SI 2016/387, reg 25(1). The period within which such an appeal may be brought is one month from the date on which notice of the decision was served on the person desiring to appeal or, if it is shorter, the period specified in the notice (see note 5): Animal Feed (Hygiene, Sampling etc and Enforcement) (England) Regulations 2015, SI 2015/454, reg 25(3); Animal Feed (Hygiene, Sampling etc and Enforcement) (Wales) Regulations 2016, SI 2016/387, reg 25(3). The procedure on such an appeal is by way of complaint for an order, and the Magistrates' Courts Act 1980 (see MAGISTRATES vol 71 (2013) PARA 522 et seq) applies to the proceedings: Animal Feed (Hygiene, Sampling etc and Enforcement) (England) Regulations 2015, SI 2015/454, reg 25(2); Animal Feed (Hygiene, Sampling etc and Enforcement) (Wales) Regulations 2016, SI 2016/387, reg 25(2). The making of a complaint for an order is deemed for these purposes to be the bringing of the appeal: Animal Feed (Hygiene, Sampling etc and Enforcement) (England) Regulations 2015, SI 2015/454, reg 25(3); Animal Feed (Hygiene, Sampling etc and Enforcement) (Wales) Regulations 2016, SI 2016/387, reg 25(3.

9   Animal Feed (Hygiene, Sampling etc and Enforcement) (England) Regulations 2015, SI 2015/454, reg 26(a); Animal Feed (Hygiene, Sampling etc and Enforcement) (Wales) Regulations 2016, SI 2016/387, reg 26(a).

10   Animal Feed (Hygiene, Sampling etc and Enforcement) (England) Regulations 2015, SI 2015/454, reg 27(1); Animal Feed (Hygiene, Sampling etc and Enforcement) (Wales) Regulations 2016, SI 2016/387, reg 27(1).

80.   Feed business prohibition orders.

If a feed business operator[1] is convicted of an offence under specified feed law[2], the court may (or, depending on the circumstances, must) impose an appropriate prohibition[3]. If the court by, or before, which the operator is convicted thinks it proper to do so in all the circumstances of the case, it may, at its discretion, by order impose a prohibition on the operator participating in the management of any feed business[4], or any feed business of a class or description specified in the order[5]. If, however, the court by or before which the operator is convicted is satisfied that the health risk condition is fulfilled[6] with respect to the feed business concerned, it is required by order to impose an appropriate prohibition commensurate to the grounds on which the health risk condition is fulfilled[7]. Such an order is referred to as a 'feed business prohibition order' and any contravention of it is an offence[8]. A feed business prohibition order ceases to have effect only on the issue by the enforcement authority of a certificate to the effect that it is satisfied that the feed business operator has taken sufficient measures to secure that the health risk condition is no longer fulfilled with respect to the feed business (in the case of a mandatory order)[9] or on the giving by the court of a direction to that effect (in the case of a discretionary order)[10]. A person who is aggrieved by any decision of a magistrates' court to make a feed business prohibition order may appeal to the Crown Court[11].

1   As to the meaning of 'feed business operator' see PARA 79 note 2.
2   Animal Feed (Hygiene, Sampling etc and Enforcement) (England) Regulations 2015, SI 2015/454, reg 28(1)(a), (4)(a); Animal Feed (Hygiene, Sampling etc and Enforcement) (Wales) Regulations 2016, SI 2016/387, reg 28(1)(a), (4)(a). As to the specified feed law for these purposes see PARA 77. For defences to offences under specified feed law see PARA 77 note 2.
3   Animal Feed (Hygiene, Sampling etc and Enforcement) (England) Regulations 2015, SI 2015/454, reg 28(1), (4); Animal Feed (Hygiene, Sampling etc and Enforcement) (Wales) Regulations 2016, SI 2016/387, reg 28(1), (4).
4   As to the meaning of 'feed business' see Council Regulation (EC) 178/2002 (OJ L031, 1.1.2002, p 1) laying down the general principles and requirements of food law, establishing the European Food Safety Authority and laying down procedures in matters of food safety, art 3(5) (definition applied by the Animal Feed (Hygiene, Sampling etc and Enforcement) (England) Regulations 2015, SI 2015/454, reg 2(2); and the Animal Feed (Hygiene, Sampling etc and Enforcement) (Wales) Regulations 2016, SI 2016/387, reg 2(2)).
5   Animal Feed (Hygiene, Sampling etc and Enforcement) (England) Regulations 2015, SI 2015/454, reg 28(4)(b); Animal Feed (Hygiene, Sampling etc and Enforcement) (Wales) Regulations 2016, SI 2016/387, reg 28(4)(b). The enforcement authority must serve a copy of the order on the relevant feed business operator as soon as practicable after making it, and in the case of an order under the Animal Feed (Hygiene, Sampling etc and Enforcement) (England) Regulations 2015, SI 2015/454, reg 28(1) or, in relation to Wales, the Animal Feed (Hygiene, Sampling etc and Enforcement) (Wales) Regulations 2016, SI 2016/387, reg 28(1) affix a copy of the order in a conspicuous position on such premises used for the purposes of the feed business as the authority considers appropriate and any person who knowingly contravenes such an order is guilty of an offence: Animal Feed (Hygiene, Sampling etc and Enforcement) (England) Regulations 2015, SI 2015/454, reg 28(5); Animal Feed (Hygiene, Sampling etc and Enforcement) (Wales) Regulations 2016, SI 2016/387, reg 28(5). As to enforcement authorities and authorised officers see PARA 78. As to the penalty for an offence see PARA 79 note 7.
6   The health risk condition is fulfilled with respect to any feed business if any of the following involves risk of injury to health (including any impairment, whether permanent or temporary), namely:
   (1)   the use for the purposes of the business of any process or treatment;
   (2)   the construction of any premises used for the purposes of the business, or the use for those purposes of any equipment; or
   (3)   the state or condition of any premises or equipment used for the purposes of the business: Animal Feed (Hygiene, Sampling etc and Enforcement) (England) Regulations 2015, SI 2015/454, reg 28(2)(a)–(c); Animal Feed (Hygiene, Sampling etc and Enforcement) (Wales) Regulations 2016, SI 2016/387, reg 28(2)(a)–(c).
   'Health' means the health of an animal or, through the consumption of the products of such animal, human health: Animal Feed (Hygiene, Sampling etc and Enforcement) (England) Regulations 2015, SI 2015/454, reg 28(2); Animal Feed (Hygiene, Sampling etc and Enforcement) (Wales) Regulations 2016, SI 2016/387, reg 28(2).

7   Animal Feed (Hygiene, Sampling etc and Enforcement) (England) Regulations 2015, SI 2015/454, reg 28(1)(b); Animal Feed (Hygiene, Sampling etc and Enforcement) (Wales) Regulations 2016, SI 2016/387, reg 28(1)(b). Thus:

    (1)   if the health risk condition is fulfilled because the use for the purposes of the business of any process or treatment involves risk of injury to health (see note 6), the appropriate prohibition is a prohibition on the use of the process or treatment for the purposes of the business (Animal Feed (Hygiene, Sampling etc and Enforcement) (England) Regulations 2015, SI 2015/454, reg 28(3)(a); Animal Feed (Hygiene, Sampling etc and Enforcement) (Wales) Regulations 2016, SI 2016/387, reg 28(3)(a));

    (2)   if the health risk condition is fulfilled because the construction of any premises used for the purposes of the business, or the use for those purposes of any equipment, involves risk of injury to health, the appropriate prohibition is a prohibition on the use of the premises or equipment for the purposes of the business or any other feed business of the same class or description (Animal Feed (Hygiene, Sampling etc and Enforcement) (England) Regulations 2015, SI 2015/454, reg 28(3)(b); Animal Feed (Hygiene, Sampling etc and Enforcement) (Wales) Regulations 2016, SI 2016/387, reg 28(3)(b)); and

    (3)   if the health risk condition is fulfilled because the state or condition of any premises or equipment used for the purposes of the business involves risk of injury to health, the appropriate prohibition is a prohibition on the use of the premises or equipment for the purposes of any feed business (Animal Feed (Hygiene, Sampling etc and Enforcement) (England) Regulations 2015, SI 2015/454, reg 28(3)(c); Animal Feed (Hygiene, Sampling etc and Enforcement) (Wales) Regulations 2016, SI 2016/387, reg 28(3)(c)).

8   Animal Feed (Hygiene, Sampling etc and Enforcement) (England) Regulations 2015, SI 2015/454, reg 28(5); Animal Feed (Hygiene, Sampling etc and Enforcement) (Wales) Regulations 2016, SI 2016/387, reg 28(5). As to offences and penalties see PARAS 78 note 11, 79 note 7.

9   Animal Feed (Hygiene, Sampling etc and Enforcement) (England) Regulations 2015, SI 2015/454, reg 28(6)(a); Animal Feed (Hygiene, Sampling etc and Enforcement) (Wales) Regulations 2016, SI 2016/387, reg 28(6)(a). A 'mandatory order' is an order under the Animal Feed (Hygiene, Sampling etc and Enforcement) (England) Regulations 2015, SI 2015/454, reg 28(1) or the Animal Feed (Hygiene, Sampling etc and Enforcement) (Wales) Regulations 2016, SI 2016/387, reg 28(1) (see the text and notes 6–7). The enforcement authority must issue a certificate under this provision within 3 days of its being satisfied as mentioned in the text, and on an application by the feed business operator for such a certificate the authority must determine, as soon as is reasonably practicable and in any event within 14 days, whether or not it is so satisfied; and, if it determines that it is not so satisfied, it must give notice to the feed business operator of the reasons for that determination: Animal Feed (Hygiene, Sampling etc and Enforcement) (England) Regulations 2015, SI 2015/454, reg 28(7); Animal Feed (Hygiene, Sampling etc and Enforcement) (Wales) Regulations 2016, SI 2016/387, reg 28(7). As to the service of notices see PARA 79 note 4.

10 Animal Feed (Hygiene, Sampling etc and Enforcement) (England) Regulations 2015, SI 2015/454, reg 28(6)(b); Animal Feed (Hygiene, Sampling etc and Enforcement) (Wales) Regulations 2016, SI 2016/387, reg 28(6)(b). A 'discretionary order' is an order under the Animal Feed (Hygiene, Sampling etc and Enforcement) (England) Regulations 2015, SI 2015/454, reg 28(4) or the Animal Feed (Hygiene, Sampling etc and Enforcement) (Wales) Regulations 2016, SI 2016/387, reg 28(4) (see the text and notes 4–5). The court must give such a direction if, on an application by the feed business operator, the court thinks it proper to do so having regard to all the circumstances of the case, including in particular the conduct of the feed business operator since the making of the order; but no such application may be entertained if it is made either within 6 months of the making of the feed business prohibition order or within 3 months of the making by the feed business operator of a previous application for such a direction: Animal Feed (Hygiene, Sampling etc and Enforcement) (England) Regulations 2015, SI 2015/454, reg 28(8); Animal Feed (Hygiene, Sampling etc and Enforcement) (Wales) Regulations 2016, SI 2016/387, reg 28(8).

11 Animal Feed (Hygiene, Sampling etc and Enforcement) (England) Regulations 2015, SI 2015/454, reg 26(b); Animal Feed (Hygiene, Sampling etc and Enforcement) (Wales) Regulations 2016, SI 2016/387, reg 26(b).

81.   Emergency prohibition notices and orders.

A 'feed business emergency prohibition notice' is a notice which may be served[1] on a feed business operator[2] if an authorised officer of an enforcement authority[3] is satisfied that there is an imminent risk of injury to health (that is, that the 'health risk condition' is fulfilled)[4] with respect to any relevant feed business[5]. A 'feed business emergency prohibition order' is an order which must be made by a magistrates' court which is satisfied, on the application of an authorised officer, that there is such a risk[6]. A feed business emergency prohibition notice may, and a feed business emergency prohibition order must, impose an appropriate prohibition commensurate to the grounds on which the health risk condition is fulfilled[7]. Emergency prohibition notices and orders cease to have effect on the issue by the enforcement authority of a certificate to the effect that it is satisfied that the feed business operator has taken sufficient measures to secure that the health risk condition is no longer fulfilled with respect to the feed business[8]; an emergency prohibition notice will also cease to have effect, if no application for a feed business emergency prohibition order is made within the period of three days beginning with the service of the notice, at the end of that period or, if such an application is so made, on the determination or abandonment of the application[9]. A person who is aggrieved by any decision of a magistrates' court to make an emergency prohibition order may appeal to the Crown Court[10].

1　As to the service of notices see PARA 79 note 4.
2　As to the meaning of 'feed business operator' see PARA 79 note 2.
3　As to enforcement authorities and authorised officers see PARA 78.
4　For these purposes the health risk condition is fulfilled with respect to any feed business if any of the following involves imminent risk of injury to health (including any impairment, whether permanent or temporary):
　　(1)　the use for the purposes of the business of any process or treatment;
　　(2)　the construction of any premises used for the purposes of the business, or the use for those purposes of any equipment; or
　　(3)　the state or condition of any premises or equipment used for the purposes of the business: Animal Feed (Hygiene, Sampling etc and Enforcement) (England) Regulations 2015, SI 2015/454, reg 28(2)(a)–(c); Animal Feed (Hygiene, Sampling etc and Enforcement) (Wales) Regulations 2016, SI 2016/387, reg 28(2)(a)–(c).
　　'Health' means the health of an animal or, through the consumption of the products of such animal, human health: Animal Feed (Hygiene, Sampling etc and Enforcement) (England) Regulations 2015, SI 2015/454, reg 28(2); Animal Feed (Hygiene, Sampling etc and Enforcement) (Wales) Regulations 2016, SI 2016/387, reg 28(2).
5　Animal Feed (Hygiene, Sampling etc and Enforcement) (England) Regulations 2015, SI 2015/454, reg 29(1); Animal Feed (Hygiene, Sampling etc and Enforcement) (Wales) Regulations 2016, SI 2016/387, reg 29(1). As to the meaning of 'feed business' see PARA 80 note 4. As soon as practicable after the service of a feed business emergency prohibition notice, an authorised officer of an enforcement authority must affix a copy of the notice in a conspicuous position on such premises used for the purposes of the feed business as he considers appropriate, and any person who contravenes such an order commits an offence: Animal Feed (Hygiene, Sampling etc and Enforcement) (England) Regulations 2015, SI 2015/454, reg 29(5); Animal Feed (Hygiene, Sampling etc and Enforcement) (Wales) Regulations 2016, SI 2016/387, reg 29(5). Where an emergency prohibition notice is served on a feed business operator, the enforcement authority must compensate him in respect of any loss suffered by reason of his complying with the notice unless an application for an emergency prohibition order is made within the period of three days beginning with the service of the notice and the court declares itself satisfied, on the hearing of the application, that the health risk condition was fulfilled with respect to the feed business at the time when the notice was served; and any disputed question as to the right to or the amount of any compensation payable must be determined by arbitration: Animal Feed (Hygiene, Sampling etc and Enforcement) (England) Regulations 2015, SI 2015/454, reg 29(10); Animal Feed (Hygiene, Sampling etc and Enforcement) (Wales) Regulations 2016, SI 2016/387, reg 29(10). As to penalties for offences see PARA 79 note 7.
6　Animal Feed (Hygiene, Sampling etc and Enforcement) (England) Regulations 2015, SI 2015/454, reg 29(2); Animal Feed (Hygiene, Sampling etc and Enforcement) (Wales) Regulations 2016, SI 2016/387, reg 29(2). An officer may not apply for a feed business emergency prohibition order unless, at least one day before the date of the application, he has served notice on the relevant feed business operator of his intention to apply for the order: Animal Feed (Hygiene, Sampling etc and Enforcement) (England) Regulations 2015, SI 2015/454, reg 29(3); Animal Feed (Hygiene, Sampling etc and Enforcement) (Wales) Regulations 2016, SI 2016/387, reg 29(3). Where a

magistrates' court makes a feed business emergency prohibition order under the Animal Feed (Hygiene, Sampling etc and Enforcement) (England) Regulations 2015, SI 2015/454, reg 29(2) or the Animal Feed (Hygiene, Sampling etc and Enforcement) (Wales) Regulations 2016, SI 2016/387, reg 29(2) with respect to any feed business, the Animal Feed (Hygiene, Sampling etc and Enforcement) (England) Regulations 2015, SI 2015/454, reg 28(1)) or, in relation to Wales, the Animal Feed (Hygiene, Sampling etc and Enforcement) (Wales) Regulations 2016, SI 2016/387, reg 28(1) (see PARA 80) apply as if the feed business operator had been convicted by the court of an offence under specified feed law: Animal Feed (Hygiene, Sampling etc and Enforcement) (England) Regulations 2015, SI 2015/454, reg 28(9); Animal Feed (Hygiene, Sampling etc and Enforcement) (Wales) Regulations 2016, SI 2016/387, reg 28(9). As to the specified feed law for these purposes see PARA 77.

As soon as practicable after the making of a feed business emergency prohibition order, an authorised officer of an enforcement authority must serve a copy of the order on the relevant feed business operator and affix a copy of the order in a conspicuous position on such premises used for the purposes of the feed business as he considers appropriate and person who knowingly contravenes such an order commits an offence: Animal Feed (Hygiene, Sampling etc and Enforcement) (England) Regulations 2015, SI 2015/454, reg 29(6); Animal Feed (Hygiene, Sampling etc and Enforcement) (Wales) Regulations 2016, SI 2016/387, reg 29(6). As to penalties see PARA 79 note 7.

7　Animal Feed (Hygiene, Sampling etc and Enforcement) (England) Regulations 2015, SI 2015/454, regs 28(3), 29(4); Animal Feed (Hygiene, Sampling etc and Enforcement) (Wales) Regulations 2016, SI 2016/387, regs 28(3), 29(4). The appropriate prohibition in either case is:

(1)　if the health risk condition is fulfilled because the use for the purposes of the business of any process or treatment involves imminent risk of injury to health (see PARA 80 note 6), a prohibition on the use of the process or treatment for the purposes of the business (Animal Feed (Hygiene, Sampling etc and Enforcement) (England) Regulations 2015, SI 2015/454, reg 28(3)(a), (4); Animal Feed (Hygiene, Sampling etc and Enforcement) (Wales) Regulations 2016, SI 2016/387, regs 28(3)(a), 29(4));

(2)　if the health risk condition is fulfilled because the construction of any premises used for the purposes of the business, or the use for those purposes of any equipment, involves imminent risk of injury to health, a prohibition on the use of the premises or equipment for the purposes of the business or any other feed business of the same class or description (Animal Feed (Hygiene, Sampling etc and Enforcement) (England) Regulations 2015, SI 2015/454, regs 28(3)(b), 29(4); Animal Feed (Hygiene, Sampling etc and Enforcement) (Wales) Regulations 2016, SI 2016/387, regs 28(3)(b), 29(4)); and

(3)　if the health risk condition is fulfilled because the state or condition of any premises or equipment used for the purposes of the business involves imminent risk of injury to health, a prohibition on the use of the premises or equipment for the purposes of any feed business (Animal Feed (Hygiene, Sampling etc and Enforcement) (England) Regulations 2015, SI 2015/454, regs 28(3)(c), 29(4); Animal Feed (Hygiene, Sampling etc and Enforcement) (Wales) Regulations 2016, SI 2016/387, regs 28(3)(c), 29(4)).

8　Animal Feed (Hygiene, Sampling etc and Enforcement) (England) Regulations 2015, SI 2015/454, reg 29(8); Animal Feed (Hygiene, Sampling etc and Enforcement) (Wales) Regulations 2016, SI 2016/387, reg 29(8). The enforcement authority must issue such a certificate within three days of being satisfied as mentioned in the text, and on an application by the feed business operator for such a certificate, the authority must determine as soon as is reasonably practicable and in any event within 14 days whether or not it is so satisfied; and, if it determines that it is not so satisfied, it must give notice to the feed business operator of the reasons for that determination: Animal Feed (Hygiene, Sampling etc and Enforcement) (England) Regulations 2015, SI 2015/454, reg 29(9); Animal Feed (Hygiene, Sampling etc and Enforcement) (Wales) Regulations 2016, SI 2016/387, reg 29(9).

9　Animal Feed (Hygiene, Sampling etc and Enforcement) (England) Regulations 2015, SI 2015/454, reg 29(7); Animal Feed (Hygiene, Sampling etc and Enforcement) (Wales) Regulations 2016, SI 2016/387, reg 29(7).

10　Animal Feed (Hygiene, Sampling etc and Enforcement) (England) Regulations 2015, SI 2015/454, reg 26(b); Animal Feed (Hygiene, Sampling etc and Enforcement) (Wales) Regulations 2016, SI 2016/387, reg 26(b).

82.　Enforcement powers of officers.

For the purposes of executing and enforcing specified feed law[1] or carrying out investigations on undesirable substances in animal feed to determine the source of specified undesirable substances[2], an authorised officer[3] may on producing, if requested to do so, some duly authenticated documentation showing his identity and authority, enter[4] any premises[5] on which he has reasonable cause to believe:

(1) that feed[6] has been, or is being, manufactured or produced, or is being kept for the purpose of being placed on the market, incorporated in another product or used[7]; or

(2) that there is any feed which the occupier of the premises has in his possession or under his control[8].

An authorised officer entering premises pursuant to these provisions, or a warrant issued under them, has the right to make inspections[9], take samples[10] and study, seize and detain records[11].

Where an officer has inspected or sampled any material pursuant to these provisions, and on such an inspection, or upon analysis of samples taken, it appears to him that the material fails to comply with the requirements of specified feed law[12], he may either:

(a) give notice to the person in charge of the material that, until the notice is withdrawn, the material or any specified portion of it is not to be used as feed and either is not to be removed or is not to be removed except to some place specified in the notice[13]; or

(b) seize the material in order to have it dealt with by a justice of the peace[14].

A justice of the peace has power to condemn the material[15].

1 As to the specified feed law for these purposes see PARA 77.
2 Ie in accordance with Council Directive (EC) 2002/32 (OJ L140, 30.5.2002, p 10) on undesirable substances in animal feed, art 4.2.
3 As to enforcement authorities and authorised officers see PARA 78.
4 The entry of premises under these provisions and otherwise than by warrant signed by a justice must take place at reasonable times and, in the case of audits where prior notification of the occupier is necessary, on prior notice of not less than 48 hours being given to the occupier: Animal Feed (Hygiene, Sampling etc and Enforcement) (England) Regulations 2015, SI 2015/454, reg 30(2); Animal Feed (Hygiene, Sampling etc and Enforcement) (Wales) Regulations 2016, SI 2016/387, reg 30(2).
   If any person discloses to any other person any information in relation to any manufacturing process or trade secret which has been obtained by him on premises he has entered by virtue of these provisions or any other information obtained by him in pursuance of these provisions he is guilty of an offence and liable on summary conviction to a fine not exceeding level 5 on the standard scale unless the disclosure was made in and for the purpose of the performance by him or any other person of functions under these provisions: Animal Feed (Hygiene, Sampling etc and Enforcement) (England) Regulations 2015, SI 2015/454, reg 32(3); Animal Feed (Hygiene, Sampling etc and Enforcement) (Wales) Regulations 2016, SI 2016/387, reg 32(3). This does not, however, apply to prevent an authorised officer who has taken a sample under these provisions from disclosing:
   (1) to the manufacturer or to the last seller of the material, information as to the place where and the person from whom the sample was taken;
   (2) to that manufacturer or last seller or to any person who had that material on his premises, information as to the results of any analysis of that sample; or
   (3) any information which it is necessary to disclose in order to prevent the occurrence of a serious risk to human or animal health or to the environment: Animal Feed (Hygiene, Sampling etc and Enforcement) (England) Regulations 2015, SI 2015/454, reg 32(4); Animal Feed (Hygiene, Sampling etc and Enforcement) (Wales) Regulations 2016, SI 2016/387, reg 32(4).
   A person guilty of an offence under the Animal Feed (Hygiene, Sampling etc and Enforcement) (England) Regulations 2015, SI 2015/454, reg 32(3) or the Animal Feed (Hygiene, Sampling etc and Enforcement) (Wales) Regulations 2016, SI 2016/387, reg 32(3) is liable on summary conviction to a fine not exceeding level 5 on the standard scale: Animal Feed (Hygiene, Sampling etc and Enforcement) (England) Regulations 2015, SI 2015/454, reg 34(3); Animal Feed (Hygiene, Sampling etc and Enforcement) (Wales) Regulations 2016, SI 2016/387, reg 34(3). As to the standard scale see PARA 14 note 2. As to offences and penalties generally see PARA 78 note 11.

5　As to the meaning of 'premises' see PARA 78 note 4. If a justice of the peace, on sworn information in writing, is satisfied that there is reasonable ground for entry into any such premises as are mentioned in the text and either:

> (1)　that admission to the premises has been refused, or a refusal is apprehended, and that notice of the intention to apply for a warrant has been given to the occupier (Animal Feed (Hygiene, Sampling etc and Enforcement) (England) Regulations 2015, SI 2015/454, reg 30(4)(a); Animal Feed (Hygiene, Sampling etc and Enforcement) (Wales) Regulations 2016, SI 2016/387, reg 30(4)(a)); or
>
> (2)　that an application for admission or the giving of such a notice would defeat the object of the entry, or that the case is one of urgency, or that the premises are unoccupied or the occupier temporarily absent (Animal Feed (Hygiene, Sampling etc and Enforcement) (England) Regulations 2015, SI 2015/454, reg 30(4)(b); Animal Feed (Hygiene, Sampling etc and Enforcement) (Wales) Regulations 2016, SI 2016/387, reg 30(4)(b)),

the justice may by warrant signed by him authorise the authorised officer to enter the premises, if need be by reasonable force (Animal Feed (Hygiene, Sampling etc and Enforcement) (England) Regulations 2015, SI 2015/454, reg 30(4); Animal Feed (Hygiene, Sampling etc and Enforcement) (Wales) Regulations 2016, SI 2016/387, reg 30(4).

Every such warrant continues in force for a period of one month: Animal Feed (Hygiene, Sampling etc and Enforcement) (England) Regulations 2015, SI 2015/454, reg 30(5); Animal Feed (Hygiene, Sampling etc and Enforcement) (Wales) Regulations 2016, SI 2016/387, reg 30(5).

An authorised officer entering premises by virtue of these powers (whether pursuant to a warrant or otherwise) may be accompanies by such other persons and take such equipment as may appear to him to be necessary, and on leaving any unoccupied premises which he has entered by virtue of a warrant, must leave them as effectively secured against unauthorised entry as he found them: Animal Feed (Hygiene, Sampling etc and Enforcement) (England) Regulations 2015, SI 2015/454, reg 30(6); Animal Feed (Hygiene, Sampling etc and Enforcement) (Wales) Regulations 2016, SI 2016/387, reg 30(6).

These provisions do not authorise any person, except with the permission of the local authority under the Animal Health Act 1981, to enter any premises on which an animal or bird affected with any disease to which the Animal Health Act 1981 applies is kept and which is situated in a place declared under the Animal Health Act 1981 to be infected with such a disease: Animal Feed (Hygiene, Sampling etc and Enforcement) (England) Regulations 2015, SI 2015/454, reg 30(17); Animal Feed (Hygiene, Sampling etc and Enforcement) (Wales) Regulations 2016, SI 2016/387, reg 30(17). As to the application of the Animal Health Act 1981 in connection with diseases of animals see ANIMALS vol 2 (2017) PARA 377 et seq.

6　As to the meaning of 'feed' see Council Regulation (EC) 178/2002 (OJ L031, 1.1.2002, p 1) laying down the general principles and requirements of food law, establishing the European Food Safety Authority and laying down procedures in matters of food safety, art 3(4) (definition applied by the Animal Feed (Hygiene, Sampling etc and Enforcement) (England) Regulations 2015, SI 2015/454, reg 2(2); Animal Feed (Hygiene, Sampling etc and Enforcement) (Wales) Regulations 2016, SI 2016/387, reg 2(2)).

7　Animal Feed (Hygiene, Sampling etc and Enforcement) (England) Regulations 2015, SI 2015/454, reg 30(1), (3)(a); Animal Feed (Hygiene, Sampling etc and Enforcement) (Wales) Regulations 2016, SI 2016/387, reg 30(1), (3)(a).

8　Animal Feed (Hygiene, Sampling etc and Enforcement) (England) Regulations 2015, SI 2015/454, reg 30(3)(b); Animal Feed (Hygiene, Sampling etc and Enforcement) (Wales) Regulations 2016, SI 2016/387, reg 30(3)(b). This power may not be exercised in respect of any premises used only as a dwelling: Animal Feed (Hygiene, Sampling etc and Enforcement) (England) Regulations 2015, SI 2015/454, reg 30(3); Animal Feed (Hygiene, Sampling etc and Enforcement) (Wales) Regulations 2016, SI 2016/387, reg 30(3).

9　An authorised officer entering premises by virtue of these provisions, or of a warrant issued under it, has the right to inspect:

> (1)　any material appearing to be feed;
>
> (2)　any article appearing to be a container or package used or intended to be used to store, wrap or package any feed, or to be a label or advertisement used or intended to be used in connection with feed; or
>
> (3)　any vehicle, plant or equipment appearing to be used, or intended to be used, in connection with the manufacture, production, storage, transport or use of feed, and any process of manufacture, production, storage, transport or use of feed: Animal Feed (Hygiene, Sampling etc and Enforcement) (England) Regulations 2015, SI 2015/454, reg 30(7); Animal Feed (Hygiene, Sampling etc and Enforcement) (Wales) Regulations 2016, SI 2016/387, reg 30(7).

10 An authorised officer entering premises by virtue of these provisions, or of a warrant issued under it, has the right to take on those premises, in the prescribed manner, a sample of any material appearing to be a feed manufactured, produced, placed on the market or intended to be placed on the market or to be material used, or intended to be used, as feed: Animal Feed (Hygiene, Sampling etc and Enforcement) (England) Regulations 2015, SI 2015/454, reg 30(8); Animal Feed (Hygiene, Sampling etc and Enforcement) (Wales) Regulations 2016, SI 2016/387, reg 30(8). Without prejudice to the authorised officer's powers and duties as to the taking of samples in the prescribed manner, an authorised officer may take a sample in a manner other than that prescribed of any material which has been sold for use as feed or which the officer has reasonable cause to believe to be intended for sale as such: Animal Feed (Hygiene, Sampling etc and Enforcement) (England) Regulations 2015, SI 2015/454, reg 30(9); Animal Feed (Hygiene, Sampling etc and Enforcement) (Wales) Regulations 2016, SI 2016/387, reg 30(9). Where, for the purpose of taking a sample under these provisions, an authorised officer takes some of it from each of one or more containers, which are exposed for sale by retail, and none of which weighs more than six kilograms, the owner of the container or containers may require the officer to purchase the container or containers on behalf of the authority for which the officer acts: Animal Feed (Hygiene, Sampling etc and Enforcement) (England) Regulations 2015, SI 2015/454, reg 30(10); Animal Feed (Hygiene, Sampling etc and Enforcement) (Wales) Regulations 2016, SI 2016/387, reg 30(10).

11 An authorised officer entering premises by virtue of these provisions, or of a warrant issued under it, has the right:

   (1)   to require any person carrying on, or appearing to be carrying on, a feed business, or any person employed in connection with such a business, to produce any record (in whatever form it is held) relating to or arising out of the exercise in the course of that business of any such activity, and of which that person has possession or control; and

   (2)   to inspect and take copies of any record, or of any entry in any record produced in pursuance of head (1): Animal Feed (Hygiene, Sampling etc and Enforcement) (England) Regulations 2015, SI 2015/454, reg 30(11); Animal Feed (Hygiene, Sampling etc and Enforcement) (Wales) Regulations 2016, SI 2016/387, reg 30(11).

An authorised officer exercising the power conferred by the above provisions in respect of a record held by means of a computer:

   (a)   is entitled at any reasonable time to have access to, and inspect and check the operation of, any computer and associated apparatus or material which is or has been, or which it appears is or has been, in use in connection with the record in question;

   (b)   may require:

      (i)   the person by whom or on whose behalf the computer is or has been so used, or

      (ii)   any person having charge of, or otherwise concerned with the operation of, the computer, apparatus or material,

      to afford the authorised officer such reasonable assistance as the officer may require for that purpose; and

   (c)   may require the record, or an extract from the record, to be produced in a form in which it may be taken away: Animal Feed (Hygiene, Sampling etc and Enforcement) (England) Regulations 2015, SI 2015/454, reg 30(12); Animal Feed (Hygiene, Sampling etc and Enforcement) (Wales) Regulations 2016, SI 2016/387, reg 30(12).

Where, in the case of a person carrying on, or appearing to carry on, a business which consists of or includes the manufacture of a compound feed a requirement is made under head (1) above in relation to any feed which is, or appears to be, intended for a particular nutritional purpose and, at the time the requirement is made, the record in respect of which it is made has been published and is available in accessible form for public use, the person of whom the requirement is made will be deemed to comply with it if, at the time it is made, that person supplies the authorised officer making it with correct and adequate details of the publication concerned, and of where a copy of it may be obtained: Animal Feed (Hygiene, Sampling etc and Enforcement) (England) Regulations 2015, SI 2015/454, reg 30(13); Animal Feed (Hygiene, Sampling etc and Enforcement) (Wales) Regulations 2016, SI 2016/387, reg 30(13).

An authorised officer entering premises by virtue of this regulation, or of a warrant issued under it, has the right to seize and detain any record which the officer has reasonable cause to believe to be a record which may be required as evidence in proceedings under specified feed law: and adequate details of the publication concerned, and of where a copy of it may be obtained: Animal Feed (Hygiene, Sampling etc and Enforcement) (England) Regulations 2015, SI 2015/454, reg 30(14); Animal Feed (Hygiene, Sampling etc and Enforcement) (Wales) Regulations 2016, SI 2016/387, reg 30(14). On seizing and detaining any such record, the authorised officer must provide to the occupier a notice containing a description of the record and a statement that the record will be detained until it is no longer required as evidence in proceedings under specified feed law: Animal Feed (Hygiene, Sampling etc and Enforcement) (England) Regulations 2015, SI 2015/454, reg 30(15); Animal Feed (Hygiene, Sampling etc and Enforcement) (Wales) Regulations 2016, SI 2016/387, reg 30(15).

As to the meanings, for these purposes, of 'compound feed' and 'feed which is, or appears to be intended for a particular nutritional purpose' see Council Regulation (EC) 767/2009 (OJ L229, 1.9.2009, p 1–28) on placing on the market and use of feed, arts 3(2)(h), (o) respectively: Animal Feed (Hygiene, Sampling etc and Enforcement) (England) Regulations 2015, SI 2015/454, reg 30(16); Animal Feed (Hygiene, Sampling etc and Enforcement) (Wales) Regulations 2016, SI 2016/387, reg 30(16).

12 Animal Feed (Hygiene, Sampling etc and Enforcement) (England) Regulations 2015, SI 2015/454, reg 31(1); Animal Feed (Hygiene, Sampling etc and Enforcement) (Wales) Regulations 2016, SI 2016/387, reg 31(1).

13 Animal Feed (Hygiene, Sampling etc and Enforcement) (England) Regulations 2015, SI 2015/454, reg 31(2)(a); Animal Feed (Hygiene, Sampling etc and Enforcement) (Wales) Regulations 2016, SI 2016/387, reg 31(2)(a). A person who knowingly contravenes the requirements of a notice under head (a) in the text commits an offence: Animal Feed (Hygiene, Sampling etc and Enforcement) (England) Regulations 2015, SI 2015/454, reg 31(2); Animal Feed (Hygiene, Sampling etc and Enforcement) (Wales) Regulations 2016, SI 2016/387, reg 31(2). An authorised officer who exercises the powers conferred by head (a) must, as soon as is reasonably practicable and in any event within 21 days, determine whether or not the officer is satisfied that the material complies with the requirements mentioned in the Animal Feed (Hygiene, Sampling etc and Enforcement) (England) Regulations 2015, SI 2015/454, reg 31(1) or the Animal Feed (Hygiene, Sampling etc and Enforcement) (Wales) Regulations 2016, SI 2016/387, reg 31(1) and if so satisfied, forthwith withdraw the notice: Animal Feed (Hygiene, Sampling etc and Enforcement) (England) Regulations 2015, SI 2015/454, reg 31(3)(a); Animal Feed (Hygiene, Sampling etc and Enforcement) (Wales) Regulations 2016, SI 2016/387, reg 31(3)(a). If the authorised office is not so satisfied, he must proceed to have the matter dealt with by a justice of the peace: Animal Feed (Hygiene, Sampling etc and Enforcement) (England) Regulations 2015, SI 2015/454, reg 31(3)(b); Animal Feed (Hygiene, Sampling etc and Enforcement) (Wales) Regulations 2016, SI 2016/387, reg 31(3)(b). If a notice under head (a) in the text is withdrawn, or the justice of the peace by whom any material falls to be dealt with under this regulation refuses to condemn it, the enforcement authority must compensate the owner of the material for any depreciation in its value resulting from the action taken by the authorised officer and any disputed question as to the right or amount of any compensation payable is to be determined by arbitration: Animal Feed (Hygiene, Sampling etc and Enforcement) (England) Regulations 2015, SI 2015/454, reg 31(6), (7); Animal Feed (Hygiene, Sampling etc and Enforcement) (Wales) Regulations 2016, SI 2016/387, reg 31(6), (7).

14 Animal Feed (Hygiene, Sampling etc and Enforcement) (England) Regulations 2015, SI 2015/454, reg 31(2)(b); Animal Feed (Hygiene, Sampling etc and Enforcement) (Wales) Regulations 2016, SI 2016/387, reg 31(2)(b). Where the authorised officer exercises these powers or otherwise refers a matter to a justice he must inform the person in charge of the material of his intention to have it dealt with by a justice and:

(1)   a person who might be liable under the provisions of specified feed law to a prosecution in respect of the material shall, if that person attends before the justice of the peace by whom the material falls to be dealt with, be entitled to be heard and to call witnesses; and

(2)   that justice of the peace may, but need not, be a member of the court before which a person is charged with an offence under those provisions in relation to that material: Animal Feed (Hygiene, Sampling etc and Enforcement) (England) Regulations 2015, SI 2015/454, reg 31(4); Animal Feed (Hygiene, Sampling etc and Enforcement) (Wales) Regulations 2016, SI 2016/387, reg 31(4).

15 Animal Feed (Hygiene, Sampling etc and Enforcement) (England) Regulations 2015, SI 2015/454, reg 31(5); Animal Feed (Hygiene, Sampling etc and Enforcement) (Wales) Regulations 2016, SI 2016/387, reg 31(5). The appropriate order is that the material is to be destroyed or to be so disposed of as to prevent it from being used as food for human consumption, or for feed, and that any expenses reasonably incurred in connection with the destruction or disposal are to be defrayed by the feed business operator: Animal Feed (Hygiene, Sampling etc and Enforcement) (England) Regulations 2015, SI 2015/454, reg 31(5); Animal Feed (Hygiene, Sampling etc and Enforcement) (Wales) Regulations 2016, SI 2016/387, reg 31(5). As to the meaning of 'feed business operator' see PARA 79 note 2. However in the case of material referred to in European Parliament and Council Regulation (EC) 1829/2003 (OJ L268, 18.10.2003, p 1) on genetically modified food and feed, art 15.1, which is the subject of an authorisation granted under European Parliament and Council Regulation (EC) 1829/2003 and has been produced in accordance with any conditions relating to that authorisation but does not bear the appropriate labelling as required by art 25, the

justice of the peace may order that the material be labelled properly as soon as reasonably practicable and at the expense of the feed business operator and may also order the release of the material into the custody of the operator: Animal Feed (Hygiene, Sampling etc and Enforcement) (England) Regulations 2015, SI 2015/454, reg 31(8); Animal Feed (Hygiene, Sampling etc and Enforcement) (Wales) Regulations 2016, SI 2016/387, reg 31(8).

83.   Sampling and analysis.

Where an authorised officer[1] obtains a sample[2] and decides to have it analysed for the purpose of ascertaining whether there is or has been any contravention of specified feed law[3], he first must divide the sample into three (or, if the person who manufactured any sampled material is not a person to whom part of the sample should be sent, four[4]) parts of as near as may be equal size and cause each part to be marked, sealed and fastened in the prescribed manner[5]. One part must be sent for analysis[6], one must be sent to the person on whose premises[7] the material was sampled or to his agent[8], one (if there are four parts) must be sent to the manufacturer[9], and the remaining part must be retained and preserved as an officially sealed reference sample[10].

Where following analysis of a part of a sample[11] proceedings are intended to be, or have been, commenced against a person for an offence under specified feed law[12], and the prosecution intends to adduce evidence of the result of that part of the sample[13], the authorised officer may be required to send the retained part of the sample to the Government Chemist for analysis[14]. The Government Chemist[15] must then analyse in the prescribed manner the part of the sample so sent to him and send to the authorised officer a certificate of the analysis[16]. The authorised officer must, immediately upon receipt of the certificate, supply a copy of it to the prosecutor (if a person other than the authorised officer) and the defendant[17].

Any person who either tampers with any material so as to procure that any sample of it taken or submitted for analysis under these provisions does not correctly represent the material, or tampers or interferes with any sample taken or submitted for analysis under these provisions, is guilty of an offence[18].

1   As to enforcement authorities and authorised officers see PARA 78.
2   As to the power to obtain samples see PARA 82).
3   As to the specified feed law for these purposes see PARA 77.
4   Animal Feed (Hygiene, Sampling etc and Enforcement) (England) Regulations 2015, SI 2015/454, reg 15(2); Animal Feed (Hygiene, Sampling etc and Enforcement) (Wales) Regulations 2016, SI 2016/387, reg 15(2).
5   Animal Feed (Hygiene, Sampling etc and Enforcement) (England) Regulations 2015, SI 2015/454, reg 15(1)(a); Animal Feed (Hygiene, Sampling etc and Enforcement) (Wales) Regulations 2016, SI 2016/387, reg 15(1)(a). 'Prescribed manner' means the manner prescribed by Commission Regulation (EC) 152/2009 (OJ L54, 26.2.2009, p 1) laying down the methods of sampling and analysis for the official control of feed: Animal Feed (Hygiene, Sampling etc and Enforcement) (England) Regulations 2015, SI 2015/454, reg 2(1); Animal Feed (Hygiene, Sampling etc and Enforcement) (Wales) Regulations 2016, SI 2016/387, reg 2(1).
6   Animal Feed (Hygiene, Sampling etc and Enforcement) (England) Regulations 2015, SI 2015/454, reg 15(1)(b); Animal Feed (Hygiene, Sampling etc and Enforcement) (Wales) Regulations 2016, SI 2016/387, reg 15(1)(b). This part must be sent, accompanied by a statement signed by the authorised office confirming that the sample was taken in a prescribed manner. to the agricultural analyst for the area of the enforcement authority from which the authorised officer derives his authority: Animal Feed (Hygiene, Sampling etc and Enforcement) (England) Regulations 2015, SI 2015/454, reg 15(1)(b), (3); Animal Feed (Hygiene, Sampling etc and Enforcement) (Wales) Regulations 2016, SI 2016/387, reg 15(1)(b), (3). The agricultural analyst must analyse the part of the sample sent to him and send a certificate of analysis to the authorised officer, who must send a copy to the person on whose premises the material was sampled or that person's agent; and, if a part of the sample was sent under the Animal Feed (Hygiene, Sampling etc and Enforcement) (England) Regulations 2015, SI 2015/454, reg 15(4) or the Animal Feed (Hygiene, Sampling etc and Enforcement) (Wales) Regulations 2016, SI 2016/387, reg 15(2), to the person to whom that part was sent: Animal Feed (Hygiene, Sampling etc and Enforcement) (England) Regulations 2015,

SI 2015/454, reg 15(4); Animal Feed (Hygiene, Sampling etc and Enforcement) (Wales) Regulations 2016, SI 2016/387, reg 15(4). Any such analysis may be performed by any person acting under the direction of the agricultural analyst: Animal Feed (Hygiene, Sampling etc and Enforcement) (England) Regulations 2015, SI 2015/454, reg 15(5); Animal Feed (Hygiene, Sampling etc and Enforcement) (Wales) Regulations 2016, SI 2016/387, reg 15(5).

If the agricultural analyst determines that an effective analysis of the sample cannot be performed by him or under his direction he must send it to the agricultural analyst for another area, together with any documents received by him with the sample: Animal Feed (Hygiene, Sampling etc and Enforcement) (England) Regulations 2015, SI 2015/454, reg 15(6); Animal Feed (Hygiene, Sampling etc and Enforcement) (Wales) Regulations 2016, SI 2016/387, reg 15(6). An agricultural analyst is not liable for acts done by him pursuant to his statutory duties and is indemnified against any damages which may be awarded: see PARA 78.

7   As to the meaning of 'premises' see PARA 78 note 4.
8   Animal Feed (Hygiene, Sampling etc and Enforcement) (England) Regulations 2015, SI 2015/454, reg 15(1)(c); Animal Feed (Hygiene, Sampling etc and Enforcement) (Wales) Regulations 2016, SI 2016/387, reg 15(1)(c).
9   The authorised officer must within 14 days of the date of sampling send the fourth part to the manufacturer, unless he does not know and is unable to ascertain after making reasonable inquiries the identity of the manufacturer or his address in the United Kingdom: Animal Feed (Hygiene, Sampling etc and Enforcement) (England) Regulations 2015, SI 2015/454, reg 15(2); Animal Feed (Hygiene, Sampling etc and Enforcement) (Wales) Regulations 2016, SI 2016/387, reg 15(2). As to the meaning of 'United Kingdom' see PARA 1 note 1.
10 Animal Feed (Hygiene, Sampling etc and Enforcement) (England) Regulations 2015, SI 2015/454, reg 15(1)(d); Animal Feed (Hygiene, Sampling etc and Enforcement) (Wales) Regulations 2016, SI 2016/387, reg 15(1)(d).
11 Ie that sample having been sent for analysis under the Animal Feed (Hygiene, Sampling etc and Enforcement) (England) Regulations 2015, SI 2015/454, reg 15(1)(b) or the Animal Feed (Hygiene, Sampling etc and Enforcement) (Wales) Regulations 2016, SI 2016/387, reg 15(1)(b) (see the text and note 6).
12 Animal Feed (Hygiene, Sampling etc and Enforcement) (England) Regulations 2015, SI 2015/454, reg 16(1)(a); Animal Feed (Hygiene, Sampling etc and Enforcement) (Wales) Regulations 2016, SI 2016/387, reg 16(1)(a). As to the specified feed law for these purposes see PARA 77.
13 Animal Feed (Hygiene, Sampling etc and Enforcement) (England) Regulations 2015, SI 2015/454, reg 16(1)(b); Animal Feed (Hygiene, Sampling etc and Enforcement) (Wales) Regulations 2016, SI 2016/387, reg 16(1)(b).
14 Animal Feed (Hygiene, Sampling etc and Enforcement) (England) Regulations 2015, SI 2015/454, reg 16(2); Animal Feed (Hygiene, Sampling etc and Enforcement) (Wales) Regulations 2016, SI 2016/387, reg 16(2). The officer may do this of his own volition, and must do so if requested by the prosecutor (if a person other than the authorised officer) or the defendant (or prospective defendant): Animal Feed (Hygiene, Sampling etc and Enforcement) (England) Regulations 2015, SI 2015/454, reg 16(2)(a)–(c), (7); Animal Feed (Hygiene, Sampling etc and Enforcement) (Wales) Regulations 2016, SI 2016/387, reg 16(2)(a)–(c), (7). Where the request is made by the defendant, the authorised officer may give him notice in writing requesting payment of a fee specified in the notice in respect of the functions of the Government Chemist under these provisions; and if the specified fee does not exceed either the cost of performing those functions or the appropriate fee (ie such fee as may be fixed in accordance with the provisions of the Agriculture Act 1970 s 78(10): see PARA 57) for the performance of any similar function under s 78 (further analysis by the Government Chemist: see PARAS 51, 57) the officer may, in the absence of agreement by the defendant to pay the fee, refuse to comply with the defendant's request: Animal Feed (Hygiene, Sampling etc and Enforcement) (England) Regulations 2015, SI 2015/454, reg 16(6), (7); Animal Feed (Hygiene, Sampling etc and Enforcement) (Wales) Regulations 2016, SI 2016/387, reg 16(6), (7). As to the service of notices see PARA 79 note 4.
15 Any analysis required to be made under the Animal Feed (Hygiene, Sampling etc and Enforcement) (England) Regulations 2015, SI 2015/454, reg 16(3) or the Animal Feed (Hygiene, Sampling etc and Enforcement) (Wales) Regulations 2016, SI 2016/387, reg 16(3) may be performed by any person acting under the direction of the Government Chemist: Animal Feed (Hygiene, Sampling etc and Enforcement) (England) Regulations 2015, SI 2015/454, reg 16(4); Animal Feed (Hygiene, Sampling etc and Enforcement) (Wales) Regulations 2016, SI 2016/387, reg 16(4).
16 Animal Feed (Hygiene, Sampling etc and Enforcement) (England) Regulations 2015, SI 2015/454, reg 16(3); Animal Feed (Hygiene, Sampling etc and Enforcement) (Wales) Regulations 2016, SI 2016/387, reg 16(3). As to the form and status of a certificate of analysis see the Animal Feed (Hygiene, Sampling etc and Enforcement) (England) Regulations 2015, SI 2015/454, reg 18 and

the Animal Feed (Hygiene, Sampling etc and Enforcement) (Wales) Regulations 2016, SI 2016/387, reg 18. As to the methods of sending a final sample see the Animal Feed (Hygiene, Sampling etc and Enforcement) (England) Regulations 2015, SI 2015/454, reg 17 and the Animal Feed (Hygiene, Sampling etc and Enforcement) (Wales) Regulations 2016, SI 2016/387, reg 17.

17 Animal Feed (Hygiene, Sampling etc and Enforcement) (England) Regulations 2015, SI 2015/454, reg 16(5); Animal Feed (Hygiene, Sampling etc and Enforcement) (Wales) Regulations 2016, SI 2016/387, reg 16(5).

18 Animal Feed (Hygiene, Sampling etc and Enforcement) (England) Regulations 2015, SI 2015/454, reg 20; Animal Feed (Hygiene, Sampling etc and Enforcement) (Wales) Regulations 2016, SI 2016/387, reg 20. The offence is punishable, in England, on summary conviction to a term of imprisonment not exceeding 3 months or to a fine not exceeding level 5 on the standard scale, or both (Animal Feed (Hygiene, Sampling etc and Enforcement) (England) Regulations 2015, SI 2015/454, reg 34(2)) and, in Wales, on summary conviction to a term of imprisonment not exceeding six months or to a fine or both (Animal Feed (Hygiene, Sampling etc and Enforcement) (Wales) Regulations 2016, SI 2016/387, reg 34(2)) As to the standard scale see PARA 14 note 2. As to offences and penalties generally see PARA 78 note 11.

(iii) Official Controls on Feed

84. Official controls.

Provision is made[1] for the verification of compliance with official controls established by EU rules in the areas of:

(1) food and food safety, integrity and wholesomeness at any stage of production, processing and distribution of food, including rules aimed at ensuring fair practices in trade and protecting consumer interests and information, and the manufacture and use of materials and articles intended to come into contact with food;

(2) deliberate release into the environment of Genetically Modified Organisms (GMOs) for the purpose of food and feed production;

(3) feed and feed safety at any stage of production, processing and distribution of feed and the use of feed, including rules aimed at ensuring fair practices in trade and protecting consumer health, interests and information;

(4) animal health requirements;

(5) prevention and minimisation of risks to human and animal health arising from animal by-products and derived products;

(6) welfare requirements for animals;

(7) protective measures against pests of plants;

(8) requirements for the placing on the market and use of plant protection products and the sustainable use of pesticides, with the exception of pesticides application equipment;

(9) organic production and labelling of organic products;

(10) use and labelling of protected designations of origin, protected geographical indications and traditional specialities guaranteed[2].

1 Provision was made by Council Regulation (EC) 882/2004 (OJ L165, 30.4.2004, p 1) on official controls performed to ensure the verification of compliance with feed and food law, animal health and animal welfare rules and was implemented in the UK by the Official Feed and Food Controls (England) Regulations 2007, SI 2007/3185 and the Official Feed and Food Controls (Wales) Regulations 2007, SI 2007/3294. Council Regulation (EU) 882/2004 (OJ L165, 30.4.2004, p 1) has been has been repealed and replaced by European Parliament and Council Regulation (EU) 2017/625 (OJ L95, 7.4.2017, p 1) on official controls and other official activities performed to ensure the application of food and feed law, rules on animal health and welfare, plant health and plant protection products.

2 See European Parliament and Council Regulation (EU) 2017/625 (OJ L95, 7.4.2017, p 1) art 1(2).

(iv) Residual Powers of Secretary of State

85. Powers of Secretary of State concerning production and distribution of feeding stuffs.
The Secretary of State[1] may for the purpose of regulating any animal feeding stuff[2], or anything done to or in relation to, or with a view to the production of, any animal feeding stuff, make an order applying, or making provision corresponding to, any provisions of the Food Safety Act 1990[3]. Such an order may make provision with a view to protecting animal health, protecting human health or for any other purpose which appears to the Secretary of State to be appropriate[4]. Before making such an order, the Secretary of State must consult such organisations as appear to him to be representative of interests likely to be substantially affected by the order[5] and must have regard to any advice given by the Food Standards Agency[6].

1 As to the Secretary of State see PARA 390.
2 For these purposes 'animal feeding stuff' means feeding stuff for any description of animals, including any nutritional supplement or other similar substance which is not administered through oral feeding (Food Standards Act 1999 s 36(1)); and 'animal' means any creature other than a bird or fish (Food Safety Act 1990 s 53(1); Food Standards Act 1999 s 36(1)).
3 Food Standards Act 1999 s 30(1), (2). Orders may include any power to make subordinate legislation or to give directions, may apply the Food Safety Act 1990 with or without modifications, and may be made by reference to the Food Safety Act 1990 as it stood immediately before 11 November 1999 (ie the day on which the Food Standards Act 1999 received the Royal Assent) or as it stands following any amendment or repeal made by the Food Standards Act 1999: s 30(2), (3). As to the Food Safety Act 1990 see FOOD AND DRINK. At the date at which this volume states the law no orders had been made under the Food Standards Act 1999 s 30.
4 Food Standards Act 1999 s 30(4).
5 Food Standards Act 1999 s 30(6)(a). This requirement does not apply in any case in which consultation is required by Council Regulation (EC) 178/2002 (OJ L031, 1.1.2002, p 1) laying down the general principles and requirements of food law, establishing the European Food Safety Authority and laying down procedures in matters of food safety, art 9: Food Standards Act 1999 s 30(9) (added by SI 2004/3254).
6 Food Standards Act 1999 s 30(6)(b). As to the Food Standards Agency see FOOD AND DRINK vol 51 (2013) PARAS 634–653.

(5) MEDICATED FEEDING STUFFS AND SPECIFIED FEED ADDITIVES

86. Incorporation of veterinary medicinal products into animal feeding stuffs.
Any person who incorporates a veterinary medicinal product[1] (or a premixture[2] containing a veterinary medicinal product) into feeding stuffs:

(1)   must do so in accordance with the summary of product characteristics, and must take account of any interactions listed there[3];

(2)   must ensure that the veterinary medicinal product does not contain the same active substance as any other additive[4];

(3)   must ensure that the veterinary medicinal product is incorporated in accordance with its marketing authorisation (unless it has been prescribed under the cascade[5]) and the prescription[6];

(4)   must ensure that the daily dose of the veterinary medicinal product is contained in a quantity of medicated feeding stuffs corresponding to at least half the daily feeding stuffs ration of the animals treated or, in the case of ruminants, corresponding to at least half the daily requirements of non-mineral complementary feedingstuffs[7].

Any person who incorporates a veterinary medicinal product into a premixture:
- (a)   must do so in accordance with the summary of product characteristics, and must take account of any interactions listed there[8]; and
- (b)   must ensure that the veterinary medicinal product does not contain the same active substance as any other additive[9].

No person may incorporate a veterinary medicinal product into a premixture or feeding stuff, or act as a distributor of premixtures or feeding stuffs containing a veterinary medicinal product, without being approved to do so by the Secretary of State[10].

A manufacturer must ensure that, so far as is reasonably practical, the veterinary medicinal product is evenly incorporated throughout the feeding stuffs[11].

Failure to comply with the above provisions is an offence[12].

1   'Veterinary medicinal product' means any substance or combination of substances presented as having properties for treating or preventing disease in animals or any substance or combination of substances that may be used in, or administered to, animals with a view either to restoring, correcting or modifying physiological functions by exerting a pharmacological, immunological or metabolic action, or to making a medical diagnosis (Veterinary Medicines Regulations 2013, SI 2013/2033, reg 2(1)); and 'animal' means all animals other than man and includes birds, reptiles, fish, molluscs, crustacea and bees (reg 2(2)). The Veterinary Medicines Regulations 2013, SI 2013/2033, apply to all veterinary medicinal products irrespective of whether or not there is other legislation controlling a product: reg 2(5).
2   'Premixture' means a mixture of a veterinary medicinal product or a specified feed additive with feeding stuffs materials, intended for further mixing with feeding stuffs before being fed to animals: Veterinary Medicines Regulations 2013, SI 2013/2033, Sch 5 para 1(3). For these purposes 'specified feed additives' are coccidiostats, histomonostats and all other zootechnical additives except digestibility enhancers, gut flora stabilisers and substances incorporated with the intention of favourably affecting the environment: Sch 5 para 1(1). 'Zootechnical additive' means any additive used to maintain animals in good health or favourably affect their performance: Sch 5 para 1(3).
    Schedule 5 applies in relation to the specified feed additives (see note 3) when used as feed additives (Sch 5 para 1(1)) and in relation to the manufacture and placing on the market of feeding stuffs containing a veterinary medicinal product (Sch 5 para 1(2)), making provision for the enforcement in England and Wales of:
    (1)   Council Regulation (EC) 178/2002 (OJ L031, 1.1.2002, p 1) laying down the general principles and requirements of food law, establishing the European Food Safety Authority and laying down procedures in matters of food safety (see in particular the Veterinary Medicines Regulations 2013, SI 2013/2033, Sch 5 para 2);
    (2)   Council Regulation (EC) 1831/2003 (OJ L268, 18.10.2003, p 29) on additives for use in animal nutrition (see in particular the Veterinary Medicines Regulations 2013, SI 2013/2033, Sch 5 para 3);
    (3)   Council Regulation (EC) 882/2004 (OJ L165, 30.4.2004, p 1) on official controls performed to ensure the verification of compliance with feed and food law, animal health and animal welfare rules (repealed and replaced by European Parliament and Council Regulation (EU) 2017/625 (OJ L95, 7.4.2017, p 1) on official controls and other official activities performed to ensure the application of food and feed law, rules on animal health and welfare, plant health and plant protection products) (see in particular the Veterinary Medicines Regulations 2013, SI 2013/2033, Sch 5 para 4);
    (4)   Council Regulation (EC) 183/2005 (OJ L38, 8.2.2005, p 1) laying down requirements for feed hygiene (see in particular the Veterinary Medicines Regulations 2013, SI 2013/2033, Sch 5 para 5); and
    (5)   Council Regulation (EC) 767/2009 (OJ L229, 1.9.2009, p 1–28) on placing on the market and use of feed (see in particular the Veterinary Medicines Regulations 2013, SI 2013/2033, Sch 5 para 6).
    Failure to comply with certain provisions mentioned in heads (1) to (5) above is an offence: see Sch 5 para 31(a)–(d). Provision is made for sampling and analysis pursuant to enforcement action taken under Sch 5: see Sch 5 para 22.
3   Veterinary Medicines Regulations 2013, SI 2013/2033, Sch 5 para 10(a).
4   Veterinary Medicines Regulations 2013, SI 2013/2033, Sch 5 para 10(b).

5   As to the meaning of the 'cascade' see Sch 4 para 1; and MEDICAL PRODUCTS AND DRUGS vol 75 (2013) PARA 423.
6   Veterinary Medicines Regulations 2013, SI 2013/2033, Sch 5 para 10(c).
7   Veterinary Medicines Regulations 2013, SI 2013/2033, Sch 5 para 10(d).
8   Veterinary Medicines Regulations 2013, SI 2013/2033, Sch 5 para 8(a).
9   Veterinary Medicines Regulations 2013, SI 2013/2033, Sch 5 para 8(b).
10 Veterinary Medicines Regulations 2013, SI 2013/2033, Sch 5 para 7(2). For the purposes of Council Directive (EC) 90/167 (OJ L092, 7.4.90, p 42) laying down the conditions governing the preparation, placing on the market and use of medicated feeding stuffs in the Community the competent authority is the Secretary of State: Veterinary Medicines Regulations 2013, SI 2013/2033, Sch 5 para 7(1). The conditions which govern approval of feed business establishments under Council Regulation (EC) 183/2005 (OJ L38, 8.2.2005, p 1) laying down requirements for feed hygiene also govern approval of manufacturers and distributors under the Veterinary Medicines Regulations 2013, SI 2013/2033, Sch 5 para 7(2): Sch 5 para 7(3). The Secretary of State must conduct inspections of manufacturers and distributors approved under Sch 5 para 7(2) basing the frequency of inspection on the risks associated with each premises' history and the nature of the products handled at the premises: Sch 5 para 7(4). The provisions of Sch 5 para 7 do not apply in relation to any person breeding or selling ornamental fish not intended for human consumption provided that the person does not use more than a total of 1kg of veterinary medicinal product annually for that purpose: Sch 5 para 7(6). In the case of the refusal, suspension or revocation of an approval under Sch 5 para 7 the appeals procedure relating to a manufacturing authorisation in reg 30 applies: Sch 5 para 7(7). The requirements of Sch 5 para 7 do not apply in relation to animals on domestic premises: see Sch 5 para 30.
11 Veterinary Medicines Regulations 2013, SI 2013/2033, Sch 5 para 7(5).
12 See the Veterinary Medicines Regulations 2013, SI 2013/2033, Sch 5 para 31(e), (f), (h). A person guilty of an offence under the Veterinary Medicines Regulations 2013, SI 2013/2033 (see the text and notes 1–11); and PARA 89 et seq) is liable on summary conviction to a fine not exceeding the statutory maximum or to imprisonment for a term not exceeding 6 months or both (reg 44(1)(a)), or on conviction on indictment to a fine or to imprisonment for a term not exceeding two years or both (reg 44(1)(b)). As to the statutory maximum see PARA 58 note 1. Where a body corporate is guilty of such an offence, and that offence is proved to have been committed with the consent or connivance of, or to have been attributable to any neglect on the part of, a qualified person appointed as such for these purposes, or any director (which in relation to a body corporate whose affairs are managed by its members, means a member of the body corporate), manager, secretary or other similar person of the body corporate, or any person who was purporting to act in any such capacity, he is guilty of the offence as well as the body corporate (reg 44(2), (4)). If such an offence committed by a partnership is shown to have been committed with the consent or connivance of a partner, or to be attributable to any neglect on their part, the partner as well as the partnership is guilty of the offence and liable to be proceeded against and punished accordingly: reg 44(3).

87. Importing feeding stuffs containing veterinary medicinal products.

It is an offence to import a feeding stuff containing a veterinary medicinal product[1] from a third country[2] or to fail to comply with restrictions placed on the bringing in of feeding stuffs containing a veterinary medicinal product from other member states[3].

1   As to the meaning of 'veterinary medicinal product' see PARA 86 note 2.
2   Veterinary Medicines Regulations 2013, SI 2013/2033, Sch 5 paras 27, 31(w). As to offences see PARA 86 note 12. A manufacturer of premixture or feeding stuffs who imports a veterinary medicinal product authorised in another Member State or third country for the purposes of incorporating it into premixture or feeding stuffs for export does not commit an offence under reg 43(q) (importation of an unauthorised veterinary medicinal product) or reg 43(r) (possession of an unauthorised veterinary medicinal product): Sch 5 para 29(1) (substituted by SI 2014/599). It is an offence for a person to place that premixture or feeding stuff on the market in the United Kingdom once the veterinary medicinal product has been incorporated into it: see the Veterinary Medicines Regulations 2013, SI 2013/2033, Sch 5 paras 29(2), 31(y).
3   No person may bring in feeding stuffs containing a veterinary medicinal product from another member state unless they have been manufactured in accordance with the provisions of Council Directive (EC) 90/167 (OJ L092, 7.4.90, p 42) laying down the conditions governing the preparation, placing on the market and use of medicated feeding stuffs in the Community and Council Regulation (EC) 183/2005 (OJ L38, 8.2.2005, p 1) laying down requirements for feed

hygiene (see PARA 71) (Veterinary Medicines Regulations 2013, SI 2013/2033, Sch 5 para 28(a)) and they only contain a veterinary medicinal product that has the same quantitative and qualitative composition as a veterinary medicinal product authorised in the United Kingdom (Sch 5 para 28(b)). It is an offence to fail to comply with Sch 5 para 28: Sch 5 para 31(x). As to the meaning of 'United Kingdom' see PARA 1 note 1.

88. Top dressing.

No person may promote or label any veterinary medicinal product[1], or anything containing a veterinary medicinal product, as being suitable for top dressing (that is, sprinkling it on to feeding stuffs without thoroughly incorporating it) unless the summary of product characteristics specifically permits this use[2].

It is an offence to fail to comply with the above provision[3].

1   As to the meaning of 'veterinary medicinal product' see PARA 86 note 2.
2   Veterinary Medicines Regulations 2013, SI 2013/2033, Sch 5 paras 9.
3   Veterinary Medicines Regulations 2013, SI 2013/2033, Sch 5 para 31(g).

89. Records.

Any person who incorporates a veterinary medicinal product[1] into a premixture[2], a premixture containing a veterinary medicinal product into feeding stuffs[3], or a veterinary medicinal product into feeding stuffs[4], must make a daily record of the types and quantities of all veterinary medicinal products (and specified feed additives[5], if any) and premixture used in the manufacturing process[6] and the quantity of feeding stuffs and premixture containing veterinary medicinal product manufactured on that day[7]. An approved distributor must make a daily record of the types and quantities of all premixtures and feeding stuffs containing veterinary medicinal products bought and sold that day[8] and the quantity held[9]; and a manufacturer and distributor must also record for each consignment supplied, as soon as reasonably practicable, the date of delivery[10], the name and address of each consignee (or, in the case of a manufacturer supplying to a distributor, the name and address of the distributor)[11], the type of feeding stuffs or premixture supplied[12], the quantity[13], the type of veterinary medicinal product incorporated into the feeding stuffs[14], and the expiry date[15]. Records must be kept for five years[16]. It is an offence to fail to comply with these provisions[17].

1   As to the meaning of 'veterinary medicinal product' see PARA 86 note 2.
2   Veterinary Medicines Regulations 2013, SI 2013/2033, Sch 5 para 11(1)(a). As to the meaning of 'premixture' see PARA 86 note 2.
3   Veterinary Medicines Regulations 2013, SI 2013/2033, Sch 5 para 11(1)(b).
4   Veterinary Medicines Regulations 2013, SI 2013/2033, Sch 5 para 11(1)(c).
5   As to the meaning of 'specified feed additive' see PARA 86 note 2.
6   Veterinary Medicines Regulations 2013, SI 2013/2033, Sch 5 para 11(1)(i).
7   Veterinary Medicines Regulations 2013, SI 2013/2033, Sch 5 para 11(1)(ii).
8   Veterinary Medicines Regulations 2013, SI 2013/2033, Sch 5 para 11(2)(a).
9   Veterinary Medicines Regulations 2013, SI 2013/2033, Sch 5 para 11(2)(b).
10   Veterinary Medicines Regulations 2013, SI 2013/2033, Sch 5 para 11(3)(a).
11   Veterinary Medicines Regulations 2013, SI 2013/2033, Sch 5 para 11(3)(b).
12   Veterinary Medicines Regulations 2013, SI 2013/2033, Sch 5 para 11(3)(c).
13   Veterinary Medicines Regulations 2013, SI 2013/2033, Sch 5 para 11(3)(d).
14   Veterinary Medicines Regulations 2013, SI 2013/2033, Sch 5 para 11(3)(e).
15   Veterinary Medicines Regulations 2013, SI 2013/2033, Sch 5 para 11(3)(f).
16   Veterinary Medicines Regulations 2013, SI 2013/2033, Sch 5 para 11(4).
17   Veterinary Medicines Regulations 2013, SI 2013/2033, Sch 5 para 31(i). As to offences see PARA 86 note 12.

90. Labelling.

A premixture[1] containing a veterinary medicinal product[2] must be clearly and legibly labelled with:

(1)   the words 'MEDICATED PREMIXTURE' (or if it is to be labelled as 'complementary feeding stuffs' 'MEDICATED COMPLEMENTARY FEEDINGSTUFFS')[3] in upper case letters[4];

(2)   the proprietary name of the veterinary medicinal product and the authorisation number[5];

(3)   the name and amount of the active substance (mg/kg) in the premixture[6];

(4)   the range of acceptable inclusion rates of the premixture into the final feeding stuffs, the range of acceptable levels of the active ingredients in the final feeding stuffs and the words 'refer to the prescription for the exact inclusion rate' or equivalent wording[7];

(5)   warnings and contra-indications[8];

(6)   withdrawal period and a statement that, if the prescription requires a longer withdrawal period, that is the one that applies[9];

(7)   the expiry date[10];

(8)   any special storage instructions[11]; and

(9)   where a prescription is required, a statement to this effect[12],

and if the premixture also contains an applicable specified feed additive[13] it must also contain the information required under the labelling requirements specified for the purposes of the Additives Regulation[14].

Feeding stuffs containing a veterinary medicinal product must be clearly and legibly labelled with:

(a)   the words 'MEDICATED FEEDINGSTUFFS' in upper case letters, or where feeding stuffs are to be labelled as a complementary feeding stuff and intended to be fed to animals without further mixing with feed materials,   the   words   'MEDICATED   COMPLEMENTARY FEEDINGSTUFF'[15];

(b)   the proprietary name, authorisation number and inclusion rate (kg/tonne or mg/kg) of the veterinary medicinal product incorporated into the feeding stuffs[16];

(c)   the name and amount of the active substance (mg/kg) in the feeding stuffs[17];

(d)   the species of animal[18] for which the feeding stuffs are intended[19];

(e)   warnings and contra-indications[20];

(f)   the withdrawal period, and a statement that, if the prescription requires a longer withdrawal period, that is the one that applies[21];

(g)   the expiry date[22];

(h)   any special storage instructions required by the marketing authorisation[23];

(i)   a statement to the effect that the feeding stuff must only be fed in accordance with its prescription[24]; and

(j)   the name and approval number of the manufacturer or the distributor[25].

In the case of feeding stuffs distributed by road tankers or in bulk the labelling requirements must be given in a document accompanying the feeding stuffs[26].

It is an offence to supply any such premixtures or feeding stuffs not labelled in accordance with these requirements and with general and specific EU mandatory requirements[27] or to fail to comply with the documentation requirements[28].

1   As to the meaning of 'premixture' see PARA **86** note 2.

2   As to the meaning of 'veterinary medicinal product' see PARA 86 note 2.

3   Ie under legislation implementing Council Directive 79/373 (OJ L86, 6.4.1979, p 30–37) on the marketing of compound feeding stuffs.

4   Veterinary Medicines Regulations 2013, SI 2013/2033, Sch 5 para 12(1)(a).

5   Veterinary Medicines Regulations 2013, SI 2013/2033, Sch 5 para 12(1)(b).

6   Veterinary Medicines Regulations 2013, SI 2013/2033, Sch 5 para 12(1)(c).

7   Veterinary Medicines Regulations 2013, SI 2013/2033, Sch 5 para 12(1)(d).

8   Veterinary Medicines Regulations 2013, SI 2013/2033, Sch 5 para 12(1)(e).

9   Veterinary Medicines Regulations 2013, SI 2013/2033, Sch 5 para 12(1)(f). The withdrawal period must be that specified in the marketing authorisation for the veterinary medicinal product, and if there is more than one veterinary medicinal product used it must be the longest: Sch 5 para 12(2).

10   Veterinary Medicines Regulations 2013, SI 2013/2033, Sch 5 para 12(1)(g).

11   Veterinary Medicines Regulations 2013, SI 2013/2033, Sch 5 para 12(1)(h).

12   Veterinary Medicines Regulations 2013, SI 2013/2033, Sch 5 para 12(1)(i).

13   Ie a specified feed additive to which the Veterinary Medicines Regulations 2013, SI 2013/2033, Sch 5 applies: see PARA 86 note 2. As to the meaning of 'specified feed additive' see PARA 86 note 2.

14   Veterinary Medicines Regulations 2013, SI 2013/2033, Sch 5 para 12(3). For the labelling requirements specified for the purposes of the Additives Regulation (ie Council Regulation (EC) 1831/2003 (OJ L268, 18.10.2003, p 29) on additives for use in animal nutrition) see art 16.

15   Veterinary Medicines Regulations 2013, SI 2013/2033, Sch 5 para 14(1)(a).

16   Veterinary Medicines Regulations 2013, SI 2013/2033, Sch 5 para 14(1)(b).

17   Veterinary Medicines Regulations 2013, SI 2013/2033, Sch 5 para 14(1)(c).

18   Veterinary Medicines Regulations 2013, SI 2013/2033, Sch 5 para 14(1)(d).

20   Veterinary Medicines Regulations 2013, SI 2013/2033, Sch 5 para 14(1)(f).

21   Veterinary Medicines Regulations 2013, SI 2013/2033, Sch 5 para 14(1)(g). If there is more than one veterinary medicinal product used, the longest withdrawal period must be shown on the label: Sch 5 para 14(2).

22   Veterinary Medicines Regulations 2013, SI 2013/2033, Sch 5 para 14(1)(h).

23   As to the meaning of 'animal' see PARA 86 note 2.

24   Veterinary Medicines Regulations 2013, SI 2013/2033, Sch 5 para 14(1)(i).

25   Veterinary Medicines Regulations 2013, SI 2013/2033, Sch 5 para 14(1)(j).

26   Veterinary Medicines Regulations 2013, SI 2013/2033, Sch 5 para 25(1). The transporter must hand over details when he delivers the feeding stuffs unless these have already been provided to the purchaser: Sch 5 para 25(1).

27   Ie with the labelling requirements of European Parliament and Council Regulation (EC) 767/2009 (OJ L 229, 1.9.2009, p 1) on the placing on the market and use of feed, arts 15, 17: Veterinary Medicines Regulations 2013, SI 2013/2033, Sch 5 paras 13, 14(3).

28   See the Veterinary Medicines Regulations 2013, SI 2013/2033, Sch 5 paras 12(4), 14(4), 25(1), 31(j), (k), (l), (u). As to offences see PARA 86 note 12.

91. Possession, placing on the market and use of feeding stuffs.

No person other than a person holding the appropriate approval[1] may be in possession of any:

(1)   specified feed additive or veterinary medicinal product[2];

(2)   premixtures[3] containing such an additive or a veterinary medicinal product[4]; or

(3)   feeding stuffs or complementary feeding stuffs containing such an additive or a veterinary medicinal product[5].

No person other than a manufacturer or distributor may be in possession of feeding stuffs incorporating a veterinary medicinal product unless it has been supplied under a prescription[6].

No person may possess, place on the market or feed to animals any feeding stuffs incorporating veterinary medicinal products or specified feed additives unless they have been incorporated in accordance with the relevant provisions[7].

No person may feed to any animal, or buy, possess or supply for the purpose of feeding to any animal, any feeding stuff containing a veterinary medicinal product or specified feed additive unless:

(a)   that veterinary medicinal product or specified feed additive is authorised for that species of animal and for the purpose for which it is used[8]; or

(b)   in the case of a veterinary medicinal product, it was prescribed for that animal[9].

It is an offence to fail to comply with the above provisions[10].

1   Ie an approval under the Veterinary Medicines Regulations 2013, SI 2013/2033, Sch 5 (see PARA 86).
2   Ie ones to which Veterinary Medicines Regulations 2013, SI 2013/2033, Sch 5 applies: Sch 5 para 21(1)(a). As to the meaning of 'veterinary medicinal product' see PARA 86 note 2. As to the meaning of 'specified feed additive' see PARA 86 note 2. As to the specified feed additives and veterinary medicinal products to which Sch 5 applies see PARA 86 note 2.
3   As to the meaning of 'premixture' see PARA 86 note 2.
4   Veterinary Medicines Regulations 2013, SI 2013/2033, Sch 5 para 21(1)(b).
5   Unless supplied under the Veterinary Medicines Regulations 2013, SI 2013/2033: Sch 5 para 21(1)(c).
6   Veterinary Medicines Regulations 2013, SI 2013/2033, Sch 5 para 21(2).
7   Ie incorporated in accordance with the Veterinary Medicines Regulations 2013, SI 2013/2033, Sch 5: Sch 5 para 26(1). This does not apply in relation to feeding stuffs if the veterinary medicinal product has been incorporated in accordance with an animal test certificate or the feeding stuff has been imported in accordance with Sch 5: Sch 5 para 26(3).
8   Veterinary Medicines Regulations 2013, SI 2013/2033, Sch 5 para 26(2)(a).
9   Veterinary Medicines Regulations 2013, SI 2013/2033, Sch 5 para 26(2)(b).
10 Veterinary Medicines Regulations 2013, SI 2013/2033, Sch 5 para 31(r), (v). As to offences see PARA 86 note 12.

92.   Supply of specified feed additives.

No person other than the person who manufactured a specified feed additive[1] or an approved distributor may supply a specified feed additive[2].

The person who manufactured the specified feed additive may only supply it to:

(1)   an approved distributor[3];

(2)   an approved premixture manufacturer or an approved complementary feeding stuffs manufacturer[4]; or

(3)   a feeding stuff manufacturer approved to mix a specified feed additive directly into feedingstuff[5].

An approved distributor may only supply it to:

(a)   another approved distributor[6];

(b)   an approved premixture manufacturer or an approved complementary feeding stuffs manufacturer[7]; or

(c)   a feeding stuff manufacturer approved to mix a specified feed additive directly into feedingstuff[8].

It is an offence to fail to comply with the above provisions[9].

1   As to the meaning of 'specified feed additive' see PARA 86 note 2. As to the specified feed additives to which the Veterinary Medicines Regulations 2013, SI 2013/2033, Sch 5 applies see PARA 86 note 2.
2   Veterinary Medicines Regulations 2013, SI 2013/2033, Sch 5 para 15(1).
3   Veterinary Medicines Regulations 2013, SI 2013/2033, Sch 5 para 15(2)(a).
4   Veterinary Medicines Regulations 2013, SI 2013/2033, Sch 5 para 15(2)(b).
5   Veterinary Medicines Regulations 2013, SI 2013/2033, Sch 5 para 15(2)(c).
6   Veterinary Medicines Regulations 2013, SI 2013/2033, Sch 5 para 15(3)(a).
7   Veterinary Medicines Regulations 2013, SI 2013/2033, Sch 5 para 15(3)(b).
8   Veterinary Medicines Regulations 2013, SI 2013/2033, Sch 5 para 15(3)(c).

9 Veterinary Medicines Regulations 2013, SI 2013/2033, Sch 5 para 31(m). As to offences see PARA
   86 note 12.

93. Supply of a premixture.

No person other than the person who manufactured a premixture[1] or an approved distributor may supply a premixture[2].

The person who manufactured the premixture may only supply it to an approved distributor or to a feeding stuff manufacturer approved to incorporate that premixture[3].

An approved distributor may only supply it to another approved distributor or to a feeding stuff manufacturer approved to incorporate that premixture[4].

It is an offence to fail to comply with the above provisions[5].

1 As to the meaning of 'premixture' see PARA **86** note 2.
2 Veterinary Medicines Regulations 2013, SI 2013/2033, Sch 5 para 16(1).
3 Veterinary Medicines Regulations 2013, SI 2013/2033, Sch 5 para 16(2).
4 Veterinary Medicines Regulations 2013, SI 2013/2033, Sch 5 para 16(3).
5 Veterinary Medicines Regulations 2013, SI 2013/2033, Sch 5 para 31(n). As to offences see PARA
   86 note 12.

94. Supply of a complementary feeding stuff.

No person other than the person who manufactured a complementary feeding stuff containing a specified feed additive, or an approved distributor, may supply a complementary feeding stuff[1] containing a specified feed additive[2].

The person who manufactured such complementary feeding stuff may only supply it to an approved distributor or to a feeding stuff manufacturer registered to incorporate that complementary feeding stuff or approved to incorporate a premixture[3].

An approved distributor may only supply it to another approved distributor or to a feeding stuff manufacturer registered to incorporate that complementary feeding stuff or approved to incorporate a premixture[4].

It is an offence to fail to comply with the above provisions[5].

1 For these purposes 'complementary feeding stuff' has the meaning given in European Parliament
   and Council Regulation (EC) 767/2009 (OJ L 229, 1.9.2009, p 1) on the placing on the market and
   use of feed, art 3: Veterinary Medicines Regulations 2013, SI 2013/2033, Sch 5 para 17(4).
2 Veterinary Medicines Regulations 2013, SI 2013/2033, Sch 5 para 17(1).
3 Veterinary Medicines Regulations 2013, SI 2013/2033, Sch 5 para 17(2). As to the meaning of
   'premixture' see PARA **86** note 2.
4 Veterinary Medicines Regulations 2013, SI 2013/2033, Sch 5 para 17(3).
5 Veterinary Medicines Regulations 2013, SI 2013/2033, Sch 5 para 31(o). As to offences see PARA
   86 note 12.

95. Supply of feeding stuffs containing a veterinary medicinal product.

No person other than the person who manufactured the feeding stuffs or an approved distributor may supply feeding stuffs containing a veterinary medicinal product[1].

The person who manufactured the feeding stuff may only supply it to an approved distributor or to a person who keeps animals for feeding to those animals[2].

A distributor may only supply it to another approved distributor or to a person who keeps animals for feeding to those animals[3].

No manufacturer or distributor may supply a feeding stuff to anyone not specified in these provisions, or otherwise than in accordance with these provisions[4].

It is an offence to fail to comply with the above provisions[5].

1　Veterinary Medicines Regulations 2013, SI 2013/2033, Sch 5 para 18(1). As to the meaning of 'veterinary medicinal product' see PARA 86 note 2.
2　Veterinary Medicines Regulations 2013, SI 2013/2033, Sch 5 para 18(2). Supply to a person who keeps animals must be in accordance with a written prescription as follows: Sch 5 para 18(4). If a prescription is for a period of longer than one month, the supplier may not provide more than one month's supply at any one time: Sch 5 para 18(5). The person supplying the feeding stuff must keep the prescription for five years: Sch 5 para 18(7).
3　Veterinary Medicines Regulations 2013, SI 2013/2033, Sch 5 para 18(3).
4　Veterinary Medicines Regulations 2013, SI 2013/2033, Sch 5 para 18(6).
5　Veterinary Medicines Regulations 2013, SI 2013/2033, Sch 5 para 31(p). As to offences see PARA 86 note 12.

96. Storage, packaging and transportation.

No person may store a veterinary medicinal product[1] intended for incorporation into feeding stuffs, or a premixture[2] or feeding stuffs containing a veterinary medicinal product, except in a suitable storage area that is locked when not in use or in a hermetic container designed to store those products[3].

No person may place on the market feeding stuffs containing a veterinary medicinal product except in packages or containers that are sealed in such a way that, when the package or container is opened, the seal is damaged[4].

Any person transporting feeding stuffs containing veterinary medicinal products or specified feed additives[5] in road tankers or similar containers must ensure that the vehicle or container is cleaned before any re-use if this is necessary to prevent undesirable interaction or contamination[6]. Any person operating an undertaking transporting feeding stuffs containing veterinary medicinal products or specified feed additives must give written instructions to drivers on how to load and unload vehicles so as to avoid cross-contamination, and take reasonable steps to ensure that the driver complies with those instructions[7].

Failure to comply with any of these requirements is an offence[8].

1　As to the meaning of 'veterinary medicinal product' see PARA 86 note 2.
2　As to the meaning of 'premixture' see PARA 86 note 2.
3　Veterinary Medicines Regulations 2013, SI 2013/2033, Sch 5 para 23.
4　Veterinary Medicines Regulations 2013, SI 2013/2033, Sch 5 para 24.
5　As to the meaning of 'specified feed additive' see PARA 86 note 2.
6　Veterinary Medicines Regulations 2013, SI 2013/2033, Sch 5 para 25(2). Where the feeding stuffs contain a veterinary medicinal product, the person transporting them must ensure that the vehicle is accompanied by documentation stating this: Sch 5 para 25(3).
7　Veterinary Medicines Regulations 2013, SI 2013/2033, Sch 5 para 25(4). There are also requirements as to the provision of documentation regarding labelling: see Sch 5 para 25(1); and PARA 90.
8　Veterinary Medicines Regulations 2013, SI 2013/2033, Sch 5 para 31(s), (t), (u). As to offences see PARA 86 note 12.

97. Prescriptions.

A prescription for feeding stuffs containing a veterinary medicinal product[1] is valid for three months or such shorter period as may be specified[2], must be sufficient for only one course of treatment[3], and must contain:

(1)　the name and address of the person prescribing the product[4];
(2)　the qualifications enabling the person to prescribe the product[5];
(3)　the name and address of the keeper of the animals to be treated[6];
(4)　the species of animal, identification and number of the animals[7];
(5)　the premises at which the animals are kept if this is different from the address of the keeper[8];
(6)　the date of the prescription[9];

(7)   the signature or other authentication of the person prescribing the product[10];

(8)   the name and amount of the product prescribed[11];

(9)   the dosage and administration instructions[12];

(10)   any necessary warnings[13];

(11)   the withdrawal period[14];

(12)   the manufacturer or the distributor of the feeding stuffs (who must be approved for the purpose)[15];

(13)   a statement that, if the validity exceeds one month, not more than 31 days' supply may be provided at any time[16];

(14)   the name, type and quantity of feeding stuffs to be used[17];

(15)   the inclusion rate of the veterinary medicinal product and the resulting inclusion rate of the active substance[18];

(16)   any special instructions[19];

(17)   the percentage of the prescribed feeding stuffs to be added to the daily ration[20]; and

(18)   if it is prescribed under the cascade, a statement to that effect[21].

The person who writes the prescription must be satisfied that there is no undesirable interaction between the veterinary medicinal product and any feed additive used in the feeding stuffs[22] and that the active substance of the veterinary medicinal product is not the same as an active substance in any feed additive used in the feeding stuffs[23]; he must also give copies of the prescription to appropriate persons[24]. The person must prescribe a veterinary medicinal product authorised for incorporation in feeding stuffs but may, if there is no veterinary medicinal product authorised for a condition in a particular species:

(a)   prescribe a veterinary medicinal product authorised for another species or for another condition in the same species, and

(b)   prescribe more than one veterinary medicinal product,

provided all veterinary medicinal products prescribed are authorised for incorporation in feedingstuffs[25].

1   As to the meaning of 'veterinary medicinal product' see PARA 86 note 2.
2   Veterinary Medicines Regulations 2013, SI 2013/2033, Sch 5 para 19(2).
3   Veterinary Medicines Regulations 2013, SI 2013/2033, Sch 5 para 19(3).
4   Veterinary Medicines Regulations 2013, SI 2013/2033, Sch 5 para 19(1)(a).
5   Veterinary Medicines Regulations 2013, SI 2013/2033, Sch 5 para 19(1)(b).
6   Veterinary Medicines Regulations 2013, SI 2013/2033, Sch 5 para 19(1)(c). As to the meaning of 'animal' see PARA 86 note 2.
7   Veterinary Medicines Regulations 2013, SI 2013/2033, Sch 5 para 19(1)(d).
8   Veterinary Medicines Regulations 2013, SI 2013/2033, Sch 5 para 19(1)(e).
9   Veterinary Medicines Regulations 2013, SI 2013/2033, Sch 5 para 19(1)(f).
10   Veterinary Medicines Regulations 2013, SI 2013/2033, Sch 5 para 19(1)(g).
11   Veterinary Medicines Regulations 2013, SI 2013/2033, Sch 5 para 19(1)(h).
12   Veterinary Medicines Regulations 2013, SI 2013/2033, Sch 5 para 19(1)(i).
13   Veterinary Medicines Regulations 2013, SI 2013/2033, Sch 5 para 19(1)(j).
14   Veterinary Medicines Regulations 2013, SI 2013/2033, Sch 5 para 19(1)(k).
15   Veterinary Medicines Regulations 2013, SI 2013/2033, Sch 5 para 19(1)(l). As to approvals see PARA 86.
16   Veterinary Medicines Regulations 2013, SI 2013/2033, Sch 5 para 19(1)(m).
17   Veterinary Medicines Regulations 2013, SI 2013/2033, Sch 5 para 19(1)(n).
18   Veterinary Medicines Regulations 2013, SI 2013/2033, Sch 5 para 19(1)(o).
19   Veterinary Medicines Regulations 2013, SI 2013/2033, Sch 5 para 19(1)(p).
20   Veterinary Medicines Regulations 2013, SI 2013/2033, Sch 5 para 19(1)(q).
21   Veterinary Medicines Regulations 2013, SI 2013/2033, Sch 5 para 19(1)(r). As to the meaning of the 'cascade' see Sch 4 para 1; and MEDICAL PRODUCTS AND DRUGS vol 75 (2013) PARA 423.
22   Veterinary Medicines Regulations 2013, SI 2013/2033, Sch 5 para 20(2)(a).

23 Veterinary Medicines Regulations 2013, SI 2013/2033, Sch 5 para 20(2)(b).
24 The person who writes the prescription must give a copy to the person incorporating the veterinary
   medicinal product into the feeding stuffs or to the distributor of the feeding stuffs (Veterinary
   Medicines Regulations 2013, SI 2013/2033, Sch 5 para 20(1)(a)) and give one copy to the keeper
   of the animals to be treated (Sch 5 para 20(1)(b)). He must also keep a copy himself: Sch 5 para
   20(1)(c).
       The requirement for a written prescription does not apply in relation to a veterinary medicinal
   product incorporated into feeding stuffs in domestic premises for feeding under Sch 5 para 30, but
   in this case Sch 3 relating to supply of a veterinary medicinal product apply in relation to the
   supply of premixture and feeding stuffs in the same way as they apply to a veterinary medicinal
   product: Sch 5 para 30(3).
25 Veterinary Medicines Regulations 2013, SI 2013/2033, Sch 5 para 20(3) (substituted by
   SI 2014/599). Failure to comply with the Veterinary Medicines Regulations 2013, SI 2013/2033,
   Sch 5 para 20 is an offence: Sch 5 para 31(q) (amended by SI 2014/599). As to offences see PARA
   86 note 12.

(6) USE OF ANIMAL BY-PRODUCTS AND CATERING WASTE IN FEEDING STUFFS AND FERTILISERS

(i) Restrictions on Use of Animal By-products

98. Restrictions on access to animal by-products.

Animal by-products, including catering waste, must not be brought on to any premises[1] if farmed animals would have access to such animal by-products[2].

The body or part of a body of any farmed animal that has not been slaughtered for human consumption must be held by an operator, pending consignment or disposal, in such manner as to ensure that no animal or bird will have access to it[3].

1 'Premises' means:
   (1)   any land, building, shed or pen;
   (2)   any receptacle or container;
   (3)   any ship; and
   (4)   a vehicle of any description: Animal By-Products (Enforcement) (England) Regulations
         2013, SI 2013/2952, reg 2(1) (amended by SI 2015/1980); Animal By-Products
         (Enforcement) (Wales) 2014, SI 2014/517, reg 2(1).
   Expressions used in the Animal By-Products (Enforcement) (England) Regulations 2013,
   SI 2013/2952 and the Animal By-Products (Enforcement) (Wales) 2014, SI 2014/517 that are also
   used in European Parliament and Council Regulation (EC) 1069/2009 (OJ L300, 14.11.2009, p 1)
   laying down health rules as regards animal by-products and derived products not intended for
   human consumption 'the EU Control Regulation' or in its implementing regulation, Commission
   Regulation (EU) 142/2011 (OJ L54, 26.2.2011, p 1) 'EU Implementing Regulation' have the same
   meaning in the animal by-products regulations as they have in the EU Control Regulation or EU
   Implementing Regulation: Animal By-Products (Enforcement) (England) Regulations 2013,
   SI 2013/2952, reg 2(1); Animal By-Products (Enforcement) (Wales) 2014, SI 2014/517, reg 2(1).
2 Animal By-Products (Enforcement) (England) Regulations 2013, SI 2013/295, reg 4(1); Animal
   By-Products (Enforcement) (Wales) 2014, SI 2014/517, reg 4(1). As to exceptions relating to
   products derived from catering waste and meat and bone meals derived from certain specified
   sources: see the Animal By-Products (Enforcement) (England) Regulations 2013, SI 2013/2952, reg
   4(2); and the Animal By-Products (Enforcement) (Wales) 2014, SI 2014/517, reg 4(2).
3 Animal By-Products (Enforcement) (England) Regulations 2013, SI 2013/2952, reg 4(3); Animal
   By-Products (Enforcement) (Wales) 2014, SI 2014/517, reg 4(3).

99. Use of organic fertilisers and soil improvers.

Where organic fertilisers or soil improvers are applied to land, no person may allow pigs to have access to that land or to be fed cut herbage from such land for a period of 60 days beginning with the day on which the organic fertiliser or soil improver is applied[1].

This does not apply to the following organic fertilisers or soil improvers:

(1)   manure;
(2)   milk;
(3)   milk-based products;
(4)   milk-derived products;
(5)   colostrum;
(6)   colostrum products; or
(7)   digestive tract content[2].

1   Animal By-Products (Enforcement) (England) Regulations 2013, SI 2013/2952, reg 5(1); Animal By-Products (Enforcement) (Wales) 2014, SI 2014/517, reg 5(1).
2   Animal By-Products (Enforcement) (England) Regulations 2013, SI 2013/2952, reg 5(2); Animal By-Products (Enforcement) (Wales) 2014, SI 2014/517, reg 5(2).

100.   Placing on the market.

The placing on the market of untreated wool and untreated hair from farms or from establishments or plants is authorised except where they present a risk of any disease communicable through those products to humans or animals[1].

1   Animal By-Products (Enforcement) (England) Regulations 2013, SI 2013/2952, reg 8; Animal By-Products (Enforcement) (Wales) 2014, SI 2014/517, reg 8.

101.   Reporting of test results.

Operators of slaughterhouses, cutting plants, game-handling establishments[1] and cold stores[2] must report to the Secretary of State or, in relation to Wales, the Welsh Ministers[3] the results of any tests carried out pursuant to EU provisions relating to the following which fail to meet the required standards:

(1)   requirements for the transformation of animal by-products and derived products into biogas and composting[4];
(2)   processing and placing on the market of animal by-products and derived products for feeding to farmed animals[5];
(3)   placing on the market and use of organic fertilisers and soil improvers[6]; and
(4)   pet food and other derived products[7].

1   The terms 'slaughterhouse', 'cutting plant' and 'game-handling establishment' have the meanings given to them in the Food Safety and Hygiene (England) Regulations 2013, SI 2013/14, reg 5(6) or, in relation to Wales, the Food Hygiene (Wales) Regulations 2006. SI 2006/31, reg 5(6) (see FOOD AND DRINK vol 51 (2013) PARA 698 et seq): Animal By-Products (Enforcement) (England) Regulations 2013, SI 2013/2952, reg 10(2)(a) (amended by SI 2013/2996); Animal By-Products (Enforcement) (Wales) 2014, SI 2014/517, reg 10(2)(a).
2   'Cold store' means any other premises used for the storage, under temperature controlled conditions, of fresh meat held for sale for human consumption: Animal By-Products (Enforcement) (England) Regulations 2013, SI 2013/2952, reg 10(2)(b); Animal By-Products (Enforcement) (Wales) 2014, SI 2014/517, reg 10(2)(b).
3   As to the Secretary of State and the Welsh Ministers see PARA 390.
4   Ie Commission Regulation (EU) 142/2011 (OJ L54, 26.2.2011, p 1) 'EU Implementing Regulation', art 10(1).
5   Ie Commission Regulation (EU) 142/2011 (OJ L54, 26.2.2011, p 1) 'EU Implementing Regulation' art 21(1).
6   Ie Commission Regulation (EU) 142/2011 (OJ L54, 26.2.2011, p 1) 'EU Implementing Regulation', art 22(1).
7   Ie Commission Regulation (EU) 142/2011 (OJ L54, 26.2.2011, p 1) 'EU Implementing Regulation', art 24(3): Animal By-Products (Enforcement) (England) Regulations 2013, SI 2013/2952, reg 9 (amended by SI 2015/1980); Animal By-Products (Enforcement) (Wales) 2014, SI 2014/517, reg 9.

102. Staining.

Operators of slaughterhouses, cutting plants, game-handling establishments[1] and cold stores[2] are required to stain certain animal by-products unless certain exceptions apply[3].

1   As to the meanings of 'slaughterhouse', 'cutting plant' and 'game-handling establishment' see PARA 101 note 1.
2   Animal By-Products (Enforcement) (England) Regulations 2013, SI 2013/2952, reg 10(1); Animal By-Products (Enforcement) (Wales) 2014, SI 2014/517, reg 10(1). As to the meaning of 'cold store' see PARA 101 note 2.
3   See the Animal By-Products (Enforcement) (England) Regulations 2013, SI 2013/2952, reg 10; and the Animal By-Products (Enforcement) (Wales) 2014, SI 2014/517, reg 10. As to the enforcement of these provisions see the Animal By-Products (Enforcement) (England) Regulations 2013, SI 2013/2952, reg 21 and the Animal By-Products (Enforcement) (Wales) 2014, SI 2014/517, reg 21.

103. Procedure for registration of plants and establishments.

Provision is made for the registration of establishments and plants which are active at any stage of the generation, transport, handling, processing, storage, placing on the market, distribution, use or disposal of animal by-products and derived products[1], along with an appeals procedure[2].

1   See the Animal By-Products (Enforcement) (England) Regulations 2013, SI 2013/2952, regs 11–15; and the Animal By-Products (Enforcement) (Wales) 2014, SI 2014/517, regs 11–15.
2   See the Animal By-Products (Enforcement) (England) Regulations 2013, SI 2013/2952, reg 16; and the Animal By-Products (Enforcement) (Wales) 2014, SI 2014/517, reg 16.

104. Offences and penalties.

A person who fails to comply with certain EU obligations relating to animal by-products ('an animal by-product requirement')[1] commits an offence[2].

It is an offence:

(1)   intentionally to obstruct an authorised person[3];
(2)   without reasonable cause, to fail to give to an authorised person any information or assistance or to provide any facilities that such person may reasonably require;
(3)   knowingly or recklessly to give false or misleading information to an authorised person; or
(4)   to fail to produce a record or document when required to do so by an authorised person[4].

1   As to the 'animal by-product requirement' see the Animal By-Products (Enforcement) (England) Regulations 2013, SI 2013/2952 Sch 1; and the Animal By-Products (Enforcement) (Wales) 2014, SI 2014/517, Sch 1.
2   Animal By-Products (Enforcement) (England) Regulations 2013, SI 2013/2952, reg 17; Animal By-Products (Enforcement) (Wales) 2014, SI 2014/517, reg 17. A person guilty of an offence under the Animal By-Products (Enforcement) (England) Regulations 2013, SI 2013/2952 or the Animal By-Products (Enforcement) (Wales) 2014, SI 2014/517 is liable on summary conviction, to a fine not exceeding the statutory maximum or to imprisonment not exceeding three months or both or, on conviction on indictment, to a fine or to imprisonment for a term not exceeding two years, or both: Animal By-Products (Enforcement) (England) Regulations 2013, SI 2013/2952, reg 20; Animal By-Products (Enforcement) (Wales) 2014, SI 2014/517, reg 20. As to provision for corporate, partnership and unincorporated association offences: see the Animal By-Products (Enforcement) (England) Regulations 2013, SI 2013/2952, reg 19; and the Animal By-Products (Enforcement) (Wales) 2014, SI 2014/517, reg 19.
3   An enforcement authority may authorise in writing such persons as the authority considers appropriate to act for the purpose of enforcing the Animal By-Products (Enforcement) (England) Regulations 2013, SI 2013/2952 or, in relation to Wales, the Animal By-Products (Enforcement) (Wales) 2014, SI 2014/517: Animal By-Products (Enforcement) (England) Regulations 2013, SI 2013/2952, reg 22; Animal By-Products (Enforcement) (Wales) 2014, SI 2014/517, reg 22. An

enforcement authority means a person exercising functions under the Animal By-Products (Enforcement) (England) Regulations 2013, SI 2013/2952, reg 21(1) or (2) (see PARA 102), or, in relation to Wales, the Animal By-Products (Enforcement) (Wales) 2014, SI 2014/517, reg 22(1) or (2): Animal By-Products (Enforcement) (England) Regulations 2013, SI 2013/2952, reg 2(1); Animal By-Products (Enforcement) (Wales) 2014, SI 2014/517, reg 2(1). As to powers of entry and additional powers of an authorised person see the Animal By-Products (Enforcement) (England) Regulations 2013, SI 2013/2952, reg 23; and the Animal By-Products (Enforcement) (Wales) 2014, SI 2014/517, reg 23. As to issue of warrants to authorise an authorised person to enter by force see the Animal By-Products (Enforcement) (England) Regulations 2013, SI 2013/2952, reg 24; and the Animal By-Products (Enforcement) (Wales) 2014, SI 2014/517, reg 24. As to notices served by an authorised person the Animal By-Products (Enforcement) (England) Regulations 2013, SI 2013/2952, reg 25; and the Animal By-Products (Enforcement) (Wales) 2014, SI 2014/517, reg 25. As to the power to disclose information for enforcement purposes: see the Animal By-Products (Enforcement) (England) Regulations 2013, SI 2013/2952, reg 26; and the Animal By-Products (Enforcement) (Wales) 2014, SI 2014/517, reg 26.

4   Animal By-Products (Enforcement) (England) Regulations 2013, SI 2013/2952, reg 18; Animal By-Products (Enforcement) (Wales) 2014, SI 2014/517, reg 18.

(ii) Collection of Catering Waste

105. Local authority powers to collect kitchen waste for animal feeding stuffs.

A local authority[1] may, whether in the discharge of its functions as to the removal of house or trade refuse or otherwise[2], collect kitchen or other waste in its area for use as animal feeding stuffs[3], with or without processing[4]. An authority collecting waste under these provisions may agree to pay for waste saved for collection, may process the waste it collects[5], and may sell it processed or unprocessed[6].

A local authority may also make bye-laws[7] regulating in its area or any part of it the collection of kitchen or other waste for use as animal feeding stuffs and the carriage of waste so collected (whether there or elsewhere)[8].

1   The Agriculture (Miscellaneous Provisions) Act 1954 s 9(9) provides that 'local authority' for these purposes means the council of a borough, urban district or rural district or an authority which is a sanitary authority for the purposes of the Public Health (London) Act 1936, but in practice this is a reference to a district or London borough council, or the Common Council of the City of London, in England, and a county or county borough council in Wales: see LOCAL GOVERNMENT vol 69 (2009) PARA 22 et seq. As to the London boroughs and their councils see LONDON GOVERNMENT vol 71 (2013) PARAS 5, 14–15, 20 et seq. As to the City of London and the Common Council see LONDON GOVERNMENT vol 71 (2013) PARAS 16–17, 34 et seq.

2   For local authority functions as to the removal of waste see ENVIRONMENTAL QUALITY AND PUBLIC HEALTH vol 46 (2010) PARA 620 et seq.

3   An authority collecting waste under these provisions may provide receptacles in which the waste may be deposited for collection, and may place any receptacles so provided in any street or public place: Agriculture (Miscellaneous Provisions) Act 1954 s 9(4). Any person (other than a person employed in connection with the local authority's collection of the waste) who removes the whole or part of the contents of any such receptacle when placed in a street or public place or set out for the purpose of its contents being removed under these provisions is liable on summary conviction to a fine not exceeding level 1 on the standard scale: s 9(5) (amended by virtue of the Criminal Justice Act 1982 ss 35, 38, 46). Moreover, any person who wilfully deposits, in any receptacle so provided or otherwise used for the deposit of waste to be collected under these provisions, anything which he knows or has reasonable cause to believe to be unsuitable for use as animal feeding stuffs, is liable on summary conviction to a fine not exceeding level 1 on the standard scale: s 9(5) (as so amended). As to the standard scale see PARA 14 note 2.

Proceedings in respect of an offence created by or under s 9 may not in general be taken by any person other than the local authority in whose area the offence is alleged to have been committed, unless taken by or with the consent of the Director of Public Prosecutions: s 9(7). Where, however, a local authority collects waste outside its area, it may without the consent of the Director of Public

Prosecutions take proceedings in respect of an offence under s 9(5) alleged to have been committed at any place within the limits of its collection: s 9(7).

4   Agriculture (Miscellaneous Provisions) Act 1954 s 9(1). Nothing in s 9 may be taken as authorising anything to be used unprocessed as animal feeding stuffs where processing is required by or under any other enactment: s 9(8).

5   An authority which processes the waste it collects may also acquire other materials for processing with it, including kitchen or other waste collected by any other local authority or person: Agriculture (Miscellaneous Provisions) Act 1954 s 9(2).

6   Agriculture (Miscellaneous Provisions) Act 1954 s 9(2).

7   Bye-laws made under the Agriculture (Miscellaneous Provisions) Act 1954 s 9(6) require confirmation of the Secretary of State: s 9(6) (amended by the Secretary of State for the Environment Order 1970, SI 1970/1681, art 2(1)). As to the Secretary of State see PARA 390.

8   Agriculture (Miscellaneous Provisions) Act 1954 s 9(6). Bye-laws may in particular be made for securing the use of suitable times, routes, vehicles and receptacles: s 9(6). The fines which may be imposed by the bye-laws on persons offending against them may be of an amount not exceeding level 1 on the standard scale or not exceeding a lesser amount, with, in the case of a continuing offence, a further sum not exceeding £2 for each day during which the offence continues after conviction therefor: s 9(6) (amended by virtue of the Criminal Justice Act 1982 ss 37, 46; and by the Decimal Currency Act 1969 s 10(1)).

(iii)   Control of Transmissible Spongiform Encephalopathies

106.   Prohibition on feeding animal proteins.

It is an offence to[1]:

(1)   feed to any ruminate animal[2];

(2)   supply for feeding to any ruminant animal[3];

(3)   to permit any ruminant animal to have access to[4],

any animal protein (or anything containing animal protein)[5].

It is an offence[6] to:

(a)   feed to any pig, poultry, horse or any farmed non-ruminant animal[7];

(b)   supply for feeding to any such animal[8]; or

(c)   allow any such animal to have access to[9],

certain animal proteins and products[10].

These provisions are enforced by the local authority[11] or, where so directed, by the Secretary of State or (as the case may be) the Welsh Ministers[12].

1   Ie an offence for the purposes of Council Regulation (EC) 999/2001 (OJ L147, 31.5.2001, p 1) laying down rules for the prevention, control and eradication of certain transmissible spongiform encephalopathies (the 'TSE Regulation'), art 7(1), Annex IV Pt I point (b). Council Regulation (EC) 999/2001 (OJ L147, 31.5.2001, p 1) is known as the 'EU TSE Regulation' and is to be read with the instruments set out in the Transmissible Spongiform Encephalopathies (England) Regulations 2010, SI 2010/801, reg 2(1); Transmissible Spongiform Encephalopathies (Wales) Regulations 2008, SI 2008/3154, reg 2(1): Transmissible Spongiform Encephalopathies (England) Regulations 2010, SI 2010/801, reg 2(1); Transmissible Spongiform Encephalopathies (Wales) Regulations 2008, SI 2008/3154, reg 2(1). These regulations (for provisions which are relevant to this title see the text and notes 2–12; and PARAS 107–110) implement the EU TSE Regulation, and expressions that are not defined in the English or Welsh regulations and occur in the EU TSE Regulation have the same meaning in the English and Welsh regulations as they have for the purposes of the EU TSE Regulation: Transmissible Spongiform Encephalopathies (England) Regulations 2010, SI 2010/801, reg 2(2); Transmissible Spongiform Encephalopathies (Wales) Regulations 2008, SI 2008/3154, reg 2(2). The Secretary of State and the Welsh Ministers are the competent authorities for the purposes of the EU TSE Regulation except as otherwise specified in the Transmissible Spongiform Encephalopathies (England) Regulations 2010, SI 2010/801, or the Transmissible Spongiform Encephalopathies (Wales) Regulations 2008, SI 2008/3154: Transmissible Spongiform Encephalopathies (England) Regulations 2010, SI 2010/801, reg 3; Transmissible Spongiform Encephalopathies (Wales) Regulations 2008, SI 2008/3154, reg 3. As to the Secretary of State and the Welsh Ministers see PARA 390.

A person guilty of an offence under the Transmissible Spongiform Encephalopathies (England) Regulations 2010, SI 2010/801, or the Transmissible Spongiform Encephalopathies (Wales)

Regulations 2008, SI 2008/3154, is liable on summary conviction to a fine not exceeding the statutory maximum or to imprisonment for a term of three months or both, or on conviction on indictment to a fine or to imprisonment for a term not exceeding two years or both: Transmissible Spongiform Encephalopathies (England) Regulations 2010, SI 2010/801, reg 18; Transmissible Spongiform Encephalopathies (Wales) Regulations 2008, SI 2008/3154, reg 18. As to corporate offences: see the Transmissible Spongiform Encephalopathies (England) Regulations 2010, SI 2010/801, reg 19; and the Transmissible Spongiform Encephalopathies (Wales) Regulations 2008, SI 2008/3154, reg 19. As to the statutory maximum see PARA 58 note 1.

2   Transmissible Spongiform Encephalopathies (England) Regulations 2010, SI 2010/801, Sch 6 para 1(1)(a); Transmissible Spongiform Encephalopathies (Wales) Regulations 2008, SI 2008/3154, Sch 6 para 1(1)(a).

3   Transmissible Spongiform Encephalopathies (England) Regulations 2010, SI 2010/801, Sch 6 para 1(1)(b); Transmissible Spongiform Encephalopathies (Wales) Regulations 2008, SI 2008/3154, Sch 6 para 1(1)(b).

4   Transmissible Spongiform Encephalopathies (England) Regulations 2010, SI 2010/801, Sch 6 para 1(1)(c); Transmissible Spongiform Encephalopathies (Wales) Regulations 2008, SI 2008/3154, Sch 6 para 1(1)(c).

5   Transmissible Spongiform Encephalopathies (England) Regulations 2010, SI 2010/801, Sch 6 para 1(1); Transmissible Spongiform Encephalopathies (Wales) Regulations 2008, SI 2008/3154, Sch 6 para 1(1). It is not an offence under these provisions to feed, supply for feeding or permit access to the proteins specified in Council Regulation (EC) 999/2001 (OJ L147, 31.5.2001, p 1) Annex IV Pt II point A(a): Transmissible Spongiform Encephalopathies (England) Regulations 2010, SI 2010/801, Sch 6 para 1(1); Transmissible Spongiform Encephalopathies (Wales) Regulations 2008, SI 2008/3154, Sch 6 para 1(1). In relation to England, the prohibition does not apply in relation to liquid milk replacers containing fishmeal provided that:

(1)   the fishmeal has been produced, labelled, transported and used in accordance with EU TSE Regulation Annex IV Part II point BA;

(2)   the liquid milk replacer is intended for, and fed only to unweaned, ruminant farmed animals in accordance with EU TSE Regulation Annex IV Part II point A(e); and

(3)   the prohibition continues to apply in relation to all other ruminant animals: Transmissible Spongiform Encephalopathies (England) Regulations 2010, SI 2010/801, Sch 6 para 1(4).

The provisions of the Transmissible Spongiform Encephalopathies (England) Regulations 2010, SI 2010/801, Sch 6 and the Transmissible Spongiform Encephalopathies (Wales) Regulations 2008, SI 2008/3154, Sch 6 (see the text and notes 6–12; and PARAS 107, 108) do not apply in relation to animals kept for the purposes of research in premises approved for that purpose by the Secretary of State or, as the case may be, the Welsh Ministers (Transmissible Spongiform Encephalopathies (England) Regulations 2010, SI 2010/801, reg 4(1); Transmissible Spongiform Encephalopathies (Wales) Regulations 2008, SI 2008/3154, reg 4(1)); and if a bovine animal, sheep or goat kept in approved research premises or its progeny dies or is killed, the occupier must dispose of it as a category 1 animal by-product in accordance with Council Regulation (EC) 1069/2009 (OJ L300, 14.11.2009, p 1) laying down health rules as regards animal by-products and derived products not intended for human consumption, and failure to do so is an offence (Transmissible Spongiform Encephalopathies (England) Regulations 2010, SI 2010/801, reg 4(2) (amended by SI 2013/2952); Transmissible Spongiform Encephalopathies (Wales) Regulations 2008, SI 2008/3154, reg 4(2) (substituted by SI 2014/517). For these purposes 'bovine animal' includes bison and buffalo (including water buffalo): Transmissible Spongiform Encephalopathies (England) Regulations 2010, SI 2010/801, reg 2(1); Transmissible Spongiform Encephalopathies (Wales) Regulations 2008, SI 2008/3154, reg 2(1). In relation to England, 'premises' includes domestic premises if they are being used for any purposes in connection with the EU TSE Regulations or the Transmissible Spongiform Encephalopathies (England) Regulations 2010, SI 2010/801, land and outbuildings, a slaughterhouse, a place that is for the purposes of the EU TSE Regulation Annex V point 4(1)(a), another place of slaughter, and any vehicle, container or structure (moveable or otherwise): Transmissible Spongiform Encephalopathies (England) Regulations 2010, SI 2010/801, reg 2(1).

6   Ie for the purposes of Council Regulation (EC) 999/2001 (OJ L147, 31.5.2001, p 1) art 7(2), Annex IV Pt I point (a).

7   Transmissible Spongiform Encephalopathies (England) Regulations 2010, SI 2010/801, Sch 6 para 2(1)(a); Transmissible Spongiform Encephalopathies (Wales) Regulations 2008, SI 2008/3154, Sch 6 para 2(1)(a).

8 Transmissible Spongiform Encephalopathies (England) Regulations 2010, SI 2010/801, Sch 6 para
    2(1)(b); Transmissible Spongiform Encephalopathies (Wales) Regulations 2008, SI 2008/3154,
    Sch 6 para 2(1)(b).
9 Transmissible Spongiform Encephalopathies (England) Regulations 2010, SI 2010/801, Sch 6 para
    2(1)(c); Transmissible Spongiform Encephalopathies (Wales) Regulations 2008, SI 2008/3154,
    Sch 6 para 2(1)(c).
10 Transmissible Spongiform Encephalopathies (England) Regulations 2010, SI 2010/801, Sch 6 para
    2(1); Transmissible Spongiform Encephalopathies (Wales) Regulations 2008, SI 2008/3154, Sch 6
    para 2(1). Ie including any feeding stuffs containing animal protein: Transmissible Spongiform
    Encephalopathies (England) Regulations 2010, SI 2010/801, Sch 6 para 2(4); Transmissible
    Spongiform Encephalopathies (Wales) Regulations 2008, SI 2008/3154, Sch 6 para 2(4). The
    prohibition set out in the text applies to processed animal protein, gelatine of ruminant origin,
    blood products, hydrolysed protein, dicalcium phosphate and tricalcium phosphate of animal
    origin pet food containing animal protein; and raw pet food consisting of animal protein:
    Transmissible Spongiform Encephalopathies (England) Regulations 2010, SI 2010/801, Sch 6 para
    2(2)(a)–(g); Transmissible Spongiform Encephalopathies (Wales) Regulations 2008, SI 2008/3154,
    Sch 6 para 2(2)(a)–(g). It does not, however, apply in relation to the protein specified in Council
    Regulation (EC) 999/2001 (OJ L147, 31.5.2001, p 1) Annex IV Pt II point A(a); fishmeal (and
    feeding stuffs containing it) that has been produced, labelled, transported and stored in accordance
    with Annex IV Pt II point B; dicalcium phosphate and tricalcium phosphate (and feeding stuffs
    containing them) that have been produced, labelled, transported and stored in accordance with
    Annex IV Pt II point C; blood products derived from non-ruminants (and feeding stuffs containing
    them) that have been produced, labelled, transported and stored in accordance with Annex IV Pt
    II point D; in the case of feeding to fish, blood meal derived from non-ruminants (and feeding stuffs
    containing it) that has been produced, labelled, transported and stored in accordance with Annex
    IV Pt II point D; and tuber and root crops (and feeding stuffs containing such products) in which
    bone spicules have been detected if authorised by the Secretary of State or the Welsh Ministers
    following a risk assessment in accordance with Annex IV Pt II point A(d): Transmissible
    Spongiform Encephalopathies (England) Regulations 2010, SI 2010/801, Sch 6 para 2(3)(a)–(f);
    Transmissible Spongiform Encephalopathies (Wales) Regulations 2008, SI 2008/3154, Sch 6 para
    2(3)(a)–(f).
11 See the Transmissible Spongiform Encephalopathies (England) Regulations 2010, SI 2010/801, reg
    20(3), (4); and the Transmissible Spongiform Encephalopathies (Wales) Regulations 2008,
    SI 2008/3154, reg 20(3), (4).
      By virtue of the Transmissible Spongiform Encephalopathies (England) Regulations 2010,
    SI 2010/801, reg 2(1), in England 'local authority' means:
      (1)   where there is a unitary authority (within the meaning of the Local Government Changes
            for England Regulations 1994, SI 1994/867), that authority; and
      (2)   where there is not a unitary authority:
            (a)   in a metropolitan district, the council of that district;
            (b)   in a non-metropolitan county, the council of that county or the council of a
                  district within the county area;
            (c)   in each London borough, the council of that borough; and
            (d)   in the City of London, the Common Council.
    By virtue of the Transmissible Spongiform Encephalopathies (Wales) Regulations 2008,
    SI 2008/3154, reg 2(1), in Wales 'local authority' means the council of any county or county
    borough. As to local government areas and authorities in England and Wales see LOCAL
    GOVERNMENT vol 69 (2009) PARA 22 et seq. As to the London boroughs and their councils see
    LONDON GOVERNMENT vol 71 (2013) PARAS 15, 20–22, 55 et seq. As to the Common Council
    of the City of London see LONDON GOVERNMENT vol 71 (2013) PARA 34 et seq.
12 The Secretary of State or, as the case may be, the Welsh Ministers may direct, in relation to cases
    of a particular description or any particular case, that an enforcement duty imposed on the local
    authority under the Transmissible Spongiform Encephalopathies (England) Regulations 2010,
    SI 2010/801, reg 20 or the Transmissible Spongiform Encephalopathies (Wales) Regulations 2008,
    SI 2008/3154, reg 20 must be discharged by the Secretary of State and not by the local authority:
    Transmissible Spongiform Encephalopathies (England) Regulations 2010, SI 2010/801, reg 20(4);
    Transmissible Spongiform Encephalopathies (Wales) Regulations 2008, SI 2008/3154, reg 20(4).

107. Movement prohibitions and slaughter.

Where an inspector[1] has reasonable grounds to believe that a TSE[2] susceptible
animal has been fed or has had access to:

(1)   specified risk material[3];
(2)   any material which the inspector has reasonable grounds to believe carries the risk of TSE infectivity[4]; or
(3)   animal protein for which he cannot establish the origin or the TSE infectivity risk[5],

then he may serve a notice[6] on the owner or person in charge of the animal:

(a)   prohibiting or restricting the movement of the animal from the premises described in the notice and, if it is bovine, seize its passport[7];
(b)   requiring that owner or person in charge of the animal kill the animal and dispose of it as specified in the notice[8]; or
(c)   requiring the owner or person to keep the animal on such premises and in such manner as the notice provides[9].

Provision is made for the payment of compensation where an animal is killed pursuant to these provisions[10].

These provisions are enforced by the local authority or, where so directed, by the Secretary of State or (as the case may be) the Welsh Ministers[11].

1   As to the appointment of inspectors see PARA 110.
2   'TSE' means transmissible spongiform encephalopathy: Transmissible Spongiform Encephalopathies (England) Regulations 2010, SI 2010/801, reg 2(1); Transmissible Spongiform Encephalopathies (Wales) Regulations 2008, SI 2008/3154, reg 2(1).
3   Transmissible Spongiform Encephalopathies (England) Regulations 2010, SI 2010/801, Sch 6 para 4(a); Transmissible Spongiform Encephalopathies (Wales) Regulations 2008, SI 2008/3154, Sch 6 para 4(a). As to the meaning of 'specified risk material' see Council Regulation (EC) 999/2001 (OJ L147, 31.5.2001, p 1) laying down rules for the prevention, control and eradication of certain transmissible spongiform encephalopathies, art 3.1(g) (definition applied by the Transmissible Spongiform Encephalopathies (England) Regulations 2010, SI 2010/801, reg 2(2); and the Transmissible Spongiform Encephalopathies (Wales) Regulations 2008, SI 2008/3154, reg 2(2)).
4   Transmissible Spongiform Encephalopathies (England) Regulations 2010, SI 2010/801, Sch 6 para 4(b); Transmissible Spongiform Encephalopathies (Wales) Regulations 2008, SI 2008/3154, Sch 6 para 4(b).
5   Transmissible Spongiform Encephalopathies (England) Regulations 2010, SI 2010/801, Sch 6 para 4(c); Transmissible Spongiform Encephalopathies (Wales) Regulations 2008, SI 2008/3154, Sch 6 para 4(c).
6   Ie in accordance with the Transmissible Spongiform Encephalopathies (England) Regulations 2010, SI 2010/801, reg 15 or, in relation to Wales, the Transmissible Spongiform Encephalopathies (Wales) Regulations 2008, SI 2008/3154, reg 15.
7   Transmissible Spongiform Encephalopathies (England) Regulations 2010, SI 2010/801, Sch 6 para 4(2); Transmissible Spongiform Encephalopathies (Wales) Regulations 2008, SI 2008/3154, Sch 6 para 4(2).
8   Transmissible Spongiform Encephalopathies (England) Regulations 2010, SI 2010/801, Sch 6 para 5(1), (2)(a); Transmissible Spongiform Encephalopathies (Wales) Regulations 2008, SI 2008/3154, Sch 6 para 5(1), (2)(a). The inspector must ensure that all the animals specified for killing in the notice are killed or disposed of: Transmissible Spongiform Encephalopathies (England) Regulations 2010, SI 2010/801, Sch 6 para 5(3); Transmissible Spongiform Encephalopathies (Wales) Regulations 2008, SI 2008/3154, Sch 6 para 5(3).
9   Transmissible Spongiform Encephalopathies (England) Regulations 2010, SI 2010/801, Sch 6 para 5(2)(b); Transmissible Spongiform Encephalopathies (Wales) Regulations 2008, SI 2008/3154, Sch 6 para 5(2)(b). If the inspector serves such a notice he must ensure that the cattle passport is stamped with the words 'Not for human consumption': Transmissible Spongiform Encephalopathies (England) Regulations 2010, SI 2010/801, Sch 6 para 5(2)(b); Transmissible Spongiform Encephalopathies (Wales) Regulations 2008, SI 2008/3154, Sch 6 para 5(2)(b). As to the meaning of 'cattle passport' see the Cattle Identification Regulations 2007, SI 2007/529, reg 2(1); the Cattle Identification (Wales) Regulations 2007, SI 2007/842, reg 2(1); and ANIMALS vol 2 (2017) PARA 412 (definition applied by the Transmissible Spongiform Encephalopathies (England) Regulations 2010, SI 2010/801, reg 2(1); and the Transmissible Spongiform Encephalopathies (Wales) Regulations 2008, SI 2008/3154, reg 2(1)). It is an offence to consign for slaughter for human consumption or to slaughter for human consumption any TSE susceptible animal the passport for which has been stamped under this provision: Transmissible Spongiform

Encephalopathies (England) Regulations 2010, SI 2010/801, Sch 6 para 7; Transmissible Spongiform Encephalopathies (Wales) Regulations 2008, SI 2008/3154, Sch 6 para 7.

10 Where an animal is killed under the Transmissible Spongiform Encephalopathies (England) Regulations 2010, SI 2010/801, Sch 6 para 5 or the Transmissible Spongiform Encephalopathies (Wales) Regulations 2008, SI 2008/3154, Sch 6 para 5, the Secretary of State or (as the case may be) the Welsh Ministers may pay compensation if he considers or they consider it appropriate in all the circumstances and he or they must give a decision on whether or not to pay compensation in writing: Transmissible Spongiform Encephalopathies (England) Regulations 2010, SI 2010/801, Sch 6 para 6(1); Transmissible Spongiform Encephalopathies (Wales) Regulations 2008, SI 2008/3154, Sch 6 para 6(1). As to the compensation value see the Transmissible Spongiform Encephalopathies (England) Regulations 2010, SI 2010/801, Sch 6 para 6(3) and, in relation to Wales, the Transmissible Spongiform Encephalopathies (Wales) Regulations 2008, SI 2008/3154, Sch 6 para 6(3). As to the Secretary of State and the Welsh Ministers see PARA 390. As to the appeals procedure in relation to this decision see the Transmissible Spongiform Encephalopathies (England) Regulations 2010, SI 2010/801, Sch 6 para 6(2) and, in relation to Wales, the Transmissible Spongiform Encephalopathies (Wales) Regulations 2008, SI 2008/3154, Sch 6 para 6(2).

11 See PARA 106 text and notes 11, 12.

108. Regulation of protein production.

The production, packaging, transportation and storage of protein and feeding stuffs is required to be carried out in accordance with the EU TSE Regulation[1]. Specific requirements, and corresponding offences for the failure to comply therewith[2], are established in relation to:

(1)   fishmeal, and feeding stuffs containing fishmeal, intended for feeding to non-ruminant farmed animals[3];

(2)   feeding stuffs containing dicalcium phosphate or tricalcium phosphate for feeding to non-ruminant farmed animals[4];

(3)   blood products or blood meal, or feeding stuffs containing blood products or blood meal[5].

Provision is also made for the bulk transportation of anything so produced[6], the prevention of cross contamination in the manufacture of feeding stuffs[7], the export of processed animal protein to third countries[8] and the manufacture and transportation of pet food and feeding stuffs[9].

These provisions are enforced by the local authority or, where so directed, by the Secretary of State or (as the case may be) the Welsh Ministers[10].

1   See the Transmissible Spongiform Encephalopathies (England) Regulations 2010, SI 2010/801, Sch 6 paras 8–20; Transmissible Spongiform Encephalopathies (Wales) Regulations 2008, SI 2008/3154, Sch 6 paras 8–20; and the text and notes 2–10. As to the EU TSE Regulation (ie Council Regulation (EC) 999/2001 (OJ L147, 31.5.2001, p 1) laying down rules for the prevention, control and eradication of certain transmissible spongiform encephalopathies) see PARA 106.
    These provisions do not apply in relation to animals kept for research: see PARA 106 note 2.

2   As to offences see PARA 106 note 1.

3   See the Transmissible Spongiform Encephalopathies (England) Regulations 2010, SI 2010/801, Sch 6 paras 8, 10; and the Transmissible Spongiform Encephalopathies (Wales) Regulations 2008, SI 2008/3154, Sch 6 paras 8, 9. In relation to England, provision is also made relating to fishmeal for feeding to unweaned, ruminant farm animals: see the Transmissible Spongiform Encephalopathies (England) Regulations 2010, SI 2010/801, Sch 6 paras 9, 10.

4   See the Transmissible Spongiform Encephalopathies (England) Regulations 2010, SI 2010/801, Sch 6 paras 11, 12; and the Transmissible Spongiform Encephalopathies (Wales) Regulations 2008, SI 2008/3154, Sch 6 paras 10, 11.

5   See the Transmissible Spongiform Encephalopathies (England) Regulations 2010, SI 2010/801, Sch 6 paras 13, 14; and the Transmissible Spongiform Encephalopathies (Wales) Regulations 2008, SI 2008/3154, Sch 6 paras 12, 13.

6   See the Transmissible Spongiform Encephalopathies (England) Regulations 2010, SI 2010/801, Sch 6 para 16; and the Transmissible Spongiform Encephalopathies (Wales) Regulations 2008, SI 2008/3154, Sch 6 para 15.

7 See the Transmissible Spongiform Encephalopathies (England) Regulations 2010, SI 2010/801, Sch 6 paras 15, 20, 21; and the Transmissible Spongiform Encephalopathies (Wales) Regulations 2008, SI 2008/3154, Sch 6 paras 14, 19, 20.

8 See the Transmissible Spongiform Encephalopathies (England) Regulations 2010, SI 2010/801, Sch 6 para 18; and the Transmissible Spongiform Encephalopathies (Wales) Regulations 2008, SI 2008/3154, Sch 6 para 17.

9 See the Transmissible Spongiform Encephalopathies (England) Regulations 2010, SI 2010/801, Sch 6 para 17; and the Transmissible Spongiform Encephalopathies (Wales) Regulations 2008, SI 2008/3154, Sch 6 para 16.

10 See PARA 106. As to the Secretary of State and the Welsh Ministers see PARA 390.

109. Approvals, authorisations, licences and registrations.

The occupier of any premises approved, authorised, licensed or registered for the purposes of the legislation concerned with transmissible spongiform encephalopathies[1] commits an offence[2] if he does not ensure that the premises are maintained and operated in accordance with any condition of the approval, authorisation, licence or registration[3] and the requirements of that legislation and the EU TSE Regulation[4], and that any person employed by him, and any person permitted to enter the premises, complies with those conditions and requirements[5].

Approvals, authorisations, licences and registrations are granted by the Secretary of State or (as the case may be) the Welsh Ministers[6] and must be granted, subject to the necessary conditions[7], if he is or they are satisfied that the provisions of the relevant legislation[8] and the EU TSE Regulation will be complied with[9]. The Secretary of State and the Welsh Ministers may suspend or amend an approval, authorisation, licence or registration so granted if any of the conditions under which it was granted is not fulfilled or if he, or they, consider it necessary in the light of technical or scientific developments[10] or if he is or they are satisfied that the provisions of the relevant legislation or the EU TSE Regulation are not being complied with[11], and may revoke an approval, authorisation, licence or registration if satisfied that the premises will not be operated in accordance with the relevant legislation or the EU TSE Regulation and:

(1) the approval, authorisation, licence or registration is currently suspended and the period for appeal[12] has expired or following such appeal the suspension has been upheld by the Secretary of State or the Welsh Ministers[13];

(2) the approval, authorisation, licence or registration has previously been suspended by the Secretary of State or the Welsh Ministers and there is further non-compliance with the relevant legislation or the EU TSE Regulation[14]; or

(3) the Secretary of State is or the Welsh Ministers are satisfied that the occupier no longer uses the premises for the purpose for which the approval, authorisation, licence or registration was granted[15].

1 Ie the Transmissible Spongiform Encephalopathies (England) Regulations 2010, SI 2010/801, and the Transmissible Spongiform Encephalopathies (Wales) Regulations 2008, SI 2008/3154.

2 As to offences see PARA 106 note 1.

3 Transmissible Spongiform Encephalopathies (England) Regulations 2010, SI 2010/801, reg 7(a)(i); Transmissible Spongiform Encephalopathies (Wales) Regulations 2008, SI 2008/3154, reg 7(a)(i).

4 Transmissible Spongiform Encephalopathies (England) Regulations 2010, SI 2010/801, reg 7(a)(ii); Transmissible Spongiform Encephalopathies (Wales) Regulations 2008, SI 2008/3154, reg 7(a)(ii). As to the EU TSE Regulation (ie Council Regulation (EC) 999/2001 (OJ L147, 31.5.2001, p 1) laying down rules for the prevention, control and eradication of certain transmissible spongiform encephalopathies) see PARA 106.

5 Transmissible Spongiform Encephalopathies (England) Regulations 2010, SI 2010/801, reg 7(b); Transmissible Spongiform Encephalopathies (Wales) Regulations 2008, SI 2008/3154, reg 7(b).

6   As to the Secretary of State and the Welsh Ministers see PARA **390**.

7   An approval, authorisation, licence or registration may be made subject to such conditions as are necessary to ensure that the provisions of the EU TSE Regulation, the Transmissible Spongiform Encephalopathies (England) Regulations 2010, SI 2010/801, and the Transmissible Spongiform Encephalopathies (Wales) Regulations 2008, SI 2008/3154, will be complied with (Transmissible Spongiform Encephalopathies (England) Regulations 2010, SI 2010/801, reg 6(3)(a); Transmissible Spongiform Encephalopathies (Wales) Regulations 2008, SI 2008/3154, reg 6(3)(a)) or to protect public or animal health (Transmissible Spongiform Encephalopathies (England) Regulations 2010, SI 2010/801, reg 6(3)(b); Transmissible Spongiform Encephalopathies (Wales) Regulations 2008, SI 2008/3154, reg 6(3)(b)).

8   See note 1.

9   Transmissible Spongiform Encephalopathies (England) Regulations 2010, SI 2010/801, reg 6(1); Transmissible Spongiform Encephalopathies (Wales) Regulations 2008, SI 2008/3154, reg 6(1). An approval, authorisation, licence or registration must be in writing and must specify the address of the premises, the name of the occupier and the purpose for which it is granted: Transmissible Spongiform Encephalopathies (England) Regulations 2010, SI 2010/801, reg 6(2); Transmissible Spongiform Encephalopathies (Wales) Regulations 2008, SI 2008/3154, reg 6(2). If the Secretary of State refuses or the Welsh Ministers refuse to grant an approval, authorisation, licence or registration, or one is granted subject to conditions, he or they must give the reasons in writing and explain the right of the applicant to make written representations to a person appointed by the Secretary of State or (as the case may be) the Welsh Ministers (Transmissible Spongiform Encephalopathies (England) Regulations 2010, SI 2010/801, reg 6(3); Transmissible Spongiform Encephalopathies (Wales) Regulations 2008, SI 2008/3154, reg 6(4)), at which point the appeals procedure applies (see PARA **107** note 9) (Transmissible Spongiform Encephalopathies (England) Regulations 2010, SI 2010/801, reg 6(5); Transmissible Spongiform Encephalopathies (Wales) Regulations 2008, SI 2008/3154, reg 6(5)).

10 Transmissible Spongiform Encephalopathies (England) Regulations 2010, SI 2010/801, reg 8(1)(a), (2); Transmissible Spongiform Encephalopathies (Wales) Regulations 2008, SI 2008/3154, reg 8(1)(a), (2). A suspension or amendment may have immediate effect if the Welsh Ministers consider it necessary for the protection of public or animal health; and otherwise may have effect after the expiration of at least 21 days: Transmissible Spongiform Encephalopathies (England) Regulations 2010, SI 2010/801, reg 8(3); Transmissible Spongiform Encephalopathies (Wales) Regulations 2008, SI 2008/3154, reg 8(3). Notification of the suspension or amendment must be in writing, state when it comes into effect, give the reasons and explain the right of the person who has been notified to make written representations to a person appointed by the Secretary of State or (as the case may be) the Welsh Ministers (Transmissible Spongiform Encephalopathies (England) Regulations 2010, SI 2010/801, reg 8(4); Transmissible Spongiform Encephalopathies (Wales) Regulations 2008, SI 2008/3154, reg 8(4)), at which point the appeals procedure applies (see PARA **107** note 9) (Transmissible Spongiform Encephalopathies (England) Regulations 2010, SI 2010/801, reg 8(5); Transmissible Spongiform Encephalopathies (Wales) Regulations 2008, SI 2008/3154, reg 8(5)). If the suspension or amendment does not have immediate effect and the appropriate representations are made, the suspension or amendment will not have effect until the final determination of the appeal by the Secretary of State or the Welsh Ministers unless he considers or they consider that it is necessary for the protection of public or animal health for the amendment or suspension to have effect before then: Transmissible Spongiform Encephalopathies (England) Regulations 2010, SI 2010/801, reg 8(6); Transmissible Spongiform Encephalopathies (Wales) Regulations 2008, SI 2008/3154, reg 8(6).

11 Transmissible Spongiform Encephalopathies (England) Regulations 2010, SI 2010/801, reg 8(1)(b); Transmissible Spongiform Encephalopathies (Wales) Regulations 2008, SI 2008/3154, reg 8(1)(b). See note 10.

12 Ie under the Transmissible Spongiform Encephalopathies (England) Regulations 2010, SI 2010/801, reg 10 or the Transmissible Spongiform Encephalopathies (Wales) Regulations 2008, SI 2008/3154, reg 10 (see PARA **107** note 9).

13 Transmissible Spongiform Encephalopathies (England) Regulations 2010, SI 2010/801, reg 9(1)(a); Transmissible Spongiform Encephalopathies (Wales) Regulations 2008, SI 2008/3154, reg 9(1)(a).

14 Transmissible Spongiform Encephalopathies (England) Regulations 2010, SI 2010/801, reg 9(1)(b); Transmissible Spongiform Encephalopathies (Wales) Regulations 2008, SI 2008/3154, reg 9(1)(b). If the Secretary of State or the Welsh Ministers revoke an approval, authorisation, licence or registration under this provision, the appeals procedure (see PARA **107** note 9) applies but the revocation remains in force during that appeals procedure: Transmissible Spongiform

Encephalopathies (England) Regulations 2010, SI 2010/801, reg 9(2); Transmissible Spongiform Encephalopathies (Wales) Regulations 2008, SI 2008/3154, reg 9(2).

15 Transmissible Spongiform Encephalopathies (England) Regulations 2010, SI 2010/801, reg 9(1)(c); Transmissible Spongiform Encephalopathies (Wales) Regulations 2008, SI 2008/3154, reg 9(1)(c). If the Secretary of State revokes or the Welsh Ministers revoke an approval, authorisation, licence or registration under this provision, the appeals procedure (see PARA 107 note 9) applies but the revocation remains in force during that appeals procedure: Transmissible Spongiform Encephalopathies (England) Regulations 2010, SI 2010/801, reg 9(2); Transmissible Spongiform Encephalopathies (Wales) Regulations 2008, SI 2008/3154, reg 9(2).

110. Inspections and notifications.

An inspector[1] may:

(1) seize any animal, body of an animal, and any parts of the body (including the blood and the hide) and any semen, embryo or ovum, or any animal protein or feeding stuffs that may contain animal protein, and dispose of them as necessary[2];

(2) carry out any inquiries, investigations, examinations and tests[3];

(3) collect, pen and inspect any animal[4];

(4) inspect any body of an animal and any parts of the body (including the blood and the hide) and any semen, embryo or ovum[5];

(5) inspect any part of a premises, any equipment, facility, operation or procedure[6];

(6) take any samples[7];

(7) have access to, and inspect and copy, any records[8] in order to determine if the relevant legislation[9] is being complied with, or remove such records to enable them to be copied[10];

(8) have access to, inspect and check the operation of, any computer and any associated apparatus or material that is or has been in use in connection with any record[11];

(9) mark anything (including an animal) whether electronically or otherwise, for identification purposes[12]; and

(10) lock or seal any container or store[13].

If it is necessary for any reason connected with the enforcement of the relevant legislation[14] an inspector may serve a notice[15]:

(a) prohibiting or requiring the movement of any animal onto or from the premises specified in the notice[16];

(b) specifying those parts of premises to which an animal may or may not be allowed access[17];

(c) requiring the killing or slaughter of any animal[18];

(d) prohibiting or requiring the movement onto or from premises specified in the notice, of the body or any part of the body (including the blood and the hide) of any animal, any animal protein or feeding stuffs that may contain animal protein, and any animal semen, embryo or ovum[19];

(e) requiring the disposal of the body or any part of the body (including the blood and the hide) of any animal (whether or not it is one that was required to be detained), and any semen, embryo or ovum as may be specified in the notice[20];

(f) requiring the disposal of any animal protein or feeding stuffs that may contain animal protein or specify how they are to be used[21]; or

(g) requiring the recall of any animal protein or feeding stuffs that may contain animal protein[22].

An inspector may serve such a notice on the owner or keeper of any animal[23], the person in possession of the body or any part of the body of an animal (including the blood and the hide) or any semen, embryo or ovum[24], or the person in possession of any animal protein or feeding stuffs that may contain animal protein[25]. In addition, if an inspector suspects that any premises, vehicle or container to which the relevant legislation[26] applies constitutes a risk to animal or public health, he may serve a notice on the occupier or person in charge of the premises, vehicle or container requiring that person to cleanse and disinfect all or any part of the premises, vehicle or container and any associated equipment[27]. Failure to comply with a notice is an offence[28].

Pursuant to his powers an inspector may enter any premises[29] for the purpose of ensuring that the relevant legislation is being complied with[30].

1   The Secretary of State (or, as the case may be, the Welsh Ministers) and the local authority must appoint inspectors for the purposes of the enforcement of the Transmissible Spongiform Encephalopathies (England) Regulations 2010, SI 2010/801, and the Transmissible Spongiform Encephalopathies (Wales) Regulations 2008, SI 2008/3154 (except as specified in the Transmissible Spongiform Encephalopathies (England) Regulations 2010, SI 2010/801, Schs 7, 8 and the Transmissible Spongiform Encephalopathies (Wales) Regulations 2008, SI 2008/3154, Sch 7, 8: see FOOD AND DRINK): see the Transmissible Spongiform Encephalopathies (England) Regulations 2010, SI 2010/801, reg 12; and the Transmissible Spongiform Encephalopathies (Wales) Regulations 2008, SI 2008/3154, reg 12 (amended by SI 2008/3266). As to the local authorities see PARA 106 note 11.
       An inspector is not personally liable for anything he does in the execution or purported execution of the Transmissible Spongiform Encephalopathies (England) Regulations 2010, SI 2010/801, or the Transmissible Spongiform Encephalopathies (Wales) Regulations 2008, SI 2008/3154, and within the scope of his employment, if he acted in the honest belief that his duty under the regulations required or entitled him to do it; but this does not affect any liability of his employer: Transmissible Spongiform Encephalopathies (England) Regulations 2010, SI 2010/801, reg 14(3); Transmissible Spongiform Encephalopathies (Wales) Regulations 2008, SI 2008/3154, reg 14(3).
       A person is guilty of an offence if he intentionally obstructs an inspector acting under the Transmissible Spongiform Encephalopathies (England) Regulations 2010, SI 2010/801, or the Transmissible Spongiform Encephalopathies (Wales) Regulations 2008, SI 2008/3154, or without reasonable cause fails to give to an inspector acting thereunder any assistance or information or to provide any facilities that the inspector may reasonably require him to give or provide for the performance of his functions thereunder, or gives false or misleading information to an inspector so acting, or fails to produce a record when required to do so by an inspector so acting: Transmissible Spongiform Encephalopathies (England) Regulations 2010, SI 2010/801, reg 17; Transmissible Spongiform Encephalopathies (Wales) Regulations 2008, SI 2008/3154, reg 17. As to offences see PARA 106 note 1.
2   Transmissible Spongiform Encephalopathies (England) Regulations 2010, SI 2010/801, reg 14(1)(a); Transmissible Spongiform Encephalopathies (Wales) Regulations 2008, SI 2008/3154, reg 14(1)(a).
3   Transmissible Spongiform Encephalopathies (England) Regulations 2010, SI 2010/801, reg 14(1)(b); Transmissible Spongiform Encephalopathies (Wales) Regulations 2008, SI 2008/3154, reg 14(1)(b).
4   Transmissible Spongiform Encephalopathies (England) Regulations 2010, SI 2010/801, reg 14(1)(c); Transmissible Spongiform Encephalopathies (Wales) Regulations 2008, SI 2008/3154, reg 14(1)(c). For this purpose an inspector may also require the keeper of any such animal to arrange for the collection and penning of the animal: Transmissible Spongiform Encephalopathies (England) Regulations 2010, SI 2010/801, reg 14(1)(c); Transmissible Spongiform Encephalopathies (Wales) Regulations 2008, SI 2008/3154, reg 14(1)(c).
5   Transmissible Spongiform Encephalopathies (England) Regulations 2010, SI 2010/801, reg 14(1)(d); Transmissible Spongiform Encephalopathies (Wales) Regulations 2008, SI 2008/3154, reg 14(1)(d).
6   Transmissible Spongiform Encephalopathies (England) Regulations 2010, SI 2010/801, reg 14(1)(e); Transmissible Spongiform Encephalopathies (Wales) Regulations 2008, SI 2008/3154, reg 14(1)(e).
7   Transmissible Spongiform Encephalopathies (England) Regulations 2010, SI 2010/801, reg 14(1)(f); Transmissible Spongiform Encephalopathies (Wales) Regulations 2008, SI 2008/3154, reg 14(1)(f).

8 Ie any records in whatever form they are held and including records kept under the EU TSE Regulation (ie Council Regulation (EC) 999/2001 (OJ L147, 31.5.2001, p 1) laying down rules for the prevention, control and eradication of certain transmissible spongiform encephalopathies) (see PARA 106), the Transmissible Spongiform Encephalopathies (England) Regulations 2010, SI 2010/801, and the Transmissible Spongiform Encephalopathies (Wales) Regulations 2008, SI 2008/3154: Transmissible Spongiform Encephalopathies (England) Regulations 2010, SI 2010/801, reg 14(1)(g); Transmissible Spongiform Encephalopathies (Wales) Regulations 2008, SI 2008/3154, reg 14(1)(g).

9 Ie the Transmissible Spongiform Encephalopathies (England) Regulations 2010, SI 2010/801, and the Transmissible Spongiform Encephalopathies (Wales) Regulations 2008, SI 2008/3154.

10 Transmissible Spongiform Encephalopathies (England) Regulations 2010, SI 2010/801, reg 14(1)(g); Transmissible Spongiform Encephalopathies (Wales) Regulations 2008, SI 2008/3154, reg 14(1)(g).

11 Transmissible Spongiform Encephalopathies (England) Regulations 2010, SI 2010/801, reg 14(1)(h); Transmissible Spongiform Encephalopathies (Wales) Regulations 2008, SI 2008/3154, reg 14(1)(h). For this purpose an inspector may also require any person having charge of, or otherwise concerned with the operation of, the computer, apparatus or material to afford him such assistance as he may reasonably require (including providing him with any necessary passwords) and, where a record is kept by means of a computer, may require the records to be produced in a form in which they may be taken away: Transmissible Spongiform Encephalopathies (England) Regulations 2010, SI 2010/801, reg 14(1)(h); Transmissible Spongiform Encephalopathies (Wales) Regulations 2008, SI 2008/3154, reg 14(1)(h).

12 Transmissible Spongiform Encephalopathies (England) Regulations 2010, SI 2010/801, reg 14(1)(i); Transmissible Spongiform Encephalopathies (Wales) Regulations 2008, SI 2008/3154, reg 14(1)(i). Any person who defaces, obliterates or removes any mark or seal, or removes any lock, applied under these provisions is guilty of an offence: Transmissible Spongiform Encephalopathies (England) Regulations 2010, SI 2010/801, reg 14(2); Transmissible Spongiform Encephalopathies (Wales) Regulations 2008, SI 2008/3154, reg 14(2).

13 Transmissible Spongiform Encephalopathies (England) Regulations 2010, SI 2010/801, reg 14(1)(j); Transmissible Spongiform Encephalopathies (Wales) Regulations 2008, SI 2008/3154, reg 14(1)(j). See note 12.

14 Ie the Transmissible Spongiform Encephalopathies (England) Regulations 2010, SI 2010/801, the Transmissible Spongiform Encephalopathies (Wales) Regulations 2008, SI 2008/3154, and the EU TSE Regulation.

15 Notices must be in writing, and must give the reasons for being served: Transmissible Spongiform Encephalopathies (England) Regulations 2010, SI 2010/801, reg 15(2); Transmissible Spongiform Encephalopathies (Wales) Regulations 2008, SI 2008/3154, reg 15(2).

16 Transmissible Spongiform Encephalopathies (England) Regulations 2010, SI 2010/801, reg 15(3)(a); Transmissible Spongiform Encephalopathies (Wales) Regulations 2008, SI 2008/3154, reg 15(3)(a). If a notice is served restricting movements, an inspector may subsequently permit movement under the authority of a licence, and the person transporting under the authority of such a licence must carry it with him during movement and produce it on demand to an inspector, failure to do so being an offence: Transmissible Spongiform Encephalopathies (England) Regulations 2010, SI 2010/801, reg 16; Transmissible Spongiform Encephalopathies (Wales) Regulations 2008, SI 2008/3154, reg 16.

17 Transmissible Spongiform Encephalopathies (England) Regulations 2010, SI 2010/801, reg 15(3)(b); Transmissible Spongiform Encephalopathies (Wales) Regulations 2008, SI 2008/3154, reg 15(3)(b).

18 Transmissible Spongiform Encephalopathies (England) Regulations 2010, SI 2010/801, reg 15(3)(c); Transmissible Spongiform Encephalopathies (Wales) Regulations 2008, SI 2008/3154, reg 15(3)(c).

19 Transmissible Spongiform Encephalopathies (England) Regulations 2010, SI 2010/801, reg 15(3)(d); Transmissible Spongiform Encephalopathies (Wales) Regulations 2008, SI 2008/3154, reg 15(3)(d).

20 Transmissible Spongiform Encephalopathies (England) Regulations 2010, SI 2010/801, reg 15(3)(e); Transmissible Spongiform Encephalopathies (Wales) Regulations 2008, SI 2008/3154, reg 15(3)(e).

21 Transmissible Spongiform Encephalopathies (England) Regulations 2010, SI 2010/801, reg 15(3)(f); Transmissible Spongiform Encephalopathies (Wales) Regulations 2008, SI 2008/3154, reg 15(3)(f).

22 Transmissible Spongiform Encephalopathies (England) Regulations 2010, SI 2010/801, reg 15(3)(g); Transmissible Spongiform Encephalopathies (Wales) Regulations 2008, SI 2008/3154, reg 15(3)(g).

23 Transmissible Spongiform Encephalopathies (England) Regulations 2010, SI 2010/801, reg 15(1)(a); Transmissible Spongiform Encephalopathies (Wales) Regulations 2008, SI 2008/3154, reg 15(1)(a).

24 Transmissible Spongiform Encephalopathies (England) Regulations 2010, SI 2010/801, reg 15(1)(b); Transmissible Spongiform Encephalopathies (Wales) Regulations 2008, SI 2008/3154, reg 15(1)(b).

25 Transmissible Spongiform Encephalopathies (England) Regulations 2010, SI 2010/801, reg 15(1)(c); Transmissible Spongiform Encephalopathies (Wales) Regulations 2008, SI 2008/3154, reg 15(1)(c).

26 See note 14.

27 Transmissible Spongiform Encephalopathies (England) Regulations 2010, SI 2010/801, reg 15(4); Transmissible Spongiform Encephalopathies (Wales) Regulations 2008, SI 2008/3154, reg 15(4).

28 Transmissible Spongiform Encephalopathies (England) Regulations 2010, SI 2010/801, reg 15(7); Transmissible Spongiform Encephalopathies (Wales) Regulations 2008, SI 2008/3154, reg 15(7). A notice must be complied with at the expense of the person on whom it is served, and if it is not complied with an inspector may arrange to have it complied with at that person's expense: Transmissible Spongiform Encephalopathies (England) Regulations 2010, SI 2010/801, reg 15(6); Transmissible Spongiform Encephalopathies (Wales) Regulations 2008, SI 2008/3154, reg 15(6). A notice may specify how it must be complied with, and specify time limits: Transmissible Spongiform Encephalopathies (England) Regulations 2010, SI 2010/801, reg 15(5); Transmissible Spongiform Encephalopathies (Wales) Regulations 2008, SI 2008/3154, reg 15(5).

29 For this purpose, in relation to Wales 'premises' includes any vehicle, container or structure (moveable or otherwise) and includes any domestic premises if they are being used for any purpose in connection with the EU TSE Regulation or the Transmissible Spongiform Encephalopathies (Wales) Regulations 2008, SI 2008/3154: reg 13(8). As to the meaning of 'premises' in relation to England see PARA 106 note 5. Entry may be secured at all reasonable hours but only on the inspector producing, if so required, some duly authenticated document showing his authority: see the Transmissible Spongiform Encephalopathies (England) Regulations 2010, SI 2010/801, reg 13(2), (3); and the Transmissible Spongiform Encephalopathies (Wales) Regulations 2008, SI 2008/3154, reg 13(2), (3). An inspector may take with him such other persons as he considers necessary and any representative of the European Commission acting for the purpose of the enforcement of an EU obligation: Transmissible Spongiform Encephalopathies (England) Regulations 2010, SI 2010/801, reg 13(4); Transmissible Spongiform Encephalopathies (Wales) Regulations 2008, SI 2008/3154, reg 13(4) (amended by SI 2011/1043). If inspectors enter any unoccupied premises or, in relation to England, where the premises are occupied, the occupier of the premises is temporarily absent, they must leave those premises (so far as reasonably practicable) as effectively secured against unauthorised entry as the inspectors found them: Transmissible Spongiform Encephalopathies (England) Regulations 2010, SI 2010/801, reg 13(5); Transmissible Spongiform Encephalopathies (Wales) Regulations 2008, SI 2008/3154, reg 13(5). A warrant valid for one month may be issued by a justice of the peace: see the Transmissible Spongiform Encephalopathies (England) Regulations 2010, SI 2010/801, reg 13(6), (7); and the Transmissible Spongiform Encephalopathies (Wales) Regulations 2008, SI 2008/3154, reg 13(6), (7).

30 Transmissible Spongiform Encephalopathies (England) Regulations 2010, SI 2010/801, reg 13(1); Transmissible Spongiform Encephalopathies (Wales) Regulations 2008, SI 2008/3154, reg 13(1).

5. PROTECTION OF CROPS

(1) PREVENTION OF TRANSMISSIBLE DISEASES IN CROPS

111. Meaning of 'pests'.
The Plant Health Act 1967 has effect for the control of pests and diseases injurious to agricultural or horticultural crops or to trees or bushes[1]; and for these purposes 'pests' extends to insects, bacteria, fungi and other vegetable or animal organisms, viruses and all other agents causative of any transmissible disease of agricultural or horticultural crops or of trees or bushes, and includes pests in any stage of existence[2].

1 Plant Health Act 1967 s 1(1) (amended by the European Communities Act 1972 Sch 4 para 8(1), (2)). References to a 'crop' in the Plant Health Act 1967 are to be taken as including references to trees and bushes: s 1(1)(b). The control of pesticides is governed by the Food and Environment Protection Act 1985 Pt III (ss 16–19): see PARAS 130–141.
2 Plant Health Act 1967 s 1(1)(a).

112. Control of introduction of pests.
A competent authority[1] may make such orders as it thinks expedient, or called for by any EU obligation[2], for preventing the introduction of pests[3] into Great Britain[4]. The orders may prohibit or regulate the landing in Great Britain[5] of articles of any description (and in particular plants, trees or bushes or any part or produce thereof) where it appears to the competent authority that their landing is likely to introduce a pest into Great Britain, and the orders may direct or authorise the destruction of such articles if landed[6]. Member states are also authorised[7] temporarily to take additional measures in this regard where authorised so to do by a decision of the European Commission[8].

1 The 'competent authorities' for these purposes are Secretary of State and the Welsh Ministers (Plant Health Act 1967 s 1(2)(a)(ii), (b) (substituted by SI 2013/755)) or, as regards the protection of forest trees and timber (which for these purposes includes all forest products), the Forestry Commissioners (Plant Health Act 1967 s 1(2)(a)(i) (as so substituted). As to the Secretary of State and the Welsh Ministers see PARA 390. As to the Forestry Commissioners see FORESTRY vol 52 (2014) PARA 37 et seq. The Forestry Commissioners in exercising their powers under the Plant Health Act 1967 must comply with any directions given by the Secretary of State as regards England: see the Forestry Act 1967 s 1(4)(a); and FORESTRY vol 52 (2014) PARA 44.
2 'EU obligation' means any obligation created or arising by or under the Treaties as defined by the European Communities Act 1972 s 1(2), Sch 1 Pt I, whether an enforceable EU obligation or not: s 1(2), Sch 1 Pt II (amended by the European Union (Amendment) Act 2008 Schedule, Pt 1).
3 As to the meaning of 'pest' see PARA 111.
4 Plant Health Act 1967 s 2(1) (amended by the European Communities Act 1972 s 4(1), Sch 4 para 8(1), (2) and SI 2011/1043). As to the meaning of 'Great Britain' see PARA 1 note 1. Notice of such orders is to be published in the London Gazette (Plant Health Act 1967 s 6(2)), and, if a competent authority sends an order to a local authority for publication, the local authority must publish it in such manner as the local authority thinks sufficient and proper to ensure publicity (s 6(3) (amended by the Local Government Act 1974 Sch 6 para 19(2), Sch 8)). As to the local authorities for these purposes see PARA 115.
5 References in the Plant Health Act 1967 s 2(2) to the landing of any article include references to its importation through the tunnel system as defined in the Channel Tunnel Act 1987 (see RAILWAYS AND TRAMWAYS vol 86 (2017) PARA 115): Plant Health Act 1967 s 2(3) (added by SI 1990/2371).
6 Plant Health Act 1967 s 2(2) (amended by the Customs and Excise Management Act 1979 Sch 4 para 12). This is without prejudice to provisions of the Customs and Excise Management Act 1979 imposing penalties or liability to forfeiture: see the Plant Health Act 1967 s 2(2) (as so amended). For those provisions see the Customs and Excise Management Act 1979 ss 49, 50; and CUSTOMS AND EXCISE vol 31 (2012) PARAS 991–992.

The following orders have been made:

(1)   the Plant Health (Forestry) Order 2005, SI 2005/2517; and the Plant Health (Forestry) (*Phytophthora ramorum*) (Great Britain) Order 2004, SI 2004/3213 (revoked in relation to England);

(2)   the Plant Health (England) Order 2015, SI 2015/610; and the Plant Health (Wales) Order 2006, SI 2006/1643 (and see also the following regulations, which were all made under the Finance Act 1973 s 56(1): the Plant Health (Fees) (England) Regulations 2014, SI 2014/601; and the Plant Health (Fees) (Wales) Regulations 2014, SI 2014/1792);

(3)   the Plant Health (*Phytophthora ramorum*) (Wales) Order 2006, SI 2006/1344.

Orders under the Plant Health Act 1967 may (without prejudice to s 4(1) (see PARA 114)) impose such reasonable fees or other charges as the competent authority may with the consent of the Treasury prescribe:

(a)   in connection with applications for and the issue of any licence or certificate which may be issued in pursuance of such an order in connection with the import or export of any article (s 4A(1) (s 4A added by the Agriculture Act 1986 s 3)); and

(b)   in respect of the performance by the authority of any service without the performance of which any requirement for the issue of such a licence would not be met (Plant Health Act 1967 s 4A(2) (as so added)).

The orders which incorporate such provision are the Plant Health (Export Certification) (England) Order 2004, SI 2004/1404; the Plant Health (Export Certification) (Wales) Order 2006, SI 2006/1701; and the Plant Health (Export Certification) (Forestry) (Great Britain) Order 2004, SI 2004/1684. As to the Treasury see CONSTITUTIONAL AND ADMINISTRATIVE LAW vol 20 (2014) PARA 263 et seq.

The competent authorities may require orders made under the Plant Health Act 1967 to be carried into effect by local authorities: see s 5; and PARA 115. Orders may also contain provisions for requiring a person to pay to a competent authority or local authority the cost to the authority of doing anything which that person has, in breach of a requirement imposed on him by or under the order, failed to do: Agriculture (Miscellaneous Provisions) Act 1972 s 20.

7   Ie pursuant to the European Communities Act 1972 s 2(2).

8   See eg the Potatoes Originating in Egypt (England) Regulations 2004, SI 2004/1165; and the Potatoes Originating in Egypt (Wales) Regulations 2004, SI 2004/2245 (both authorised by Commission Decision (EC) 2004/4 (OJ L2, 6.1.2004, p 38) authorising member states temporarily to take emergency measures against the dissemination of *Pseudomonas solanacearum (Smith) Smith* as regards Egypt).

113.   Control of spread of pests.

A competent authority[1] may make such orders as it thinks expedient or called for by any EU obligation[2] for preventing the spread of pests[3] in Great Britain or the conveyance of pests by articles exported from Great Britain[4]. Such an order may prohibit the selling, or exposing or offering for sale, or the keeping, of living specimens of a pest, or the distribution in any manner of such specimens[5], and may also direct or authorise:

(1)   the removal, treatment or destruction of any crop[6], or any seed, plant or part thereof or any container, wrapping or other article or any substance which has on it, or is infected with, a pest, or to or by means of which a pest is in the opinion of the competent authority likely to spread[7]; and

(2)   the entering on any land or elsewhere for the purpose of any removal, treatment or destruction authorised by the orders, or any examination or inquiry so authorised, or for any other purpose of the orders[8].

Orders may provide for the punishment of persons guilty of an offence against them[9], proceedings for which may be instituted at any time within 12 months of the alleged offence[10].

Member states are also authorised[11] temporarily to take additional measures in this regard where authorised so to do by a decision of the European Commission[12].

1   As to the competent authorities for these purposes see PARA 112 note 1.

2   As to the meaning of 'EU obligation' see PARA 112 note 2.

3   As to the meaning of 'pests' see PARA **111**.
4   Plant Health Act 1967 s 3(1) (amended by the European Communities Act 1972 Sch 4 para 8(1), (2)). As to the meaning of 'Great Britain' see PARA **1** note 1.
5   Plant Health Act 1967 s 3(3).
6   As to the meaning of 'crop' see PARA **111** note 1.
7   Plant Health Act 1967 s 3(2)(a) (s 3(2) amended by the European Communities Act 1972 Sch 4 para 8(1), (3)).
8   Plant Health Act 1967 s 3(2)(b) (as amended: see note 7).
9   Orders may provide that a person guilty of an offence against them is to be liable on summary conviction to a fine of an amount not exceeding level 5 on the standard scale, or not exceeding a lesser amount: Plant Health Act 1967 s 3(4) (s 3(4) substituted, and s 3(4A) added, by the Criminal Justice Act 1982 s 42). As to the standard scale and the powers of magistrates' courts to issue fines on summary conviction see SENTENCING vol 92 (2015) PARA 176. Until a day to be appointed an order made for the purposes of preventing the spread in Great Britain of the Colorado beetle (*Leptinotarsa decemlineata* (Say)) may provide that a person guilty of an offence against it relating to the keeping of living specimens of this beetle (in any stage of existence), or to the distribution in any manner of such specimens, is liable on summary conviction to imprisonment for not more than three months as well as, or as an alternative to, a fine not exceeding level 5 on the standard scale (Plant Health Act 1967 s 3(4A) (as so added)); as from that day the term of imprisonment to which a person may (additionally or alternatively) be liable under this provision is increased to a term not exceeding 51 weeks (Plant Health Act 1967 s 3(4A), (4B)(a) (s 3(4A) as so added; s 3(4A) prospectively amended, and s 3(4B) prospectively added, by the Criminal Justice Act 2003 s 283, Sch 27 paras 1(1)–(3))). At the date at which this volume states the law no such day had been appointed.
10 Plant Health Act 1967 s 3(5) (amended by the European Communities Act 1972 Sch 4 para 8(1), (2)). The following orders have been made:
     (1)   the Dutch Elm Disease (Local Authorities) Order 1984, SI 1984/687;
     (2)   the Plant Health (Forestry) Order 2005, SI 2005/2517; and the Plant Health (Forestry) (*Phytophthora ramorum*) (Great Britain) Order 2004, SI 2004/3213 (revoked in relation to England);
     (3)   the Plant Health (England) Order 2015, SI 2015/610; and the Plant Health (Wales) Order 2006, SI 2006/1643 (and see also the following regulations, which were all made under the Finance Act 1973 s 56(1): the Plant Health (Fees) (England) Regulations 2014, SI 2014/601; and the Plant Health (Fees) (Wales) Regulations 2014, SI 2014/1792));
     (4)   the Plant Health (England) Order 2015, SI 2015/610; and the Plant Health (*Phytophthora ramorum*) (Wales) Order 2006, SI 2006/1344;
     (5)   the Plant Health (Sweet Chestnut Blight) (England) Order 2017, SI 2017/178;
     (6)   the Plant Health (Export Certification) (England) Order 2004, SI 2004/1404; the Plant Health (Export Certification) (Wales) Order 2006, SI 2006/1701; and the Plant Health (Export Certification) (Forestry) (Great Britain) Order 2004, SI 2004/1684 (also making provision pursuant to the Plant Health Act 1967 s 4A (see PARA 112 note 6)).
     The competent authorities may require orders made under the Plant Health Act 1967 to be carried into effect by local authorities: see s 5; and PARA 115. Orders may also contain provisions for requiring a person to pay to a competent authority or local authority the cost to the authority of doing anything which that person has, in breach of a requirement imposed on him by or under the order, failed to do: Agriculture (Miscellaneous Provisions) Act 1972 s 20. The orders which incorporate such provision are those listed above as having been made partly under the Plant Health Act 1967 s 3, with the exception of, the Dutch Elm Disease (Local Authorities) Order 1984, SI 1984/687, and the Plant Health (*Phytophthora ramorum*) (Wales) Order 2006, SI 2006/1344.
11 Ie pursuant to the European Communities Act 1972 s 2(2).
12 See eg the Potatoes Originating in Egypt (England) Regulations 2004, SI 2004/1165; and the Potatoes Originating in Egypt (Wales) Regulations 2004, SI 2004/2245 (both authorised by Commission Decision (EC) 2004/4 (OJ L2, 6.1.2004, p 38) authorising member states temporarily to take emergency measures against the dissemination of *Pseudomonas solanacearum (Smith) Smith* as regards Egypt).

114. Dealing with infected crops.

Orders relating to the control of pests[1] may enable an inspector authorised by the Secretary of State and the Welsh Ministers[2]:

(1)   in the case of any specified pest which has been introduced into Great Britain, to remove or destroy any crop[3], or any seed, plant or part thereof, which has on it or is infected with the pest, or to or by means of which the pest is likely to spread[4], and generally to take such steps as he may think expedient in connection with any crop, or any seed, plant or part thereof, for preventing the spread of the pest[5]; and

(2)   to enter on any land or elsewhere for those purposes or for the purpose of any examination or inquiry authorised by the orders, or for any other purpose of the orders[6].

Orders may also impose in respect of any certificate given after an inspection such fee or other charge as may be prescribed by the Secretary of State or the Welsh Ministers with the consent of the Treasury[7].

The Secretary of State and the Welsh Ministers may pay compensation in respect of any crop, or any seed, plant or part thereof, which is removed or destroyed by or under the instructions of an inspector[8].

1   Ie orders under the Plant Health Act 1967: see ss 2, 3; and PARAS 112–113. As to the meaning of 'pests' see PARA 111.
2   As to the Secretary of State and the Welsh Ministers see PARA 390.
3   As to the meaning of 'crop' see PARA 111 note 1.
4   Plant Health Act 1967 s 4(1)(a)(i). Orders made for the control of pests which have made such provision as is referred to in s 4(1) are:
     (1)   the Plant Health (England) Order 2015, SI 2015/610; and the Plant Health (Wales) Order 2006, SI 2006/1643;
     (2)   the Plant Health (*Phytophthora ramorum*) (Wales) Order 2006, SI 2006/1344;
     (3)   the Plant Health (Sweet Chestnut Blight) (England) Order 2017, SI 2017/178.
     As to the enforcement of these orders by local authorities see PARA 115.
5   Plant Health Act 1967 s 4(1)(a)(ii). See note 4. As to the meaning of 'Great Britain' see PARA 1 note 1.
6   Plant Health Act 1967 s 4(1)(b) (amended by the European Communities Act 1972 Sch 4 para 8(1), (3)). See note 4.
7   Plant Health Act 1967 s 4(1). In connection with the levying of charges relating to import and export licences and certificates, see also the orders made under the Plant Health Act 1967 s 4A; and PARA 112 note 6. As to the Treasury see CONSTITUTIONAL AND ADMINISTRATIVE LAW vol 20 (2014) PARA 263 et seq.
8   Plant Health Act 1967 s 4(2). The value of the crop, seed or plant is to be that which it has at the time of the removal or destruction and, if the Secretary of State requires or the Welsh Ministers require, is to be ascertained by officers or by arbitration: s 4(2). The expenses of the Secretary of State and the Welsh Ministers in the execution of the Plant Health Act 1967, including any compensation under s 4(2), are to be paid out of money provided by Parliament but are not without the consent of the Treasury to exceed £2,000 in any year: s 4(3).

115. Execution of control by local authorities.

A competent authority[1] may require a local authority[2] to carry into effect any order relating to the control of pests[3] and may, with the consent of the local authority, require a local authority to pay compensation in respect of any crop[4], or any seed, plant or part thereof, which is removed or destroyed in pursuance of any such order[5]. The local authority may, however, withhold compensation in respect of anything removed or destroyed if, in relation thereto, the owner or person having charge thereof has, in its judgment, done anything in contravention of, or failed to do anything in compliance with, any order[6]. The value of anything removed or destroyed is to be taken to be the value which it has at the time of removal or destruction and, if the local authority so requires, is to be ascertained by its officers or by arbitration[7].

Every local authority must keep a record relative to proceedings under any order relating to the control of pests made by the competent authority; and the record must state the date of any removal or destruction under the order, and other proper particulars, and is to be admitted in evidence[8].

1   As to the competent authorities for these purposes see PARA 112 note 1.
2   The local authorities for the purposes of the Plant Health Act 1967 are the councils of non-metropolitan counties, metropolitan districts and London boroughs and the Common Council of the City of London (in relation to England) and the councils of counties and county boroughs (in relation to Wales): s 5(3) (substituted by the Local Government Act 1972 Sch 29 para 34; and amended by the Local Government (Wales) Act 1994 Sch 16 para 28). As to the counties and districts in England and their councils see LOCAL GOVERNMENT vol 69 (2009) PARA 22 et seq. As to the London boroughs and their councils see LONDON GOVERNMENT vol 71 (2013) PARAS 5, 14–15, 20 et seq. As to the Common Council of the City of London see LONDON GOVERNMENT vol 71 (2013) PARA 34 et seq. As to local authorities in Wales see LOCAL GOVERNMENT vol 69 (2009) PARAS 22–23, 37 et seq.
3   Ie any order under the Plant Health Act 1967: s 5(1). As to those orders see PARAS 112–114. Note in particular the provisions as to the payment of a local authority's costs (see the Agriculture (Miscellaneous Provisions) Act 1972 s 20; and PARAS 112 note 6, 113 note 10).
4   As to the meaning of 'crop' see PARA 111 note 1.
5   Plant Health Act 1967 s 5(1). See the Dutch Elm Disease (Local Authorities) Order 1984, SI 1984/687.
6   Plant Health Act 1967 s 5(1)(a).
7   Plant Health Act 1967 s 5(1)(b).
8   Plant Health Act 1967 s 5(2) (amended by the Local Government Act 1974 Sch 6 para 19(1), Sch 8).

(2) PREVENTION OF DAMAGE BY DESTRUCTIVE ANIMALS

(i) Wild Animals and Birds

116. Prevention of damage by wild animals and birds.
The Secretary of State and the Welsh Ministers[1] may serve, on any person having the right so to do, a written notice requiring that person to take, within such time as may be specified in the notice, such steps as may be necessary for the killing, taking or destruction on specified land of specified animals[2] or birds[3], or the eggs of specified birds, if it appears expedient to do so for the purpose of preventing damage to crops, pasture, animal or human foodstuffs, livestock, trees, hedges, banks or any works on land[4]. Failure to comply with such a requirement is an offence[5], and steps may be taken to secure compliance[6]. The Secretary of State and the Welsh Ministers cannot, however, require any killing, taking or destruction which would otherwise be prohibited by law[7], except in the case of game out of season[8], and cannot serve a notice requiring the destruction of rats and mice where the local authority has power[9] to require the necessary steps to be taken[10].

Poisonous gas may be used in holes, burrows and earths for the purpose of killing the animals in question[11] (although, if other animals are prescribed, the regulations specifying them may exclude this power[12]). A licence permitting the use of a spring trap for killing or taking hares or rabbits elsewhere than in a rabbit hole[13] may be embodied in a notice of the kind described above[14].

The Secretary of State and the Welsh Ministers may, with the approval of the Treasury[15], contribute towards the expenses incurred or to be incurred by any person in killing, taking or destroying the animals, birds or eggs in question[16], and may supply services, equipment, appliances and other material for these purposes and make reasonable charges for such assistance[17].

1   As to the Secretary of State and the Welsh Ministers see PARA 390.
2   The animals are rabbits, hares and other rodents, deer, foxes, moles and such other animals as may be prescribed by regulations made by the Secretary of State or the Welsh Ministers: Agriculture Act 1947 s 98(4). At the date at which this volume states the law no such regulations were in force. The Secretary of State and the Welsh Ministers may also give such directions as appear expedient authorising the keeping and disposal of such animals as may be killed or taken: s 100(3).
    For further provisions relating to the control of rabbits see PARAS **117–118**. See also the Forestry Act 1967 s 7; and FORESTRY vol 52 (2014) PARA 63. By the Pests Act 1954 s 1(6), the making of a rabbit clearance order under that Act (see PARA **118**) does not prevent the giving, in relation to land in the rabbit clearance area designated by the order, of notices under the Agriculture Act 1947 s 98; and as respects rabbits a notice may be given under s 98 to the occupier of any such land, whether or not he has the right apart from the notice, to take the steps required by it. For further provisions relating to the control of rats and mice see the Prevention of Damage by Pests Act 1949; and ENVIRONMENTAL QUALITY AND PUBLIC HEALTH vol 46 (2010) PARAS 873–876. See also the Forestry Act 1967 s 7; and FORESTRY vol 52 (2014) PARA 63.
3   The birds which may be specified in such a notice comprise all wild birds, save those which are protected in the area to which the notice relates by virtue of the Wildlife and Countryside Act 1981 Sch 1 (see ANIMALS vol 2 (2017) PARA 325), as it applies in relation to any area whether by virtue of the terms thereof or by virtue of an order of the Secretary of State or the Welsh Ministers, and such other birds as may be prescribed by regulations made by the Secretary of State or the Welsh Ministers: Agriculture Act 1947 s 98(4) (amended by the Protection of Birds Act 1954 Sch 5 para 1). At the date at which this volume states the law no such regulations were in force. The Secretary of State and the Welsh Ministers may also give such directions as appear expedient authorising the keeping and disposal of such birds or eggs as may be killed or taken: Agriculture Act 1947 s 100(3).
4   Agriculture Act 1947 s 98(1). Any notice or other document required or authorised by or under the Agriculture Act 1947 to be given to or served on any person is duly given or served if it is delivered to him, or left at his proper address, or sent to him by post in a registered letter, and any such document required or authorised to be given to or served on an incorporated company or body is duly given or served if given to or served on the secretary or clerk of the company or body: s 107(1), (2). For these purposes the proper address of any person to or on whom any such document is to be given or served is, in the case of the secretary or clerk of any incorporated company or body, that of the registered or principal office of the company or body, and in any other case is the last known address of the person in question: s 107(3). Where any document is to be given to or served on a person as being the person having any interest in land, and it is not practicable after reasonable inquiry to ascertain his name or address, the document may be given or served by addressing it to him by the description of the person having that interest in the land (naming it), and delivering the document to some responsible person on the land or by affixing it, or a copy of it, to some conspicuous object on the land: s 107(4). Where any such document or notice is to be given or served on any person as being the owner of the land and the land is vested in the incumbent of a benefice of the Church of England, a copy must be served on the Diocesan Board of Finance for the diocese in which the land is situated: s 107(5) (amended by the Church of England (Miscellaneous Provisions) Measure 2006 s 14, Sch 5 para 2). In the case of land used for agriculture a notice under the Agriculture Act 1947 s 98 may be served upon an agent or servant of the occupier where the agent or servant is responsible for the control of the farming of the land: s 100(6). As to the meaning of 'agriculture' for these purposes see PARA 10. For the purpose of enabling them to perform their functions under s 98 the Secretary of State and the Welsh Ministers may require any person who is the occupier of land, or who appears to have an interest in land, or who receives rent in respect of land, to state in writing the nature of his own interest in the land, and the name and address of any other person known to him as having an interest in it or as having the right to kill on the land any animals or birds to which s 98 applies; and any person who, having been required to give such information, fails to give it or knowingly makes any misstatement is liable on summary conviction to a fine not exceeding level 1 on the standard scale: Pests Act 1954 s 4(1), (2) (s 4(2) amended by virtue of the Criminal Justice Act 1982 ss 38, 46). As to the standard scale and the powers of magistrates' courts to issue fines on summary conviction see SENTENCING vol 92 (2015) PARA 176.

5 Agriculture Act 1947 s 100(1). A person who commits an offence under s 98 or s 99 (see PARA 119) is liable on summary conviction to a maximum fine of level 2 on the standard scale, and to a further maximum fine of £5 for each day after conviction on which the failure continues: s 100(1) (amended by the Criminal Justice Act 1982 s 46).

6 The Secretary of State and the Welsh Ministers may authorise a person to enter the land at any time to secure compliance with any requirements under the Agriculture Act 1947 s 98 or s 99 (see PARA 119), and may recover the reasonable cost of so doing: s 100(2). Any person who obstructs a person exercising these powers is liable on summary conviction to a fine not exceeding level 2 on the standard scale: s 106(7) (amended by the Pests Act 1954 s 5(1); and by virtue of the Criminal Justice Act 1982 s 46). For provisions as to entry and inspection generally see PARA 392. In the event of dispute, costs are to be determined by the arbitration of an arbitrator appointed in default of agreement by the President of the Royal Institution of Chartered Surveyors: Agriculture Act 1947 s 100(2). As to the Royal Institution of Chartered Surveyors generally see BUILDING CONTRACTS vol 6 (2011) PARA 490. If a person alleges that the cost of complying with the requirements of the Secretary of State or the Welsh Ministers ought to have been borne wholly or in part by some other person having an interest in the land, he may apply to the court for such indemnity as it may consider just and equitable: s 100(5).

7 Agriculture Act 1947 s 98(2). As to the protection of animals in law see generally ANIMALS. The stalking or flushing out of a wild mammal for the purpose of preventing or reducing serious damage which the wild mammal would otherwise cause to livestock, food for livestock, crops, vegetables, fruit or other property is, subject to conditions relating to the means of stalking or flushing out, 'exempt hunting' for the purposes of the Hunting Act 2004: see s 2(1), Sch 1 para 1(1), (2)(a)(i), (iii), (iv), (vii), (4)–(7); and ANIMALS vol 2 (2017) PARAS 325–371.

8 Agriculture Act 1947 s 98(2) proviso.

9 Ie under the Prevention of Damage by Pests Act 1949 s 4 (see ENVIRONMENTAL QUALITY AND PUBLIC HEALTH vol 46 (2010) PARA 875).

10 Prevention of Damage by Pests Act 1949 s 20(1). See, however, note 17.

11 A person is not guilty of an offence under the Protection of Animals Act 1911 s 8 (see ANIMALS vol 2 (2017) PARA 161) by reason only that he uses poisonous gas in a rabbit hole, or places in a rabbit hole a substance which, by evaporation or in contact with moisture, generates poisonous gas: Prevention of Damage by Rabbits Act 1939 s 4; Agriculture Act 1947 s 98(3).

12 Agriculture Act 1947 s 98(4) (proviso).

13 Such a licence may be granted under the Pests Act 1954 s 9(3) (see ANIMALS vol 2 (2017) PARA 364).

14 Pests Act 1954 s 9(4)(a).

15 As to the Treasury see CONSTITUTIONAL AND ADMINISTRATIVE LAW vol 20 (2014) PARA 263 et seq.

16 Pests Act 1954 s 3(1).

17 Agriculture Act 1947 s 101(1), (2). The powers of the Secretary of State and the Welsh Ministers of giving and charging for assistance under s 101 may be exercised in relation to the destruction of rats and mice notwithstanding the restriction on serving notice requiring such steps to be taken for that purpose: Prevention of Damage by Pests Act 1949 s 20(1). The Secretary of State and the Welsh Ministers may also render assistance in the prevention or treatment of any infestation of food by rats, mice, insects or mites: see ss 20(2), 28(1).

117. Further powers concerning rabbits.

In addition to their power to serve notice requiring the taking of certain measures against specified wild animals and birds[1] the Secretary of State and the Welsh Ministers[2] have power, where it appears expedient for preventing damage by rabbits to crops, pasture, trees, hedges, banks or any works on land, to serve notice on the occupier (or, in the case of unoccupied land, the person entitled to occupy it) requiring him to take on the land, within the time specified in the notice, such steps as may be specified to destroy or reduce the breeding places or cover for rabbits, or to exclude rabbits therefrom, or to prevent the rabbits living in any place on the land from spreading to or doing damage in any other place[3]. Failure to comply with such a requirement is an offence[4], and steps may be taken to secure compliance[5].

The Secretary of State and the Welsh Ministers may also, with the approval of the Treasury[6], contribute towards the expenses incurred or to be incurred by any person in destroying or reducing breeding places or cover for rabbits or in excluding rabbits therefrom, or in preventing the rabbits living in any place from spreading to or doing damage in any other place[7], and may supply services, equipment, appliances and other material for these purposes and may make reasonable charges for such assistance[8].

1　See PARA 116.

2　As to the Secretary of State and the Welsh Ministers see PARA 390.

3　Agriculture Act 1947 s 98(7) (added by the Pests Act 1954 s 2(1)). As to the service of notices see PARA 116 note 4. Every such notice must specify a time within which the occupier or any person interested in the land may submit to the Secretary of State or the Welsh Ministers written objections to the notice, and is to be provisional only and of no effect unless confirmed after the expiration of that time by a further notice served on the occupier; and, where the occupier holds the land under a contract of tenancy, a copy of any notice is to be served on any person to whom the occupier pays rent under the tenancy: Agriculture Act 1947 s 98(7) (as so added). A provisional notice may be confirmed either without modifications or with such modifications as appear to the Secretary of State or the Welsh Ministers desirable having regard to any objections submitted to him or them: s 98(7) (as so added).

　　The Secretary of State and the Welsh Ministers may also give such directions as appear expedient authorising the keeping and disposal of such animals as may be killed or taken for these purposes: s 100(3).

4　See the Agriculture Act 1947 s 100(1); and PARA 116.

5　See the Agriculture Act 1947 s 100(2); and PARA 116.

6　As to the Treasury see CONSTITUTIONAL AND ADMINISTRATIVE LAW vol 20 (2014) PARA 263 et seq.

7　Pests Act 1954 s 3(1).

8　Agriculture Act 1947 s 101(1), (2); Pests Act 1954 s 2(2).

118. Rabbit clearance areas and rabbit clearance orders.

The Secretary of State and the Welsh Ministers[1] have power to make rabbit clearance orders designating areas as 'rabbit clearance areas' to be freed, so far as practicable, of wild rabbits, and providing for or regulating the steps to be taken for that purpose[2]. The occupier[3] of any land in a rabbit clearance area must take such steps as may from time to time be necessary for the killing or taking of wild rabbits living on or resorting to the land[4] and, where it is not reasonably practicable to destroy the rabbits living on any part of the land, for the prevention of damage by those rabbits, and must in particular comply with any directions contained in the rabbit clearance order as to the steps to be so taken or as to the time for taking them[5]. Failure to comply with the requirements of a rabbit clearance order is an offence[6], and steps may be taken to secure compliance[7]. Any person authorised by the Secretary of State or the Welsh Ministers may at all reasonable times enter on and inspect land for the purpose of determining whether, and if so in what manner, these powers are to be exercised in relation to the land or whether, and if so in what manner, any requirement imposed under these provisions has been complied with[8].

1　As to the Secretary of State and the Welsh Ministers see PARA 390.

2　Pests Act 1954 s 1(1). Rabbit clearance orders are not made by statutory instrument and are not recorded in this work. The Secretary of State and the Welsh Ministers may vary or revoke a rabbit clearance order: s 1(1). An order is to be published in such manner as the Secretary of State thinks or the Welsh Ministers think fit, and the Secretary of State or the Welsh Ministers must take reasonable steps to bring an order to the notice of persons likely to be affected and to enable them to purchase copies: s 1(10). Before making an order the Secretary of State or the Welsh Ministers:

(1)   must (unless satisfied that to do so would be unreasonable in the circumstances) consult persons representative of the interests in the area concerned of farmers, owners of agricultural land, and workers employed in agriculture and of the forestry interests, if any, in the area, and

(2)   must give notice of the proposal in such a manner as he thinks or they think reasonable for the purpose of informing the persons interested in land in the area: s 1(11).

The requirement in head (1) does not apply to an order which applies only in relation to England: s 1(11A) (added by the Deregulation Act 2015 Sch 22 para 2). Any such notice must indicate the nature of any directions proposed to be included in the order and must specify a time (not being less than 14 days) within which persons interested in land in the area concerned may make representations to the Secretary of State or the Welsh Ministers, and any order may give effect to the proposals either without modifications or with such modifications as appear desirable having regard to such representations: Pests Act 1954 s 1(12). As to the giving of notices under the Agriculture Act 1947 s 98 in relation to land in rabbit clearance areas see the Pests Act 1954 s 1(6); and PARA **116** note 2.

3   In relation to unoccupied land 'occupier' means the person entitled to occupy the land: Pests Act 1954 s 1(13). In the case of land used for agriculture notice may be served upon an agent or servant of the occupier where the agent or servant is responsible for the control of the farming of the land: Agriculture Act 1947 s 100(6); Pests Act 1954 s 1(9). As to the service of notices see PARA **116** note 4.

4   A person who is duly authorised by the occupier of land in a rabbit clearance area to kill or take rabbits for the purpose of complying with any requirement imposed pursuant to a rabbit clearance order, and who acts in accordance with that authorisation, does not thereby commit an offence under any enactment relating to the unlawful destruction or pursuit of game: s 1(7). The Secretary of State and the Welsh Ministers may also give such directions as appear expedient authorising the keeping and disposal of such rabbits as may be killed or taken: Agriculture Act 1947 s 100(3).

     A licence permitting the use of a spring trap for killing or taking hares or rabbits elsewhere than in a rabbit hole (which may be granted under the Pests Act 1954 s 9(3): see ANIMALS VOL 2 (2017) PARA 364) may be embodied in a rabbit clearance order: s 9(4)(a).

5   Pests Act 1954 s 1(2). Nothing in s 1(1) (see the text and notes 1–2) or s 1(2), or in any order thereunder, confers on the occupier any additional right to authorise persons to kill rabbits on the land with firearms: s 1(3). However, the Secretary of State and the Welsh Ministers may, on the occupier's application, sanction the authorisation by the occupier of a reasonable number of persons to kill rabbits on the land with firearms, in addition to any person so authorised under the Ground Game Act 1880 s 1 (see ANIMALS VOL 2 (2017) PARA 73), if satisfied that the circumstances necessitate a greater use of firearms than the occupier can authorise, that the occupier has attempted to obtain the sanction of the persons having, apart from the Ground Game Act 1880, the right to kill and take rabbits on the land, and that their sanction has been unreasonably withheld: Pests Act 1954 s 1(4). Persons having the right to kill or take rabbits on any land are not treated as having unreasonably withheld the sanction for these purposes if, in so far as the use of firearms is required, they are themselves taking or proposing to take adequate steps for the destruction of the wild rabbits on the land: s 1(5). The Ground Game Act 1880 s 1 applies for these purposes: Pests Act 1954 s 1(4).

6   Agriculture Act 1947 s 100(1). A person who commits such an offence is liable on summary conviction to a maximum fine of level 2 on the standard scale, and to a further maximum fine of £5 for each day after conviction on which the failure continues: Agriculture Act 1947 s 100(1) (amended by the Criminal Justice Act 1982 s 46). As to the standard scale and the powers of magistrates' courts to issue fines on summary conviction see SENTENCING VOL 92 (2015) PARA 176.

7   The Secretary of State and the Welsh Ministers may authorise a person to enter the land at any time to secure compliance with any requirements of a rabbit clearance order, and may recover the reasonable cost of so doing: Agriculture Act 1947 s 100(2). Any person who obstructs a person exercising these powers is liable on summary conviction to a fine not exceeding level 2 on the standard scale: Agriculture Act 1947 s 106(7) (amended by the Pests Act 1954 s 5(1); and by virtue of the Criminal Justice Act 1982 s 46). For provisions as to entry and inspection generally see PARA 392. In the event of dispute, costs are to be determined by the arbitration of an arbitrator appointed in default of agreement by the President of the Royal Institution of Chartered Surveyors: Agriculture Act 1947 s 100(2). As to the Royal Institution of Chartered Surveyors generally see BUILDING CONTRACTS VOL 6 (2011) PARA 490. If a person alleges that the cost of complying with the requirements of the Secretary of State or the Welsh Ministers ought to have been borne wholly

or in part by some other person having an interest in the land, he may apply to the court for such indemnity as it may consider just and equitable: s 100(5).

8   Pests Act 1954 s 1(8).

(ii) Captive Animals

119.   Prevention of escape of captive animals.

If it appears to the Secretary of State or the Welsh Ministers[1] expedient to do so in order to prevent damage to crops, pasture, animal or human foodstuffs, livestock, trees, hedges, banks or any works on land, he or they may serve written notice on the occupier of any land requiring him to take the necessary steps to prevent the escape from captivity of any animals which are kept there[2]. Failure to comply with such a requirement is an offence[3], and steps may be taken to secure compliance[4].

1   As to the Secretary of State and the Welsh Ministers see PARA 390.
2   Agriculture Act 1947 s 99. As to the service of notices see PARA 116 note 4. In the case of land used for agriculture the notice may be served upon an agent or servant of the occupier where the agent or servant is responsible for the control and farming of the land: s 100(6). As to the meaning of 'agriculture' for these purposes see PARA 10.
3   See the Agriculture Act 1947 s 100(1); and PARA 116.
4   See the Agriculture Act 1947 s 100(2); and PARA 116.

(iii) Destructive Imported Animals and Species

120.   Prevention of importation and keeping of destructive animals.

If at any time the Secretary of State is, or the Welsh Ministers[1] are, satisfied with respect to animals of any non-indigenous mammalian species[2] that by reason of their destructive habits it is desirable to prohibit or control their importation[3] or keeping, and to destroy any which may be at large or keep under review whether any which may be at large should be destroyed, he or they may prohibit by order[4], either absolutely or except under licence[5], the importation into and the keeping within Great Britain of any animals of that species[6]. Pursuant to this power, the importation and keeping of musk rats[7], grey squirrels[8] and non-indigenous rabbits[9], and the keeping (but not the importation) of coypus[10], and the keeping of mink[11] are prohibited[12].

The importation, or attempted importation, into Great Britain of any destructive animal, the importation or keeping of which is absolutely prohibited, or the importation, attempted importation or keeping of any destructive animal without a licence at a time when a licence is required for such importation or keeping, is an offence[13].

Compensation may be payable to a person keeping any such animal whose custody is subsequently absolutely prohibited under these provisions[14].

1   As to the Secretary of State and the Welsh Ministers see PARA 390.
2   'Non-indigenous mammalian species' means a mammalian species which on 17 March 1932 (ie the date of the commencement of the Destructive Imported Animals Act 1932) was not established in a wild state in Great Britain, or had only become so established during the preceding 50 years, other than any species which was on that date commonly kept in Great Britain in a domesticated state: s 10(2). As to the meaning of 'Great Britain' see PARA 1 note 1.
3   References to the importation into Great Britain do not include a reference to importation from a member state: Destructive Imported Animals Act 1932 s 11(2) (added by SI 1992/3302). As to the control of the introduction of new species of animals into Great Britain see further the Wildlife and Countryside Act 1981 s 14; and ANIMALS vol 2 (2017) PARA 280. The importation of animals

may also be controlled for the purpose of preventing the introduction of disease: see the Animal Health Act 1981 s 10; and ANIMALS vol 2 (2017) PARAS 413–417.

4   An order under the Destructive Imported Animals Act 1932 s 1(1) may prohibit absolutely the importation of musk rats notwithstanding that the keeping of them is not prohibited absolutely: s 1(1) (proviso). Where the Destructive Imported Animals Act 1932 is applied to animals other than musk rats, its provisions apply subject to such exceptions and other modifications, if any, as may be specified in the relevant order: s 10(1).

5   Licences are granted under the Destructive Imported Animals Act 1932 ss 2, 3: see PARA 121.

6   Destructive Imported Animals Act 1932 ss 1(1), 10(1) (s 10(1) amended by the Deregulation Act 2015 Sch 13 para 1(2), (2)). The power in the Destructive Imported Animals Act 1932 s 10(1) (like the power in s 1(1)) includes power to revoke or amend an order made under that provision: s 10(1A) (added by the Deregulation Act 2015 Sch 13 para 1(1), (3)).

7   Ie animals of the species designated *fiber zibethicus* or *ondatra zibethica* and commonly known as the musk rat or musquash: see the Musk Rats (Prohibition of Importation and Keeping) Order 1933, SR & O 1933/106.

8   Ie animals of the species designated *sciurus carolinensis* and commonly known as the grey squirrel: see the Grey Squirrels (Prohibition of Importation and Keeping) Order 1937, SR & O 1937/478.

9   Ie rabbits other than the species designated *oryctolagus cuniculus* (European rabbit): see the Non-Indigenous Rabbits (Prohibition of Importation and Keeping) Order 1954, SI 1954/927.

10 Ie animals of the species designated *myocastor coypus*: see the Coypus (Prohibition on Keeping) Order 1987, SI 1987/2195.

11 Ie animals of the species designated *mustela vison*.

12 See the Mink Keeping (Prohibition) (England) Order 2004, SI 2004/100; and the Mink Keeping (Prohibition) (Wales) Order 2012, SI 2012/1427.

13 Destructive Imported Animals Act 1932 ss 6(1)(a), (b), 10(1). The offender is liable on summary conviction to a penalty of level 2 on the standard scale, or, if the offence was committed in respect of more than four animals, to a penalty of level 1 on the standard scale in respect of each animal: s 6(1) (amended by the Criminal Law Act 1977 s 31(6); and by virtue of the Criminal Justice Act 1982 s 46). As to the standard scale and the powers of magistrates' courts to issue fines on summary conviction see SENTENCING vol 92 (2015) PARA 176. The court has power in the case of a conviction for these offences to order the forfeiture and destruction of the animals concerned in the offence: Destructive Imported Animals Act 1932 s 6(1). Where an officer of police or any person duly authorised by the Secretary of State or the Welsh Ministers has reason to believe that an offence under s 6(1)(a) has been committed, he may seize the animals concerned and detain them pending the determination of proceedings or until the Secretary of State is or the Welsh Ministers are satisfied that no proceedings are likely to be instituted: ss 6(2), 11(1) (s 11(1) renumbered by SI 1992/3302). The obstruction of authorised officers or of persons authorised by or employed by or on behalf of the Secretary of State or the Welsh Ministers in the execution of their duty is an offence punishable on summary conviction by a penalty of level 2 on the standard scale: Destructive Imported Animals Act 1932 s 6(1)(e).

    Proceedings in England and Wales for an offence under s 6 may be brought within the period of six months beginning with the date on which evidence sufficient in the opinion of the prosecutor to warrant the proceedings came to his knowledge (s 6(3) (s 6(3)–(6) added by the Natural Environment and Rural Communities Act 2006 Sch 6 para 1)), although this does not authorise the commencement of proceedings for an offence more than two years after the date on which the offence was committed (Destructive Imported Animals Act 1932 s 6(4) (as so added)). For these purposes a certificate signed by or on behalf of the prosecutor and stating the date on which evidence sufficient in his opinion to warrant the proceedings came to his knowledge is conclusive evidence of that fact (s 6(5) (as so added)); and a certificate stating that matter and purporting to be so signed is to be deemed to be so signed unless the contrary is proved (s 6(6) (as so added)).

14 See PARA 123.

121. Regulations and licences for the importation and keeping of destructive animals.

The Secretary of State and the Welsh Ministers[1] may make regulations with respect to ports of importation, the form of containers for transport, the premises where the animals may be kept and establishing precautions against escape[2]. They may also prescribe forms and conditions of licences[3] and, with the approval of the Treasury[4], fees for the grant or renewal of licences[5]. Pursuant to these powers regulations have been made in connection with the keeping of mink[6]. The Secretary of State and the Welsh Ministers may grant or renew licences and revoke licences for breach of the terms thereof, or breach of any regulations, or following conviction for an offence[7]. Special licences may be granted, on application, to persons wishing to keep prohibited destructive animals for exhibition, scientific research or other exceptional purposes; these licences may authorise the importation and keeping of limited numbers of the animals and may be revoked at any time[8]. Regulations enabling the granting of special licences for the keeping of coypus have been made[9]. A licence holder who contravenes or fails to comply with any regulation or term of his licence commits an offence[10]. Certain powers of wildlife inspectors and constables are exercisable in relation to licences for the importation and keeping of destructive animals and related offences[11].

1 As to the Secretary of State and the Welsh Ministers see PARA 390.
2 Destructive Imported Animals Act 1932 ss 2(a), 10(1).
3 Destructive Imported Animals Act 1932 s 2(b).
4 As to the Treasury see CONSTITUTIONAL AND ADMINISTRATIVE LAW vol 20 (2014) PARA 263 et seq.
5 Destructive Imported Animals Act 1932 s 2(c).
6 See the Mink (Keeping) Regulations 1975, SI 1975/2223 (revoked in relation to England).
7 Destructive Imported Animals Act 1932 s 3.
8 Destructive Imported Animals Act 1932 s 8.
9 See the Coypus (Special Licence) (Fees) Regulations 1997, SI 1997/2751 (revoked in relation to Wales).
10 Destructive Imported Animals Act 1932 s 6(1)(c). A person who commits such an offence is liable on summary conviction to a penalty of level 1 on the standard scale, and to a further penalty of £2 for every day on which the offence continues after conviction: s 6(1) (amended by the Criminal Law Act 1977 s 31(8); the Decimal Currency Act 1969 s 10(1); and by virtue of the Criminal Justice Act 1982 s 46). Forfeiture and destruction of the animals concerned may be ordered by the court on a conviction for this offence: Destructive Imported Animals Act 1932 s 6(1). As to the bringing of proceedings see PARA 120 note 13. As to the standard scale and the powers of magistrates' courts to issue fines on summary conviction see SENTENCING vol 92 (2015) PARA 176.
11 See the Wildlife and Countryside Act 1981 ss 18A–18C, 18F, 19XB(1), (4), 19(3), 21(4AA)–(4C) (applied to licences and offences under the Destructive Imported Animals Act 1932 by the Natural Environment and Rural Communities Act 2006 s 52, Sch 5 paras 7, 8, 13); and ANIMALS vol 2 (2017) PARA 299 et seq.

122. Destruction of animals at large.
Turning loose or wilfully allowing the escape of prohibited destructive animals is an offence[1]. The occupier[2] of any land[3] who knows that any animals in respect of which a prohibition order is in force[4] are to be found on his land, not being either mink (in England) or any prohibited animals kept by him under a licence[5], must forthwith give notice to the Secretary of State or the Welsh Ministers[6]. As soon as the Secretary of State becomes, or the Welsh Ministers become, aware of the existence of prohibited animals on land (other than animals kept under a licence, but including for these purposes mink), he or they may take such steps as are considered necessary for the animals' destruction[7]; and the occupier must afford all such facilities as are in his power to any persons authorised in this matter[8].

1 Destructive Imported Animals Act 1932 ss 6(1)(d), 10(1). The offender is liable on summary conviction to a penalty of level 2 on the standard scale, or, if the offence was committed in respect of more than four animals, to a penalty of level 1 on the standard scale in respect of each animal: s 6(1) (amended by the Criminal Law Act 1977 s 31(6); and by virtue of the Criminal Justice Act

1982 s 46). As to the bringing of proceedings see PARA 120 note 13. As to the standard scale and the powers of magistrates' courts to issue fines on summary conviction see SENTENCING vol 92 (2015) PARA 176.

2   In the case of land not occupied by any tenant or other person 'occupier' means the owner of the land: Destructive Imported Animals Act 1932 s 11(1) (renumbered by SI 1992/3302).

3   'Land' includes land covered with water and any buildings and any other erection on land and any cellar, sewer, drain or culvert in or under land: Destructive Imported Animals Act 1932 s 11(1) (as renumbered: see note 2).

4   Ie an order prohibiting the importation and keeping of specified animals under the Destructive Imported Animals Act 1932 s 1 (see PARA 120). Orders have been made, specifying varying degrees of prohibition, in respect of musk rats, grey squirrels, non-indigenous rabbits, coypus, and mink: see PARA 120.

5   As to the licensing of the keeping of animals of prohibited species see PARA 121.

6   Destructive Imported Animals Act 1932 ss 5(1), (2), 11(1) (s 11(1) as renumbered: see note 2); Mink Keeping (Prohibition) (England) Order 2004, SI 2004/100, art 2(2)(a). As to the Secretary of State and the Welsh Ministers see PARA 390. Failure to give the notice required is an offence punishable on summary conviction by a fine of level 1 on the standard scale: Destructive Imported Animals Act 1932 s 6(1)(f); Mink Keeping (Prohibition) (England) Order 2004, SI 2004/100, art 2(2)(a).

7   Destructive Imported Animals Act 1932 s 5(3). No action for damages lies in respect of the killing or wounding of prohibited destructive animals found at large: s 5(5). Compensation may, however, be payable: see PARA 123.

8   Destructive Imported Animals Act 1932 s 5(3) (s 5(3) amended, and s 5(3A) added, by the Natural Environment and Rural Communities Act 2006 Sch 11 para 1). In relation to England and Wales an 'authorised person' for this purpose is a person authorised in writing by the appropriate department to exercise powers under the Destructive Imported Animals Act 1932 s 5(3): s 5(3A)(a) (as so added). As to the obstruction of officers see s 6(1)(e); and PARA 120 note 13.

123. Compensation.

Compensation is payable by the Secretary of State and the Welsh Ministers[1] in respect of pecuniary loss suffered by persons by reason of their being required, in consequence of the making of an order prohibiting absolutely the keeping of any destructive animal[2], to destroy animals kept for profit and in respect of the value of any structure or equipment which is rendered useless or of less utility by reason of such a prohibition[3].

1   As to the Secretary of State and the Welsh Ministers see PARA 390.

2   As to such orders see PARA 120.

3   See the Destructive Imported Animals Act 1932 ss 7, 10(1), 11(1) (s 11(1) renumbered by SI 1992/3302). Compensation is payable to persons keeping the relevant prohibited animal on the date of the order and must be claimed within three months of that date; accordingly, until such time as orders prohibiting further species are made under the Destructive Imported Animals Act 1932 s 10(1) (see PARA 120), these provisions must be considered to be of no continuing effect, since the orders prohibiting the keeping of musk rats, grey squirrels, non-indigenous rabbits and coypus have been in force since 1933, 1937, 1954 and 1987 respectively (see PARA 120 notes 7–10), and the orders prohibiting the keeping of mink (see PARA 120 notes 11–12) continue the effect of an order originally made in 1962 (ie the Mink (Importation and Keeping) Order 1962, SI 1962/1666 (revoked)).

(3) PREVENTION OF SPREAD OF INJURIOUS WEEDS

124. Occupier's duty.

Although at common law an occupier of land is under no duty to an adjoining occupier to cut thistles naturally growing on his land so as to prevent them seeding on the adjoining land[1], an occupier of land[2] may be required to take action to prevent the spread of spear thistle[3], creeping or field thistle[4], curled dock[5], broad-leaved dock[6], ragwort[7], and such additional weeds as the Secretary of State or the Welsh Ministers may by regulations prescribe[8]. If satisfied that there are injurious weeds of any of these kinds growing upon any land, the Secretary of State, the Welsh Ministers or an authorised local authority[9] may serve a written notice on the occupier[10] requiring him, within the time specified in the notice, to take such action as may be necessary to prevent the weeds from spreading[11].

A person who plants or otherwise causes to grow in the wild, or sells, offers or exposes for sale, or has in his possession or transports for the purposes of sale, certain plants, including Japanese knotweed, or hybrids of those plants, commits an offence[12].

1 *Giles v Walker* (1890) 24 QBD 656. Failure to do so can in some circumstances, however, constitute an actionable nuisance: *French v Auckland City Council* [1974] 1 NZLR 340.
2 In the case of any public road, 'occupier' means the authority by whom the road is being maintained, and in the case of unoccupied land it means the person entitled to the occupation thereof: Weeds Act 1959 s 11(2).
3 Ie *cirsium vulgare* (Savi) Ten.
4 Ie *cirsium arvense* (L) Scop.
5 Ie *rumex crispus* L.
6 Ie *rumex obtusifolius* L.
7 Ie *seneccio jacobaca* L. The Secretary of State and the Welsh Ministers may make, and revise, a code of practice for the purpose of providing guidance on how to prevent the spread of ragwort: Weeds Act 1959 s 1A(1), (4) (s 1A added by the Ragwort Control Act 2003 s 1). As to the Secretary of State and the Welsh Ministers see PARA 390. Before making or revising the code the Secretary of State and the Welsh Ministers must consult such persons as they consider appropriate: Weeds Act 1959 s 1A(2) (as so added). The code is admissible in evidence (s 1A(5) (as so added)); and is to be taken into account in determining any question arising in proceedings if it appears to the court to be relevant (s 1A(6) (as so added)).
8 Weeds Act 1959 s 1(1), (2). At the date at which this volume states the law no regulations had been made under s 1(1) specifying any such additional injurious weeds.
9 The Secretary of State and the Welsh Ministers may authorise the council of any county, county borough or metropolitan district to exercise on his or their behalf any of the powers (other than the power to make regulations) conferred by the Weeds Act 1959: s 5 (amended by the Local Government (Wales) Act 1994 Sch 16 para 15; the Local Government Act 1972 Sch 30; and the Local Government Act 1985 Sch 8 para 21). As to the counties and districts in England and their councils see LOCAL GOVERNMENT vol 69 (2009) PARA 22 et seq. As to local authorities in Wales see LOCAL GOVERNMENT vol 69 (2009) PARAS 22–23, 37 et seq.
10 Any notice required or authorised by the Weeds Act 1959 to be served on any person is duly served if it is delivered to him, or left at his proper address, or sent to him by post in a registered letter, and any such notice required or authorised to be served on an incorporated company or body is duly served if served on the secretary or clerk of the company or body: s 6(1), (2). The proper address of any person on whom any such notice is to be served is, in the case of the secretary or clerk of any incorporated company or body, that of the registered or principal office of the company or body, and in any other case is the last known address of the person in question: s 6(3). Where any such notice is to be served on a person as being the person having any interest in land, and it is not practicable after reasonable inquiry to ascertain his name or address, the notice may be served by addressing it to him by the description of the person having that interest in the land (naming it), and delivering the notice to some responsible person on the land or by affixing it, or a copy of it, to some conspicuous object on the land: s 6(4). Where any such notice is to be served on a tenant a copy thereof must be served on the landlord: s 6(5). Where any such notice is to be given or served on any person as being the owner of the land and the land is vested in the incumbent of a benefice of the Church of England, a copy must be served on the Diocesan Board of Finance for the diocese in which the land is situated: s 6(6) (amended by the Church of England (Miscellaneous Provisions) Measure 2006 s 14, Sch 5 para 7).
11 Weeds Act 1959 s 1(1).
12 See the Wildlife and Countryside Act 1961 ss 14, 14ZA, Sch 9 Pt II; and OPEN SPACES AND COUNTRYSIDE vol 78 (2010) PARA 712A.

125. Penalty for non-compliance and default powers.

An occupier of land[1] who unreasonably fails to comply with a notice to take action to prevent the spread of injurious weeds[2] commits an offence[3]. Where such a notice has been served on the occupier of land and he has not taken the action required within the time specified in the notice, the Secretary of State or the Welsh Ministers may take that action and recover the reasonable cost of so doing from the occupier or, if it is not practicable after reasonable inquiry to ascertain his name or address and he is not the owner[4], from the owner[5].

1   As to the meaning of 'occupier' see PARA 124 note 2.
2   Ie a notice served under the Weeds Act 1959 s 1: see PARA 124.
3   Weeds Act 1959 s 2(1). The offender is liable on summary conviction to a fine not exceeding level 2 on the standard scale: s 2(1) (amended by virtue of the Criminal Justice Act 1982 ss 35, 37, 38). As to the standard scale and the powers of magistrates' courts to issue fines on summary conviction see SENTENCING vol 92 (2015) PARA 176. If such a failure in respect of which a person is convicted is not remedied within 14 days after the conviction, he is guilty of a further offence and may be punished accordingly: Weeds Act 1959 s 2(2). Proceedings for an offence under s 2(1) may only be instituted by the Secretary of State or the Welsh Ministers: s 2(3). As to the Secretary of State and the Welsh Ministers see PARA 390. For the power of the Secretary of State and the Welsh Ministers to delegate their powers to local authorities see PARA 124 note 9.
4   'Owner' includes a person entitled for a term of years certain or other limited estate: Weeds Act 1959 s 11(2).
5   Weeds Act 1959 s 3(1). Where the Secretary of State is or the Welsh Ministers are unable after reasonable inquiry to ascertain the name and address of the owner, he or they may apply to the High Court (or, if the sum involved does not exceed the county court limit, the county court) for an order imposing on the land a charge for securing the payment of the sum he is or they are entitled to recover from the owner: s 3(2). Such a charge is a local land charge: s 3(3) (amended by the Local Land Charges Act 1975 Sch 2). As to the county court limit see COURTS AND TRIBUNALS vol 24 (2010) PARA 767. As to local land charges see REAL PROPERTY AND REGISTRATION vol 87 (2017) PARA 706 et seq.
    Where, by reason of the default of the occupier, the owner of any land has been required to pay any sum to the Secretary of State or the Welsh Ministers or has, by reason of such a charge, otherwise suffered loss he is entitled to recover the amount of his loss from the occupier: s 3(4).

126.   Entry and inspection.

Any person authorised by the Secretary of State, the Welsh Ministers[1] or an authorised local authority[2] may, on the production, if required, of his authority, enter on and inspect any land for the purpose of carrying into effect the statutory provisions for the prevention of the spread of injurious weeds[3]. Entry and inspection may be carried out only after service on the occupier[4] of notice of the date when the inspection is to take place[5]. Any person preventing or obstructing such entry commits an offence[6].

1   As to the Secretary of State and the Welsh Ministers see PARA 390.
2   For the power of the Secretary of State and the Welsh Ministers to delegate their powers to local authorities see PARA 124 note 9. Where a local authority is accordingly authorised to discharge the functions of the Secretary of State or the Welsh Ministers under these provisions, its authorisation extends only in relation to land in its area: Weeds Act 1959 s 5 (amended by the Local Government (Wales) Act 1994 Sch 16 para 15; the Local Government Act 1972 Sch 30; and the Local Government Act 1985 Sch 8 para 21).
3   Weeds Act 1959 s 4(1). The statutory provisions for the prevention of the spread of injurious weeds are those contained in the Weeds Act 1959: see PARAS 124–125.
4   As to the meaning of 'occupier' see PARA 124 note 2.
5   Weeds Act 1959 s 4(1).
6   Weeds Act 1959 s 4(2). A person who commits such an offence is liable on summary conviction to a fine not exceeding level 3 on the standard scale: s 4(2) (amended by virtue of the Criminal Justice Act 1982 ss 38, 46). As to the standard scale and the powers of magistrates' courts to issue fines on summary conviction see SENTENCING vol 92 (2015) PARA 176.

(4) PROTECTION OF WILD PLANTS

127. Restrictions on the sale etc of wild plants.
It is an offence to deliberately pick, collect, cut, uproot or destroy certain wild plants unless done in accordance with the terms of a licence[1] and to plant or otherwise grow in the wild certain plants[2]. It is also an offence to sell certain plants[3].

1 See OPEN SPACES AND COUNTRYSIDE vol 78 (2010) PARAS 712, 713.
2 See OPEN SPACES AND COUNTRYSIDE vol 78 (2010) PARA 712A.
3 See OPEN SPACES AND COUNTRYSIDE vol 78 (2010) PARA 712B.

(5) PREVENTION OF CROSS-POLLINATION

128. Prevention of injurious cross-pollination affecting seed crops.
For the purpose of maintaining the purity of seed of any types and varieties of plants of any species of the genus *Allium, Beta* or *Brassica*[1], the Secretary of State and the Welsh Ministers[2] may serve on the occupier of land[3] on which controlled crops or plants are growing[4] a notice requiring him to take specified steps to prevent injurious cross-pollination in the protected crop[5]. Such notices may be served only on an application to the Secretary of State or the Welsh Ministers[6], who must be satisfied that the controlled crops or plants are causing or may cause injurious cross-pollination in a protected crop being grown in the area[7] and, in the case of controlled crops or plants which are not self-sown, that the grower did not give the persons responsible for the arrangements for isolation of their crops such notice of his intention to grow the crops or plants to the flowering stage as would have enabled them to take any appropriate steps to alter the arrangements[8]. On failure to comply with such a notice, the Secretary of State or the Welsh Ministers may enter and do what that person has failed to do, or take other appropriate action[9]. Unreasonable failure to comply with a notice is an offence[10].

These powers are not of general application. They may be brought into force by order of the Secretary of State or the Welsh Ministers in an area where crops of seeds of any types or varieties of plants of any species of the genus *Allium, Beta* or *Brassica* are being grown if the Secretary of State is or the Welsh Ministers are satisfied that in that area satisfactory arrangements have been made for locating such crops so as to isolate them from crops or plants which might cause injurious cross-pollination[11].

1 Plant Varieties and Seeds Act 1964 s 33(1).
2 As to the Secretary of State and the Welsh Ministers see PARA 390.
3 'Occupier' means, in the case of unoccupied land, the person entitled to occupy the land: Plant Varieties and Seeds Act 1964 s 33(11).
4 'Controlled crops or plants' are crops, grown for any purpose, of the types or varieties of plants which are protected by the order in the relevant area (see the text and note 11), and such additional kinds of crops or plants, whether grown or self-sown and whether of those or any other types or varieties, as may be specified in the order for these purposes in that area: Plant Varieties and Seeds Act 1964 s 33(4)(ii). A person duly authorised by the Secretary of State or the Welsh Ministers may, on production if so required of his authority, at all reasonable hours enter on any land (but not into any dwelling house) in an area where these provisions are in force (see the text and note 11) for the purpose of ascertaining whether controlled crops or plants are growing on the land or of inspecting and taking samples of any controlled crops or plants growing on the land: s 33(8). A person who obstructs or impedes a person acting in the exercise of these powers or those conferred by s 33(6) (see the text and note 9) is liable on summary conviction to a fine not exceeding level 1 on the standard scale: s 33(10) (amended by virtue of the Criminal Justice Act

1982 ss 38, 46). As to the standard scale and the powers of magistrates' courts to issue fines on summary conviction see SENTENCING vol 92 (2015) PARA 176.
5 Plant Varieties and Seeds Act 1964 s 33(5). 'Protected crop' means a crop of a type or a variety of plant which is protected by the order in the relevant area (see the text and note 11), being a crop grown to produce seeds: s 33(4)(i). A notice under s 33 or Sch 7 (see the text and note 6) may be served by leaving it at, or sending it by post addressed to, the last known address of the person on whom it is to be served, and if it is not practicable after reasonable inquiry to ascertain his name and address, the notice may be served by addressing it to him as the 'occupier' of the land and affixing it or a copy of it to some conspicuous object on the land: s 33(9).
6 An application seeking the issue of such a notice must be made in accordance with the Plant Varieties and Seeds Act 1964 Sch 7, which provides for notifying the occupier and affording the applicant and the occupier an opportunity to make representations, and specifies the matters which the Secretary of State or the Welsh Ministers must consider.
7 Plant Varieties and Seeds Act 1964 s 33(5)(a).
8 Plant Varieties and Seeds Act 1964 s 33(5)(b).
9 If the person served with a notice under the Plant Varieties and Seeds Act 1964 s 33 does not comply with any requirement in the notice, the Secretary of State or the Welsh Ministers may enter and do what that person has failed to do or, if in the opinion of the Secretary of State or the Welsh Ministers that would no longer serve the purpose for which the notice was served, may take such other action as appears appropriate for that purpose; and where, when the default occurs, further obligations remain under the notice, the Secretary of State or the Welsh Ministers may also take such action as appears appropriate to meet the purposes for which those further obligations were imposed: s 33(6). The Secretary of State and the Welsh Ministers may recover from the person on whom the notice was served a sum equal to the reasonable cost incurred in taking any such action: s 33(6). Obstructing an authorised person acting pursuant to s 33(6) is an offence: see note 4.
10 Plant Varieties and Seeds Act 1964 s 33(7). The offence is punishable on summary conviction with a fine not exceeding level 3 on the standard scale: s 33(7) (amended by virtue of the Criminal Justice Act 1982 ss 38, 46).
11 Plant Varieties and Seeds Act 1964 s 33(2). An order must be made after consultation with the persons responsible for the arrangements for locating the crops and persons representative of other interests concerned (s 33(3)(a)), and must state which types and varieties of plants are protected (s 33(4)(a)) and specify the kinds of crops and plants which are to be controlled (s 33(4)(b)). Orders may relate to more than one area and may make different provision for the different areas to which they relate: s 33(4)(c). Such orders, being of local application only, are not recorded in this work.

129. Prevention of injurious cross-pollination affecting hop plants.

For the purpose of facilitating the production of seedless hops in England[1], the Secretary of State[2] may serve on the occupier of land[3] on which any male hop plants are growing a notice requiring him to take, within such time as may be specified in the notice, such steps for the removal, treatment or destruction of those plants as may be so specified for the purpose of preventing those plants from becoming or remaining an actual or potential cause of pollination in female hop plants in the area[4]. On failure to comply with such a notice, the Secretary of State may enter and do what that person has failed to do, or take other appropriate action[5]. Unreasonable failure to comply is an offence[6].

These powers are not of general application, but may be brought into force by order of the Secretary of State in any area in England in which persons are engaged in growing hops where the Secretary of State is satisfied that it is reasonable to make such an order[7].

1 Agriculture (Miscellaneous Provisions) Act 1976 s 5(1). These provisions do not apply in Wales: see s 5(2).
2 As to the Secretary of State see PARA 390.
3 'Occupier' means, in the case of unoccupied land, the person entitled to occupy the land: Agriculture (Miscellaneous Provisions) Act 1976 s 5(6).
4 Agriculture (Miscellaneous Provisions) Act 1976 s 5(6). A notice under s 5 may be served by leaving it at, or sending it by post addressed to, the last known address of the person on whom it is to be served, and if it is not practicable after reasonable inquiry to ascertain his name and address, the notice may be served by addressing it to him as the 'occupier' of the land and affixing it or a copy of it to some conspicuous object on the land: s 5(10). If the person served with a notice

does not comply with any requirement in the notice, the Secretary of State may enter and do what that person has failed to do: s 5(7). The Secretary of State may recover from the person on whom the notice was served a sum equal to the reasonable cost incurred by him in taking any such action: s 5(7).

A person duly authorised by the Secretary of State may, on production if so required of his authority, at all reasonable hours enter on any land (but not into any dwelling house) in an area where these provisions are in force (see the text and note 7) for the purpose of ascertaining whether male hop plants are growing on the land: s 5(9).

A person who obstructs or impedes a person acting in the exercise of these powers is liable on summary conviction to a fine not exceeding level 3 on the standard scale: s 5(11) (amended by virtue of the Criminal Justice Act 1982 ss 38, 46). As to the standard scale and the powers of magistrates' courts to issue fines on summary conviction see SENTENCING vol 92 (2015) PARA 176.

5　See note 4.

6　Agriculture (Miscellaneous Provisions) Act 1976 s 5(8). The offence is punishable on summary conviction with a fine not exceeding level 3 on the standard scale: s 5(8) (amended by virtue of the Criminal Justice Act 1982 ss 38, 46).

7　Agriculture (Miscellaneous Provisions) Act 1976 s 5(2). An order must be made after consultation with such organisations as appear to the Secretary of State appropriate as representing persons carrying on in the area the business of producing hops (s 5(2)(a)) and with such persons as are known to him to be carrying on that business in the area (s 5(2)(b)), and may be varied or revoked by subsequent order, after consultation with such organisations and persons, if the Secretary of State is satisfied that it is reasonable to make such an order (s 5(3)(a), (b)).

Before making an order the Secretary of State must publish, in such manner as he considers appropriate for informing persons likely to be affected, a notice of his intention to do so, stating where a draft of the order may be inspected and copies obtained (s 5(4)(a)) and the time (not being less than 28 days from the publication of the notice) within which and the manner in which objections to the proposed order can be made (s 5(4)(b)). Before making the order the Secretary of State must consider any objections duly made, and, if he decides to make the order, may do so either in the form of the draft or with such modifications as he thinks fit: s 5(4). At the date at which this volume states the law no such orders had been made.

6. PESTICIDES AND PLANT PROTECTION PRODUCTS

(1) CONTROL AND REGULATION OF PESTICIDES ETC

130. Power to control pesticides and plant protection products.
Provision is made[1] with a view to the continuous development of means to protect the health of human beings, creatures[2] and plants[3], to safeguard the environment[4], and to secure safe, efficient and humane methods of controlling pests[5], and with a view to making information about pesticides[6] available to the public[7]. These provisions apply to any substance, preparation or organism prepared or used as if it were a pesticide for the purpose of:

(1)   protecting plants or wood or other plant products from harmful organisms[8];

(2)   regulating the growth of plants[9];

(3)   giving protection against harmful creatures[10];

(4)   rendering such creatures harmless[11];

(5)   controlling organisms with harmful or unwanted effects on water systems, buildings or other structures, or on manufactured products[12]; and

(6)   protecting plants against ectoparasites[13].

Provision is also made[14] restricting the marketing and use of a plant protection product, that is, a product, in the form in which it is supplied to the user, consisting of or containing active substances[15], safeners or synergists, and intended for one of the following uses:

(a)   protecting plants or plant products against all harmful organisms or preventing the action of such organisms, unless the main purpose of these products is considered to be for reasons of hygiene rather than for the protection of plants or plant products;

(b)   influencing the life processes of plants, such as substances influencing their growth, other than as a nutrient;

(c)   preserving plant products, in so far as such substances or products are not subject to special Community provisions on preservatives;

(d)   destroying undesired plants or parts of plants, except algae unless the products are applied on soil or water to protect plants; or

(e)   checking or preventing undesired growth of plants, except algae unless the products are applied on soil or water to protect plants[16].

Certain plant protection products that are pesticides are subject to further regulation[17].

1   Ie under the Food and Environment Protection Act 1985 Pt III (ss 16–19).
2   'Creature' means any living organism other than a human being or a plant: Food and Environment Protection Act 1985 s 24(1).
3   Food and Environment Protection Act 1985 s 16(1)(a)(i). 'Plants' means any form of vegetable matter, while it is growing and after it has been harvested, gathered, felled or picked, including in particular agricultural crops, trees and bushes grown for purposes other than those of agriculture, wild plants and fungi: s 24(1). As to the meaning of 'agricultural' see PARA 10. 'Crops' includes any form of vegetable produce: s 24(1).
4   Food and Environment Protection Act 1985 s 16(1)(a)(ii).
5   Food and Environment Protection Act 1985 s 16(1)(a)(iii). For these purposes 'pest' means:
      (1)   any organism harmful to plants or to wood or other plant products;
      (2)   any undesired plant; and
      (3)   any harmful creature: s 16(15).

6   'Pesticide' means any substance, preparation or organism prepared or used for destroying any pest: Food and Environment Protection Act 1985 s 16(15). Pesticides may be identified in any way: s 16(4).

7   Food and Environment Protection Act 1985 s 16(1)(b). For the power of the Secretary of State and the Welsh Ministers to regulate the manufacture and use of pesticides see PARA 131. As to the Secretary of State and the Welsh Ministers see PARA 390.

8   Food and Environment Protection Act 1985 s 16(16)(a).

9   Food and Environment Protection Act 1985 s 16(16)(b).

10   Food and Environment Protection Act 1985 s 16(16)(c).

11   Food and Environment Protection Act 1985 s 16(16)(d).

12   Food and Environment Protection Act 1985 s 16(16)(e).

13   Food and Environment Protection Act 1985 s 16(16)(f).

14   Ie under the Plant Protection Products Regulations 2011, SI 2011/2131: see PARA 132 et seq. These regulations implement European Parliament and Council Regulation (EC) 1107/2009 (OJ L309, 24.11.2009, p 1) concerning the placing of plant protection products on the market, which lays down rules for the authorisation of plant protection products in commercial form and for their placing on the market, use and control within the EU and rules for the approval of active substances, safeners and synergists, which plant protection products contain or consist of, and rules for adjuvants and co-formulant (arts 1.1, 1.2).

15   For definitions see European Parliament and Council Regulation (EC) 1107/2009 (OJ L309, 24.11.2009, p 1) art 3.

16   European Parliament and Council Regulation (EC) 1107/2009 (OJ L309, 24.11.2009, p 1) art 2.

17   Ie under the Plant Protection Products (Sustainable Use) Regulations 2012, SI 2012/1657: see PARAS 136–137. These regulations apply to pesticides that are plant protection products as defined in European Parliament and Council Regulation (EC) 1107/2009 (OJ L309, 24.11.2009, p 1) (see the text to and note 14) and implement European Parliament and Council Directive (EC) 2009/128 (OJ L309, 24.11.2009, p 71) establishing a framework for Community action to achieve the sustainable use of pesticides.

131.   Regulation of manufacture and use of pesticides.

The Secretary of State and the Welsh Ministers[1] may jointly by regulations[2]:

(1)   impose specified prohibitions[3] in relation to pesticides[4], but exclude from them pesticides of a description specified in the regulations[5];

(2)   provide that they may jointly give their approval[6], in relation to pesticides of a description specified in the regulations, to the doing of anything that would otherwise be prohibited by virtue of the specified prohibitions[7];

(3)   provide for the imposition of conditions on an approval when or after it is given[8];

(4)   provide for the giving of consent by the Secretary of State and the Welsh Ministers, or either of them, to the doing of anything contrary to a specified prohibition[9];

(5)   provide that such a consent may be given either with or without conditions[10];

(6)   provide for the review, revocation or suspension of an approval and the amendment of conditions imposed on an approval[11];

(7)   direct that, if there has been a breach, in relation to any pesticide, of any of the specified prohibitions or conditions imposed, the Secretary of State and the Welsh Ministers, and any local authority[12], will have the power to seize or dispose of the pesticide or anything treated with it or to require some other person to do so and to direct some other person to take such remedial action as appears to the Secretary of State, the Welsh Ministers or the local authority necessary as a result of the contravention[13];

(8) provide that if any pesticide has been imported in contravention of any specified prohibitions or conditions, either the Secretary of State or the Welsh Ministers may require its removal from the United Kingdom[14];

(9) provide for information[15] to be made available to the public[16];

(10) specify how much pesticide or pesticide residue[17] may be left in any crop[18], food[19] or feeding stuff[20]; and

(11) direct that, if there is more than the permitted pesticide or pesticide residue in any crop, food or feeding stuff, either the Secretary of State or the Welsh Ministers may seize or dispose of such crop, food or feeding stuff or require that some other person does so and direct that some other person takes such remedial action as appears to the Secretary of State or the Welsh Ministers to be necessary as a result of the contravention[21].

A person who without reasonable excuse contravenes, or causes or permits another person to contravene, any provision or requirement of any regulations, any condition of approval of a pesticide or any requirement imposed by virtue of regulations is guilty of an offence[22].

Provision as to the enforcement of the relevant regulations is also made[23].

1 As to the Secretary of State and the Welsh Ministers see PARA 390. For the power of the Secretary of State to require the provision of information necessary to the discharge of his functions under these provisions see PARA 140. As to the duty of the Secretary of State see *R (on the application of Downs) v Secretary of State for Environment, Food and Rural Affairs* [2009] EWCA Civ 664, [2009] 3 CMLR 1544, [2009] All ER (D) 71 (Jul).

2 The Secretary of State and the Welsh Ministers must consult the Food Standards Agency as to regulations which he or they contemplate making (Food and Environment Protection Act 1985 s 16(9A)(a) (s 16(9A) added by the Food Standards Act 1999 Sch 3 para 16(5))), and must consult the Health and Safety Executive when contemplating making regulations likely to affect the health or safety of persons at work (Food and Environment Protection Act 1985 s 16(10) (amended by SI 2008/90). As to the Food Standards Agency see FOOD AND DRINK vol 51 (2013) PARAS 634–653. As to the Health and Safety Commission see HEALTH AND SAFETY AT WORK vol 52 (2014) PARA 326 et seq.

3 Ie prohibitions of:
  (1) importation;
  (2) sale, offer or exposure for sale or possession for the purpose of sale;
  (3) supply or offer to supply;
  (4) storage;
  (5) use;
  (6) advertisement: Food and Environment Protection Act 1985 s 16(3).
 See the Control of Pesticides Regulations 1986, SI 1986/1510, reg 4.

4 As to the meaning of 'pesticide' see PARA 130 note 6.

5 Food and Environment Protection Act 1985 s 16(2)(a). As to the pesticides and other substances to which the Control of Pesticides Regulations 1986, SI 1986/1510, apply see reg 3(1) (reg 3 substituted by SI 1997/188; and amended by SI 2001/880, SI 2011/2131, SI 2013/1478, SI 2013/150); and as to the pesticides and substances to which the Control of Pesticides Regulations 1986, SI 1986/1510, do not apply see reg 3(2) (as so substituted and amended). See the Plant Protection Regulations 2011, SI 2011/2131; and PARAS 130, 136–137.

6 'Approval' means approval under regulations: Food and Environment Protection Act 1985 s 16(2).

7 Food and Environment Protection Act 1985 s 16(2)(b). Approvals may be given in the form of:
  (1) experimental permits;
  (2) provisional approvals; and
  (3) full approvals,
 and may be reviewed, revoked or suspended: see the Control of Pesticides Regulations 1986, SI 1986/1510, reg 5(1)–(3), (5)(a) (reg 5(2) substituted by SI 1997/188). See also the text and note 11. Payment of a fee for approval of a pesticide may be required: see the Food and Environment Protection Act 1985 s 18(1), (2)(a), (3)–(8) (s 18 substituted by the Pesticides (Fees and Enforcement) Act 1989 s 1(1)). The Secretary of State and the Welsh Ministers must from time to time consult the Food Standards Agency as to the general approach to be taken in relation to the

giving, revocation or suspension of approvals and the imposition of conditions on approvals (including the identification of circumstances in which it may be desirable for the Agency to be consulted in relation to particular cases) (s 16(9A)(b) (as added: see note 2)). It is a defence in proceedings for an offence under the Protection of Animals Act 1911 s 8(b) (which restricts the placing on land of poison and poisonous substances: see ANIMALS vol 2 (2017) PARA 161) for the person charged to show that he acted in accordance with an approval: Food and Environment Protection Act 1985 s 16(14)(a).

8   Food and Environment Protection Act 1985 s 16(2)(c). As to conditions on approvals and the amendment thereof see the Control of Pesticides Regulations 1986, SI 1986/1510, reg 5(4), (5)(b). As to the duty to consult see note 7.

9   Food and Environment Protection Act 1985 s 16(2)(d). Provision is made for the giving of consent to the advertisement, sale, supply, storage and use of pesticides: see the Control of Pesticides Regulations 1986, SI 1986/1510, reg 6 (substituted by SI 1997/188).

10 Food and Environment Protection Act 1985 s 16(2)(e). As to conditions for the giving of consents to the advertisement, sale, supply, storage and use of pesticides see the Control of Pesticides Regulations 1986, SI 1986/1510, Schs 1–4 (substituted by SI 1997/188; and SI 1986/1510 Sch 4 further amended by SI 2013/755).

11 Food and Environment Protection Act 1985 s 16(2)(f). As to the review, revocation and suspension of approvals see the Control of Pesticides Regulations 1986, SI 1986/1510, reg 5(5)(a). As to conditions see note 10.

12 For these purposes 'local authority' means any local authority, as defined in the Local Government Act 1972 (see s 270(1); and LOCAL GOVERNMENT vol 69 (2009) PARA 23), except a parish or community council, or a port health authority: Food and Environment Protection Act 1985 ss 16(2A)(a), 19(8)(a), (d) (s 16(2A) added by the Pesticides Act 1998 s 1(4); Food and Environment Protection Act 1985 s 19(8) added by the Pesticides (Fees and Enforcement) Act 1989 s 2). As to local authorities in England and Wales see LOCAL GOVERNMENT vol 69 (2009) PARA 22 et seq. As to port health authorities and port health districts see ENVIRONMENTAL QUALITY AND PUBLIC HEALTH vol 45 (2010) PARA 102.

13 Food and Environment Protection Act 1985 s 16(2)(g) (amended by the Pesticides Act 1998 s 1(2)(b)). As to seizure and disposal see the Control of Pesticides Regulations 1986, SI 1986/1510, reg 7(1) (reg 7 substituted by SI 1997/188).

14 Food and Environment Protection Act 1985 s 16(2)(h). As to the power to require the removal of imported goods see the Control of Pesticides Regulations 1986, SI 1986/1510, reg 7(2) (reg 7 substituted by SI 1997/188). As to the meaning of 'United Kingdom' see PARA 1 note 1.

15 For these purposes 'information' means any information which has been supplied to a government department or other authority at any time for the purposes of, or otherwise in connection with, any provision made under the Food and Environment Protection Act 1985 s 16, the United Kingdom Pesticides Safety Precautions Scheme, or the Agricultural Chemicals Approval Scheme: s 16(2A)(b) (as added: see note 12). The United Kingdom Pesticides Safety Precautions Scheme is a voluntary scheme operated jointly between the Department for the Environment, Food and Rural Affairs and the Health and Safety Executive; the Agricultural Chemicals Approval Scheme was a voluntary scheme which was in operation until the enactment of the Control of Pesticides Regulations 1986, SI 1986/1510.

16 Food and Environment Protection Act 1985 s 16(2)(j) (substituted by the Pesticides Act 1998 s 1(3)). Provision may be made for the information to be made available subject to any condition that the Secretary of State considers or the Welsh Ministers consider appropriate (Food and Environment Protection Act 1985 s 16(2)(j)(i) (as so substituted)) and for the payment of such amounts as the Secretary of State or the Welsh Ministers may, with the consent of the Treasury, determine as representing the cost reasonably attributable to the supply of the information (s 16(2)(j)(ii) (as so substituted)). As to the Treasury see CONSTITUTIONAL AND ADMINISTRATIVE LAW vol 20 (2014) PARA 263 et seq. The Secretary of State and the Welsh Ministers must have regard to the interests of persons supplying information when making such regulations: s 16(5). For provision as to the release of information to the public see the Control of Pesticides Regulations 1986, SI 1986/1510, reg 8 (substituted by SI 1997/188; and amended by SI 2011/2131).

17 'Pesticide residue' means any substance resulting from the use of a pesticide, including any such derivative as regulations may specify in relation to a particular pesticide: Food and Environment Protection Act 1985 s 16(15).

18 As to the meaning of 'crops' see PARA 130 note 3.

19 As to the meaning of 'food' see the Food Safety Act 1990 s 1(1), (2); and FOOD AND DRINK vol 51 (2013) PARA 608 (definition applied by the Food and Environment Protection Act 1985 s 24(1) (substituted by the Food Safety Act 1990 Sch 3 para 29(c))).
20 Food and Environment Protection Act 1985 s 16(2)(k). See the Pesticides (Maximum Residue Levels) (England and Wales) Regulations 2008, SI 2008/2570; and FOOD AND DRINK vol 51 (2013) PARA 719.
21 Food and Environment Protection Act 1985 s 16(2)(l).
22 Food and Environment Protection Act 1985 s 16(12)(a)(i)–(iii). 'Contravenes' includes 'fails to comply with': s 16(13). The penalty on summary conviction is a fine not exceeding the statutory maximum and on conviction on indictment is a fine: s 21(3), (4). As to the statutory maximum see PARA 58 note 1. If the Secretary of State or the Welsh Ministers do anything in consequence of a failure on the part of any person to comply with regulations, he or they may recover from that person expenses reasonably incurred by him or them in doing it: s 16(13A) (added by the Pesticides (Fees and Enforcement) Act 1989 s 1(2)).
23 See the Food and Environment Protection Act 1985 s 19; and PARA 139.

(2) PLANT PROTECTION PRODUCTS

132. Marketing and use of plant protection products.

A plant protection product[1] must not be placed on the market or used unless it has been authorised in the member state concerned in accordance with the relevant EU provisions[2]. A person must not place on the market or use a plant protection product in contravention of this prohibition[3], or cause or permit another person to do so[4].

By way of derogation from the above prohibition[5], experiments or tests for research or development purposes involving the release into the environment of an unauthorised plant protection product or involving unauthorised use of a plant protection product may be carried out if the member state in whose territory the experiment or test is to be carried out has assessed the available data and granted a permit for trial purposes[6]. A person must not place on the market or use a plant protection product in contravention of one or more conditions in a permit granted for such trial purposes, or cause or permit another person to do so[7].

A person must use a plant protection product in compliance with conditions established in accordance with EU provisions[8] and specified on the labelling as required[9] by EU provisions[10].

A plant protection product for which a parallel trade permit has been issued must be placed on the market and used only in accordance with the provisions of the authorisation of the reference product[11]. A person must not place on the market or use a plant protection product in contravention of this provision[12], or cause or permit another person to do so[13].

A person who contravenes or fails to comply with the above provisions[14] is guilty of an offence[15].

1 As to the meaning of 'plant protection product' see PARA 130.
2 Ie in accordance with European Parliament and Council Regulations (EC) 1107/2009 (OJ L309, 24.11.2009, p 1) concerning the placing of plant protection products on the market: see art 28(1). By way of derogation from this restriction, no authorisation is required in certain cases: see art 28(2).
3 Ie in contravention of European Parliament and Council Regulations (EC) 1107/2009 (OJ L309, 24.11.2009, p 1), art 28.
4 Plant Protection Products Regulations 2011, SI 2011/2131, reg 9. The authorisation holder is responsible for providing information on potentially harmful or unacceptable effects: see reg 13. Specific provision is made for the tests and studies involving vertebrate animals and the sharing of information from such tests: see reg 15. As to what constitutes a vertebrate study subject to data

sharing see *R (on the application of Chiltern Farm Chemical Ltd v Health and Safety Executive* [2017] EWHC 2491 (Admin), [2017] All ER (D) 160 (Oct).

5   Ie by way of derogation from European Parliament and Council Regulations (EC) 1107/2009 (OJ L309, 24.11.2009, p 1), art 28.

6   European Parliament and Council Regulations (EC) 1107/2009 (OJ L309, 24.11.2009, p 1), art 54(1).

7   Plant Protection Products Regulations 2011, SI 2011/2131, reg 11(2).

8   Ie established in accordance with European Parliament and Council Regulations (EC) 1107/2009 (OJ L309, 24.11.2009, p 1) art 31.

9   Ie as specified on the labelling as required in European Parliament and Council Regulations (EC) 1107/2009 (OJ L309, 24.11.2009, p 1) art 55.

10   Plant Protection Products Regulations 2011, SI 2011/2131, reg 12.

11   European Parliament and Council Regulations (EC) 1107/2009 (OJ L309, 24.11.2009, p 1), art 52(5).

12   Ie in contravention of European Parliament and Council Regulations (EC) 1107/2009 (OJ L309, 24.11.2009, p 1) art 52(5).

13   Plant Protection Products Regulations 2011, SI 2011/2131, reg 11(1).

14   Ie who fails to comply with the Plant Protection Products Regulations 2011, SI 2011/2131, regs 9, 11, 12.

15   Plant Protection Products Regulations 2011, SI 2011/2131, reg 23. Such a person is liable, on summary conviction, to a fine not exceeding the statutory maximum, and, on indictment, to a fine: reg 26(1). In any proceedings for an offence under the Plant Protection Products Regulations 2011, SI 2011/2131, other than in relation to reg 15(2), 22(1)(a) or 22(2), it is a defence for the person charged to prove that they took all reasonable precautions and exercised all due diligence to avoid the commission of the offence: reg 25(1). A person is to be taken to have established the defence provided by reg 25(1) if they prove:

    (1)   that they acted under instructions given to them by their employer; or

    (2)   that they acted in reliance on information supplied by another person without any reason to suppose that the information was false or misleading,

and in either case that they took all such steps as were reasonably open to them to ensure that no offence would be committed: reg 25(2).

If, in any case, the defence provided by reg 25(1) involves an allegation that the commission of the offence was due to:

    (a)   an act or omission by another person, other than the giving of instructions to the person charged with the offence by their employer; or

    (b)   reliance on information supplied by another person,

the person charged must not, without leave of the court, be entitled to rely on that defence unless within a period ending seven clear days before the hearing, they have served on the prosecutor a notice giving such information identifying or assisting in the identification of that other person as was then in their possession: reg 25(3).

It is a defence in proceedings for an offence under the Protection of Animals Act 1911 s 8(b) (which restricts the placing on land of poison and poisonous substances: see ANIMALS vol 2 (2017) PARA 161) for the person charged to show that they acted in accordance with an authorisation or permission granted, or deemed to be granted, in accordance with European Parliament and Council Regulations (EC) 1107/2009 (OJ L309, 24.11.2009, p 1): Plant Protection Products Regulations 2011, SI 2011/2131, reg 25(4).

133. Marketing and use of adjuvants.

A person must not place on the market or use an adjuvant[1] unless it has been authorised in accordance with the relevant EU provisions[2], or cause or permit another person to do so[3]. Until the adoption of detailed rules[4], the national provisions for authorisation of adjuvants are as follows[5].

An adjuvant is authorised for use with an authorised plant protection product in England and Wales if it is included in a list of adjuvants published by the Secretary of State from time to time ('the English and Welsh list')[6] or, if not included in the English and Welsh list, if it is used with an authorised plant protection product for the sole purpose of research and development[7].

The Secretary of State may, in relation to any adjuvant for which an application has been made for inclusion on the England and Welsh list or which is included in the list, at any time:

(1)   determine data requirements (concerning human safety or environmental protection) to which the inclusion, or the continued inclusion, of that adjuvant in the list must be subject[8];

(2)   determine requirements to which the use of that adjuvant with authorised plant protection products must be subject[9]; and

(3)   for reasons of human safety or environmental protection, or with the consent of the applicant, amend any requirement which has been determined under head (1) or (2)[10].

1   'Adjuvants' are: substances or preparations which consist of co-formulants or preparations containing one or more co-formulants, in the form in which they are supplied to the user and placed on the market to be mixed by the user with a plant protection product and which enhance its effectiveness or other pesticidal properties: European Parliament and Council Regulations (EC) 1107/2009 (OJ L309, 24.11.2009, p 1) concerning the placing of plant protection products on the market: see art 2(3)(d).

2   Ie authorised in accordance with European Parliament and Council Regulations (EC) 1107/2009 (OJ L309, 24.11.2009, p 1), art 58.

3   Plant Protection Products Regulations 2011, SI 2011/2131, reg 14(1).

4   Ie as referred to in European Parliament and Council Regulations (EC) 1107/2009 (OJ L309, 24.11.2009, p 1) art 58(2).

5   Plant Protection Products Regulations 2011, SI 2011/2131, reg 14(2), (4).

6   A person may apply to the Secretary of State for an adjuvant to be included on the English and Welsh list: Plant Protection Products Regulations 2011, SI 2011/2131, Sch 2 para 1.

7   Plant Protection Products Regulations 2011, SI 2011/2131, Sch 2 para 1.

8   The Secretary of State may, in relation to any adjuvant included in the list, remove that adjuvant from it:

(1)   if it appears to him that the applicant has failed to comply with any data requirement which has been determined in relation to that adjuvant under head (1) or amended under head (3);

(2)   if it appears to the Secretary of State that any literature relating to the adjuvant is not in accordance with any requirement to which the use of that adjuvant is subject, as determined under head (2) or amended under head (3);

(3)   if it appears to the Secretary of State that:

(a)   any literature relating to the adjuvant refers to a plant protection product; and

(b)   the use of that adjuvant with that plant protection product is not in accordance with the conditions of the authorisation given in relation to that plant protection product;

(4)   for reasons of human safety or environmental protection; or

(5)   at the request of the applicant: Plant Protection Products Regulations 2011, SI 2011/2131, Sch 2 para 5.

The Secretary of State must, upon a decision to remove an adjuvant from the list, include in the list that decision and the date on which, any conditions in accordance with which, the removal is to take effect: Sch 2 para 6. For the purposes of head (3)(a) above 'literature relating to the adjuvant' means the labelling of the packaging in which the adjuvant is contained, any leaflet accompanying that package or any other material in writing produced by, or on behalf of, the applicant describing the adjuvant or how to use it: Sch 2 para 7(1). For the purposes of head (3)(b) above 'authorisation' means any authorisation or permission granted, or deemed to be granted, in accordance with European Parliament and Council Regulations (EC) 1107/2009 (OJ L309, 24.11.2009, p 1) and in head (2) in the text 'authorised' is to be construed accordingly: Plant Protection Products Regulations 2011, SI 2011/2131, Sch 2 para 7(2).

9   The Secretary of State must, in relation to any adjuvant included in the list, also state any requirements which they have determined under head (2) in the text and any amendments to such requirements that have been made under head (3) in the text: Plant Protection Products Regulations 2011, SI 2011/2131, Sch 2 para 4.

10 Plant Protection Products Regulations 2011, SI 2011/2131, Sch 2 para 3.

134.   Seeds treated with plant protection products.

A person must not place on the market or use seeds treated with plant protection products[1] that are not authorised for use on such seeds in any member state, or cause or permit another person to do so[2]. Nor may a person place on the market treated seeds[3] in contravention of EU provisions relating to the labelling of such seeds[4], or cause or permit another person to do so[5].

Where the Secretary of State reasonably considers that treated seeds are likely to constitute a serious risk to human or animal health or to the environment, he may issue a notice in writing restricting or prohibiting their sale or use, or both[6].

1   As to the meaning of 'plant protection product' see PARA 130.
2   Plant Protection Products Regulations 2011, SI 2011/2131, reg 10(1).
3   For these purposes 'treated seeds' means seeds treated with plant protection products authorised for that use in at least one member state: Plant Protection Products Regulations 2011, SI 2011/2131, reg 10(3).
4   Ie in contravention of European Parliament and Council Regulation (EC) 1107/2009 (OJ L309, 24.11.2009, p 1) concerning the placing of plant protection products on the market, art 49(4).
5   Plant Protection Products Regulations 2011, SI 2011/2131, reg 10(2).
6   Plant Protection Products Regulations 2011, SI 2011/2131, reg 5(1). The notice must set out the grounds for issuing the notice and give a time limit for compliance: reg 5(3). Failure to comply is an offence for which a person is liable on summary conviction to a fine of an amount not exceeding level 5 on the standard scale: see regs 21(1)(a), 23(d), 26(2). As to the standard scale and the powers of magistrates' courts to issue fines on summary conviction see SENTENCING vol 92 (2015) PARA 176.

135.   Packaging and labelling requirements.

A plant protection product[1] or an adjuvant that may be mistaken for food, drink or feed must be packaged in such a way as to minimise the likelihood of such a mistake being made[2] and a person may not package such a plant protection product or an adjuvant in contravention of this provision, or cause or permit another person to do so[3].

Plant protection products and adjuvants available to the general public that may be mistaken for food, drink or feed must contain components to discourage or prevent their consumption[4]. A person must not make available to the general public a plant protection product or adjuvant in contravention of this provision, or cause or permit another person to do so[5].

The labelling of plant protection products must meet certain classification, labelling and packaging requirements[6] and a person must not place on the market a plant protection product in contravention of those requirements, or cause or permit another person to do so[7].

1   As to the meaning of 'plant protection product' see PARA 130.
2   See European Parliament and Council Regulation (EC) 1107/2009 (OJ L309, 24.11.2009, p 1) concerning the placing of plant protection products on the market, art 64(1).
3   Plant Protection Products Regulations 2011, SI 2011/2131, reg 16(1). A person who fails to comply with regs 16, 17 is guilty of an offence and liable on summary conviction to a fine not exceeding the statutory maximum or on conviction on indictment to a fine: see regs 23, 26(1).
4   See European Parliament and Council Regulation (EC) 1107/2009 (OJ L309, 24.11.2009, p 1) art 64(2).
5   Plant Protection Products Regulations 2011, SI 2011/2131, reg 16(2).
6   See European Parliament and Council Regulation (EC) 1107/2009 (OJ L309, 24.11.2009, p 1) art 65(1).
7   Plant Protection Products Regulations 2011, SI 2011/2131, reg 17. Exceptions apply: see reg 17(a)–(c). See note 2.

136. Prohibition on advertisement.

Plant protection products[1] which are not authorised must not be advertised[2]. Every advertisement for a plant protection product must be accompanied by certain wording and warnings[3] and must not include information in text or graphic form which could be misleading as regards possible risks to human or animal health or to the environment, such as the terms 'low risk', 'non-toxic' or 'harmless'[4]. Nor may advertisements contain any visual representation of potentially dangerous practices, such as mixing or application without sufficient protective clothing, nor any use near food or use by or in the vicinity of children[5].

All statements used in advertising must be technically justifiable[6].

A person must not advertise a plant protection product in contravention of the above provisions[7], or cause or permit another person to do so[8].

1   As to the meaning of 'plant protection product' see PARA 130.
2   See European Parliament and Council Regulation (EC) 1107/2009 (OJ L309, 24.11.2009, p 1) concerning the placing of plant protection products on the market, art 66(1).
3   See European Parliament and Council Regulation (EC) 1107/2009 (OJ L309, 24.11.2009, p 1) art 66(1), (2). Advertising or promotional material must draw attention to the appropriate warning phrases and symbols as laid down in the labelling: art 66(6).
4   See European Parliament and Council Regulation (EC) 1107/2009 (OJ L309, 24.11.2009, p 1) art 66(2).
5   See European Parliament and Council Regulation (EC) 1107/2009 (OJ L309, 24.11.2009, p 1) art 66(5).
6   See European Parliament and Council Regulation (EC) 1107/2009 (OJ L309, 24.11.2009, p 1) art 66(4).
7   Ie in contravention of European Parliament and Council Regulation (EC) 1107/2009 (OJ L309, 24.11.2009, p 1) art 66(1), (2), (4) (5) or (6).
8   Plant Protection Products Regulations 2011, SI 2011/2131, reg 18.

137. Enforcement.

The Secretary of State, in relation to England, and the Welsh Ministers[1], in relation to Wales, are responsible for the enforcement of provisions[2] relating to plant protection products[3] but may authorise, in writing, any person (an 'authorised person')[4] to exercise certain enforcement powers[5].

An authorised person may enter any premises[6] (except any premises used wholly or mainly as a private dwelling) if he has reasonable grounds to believe that any plant protection product is being, or has been, applied to, or stored on or in them, or transported on or applied by means of them and that it is necessary to enter for the purpose of ensuring that the Plant Protection Regulations 2011 are complied with[7].

A justice of the peace may issue a warrant[8] permitting an authorised person to enter any premises[9] if necessary by reasonable force, for the purposes of the enforcement provisions relating to plant protection products[10] if satisfied that the authorised person has reasonable grounds[11] for requiring entry and certain conditions[12] are satisfied[13].

Entry and search under a warrant must be within three months from the date of its issue[14]. Where the occupier of the premises to be entered and searched is present at the time when an authorised person seeks to execute a warrant to enter and search it, the authorised person must:

(1)   identify himself to the occupier and must produce to the occupier evidence of his authority;
(2)   produce the warrant to the occupier; and
(3)   supply the occupier with a certified copy of it[15].

A search under a warrant may only be a search to the extent required for the purpose for which the warrant was issued[16]. An authorised person executing a warrant must make an endorsement on it stating whether what was sought was found[17].

If an authorised person is of the opinion that a person is committing, has committed or is likely to commit an offence contrary to provisions relating to plant protection products, he has certain powers to authorise the seizure and disposal of products and to serve notice on the holder take certain remedial action, including recovery of the product[18]. In certain circumstances where the authorised person suspects an offence has been committed he may serve an enforcement notice directing that any premises on or in which it appears that the offence was being committed or anything which is on or in it, is left undisturbed (whether generally or in particular respects) for as long as it appears to be reasonably necessary; or that remedial or preventative action measures are taken[19].

1   For the purposes of the Plant Protection Products Regulations 2011, SI 2011/2131 the Secretary of State is both the designated competent authority and the coordinating national authority and as such is responsible for carrying out the obligations laid down in European Parliament and Council Regulation (EC) 1107/2009 (OJ L309, 24.11.2009, p 1) concerning the placing of plant protection products on the market, and for coordinating and ensuring all necessary contacts with applicants, other member states, the Commission and the European Food Safety Authority: see art 75(1), (2); and the Plant Protection Products Regulations 2011, SI 2011/2131, regs 3, 4. As to the Secretary of State and the Welsh Ministers see PARA 390.
2   Ie the Plant Protection Products Regulations 2011, SI 2011/2131.
3   See the Plant Protection Products Regulations 2011, SI 2011/2131, reg 6(1)(a), (b) (renumbered as such by SI 2012/1657). The Secretary of State may delegate to the Director of Public Prosecutions functions in relation to the prosecution of offences under the Plant Protection Regulations 2011, SI 2011/2131 in so far as those functions relate to offences committed in England: reg 6(2) (added by SI 2012/1657). As to the meaning of 'plant protection product' see PARA 130.
4   For the purposes of the Plant Protection Regulations 2011, SI 2011/2131, 'authorised person' means a person authorised under reg 7(1) or 7(7) (see note 5): reg 2(1).
5   See the Plant Protection Regulations 2011, SI 2011/2131, reg 7(1), (4), (8), (9). As to the requirement for an authorised person to produce evidence of their authorisation: see reg 8. A person may be authorised for specific purposes: reg 7(3). The Secretary of State and the Welsh Ministers acting jointly in relation to local authority officers in England and Wales, may specify in writing descriptions of local authority officers who may be authorised to exercise enforcement powers and may direct in writing that an officer of a particular description may only be appointed to exercise them for a specified purpose: reg 7(5), (6). If the Secretary of State and Welsh Ministers specify a description of local authority officers under reg 7(5), a local authority may authorise any of its officers falling within that description to exercise enforcement powers: reg 7(7). For the purposes of reg 7 'local authority' means:
    (1)   in relation to England:
        (a)   where there is a unitary authority, within the meaning of the Local Government Changes for England Regulations 1994, SI 1994/867 (see LOCAL GOVERNMENT vol 69 (2009) PARA 56), that authority;
        (b)   where there is not a unitary authority:
            (i)   in a metropolitan district, the council of that district;
            (ii)   in a non-metropolitan district, the council of that county or the council of a district within the county area;
            (iii)   in each London borough, the council of that borough;
        (c)   in the City of London, the Common Council; or
        (d)   the Council of the Isles of Scilly;
    (2)   in relation to Wales, a county council or a county borough council: reg 7(10).
6   An authorised person must exercise powers of entry at a reasonable hour unless it appears to the authorised person that there are grounds for suspecting that the exercise of the power of entry may be frustrated if he or she seeks to exercise them at a reasonable hour: Plant Protection Products Regulations 2011, SI 2011/2131, Sch 1 para 1(2) (Sch 1 para 1 amended by SI 2012/1657). An authorised person who enters any unoccupied premises must leave it as effectively secured against

unauthorised entry as it was before his or her entry: Plant Protection Products Regulations 2011, SI 2011/2131, Sch 1 para 1(3) (as so amended). 'Premises' includes any place and, in particular, includes any vehicle, vessel, aircraft, hovercraft or marine structure and any tent or moveable structure: reg 2(1) (definition added by SI 2012/1657).

7   Plant Protection Products Regulations 2011, SI 2011/2131, Sch 1 para 1(1) (as amended: see note 6).

8   An application for a warrant under the Plant Protection Products Regulations 2011, SI 2011/2131, Sch 1 para 2(1) must be supported by an information in writing: Sch 1 para 2(1A) (added by SI 2012/1657). The warrant must specify the name of the person who applies for it, the date on which it is issued, that it is issued under the Plant Protection Products Regulations 2011, SI 2011/2131, Sch 1, the address of the premises to be entered and search and it should identify, so far as practicable, what is to be sought: Sch 1 para 2(7) (amended by SI 2012/1657). The court must provide two copies of the warrant certified as such: Plant Protection Products Regulations 2011, SI 2011/2131, Sch 1 para 2(8).

9   A warrant must authorise entry on one occasion only: Plant Protection Products Regulations 2011, SI 2011/2131, Sch 1 para 2(6). An authorised person is not liable in any civil or criminal proceedings for anything done in the purported performance of his functions as an authorised person if the court is satisfied that the act was done in good faith and that there were reasonable grounds for doing it: Sch 1 para 6.

10   Ie for the purposes of the enforcement of the Plant Protection Products Regulations 2011, SI 2011/2131.

11   Where an authorised person applies for a warrant under the Plant Protection Products Regulations 2011, SI 2011/2131, Sch 1 para 2(1), he must state the grounds upon which the application is made, that the warrant would be issued under Sch 1 and what is being sought: Sch 1 para 1(2).

12   Ie any of the conditions set out below:
     (1)   admission has been refused, or a refusal is expected, and (in either case) that notice to apply for a warrant has been given to the occupier;
     (2)   asking for admission, or the giving of such a notice, would defeat the object of the entry;
     (3)   the case is one of urgency; or
     (4)   the premises are unoccupied or the occupier is temporarily absent: Plant Protection Products Regulations 2011, SI 2011/2131, Sch 1 para 2(1A) (Sch 1 para 2 amended by SI 2012/1657).
     An application for a warrant under Sch 1 para 2(1), where the condition satisfied is set out at head (1), must be made on notice and, where the condition satisfied is set out in head (2), (3) or (4), it must be made without notice: Sch 1 para 2(4) (substituted by SI 2012/1657).

13   Plant Protection Products Regulations 2011, SI 2011/2131, Sch 1 para 2(1) (substituted by SI 2012/1657). An authorised person exercising his powers of entry under the Plant Protection Products Regulations 2011, SI 2011/2131, Sch 1 para 1(1), or in accordance with a warrant under Sch 1 para 2(1) may:
     (1)   search for any item, if necessary using reasonable force;
     (2)   open or examine, or both, anything that is on, attached to or otherwise forms part of the premises, if necessary using reasonable force;
     (3)   take with him any persons and equipment or materials he considers necessary for the enforcement of the Plant Protection Products Regulations 2011, SI 2011/2131;
     (4)   open any container, if necessary using reasonable force;
     (5)   carry out any searches, inspections, measurements and tests;
     (6)   take samples;
     (7)   have access to, and inspect and copy any documents, books or records (in whatever form they are held) which the authorised person has reason to believe may be relevant in connection with the enforcement of the Plant Protection Products Regulations 2011, SI 2011/2131 and remove them to enable them to be copied;
     (8)   photograph or copy anything which the authorised person has reasonable cause to believe may be relevant in connection with the enforcement of these Regulations; and
     (9)   seize any computers and associated equipment for the purpose of copying documents provided that they are returned as soon as practicable: Sch 1 para 4(1) (substituted by SI 2012/1657).
     Any person who accompanies an authorised person in accordance with head (3) above may perform any of the authorised person's functions but only under the supervision of that authorised person: Plant Protection Products Regulations 2011, SI 2011/2131, Sch 1 para 4(2) (Sch 4 (2)–(4) amended by SI 2012/1657). Where an authorised person takes samples under head (6) he may only take an amount that is reasonably needed for the performance of his functions under the Plant Protection Products Regulations 2011, SI 2011/2131, Sch 1 para 4(3) as so amended). Nothing in head (7), (8) or (9) is to be taken to compel the production by any person of a document which

he would be entitled to refuse to produce on grounds of legal professional privilege in proceedings in the High Court in England and Wales: Sch 1 para 4(4) (as so amended).

An authorised person may require any person to give him information as to the formulation, effects or use of any substance: Sch 1 para 4(5). An authorised person performing functions under the Plant Protection Products Regulations 2011, SI 2011/2131 may require a person whom he has reasonable cause to believe is able to give information which will assist in the execution of those provisions to answer such questions as the authorised person thinks it appropriate to ask and to sign a declaration of the truth of the answers provided: Sch 1 para 4(6).

Any person to whom any such questions are put may nominate a person to be with him when he answers and, when a person answers any such questions the only other persons who may be present, apart from the questioner, are the person (if any) so nominated and any person authorised by the authorised person to be present: Sch 1 para 4(7), (8). No answer given by a person in pursuance of a requirement imposed under Sch 1 para 4(6) is admissible in evidence in Great Britain against that person, his or her spouse, or his or her civil partner in proceedings for any offence: Sch 1 para 4(9).

14 Plant Protection Products Regulations 2011, SI 2011/2131, Sch 1 para 3(1). A search under a warrant may only be a search to the extent required for the purpose for which the warrant was issued: Sch 1 para 3(5).

15 Plant Protection Products Regulations 2011, SI 2011/2131, Sch 1 para 3(2) (amended by SI 2012/1657). Where the occupier of the premises is not present at the time when an authorised person seeks to execute such a warrant; but some other person who appears to the authorised person to be in charge of the premises is present, the Plant Protection Products Regulations 2011, SI 2011/2131, Sch 1 para 3(2) has effect as if any reference to the occupier were a reference to that other person: Sch 1 para 3(3) (amended by SI 2012/1657). If there is no person present who appears to the authorised person to be in charge of the premises, the authorised person must leave a copy of the warrant in a prominent place on the premises: Plant Protection Products Regulations 2011, SI 2011/2131, Sch 1 para 3(4) (amended by SI 2012/1657).

16 Plant Protection Products Regulations 2011, SI 2011/2131, Sch 1 para 3(5).

17 Plant Protection Products Regulations 2011, SI 2011/2131, Sch 1 para 3(6). A warrant must be returned to the designated officer for the local justice area in which the justice of the peace was acting when the warrant was issued when it has been executed or in the case of a warrant which has not been executed, upon the expiry of three months from the date of its issue or sooner: Sch 1 para 3(7). Such a warrant must be retained for 12 months from its return: Sch 1 para 3(9).

18 See the Plant Protection Products Regulations 2011, SI 2011/2131, Sch 1 para 7. Failure to comply with a notice served under Sch 1 para 7(1), (3) or (8) or para 8(1), (3) or (6) is an offence for which a person is liable on summary conviction to a fine of an amount not exceeding level 5 on the standard scale: reg 21(1)(b), (c), 23(d), 26(2).

19 See the Plant Protection Products Regulations 2011, SI 2011/2131, Sch 1 para 8(1), (2) (amended by SI 2012/1657). See also the Plant Protection Products Regulations 2011, SI 2011/2131, Sch 1 para 8(3)–(6). As to the standard scale and the powers of magistrates' courts to issue fines on summary conviction see SENTENCING vol 92 (2015) PARA 176.

(3) PROTECTION OF WILDLIFE

138. Restriction on possession or use of pesticides harmful to wildlife.
The Secretary of State[1], where he is satisfied that it is necessary or expedient so to do in the interests of protecting wild birds[2] or wild animals[3] from harm[4], may make an order prescribing ingredients contained in pesticides[5], and a person is guilty of an offence (subject to specified statutory defences[6]) if he has in his possession a pesticide containing an ingredient which has been so prescribed[7]. The Secretary of State must take such steps as are reasonably practicable to bring information about the effect of such an order to the attention of persons likely to be affected by it[8]. The court by which a person is convicted of an offence under these provisions may order the forfeiture of the pesticide in respect of which the offence was committed[9].

1 As to the Secretary of State see PARA 390.

2   For these purposes 'wild bird' means any bird of a species which is ordinarily resident in or is a visitor to the European territory of any member state in a wild state but does not include poultry: see the Wildlife and Countryside Act 1981 s 27(1) (definition amended by SI 2004/1487; and SI 2004/1733); definition applied by the Natural Environment and Rural Communities Act 2006 s 46(1), (3).

3   'Wild animal' means any animal (other than a bird) which is or (before it was killed or taken) was living wild: see the Wildlife and Countryside Act 1981 s 27(1); definition applied by the Natural Environment and Rural Communities Act 2006 s 46(3).

4   Natural Environment and Rural Communities Act 2006 s 43(2).

5   'Pesticide' means a pesticide as defined by the Food and Environment Protection Act 1985 s 16(15) (see PARA 130 note 6) and anything to which Pt III (ss 16–19) (see PARAS 130–131, 140–141) applies (by virtue of s 16(16): see PARA 130) as if it were a pesticide: Natural Environment and Rural Communities Act 2006 s 46(2).

6   It is a defence for a person charged with an offence under these provisions to prove that his possession of the pesticide was for the purposes of doing anything in accordance with provision made by or under the Poisons Act 1972 (see MEDICAL PRODUCTS AND DRUGS vol 75 (2013) PARAS 528–555) (Natural Environment and Rural Communities Act 2006 s 43(3)(a)), regulations made under the Food and Environment Protection Act 1985 s 16(2) (see PARA 131) (Natural Environment and Rural Communities Act 2006 s 43(3)(b)), European Parliament and Council Regulation (EU) 528/2012 (OJ L309, 24.11.2009, p 1) (Natural Environment and Rural Communities Act 2006 s 46(3)(c) (substituted by SI 2013/1506)), or European Parliament and Council Regulation (EU) 1107/2009 (Natural Environment and Rural Communities Act 2006 s 43(3)(d) (substituted by SI 2017/304)).

7   Natural Environment and Rural Communities Act 2006 s 43(1). This offence is punishable on summary conviction by imprisonment for a term not exceeding 51 weeks or a fine not exceeding level 5 on the standard scale (or both) (s 43(4)) except in relation to an offence committed before the day appointed for the commencement of the Criminal Justice Act 2003 s 281(5) (not yet in force), in respect of which the maximum term of imprisonment is six months (Natural Environment and Rural Communities Act 2006 s 43(6)). At the date at which this volume states the law no such day had been appointed. As to the standard scale and the powers of magistrates' courts to issue fines on summary conviction see SENTENCING vol 92 (2015) PARA 176.

8   Natural Environment and Rural Communities Act 2006 s 43(8).

9   Natural Environment and Rural Communities Act 2006 s 43(5).

139. Enforcement.

The Secretary of State and the Welsh Ministers[1] may authorise inspectors[2] to enforce in England and Wales the statutory provisions concerned with the restrictions on the use of pesticides harmful to wildlife[3]. Pursuant to this an inspector may enter any premises[4] if he has reasonable grounds to suspect that he may find there evidence that an offence is being committed under those provisions[5], require any person whom he reasonably believes has information about the formulation, effects or use of any substance found on the premises to give him that information[6], and seize any substance found on the premises if he has reasonable grounds for believing that it is evidence of such an offence[7].

When discharging any function under any of these provisions[8] an inspector must have regard to any relevant provision of the relevant code of practice[9], although failure so to do does not make an inspector liable to criminal or civil proceedings[10].

Any authorised person[11] may enter any land, vehicle, vessel[12], aircraft, hovercraft or marine structure[13] if he has reasonable grounds to believe that any pesticide[14] is being applied or stored there (in the case of land)[15] or is being or has been stored in, transported on or applied by means of it (in the other cases)[16], and that it is necessary for him to enter for any general purpose[17].

If any authorised person is of the opinion that a person is contravening any provision of regulations[18], any condition of approval of a pesticide or of a plant protection product[19] or any requirement imposed by regulations[20], or has committed such an offence in such circumstances that it is likely to be repeated, he may serve a notice on that person stating that he is of that opinion, specifying particulars of the offence, why he is of the opinion that the offence is or has been committed and directing that any land, vehicle, vessel, aircraft, hovercraft or marine structure on, or in, which the offence is or has been committed, must be left undisturbed for as long as he considers necessary or that any reasonable remedial or preventative measures must be taken[21]. A similar notice may also be served if the authorised person is of the opinion that any activities carried on, or about to be carried on, by or under the control of any person, involve, or as the case may be, will involve, a risk of the commission of such an offence[22].

1   As to the Secretary of State and the Welsh Ministers see PARA 390.
2   An authorisation must be in writing (Natural Environment and Rural Communities Act 2006 s 44(2)) and is subject to any conditions or limitations specified in it (s 44(3)). The Food and Environment Protection Act 1985 Sch 2 (officers and their powers: see FOOD AND DRINK vol 51 (2013) PARA 718), other than Sch 2 para 2A(1)(b), has effect with respect to inspectors as it has effect with respect to persons authorised to enforce Pt III (ss 16–19) (see PARAS 130–131, 140–141): Natural Environment and Rural Communities Act 2006 s 44(4).
3   Natural Environment and Rural Communities Act 2006 s 44(2). The statutory provisions concerned with the restrictions on the use of pesticides harmful to wildlife are those of s 43 (see PARA 138).
4   'Premises' includes land (including buildings), movable structures, vehicles, vessels, aircraft and other means of transport: Natural Environment and Rural Communities Act 2006 s 46(4).
5   Natural Environment and Rural Communities Act 2006 s 44(1)(a).
6   Natural Environment and Rural Communities Act 2006 s 44(1)(b).
7   Natural Environment and Rural Communities Act 2006 s 44(1)(c). An inspector who seizes a substance under this provision must give to a person on the premises, or affix conspicuously to some object on the premises, a notice stating what he has seized and the ground for seizing it (s 44(5), (6)(a)) and the address for service for any claim for the return of the substance (s 44(6)(b)). He may then retain the substance for so long as is reasonably necessary for the purposes of any investigation or proceedings in respect of an offence under s 43 (s 44(7)(a)) and, subject to any order for forfeiture under s 43(5) (see PARA 138) or any claim made within the relevant period by a person entitled to the return of the substance, may retain the substance or, after the relevant period, destroy or otherwise dispose of it (s 44(7)(b)). 'Relevant period' means the period ending 28 days after any proceedings in respect of an offence under s 43 are finally determined (s 44(8)(a)) or, if no such proceedings are brought, the time for bringing such proceedings expires (s 44(8)(b)).
8   Ie under the Natural Environment and Rural Communities Act 2006 s 44 and the Food and Environment Protection Act 1985 Sch 2 (as applied by the Natural Environment and Rural Communities Act 2006 s 44(4)) (see the text and notes 1–7).
9   Natural Environment and Rural Communities Act 2006 s 45(1)(a), (2). The Secretary of State may issue, revise and replace such a code of practice: s 45(1)(a), (b). Such a code is admissible in evidence in any proceedings (s 45(4)(a)) and must be taken into account by a court in any case in which it appears to the court to be relevant (s 45(4)(b)).
10 Natural Environment and Rural Communities Act 2006 s 45(3).
11 The Secretary of State and the Welsh Ministers may specify descriptions of local authority officers who may be authorised to exercise the powers conferred by the Food and Environment Protection Act 1985 s 19, Sch 2 (the 'enforcement powers') (as to which see FOOD AND DRINK vol 51 (2013) PARA 718), but may direct that an officer of a particular description may be authorised to exercise them only for specified purposes (s 19(1B), (7) (s 19(1A)–(1D) added by the Pesticides (Fees and Enforcement) Act 1989 s 2)); and if either the Secretary of State or the Welsh Ministers so specify a description of local authority officers, a local authority may by instrument in writing authorise any of its officers falling within that description to exercise those powers (Food and Environment Protection Act 1985 s 19(1C) (as so added)). Thus the enforcement powers may be exercised by a person whom the Secretary of State has or the Welsh Ministers have by instrument in writing (which may provide that the person to whom it is issued may only exercise the enforcement powers for specified purposes) authorised to exercise them (s 19(1)(a) (s 19(1) substituted by the Pesticides (Fees and Enforcement) Act 1989 s 2); Food and Environment Protection Act 1985 s 19(1A) (as so added)) or by an officer of a local authority who is authorised to exercise them under s 19(1C) (s 19(1)(b) (as so substituted)); and the provisions of s 19(2)–(8) (see the text and notes 2–13) are to be construed in reference to a person authorised to exercise the enforcement powers as subject

to the terms of the instrument which authorises him to exercise them (s 19(1D) (as so added)). As to the Secretary of State and the Welsh Ministers see PARA 390. As to the meaning of 'local authority' see PARA 131 note 12. For the power of an authorised person to require the provision of information necessary to the discharge of his functions under these provisions see Sch 2; and FOOD AND DRINK vol 51 (2013) PARA 718.

12 'Vessel' includes every description of vessel used in navigation: Food and Environment Protection Act 1985 s 24(1) (amended by the Merchant Shipping Act 1995 Sch 13 para 75); Merchant Shipping Act 1995 s 313(1). See SHIPPING AND MARITIME LAW vol 93 (2017) PARA 229.

13 'Marine structure' means a platform or other man-made structure at sea, other than a pipe-line: Food and Environment Protection Act 1985 s 24(1).

14 As to the meaning of 'pesticide' see PARA 130 note 6.

15 Food and Environment Protection Act 1985 s 19(2)(a).

16 Food and Environment Protection Act 1985 s 19(3)(a).

17 Food and Environment Protection Act 1985 s 19(2)(b), (3)(b). References to the general purposes of Pt III (ss 16–19) are references to the purposes mentioned in s 16(1) (see PARA 130): s 16(1). For any of those purposes, an authorised person may require any person to give him information as to the formulation, effects or use of any substance: s 19(4).

18 Ie regulations made under the Food and Environment Protection Act 1985 s 16(2) (see PARA 131).

19 As to the meaning of 'approval' in relation to pesticides see PARA 131 note 6.

20 Ie is committing an offence under the Food and Environment Protection Act 1985 s 16(12)(a) (see PARAS 131, 140).

21 Food and Environment Protection Act 1985 s 19(5). A notice under s 19(5) or s 19(6) (see the text and note 13) may at any time be withdrawn by a person so authorised (s 19(6A) (s 19(6A), (6B) added by the Pesticides Act 1998 s 2(1))), although withdrawal will not affect the power to serve a fresh notice under the Food and Environment Protection Act 1985 s 19(5) or s 19(6) (s 19(6B) (as so added)). Any notice served under these provisions by an authorised person must be entered in a public register which is to be maintained by the authorised person: see the Environment and Safety Information Act 1988 s 1; and HEALTH AND SAFETY AT WORK vol 52 (2014) PARA 341. Entries must remain in the register for at least three years: see s 3(5). Provision is made for the protection of trade secrets from disclosure through entries made in the register: see s 4.

22 Food and Environment Protection Act 1985 s 19(6). See note 12. Such a notice must state that the authorised person is of the requisite opinion, specify the matters which in his opinion give or, as the case may be, will give rise to the said risk, and direct that the activities to which the notice relates must not be carried on by or under the control of the person on whom the notice is served unless the matters specified in the notice have been remedied: Food and Environment Protection Act 1985 s 19(6).

140. Power to require information.

The Secretary of State and the Welsh Ministers[1] may require the provision of such information by importers, exporters, manufacturers, distributors or users of a pesticide[2] as he or they consider necessary:

(1)   for the purpose of controlling pesticides in the United Kingdom[3];

(2)   for fulfilling any international obligations to provide information[4]; or

(3)   for enabling the United Kingdom government to determine what action it should take to fulfil an international obligation of any other description[5].

Contravention of any such requirement, or misstatement or non-disclosure pursuant to such a requirement, is an offence[6].

1 As to the Secretary of State and the Welsh Ministers see PARA 390.

2 As to the meaning of 'pesticide' see PARA 130 note 6.

3 Food and Environment Protection Act 1985 s 16(11)(a). Payment of a fee for the collection and processing of information under s 16(11) may be required: see s 18(1), (2)(b), (3)–(8) (s 18 substituted by the Pesticides (Fees and Enforcement) Act 1989 s 1(1)); and the Plant Protection Products (Payments) Regulations 2001, SI 2001/3898, reg 2. As to the meaning of 'United Kingdom' see PARA 1 note 1.

4 Food and Environment Protection Act 1985 s 16(11)(b). See note 3.

5 Food and Environment Protection Act 1985 s 16(11)(c). See note 3.

6   See the Food and Environment Protection Act 1985 s 16(12)(a)(iii), (b)(i)–(iii). Under these
      provisions a person who without reasonable excuse contravenes, or causes or permits any other
      person to contravene, any requirement imposed by virtue of s 16(11), or in purporting to give
      information required by virtue of s 16(11) makes a statement which he knows to be false in a
      material particular, recklessly makes a statement which is false in a material particular, or
      intentionally fails to disclose any material particular, is guilty of an offence. As to offences, and the
      service of notices in connection with them, see further PARA 139.

141. Codes of practice.

After consultation with persons representative of the interests concerned, the
Secretary of State and the Welsh Ministers[1] may from time to time prepare and
issue codes of practice for the purpose of providing practical guidance in respect
of the statutory provisions regulating the manufacture and use of pesticides[2]. Any
such code must be printed and distributed, and may be put on sale to the public[3].

1   As to the Secretary of State and the Welsh Ministers see PARA 390.
2   Food and Environment Protection Act 1985 s 17(1)(a). The statutory provisions regulating the
      manufacture and use of pesticides are Pt III (ss 16–19) and regulations made thereunder: see PARAS
      130–140. Any such code may be revised by revoking, varying, amending or adding to its
      provisions: s 17(1)(b).
3   Food and Environment Protection Act 1985 s 17(5). A failure by any person to follow any
      guidance contained in a code does not of itself render that person liable to proceedings of any kind:
      s 17(6). In all criminal proceedings any such code is admissible in evidence, and if any provision
      of a code appears to the court conducting the proceedings to be relevant to any question arising
      in the proceedings, it is to be taken into account in determining that question: s 17(7).

7. LIVESTOCK

(1) IDENTIFICATION AND MOVEMENT OF LIVESTOCK

(i) Restrictions on the Movement of Farm Animals

142. Restrictions on the movement of pigs, cattle, goats and sheep.

No one may move a pig from any premises if any pig has been moved on to those premises during the previous 20 days or if any cattle, goats or sheep have been moved on to those premises during the previous 6 days[1].

No one may move any sheep, goats or cattle from any premises if any sheep, goats, cattle or pigs have been moved on to those premises during the previous 6 days[2].

Provision is made for the movement of animals to be restricted to control or prevent the spread of certain diseases such as tuberculosis[3].

1   Disease Control (England) Order 2003, SI 2003/1729, art 5; Disease Control (Wales) Order 2003, SI 2003/1966, art 5. As to the meaning of 'premises' see PARA 147 note 2. As to movements that are permitted see PARA 143 and as to movements that do not trigger a standstill period see PARA 144. As to the issue of a general licence for the movement of animals see PARA 147 et seq.
2   Disease Control (England) Order 2003, SI 2003/1729, art 4; Disease Control (Wales) Order 2003, SI 2003/1966, art 4.
3   See ANIMALS vol 2 (2017) PARA 409.

143. Permitted movement during standstill.

Notwithstanding restrictions on the movement of cattle, sheep, goats[1] and pigs[2], animals[3] may be moved off premises during the standstill period[4] if the movement is one that is permitted under the following provisions or if a permit disapplying the standstill period has been issued by a veterinary inspector[5].

The following movement are permitted off premises during the standstill period:

(1)   the movement of an animal to a place for veterinary treatment[6];
(2)   the movement of an animal from a place for veterinary treatment provided the animal has not come into contact with other animals while at the place of treatment[7];
(3)   the movement of an animal to a laboratory for diagnostic tests to be carried out to ascertain whether the animal is affected by or has been exposed to a disease[8];
(4)   the movement of an animal direct to a slaughterhouse[9];
(5)   the movement of a pig to a market for pigs intended for immediate slaughter[10];
(6)   the movement of an animal to a collecting centre[11] for animals intended for immediate slaughter, provided that:
         (a)   the collecting centre premises have not been and will not be used on the same day for a show or exhibition or for the sale or trading of animals otherwise than for immediate slaughter; and
         (b)   all animals moved to the collecting centre are moved from there direct to a slaughterhouse[12];
(7)   the movement of pigs, or in relation to England pigs or cattle, to an artificial insemination centre[13];

(8)   in relation to England only, the movement of sheep or goats to an artificial insemination centre provided they have been isolated from all other animals for six days before departure[14];

(9)   the movement of an animal for direct export or to a collecting centre or assembly centre[15] prior to such export[16];

(10)   the movement of animals between premises in a sole occupancy group[17];

(11)   the movement of an animal between land[18] over which the owner or keeper of the animal has a registered right of common[19] and:

     (a)   premises occupied by the owner or keeper of the animal and in relation to which the registered right of common is customarily exercised; or

     (b)   premises occupied by any other person who has a registered right of common over that land and in relation to which the registered right of common is customarily exercised[20];

(12)   the movement of an animal between premises occupied by the owner or keeper of the animal and in relation to which a registered right of common over land is customarily exercised and premises occupied by any other person who has a registered right of common over that land and in relation to which the registered right of common of that other person is customarily exercised[21];

(13)   the movement of a pig intended for breeding or growing[22];

(14)   in relation to England only, the movement of rams and bulls intended for breeding to a market, provided that they have been placed in an isolation facility approved for this purpose by a veterinary inspector for 6 days prior to the movement[23];

(15)   the movement of cattle, sheep and goats to shows and exhibitions[24];

(16)   movement of an animal which is on a vehicle which enters premises to drop off other animals, provided it has not left the means of transport while on the premises[25].

1   Ie notwithstanding the Disease Control (England) Order 2003, SI 2003/1729, art 4 or, in relation to Wales, the Disease Control (Wales) Order 2003, SI 2003/1966, art 4.

2   Ie notwithstanding the Disease Control (England) Order 2003, SI 2003/1729, art 5 or, in relation to Wales, the Disease Control (Wales) Order 2003, SI 2003/1966, art 5.

3   'Animals' means cattle (excluding bison and yak), deer, goats, pigs and sheep: Disease Control (England) Order 2003, SI 2003/1729, art 2; Disease Control (Wales) Order 2003, SI 2003/1966, art 2.

4   'Standstill period' means a period when animals may not be moved off premises because of the provisions of the Disease Control (England) Order 2003, SI 2003/1729, art 4 or 5 or, in relation to Wales, the Disease Control (Wales) Order 2003, SI 2003/1966, art 4 or 5: Disease Control (England) Order 2003, SI 2003/1729, art 2; Disease Control (Wales) Order 2003, SI 2003/1966, art 2. As to the meaning of 'premises' see PARA 147 note 2.

5   Disease Control (England) Order 2003, SI 2003/1729, art 6; Disease Control (Wales) Order 2003, SI 2003/1966, art 6.

6   Disease Control (England) Order 2003, SI 2003/1729, Sch 1 para 1(1); Disease Control (Wales) Order 2003, SI 2003/1966, Sch 1 para 1(1). 'Veterinary treatment' includes, in the case of goats, the collection of semen: Disease Control (England) Order 2003, SI 2003/1729, art 2; Disease Control (Wales) Order 2003, SI 2003/1966, art 2.

7   Disease Control (England) Order 2003, SI 2003/1729, Sch 1 para 1(2); Disease Control (Wales) Order 2003, SI 2003/1966, Sch 1 para 1(2).

8   Disease Control (England) Order 2003, SI 2003/1729, Sch 1 para 1(3); Disease Control (Wales) Order 2003, SI 2003/1966, Sch 1 para 1(3).

9   Disease Control (England) Order 2003, SI 2003/1729, Sch 1 para 2; Disease Control (Wales) Order 2003, SI 2003/1966, Sch 1 para 2. As to the meaning of 'slaughterhouse' see the Food Safety and Hygiene (England) Regulations 2013, SI 2013/2996 or, in relation to Wales, the Food Hygiene (Wales) Regulations 2006, SI 2006/31: Disease Control (England) Order 2003, SI 2003/1729, art 2; Disease Control (Wales) Order 2003, SI 2003/1966, art 2.

10 Disease Control (England) Order 2003, SI 2003/1729, Sch 1 para 3; Disease Control (Wales) Order 2003, SI 2003/1966, Sch 1 para 3.
11 'Collecting centre' means premises used for the intermediate reception of animals intended to be moved elsewhere (but does not include a market or other place used for the sale or trading of animals unless all the animals there are intended for immediate slaughter): Disease Control (England) Order 2003, SI 2003/1729, art 2; Disease Control (Wales) Order 2003, SI 2003/1966, art 2.
12 Disease Control (England) Order 2003, SI 2003/1729, Sch 1 para 4; Disease Control (Wales) Order 2003, SI 2003/1966, Sch 1 para 4.
13 Disease Control (England) Order 2003, SI 2003/1729, Sch 1 para 5; Disease Control (Wales) Order 2003, SI 2003/1966, Sch 1 para 5 (amended by SI 2017/674).
14 Disease Control (England) Order 2003, SI 2003/1729, Sch 1 para 6.
15 Ie approved under the Trade in Animals and Related Products Regulations 2011, SI 2011/1197, Sch 2 Pt 1 or, in relation to Wales, the Trade in Animals and Related Products (Wales) Regulations 2011, SI 2011/2379, Sch 2 Pt 1.
16 Disease Control (England) Order 2003, SI 2003/1729, Sch 1 para 7 (amended by SI 2016/280); Disease Control (Wales) Order 2003, SI 2003/1966, Sch 1 para 7.
17 Disease Control (England) Order 2003, SI 2003/1729, Sch 1 para 8; Disease Control (Wales) Order 2003, SI 2003/1966, Sch 1 para 8. The Secretary of State and the Welsh Ministers may authorise sets of premises as sole occupancy groups if satisfied that the premises are linked in terms of their control: Disease Control (England) Order 2003, SI 2003/1729, art 11; Disease Control (Wales) Order 2003, SI 2003/1966, art 11.
18 As to the meaning of 'land' see PARA 147 note 2.
19 For these purposes 'registered right of common' means a right of common registered under the Commons Registration Act 1965 or a right of common which is exempt from such registration but which is registered, designated, attached, or otherwise recognised, continued or preserved under and in accordance with any of the New Forest Acts 1854, 1949, 1964 and 1970, the Epping Forest Acts 1878 and 1880 or the City of London (Various Powers) Act 1977 or any like right or permission exercised in the Forest of Dean: Disease Control (England) Order 2003, SI 2003/1729, Sch 1 para 9(3); Disease Control (Wales) Order 2003, SI 2003/1966, Sch 1 para 9(3).
20 Disease Control (England) Order 2003, SI 2003/1729, Sch 1 para 9(1); Disease Control (Wales) Order 2003, SI 2003/1966, Sch 1 para 9(1).
21 Disease Control (England) Order 2003, SI 2003/1729, Sch 1 para 9(2); Disease Control (Wales) Order 2003, SI 2003/1966, Sch 1 para 9(2).
22 Disease Control (England) Order 2003, SI 2003/1729, Sch 1 para 10 (amended by SI 2016/280); Disease Control (Wales) Order 2003, SI 2003/1966, Sch 1 para 10. This must either be in accordance with the Pigs (Records, Identification and Movement) Order 2011, SI 2011/2154, art 21 or, in relation to Wales, the Pigs (Records, Identification and Movement) (Wales) Order 2011, SI 2011/2830, art 21 or if the pig has been placed in an isolation facility approved for this purpose by a veterinary inspector for 20 days prior to the movement: see the Disease Control (England) Order 2003, SI 2003/1729, Sch 1 para 10; and the Disease Control (Wales) Order 2003, SI 2003/1966, Sch 1 para 10.
23 Disease Control (England) Order 2003, SI 2003/1729, Sch 1 para 12(1). To qualify for this exemption:
    (1)   the movement must take place on or after 1st August and before 1st December;
    (2)   the animals must not have shared the isolation facility with animals isolated for any other purpose; and
    (3)   the person sending the animal must submit, in accordance with the terms of the licence under which the animal is moved, and without undue delay, a declaration that the animal is intended for sale for breeding: Sch 1 para 12(2) (amended by SI 2005/3100, SI 2016/280).
24 Disease Control (England) Order 2003, SI 2003/1729, Sch 1 para 13; Disease Control (Wales) Order 2003, SI 2003/1966, Sch 1 para 13 (substituted by SI 2017/674). In relation to England, head (15) in the text applies provided that the cattle, Sheep and goats have been isolated for 6 days in a facility approved for this purpose by a veterinary inspector before travelling to a show or exhibition or they have moved into the isolation facility from another show or exhibition and have not left that isolation facility since being taken on to it: Disease Control (England) Order 2003, SI 2003/1729, Sch 1 para 13. In relation to Wales this applies provided where they have moved from another show or exhibition within the last 6 days they have been held in a quarantine unit and have not left that quarantine unit since being taken into it: Disease Control (Wales) Order 2003, SI 2003/1966, Sch 1 para 13 (as so substituted).
25 Disease Control (England) Order 2003, SI 2003/1729, Sch 1 para 14; Disease Control (Wales) Order 2003, SI 2003/1966, Sch 1 para 14.

144.   Movements that do not triggers a standstill period.

The standstill period[1] is not triggered by a movement on to premises[2] if it is a movement as follows[3]:

(1)   in relation to Wales only, the arrival of cattle, sheep and goats on to the premises provided they are quarantined for six days after their arrival in a quarantine unit[4];

(2)   the movement of an animal[5] on to any premises licensed for an animal gathering[6] if the movement is for the purposes of a gathering so licensed[7];

(3)   the movement of an animal on to an artificial insemination centre[8];

(4)   movement approved by the Secretary of State or Welsh Ministers[9] of a pig on to a holding[10];

(5)   arrival of a pig for breeding (other than one being moved under provisions relating to head (4))[11] on the breeding premises provided that certain conditions are met[12];

(6)   movement of a pig (other than one being moved under provisions relating to head (4))[13] which is being returned to those premises from a place to which it had been moved for breeding, provided that certain conditions are met[14];

(7)   the return of pigs, cattle, sheep or goats from a show or exhibition to the premises from which they were consigned to that show or exhibition provided that certain conditions are met[15];

(8)   in relation to England only, return of rams and bulls from a market provided that the animals are isolated for six days after their return in premises approved by a veterinary inspector[16];

(9)   in relation to England only, arrival of rams and bulls for the purpose of breeding provided they are isolated for six days after their arrival in a facility approved for this purpose by a veterinary inspector[17];

(10)   in relation to England only, arrival of goats for the purpose of breeding provided that they have been isolated on the premises of origin for six days prior to leaving in a facility approved for this purpose by a veterinary inspector[18];

(11)   arrival of cattle which are being returned to those premises from an artificial insemination centre provided in relation to Wales, that they are quarantined for six days after their return in a quarantine unit[19];

(12)   arrival of pigs which are being returned to those premises from an artificial insemination centre provided they are isolated from all other animals for 20 days after their return[20];

(13)   arrival of sheep or goats which are returning from an artificial insemination centre provided that they are isolated from all other animals for six days after their return; and, in relation to England, they were isolated from all other animals while at the artificial insemination centre[21];

(14)   the arrival of an imported animal at its point of entry into England or Wales[22];

(15)   movement of an animal from its point of entry into the United Kingdom following its import from another member state[23];

(16)   the movement of animals between premises in a sole occupancy group[24];

(17)   movement of an animal brought on to premises in a vehicle to collect other animals provided that the animal is not unloaded at those premises[25];

(18) the arrival of sheep, goats, cattle or pigs being returned to those premises from a place for veterinary treatment or of any offspring to which they have given birth while there provided that, in the case of pigs, they are isolated from other animals for 20 days following their return[26].

1 As to the meaning of 'standstill period' see PARA 143 note 4.
2 As to the meaning of 'premises' see PARA 147 note 2.
3 Disease Control (England) Order 2003, SI 2003/1729, art 7; Disease Control (Wales) Order 2003, SI 2003/1966, art 7.
4 Disease Control (Wales) Order 2003, SI 2003/1966, Sch 2 para Z1 (added by SI 2017/674).
5 As to the meaning of 'animal' see PARA 143 note 3.
6 Ie licensed under the Animal Gatherings Order 2010, SI 2010/460 or, in relation to Wales, the Animal Gatherings (Wales) Order 2010, SI 2010/900 (see ANIMALS vol 2 (2017) PARA 170.
7 Disease Control (England) Order 2003, SI 2003/1729, Sch 2 para 1 (amended by SI 2016/280); Disease Control (Wales) Order 2003, SI 2003/1966, Sch 2 para 1 (amended by SI 2017/674).
8 Disease Control (England) Order 2003, SI 2003/1729, Sch 2 para 2; Disease Control (Wales) Order 2003, SI 2003/1966, Sch 2 para 2.
9 Ie movement referred to in the Pigs (Records, Identification and Movement) Order 2011, SI 2011/2154, art 21 or, in relation to Wales, the Pigs (Records, Identification and Movement) (Wales) Order 2011, SI 2011/2830, art 21.
10 Disease Control (England) Order 2003, SI 2003/1729, Sch 2 para 3 (amended by SI 2016/280); Disease Control (Wales) Order 2003, SI 2003/1966, Sch 2 para 3.
11 Ie other than one being moved under the Pigs (Records, Identification and Movement) Order 2011, SI 2011/2154, art 21 or, in relation to Wales, the Pigs (Records, Identification and Movement) (Wales) Order 2011, SI 2011/2830, art 21.
12 Disease Control (England) Order 2003, SI 2003/1729, Sch 2 para 4(1) (amended by SI 2016/280); Disease Control (Wales) Order 2003, SI 2003/1966, Sch 2 para 4(1) (amended by SI 2017/674). The conditions mentioned in the text are that:
    (1) prior to being moved, either there is no standstill period on the premises of departure, or alternatively it has been isolated for 20 days prior to the movement taking place in a facility approved for this purpose by a veterinary inspector;
    (2) it is isolated while on the breeding premises (or for 20 days, whichever is shorter) in an isolation facility approved for this purpose by a veterinary inspector;
    (3) any pig placed in the isolation facility with the pig brought on to the premise for breeding purposes has been on the breeding premises for at least 20 days before being placed in that facility;
    (4) any other pig placed into the isolation facility on the breeding premises with the one brought on to those premises remains in isolation for 20 days after the arrival of the pig being brought into the premises, or for 20 days after being placed into isolation with it whichever is later; and
    (5) the recipient of the breeding pig submits, in accordance with the terms of the licence under which the pig is moved, and without undue delay a declaration that the pig is intended for breeding on those premises: Disease Control (England) Order 2003, SI 2003/1729, Sch 2 para 4(1)(a)–(e) (amended by SI 2016/280); Disease Control (Wales) Order 2003, SI 2003/1966, Sch 2 para 4(1)(a)–(e) (amended by SI 2017/674).
13 Ie other than one being moved under the Pigs (Records, Identification and Movement) Order 2011, SI 2011/2154, art 21 or, in relation to Wales, the Pigs (Records, Identification and Movement) (Wales) Order 2011, SI 2011/2830, art 21.
14 Disease Control (England) Order 2003, SI 2003/1729, Sch 2 para 4(2) (amended by SI 2016/280); Disease Control (Wales) Order 2003, SI 2003/1966, Sch 2 para 4(2) (amended by SI 2017/674). The conditions mentioned in the text are that it is isolated for 20 days after the date of its return from all other animals and that the occupier of the premises from which the pig has returned from breeding has submitted the declaration required in head (5) in note 12: Disease Control (England) Order 2003, SI 2003/1729, Sch 2 para 4(2) (as so amended); Disease Control (Wales) Order 2003, SI 2003/1966, Sch 2 para 4(2) (as so amended).
15 Disease Control (England) Order 2003, SI 2003/1729, Sch 2 para 5; Disease Control (Wales) Order 2003, SI 2003/1966, Sch 2 para 5 (substituted by SI 2017/674). The conditions mentioned in the text are in relation to pigs that the animals are isolated for 20 after their return in premises approved for this purpose by a veterinary inspector: Disease Control (England) Order 2003, SI 2003/1729, Sch 2 para 5; Disease Control (Wales) Order 2003, SI 2003/1966, Sch 2 para 5(2) (as so substituted). In relation to Wales, the return of cattle, sheep or goats from a show or

exhibition to the premises from which they were consigned to that show or exhibition provided that the animals are quarantined for 6 days after their return in a quarantine unit: Sch 2 para 5(1) (as so substituted).

16 Disease Control (England) Order 2003, SI 2003/1729, Sch 2 para 6(1). To qualify for this exemption the movement must take place on or after 1st August and before 1st December and the animals must not have shared the isolation facility with animals isolated for any other purpose: Sch 2 para 6(2) (amended by SI 2005/3100; SI 2016/280).

17 Disease Control (England) Order 2003, SI 2003/1729, Sch 2 para 7(1). To qualify for this exemption the movement must take place on or after 1st August and before 1st December, the recipient of the breeding animal must submit, in accordance with the terms of the licence under which the animal is moved, and without undue delay a declaration that the animal is intended for breeding on those premises and any ewes placed with that ram must be isolated for six days in that facility: Sch 2 para 7(2) (amended by SI 2005/3100; SI 2016/280).

18 Disease Control (England) Order 2003, SI 2003/1729, Sch 2 para 8(1). To qualify for this exemption the recipient of the breeding animal must submit, in accordance with the terms of the licence under which the animal is moved, and without undue delay a declaration that the animal is intended for breeding on those premises: Sch 2 para 8(2) (amended by SI 2005/3100; SI 2016/280).

19 Disease Control (England) Order 2003, SI 2003/1729, Sch 2 para 9; Disease Control (Wales) Order 2003, SI 2003/1966, Sch 2 para 9 (substituted by SI 2017/674).

20 Disease Control (England) Order 2003, SI 2003/1729, Sch 2 para 10; Disease Control (Wales) Order 2003, SI 2003/1966, Sch 2 para 10.

21 Disease Control (England) Order 2003, SI 2003/1729, Sch 2 para 11; Disease Control (Wales) Order 2003, SI 2003/1966, Sch 2 para 9 (as substituted: see note 19).

22 Disease Control (England) Order 2003, SI 2003/1729, Sch 2 para 12(1); Disease Control (Wales) Order 2003, SI 2003/1966, Sch 2 para 12(1).

23 Disease Control (England) Order 2003, SI 2003/1729, Sch 2 para 12(2); Disease Control (Wales) Order 2003, SI 2003/1966, Sch 2 para 12(2).

24 Disease Control (England) Order 2003, SI 2003/1729, Sch 2 para 13; Disease Control (Wales) Order 2003, SI 2003/1966, Sch 2 para 13. As to sole occupancy groups see PARA 143 note 17.

25 Disease Control (England) Order 2003, SI 2003/1729, Sch 2 para 14; Disease Control (Wales) Order 2003, SI 2003/1966, Sch 2 para 14.

26 Disease Control (England) Order 2003, SI 2003/1729, Sch 2 para 15; Disease Control (Wales) Order 2003, SI 2003/1966, Sch 2 para 15.

145. Isolation facilities and quarantine units.

Pigs may not share an isolation facility with animals of any other species[1].

In relation to England, where animals are held in an isolation facility under certain disease control provisions[2], and other animals are moved in before they are released from the isolation facility, no animal may be removed from the isolation facility before the last date of release of the last animals moved into the isolation facility[3].

In relation to Wales, an isolation facility may not be used to hold any animals other than pigs[4] and where pigs are held in an isolation facility under the disease control provisions[5], and other pigs are moved in before they are released from the isolation facility, no pig may be removed from the isolation facility before the last date of release of the last pigs moved into the isolation facility[6].

In relation to Wales, a quarantine unit[7] may only be used to hold cattle, sheep and goats[7]. Where animals are held in a quarantine unit under the disease control provisions[8], and other animals are moved in before they are released from the quarantine unit, no animal may be removed from the quarantine unit before the last date of release of the last animal moved into the quarantine unit[9].

Where the Welsh Ministers[10] have served on the keeper of cattle a notice requiring the keeper to have any such cattle tested for tuberculosis[11] with a relevant test[12] before a date specified in the notice, no cattle may be held in, or moved into, a quarantine unit on the date of the relevant test unless a skin test has been applied to those cattle no more than 60 days before the date of the relevant test, and the results of the test have been read by a veterinary inspector or an approved veterinary surgeon[13] and are negative[14]. Where a relevant test for tuberculosis has been applied to such cattle as specified in such a notice but before the result of that test has been read by an inspector, or an approved veterinary surgeon, the keeper of the cattle may move any animal into a quarantine unit[15].

1 Disease Control (England) Order 2003, SI 2003/1729, art 8(2); Disease Control (Wales) Order 2003, SI 2003/1966, art 8(2).
2 Ie under the Disease Control (England) Order 2003, SI 2003/1729.
3 Disease Control (England) Order 2003, SI 2003/1729, art 8(1).
4 Disease Control (Wales) Order 2003, SI 2003/1966, art 8(3) (art 8(1), (3) substituted by SI 2017/674).
5 Ie under the Disease Control (Wales) Order 2003, SI 2003/1966.
6 Disease Control (Wales) Order 2003, SI 2003/1966, art 8(1) (as substituted: see note 4).
7 'Quarantine unit' means a facility or premises approved in writing for quarantine purposes by a body accredited by the United Kingdom Accreditation Service (UKAS): Disease Control (Wales) Order 2003, SI 2003/1966, art 2 (definition added by SI 2017/674). Approval of a quarantine unit may be made subject to conditions and may be suspended, amended or revoked by notice in writing at any time by a body accredited by UKAS or by the Welsh Ministers: Disease Control (Wales) Order 2003, SI 2003/1966, art 8A(7) (added by SI 2017/674).
8 See note 5.
9 Disease Control (Wales) Order 2003, SI 2003/1966, art 8A(2) (as added: see note 6). No person may move any animal off premises direct from a quarantine unit unless the movement is one specified in Sch 1 paras 1, 2, 4, 13 or 14 (see PARA 143): art 8A(3) (as so added).
10 As to the Welsh Ministers see PARA 390.
11 For these purposes 'tuberculosis' means infection with *Mycobacterium bovis*: Disease Control (Wales) Order 2003, SI 2003/1966, art 8A(8) (as added: see note 6).
12 For these purposes 'relevant test' means a skin test or any other diagnostic test for tuberculosis approved by the Welsh Ministers and 'skin test' means a single intradermal comparative cervical tuberculin test for tuberculosis using bovine and avian tuberculin: Disease Control (Wales) Order 2003, SI 2003/1966, art 8A(8) (as added: see note 6).
13 For these purposes 'approved veterinary surgeon' means a veterinary surgeon who is approved in accordance with the Tuberculosis (Wales) Order 2010, SI 2010/1379, art 2A: Disease Control (Wales) Order 2003, SI 2003/1966, art 8A(8) (as added: see note 6).
14 Disease Control (Wales) Order 2003, SI 2003/1966, art 8A(4) (as added: see note 6).
15 Disease Control (Wales) Order 2003, SI 2003/1966, art 8A(5) (as added: see note 6). A keeper must record:
    (1)   movement of an animal into a quarantine unit within 24 hours of the movement;
    (2)   movement of an animal out of a quarantine unit within 3 days of the movement; and
    (3)   all movements in the holding register within 36 hours of the movement: s 8A(6) (as so added).
For these purposes 'record' means notifying or reporting the movement of an animal in accordance with the Cattle Identification (Wales) Regulations 2007, SI 2007/842 or the Sheep and Goats (Records, Identification and Movement) (Wales) Order 2015, SI 2015/1992: Disease Control (Wales) Order 2003, SI 2003/1966, art 8A(8) (as so added).

146. Restrictions on movements to and from slaughterhouses.

No one may:
(1)   move any animal[1] to a slaughterhouse[2] save for the purpose of slaughter within 48 hours of its arrival there; or
(2)   receive any animal from a slaughterhouse unless, in the case of any animal other than a pig, under the authority of a licence issued by a veterinary inspector[3].

1 As to the meaning of 'animal' see PARA 143 note 3.
2 As to the meaning of 'slaughterhouse' see the Food Safety and Hygiene (England) Regulations 2013, SI 2013/2996 or, in relation to Wales, the Food Hygiene (Wales) Regulations 2006, SI 2006/31: Disease Control (England) Order 2003, SI 2003/1729, art 2; Disease Control (Wales) Order 2003, SI 2003/1966, art 2.
3 Disease Control (England) Order 2003, SI 2003/1729, art 10; Disease Control (Wales) Order 2003, SI 2003/1966, art 10.

(ii) Licences to Move Animals

147. Requirement for a general licence to move animals.

No one may move an animal[1] from any premises[2] unless the movement is made under the authority of a licence issued by the Welsh Ministers, the Secretary of State[3] or an inspector[4]. This does not apply to any movement authorised by a walking licence[5] issued to a keeper of a pet pig[6].

The licence, permit or authorisation must be in writing, may be general or specific, may be subject to conditions and may be varied, suspended or revoked at any time by notice in writing issued:

(1)   by the Secretary of State or the Welsh Ministers, in the case of a licence, permit or authorisation issued by the Secretary of State or an inspector of any kind;

(2)   by a veterinary inspector, in the case of a licence or permit issued by a veterinary inspector or any other inspector of the Secretary of State or the Welsh Ministers;

(3)   by an inspector of the Secretary of State or the Welsh Ministers (other than a veterinary inspector), in the case of a licence issued by any such inspector; or

(4)   by an inspector of a local authority, in the case of a licence issued by an inspector of that local authority[7].

In deciding whether to issue a licence[8] or a permit[9] an inspector or a veterinary inspector must comply with any instructions issued by the Secretary of State[10].

General licences have been granted for the movement of deer, cattle, sheep, goats and pigs[11].

1   As to the meaning of 'animals' see PARA 143 note 3.
2   'Premises' includes land, with or without buildings and 'land' includes common or unenclosed land: Disease Control (England) Order 2003, SI 2003/1729, art 2; Disease Control (Wales) Order 2003, SI 2003/1966, art 2. These provisions do not apply in relation to a movement to or from a zoo licensed under the Zoo Licensing Act 1981 (see ANIMALS vol 2 (2017) PARA 261): Disease Control (England) Order 2003, SI 2003/1729, art 3 (substituted by SI 2006/182); Disease Control (Wales) Order 2003, SI 2003/1966, art 3 (substituted by SI 2006/179)
3   As to the Secretary of State and the Welsh Ministers see PARA 390.
4   Disease Control (England) Order 2003, SI 2003/1729, art 12(1); Disease Control (Wales) Order 2003, SI 2003/1966, art 12(1). Where an inspector of a local authority issues a licence under the Disease Control (England) Order 2003, SI 2003/1729, art 12(1) or the Disease Control (Wales) Order 2003, SI 2003/1966, art 12(1), he must retain a copy of the licence for 6 months: Disease Control (England) Order 2003, SI 2003/1729, art 16; Disease Control (Wales) Order 2003, SI 2003/1966, art 16. If any person fails to comply with a licence an officer of the Secretary of State or the Welsh Ministers or an inspector may arrange for it to be complied with at the expense of the person in default: Disease Control (England) Order 2003, SI 2003/1729, art 17; Disease Control (Wales) Order 2003, SI 2003/1966, art 17.
5   Ie authorised by a licence under the Pigs (Records, Identification and Movement) Order 2011, SI 2011/2154, art 20 or, in relation to Wales, the Pigs (Records, Identification and Movement) (Wales) Order 2011, SI 2011/2830, art 20.
6   Disease Control (England) Order 2003, SI 2003/1729, art 12(2) (amended by SI 2016/280); Disease Control (Wales) Order 2003, SI 2003/1966, art 12(2) (amended by SI 2011/2830).
7   Disease Control (England) Order 2003, SI 2003/1729, art 19(1); Disease Control (Wales) Order2003, SI 2003/1966, art 19(1).
8   Ie a licence under the Disease Control (England) Order 2003, SI 2003/1729, art 12(1) or the Disease Control (Wales) Order 2003, SI 2003/1966, art 12(1).
9   Ie a permit under Disease Control (England) Order 2003, SI 2003/1729, art 6(b); Disease Control (Wales) Order 2003, SI 2003/1966, art 6(b).
10 Disease Control (England) Order 2003, SI 2003/1729, art 19(2); Disease Control (Wales) Order 2003, SI 2003/1966, art 19(2).

11 Eg General Licence for the Movement of Deer within Wales granted by the Welsh Ministers on 12
    July 2016. The general licences are published on the UK Government Website or, in relation to
    Wales, on the Welsh Government website.

148. Notices prohibiting movement under a general licence.

Where a general licence has been issued[1], the Secretary of State or the Welsh
Ministers[2] may issue a notice[3] prohibiting:

(1)   the movement under the authority of that licence of any animal[4] from
         any premises[5] specified in the notice[6]; or

(2)   any person specified in the notice from moving animals under the
         authority of that licence either generally or to or from any premises
         specified in the notice[7].

A notice may only be issued under the above provisions on the advice of an
inspector, who must be of the opinion that:

(a)   the disease control provisions[8] are not being or have not been complied
         with in relation to animals moved to or from the premises in question or
         in relation to the movement of any other animals of which the person on
         whom the notice is to be served is or has at any time been the keeper[9];
         and

(b)   the service of a notice is necessary to prevent a possible spread of
         disease[10].

1   Ie issued under the Disease Control (England) Order 2003, SI 2003/1729, art 12 (in relation to
    England) or the Disease Control (Wales) Order 2003, SI 2003/1966, art 12 (in relation to Wales)
    (see PARA 146). A licence issued by a competent authority in Scotland or England for the purposes
    the movement of animals operates in Wales as if it had been issued under the Disease Control
    (Wales) Order 2003, SI 2003/1966: art 18. As to cross-border movements of animals into England
    see the Disease Control (England) Order 2003, SI 2003/1729, art 18 (substituted by
    SI 2012/2897).
2   As to the Secretary of State and the Welsh Ministers see PARA 390.
3   A notice must be in writing, may be subject to conditions and may be amended, suspended or
    revoked at any time by further notice by the Secretary of State or the Welsh Ministers: Disease
    Control (England) Order 2003, SI 2003/1729, art 13(5); Disease Control (Wales) Order 2003,
    SI 2003/1966, art 13(5).
4   As to the meaning of 'animal' see PARA 143 note 3.
5   As to the meaning of 'premises' see PARA 147 note 2.
6   Disease Control (England) Order 2003, SI 2003/1729, art 13(1)(a); Disease Control (Wales)
    Order2003, SI 2003/1966, art 13(1)(a). A notice issued under head (1) in the text must be served
    on the occupiers of each of the premises specified in the notice and in any other way that the
    Secretary of State or the Welsh Ministers thinks fit to draw the notice to the attention of persons
    affected by it: Disease Control (England) Order 2003, SI 2003/1729, art 13(3); Disease Control
    (Wales) Order 2003, SI 2003/1966, art 13(3).
7   Disease Control (England) Order 2003, SI 2003/1729, art 13(1)(b); Disease Control (Wales) Order
    2003, SI 2003/1966, art 13(1)(b). A notice issued under head (2) in the text must be served on the
    person prohibited from moving animals by the notice and on the occupiers of any premises
    individually named in the notice: Disease Control (England) Order 2003, SI 2003/1729, art 13(4);
    Disease Control (Wales) Order 2003, SI 2003/1966, art 13(4). If any person fails to comply with
    a notice an officer of the Secretary of State or the Welsh Ministers or an inspector may arrange for
    it to be complied with at the expense of the person in default: Disease Control (England) Order
    2003, SI 2003/1729, art 17; Disease Control (Wales) Order 2003, SI 2003/1966, art 17.
8   Ie the provisions in the Disease Control (England) Order 2003, SI 2003/1729, or, in relation to
    Wales, the Disease Control (Wales) Order 2003, SI 2003/1966.
9   Disease Control (England) Order 2003, SI 2003/1729, art 13(2)(a); Disease Control (Wales) Order
    2003, SI 2003/1966, art 13(2)(a).
10 Disease Control (England) Order 2003, SI 2003/1729, art 13(2)(b); Disease Control (Wales) Order
    2003, SI 2003/1966, art 13(2)(b).

149. Specific licences.

An animal[1] moved under a specific licence must be moved by the most direct route available to the place of destination specified in the licence and must be accompanied throughout the movement by the licence[2].

The person in charge of any animal moved under a specific licence must, on demand made by a constable or by an inspector or other officer of the Secretary of State or the Welsh Ministers, or of a local authority produce the licence, allow a copy or an extract to be taken and, if so required, furnish his name and address[3].

Every animal which is moved under a specific licence must be kept separate throughout such movement from any animal which is not being moved under that licence[4].

Where animals are moved under a specific licence, then, unless the licence provides otherwise, the occupier of premises which they are moved on to must ensure that he or his representative is given the licence before allowing the animals to be unloaded and keep the licence for six months and during that period produce it to an inspector on request[5].

1   As to the meaning of 'animal' see PARA 143 note 3.
2   Disease Control (England) Order 2003, SI 2003/1729, art 14(1); Disease Control (Wales) Order 2003, SI 2003/1966, art 14(1).
3   Disease Control (England) Order 2003, SI 2003/1729, art 14(2); Disease Control (Wales) Order 2003/1966, art 14(2). If any person fails to comply with a licence an officer of the Secretary of State or the Welsh Ministers or an inspector may arrange for it to be complied with at the expense of the person in default: Disease Control (England) Order 2003, SI 2003/1729, art 17; Disease Control (Wales) Order 2003, SI 2003/1966, art 17.
4   Disease Control (England) Order 2003, SI 2003/1729, art 14(3) (substituted by SI 2008/1066); Disease Control (Wales) Order 2003, SI 2003/1966, art 14(3) (substituted by SI 2008/1314).
5   Disease Control (England) Order 2003, SI 2003/1729, art 14(4); Disease Control (Wales) Order 2003, SI 2003/1966, art 14(4).

150. Movement documents for deer.

Where deer are moved under a general licence[1], and that licence requires the person moving the deer to have a movement document, the occupier of premises[2] which they are moved on to must comply with the conditions of the licence relating to the reporting of movement information and keep a copy of the completed movement document for six months and during that period produce it to an inspector on request[3].

In relation to England, a person must not move a deer[4] on to or off any premises[5] unless:

(1)   the deer is identified by an ear tag in a manner that has been approved by the Secretary of State[6];
(2)   the move is made under the authority of a licence[7]; and
(3)   the move is recorded[8] in the appropriate manner[9].

A person must not expose a deer for sale or cause or permit it to be exposed for sale in any market or sale-yard unless the deer has been marked or identified in accordance with head (1) and such mark or identification is so maintained as to be clearly legible[10].

A person must not move the carcase[11] of any deer on to or off any premises other than in a manner approved by the Secretary of State[12].

In relation to Wales, the keeper of a deer must mark or identify it in a manner approved by the Welsh Ministers[13].

1   As to the issue of general licences see PARA 147.
2   As to the meaning of 'premises' see PARA 147 note 2.

3 Disease Control (England) Order 2003, SI 2003/1729, art 15A (added by SI 2016/280); Disease Control (Wales) Order 2003, SI 2003/1966, art 15A (added by SI 2017/674).
4 For these purposes of the Tuberculosis (Deer and Camelid) (England) Order 2014, SI 2014/2337 'deer' means deer of any species that are managed by a keeper (including deer that are managed on enclosed park land) and 'keeper' means any person who owns or is responsible for a deer or camelid (as applicable), whether on a permanent or temporary basis, but it does not include a person solely responsible for transporting such an animal: see art 2.
5 For these purposes ''premises' includes land with or without buildings: Tuberculosis (Deer and Camelid) (England) Order 2014, SI 2014/2337, art 2. See also PARA 147 note 2.
6 As to the Secretary of State see PARA 390.
7 Ie a licence granted under the Disease Control (England) Order 2003, SI 2003/1729.
8 Ie it is recorded in accordance with the Movement of Animals (Records) Order 1960, SI 1960/105 (see ANIMALS).
9 Tuberculosis (Deer and Camelid) (England) Order 2014, SI 2014/2337, art 10(1).
10 Tuberculosis (Deer and Camelid) (England) Order 2014, SI 2014/2337, art 10(3).
11 For these purposes 'carcase' includes any part of an animal: Tuberculosis (Deer and Camelid) (England) Order 2014, SI 2014/2337, art 2.
12 Tuberculosis (Deer and Camelid) (England) Order 2014, SI 2014/2337, art 10(2).
13 See the Tuberculosis (Wales) Order 2011, SI 2011/692, art 5. As to the Welsh Ministers see PARA 390.

(iii) Transport of Animals

151.   Notification requirements when moving pigs.

Keepers[1], other than markets, must notify the Agriculture and Horticulture Development Board ('BPEX')[2] of all movements of pigs from their holdings[3] before those movements take place[4]. Keepers may notify BPEX electronically[5] by entering specified information onto the BPEX movement recording system[6]. When pigs are moved from a market the market must notify BPEX of the specified information in relation to those pigs electronically on the day of the movement[7].

A keeper moving pigs to a market need not notify the movement in advance if the market notifies BPEX electronically of the specified information on the day of the pigs arrival at the market[8].

A keeper moving pigs to a collection centre need not notify the movement in advance if the collection centre has agreed with the keeper to notify BPEX electronically of the specified information on the day of the pigs arrival at the collection centre[9].

A keeper moving a pig to a veterinary practice for emergency treatment need not notify the movement[10].

When a keeper intends to move a pig from their holding to a show and knows which holding they intend to move the pig to after the show, they must notify both the movement to the show and the movement from the show before moving the pig to the show[11].

When a keeper moves a pig to a show without knowing which holding they intend to move the pig to after the show, they must provide, in relation to the movement from the show, the specified information to BPEX or report to Meat and Livestock Commercial Services Limited ('MLCSL') within three days of the move from the show[12].

Any person transporting pigs must carry documentation containing certain information and give two copies to the keeper at the holding of destination if that new keeper is not able to notify BPEX electronically that the new keeper has received those animals[13]. In the case of a pig moved from a holding to a port and intended for consignment outside Great Britain the keeper at that holding must send a copy of documentation to MLCSL within three days of the animal leaving the holding[14].

1 'Keeper' means any person having care and control of pigs, whether on a temporary or permanent basis, but does not include a person who only transports pigs: Pigs (Records, Identification and Movement) Order 2011, SI 2011/2154, art 2; Pigs (Records, Identification and Movement) (Wales) Order 2011, SI 2011/2830, art 2.

2 As to the Agriculture and Horticulture Development Board see PARAS 393–396.

3 As to the meaning of 'holding' see PARA 155 note 1.

4 Pigs (Records, Identification and Movement) Order 2011, SI 2011/2154, arts 2, 12(1); Pigs (Records, Identification and Movement) (Wales) Order 2011, SI 2011/2830, arts 2, 12(1).

5 If a keeper does not notify BPEX electronically they must provide the information by telephone or in writing to Meat and Livestock Commercial Services Limited ('MLCSL') and may not move those pigs until they have received a document from MLCSL recording that information: Pigs (Records, Identification and Movement) Order 2011, SI 2011/2154, arts 2, 12(3); Pigs (Records, Identification and Movement) (Wales) Order 2011, SI 2011/2830, arts 2, 12(3). When MLCSL receives notification of movement information it must, within one working day of receipt excluding weekends, send the keeper sufficient copies of a document recording that information to enable the keeper, and any transporter and the keeper at the holding of destination to meet their recording obligations: Pigs (Records, Identification and Movement) Order 2011, SI 2011/2154, art 12(4); Pigs (Records, Identification and Movement) (Wales) Order 2011, SI 2011/2830, art 12(4).

6 Pigs (Records, Identification and Movement) Order 2011, SI 2011/2154, arts 2, 12(2); Pigs (Records, Identification and Movement) (Wales) Order 2011, SI 2011/2830, arts 2, 12(2). As to the information to be entered see the Pigs (Records, Identification and Movement) Order 2011, SI 2011/2154, art 12(2) (a)–(d); Pigs (Records, Identification and Movement) (Wales) Order 2011, SI 2011/2830, art 12(a)–(d). For these purposes 'BPEX movement recording system' means the electronic movement recording system maintained for the purpose of notifications under this Order by BPEX and "working day' means a day which is not a Saturday or a Sunday, Christmas Day, Good Friday or a bank holiday in England and Wales under the Banking and Financial Dealings Act 1971: Pigs (Records, Identification and Movement) Order 2011, SI 2011/2154, art 12(6); Pigs (Records, Identification and Movement) (Wales) Order 2011, SI 2011/2830, art 12(6).

7 Pigs (Records, Identification and Movement) Order 2011, SI 2011/2154, art 12(5); Pigs (Records, Identification and Movement) (Wales) Order 2011, SI 2011/2830, art 12(5).

8 Pigs (Records, Identification and Movement) Order 2011, SI 2011/2154, art 14(1); Pigs (Records, Identification and Movement) (Wales) Order 2011, SI 2011/2830, art 14(1).

9 Pigs (Records, Identification and Movement) Order 2011, SI 2011/2154, art 14(2); Pigs (Records, Identification and Movement) (Wales) Order 2011, SI 2011/2830, art 14(2).

10 Pigs (Records, Identification and Movement) Order 2011, SI 2011/2154, art 15; Pigs (Records, Identification and Movement) (Wales) Order 2011, SI 2011/2830, art 15.

11 Pigs (Records, Identification and Movement) Order 2011, SI 2011/2154, art 16(1); Pigs (Records, Identification and Movement) (Wales) Order 2011, SI 2011/2830, art 16(1).

12 Pigs (Records, Identification and Movement) Order 2011, SI 2011/2154, art 16(2); Pigs (Records, Identification and Movement) (Wales) Order 2011, SI 2011/2830, art 16(2).

13 See the Pigs (Records, Identification and Movement) Order 2011, SI 2011/2154, art 17(1), (2); and the Pigs (Records, Identification and Movement) (Wales) Order 2011, SI 2011/2830, art 17(1), (2). As to how long the keeper must keep the documentation for and his notification duties see the Pigs (Records, Identification and Movement) Order 2011, SI 2011/2154, art 18 and the Pigs (Records, Identification and Movement) (Wales) Order 2011, SI 2011/2830, art 18.

14 Pigs (Records, Identification and Movement) Order 2011, SI 2011/2154, art 19; Pigs (Records, Identification and Movement) (Wales) Order 2011, SI 2011/2830, art 19.

(iv) Identification and Registration of Animals

152. Marking of livestock.

The marking of livestock may be required for the purposes of subsidies or guaranteed prices to distinguish imported from home-produced livestock[1], or to ensure that a home-produced animal is not presented more than once[2]. Marking may also be required to indicate that an animal is suitable, or unsuitable, for breeding[3], or in connection with the control of the spread of diseases among animals[4].

1 See the Agriculture Act 1957 s 6; the Imported Livestock Order 1958, SI 1958/558, art 6; and PARA 169.
2 See the Agriculture Act 1957 s 5; the Sheep Variable Premium (Protection of Payments) (No 2) Order 1980, SI 1980/1811; and PARA 169.
3 See the Hill Farming Act 1946 s 18(1)(d); and PARA 156.
4 See the Animal Health Act 1981 s 8(1); and ANIMALS vol 2 (2017) PARA 409.

153. Cattle identification and registration.

An occupier of a holding who begins to keep bovine animals, including bison and buffalo, on that holding, and any person who takes over the occupation of a holding where cattle are kept, must notify the Secretary of State or, in relation to Wales, the Welsh Ministers, within one month of his name and address and the address of the holding[1], whereon they will be issued with a herdmark for each holding[2].

The Secretary of State or, in relation to Wales, the Welsh Ministers are responsible for approving and issuing ear tags with a unique identification number which must be applied, by the person responsible for identifying cattle by means of an ear tag, to a calf within a specified time[3]. It is an offence to move from a holding cattle that should have been tagged and that are not[4].

An application for registration by means of an application for a passport must be made within a certain time frame for all calves, and for cattle brought in from another member state, the Channel Islands, the Isle of Man or Northern Ireland[5]. The Secretary of State or, in relation to Wales, the Welsh Ministers, will then issue a cattle passport for that animal[6].

Movement of cattle on to or off a holding and the death of an animal must be notified to the Secretary of State or, as appropriate, the Welsh Ministers[7].

1 See the Cattle Identification Regulations 2007, SI 2007/529, regs 2(1), 3(1); the Cattle Identification (Wales) Regulations 2007, SI 2007/842, regs 2(1), 3(1); and ANIMALS vol 2 (2017) PARA 412.
2 See the Cattle Identification Regulations 2007, SI 2007/529, reg 3(2); the Cattle Identification (Wales) Regulations 2007, SI 2007/842, reg 3(2); and ANIMALS vol 2 (2017) PARA 412. As to the Secretary of State and the Welsh Ministers see PARA 390.
3 See the Cattle Identification Regulations 2007, SI 2007/529, Sch 1 para 1; the Cattle Identification (Wales) Regulations 2007, SI 2007/842, Sch 1 para 1; and ANIMALS vol 2 (2017) PARA 412.
4 See the Cattle Identification Regulations 2007, SI 2007/529, Sch 1 para 3; the Cattle Identification (Wales) Regulations 2007, SI 2007/842, Sch 1 para 3; and ANIMALS vol 2 (2017) PARA 412.
5 See the Cattle Identification Regulations 2007, SI 2007/529, Sch 2; the Cattle Identification (Wales) Regulations 2007, SI 2007/842, Sch 2; and ANIMALS vol 2 (2017) PARA 412.
6 See the Cattle Identification Regulations 2007, SI 2007/529, Sch 3 para 1; the Cattle Identification (Wales) Regulations 2007, SI 2007/842, Sch 3 para 1; and ANIMALS vol 2 (2017) PARA 412.
7 See the Cattle Identification Regulations 2007, SI 2007/529, Sch 4; the Cattle Identification (Wales) Regulations 2007, SI 2007/842, Sch 4; and ANIMALS vol 2 (2017) PARA 412.

154. Identification of sheep and goats.

Provision is made for the identification of sheep and goats[1] and for the recording of certain information when an animal is moved onto or from its holding[2]. An animal may only be received by a market operator onto a market if it is correctly identified as per these provisions and accompanied by a movement document[3].

1   See the Sheep and Goats (Records, Identification and Movement) (England) Order 2009, SI 2009/3219; and the Sheep and Goats (Records, Identification and Movement) (Wales) Order 2015, SI 2015/1992.

2   See the Sheep and Goats (Records, Identification and Movement) (England) Order 2009, SI 2009/3219, art 23; and the Sheep and Goats (Records, Identification and Movement) (Wales) Order 2015, SI 2015/1992, art 23. As to a computerised central database which permits such movement to be recorded electronically see the Sheep and Goats (Records, Identification and Movement) (England) Order 2009, SI 2009/3219, art 24 and the Sheep and Goats (Records, Identification and Movement) (Wales) Order 2015, SI 2015/1992, art 24.

3   See the Sheep and Goats (Records, Identification and Movement) (England) Order 2009, SI 2009/3219, art 29(4); and the Sheep and Goats (Records, Identification and Movement) (Wales) Order 2015, SI 2015/1992, art 29(4).

155. Identification of pigs.

An occupier of a holding[1] who begins to keep pigs on that holding, and any person who takes over the occupation of a holding where pigs are kept, must notify the Secretary of State or, in relation to Wales, the Welsh Ministers[2] within one month of their name and address and the address of the holding, after which the Secretary of State or Welsh Ministers must issue a herdmark[3].

No person may move a pig off a holding unless it has an ear tag[4] with the letters 'UK' followed by the herdmark of the holding from which it is being moved or it has a tattoo[5] showing that herdmark (with or without the letters 'UK')[6]. This does not apply in relation to a pig less than one year old provided that it is identified with a temporary mark[7], unless the pig is being moved to a market, slaughterhouse, show or for the purposes of intra-Community trade or export[8].

No person may move a pig off a holding to a show or to an exhibition, or for breeding purposes with the intention of returning the pig to the holding from which it was moved, or for the purpose of collection of semen at a porcine semen centre, unless the pig is marked in accordance with the above provisions relating to ear tags and tattoos[9] or with a herdmark that includes a unique individual identification number[10].

No person may move a pig off a holding for the purposes of intra-Community trade or export unless it has an ear tag or tattoo in its ear, in either case bearing the letters 'UK' followed by a herdmark and a unique individual identification number[11].

Any person importing a pig from outside the EU must apply an ear tag or tattoo[12] within 30 days of its arrival at the holding destination unless the pig is moved directly to a slaughterhouse and is slaughtered within 30 days of its arrival from outside the EU[13].

1   'Holding' means any establishment, construction or, in the case of an open air farm, any place in which pigs are held, kept or handled: Pigs (Records, Identification and Movement) Order 2011, SI 2011/2154, art 2; Pigs (Records, Identification and Movement) (Wales) Order 2011, SI 2011/2830, art 2.

2   As to the Secretary of State and the Welsh Ministers see PARA 390.

3   Pigs (Records, Identification and Movement) Order 2011, SI 2011/2154, art 4(1), (2); Pigs (Records, Identification and Movement) (Wales) Order 2011, SI 2011/2830, art 4(1), (2).

4   An ear tag must be:

    (1)   easy to read during the pig's lifetime;

    (2)   made of either metal or plastic or a combination of metal and plastic;

    (3)   tamper-resistant;

    (4)   incapable of re-use;

    (5)   sufficiently heat-resistant that neither the ear tag nor the information printed or stamped on it can be damaged by the processing of the carcase following slaughter; and

(6)   designed to remain attached to the pig without harming it: Pigs (Records, Identification and Movement) Order 2011, SI 2011/2154, art 6(1); Pigs (Records, Identification and Movement) (Wales) Order 2011, SI 2011/2830, art 6(1).

A keeper may mark a pig with any further information, or add further information to the ear tag or tattoo provided that the further information is clearly distinguished from the information required under the relevant Order: Pigs (Records, Identification and Movement) Order 2011, SI 2011/2154, art 6(4); Pigs (Records, Identification and Movement) (Wales) Order 2011, SI 2011/2830, art 6(4).

5   A tattoo must be applied either by tattoo forceps, in which case it must be on an ear, or by slap-marking equipment, in which case it must be on each shoulder and must, in either case, be easy to read: Pigs (Records, Identification and Movement) Order 2011, SI 2011/2154, art 6(2); Pigs (Records, Identification and Movement) (Wales) Order 2011, SI 2011/2830, art 6(2). As an alternative to applying a tattoo by the methods referred to in the text a keeper may apply a tattoo to each shoulder by means of equipment which uses compressed air to drive the tattooing pins into the skin of the pig provided the tattoo is easy to read: Pigs (Records, Identification and Movement) Order 2011, SI 2011/2154, art 6(3); Pigs (Records, Identification and Movement) (Wales) Order 2011, SI 2011/2830, art 6(3). Unless authorised by the Secretary of State or, in relation to Wales, the Welsh Ministers, no person may remove or deface an eartag or tattoo which complies with the Pigs (Records, Identification and Movement) Order 2011, SI 2011/2154, art 6 or Pigs (Records, Identification and Movement) (Wales) Order 2011, SI 2011/2830, art 6: Pigs (Records, Identification and Movement) Order 2011, SI 2011/2154, art 22; Pigs (Records, Identification and Movement) (Wales) Order 2011, SI 2011/2830, art 22.

6   Pigs (Records, Identification and Movement) Order 2011, SI 2011/2154, art 7(1); Pigs (Records, Identification and Movement) (Wales) Order 2011, SI 2011/2830, art 7(1). Subject to the Disease Control Order (England) 2003, SI 2003/1729 or, in relation to Wales, the Disease Control (Wales) Order 2003, SI 2003/1966, in the case of a market:

(1)   a pig may be moved off if it is marked with the herdmark of the holding from which it arrived;

(2)   if the pig is not correctly identified when it arrives at a market a keeper may correct the identification so that it is identified with the herdmark of the holding from which it arrived, but if he does not do so it may only be returned to the holding from which it came: see the Pigs (Records, Identification and Movement) Order 2011, SI 2011/2154, art 7(2); Pigs (Records, Identification and Movement) (Wales) Order 2011, SI 2011/2830, art 7(2).

7   The temporary mark must either by itself or by reference to a document accompanying the pig during the movement enables the holding from which the pig was last moved to be identified and that lasts until the pig reaches its destination: Pigs (Records, Identification and Movement) Order 2011, SI 2011/2154, art 8(1)(a), (b); Pigs (Records, Identification and Movement) (Wales) Order 2011, SI 2011/2830, art 8(1)(a), (b).

8   Pigs (Records, Identification and Movement) Order 2011, SI 2011/2154, art 8(1), (2); Pigs (Records, Identification and Movement) (Wales) Order 2011, SI 2011/2830, art 8(1), (2).

9   Ie in accordance with the Pigs (Records, Identification and Movement) Order 2011, SI 2011/2154, art 7 or the Pigs (Records, Identification and Movement) (Wales) Order 2011, SI 2011/2830, art 7.

10 Pigs (Records, Identification and Movement) Order 2011, SI 2011/2154, art 9(1); Pigs (Records, Identification and Movement) (Wales) Order 2011, SI 2011/2830, art 9(1).

11 Pigs (Records, Identification and Movement) Order 2011, SI 2011/2154, art 10; Pigs (Records, Identification and Movement) (Wales) Order 2011, SI 2011/2830, art 10.

12 The ear tag or tattoo must contain the following information, in the following order:

(1)   the letters 'UK';

(2)   the herdmark of the herd into which the imported pig is introduced;

(3)   any other information, if the keeper wishes to apply such information; and

(4)   the letter 'F': Pigs (Records, Identification and Movement) Order 2011, SI 2011/2154, art 11(1)(a)–(d); Pigs (Records, Identification and Movement) (Wales) Order 2011, SI 2011/2830, art 11(1) (a)–(d).

13 See the Pigs (Records, Identification and Movement) Order 2011, SI 2011/2154, art 11; and the Pigs (Records, Identification and Movement) (Wales) Order 2011, SI 2011/2830, art 11.

(2) BREEDING

156. Control of rams.

In order to improve the quality of sheep, the Secretary of State and the Welsh Ministers[1] may make regulations[2] controlling the keeping of rams and uncastrated ram lambs on land of any specified description and providing for matters incidental thereto[3]. In particular the regulations may prohibit the keeping of such rams or lambs in certain areas unless approved for breeding purposes, or the keeping of them during specified periods unless licensed[4]. They may also provide for the inspection or marking of such rams and lambs, and can include provisions for requiring[5] them to be slaughtered or castrated where they appear to be of defective or inferior conformation and likely to beget defective or inferior progeny, or are permanently affected with any contagious or infectious disease, or any other disease rendering them unsuitable for breeding purposes[6]. Further, they may provide for the seizure and sale of any such rams or lambs kept in contravention of the regulations, and may enable a court by or before which anyone is convicted of such a contravention to direct that the proceeds of the sale be applied towards the payment of any fine imposed, or that the animal or the proceeds of sale be returned to the owner of the animal in question[7]. Regulations may also be made providing that where, as a result of refusal to approve a ram or lamb for breeding purposes, a person is prohibited from keeping it on any land, or where a notice requiring slaughter or castration has been served, the person in question may apply for a referee's inspection of the ram or lamb, and that the refusal or notice must be confirmed or withdrawn in accordance with the referee's recommendation[8].

If any person permits a ram or lamb to be on any land in contravention of these regulations he is guilty of an offence[9]. Penalties are laid down for allowing licences to be used by others, for making or having possession of a document so closely resembling a licence as to be calculated to deceive, and for altering or defacing marks on rams or lambs[10], or wrongfully marking them[11].

1 As to the Secretary of State and the Welsh Ministers see PARA 390.
2 At the date at which this volume states the law no regulations under these provisions are in force.
3 See the Hill Farming Act 1946 s 18 (amended by SI 1955/554). The penalty on summary conviction for obstructing a person exercising a power conferred by the Hill Farming Act 1946 s 18 is a fine not exceeding level 2 on the standard scale: s 19(6) (amended by virtue of the Criminal Justice Act 1982 ss 35, 37, 46). As to the standard scale and the powers of magistrates' courts to issue fines on summary conviction see SENTENCING vol 92 (2015) PARA 176.
4 See the Hill Farming Act 1946 s 18(1)(a), (b).
5 There is a penalty on summary conviction for not complying with this requirement of a fine not exceeding level 2 on the standard scale, and the offender is liable to a further fine of £5 for every day after his conviction on which the failure continues: Hill Farming Act 1946 s 19(4) (amended by virtue of the Criminal Justice Act 1982 s 46). On summary conviction of moving, after service of such a requirement, a ram or lamb without permission to any place except a slaughterhouse there is a penalty of a fine not exceeding level 2 on the standard scale: Hill Farming Act 1946 s 19(5) (amended by virtue of the Criminal Justice Act 1982 ss 35, 46; and by SI 1955/554).
6 See the Hill Farming Act 1946 s 18(1)(c)–(e).
7 See the Livestock Rearing Act 1951 s 7(1)(a) (amended by SI 1955/554).
8 See the Livestock Rearing Act 1951 s 7(1)(b) (amended by SI 1955/554). No requisition for slaughter or castration can take effect until the time for this application has elapsed, or an application has been made and the requisition confirmed: Livestock Rearing Act 1951 s 7(2).
9 See the Hill Farming Act 1946 s 19(1). Any person guilty of such an offence is liable on summary conviction to a fine not exceeding level 1 on the standard scale, and to a further fine of £5 for every day upon which the contravention continues: s 19(1) (amended by virtue of the Criminal Justice Act 1982 s 46).

10 Hill Farming Act 1946 s 19(2) (amended by the Forgery and Counterfeiting Act 1981 Schedule Pt I). Intent to deceive must be proved in all these cases: see the Hill Farming Act 1946 s 19(2) (as so amended). Until a day to be appointed the penalty on summary conviction is a fine not exceeding level 2 on the standard scale or imprisonment not exceeding three months or both (s 19(2) (amended by virtue of the Criminal Justice Act 1982 s 46)); as from that day a person guilty of an offence under the Hill Farming Act 1946 s 19(2) may no longer be sentenced to a term of imprisonment, whether as an alternative or in addition to the specified fine (s 19(2) (as so amended; prospectively amended by the Criminal Justice Act 2003 s 332, Sch 37 Pt 9)). At the date at which this volume states the law no such day had been appointed.

11 Ie placing upon them a mark prescribed by regulations otherwise than in pursuance of the regulations, or placing a mark so closely resembling a prescribed mark as to be calculated to deceive: Hill Farming Act 1946 s 19(3). Until a day to be appointed the penalty on summary conviction for this offence is a fine not exceeding level 2 on the standard scale or imprisonment not exceeding three months or both (s 19(3) (amended by virtue of the Criminal Justice Act 1982 s 46)); as from that day a person guilty of an offence under the Hill Farming Act 1946 s 19(3) may no longer be sentenced to a term of imprisonment, whether as an alternative or in addition to the specified fine (s 19(3) (as so amended; prospectively amended by the Criminal Justice Act 2003 s 332, Sch 37 Pt 9)). At the date at which this volume states the law no such day had been appointed.

157. Breeding of pigs.

The Secretary of State or, in relation to Wales, the Welsh Ministers[1] may approve a holding[2] for the purposes of movements of pigs[3] intended for breeding or growing[4].

The approval must specify which holdings pigs may be moved from and which holdings they may be moved to[5].

1 As to the Secretary of State and the Welsh Ministers see PARA 390.
2 As to the meaning of 'holding' see PARA 155 note 1.
3 As to requirements relating to the movement of pigs see PARA 151.
4 Pigs (Records, Identification and Movement) Order 2011, SI 2011/2154, art 21(1); Pigs (Records, Identification and Movement) (Wales) Order 2011, SI 2011/2830, art 21(1). A movement of pigs between holdings approved under these provisions does not trigger the standstill period in the Disease Control Order (England) 2003, SI 2003/1729 or, in relation to Wales, the Disease Control (Wales) Order 2003, SI 2003/1966: Pigs (Records, Identification and Movement) Order 2011, SI 2011/2154, art 21(3); Pigs (Records, Identification and Movement) (Wales) Order 2011, SI 2011/2830, art 21(3).
5 Pigs (Records, Identification and Movement) Order 2011, SI 2011/2154, art 21(2); Pigs (Records, Identification and Movement) (Wales) Order 2011, SI 2011/2830, art 21(2).

158. Pure-bred animals for breeding.

EU member states are required to ensure that intra-community trade in pure-bred breeding animals of the bovine species, the semen, ova and embryos thereof, and bulls used for artificial insemination, along with the establishment of herd books and the recognition of organisations and associations which maintain herd books, are not prohibited, impeded or restricted on zootechnical grounds[1]. This requirement has been implemented by domestic legislation[2]. Provision is also made in connection with the importation of pure-bred breeding animals from third countries[3].

1 See Council Directive (EC) 2009/157 (OJ L323, 10.12.2009, p 1) on pure-bred breeding animals of the bovine species, art 2.
2 See the Zootechnical Standards (England) Regulations 2012, SI 2012/2665; and the Zootechnical Standards (Wales) Regulations 2015, SI 2015/1686.
3 See European Parliament and Council Regulation (EU) 2016/1012 (OJ L171, 29.6.2016, p 66) on zootechnical and genealogical conditions for the breeding, trade in and entry into the EU of purebred breeding animals, hybrid breeding pigs and the germinal products thereof.

159.   Artificial breeding of livestock.

The Secretary of State and the Welsh Ministers[1] may make regulations[2] controlling the practice of artificial breeding, including artificial insemination and transfer of ova or embryos, of livestock[3]. For the purpose of controlling the use for artificial breeding of any specified kind of livestock or of semen, ova or embryos of livestock, regulations may prohibit the carrying on of any specified activity in connection with livestock except under the authority of a licence or approval issued under the regulations[4], and may also prohibit the importation of semen, ova or embryos of any specified kind of livestock except under the authority of a licence[5]. Accordingly, regulations may make provision in respect of the issue, modification, suspension and revocation of licences or approvals including the conditions subject to which they may be issued[6].

For the purpose of ascertaining whether the provisions of regulations, or the conditions of any licence or approval under them, are being or have been contravened, a person authorised in writing by the Secretary of State or the Welsh Ministers may, on producing his authority, enter certain premises[7] at all reasonable times[8]. The authorised person may inspect the premises and any livestock or articles on them and carry out such test or other investigation as he thinks fit[9]. For the purposes of any test or investigation the authorised person may require any person on the premises to give such information as it is in his power to give[10].

Any person who contravenes any provision of regulations or the conditions of a licence or approval[11], or who intentionally obstructs any person in the exercise of his powers, or who refuses to give information which he is required to give, is guilty of an offence[12].

With a view to developing and improving the breeding of livestock (including poultry and bees) by the practice of artificial insemination, the Secretary of State or the Welsh Ministers may make contributions towards expenditure incurred with his or their approval by societies and persons engaged in research therein, and may establish and operate centres providing artificial insemination services for such research[13].

1   As to the Secretary of State and the Welsh Ministers see PARA 390.
2   As to regulations in force under the Animal Health and Welfare Act 1984 s 10 see: the Importation of Embryos, Ova and Semen Order 1980, SI 1980/12; the Bovine Semen (England) Regulations 2007, SI 2007/1319; the Bovine Semen (England) Regulations 2007, SI 2007/1319; the Bovine Semen (Wales) Regulations 2008, SI 2008/1040; the Artificial Insemination of Pigs (England and Wales) Regulations 1964, SI 1964/1172 (revoked for certain purposes by SI 1992/3161); and the Artificial Insemination of Pigs (EEC) Regulations 1992, SI 1992/3161. The Artificial Insemination of Pigs (England and Wales) Regulations 1964, SI 1964/1172 were made under the Agriculture (Miscellaneous Provisions) Act 1943 s 17 (repealed by the Animal Health and Welfare Act 1984 Sch 2) but, by virtue of the Animal Health and Welfare Act 1984 s 11(3), regulations made under the Agriculture (Miscellaneous Provisions) Act 1943 continue to have effect. See also the Bovine Embryo Collection and Transfer Regulations 1995, SI 1995/2478; and as to fees see the Animal Health (Miscellaneous Fees) Regulations 2013, SI 2013/1240 and the Animal Health (Miscellaneous Fees) (Wales) Regulations 2012, SI 2013/1241 (which specifies the fees which are payable in relation to approvals for the purpose of obtaining porcine semen in accordance with the Artificial Insemination of Pigs (England and Wales) Regulations 1964, SI 1964/1172; and fees payable in relation to approvals for the purpose of collection, production and transfer of bovine embryos in accordance with the Bovine Embryo (Collection, Production and Transfer) Regulations 1995, SI 1995/2478), and the Artificial Insemination of Pigs (EEC) Regulations 1992, SI 1992/3161).
3   Animal Health and Welfare Act 1984 s 10(1). 'Livestock' includes any animal or bird not in the wild state: s 10(8).
4   Animal Health and Welfare Act 1984 s 10(2)(a).
5   Animal Health and Welfare Act 1984 s 10(2)(b).

6 Animal Health and Welfare Act 1984 s 10(2). Without prejudice to the generality of the power to make regulations for controlling the practice of artificial breeding of livestock, regulations may include provision in respect of advertisements in connection with artificial breeding; and for the seizure and detention of anything imported in contravention of any provision of the regulations or of any conditions of any licence under them, and for dealing with anything so imported: s 10(3)(a), (b). Regulations may also provide for the payment of fees in connection with the issue of licences or approvals, and tests or examinations carried out for the purposes of the regulations: see s 10(3)(c). See note 2.

7 The premises concerned are any premises used by the holder of a licence or approval under the regulations, being premises used for or in connection with any of the purposes authorised by the licence or approval; and any premises on which there are reasonable grounds for suspecting that an offence relating to artificial breeding of livestock is being committed: Animal Health and Welfare Act 1984 s 10(4)(a), (b). 'Premises' includes any description of vehicle: s 10(8).

8 Animal Health and Welfare Act 1984 s 10(4).

9 Animal Health and Welfare Act 1984 s 10(4).

10 Animal Health and Welfare Act 1984 s 10(5).

11 This is subject to a defence of proving that the accused took all reasonable steps and exercised all due diligence: Animal Health and Welfare Act 1984 s 10(7).

12 See the Animal Health and Welfare Act 1984 s 10(6). Until a day to be appointed a person guilty of such an offence is liable on summary conviction to imprisonment for a term not exceeding three months or to a fine not exceeding level 3 on the standard scale or both (s 10(6)); as from that day the maximum term of imprisonment to which such a person is liable, either as an alternative or in addition to the specified fine, is increased to 51 weeks (s 10(6) (prospectively amended by the Criminal Justice Act 2003 s 280(2), (3), Sch 26 para 34)). At the date at which this volume states the law no such day had been appointed. As to the standard scale and the powers of magistrates' courts to issue fines on summary conviction see SENTENCING vol 92 (2015) PARA 176.

13 Agriculture (Artificial Insemination) Act 1946 s 1.

(3) WELFARE OF FARMED ANIMALS

160. Welfare of animals kept for farming purposes.

To ensure the welfare of farmed animals, regulations have been made that place keepers of farmed animals under certain specified duties[1]. Such duties cover matters such as: staffing; regular inspections of a frequency that depends on whether or not the welfare of the animal depends on frequent human attention; record keeping; freedom of movement having regard to the species of the animal; buildings and accommodation; inspections of automatic or mechanical equipment essential for the health and well-being of the animal; the food, water and other substances to be provided for the animal; breeding procedures; and the prohibition of the application of an electrical current to an animal for the purpose of immobilisation[2]. Additional conditions apply to the keeping of hens[3], calves confined for rearing and fattening[4], cattle[5], pigs[6] and rabbits[7].

Inspections may be carried out by inspectors to check compliance with the above provisions and to ascertain whether any offence under or by virtue of the Animal Welfare Act 2006 has been or is being committed[8].

1 See the Welfare of Farmed Animals (England) Regulations 2007, SI 2007/2078, reg 4; and the Welfare of Farmed Animals (Wales) Regulations 2007, SI 2007/3070, reg 4; and ANIMALS vol 2 (2017) PARA 163.

2 See the Welfare of Farmed Animals (England) Regulations 2007, SI 2007/2078, Sch 1; and the Welfare of Farmed Animals (Wales) Regulations 2007, SI 2007/3070, Sch 1; and ANIMALS vol 2 (2017) PARA 163.

3 See the Welfare of Farmed Animals (England) Regulations 2007, SI 2007/2078, Sch 2–5A; and the Welfare of Farmed Animals (Wales) Regulations 2007, SI 2007/3070, Sch 2–5A; and ANIMALS vol 2 (2017) PARA 163.

4   See the Welfare of Farmed Animals (England) Regulations 2007, SI 2007/2078, Sch 6; and the
    Welfare of Farmed Animals (Wales) Regulations 2007, SI 2007/3070, Sch 6; and ANIMALS vol 2
    (2017) PARA 163.

5   See the Welfare of Farmed Animals (England) Regulations 2007, SI 2007/2078, Sch 7; and the
    Welfare of Farmed Animals (Wales) Regulations 2007, SI 2007/3070, Sch 7; and ANIMALS vol 2
    (2017) PARA 163.

6   See the Welfare of Farmed Animals (England) Regulations 2007, SI 2007/2078, Sch 8; and the
    Welfare of Farmed Animals (Wales) Regulations 2007, SI 2007/3070, Sch 8; and ANIMALS vol 2
    (2017) PARA 163.

7   See the Welfare of Farmed Animals (England) Regulations 2007, SI 2007/2078, Sch 9; and the
    Welfare of Farmed Animals (Wales) Regulations 2007, SI 2007/3070, Sch 9; and ANIMALS vol 2
    (2017) PARA 163.

8   See the Animal Welfare Act 2006 s 28(1); and ANIMALS vol 2 (2017) PARA 164.

161.   Fur farming.

It is an offence to keep animals solely or primarily for slaughter for the value of their fur or for breeding progeny for such slaughter[1] and importing, exporting to or from the EU of cat and dog fur is also prohibited[2].

1   See the Fur Farming (Prohibition) Act 2000 s 1; and ANIMALS vol 2 (2017) PARA 165.

2   See the Cat and Dog Fur (Control of Import, Export and Placing on the Market) Regulations 2008,
    SI 2008/2795; and ANIMALS vol 2 (2017) PARA 166.

162.   Control and eradication of disease.

The Animal Health Act 1981 makes provision for the control and eradication of diseases in animals, including those specifically associated with farm animals[1]. Particular provision is made in relation to the establishment of preventative measures and contingency plans[2], the separation and treatment of diseased animals[3], the import and export of animals[4], the movement of diseased animals and the control of infected areas[5], slaughter and compensation[6], and enforcement[7]. Specific provision is also made in connection with individual diseases namely rabies[8], foot-and-mouth disease[9], African horse sicknes[10], bluetongue[11] and transmissible spongiform encephalopathies[12], and for the eradication of brucellosis[13]. Provision is also made in connection with the spreading of disease by animals of non-dangerous species, including farm animals[14].

1   See the Animal Health Act 1981 Pts I, II (ss 1–14, 14A–36); regulations made and having effect
    thereunder; and ANIMALS vol 2 (2017) PARA 374 et seq. 'Animals' for these purposes means
    cattle, sheep and goats and all other ruminating animals and swine, and 'disease' means cattle
    plague or rinderpest, contagious pleuro-pneumonia of cattle, foot-and-mouth disease, sheep-pox,
    sheep scab or swine fever, although both these definitions can be and have been extended to
    include other mammals or other diseases: see ss 87(1), 88(1), 89(1); and ANIMALS vol 2 (2017)
    PARAS 375–376. These provisions also apply to poultry: see ANIMALS vol 2 (2017)
    PARAS 433–442.

2   See the Animal Health Act 1981 s 3 et seq; and ANIMALS vol 2 (2017) PARAS 377–383.

3   See the Animal Health Act 1981 ss 7, 14–16; and ANIMALS vol 2 (2017) PARAS 384–388.

4   See the Animal Health Act 1981 ss 10, 10A; and ANIMALS vol 2 (2017) PARAS 413–419.

5   See the Animal Health Act 1981 ss 7, 8, 17, 18; and ANIMALS vol 2 (2017) PARAS 404–412.

6   See the Animal Health Act 1981 s 31 et seq; and ANIMALS vol 2 (2017) PARAS 420–425.

7   See the Animal Health Act 1981 s 60 et seq; and ANIMALS vol 2 (2017) PARAS 426–432.

8   See the Animal Health Act 1981 ss 1, 24; and ANIMALS vol 2 (2017) PARAS 389–391.

9   See the Animal Health Act 1981 ss 6A, 6B, 14A, 14B, 16A, 31 et seq; and ANIMALS vol 2 (2017)
    PARAS 392–400. In connection with preventing the spread of disease through markets see also
    PARA 164.

10 See the African Horse Sickness (England) Regulations 2012, SI 2012/2629; and ANIMALS vol 2 (2017) PARA 401.
11 See the Bluetongue Regulations 2008, SI 2008/962; the Bluetongue (Wales) Regulations 2008, SI 2008/1090; and ANIMALS vol 2 (2017) PARA 402.
12 See the Transmissible Spongiform Encephalopathies (England) Regulations 2010, SI 2010/801; the Transmissible Spongiform Encephalopathies (Wales) Regulations 2008, SI 2008/3154; and ANIMALS vol 2 (2017) PARA 403.
13 See the Agriculture Act 1970 s 106; and ANIMALS vol 2 (2017) PARA 378.
14 See ANIMALS vol 2 (2017) PARA 50.

163. Worrying and injuring livestock.

If a dog worries livestock[1] on any agricultural land[2], the owner of the dog and, if it is in the charge of anyone other than its owner, that person also, is (subject to statutory defences) guilty of an offence[3]. Further, a person who keeps a dog which causes damage by killing or injuring livestock is absolutely liable for the damage[4]. Statutory defences also apply to this offence[5]. There are also restrictions on taking dogs onto access land[6], or allowing them to remain there, where they are in the vicinity of livestock[7].

1 'Livestock' for this purpose means cattle, sheep, goats, swine, horses or poultry; 'cattle' means bulls, cows, oxen, heifers or calves; 'horses' includes asses and mules; and 'poultry' means domestic fowls, turkeys, geese or ducks: Dogs (Protection of Livestock) Act 1953 s 3(1). Rabbits are not included, even if kept commercially: see *Tallents v Bell and Goddard* [1944] 2 All ER 474, CA. 'Worrying livestock' means attacking livestock, chasing it in such a way as may be reasonably expected to cause it injury or suffering, or, in the case of females, abortion or loss of or diminution in their produce, or being at large, that is not on a leash or under close control, in a field or enclosure where there are sheep: Dogs (Protection of Livestock) Act 1953 s 1(2). See further ANIMALS vol 2 (2017) PARA 238.
2 'Agricultural land' means land used as arable, meadow or grazing land, or for the purpose of poultry or pig farming, market gardens, allotments, nursery grounds or orchards: Dogs (Protection of Livestock) Act 1953 s 3(1). See further ANIMALS vol 2 (2017) PARA 238.
3 See the Dogs (Protection of Livestock) Act 1953 s 1(1); and ANIMALS vol 2 (2017) PARA 238. Provision is also made for damage caused by trespassing livestock and nuisance caused by livestock generally (see ANIMALS vol 2 (2017) PARAS 51–63) and in connection with the causing of injury or the spread of disease by animals of non-dangerous species, including farm animals (see ANIMALS vol 2 (2017) PARAS 47–50).
4 See the Animals Act 1971 s 3; and ANIMALS vol 2 (2017) PARAS 236–237. 'Livestock' for this purpose means cattle, horses, hinnies, sheep, pigs, goats, poultry, deer not in a wild state, and also, while in captivity, pheasants, partridges and grouse; 'poultry' means the domestic varieties of fowls, turkeys, geese, ducks, guinea-fowls, pigeons, peacocks and quails; and 'horse' means ass, mule or hinny: Animals Act 1971 s 11 (amended by the Control of Horses Act 2015 s 1(3)).
5 See the Animals Act 1971 s 3; and ANIMALS vol 2 (2017) PARAS 236–237.
6 Ie pursuant to the Countryside and Rights of Way Act 2000 s 2 (see OPEN SPACES AND COUNTRYSIDE vol 78 (2010) PARA 583).
7 See the Countryside and Rights of Way Act 2000 s 21(3)(c), Sch 2 paras 4, 5; and ANIMALS vol 2 (2017) PARA 214.

164. Welfare of animals in transit and at markets.

Provision is made for the protection of animals, including farm animals, during transport[1], under which it is required that:
(1) no person may transport animals or cause animals to be transported in a way likely to cause injury or undue suffering to them[2];
(2) transported animals are fit for the journey[3];
(3) arrangements are made to minimise the length of the journey and meet the animals' needs during the journey[4];

(4)　　　the means of transport and loading and unloading facilities are designed, constructed, maintained and operated so as to avoid injury and suffering and ensure the safety of the animals[5];

(5)　　　the personnel handling the animals are trained or competent and carry out their tasks without using violence or any method likely to cause unnecessary fear, injury or suffering[6];

(6)　　　the transport is carried out without delay and the welfare conditions of the animals are regularly checked and maintained[7];

(7)　　　sufficient floor area and height is provided for the animals, appropriate to their size and the intended journey[8]; and

(8)　　　water, feed and rest are offered to the animals at suitable intervals and are appropriate in quality and quantity to their species and size[9].

These provisions have been implemented in England and Wales by statutory instrument[10].

Duties are imposed on market authorities to provide facilities for the weighing of cattle at markets[11] and to prevent the spread of disease[12].

1　See Council Regulation (EC) 1/2005 (OJ L3, 05.01.2005, p 1) on the protection of animals during transport and related operations.
2　Council Regulation (EC) 1/2005 (OJ L3, 05.01.2005, p 1) art 3.
3　Council Regulation (EC) 1/2005 (OJ L3, 05.01.2005, p 1) art 3(b).
4　Council Regulation (EC) 1/2005 (OJ L3, 05.01.2005, p 1) art 3(a).
5　Council Regulation (EC) 1/2005 (OJ L3, 05.01.2005, p 1) art 3(c), (d).
6　Council Regulation (EC) 1/2005 (OJ L3, 05.01.2005, p 1) art 3(e).
7　Council Regulation (EC) 1/2005 (OJ L3, 05.01.2005, p 1) art 3(f).
8　Council Regulation (EC) 1/2005 (OJ L3, 05.01.2005, p 1) art 3(g).
9　Council Regulation (EC) 1/2005 (OJ L3, 05.01.2005, p 1) art 3(h).
10　See the Welfare of Animals (Transport) (England) Order 2006, SI 2006/3260, and the Welfare of Animals (Transport) (Wales) Order 2007, SI 2007/1047. See generally in connection with animal welfare during transport ANIMALS vol 2 (2017) PARAS 167–169.
11　See the Markets and Fairs (Weighing of Cattle) Acts 1887, 1891 and 1926; the Food Act 1984 s 57; and MARKETS vol 71 (2013) PARAS 900–902.
12　See the Animals Act 1981 ss 7, 8, 10, 17, 25, 26; the Foot-and-Mouth Disease (England) Order 2006, SI 2006/182; the Foot-and-Mouth Disease (Wales) Order 2006, SI 2006/179; and MARKETS vol 71 (2013) PARA 904.

165. Regulation of slaughterhouses.

The welfare of animals which are to be slaughtered, the methods of slaughter, the conditions for slaughter and killing, and the conditions and requirements to be observed in slaughterhouses and knackers' yards are the subject of detailed regulation which is considered elsewhere in this work[1].

Provision is also made in connection with the use of slaughter as a means to control or prevent the spread of disease, and the payment of compensation when such slaughter is carried out[2].

1　See FOOD AND DRINK vol 51 (2013) PARA 932 et seq. As to the export of animals for slaughter to other member states see Case C-5/94 *R v Ministry of Agriculture, Fisheries and Food, ex p Hedley Lomas (Ireland) Ltd* [1997] QB 139, [1996] All ER (EC) 493, [1996] ECR I-2556, ECJ. Persons authorised to conduct and regulate markets and fairs are also empowered to make provision for slaughterhouses: see the Markets and Fairs Clauses Act 1847 ss 17–19; and MARKETS vol 71 (2013) PARAS 893–894.
2　See PARA 162; and ANIMALS vol 2 (2017) PARAS 394 et seq, 420–425, 439.

(4) RED MEAT INDUSTRY IN WALES

166. Objectives of the Meat Industry (Wales) Measure 2010.

Provision is made for the regulation of the red meat industry in Wales by the Red Meat Industry (Wales) Measure 2010[1].

The objectives of the Red Meat Industry (Wales) Measure 2010 are:

(1)   increasing efficiency or productivity in the red meat industry;

(2)   improving marketing in the industry;

(3)   improving or developing services that the industry provides or could provide to the community; and

(4)   improving the ways in which the industry contributes to sustainable development[2].

1   'The red meat industry' means:

     (1)   activities comprised in breeding, keeping, processing, marketing and distributing any of the following animals:

        (a)   cattle;

        (b)   sheep; or

        (c)   pigs; and

     (2)   activities comprised in producing, processing, marketing, manufacturing and distributing products derived to any substantial extent from those animals (apart from milk and milk products, fleece wool and hides); and

     (3)   slaughterhouses, auctions and markets used wholly or partly for activities falling within head (1) or (2): s 1(1).

Any reference in the Red Meat Industry (Wales) Measure 2010 to animals includes (where the context requires) a reference to animals that are dead: s 1(4). 'Cattle' means bovine animals, including bison and buffalo: s 14. 'Pigs' means porcine animals, including wild boar and other feral pigs: s 14.

2   Red Meat Industry (Wales) Measure 2010 s 2.

167. Functions of the Welsh Ministers.

The Welsh Ministers[1] may do anything that they consider appropriate to further the objectives[2] of the Red Meat Industry (Wales) Measure 2010[3].

For the purpose of furthering the objectives, the Welsh Ministers may, among other things, establish a reserve fund[4].

They may also exercise any of the following functions in relation to the red meat industry[5]:

(1)   promoting or undertaking scientific research[6];

(2)   promoting or undertaking inquiry into:

     (a)   materials and equipment, and

     (b)   methods of production, management and use of labour[7];

(3)   promoting or undertaking inquiry under head (2) includes promoting or undertaking:

     (a)   the discovery and development of new materials, equipment and methods, and of improvements in those already in use;

     (b)   the assessment of the advantages of different options; and

     (c)   the conduct of experimental establishments and of tests on a commercial scale[8];

(4)   promoting the production and marketing of standard products[9];

(5)   promoting the better definition of trade descriptions and consistency in the use of trade descriptions[10];

(6)   developing, promoting, marketing or operating:

     (a)   standards relating to the quality of products, or

     (b)   systems for the classification of products[11];

(7)   developing, reviewing or operating schemes for the certification of products or of operations connected with production or supply of products[12];

(8)   undertaking the certification of products, the registration of certification trade marks, and the functions of proprietors of those marks[13];

(9)   providing or promoting the provision of:
          (a)   training for persons engaged in or proposing to be engaged in the red meat industry; and
          (b)   their education in subjects relevant to the industry[14];

(10)   promoting:
          (a)   the adoption of measures for securing safer and better working conditions; and
          (b)   the provision and improvement of amenities for persons employed in the red meat industry[15];

(11)   promoting or undertaking inquiry as to measures for securing safer and better working conditions[16];

(12)   promoting or undertaking research into the incidence, prevention and cure of industrial diseases[17];

(13)   promoting or undertaking arrangements for encouraging the entry of persons into the red meat industry[18];

(14)   promoting or undertaking research for improving arrangements for marketing and distributing products[19];

(15)   promoting or undertaking research into matters relating to the consumption or use of goods and services supplied by the red meat industry[20];

(16)   promoting arrangements:
          (a)   for co-operative organisations;
          (b)   for supplying materials and equipment; and
          (c)   for marketing and distributing products[21];

(17)   promoting the development of export trade, including promoting or undertaking arrangements for publicity overseas[22];

(18)   promoting or undertaking arrangements for better acquainting the public in the United Kingdom with the goods and services supplied by the red meat industry and methods of using them[23];

(19)   promoting or undertaking the collection and formulation of statistics[24];

(20)   advising on any matters relating to the red meat industry and undertaking inquiry for those purposes[25];

(21)   undertaking arrangements for making information relating to the red meat industry available[26];

(22)   engaging in any form of collaboration or co-operation with other persons in performing any of the functions[27].

The powers conferred on the Welsh Ministers by the Red Meat Industry (Wales) Measure 2010 may be exercised in relation to the red meat industry as a whole or in relation to only some sectors of the industry; and may be exercised differently in relation to different sectors of the industry[28].

1   As to the Welsh Ministers see PARA 390.
2   As to the objectives of the Red Meat Industry (Wales) Measure 2010 see PARA 166.
3   Red Meat Industry (Wales) Measure 2010 s 3(1).
4   Red Meat Industry (Wales) Measure 2010 s 3(2)(b).
5   Red Meat Industry (Wales) Measure 2010 s 3(2)(a). As to the meaning of 'red meat industry' see PARA 166 note 1.

6   Red Meat Industry (Wales) Measure 2010 Sch 1 para 1. The Welsh Ministers may by order amend Sch 1 by:
     (1)   amending or omitting provisions;
     (2)   adding provisions; or
     (3)   amending or omitting any provisions which have been added: s 3(3).
   Any power of the Welsh Ministers to make an order or regulations under the Red Meat Industry (Wales) Measure 2010 is exercisable by statutory instrument: s 17(1). Any power of the Welsh Ministers to make an order or regulations under this Measure includes power:
     (a)   to make different provision for different cases, different activities relating to the red meat industry, or different sectors of the industry;
     (b)   to make provision generally or in relation to specific cases;
     (c)   to make such incidental, supplementary, consequential, transitory, transitional or saving provision as the Welsh Ministers think fit: s 17(2).
   As to orders and regulations under the Red Meat Industry (Wales) Measure 2010 see further s 17(3), (4).
7   Red Meat Industry (Wales) Measure 2010 Sch 1 para 2.
8   Red Meat Industry (Wales) Measure 2010 Sch 1 para 3.
9   Red Meat Industry (Wales) Measure 2010 Sch 1 para 4.
10   Red Meat Industry (Wales) Measure 2010 Sch 1 para 5.
11   Red Meat Industry (Wales) Measure 2010 Sch 1 para 6.
12   Red Meat Industry (Wales) Measure 2010 Sch 1 para 7.
13   Red Meat Industry (Wales) Measure 2010 Sch 1 para 8.
14   Red Meat Industry (Wales) Measure 2010 Sch 1 para 9.
15   Red Meat Industry (Wales) Measure 2010 Sch 1 para 10.
16   Red Meat Industry (Wales) Measure 2010 Sch 1 para 11.
17   Red Meat Industry (Wales) Measure 2010 Sch 1 para 12.
18   Red Meat Industry (Wales) Measure 2010 Sch 1 para 13.
19   Red Meat Industry (Wales) Measure 2010 Sch 1 para 14.
20   Red Meat Industry (Wales) Measure 2010 Sch 1 para 15.
21   Red Meat Industry (Wales) Measure 2010 Sch 1 para 16.
22   Red Meat Industry (Wales) Measure 2010 Sch 1 para 17.
23   Red Meat Industry (Wales) Measure 2010 Sch 1 para 18.
24   Red Meat Industry (Wales) Measure 2010 Sch 1 para 19.
25   Red Meat Industry (Wales) Measure 2010 Sch 1 para 20.
26   Red Meat Industry (Wales) Measure 2010 Sch 1 para 21.
27   Red Meat Industry (Wales) Measure 2010 Sch 1 para 22.
28   Red Meat Industry (Wales) Measure 2010 s 1(3).

168. Delegation of Welsh Ministers' powers.

The Welsh Ministers[1] may, to any extent and subject to any conditions as they think appropriate, delegate[2] any of their functions under the Red Meat Industry (Wales) Measure 2010 (other than excepted functions) to any person[3].

The Welsh Ministers may acquire or establish subsidiaries to carry out any of their functions under the Red Meat Industry (Wales) Measure 2010 (other than excepted functions)[4].

Any agreement or arrangement made under these provisions by the Welsh Ministers for delegating a function, or for arranging that a subsidiary will carry out a function, does not prevent the Welsh Ministers from exercising the function, if they consider that it is necessary or expedient for them to do so[5].

1   As to the Welsh Ministers see PARA 390.
2   A delegation under Red Meat Industry (Wales) Measure 2010 s 7(1) may be varied or revoked at any time: s 7(4).
3   Red Meat Industry (Wales) Measure 2010 s 7(1). As to the functions of the Welsh Ministers see in particular PARA 167.
4   Red Meat Industry (Wales) Measure 2010 s 7(2). An excepted function is any function relating to making regulations or orders and giving directions: s 7(3). As to the power of the Welsh Ministers to make regulations and orders see s 17; and PARA 167 note 6. Any direction given by the Welsh Ministers under the Red Meat Industry (Wales) Measure 2010 may be varied or revoked by a later

direction and must be given in writing: s 16(1). Any power of the Welsh Ministers to give directions under the Red Meat Industry (Wales) Measure 2010 includes power:

    (1)   to make different provision for different cases, different activities relating to the red meat industry, or different sectors of the industry;

    (2)   to make provision generally or in relation to specific cases: s 16(2).

5   Red Meat Industry (Wales) Measure 2010 s 7(5).

8. MARKETING OF AGRICULTURAL PRODUCE

(1) REGULATION OF MARKETING OF AGRICULTURAL PRODUCE

169. Regulation of marketing of agricultural produce in the United Kingdom.
The marketing of agricultural produce in the United Kingdom is principally governed by the Common Agricultural Policy of the European Union (CAP) and by directly applicable European legislation on price support and maintenance[1]. Although certain elements of the domestic legislation providing for guaranteed prices and markets for produce remain in force[2], their effect is largely superseded by the European legislation, and domestic provision in this field is now focused on improving the efficiency of the marketing of agricultural and horticultural produce as outlined below:

(1)   The Agricultural Marketing Act 1958 provides a framework within which the marketing of agricultural or horticultural products by the producers thereof may be regulated by schemes administered by marketing boards[3]. Schemes of this type continue to apply only in connection with the marketing of wool[4].

(2)   The Agriculture and Horticulture Development Board has been established for the purposes of increasing efficiency or productivity in the industry, improving marketing in the industry, improving or developing services that the industry provides or could provide to the community and improving the ways in which the industry contributes to sustainable development[5].

Agreements relating to the production of or trade in agricultural products[6] are in general exempt from the statutory prohibitions on agreements affecting competition[7].

EU legislation makes provision for member states to recognise producer organisations formed on the initiative of the producers[8]. Several producer organisations have been created in the UK[9].

1 As to the Common Agricultural Policy see PARA **1** et seq.
2 See the Agriculture Act 1957 Pt I (ss 5–7, 9, 11), which makes continuing provision for supporting price guarantee arrangements made under s 1 (repealed). The subordinate legislation which remain in force under Pt I (supplemented, where noted, by subsequent orders made under the European Communities Act 1972 s 2(2)) are the Imported Livestock Order 1958, SI 1958/558; the Sheep Variable Premium (Protection of Payments) (No 2) Order 1980, SI 1980/1811 (supplemented by the Sheep Variable Premium (Recovery Powers) Regulations 1983, SI 1983/1010); the Potatoes (Protection of Guarantees) Order 1985, SI 1985/64; and the Beef Special Premium (Protection of Payments) Order 1989, SI 1989/574 (supplemented by the Beef Special Premium (Recovery Powers) Regulations 1989, SI 1989/575).
3 See in particular the Agricultural Marketing Act 1958 Pt I (ss 1–32); and PARA **171** et seq. A marketing board established by such a scheme may be a fully trading board, in the sense that the producer may sell only to or through the board, or a board with more limited powers: see further PARA **173** et seq.
4 See PARAS **199–200**.
5 See the Agriculture and Horticulture Development Board Order 2008, SI 2008/576 (made under the Natural Environment and Rural Communities Act 2006); and PARA **393** et seq. See also TRADE AND INDUSTRY vol 97 (2015) PARA 1070 et seq.
6 Ie products of a kind listed in the Treaty on the Functioning of the European Union (Rome, 25 March 1957; TS 1 (1973); Cmnd 5179) Annex I: Competition Act 1998 Sch 3 para 9(9) (amended by SI 2004/1261). The TFEU was formerly known as the Treaty Establishing the European Community (often abbreviated to TEC and also known as the 'EC Treaty' or the Treaty of Rome) and was renamed by the Treaty of Lisbon Amending the Treaty Establishing the European Union

and the Treaty Establishing the European Community (Lisbon, 13 December 2007, ECS 13 (2007); Cm 7294) (often referred to as the 'Lisbon Treaty'), which came into force on 1 December 2009: see CONSTITUTIONAL AND ADMINISTRATIVE LAW vol 20 (2014) PARA 25 et seq.

7 See the Competition Act 1998 s 3(1)(c), Sch 3 para 9; and COMPETITION vol 18 (2009) PARAS 117, 120.

8 See European Parliament and Council Regulation (EU) 1308/2013 (OJ L347, 20.12.2013, p 671–854) establishing a common organisation of the markets in agricultural products, art 152; Commission Delegated Regulation (EU) 880/2012 (OJ L263, 28.9.2012, p 8) as regards transnational cooperation and contractual negotiations of producer organisations in the milk and milk products sector; and Commission Implementing Regulation (EU) 543/2011 (OJ L157, 15.6.2011, p 1) laying down detailed rules for the application of Council Regulation (EC) 1234/2007 in respect of the fruit and vegetables and processed fruit and vegetables sectors.

9 Eg Dairy Producer Organisations which are formed on the initiative of a group of farmers to negotiate contracts for the delivery of raw milk on behalf of its members.

170.   Agricultural Marketing Reorganisation Commissions.

The Secretary of State and the Welsh Ministers[1] are empowered to constitute Agricultural Marketing Reorganisation Commissions[2]. By direction of the Secretary of State or the Welsh Ministers the commissions may be charged with the duty of preparing schemes for regulating the marketing of such agricultural products (other than certain specified products[3]) as may be specified, and of investigating any matter affecting the operation of a scheme prepared or in the course of preparation by them or any other scheme[4]. The Secretary of State and the Welsh Ministers may also direct the commissions to investigate the operation of schemes and of other schemes, and to make recommendations for facilitating their operation[5]. The commissions each consist of a chairman and four other members appointed by the Secretary of State or the Welsh Ministers[6], and may hold such inquiries as they think necessary or desirable for the discharge of their functions[7].

1 As to the Secretary of State and the Welsh Ministers see PARA 390.
2 Agricultural Marketing Act 1958 s 26(1). At the date at which this volume states the law no such commissions had been established.
3 The Agricultural Marketing Act 1958 s 26 was repealed in relation to milk and potatoes by the Agriculture Act 1993 ss 21(1), (2), 46. The whole Act has been disapplied in relation to horticultural products and bananas: see PARA 171 note 2.
4 Agricultural Marketing Act 1958 s 26(1). Marketing schemes need not necessarily be prepared by a commission but may be submitted to the Secretary of State or the Welsh Ministers by bodies representative of producers under the Agricultural Marketing Act 1958 s 1 (see PARA 176).
5 Agricultural Marketing Act 1958 s 26(3). No information with respect to any particular undertaking (other than the undertaking of a marketing board) is, without the consent of the owner thereof, to be included in any published recommendations of a commission: s 47(1).
6 Agricultural Marketing Act 1958 s 26(4).
7 Agricultural Marketing Act 1958 s 26(5). For general provisions as to the constitution and operation of commissions and committees see s 32 (amended by the Natural Environment and Rural Communities Act 2006 Sch 11 para 30, Sch 12; and repealed in relation to milk and potatoes by the Agriculture Act 1993 ss 21(1), (2), 46). The meetings, quorum and procedure of the commissions are governed by the Agricultural Marketing (Reorganisation Commission) Regulations 1950, SI 1950/1869. As to payment of the expenses of the commissions see the Agricultural Marketing Act 1958 s 28(1), (3)–(5).

(2) AGRICULTURAL MARKETING SCHEME

(i) Power to Make Schemes

171. Schemes for the marketing of agricultural products.
The Agricultural Marketing Act 1958 makes provision for regulating the marketing of agricultural products[1] other than certain specified products[2], providing for persons substantially representative of producers of an agricultural product in an area to prepare and submit schemes, subject to the approval of the Secretary of State and the Welsh Ministers[3], for regulating the marketing of that product[4]. Schemes are administered by boards[5], and may apply to Great Britain[6] or any part thereof, or to Great Britain or part thereof together with Northern Ireland or part thereof, but not exclusively to Northern Ireland or part thereof[7]. At the date at which this volume states the law the only scheme remaining in force is that relating to the marketing of wool[8].

1 'Agricultural product' includes:
   (1)   any product of agriculture or horticulture;
   (2)   any article of food or drink wholly or partly manufactured or derived from any such product; and
   (3)   fleeces (including all kinds of wool, whether from a living animal or from a dead animal or from the skin of a dead animal) and the skins of animals: Agricultural Marketing Act 1958 s 52(1).
2 The Agricultural Marketing Act 1958 was repealed in relation to milk as from 1 November 1994 (Agriculture Act 1993 s 21; and see also the Agricultural Marketing Act 1958 Part I (Certification of Cessation of Effect in Relation to Milk) Order 1994, SI 1994/2922 (now lapsed)) and in relation to potatoes as from 1 July 1997 (Agriculture Act 1993 s 46). The Agricultural Marketing Act 1958 does not apply to certain horticultural produce (see the Marketing of Fresh Horticultural Produce Regulations 2009, SI 2009/1361, reg 22(c); and the Marketing of Fresh Horticultural Produce (Wales) Regulations 2009, SI 2009/1551, reg 22(c)) or bananas (see the Quality Standards for Green Bananas (England and Wales) Regulations 2012, SI 2012/947, reg 22(c)). As to the meaning of 'horticultural produce' see PARA 214 note 5. As to marketing schemes in relation to horticultural produce see PARA 218 et seq.
3 As to the Secretary of State and the Welsh Ministers see PARA 390.
4 See the Agricultural Marketing Act 1958 ss 1, 2; and PARA 176.
5 See the Agricultural Marketing Act 1958 s 3; and PARAS 184–185. An explanatory pamphlet issued by a board for promoting a scheme to producers, containing a statement of what the scheme will achieve, if it amounts to a representation at all, is only a representation as to the future, and failure to achieve the results stated does not make the board liable for damages for breach of duty: *Milk Marketing Board v Warman & Sons* [1937] 3 All ER 541.
6 As to the meaning of 'Great Britain' see PARA 1 note 1.
7 Agricultural Marketing Act 1958 s 1(2). Provision for the application of the agricultural marketing legislation to Northern Ireland is made by s 53.
8 See the British Wool Marketing Scheme (Approval) Order 1950, SI 1950/1326; and PARAS 199–200.

(ii) Provisions which may be Included in Schemes

172. Contents of marketing schemes.
A scheme regulating the marketing of an agricultural product[1] may contain provisions relating to:
   (1)   the constitution of a board to administer the scheme and the appointment by the board of an executive committee and the delegation of functions to that committee[2];

(2)　　the registration of producers and the taking of a poll of registered producers on the question whether the scheme should remain in force[3];

(3)　　the sale and marketing of the regulated product[4] and miscellaneous other matters[5];

(4)　　disciplinary procedures by which penalties may be imposed for contraventions of the scheme[6]; and

(5)　　the financial powers and duties of marketing boards[7].

Every scheme may also provide for such matters as are incidental to or consequential on the provisions of the Agricultural Marketing Act 1958 relating to the contents of schemes or are necessary for giving effect to those provisions[8].

Certain of these provisions must appear in all schemes, while many other provisions are optional. Power to buy and sell the regulated product is among the optional provisions, so that marketing boards may be either trading or non-trading bodies[9].

A scheme does not of necessity satisfy the statutory provisions if it contains all the mandatory provisions together with one or more of the optional provisions; it is a question to be considered, on a consideration of the scheme as a whole, whether it can properly be described as a scheme regulating the marketing of an agricultural product, and no special rules can be laid down[10]. It is fundamental to the operation of the statutory provisions that a scheme regulating the marketing of an agricultural product is one which introduces some orderly system of marketing that product, and a scheme which is from start to finish purely discretionary cannot properly be described as a scheme regulating the marketing of an agricultural produce[11].

1　As to the meaning of 'agricultural product' see PARA 171 note 1. The Agricultural Marketing Act 1958 no longer applies to the marketing of milk and potatoes and has been disapplied in relation to horticultural products and bananas: see PARA 171 note 2.

2　See the Agricultural Marketing Act 1958 s 3, Sch 2; and PARAS 184–185.

3　See the Agricultural Marketing Act 1958 s 4; and PARA 187.

4　'Regulated product' means, in relation to any scheme, any product the marketing of which is regulated by the scheme, but does not (except in the expression 'consumers of the regulated product') include any product in so far as it is produced outside the area to which the scheme is applicable: Agricultural Marketing Act 1958 s 52(1).

5　See the Agricultural Marketing Act 1958 ss 6–8; and PARAS 173–175.

6　See the Agricultural Marketing Act 1958 s 9; and PARA 186.

7　See the Agricultural Marketing Act 1958 ss 13–16; and PARAS 194–196.

8　Agricultural Marketing Act 1958 s 8(4).

9　See the Agricultural Marketing Act 1958 s 7(1)(a); and PARA 174.

10　*Tuker v Ministry of Agriculture, Fisheries and Food* [1960] 2 All ER 834, [1960] 1 WLR 819, CA.

11　*Tuker v Ministry of Agriculture, Fisheries and Food* [1960] 2 All ER 834, [1960] 1 WLR 819, CA.

173.　Regulation of sales.

Every marketing scheme[1] must prohibit sales of the regulated product[2] by any producer[3] who is neither registered nor exempted from registration by or under the scheme[4]. Schemes may also, with the approval of the Secretary of State and the Welsh Ministers[5], include additional provision:

(1)　　requiring registered producers[6] to sell the regulated product or certain descriptions or quantities thereof only to, or through the agency of, the board[7];

(2)　　for the determination from time to time of quantities or descriptions of the regulated product which may be sold, and of the price at, below or above which, the terms on which, and the persons to or through whom, sales may be made[8]; and

(3)   empowering the board to receive the purchase price in whole or in part and to distribute it to the sellers in a manner specified in the scheme or prescribed by the board[9].

A scheme may also provide that the sale of a product wholly or partly manufactured or derived from the regulated product is to be deemed to be a sale of the regulated product if the substance of the transaction is that the seller, being in possession of the regulated product, agrees to subject it, or cause it to be subjected to, a process and to sell the resulting product; in particular, where the regulated product is livestock, the sale of carcasses may be treated as a sale of the regulated product[10].

1   Ie a scheme under the Agricultural Marketing Act 1958: see PARA 171. The Agricultural Marketing Act 1958 no longer applies to the marketing of milk and potatoes and has been disapplied in relation to horticultural products and bananas: see PARA 171 note 2.
2   As to the meaning of 'regulated product' see PARA 172 note 4.
3   'Producer' means, in relation to any scheme, any person who produces the regulated product: Agricultural Marketing Act 1958 s 52(1). As to the registration of producers see note 6; and PARA 187.
4   Agricultural Marketing Act 1958 s 6(1). Except in the case of a substitutional scheme (see PARA 180) the operation of s 6(1)–(3) is to be suspended until the end of the suspensory period (see PARA 177): s 6(4). Every scheme must provide for exempting, from all or any of its provisions, producers and sales of such classes or descriptions as may be specified in the scheme or determined by the board: s 8(1)(a). 'Board' means a board administering a scheme and, in relation to any scheme, means the board administering that scheme: s 52(1). A producer who sells the regulated product in contravention of s 6(1) is guilty of an offence and is liable on summary conviction to a fine not exceeding the prescribed sum, or on conviction on indictment to a fine, and in either case to an additional fine not exceeding half the price at which the product was sold: s 6(6) (amended by the Criminal Law Act 1977 s 28(2); and the Magistrates' Courts Act 1980 s 32(2)). A court other than a magistrates' court may direct that part or all of the fine is to be paid to the board administering the scheme: see the Agricultural Marketing Act 1958 s 6(7). Where any offence committed by a body corporate under the Agricultural Marketing Act 1958 is proved to have been committed with the consent or approval of any director, manager, secretary or other officer of the body corporate he, as well as the body corporate, is deemed to be guilty of the offence and is liable to be proceeded against and punished accordingly: s 48. As to the prescribed sum see PARA 58 note 1.
5   As to the Secretary of State and the Welsh Ministers see PARA 390.
6   'Registered producer' means, in relation to any scheme, a producer registered under the scheme: Agricultural Marketing Act 1958 s 52(1). Subject to the approval of the Secretary of State and the Welsh Ministers, a scheme may make provision for securing that where, by reason of a registered producer dying, or becoming subject to some legal disability, or entering into a composition or scheme of arrangement with his creditors, any property in, or control of, the regulated product is transferred from the registered producer to a personal representative, trustee, committee or other person, the personal representative, trustee, committee or other person, as the case may be, is, in such circumstances and in respect of such matters as may be specified in the scheme, deemed to be a producer: s 8(3).
7   Agricultural Marketing Act 1958 s 6(2)(a). As to the initial suspension of these provisions see note 4.
8   Agricultural Marketing Act 1958 s 6(2)(b), (c). If the quantity which may be sold is restricted, the scheme must either specify or require the board to prescribe the manner in which the permitted quantity is to be determined; and the method of determination may be by reference, wholly or partly, to quantities or descriptions produced, sold or otherwise dealt with in some past period on some particular land or premises or by particular persons: s 6(3). As to the initial suspension of these provisions see note 4.
9   Agricultural Marketing Act 1958 s 6(2)(d). As to the initial suspension of these provisions see note 4. Where in conformity with a marketing scheme any contract for the sale of the regulated product by a registered producer otherwise than to, or through the agency of, the board purports to confer on the board any right to receive from the purchaser the whole or part of the purchase price, or of any damages for which the purchaser may be liable in respect of a wrongful rejection of articles tendered in accordance with the contract, the board may enforce that right against the purchaser:

s 17(4). This is so notwithstanding that the board is not a party to the contract and notwithstanding that, as between the board and the purchaser, there is no consideration: s 17(4).
10 Agricultural Marketing Act 1958 s 6(5).

174. Board's trading powers and ancillary provisions.

Subject to the approval of the Secretary of State and the Welsh Ministers[1], a marketing scheme[2] may make provision empowering the board[3] to buy the regulated product[4], to produce specified commodities from that product, and to sell, grade, pack, store, adapt for sale, insure, advertise and transport the regulated product and any commodity produced from it by the board[5]. The board may also be empowered to buy from a board administering a corresponding scheme[6], and to exercise powers similar to those mentioned above in respect of anything so bought, or act as agent for the board administering the other scheme[7]. There may be further powers to provide equipment and services to producers[8] and others[9], to co-operate with others in doing things which the board has or could have power to do[10], to procure, promote or facilitate the doing of such things by others[11], to regulate the grading, marking, packing, storing, adaptation for sale, insurance, advertisement or transportation of the regulated product[12] and to encourage, promote or conduct agricultural co-operation, research and education[13].

Schemes must make provision for arbitration in cases where a producer is aggrieved by an act or omission of the board or its disciplinary committee[14].

1 As to the Secretary of State and the Welsh Ministers see PARA 390.
2 Ie a scheme under the Agricultural Marketing Act 1958: see PARA 171. The Agricultural Marketing Act 1958 no longer applies to the marketing of milk and potatoes and has been disapplied in relation to horticultural products and bananas: see PARA 171 note 2.
3 As to the meaning of 'board' see PARA 173 note 4.
4 As to the meaning of 'regulated product' see PARA 172 note 4.
5 Agricultural Marketing Act 1958 s 7(1)(a). The operation of all provisions included in schemes (other than substitutional schemes, as to which see PARA 180) pursuant to s 7(1), (2) is to be suspended until the end of the suspensory period (see PARA 177): s 7(3). A scheme may not empower a board to grade, or regulate the grading or marking, of graded horticultural produce: see the Agriculture and Horticulture Act 1964 s 22(3); and PARA 229.
6 Ie any other scheme under the Agricultural Marketing Act 1958 or any scheme under corresponding legislation enacted by the Parliament of Northern Ireland, being in either case a scheme for regulating the marketing of the same product as the product the marketing of which is regulated by the first-mentioned scheme: s 7(4).
7 Agricultural Marketing Act 1958 s 7(1)(b), (c). See note 5.
8 As to the meaning of 'producer' see PARA 173 note 3.
9 Agricultural Marketing Act 1958 s 7(1)(d), (e). See note 5. Such powers must be so framed as to secure that things sold or let and services rendered are sold, let or rendered in such circumstances as to be likely to be utilised wholly or mainly by registered producers, or in connection with the regulated product produced by them: s 7(2). As to the meaning of 'registered producer' see PARA 173 note 6. No provision of a scheme made pursuant to s 8(4) (incidental and consequential powers: see PARA 172) is deemed to empower the board to establish any market or slaughterhouse, unless that provision in terms confers on the board a specific power to establish markets or slaughterhouses, as the case may be: s 8(4) (proviso).
10 Agricultural Marketing Act 1958 s 7(1)(f). See note 5. Every board has power to negotiate with any other person in respect of any matter concerning the marketing of the regulated product, agricultural products from which it is wholly or partly derived, or commodities which are wholly or partly derived from it; and persons agreed between the parties or, failing agreement, persons nominated by the Secretary of State or the Welsh Ministers, may be brought into consultation: s 31(1). Boards have power to pay the remuneration and expenses of advisers and consultants in whole or in part, and such payments are deemed to be expenses under the scheme: s 31(2), (3).
11 Agricultural Marketing Act 1958 s 7(1)(g). See notes 5, 10.
12 Agricultural Marketing Act 1958 s 7(1)(h). See notes 5, 10.

13 Agricultural Marketing Act 1958 s 7(1)(i). See notes 5, 10.
14 Agricultural Marketing Act 1958 ss 8(1)(b), 9(5). As to the disciplinary committee see PARA **186**.

175. Powers of entry and inspection of accounts.

Subject to the approval of the Secretary of State and the Welsh Ministers[1], a marketing scheme[2] may contain powers of entry by authorised persons on to premises occupied by registered producers[3] and believed to be used for producing the regulated product[4] or for certain activities regulated by the scheme[5], and may require registered producers to furnish such estimates, returns, accounts and other information as the board[6] considers necessary[7].

1   As to the Secretary of State and the Welsh Ministers see PARA **390**.
2   Ie a scheme under the Agricultural Marketing Act 1958: see PARA **171**. The Agricultural Marketing Act 1958 no longer applies to the marketing of milk and potatoes and has been disapplied in relation to horticultural products and bananas: see PARA **171** note 2.
3   As to the meanings of 'producer' and 'registered producer' see PARA **173** notes 3, 6.
4   As to the meaning of 'regulated product' see PARA **172** note 4.
5   Agricultural Marketing Act 1958 s 8(2)(a). Except in the case of a substitutional scheme (see PARA **180**), the operation of any provision of a scheme made pursuant to s 8(2) is to be suspended until the expiration of the suspensory period (see PARA **177**): s 8(2) proviso.
6   As to the meaning of 'board' see PARA **173** note 4.
7   Agricultural Marketing Act 1958 s 8(2)(b). See note 5.

(iii) Making, Amendment and Revocation of Schemes

176. Submission and approval of marketing schemes.

A marketing scheme[1] may be submitted by any persons who satisfy the Secretary of State or the Welsh Ministers[2] that they are substantially representative of the persons who produce the product in question in the area to which the scheme is applicable[3]. Before approving the scheme the Secretary of State or the Welsh Ministers must publish[4] notice of the submission, and of the place where copies of the scheme may be obtained, on payment of the fees specified in the notice, and inspected[5]. The notice must also specify the period, being not less than six weeks after publication, within which objections and representations with respect to the scheme may be made; and objections in writing, stating their grounds and the specific modifications required, may be sent to the Secretary of State or the Welsh Ministers within that time[6].

Where an objection has been duly made and has not been withdrawn, the Secretary of State or the Welsh Ministers must, before taking any further action, direct a public inquiry[7] to be held and consider the report of the person who held it, unless he considers or they consider the objection frivolous or he proposes or they propose to modify the scheme to meet the objection[8]. After considering the scheme and the objections and representations, and after holding such inquiries, if any, as he thinks or they think fit or as he is or they are required to hold, the Secretary of State or the Welsh Ministers may modify the scheme as he thinks or they think proper[9], but not so as to apply it to other areas[10]. Once satisfied that the scheme will be conducive to more efficient production and marketing, the Secretary of State or the Welsh Ministers may lay a draft of the scheme and a report as to the evidence by which he has or they have been satisfied that the persons submitting it are duly representative, and following approval of the draft must make an order approving the scheme[11].

1　Ie a scheme under the Agricultural Marketing Act 1958: see PARA 171. The Agricultural Marketing Act 1958 no longer applies to the marketing of milk and potatoes and has been disapplied in relation to horticultural products and bananas: see PARA 171 note 2.

2　As to the Secretary of State and the Welsh Ministers see PARA 390. In carrying out his functions under the Agricultural Marketing Act 1958 s 2, the Secretary of State acts as an officer representing the Crown and consequently cannot be restrained by injunction: *Merricks v Heathcoat-Amory* [1955] Ch 567, [1955] 2 All ER 453. The granting of an injunction in such a case is precluded by the Crown Proceedings Act 1947 s 21, but that provision permits the making of a declaratory order: see further CROWN AND CROWN PROCEEDINGS vol 29 (2014) PARA 110.

3　Agricultural Marketing Act 1958 s 1(1). When considering whether they are so satisfied, the Secretary of State and the Welsh Ministers must have regard both to the number of persons represented and to the quantity of the product they produce in that area: s 1(3).

4　Ie in the London Gazette, and in such other manner as the Secretary of State thinks or the Welsh Ministers think best for informing persons affected: Agricultural Marketing Act 1958 ss 2(1), 52(1).

5　Agricultural Marketing Act 1958 s 2(1).

6　Agricultural Marketing Act 1958 s 2(1), (2).

7　The inquiry is to be held by a competent and impartial person appointed by the Secretary of State or the Welsh Ministers and in accordance with the Agricultural Marketing (Public Inquiry) Rules 1949, SI 1949/2094: Agricultural Marketing Act 1958 s 2(13).

8　Agricultural Marketing Act 1958 s 2(3). Before making any modifications to a scheme, the Secretary of State or the Welsh Ministers must give notice of the proposed modifications to such persons (not less than nine nor more than 21) as the persons submitting it may have nominated at the time of the submission of the scheme; and if more than half of the nominees do not agree to the modifications within four weeks or such longer time as the Secretary of State or the Welsh Ministers may allow them, no further action can be taken: s 2(6).

9　Agricultural Marketing Act 1958 s 2(4). As to modifications see note 8.

10　Agricultural Marketing Act 1958 s 2(5).

11　Agricultural Marketing Act 1958 s 2(7), (8). The order must be published in the London Gazette and in such other manner as seems best for informing persons affected: s 2(12). The scheme will come into force on a date specified in the order: s 2(11). A substitutional scheme is treated as an amendment of the scheme which it replaces and the requirement of a report as to evidence is modified in that case: see PARA 180. The making of an order is conclusive evidence that the statutory requirements have been complied with, and that the order and scheme have been duly made and approved and are within the powers described: s 2(11). If a government motion to approve the draft is negatived or withdrawn, the expenses of the promoters are payable out of the appropriate agricultural marketing fund (as to which see PARA 197): s 29. If the scheme is approved those expenses are payable by the board: see s 28(2)–(4). As to the meaning of 'board' see PARA 173 note 4.

177. Poll of registered producers.

Every marketing scheme[1], other than a substitutional scheme[2], must require a poll of the registered producers[3] on the question whether the scheme should remain in force to be taken within such time as may be specified in the scheme[4]. There is a 'suspensory period' following approval of a scheme[5], pending the poll of registered producers, during which the powers conferred by the scheme to regulate sales and the marketing of the regulated product[6] cannot be exercised: if not less than two-thirds of those voting (in terms of both numbers and productive capacity)[7] support the scheme, the provisions of the scheme, suspended during the suspensory period, will come into force at the end of that period; if, however, the requisite majority does not favour the continuance of the scheme, it ceases to have effect at the date on which the result of the poll is declared[8]. If it is proved to the satisfaction of the Secretary of State or the Welsh Ministers[9], before the expiration of the suspensory period, that less than half of those entitled to vote used their vote, he or they must forthwith revoke the scheme by order[10].

1 Ie every scheme under the Agricultural Marketing Act 1958: see PARA 171. The Agricultural Marketing Act 1958 no longer applies to the marketing of milk and potatoes and has been disapplied in relation to horticultural products and bananas: see PARA 171 note 2.
2 As to substitutional schemes see PARA 180.
3 As to the meanings of 'producer' and 'registered producer' see PARA 173 notes 3, 6. A person who is registered as a producer notwithstanding that he has been exempted from registration is not deemed to be a registered producer for these purposes: Agricultural Marketing Act 1958 s 4(6).
4 Agricultural Marketing Act 1958 s 4(2). If the scheme regulates the marketing of two or more separate products a poll must be taken in respect of each product as if there were a scheme for each; and the question whether any product is to be treated as a separate product is to be determined by the provisions of the scheme: s 4(5). The scheme must detail the manner in which the polls are to be taken, and for this purpose may apply with any necessary modifications any enactments relating to parliamentary or local government elections, including their penal provisions: s 4(4)(a). It may prescribe the manner in which the productive capacity of registered producers is to be determined (s 4(4)(b)), and what information is to be furnished by registered producers and how it is to be furnished (s 4(4)(c)); and it must prescribe the manner in which the result of the poll is to be declared and published (s 4(4)(d)).
5 As to the approval of a scheme see PARA 176. The 'suspensory period', in relation to a scheme, is a period beginning on the date when the scheme is approved and ending at the expiration of such period (not being less than one month or more than two months) beginning on the date of the declaration of the result of the initial poll, as may be provided by the scheme: Agricultural Marketing Act 1958 s 52(1).
6 As to the meaning of 'regulated product' see PARA 172 note 4.
7 Ie the 'requisite majority': Agricultural Marketing Act 1958 s 52(1).
8 Agricultural Marketing Act 1958 s 4(3).
9 As to the Secretary of State and the Welsh Ministers see PARA 390.
10 Agricultural Marketing Act 1958 s 4(3) proviso.

178. Amendment and revocation of schemes.

An amendment of a marketing scheme[1] may be submitted by the board[2] to the Secretary of State or the Welsh Ministers[3] for approval, provided it has been previously published in the manner prescribed by the scheme to all producers registered[4] under the scheme[5]. When an amendment is duly submitted, the provisions relating to the publication, modification and approval of original schemes[6] apply to it with suitable modifications[7]. No scheme may be amended so as to apply to any area to which it would not have applied without the amendment[8].

A poll on the question whether a scheme should be revoked may also be demanded, and the Secretary of State or the Welsh Ministers must by order revoke the scheme if more than half of the total number of registered producers voting, who can produce more than half the quantity of the regulated product which all the producers voting can produce, vote in favour of revocation[9]. A scheme may also be revoked by a subsequent scheme[10], and the Secretary of State or the Welsh Ministers must revoke a scheme if an order is made for the winding up of the board[11].

There are also provisions under which a scheme may be amended or revoked where any provision of it or any act or omission of a board is contrary to the interests of consumers, or is contrary to the interests of persons affected by the scheme and is not in the public interest[12].

1 Ie a scheme under the Agricultural Marketing Act 1958: see PARA 171. The Agricultural Marketing Act 1958 no longer applies to the marketing of milk and potatoes and has been disapplied in relation to horticultural products and bananas: see PARA 171 note 2.
2 As to the meaning of 'board' see PARA 173 note 4.

3 As to the Secretary of State and the Welsh Ministers see PARA 390.
4 As to the meanings of 'producer' and 'registered producer' see PARA 173 notes 3, 6.
5 Agricultural Marketing Act 1958 s 2(15), Sch 1 para 1(1), (2) (s 2(15) amended by the Agriculture Act 1986 Sch 3 para 1). Where a poll on the question whether the amendment be submitted is demanded within a time prescribed in the scheme by a number or proportion of registered producers so prescribed, the amendment may not be so submitted unless approved by the requisite majority: Agricultural Marketing Act 1958 Sch 1 para 1(2). As to the meaning of 'requisite majority' see PARA 177 text and note 7. As to the conduct of polls see PARA 177.
6 Ie the provisions of the Agricultural Marketing Act 1958 s 2(1)–(4), (6), (7), (11), (13), (14), as to which see PARA 176.
7 Agricultural Marketing Act 1958 Sch 1 para 1(4).
8 Agricultural Marketing Act 1958 Sch 1 para 1(3).
9 Agricultural Marketing Act 1958 Sch 1 para 2. No such poll may be taken within two years of the date of the declaration of the result of any previous poll or within a period prescribed by the scheme from the date of the declaration, unless the board consents: Sch 1 para 2 proviso. In the case of a substitutional scheme (see PARA 180) the time limit of two years does not apply: Sch 1 para 2 proviso (i).
10 Agricultural Marketing Act 1958 Sch 1 para 3. Where a scheme is so revoked the subsequent scheme may provide for the transfer of property, rights and liabilities and for the continuation of legal proceedings: Sch 1 para 3.
11 Agricultural Marketing Act 1958 Sch 1 para 4. As to the winding up and dissolution of marketing boards see Sch 2 paras 4–6 (Sch 2 para 4 substituted by the Insolvency Act 1986 Sch 14).
12 See the Agricultural Marketing Act 1958 Sch 1 para 5. See also s 19(6)–(9); and PARA 191.

179. Consolidation of schemes.

The Secretary of State and the Welsh Ministers[1] are also empowered to prepare a consolidation of any marketing scheme[2], as it has effect with amendments, and by order to revoke the amended scheme and replace it with the consolidated scheme[3]. Any order made pursuant to this power must, however, state that it is made only for the purposes of consolidation, although it may legitimately contain such transitional and consequential provision as the Secretary of State considers or the Welsh Ministers consider necessary or expedient[4].

1 As to the Secretary of State and the Welsh Ministers see PARA 390.
2 Ie a scheme under the Agricultural Marketing Act 1958: see PARA 171. The Agricultural Marketing Act 1958 no longer applies to the marketing of milk and potatoes and has been disapplied in relation to horticultural products and bananas: see PARA 171 note 2.
3 Agricultural Marketing Act 1958 Sch 1 para 5A(1) (added by the Agriculture Act 1986 Sch 3 para 1).
4 Agricultural Marketing Act 1958 Sch 1 para 5A(2) (as added: see note 3).

180. Substitutional schemes.

A substitutional scheme is a scheme which revokes one or more existing marketing schemes[1] and is such that, at the time when it comes into force:

(1)   every person who was entitled to be registered as a producer[2] under the existing scheme or one or more of the existing schemes is entitled to be registered as a producer under the new scheme[3]; and

(2)   no person who was not entitled to be registered as a producer under the existing scheme or any of the existing schemes is entitled to be registered as a producer under the new scheme[4].

A substitutional scheme may be submitted by the board or boards[5] administering the scheme or schemes revoked by the substitutional scheme to the Secretary of State or the Welsh Ministers[6] for approval[7]. Before it is submitted it must be published, in the manner prescribed by the revoked scheme or schemes, to all producers registered under the revoked scheme or schemes, and a poll may then be demanded[8]. When a draft of a substitutional scheme is laid, the Secretary of State or the Welsh Ministers must also lay a report showing that these requirements have been complied with[9]. The declaration of the Secretary of State or the Welsh Ministers, contained in an order approving a scheme, that the scheme is a substitutional scheme, is conclusive[10].

1   Ie schemes under the Agricultural Marketing Act 1958: see PARA 171. The Agricultural Marketing Act 1958 no longer applies to the marketing of milk and potatoes and has been disapplied in relation to horticultural products and bananas: see PARA 171 note 2.
2   As to the meaning of 'producer' see PARA 173 note 3. As to the registration of producers see PARA 187.
3   Agricultural Marketing Act 1958 s 52(1).
4   Agricultural Marketing Act 1958 s 52(1).
5   As to the meaning of 'board' see PARA 173 note 4.
6   As to the Secretary of State and the Welsh Ministers see PARA 390.
7   Agricultural Marketing Act 1958 s 1(1).
8   Agricultural Marketing Act 1958 s 1(4). The provisions as to this poll and the majority required for submission to the Secretary of State or the Welsh Ministers are the same as those applicable to the case of an amendment: see s 1(4); and PARA 178.
9   Agricultural Marketing Act 1958 s 2(8).
10 Agricultural Marketing Act 1958 s 52(2).

(iv) Effect of Schemes on Contracts

181. Annulment of certain contracts.

In order to ensure that transactions in regulated agricultural products[1] are conducted only in accordance with the relevant agricultural marketing scheme[2], mechanisms exist for the annulment (in certain circumstances) of contracts made in contravention of a scheme, or whose performance would infringe a scheme. Where a scheme either requires registered producers[3] to sell the regulated product or any description of it only to, or through the agency of, the board[4], or provides for the determination of the quantity of the regulated product or any description of it which may be sold by any registered producer, every contract whereby a registered producer undertakes to sell, otherwise than to, or through the agency of, the board, a quantity of an agricultural product determined by reference to the total quantity he produces, is void and unenforceable so far as the performance of the contract is prohibited by the scheme[5].

1   As to the meaning of 'agricultural product' see PARA 171 note 1; and as to the meaning of 'regulated product' see PARA 172 note 4.
2   Ie a scheme under the Agricultural Marketing Act 1958: see PARA 171. The Agricultural Marketing Act 1958 no longer applies to the marketing of milk and potatoes and has been disapplied in relation to horticultural products and bananas: see PARA 171 note 2.
3   As to the meanings of 'producer' and 'registered producer' see PARA 173 notes 3, 6.
4   As to the meaning of 'board' see PARA 173 note 4.
5   Agricultural Marketing Act 1958 s 17(3). Such contracts cannot be registered: see s 18(1); and PARA 183. Other contracts are not annulled and can be registered: see PARAS 182–183.

182. Saving for certain contracts.

In the absence of requirements in a marketing scheme[1] that producers[2] sell regulated product[3] to or by the agency of the board[4], or provisions restricting the quantity that may be sold[5], if neither the making nor the performance of a contract was, at the time when the contract was made, prohibited by a marketing scheme, it will not, unless the contract otherwise provides, be void or unenforceable by reason of the fact that, at the time for performance, the latter has become prohibited by a scheme[6]. This protection is, however, time-limited[7].

1   Ie a scheme under the Agricultural Marketing Act 1958: see PARA 171. The Agricultural Marketing Act 1958 no longer applies to the marketing of milk and potatoes and has been disapplied in relation to horticultural products and bananas: see PARA 171 note 2.
2   As to the meaning of 'producer' see PARA 173 note 3.
3   As to the meaning of 'regulated product' see PARA 172 note 4.
4   As to the meaning of 'board' see PARA 173 note 4.
5   Ie otherwise than in the circumstances set out in PARA 181.
6   Agricultural Marketing Act 1958 s 17(1). Penalties are not incurred for the doing of acts which contravene the scheme but which are necessary for the performance of such contracts: s 17(5).
7   See the Agricultural Marketing Act 1958 s 17(2); and PARA 183.

183. Registration of protected contracts.

The statutory protection of contracts whose execution might otherwise be prohibited by a marketing scheme[1] is extended only until the expiration of three months from the date the prohibition first takes effect, unless the contracts are registered[2]. If, before the expiration of that time, any party to such a contract applies for registration, the board[3] is, subject to statutory anti-evasion provisions[4], obliged to register it[5].

Any contracting party who is aggrieved by an omission of the board to register a contract may, within a further 21 days, appeal to any county court within the district of which any party to the contract has dwelt or carried on business during the time for appeal[6]. The board and any party to the contract may appear and be heard, and the court must by order direct registration[7] if it finds that the application to register the contract was made before the expiration of the three month period after the scheme's prohibition came into effect[8], provided that if the contract was made within the period during which the anti-evasion provisions are applicable[9], it must not have been made with a view to evading the scheme[10].

1   Ie a scheme under the Agricultural Marketing Act 1958: see PARA 171. As to the statutory protection mentioned in the text see PARA 182. The Agricultural Marketing Act 1958 no longer applies to the marketing of milk and potatoes and has been disapplied in relation to horticultural products and bananas: see PARA 171 note 2.
2   Agricultural Marketing Act 1958 s 17(2).
3   As to the meaning of 'board' see PARA 173 note 4.
4   The board's obligation to register a contract does not apply if the contract was made within a period beginning 12 months before the date when notice of the submission of the scheme was published (see PARA 176) and ending six months after the expiration of the suspensory period (see PARA 177) or, in the case of a substitutional scheme (see PARA 180), ending six months after the date when the scheme comes into force, and was made with a view to evading the operation of the scheme: Agricultural Marketing Act 1958 s 18(1), (6). The registration procedure is not applicable to contracts which are void by virtue of s 17(3) (see PARA 181): s 18(1).
5   Agricultural Marketing Act 1958 s 18(1). Registration must take place within 14 days of the application: s 18(1).
6   Agricultural Marketing Act 1958 s 18(2). The appeal may instead be brought in the High Court by consent, or may be removed from the county court to the High Court in the same way as any matter commenced in the county court: s 18(5) (amended by the Crime and Courts Act 2013 Sch 9 para 57). As to the transfer of proceedings see CIVIL PROCEDURE vol 11 (2015) PARA 105.
    The disputed contract continues to be effective pending determination of the appeal: s 18(2).
7   If the court directs its registration, a contract is to be deemed to have been registered as from the date of the order: Agricultural Marketing Act 1958 s 18(3).
8   Agricultural Marketing Act 1958 s 18(3)(a). As to this period see the text and notes 1–2.
9   Ie the period described in note 4.
10 Agricultural Marketing Act 1958 s 18(3)(b). If, however, the court does not direct the registration of a contract made during the period during which the anti-evasion provisions are applicable, it may certify that a party to that contract entered into it in good faith and without a view to evading

the operation of the scheme; and in that case the party may recover the amount of any damage he has suffered by reason of the avoidance of the contract from any party certified by the court to have entered into it with a view to such evasion: s 18(4).

(v) Administration

A. BOARDS AND COMMITTEES

184. Constitution of marketing boards.

Every marketing scheme[1] must constitute a board[2] to administer it[3], and must be so framed as to secure that the total number of members is not less than eight, nor, unless the Secretary of State allows or the Welsh Ministers[4] allow a greater number, more than 24[5]. Of these members not less than two nor, subject to that minimum, more than one-fifth of the total are to be appointed by the Secretary of State or the Welsh Ministers as persons who have had experience and shown capacity in commerce, finance, administration, public affairs or the organisation of workers, or who are specially conversant with the interests of consumers of the regulated product[6]. The remaining members are to be named in the scheme, but they can hold office only for a year or less from the date on which the scheme comes into force, and after that they must be elected in accordance with the scheme either by the producers[7] or by a body or bodies elected by them[8]. The scheme may, however, permit the board to act notwithstanding any vacancy in its membership[9]. The board must be a body corporate, and the Secretary of State and the Welsh Ministers must keep its address for service in a register open for inspection by the public[10]. There are also provisions relating to the winding up and dissolution of boards[11].

1 Ie every scheme under the Agricultural Marketing Act 1958: see PARA 171. The Agricultural Marketing Act 1958 no longer applies to the marketing of milk and potatoes and has been disapplied in relation to horticultural products and bananas: see PARA 171 note 2.
2 As to the meaning of 'board' see PARA 173 note 4.
3 Agricultural Marketing Act 1958 s 3(1).
4 As to the Secretary of State and the Welsh Ministers see PARA 390.
5 Agricultural Marketing Act 1958 s 3(3), Sch 2 para 2(1)(a).
6 Agricultural Marketing Act 1958 Sch 2 para 2(1)(b). As to the meaning of 'regulated product' see PARA 172 note 4. For these purposes 'consumers of the regulated product' means persons who purchase the product, or commodities produced wholly or partly therefrom, for their own consumption or use and not persons who purchase the product, or such commodities, for the purpose of any trade or industry carried on by them: Sch 2 para 2(3).
     Members of the board appointed by the Secretary of State are disqualified for membership of the House of Commons: see the House of Commons Disqualification Act 1975 s 1(1)(f), Sch 1 Pt III; and PARLIAMENT vol 78 (2010) PARA 908.
7 As to the meaning of 'producer' see PARA 173 note 3.
8 Agricultural Marketing Act 1958 Sch 2 para 2(1)(c).
9 Agricultural Marketing Act 1958 Sch 2 para 2(2).
10 Agricultural Marketing Act 1958 Sch 2 paras 1, 3 (Sch 2 para 1 amended by the Charities Act 1960 Sch 7 Pt II).
11 See the Agricultural Marketing Act 1958 Sch 2 paras 4–6 (Sch 2 para 4 substituted by the Insolvency Act 1986 Sch 14).

185. Executive committees.

Every marketing scheme[1] must require the board[2] to appoint an executive committee from its members[3]. This committee is to consist of not more than seven members, of whom at least one must be a member appointed by the Secretary of

State or the Welsh Ministers[4], and is to have delegated to it all the functions of the board except such functions as may be specified in the scheme[5].

1   Ie every scheme under the Agricultural Marketing Act 1958: see PARA 171. The Agricultural Marketing Act 1958 no longer applies to the marketing of milk and potatoes and has been disapplied in relation to horticultural products and bananas: see PARA 171 note 2.
2   As to the meaning of 'board' see PARA 173 note 4.
3   Agricultural Marketing Act 1958 s 3(2).
4   As to the Secretary of State and the Welsh Ministers see PARA 390.
5   Agricultural Marketing Act 1958 Sch 2 para 2(1)(d).

186.   Establishment of disciplinary committees.
Every marketing scheme[1] must be framed so as to secure that there is a committee of the board[2], to be known as the disciplinary committee, constituted of not less than four nor more than six members of the board and an independent chairman[3]. Every scheme is also to require the disciplinary committee to impose on, and the board to recover from, any registered producer[4] who contravenes[5] certain provisions of the scheme[6] such monetary penalties as may be specified by the scheme[7].

1   Ie every scheme under the Agricultural Marketing Act 1958: see PARA 171. The Agricultural Marketing Act 1958 no longer applies to the marketing of milk and potatoes and has been disapplied in relation to horticultural products and bananas: see PARA 171 note 2.
2   As to the meaning of 'board' see PARA 173 note 4.
3   Agricultural Marketing Act 1958 s 9(1). The chairman must:
    (1)   have a seven year general qualification, within the meaning of the Courts and Legal Services Act 1990 s 71 (see LEGAL PROFESSIONS vol 65 (2015) PARA 540) (Agricultural Marketing Act 1958 s 9(1)(a));
    (2)   be an advocate or solicitor in Scotland of at least seven years' standing (s 9(1)(b)); or
    (3)   be a member of the Bar of Northern Ireland or solicitor of the Court of Judicature of Northern Ireland of at least seven years' standing (s 9(1)(c) (amended by the Constitutional Reform Act 2005 Sch 11 para 5),
    and be approved by the Secretary of State or the Welsh Ministers (Agricultural Marketing Act 1958 s 9(1)). As to the Secretary of State and the Welsh Ministers see PARA 390.
        Although independent, the chairman may receive a fee from the board: *Potato Marketing Board v Merricks* [1958] 2 QB 316, [1958] 2 All ER 538.
4   As to the meaning of 'registered producer' see PARA 173 note 6.
5   'Contravention' includes, in relation to a provision of the Agricultural Marketing Act 1958 or of a scheme, a failure to comply with the provision; and 'contravene' is to be construed accordingly: s 52(1).
6   The provisions in question are those made in pursuance of the Agricultural Marketing Act 1958 ss 6(2), 7(1)(a)–(c), (h), (i), 8(2): s 9(2), (3). As to those provisions see PARAS 173–175.
7   Agricultural Marketing Act 1958 s 9(2). No such penalty may be imposed in respect of a contravention which constitutes an offence under the Agricultural Marketing Act 1958 or any other Act, and, except in the case of a substitutional scheme (see PARA 180), the operation of any provision for the imposition of penalties is suspended until the end of the suspensory period (see PARA 177): s 9(2).

B. REGISTRATION AND PENALTIES UNDER SCHEMES

187.   Registration of producers.
Every marketing scheme[1] must provide for the registration of any producer[2] of the regulated product[3] who makes an application for that purpose[4]. As soon as practicable after any scheme, other than a substitutional scheme[5], comes into force, the board[6] must publish[7] a form of application for registration as a producer under the scheme[8]. With this it must also publish a notice stating:
    (1)   the nature of the regulated product and the area to which the scheme applies[9];

(2)   the classes or descriptions of producers who are exempted from registration and the procedure required, if any, for securing exemption[10];

(3)   that a poll of registered producers[11] (other than producers exempted from registration) is to be taken on the question whether the scheme should remain in force, and that no person will be allowed to vote unless registered[12];

(4)   that no person will incur any financial liability as a result of registration if it is decided that the scheme should not remain in force[13];

(5)   that, if it is decided that the scheme should remain in force, every producer who is not registered or exempted from registration will be prohibited from selling the regulated product[14]; and

(6)   where copies of the scheme may be obtained on payment[15],

and giving such other particulars as the board may think fit[16].

At the same time the Secretary of State and the Welsh Ministers must compile a list of the names and addresses of all persons they believe are producers, and forward a copy of it to the board[17]. The board must then send to everyone named in the list, and to everyone who it has reason to believe is a producer, a notice stating the particulars described above and a form of application for registration[18].

1 Ie every scheme under the Agricultural Marketing Act 1958: see PARA 171. The Agricultural Marketing Act 1958 no longer applies to the marketing of milk and potatoes and has been disapplied in relation to horticultural products and bananas: see PARA 171 note 2.

2 As to the meaning of 'producer' see PARA 173 note 3.

3 As to the meaning of 'regulated product' see PARA 172 note 4.

4 Agricultural Marketing Act 1958 s 4(1). Registration of the name or style of a partnership operates as the registration of all the partners, but for the purposes of voting and the assessment of contributions on registered producers all the partners count as a single registered producer: s 4(7). A producer may apply for registration in writing, orally or by conduct: *R v Milk Marketing Board, ex p Wenham* (1935) unreported. Schemes must provide for the register to be open for inspection, for copies of it to be available upon demand and payment of a fee, and for removal from it of the names of persons who have ceased to be producers or are exempted from registration: Agricultural Marketing Act 1958 s 8(1)(c), (d).

5 As to substitutional schemes see PARA 180.

6 As to the meaning of 'board' see PARA 173 note 4.

7 Ie in such newspapers circulating in the area to which the scheme applies as the Secretary of State or the Welsh Ministers may direct: Agricultural Marketing Act 1958 s 5(1). As to the Secretary of State and the Welsh Ministers see PARA 390.

8 Agricultural Marketing Act 1958 s 5(1).

9 Agricultural Marketing Act 1958 s 5(1)(a).

10 Agricultural Marketing Act 1958 s 5(1)(b). The classes or descriptions of producers who are exempted from registration are presumably those who are exempted from registration in pursuance of s 6(1): see PARA 173. A producer who is exempt from registration may nevertheless be registered if he wishes to be and if the scheme so provides; he is then subject to the provisions of the scheme: *Milk Marketing Board v Williams* (1935) 153 LT 115, CA.

11 As to the meaning of 'registered producer' see PARA 173 note 6.

12 Agricultural Marketing Act 1958 s 5(1)(c), (d). As to this poll see PARA 177.

13 Agricultural Marketing Act 1958 s 5(1)(d).

14 Agricultural Marketing Act 1958 s 5(1)(e).

15 Agricultural Marketing Act 1958 s 5(1)(f).

16 Agricultural Marketing Act 1958 s 5(1)(g).

17 Agricultural Marketing Act 1958 s 5(2)(a). If the Secretary of State or the Welsh Ministers have so little information at his or their disposal that such a list would serve no useful purpose, he or they may tell the board so instead of compiling one: s 5(2)(b). The Secretary of State and the Welsh Ministers may also cause such a list to be compiled at the request of any person if he thinks or they think it would facilitate the due submission of a scheme and on payment of a fee representing the cost of compiling the list: s 5(4) (amended by the Agricultural Statistics Act 1979 Sch 1 para 1).

Information obtained under the Agricultural Statistics Act 1979 s 1 may be used for the purpose of compiling any list for these purposes: see s 3(2); and PARA 404.

18 Agricultural Marketing Act 1958 s 5(3).

188. Proceedings and penalties for contraventions of schemes.

Every marketing scheme[1] must be framed so as to secure that, before a penalty is imposed for contravening[2] any of the specified provisions of the scheme[3], there is a hearing by the disciplinary committee[4] and a decision is taken in accordance with the opinion of all or the majority of its members[5]. Schemes must also secure that, at least 14 days before the hearing, notice of the time and place of the hearing and a written statement of the charge are served personally, or by registered post or recorded delivery, upon the producer[6], and that no penalty is imposed for a contravention which occurred more than six years, or such less time as the scheme specifies, before the service of that written statement[7]. Moreover, every scheme must secure that, where the charge is withdrawn or is not substantiated, the board has the power and, to such extent as the committee decides, the duty, to make payments to the producer in respect of his costs[8], and that, in such circumstances and subject to such conditions as may be specified in the scheme, the committee has the power and the duty to reconsider and vary its decisions[9].

1 Ie every scheme under the Agricultural Marketing Act 1958: see PARA 171. The Agricultural Marketing Act 1958 no longer applies to the marketing of milk and potatoes and has been disapplied in relation to horticultural products and bananas: see PARA 171 note 2.

2 As to the meaning of 'contravening' see PARA 186 note 5.

3 As to the specified provisions see PARA 186 note 6.

4 As to the establishment of the disciplinary committee see PARA 186. In the absence of special reasons the hearing must be in public (Agricultural Marketing Act 1958 s 9(6)); and the chairman may direct that evidence be given on oath and may administer the oath (s 9(7)).

5 Agricultural Marketing Act 1958 s 9(4)(a). In the event of an equality of votes, the opinion of the chairman prevails: s 9(8). Judicial review by way of a quashing order lies against a marketing board which fails to act judicially in determining to impose a penalty: *R v Milk Marketing Board, ex p North* (1934) 50 TLR 559. The committee may also postpone the imposition of a penalty for such period, not exceeding 12 months, as may be specified in the scheme: Agricultural Marketing Act 1958 s 11.

6 Agricultural Marketing Act 1958 s 9(4)(b); Recorded Delivery Service Act 1962 s 1(2), Schedule para 5. As to the meaning of 'producer' see PARA 173 note 3.

7 Agricultural Marketing Act 1958 s 9(4)(c).

8 Agricultural Marketing Act 1958 s 9(4)(d).

9 Agricultural Marketing Act 1958 s 9(4)(e).

189. Enforcement and recovery.

Decisions of disciplinary committees[1] are enforceable as if the proceedings were an arbitration under arbitral proceedings to which the board[2] and the producer[3] were parties and as if the disciplinary committee were the arbitrator or umpire appointed by the agreement[4].

Where a contravention[5] (being a contravention in respect of which the disciplinary committee has the duty to impose, and the board the duty to recover, a penalty) causes a loss to the board, the disciplinary committee may, if the written statement of charge embodies an estimate of the loss and the grounds on which the estimate is based, require the loss to be paid in addition to any penalty imposed[6]. If an estimate of loss is thus embodied in the statement of charge, no loss caused by the contravention is recoverable from the producer in any other manner and, whether or not such an estimate is so embodied, the penalty must not be fixed with a view to recovering the whole or any part of any loss suffered by the board[7]. Where the contravention relates to the giving of information or making of returns to the board and results in failure to assess or demand a contribution or other payment, or the full amount of a contribution or payment, from producers, the amount not assessed or demanded is, if the board so elects by including an estimate in the written statement of charge, to be treated for these purposes as lost by reason of the contravention[8].

1 As to the establishment of the disciplinary committee see PARA 186.
2 As to the meaning of 'board' see PARA 173 note 4.
3 As to the meaning of 'producer' see PARA 173 note 3.
4 Agricultural Marketing Act 1958 s 12(1) (amended by the Arbitration Act 1996 Sch 3 para 12). The Arbitration Act 1996 ss 45, 69 (determination of preliminary points of law and appeals therefrom: see ARBITRATION vol 2 (2017) PARAS 555, 578) and s 66 (enforcement: see ARBITRATION vol 2 (2017) PARA 574) apply in relation to a hearing before a disciplinary committee and a determination of the matters referred to a committee: Agricultural Marketing Act 1958 s 12(1) (as so amended).
5 As to the meaning of 'contravention' see PARA 186 note 5.
6 Agricultural Marketing Act 1958 s 10(1). The sum to be paid in respect of the loss must not exceed either that which justly represents the amount of the loss or the amount stated in the estimate contained in the statement of charge: s 10(1).
7 Agricultural Marketing Act 1958 s 10(2).
8 Agricultural Marketing Act 1958 s 10(3).

190. Restrictions on disclosing information.

The disclosure by any person of any information obtained in the exercise of powers conferred on him relating to polls[1], or conferred on any board[2] or reorganisation commission[3] in connection with agricultural marketing schemes[4], is prohibited[5] unless the disclosure is:

(1)   made by a board in compliance with a requirement of the Secretary of State and the Welsh Ministers[6] under the legislation relating to diseases of animals[7];

(2)   made to the Competition and Markets Authority[8], if it is made for the purpose of enabling the exercise of its statutory functions[9];

(3)   made for the purposes of legal proceedings, including arbitrations, under agricultural marketing schemes, or the statutory provisions relating thereto[10], or for the purpose of any report of such proceedings[11];

(4)   required or authorised by any such scheme or statutory provision[12].

Information obtained by the Secretary of State or the Welsh Ministers pursuant to the statutory power to obtain agricultural statistics[13] may be disclosed to marketing authorities[14].

1 As to obtaining information for the purposes of polls see PARA 177.
2 As to the meaning of 'board' see PARA 173 note 4.
3 As to Agricultural Marketing Reorganisation Commissions see PARA 170.
4 Ie conferred under the Agricultural Marketing Act 1958 Pt I (ss 1–32) (see PARA 171 et seq).
5 The penalties for unauthorised disclosure are, in the case of conviction on indictment, imprisonment for a term not exceeding two years or a fine or both and, in the case of summary conviction, imprisonment for a term not exceeding three months or a fine not exceeding the prescribed sum or both: Agricultural Marketing Act 1958 s 47(3) (amended by the Criminal Law Act 1977 s 32(1); and by virtue of the Magistrates' Courts Act 1980 s 32(2)). As to the prescribed sum see PARA 58 note 1. As to offences by bodies corporate see PARA 173 note 4.
6 As to the Secretary of State and the Welsh Ministers see PARA 390.
7 Agricultural Marketing Act 1958 s 47(2)(a) (s 47(2) amended by the Statute Law (Repeals) Act 2004; and by the Natural Environment and Rural Communities Act 2006 Sch 11 para 31, Sch 12). The legislation relating to diseases of animals is the Animal Health Act 1981, the relevant provision of which for these purposes is s 82 (which requires every board administering a scheme under the Agricultural Marketing Act 1958 to give to the Secretary of State or the Welsh Ministers such information as may reasonably be required for the purposes of his or their functions under the Animal Health Act 1981).

8 As to the Competition and Markets Authority see COMPETITION vol 18 (2009) PARA 8A et seq.
9 Agricultural Marketing Act 1958 s 47(2)(aa) (added by the Fair Trading Act 1973 Sch 12; and
   substituted by SI 2014/892). The statutory functions referred to in the text are any of the functions
   of the Competition and Markets Authority under the Fair Trading Act 1973, the Competition Act
   1980, the Enterprise Act 2002 or the Enterprise and Regulatory Reform Act 2013 Pt 3 (see
   COMPETITION vol 18 (2009) PARA 1 et seq): Agricultural Marketing Act 1958 s 47(2)(aa) (as so
   added and substituted).
10 Ie the Agricultural Marketing Act 1958 Pt I (ss 1–32) (see PARA 171 et seq).
11 Agricultural Marketing Act 1958 s 27(2)(c). Information obtained under the Agricultural
   Marketing Act 1958 is privileged from production in any legal proceedings other than those
   specifically mentioned in s 47(2): *Rowell v Pratt* [1938] AC 101, [1937] 3 All ER 660, HL.
12 Agricultural Marketing Act 1958 s 27(2)(d).
13 Ie under the Agricultural Statistics Act 1979 s 1 (see PARA 403).
14 See the Agricultural Statistics Act 1979 s 3(2)(a); and PARA 404.

C. PARLIAMENTARY SUPERVISION

191. Intervention on competition grounds.
If in relation to an agricultural marketing scheme[1]:

(1)   the Competition and Markets Authority[2] has decided, in a report on a
      market investigation reference[3], that there is one, or more than one,
      adverse effect on competition[4]; or

(2)   the Secretary of State has decided[5] that an eligible public interest
      consideration[6] is relevant[7],

and whatever is to be remedied, mitigated or prevented relates to any provision of
a marketing scheme or any act of omission of a board[8], the Secretary of State and
the Welsh Ministers[9] may by order[10] make such amendments in the scheme as he
considers or they consider expedient for the purpose of rectifying the matter[11],
revoke the scheme[12] or, where the board can rectify the matter, direct it to take any
specified steps to do so[13].

1 Ie a scheme under the Agricultural Marketing Act 1958 Pt I (ss 1–32): see PARA 171 et seq. The
   Agricultural Marketing Act 1958 no longer applies to the marketing of milk and potatoes and has
   been disapplied in relation to horticultural products and bananas: see PARA 171 note 2.
2 As to the Competition and Markets Authority see COMPETITION vol 18 (2009) PARA 8A et seq.
3 Ie a report under the Enterprise Act 2002 s 136: see COMPETITION vol 18 (2009) PARA 281.
4 Agricultural Marketing Act 1958 s 19A(1), (1A) (s 19A added by the Fair Trading Act 1973 s 127;
   Agricultural Marketing Act 1958 s 19A(1) substituted, s 19A(1A), (1B), (3) added, and s 19A(2)
   amended, by the Enterprise Act 2002 Sch 25 para 2, Sch 26; Agricultural Marketing Act 1958 s
   19A(1B) , (1C) amended by SI 2014/892). As to the meaning of 'adverse effect on competition' see
   the Enterprise Act 2002 s 134(2); and COMPETITION vol 18 (2009) PARA 1 et seq.
5 Ie under the Enterprise Act 2002 s 147(2) or 147A(2): see COMPETITION vol 18 (2009)
   PARA 291.
6 As to the meaning of 'public interest consideration' see the Enterprise Act 2002 s 139(5); and
   COMPETITION vol 18 (2009) PARA 283.
7 Agricultural Marketing Act 1958 s 19A(1B) (as added and amended: see note 4).
8 As to the meaning of 'board' see PARA 173 note 4.
9 As to the Secretary of State and the Welsh Ministers see PARA 390.
10 These powers may be exercised as if a report of a committee of investigation had contained the
    conclusion that the provision of the scheme in question, or the act or omission in question, is
    contrary to the interests of consumers of the regulated product: Agricultural Marketing Act 1958
    s 19A(2) (as added and amended: see note 4). As to the meaning of 'regulated product' see PARA
    172 note 4. Committees of investigation were established under s 19(1) (repealed) and constituted
    under the Agricultural Marketing (Committee of Investigation) Regulations 1949, SI 1949/2452
    (amended by SI 1962/2320) (now spent). There are now no powers to establish committees of
    investigation for these purposes and any committees so established have been abolished (see the
    Natural Environment and Rural Communities Act 2006 s 101(d)).

For an order made under the Agricultural Marketing Act 1958 s 19(6) see the British Wool Marketing Scheme (Directions) Order 1958, SI 1958/2126; and see also PARAS **199–200**. Before taking any such action, the Secretary of State or the Welsh Ministers must give the board notice of his or their intention, and must consider any representations the board may make within 14 days of the notice: Agricultural Marketing Act 1958 s 19(6).

An order made by virtue of s 19A in a case mentioned in s 19A(1A) (see head (1) in the text) or s 19A(1B) (see head (2) in the text) is treated, for the purposes of the Enterprise Act 2002 ss 162(1), 166(3) (duties to register and keep under review enforcement orders etc: see COMPETITION vol 18 (2009) PARAS 304–307), as if it were made under the relevant power in Pt 4 (ss 168–184) to make an enforcement order (within the meaning of Pt 4): Agricultural Marketing Act 1958 s 19A(3) (as so added).

11 Agricultural Marketing Act 1958 ss 19(6)(a), 19A(2) (s 19A(2) as added and amended: see note 4).
12 Agricultural Marketing Act 1958 s 19(6)(b).
13 Agricultural Marketing Act 1958 s 19(6)(c). Orders giving directions to boards may be revoked or varied in certain ways by order made by the Secretary of State or the Welsh Ministers after consultation with the board: s 19(7).

192. Intervention in the public interest.

The powers of the Secretary of State and the Welsh Ministers[1] by order to revoke agricultural marketing schemes[2] are also exercisable where the Secretary of State has referred to the Competition and Markets Authority[3] any question relating to the efficiency and costs of, or the service provided by, a board[4], and the Authority's report contains conclusions[5] to the effect that certain matters consisting of or including any provision of a scheme or any act or omission of a board operate against the public interest[6]. Similarly, if it appears to the Secretary of State or the Welsh Ministers that certain acts or omissions, or intended acts or omissions of the board[7] have resulted or will result in certain restrictions, limitations or prices which are or will be contrary to the public interest[8], he or they may by order give such directions to the board as he considers or they consider necessary or expedient for preventing that result or preventing or mitigating the damage to the public interest thereby entailed[9]. The Secretary of State and the Welsh Ministers must give at least 28 days' notice of the action they propose to take and their reasons[10]. Any order thus made may be varied or revoked in certain ways by order made by the Secretary of State or the Welsh Ministers after consultation with the relevant board[11].

If the Secretary of State is, or the Welsh Ministers are, of opinion that any provision of an agricultural marketing scheme or any act or omission of a board is contrary to the interests of consumers of the regulated product, or contrary to the interests of a substantial number of persons affected by the scheme and is not in the public interest, he or they may order that the scheme be revoked[12].

1 As to the Secretary of State and the Welsh Ministers see PARA **390**.
2 Ie under the Agricultural Marketing Act 1958 s 19 (see PARA **191**). The schemes in question are those having effect under the Agricultural Marketing Act 1958: see PARA **171**. The Agricultural Marketing Act 1958 no longer applies to the marketing of milk and potatoes and has been disapplied in relation to horticultural products and bananas: see PARA **171** note 2.
3 Ie under the Competition Act 1980 s 11(1), (3)(d): see COMPETITION vol 18 (2009) PARA **10**. As to the Competition and Markets Authority see COMPETITION vol 18 (2009) PARA **8A** et seq.
4 As to the meaning of 'board' see PARA **173** note 4.
5 For these purposes it is necessary that none of the Authority's conclusions are to be disregarded by virtue of the Competition Act 1980 s 11C(3) (requirement for two-thirds majority: see COMPETITION vol 18 (2009) PARA **10**): Agricultural Marketing Act 1958 s 19A(1C)(b) (s 19A added by the Fair Trading Act 1973 s 127; and the Agricultural Marketing Act 1958 s 19A(1C) added by the Enterprise Act 2002 Sch 25 para 2(1), (2)(a)).
6 Agricultural Marketing Act 1958 s 19A(1C)(a) (as added (see note 5); amended by SI 2014/892).

7 Ie acts or omissions, or intended acts or omissions, of the board in respect of the provisions of the scheme providing for empowering the board to buy, produce commodities from and sell the regulated product and to sell any commodity so produced, or for determining the quantity or descriptions of that product which may be sold by registered producers, or the price at, below or above which, the terms on which, and the persons to whom, or through the agency of whom, the product may be sold by those producers: Agricultural Marketing Act 1958 s 20(1). As to the meaning of 'regulated product' see PARA 172 note 4. As to the meanings of 'producer' and 'registered producer' see PARA 173 notes 3, 6.
8 Agricultural Marketing Act 1958 s 20(1), (2).
9 Agricultural Marketing Act 1958 s 20(2). This power may be exercised where it appears that the result, or one of the results, of any act or omission of the board or intended act or omission of the board is or will be both contrary to the public interest and: (1) to restrict the purposes for which the regulated product is used or to limit the quantity of the product which is used for any particular purpose; (2) to limit the quantity of the regulated product or of any commodity produced from it which is produced or sold; (3) to regulate the price at which the regulated product or any commodity produced from it is sold; or (4) to limit the classes of persons to whom or through the agency of whom the regulated product or any commodity produced from it is sold: s 20(2). Any order made must state the general nature of the reasons for its making: s 20(6).

When serving notice on the board of an intention to give directions, the Secretary of State and the Welsh Ministers may, if they consider it necessary to take immediate action for preventing injury to the public interest, make a temporary order directing the board as to the course of action they consider it necessary that the board should take: s 21(1) (s 21(1), (2), (4) amended by the Natural Environment and Rural Communities Act 2006 Sch 11 para 29, Sch 12). Such a temporary order must be limited to expire in accordance with the provisions of the Agricultural Marketing Act 1958 s 21(2) (as so amended). The order may be revoked or varied but not so as to extend its operation beyond the periods prescribed by this provision: s 21(4) (as so amended). Any order made is to state the general nature of the reasons for the making thereof: s 21(5).
10 Agricultural Marketing Act 1958 s 20(3) (amended by the Natural Environment and Rural Communities Act 2006 Sch 11 para 28, Sch 12).
11 Agricultural Marketing Act 1958 s 20(5). As to such orders see also s 20(6); and note 9.
12 Agricultural Marketing Act 1958 Sch 1 para 5.

193. Reports to Parliament and the National Assembly for Wales.

The Secretary of State[1] is required to lay before Parliament[2], and the Welsh Ministers[3] are required to lay before the National Assembly for Wales[4], an annual report upon the operation of marketing schemes[5] in force and upon schemes submitted since the previous report but not in force at the date of the report[6]. No information as to a particular undertaking, other than the undertaking of a marketing board[7], is to be included in any such report without the consent of the owner of the undertaking[8].

1 As to the Secretary of State see PARA 390.
2 As to the laying of documents before Parliament see the Laying of Documents before Parliament (Interpretation) Act 1948; and STATUTES AND LEGISLATIVE PROCESS vol 96 (2012) PARAS 1048, 1052.
3 As to the Welsh Ministers see PARA 390.
4 For provisions as to the laying of reports before the National Assembly for Wales see the Government of Wales Act 2006 s 162(1), Sch 11 para 36; and STATUTES AND LEGISLATIVE PROCESS vol 96 (2012) PARA 1036.
5 Ie schemes having effect under the Agricultural Marketing Act 1958: see PARA 171. The Agricultural Marketing Act 1958 no longer applies to the marketing of milk and potatoes and has been disapplied in relation to horticultural products and bananas: see PARA 171 note 2.
6 Agricultural Marketing Act 1958 s 30.
7 As to the meaning of 'board' see PARA 173 note 4.
8 Agricultural Marketing Act 1958 s 47(1).

(vi) Finance under Schemes

194. Payments, contributions, accounts and compensation.

Every marketing scheme[1] must establish a fund, to be administered and controlled by the board[2], into which all money received by the board is to be paid and from which money is to be disbursed to operate the scheme[3]. Provision must similarly be made for the payment by registered producers[4] of contributions to the fund of such amounts as may be necessary for the operation of the scheme[5], for the assessment of such contributions[6], for the distribution of surplus funds[7], for the keeping and auditing of accounts[8], for the furnishing by the board to the Secretary of State or the Welsh Ministers[9] and to registered producers of accounts, returns and other information[10], and for the furnishing by the board of a copy of the balance sheets to any person requiring it[11].

Compensation is payable under a scheme by the board to registered producers in such class of cases as may be specified in the scheme, and any scheme may provide for the payment by the board of compensation, in such class of cases as may be so specified, to registered producers in respect of any loss occasioned to those producers by the operation of any scheme, whether administered by that board or not[12].

1   Ie every scheme under the Agricultural Marketing Act 1958: see PARA 171. The Agricultural Marketing Act 1958 no longer applies to the marketing of milk and potatoes and has been disapplied in relation to horticultural products and bananas: see PARA 171 note 2.
2   As to the meaning of 'board' see PARA 173 note 4.
3   Agricultural Marketing Act 1958 s 13(1)(a). Provision is made by the Income and Corporation Taxes Act 1988 s 509 for the computing for tax purposes of profits or gains or losses on trade carried on by marketing boards etc, which are required to pay surplus money derived from dealings into a reserve fund satisfying certain conditions: see INCOME TAXATION vol 59 (2014) PARA 1931.
4   As to the meanings of 'producer' and 'registered producer' see PARA 173 notes 3, 6.
5   Agricultural Marketing Act 1958 s 13(1)(b). Except in the case of a substitutional scheme (as to which see PARA 180), the operation of any provision made in pursuance of s 13(1)(b), (c), and of the provisions relating to the payment of compensation (see the text and note 12), is to be suspended until the end of the suspensory period: s 13(3).
6   Agricultural Marketing Act 1958 s 13(1)(b). See note 5.
7   Agricultural Marketing Act 1958 s 13(1)(c). See note 5.
8   Agricultural Marketing Act 1958 s 13(1)(d).
9   As to the Secretary of State and the Welsh Ministers see PARA 390.
10 Agricultural Marketing Act 1958 s 13(1)(e).
11 Agricultural Marketing Act 1958 s 13(1)(f).
12 Agricultural Marketing Act 1958 s 13(2). As to the suspension of the operation of provisions relating to compensation see note 5.

195. Loans and grants by or to marketing boards.

A marketing scheme[1] may empower the board[2] to lend to any registered producer[3] a portion of the amount it is estimated he will receive from the sale of the regulated product[4] which he has produced or is producing[5], and to guarantee payment of any sums secured by an agricultural charge[6].

A scheme may also empower the board to lend or grant money to any other board[7], and to guarantee the loans of any other board[8], but, if the loan, grant or guarantee is not specifically authorised by the scheme, the scheme may provide that the payment is not to be made or given without a resolution which has been notified to, and approved by, the registered producers[9].

Every scheme must provide for empowering the board to borrow money for the purposes of its functions[10], and a board has power to accept grants to be applied for purposes for which it may expend money[11]. In cases where it is proposed to make a loan or a grant to a board, the scheme may also empower the board to agree with the person so proposing, or with anyone proposing to guarantee the repayment of a loan, that it will apply the loan or grant in a specified manner[12]. Any scheme making such provision must impose on the board the duty of carrying it out[13], and may exclude the right of registered producers to arbitration in relation to anything done or omitted to be done under the agreement if the agreement contains a condition requiring the board to act on the advice of specified persons[14].

A debenture issued by the board may create, in favour of a bank[15], a floating charge on any farming stock[16] owned by the board; such a charge must be registered as an agricultural charge[17] and, if so registered, must not be deemed to be a bill of sale[18].

1   Ie a scheme under the Agricultural Marketing Act 1958: see PARA 171. The Agricultural Marketing Act 1958 no longer applies to the marketing of milk and potatoes and has been disapplied in relation to horticultural products and bananas: see PARA 171 note 2.
2   As to the meaning of 'board' see PARA 173 note 4.
3   As to the meanings of 'producer' and 'registered producer' see PARA 173 notes 3, 6.
4   As to the meaning of 'regulated product' see PARA 172 note 4.
5   Agricultural Marketing Act 1958 s 14(1)(a). Except in the case of a substitutional scheme (see PARA 180), the operation of any provision made in pursuance of s 14(1) is to be suspended until the end of the suspensory period (see PARA 177): s 14(1).
6   Agricultural Marketing Act 1958 s 14(1)(b). As to agricultural charges see the Agricultural Credits Act 1928 Pt II (ss 5–14); and PARAS 406–411. See note 5.
7   Agricultural Marketing Act 1958 s 14(2)(a).
8   Agricultural Marketing Act 1958 s 14(2)(b).
9   Agricultural Marketing Act 1958 s 14(3). As to the meanings of 'producer' and 'registered producer' see PARA 173 notes 3, 6.
10 Agricultural Marketing Act 1958 s 15(1).
11 Agricultural Marketing Act 1958 s 15(2).
12 Agricultural Marketing Act 1958 s 15(3).
13 Agricultural Marketing Act 1958 s 15(4)(a).
14 Agricultural Marketing Act 1958 s 15(4)(b).
15 As to the meaning of 'bank' see the Agricultural Credits Act 1928 s 5(7); and PARA 406 note 4 (definition applied by the Agricultural Marketing Act 1958 s 15(5)).
16 As to the meaning of 'farming stock' see the Agricultural Credits Act 1928 s 5(7); and PARA 406 note 5 (definition applied by the Agricultural Marketing Act 1958 s 15(5)).
17 Ie under the Agricultural Credits Act 1928 Pt II: see PARAS 406–411.
18 Agricultural Marketing Act 1958 s 15(5).

196. Investment of surplus funds.

Every marketing scheme[1] must provide for the manner in which the money of the board[2] may be invested, and must be so framed as to secure that money not for the time being required for the purposes of the board's functions is not, except with the approval of the Secretary of State and the Welsh Ministers[3], invested otherwise than pursuant to trustees' general statutory powers of investment[4].

1   Ie every scheme under the Agricultural Marketing Act 1958: see PARA 171. The Agricultural Marketing Act 1958 no longer applies to the marketing of milk and potatoes and has been disapplied in relation to horticultural products and bananas: see PARA 171 note 2.
2   As to the meaning of 'board' see PARA 173 note 4.
3   As to the Secretary of State and the Welsh Ministers see PARA 390.
4   Agricultural Marketing Act 1958 s 16(a) (substituted by the Trustee Act 2000 Sch 2 para 31(1)). Trustees' general statutory powers of investment are set out in the Trustee Act 2000 s 3, and are restricted by ss 4, 5: see TRUSTS AND POWERS vol 98 (2013) PARAS 453–455. The scheme must also provide that a statement of these investments is to be included in an annual report made to

the Secretary of State and the Welsh Ministers and registered producers: Agricultural Marketing Act 1958 s 16(b). As to the meanings of 'producer' and 'registered producer' see PARA **173** notes 3, 6.

197. Agricultural Marketing Fund.

An Agricultural Marketing Fund, administered and controlled by the Secretary of State[1], has been established for the purpose of making loans to boards administering agricultural marketing schemes[2]. Such sums as Parliament may from time to time determine may be paid into the fund out of money provided by Parliament[3]; the fund may also be reduced if the Secretary of State thinks fit[4], although he is not thereby authorised to wind up the fund[5]. The Treasury has power to write off the account of the assets of the fund any loan which appears unlikely to be recovered; loans which are repaid after being written off are paid to the Treasury, not to the fund[6]. The Secretary of State must send annual accounts[7] to the Comptroller and Auditor General who must then certify and report on the accounts, which must be laid before Parliament on or before the following 31 January[8].

1 As to the Secretary of State see PARA **390**.
2 Agricultural Marketing Act 1958 s 22(1), (2), (4). Agricultural marketing schemes are schemes under the Agricultural Marketing Act 1958: see PARA **171**. The Agricultural Marketing Act 1958 no longer applies to the marketing of milk and potatoes and has been disapplied in relation to horticultural products and bananas: see PARA **171** note 2. The fund was originally established by the Agricultural Marketing Act 1931 s 11 (repealed) and is continued in existence by the Agricultural Marketing Act 1958 s 22(1). Similarly an Agricultural Marketing (Scotland) Fund has been established, and in cases where a scheme is applicable to both England and Scotland the loans are to be made out of both funds in such proportion as may be determined by the Secretary of State: s 22(1), (4)(a).
3 Agricultural Marketing Act 1958 s 22(3) (amended by the Agriculture (Miscellaneous Provisions) Act 1972 s 12(2)). Interest on loans must be paid to the Treasury, but the principal is repaid to the fund or funds concerned: Agricultural Marketing Act 1958 s 22(5). As to the Treasury see CONSTITUTIONAL AND ADMINISTRATIVE LAW vol 20 (2014) PARA 263 et seq.
4 If the Secretary of State considers that the sums standing to the credit of the Agricultural Marketing Fund should be reduced, he may pay such sums as he thinks fit out of that fund into the Consolidated Fund: Agriculture (Miscellaneous Provisions) Act 1972 s 12(1).
5 Agriculture (Miscellaneous Provisions) Act 1972 s 12(1) proviso.
6 Agricultural Marketing Act 1958 s 22(6) (amended by the Agriculture (Miscellaneous Provisions) Act 1972 Sch 6).
7 The Secretary of State must send the accounts to the Comptroller and Auditor General every year on or before 30 November in respect of the financial year ending on the preceding 31 March, and in them he must give reasons why any sums have been written off: Agricultural Marketing Act 1958 s 22(7).
8 Agricultural Marketing Act 1958 s 22(7). If Parliament is not then sitting the accounts and report must be laid before it within a week after it is next assembled: s 22(7).

198. Loans to marketing boards.

The Secretary of State and the Welsh Ministers[1] may make either short term or long term loans to agricultural marketing boards. Short term loans are made for the purpose of providing for the expenses of the initial working of a marketing scheme[2], are to be repaid within two years unless renewed and may be made free of interest during any period before renewal[3], and may be renewed for further periods if the Secretary of State or the Welsh Ministers are satisfied that renewal is required to provide for additional services which the board proposes to undertake[4]; while long term loans are made for a period exceeding two years and must be secured in the manner prescribed by regulations[5] and are of such sums as the Secretary of State thinks or the Welsh Ministers think fit[6].

1 As to the Secretary of State and the Welsh Ministers see PARA **390**.

2   Ie a scheme under the Agricultural Marketing Act 1958: see PARA 171. The Agricultural Marketing Act 1958 no longer applies to the marketing of milk and potatoes and has been disapplied in relation to horticultural products and bananas: see PARA 171 note 2.

3   See the Agricultural Marketing Act 1958 s 24(1)–(3) (s 24(1) amended by the Agriculture (Miscellaneous Provisions) Act 1972 s 12(3)(b), Sch 6). The Agricultural Marketing Act 1958 s 24(2) defines the expenses which are deemed to be incurred in connection with the initial working of a scheme, and s 24(3) makes provision for the deduction from the amount repayable of expenditure incurred under schemes which cease to have effect at or before the expiration of the suspensory period (see PARA 177). The terms of loans are prescribed by the Agricultural Marketing (Loans) (England) Regulations 1932, SR & O 1932/527.

4   Agricultural Marketing Act 1958 s 24(4) (amended by the Agriculture (Miscellaneous Provisions) Act 1972 s 12(3)(b)). The Secretary of State (or, as the case may be, the Welsh Ministers) must be satisfied that the board is in a position to repay the loan forthwith and that adequate arrangements have been or will be made for its repayment at the end of the renewal period: Agricultural Marketing Act 1958 s 24(4) (as so amended). As to the meaning of 'board' see PARA 173 note 4.

5   Agricultural Marketing Act 1958 s 25 (amended by the Agriculture (Miscellaneous Provisions) Act 1972 s 12(3)(c)(i), Sch 6).

6   Agricultural Marketing Act 1958 s 25 (as amended: see note 5). The aggregate of long term loans outstanding at any time is not to exceed £100,000 in the case of loans made out of the Agricultural Marketing Fund: s 25 (as so amended). As to the Agricultural Marketing Fund see PARA 197.

(vii) The British Wool Marketing Scheme

199. Control of sales.

The production and sale of wool in the United Kingdom is regulated by the British Wool Marketing Scheme[1]. A producer of wool is prohibited from selling it unless he is registered, or exempt from registration, under the scheme[2], and to sell wool contrary to this prohibition is an offence[3]. A registered producer may sell wool only through the agency of the board or, if the board so prescribes, to the board[4], and he is required to comply with the board's directions as to the persons to whom and the places to which any wool for sale is to be delivered, although the board must give due consideration to any application by him, on such notice as the board may require, as to those matters[5]. The board may prescribe the manner in which wool is to be adapted for sale, marked, packed, stored, transported or insured by registered producers, and the period within which it is to be delivered after it is produced[6].

The board is required to accept all wool duly tendered by a registered producer, being wool produced by him, and to sell it[7]. The board must value the wool in relation to a schedule of maximum prices for different classes of wool published annually by the board, and pay the producer according to the valuation[8]. Additional payments may be made to registered producers in the interests of efficient handling and marketing, and supplementary sums may be paid to them if the board thinks fit[9].

1   The British Wool Marketing Scheme 1950 is scheduled to, and approved by, the British Wool Marketing Scheme (Approval) Order 1950, SI 1950/1326. This has effect under the Agricultural Marketing Act 1958 Pt I (ss 1–32) (see PARA 171 et seq): s 54(2). The scheme establishes the British Wool Marketing Board as the board to administer the scheme (British Wool Marketing Scheme (Approval) Order 1950, SI 1950/1326, Schedule para 4) and is stated to apply to the whole of the United Kingdom except the administrative County of Zetland (now the district of the Island Council of Shetland) (Schedule para 1). Provision is made for the constitution of the board (see Schedule para 6 (substituted by SI 2000/1709)) and the election of members (see the British Wool Marketing Scheme (Approval) Order 1950, SI 1950/1326, Schedule para 7 (substituted by SI 2000/1709)). For the purposes of the Companies Act 2006 s 1157 (power of court to grant relief in certain cases: see COMPANIES vol 14 (2016) PARA 645), the British Wool Marketing Board is

treated as a company and its members as officers of it: Agriculture Act 1993 s 57 (amended by SI 2008/948).

2 British Wool Marketing Scheme (Approval) Order 1950, SI 1950/1326, Schedule para 69. The board has power to exempt any description of producers, wool or sales of wool from any provisions of the scheme; and sales of skin wool by fellmongers are exempt from the marketing provisions if the wool was produced in the course of their business as such: Schedule para 70. A producer is exempt from registration if he has not had in his possession more than four sheep aged over four months at any one time in either the current or preceding calendar year, or if he is a fellmonger and produces wool only in the course of his business as such: Schedule para 53.

3 See the Agricultural Marketing Act 1958 s 6(6); and PARA **173**. The scheme provides that the sale of any product wholly or partly manufactured or derived from wool is deemed to be a sale of wool if the substance of the transaction is that the seller agrees to subject it to some process and to sell the resulting product to the buyer: British Wool Marketing Scheme (Approval) Order 1950, SI 1950/1326, Schedule para 89.

4 British Wool Marketing Scheme (Approval) Order 1950, SI 1950/1326, Schedule para 71(1), (2).

5 British Wool Marketing Scheme (Approval) Order 1950, SI 1950/1326, Schedule para 71(3). The Secretary of State has directed that such applications must be made before the end of November and relate to wool to be delivered on or after the following 1 May: British Wool Marketing Scheme (Directions) Order 1958, SI 1958/2126. As to the Secretary of State see PARA **390**.

6 British Wool Marketing Scheme (Approval) Order 1950, SI 1950/1326, Schedule para 71(4), (5) (amended by SI 1977/1695).

7 British Wool Marketing Scheme (Approval) Order 1950, SI 1950/1326, Schedule para 72(2) (amended by SI 1962/622).

8 British Wool Marketing Scheme (Approval) Order 1950, SI 1950/1326, Schedule para 72(2)–(6) (amended by SI 1962/622; SI 1966/828). There is an appeal tribunal to deal with objections to valuations: see the British Wool Marketing Scheme (Approval) Order 1950, SI 1950/1326, Schedule paras 72(5), 91 (amended by SI 1966/828; SI 2000/1709). The tribunal must act judicially: *Barrs v British Wool Marketing Board* 1957 SC 72, Ct of Sess.

9 British Wool Marketing Scheme (Approval) Order 1950, SI 1950/1326, Schedule para 72(7), (8) (amended by SI 1962/622).

200. Penalties.

If a registered producer contravenes the control of marketing established by the British Wool Marketing Scheme[1] he incurs liability to a penalty of such amount, not exceeding £100 plus half the PRICE of any wool sold in contravention of the scheme, as the disciplinary committee[2] thinks just[3]. For other offences the maximum penalty is £100[4]. No such penalty may be imposed, however, in respect of a contravention which constitutes an offence under the Agricultural Marketing Act 1958 or any other Act[5].

1 As to the scheme and the system of marketing control established thereunder see PARA **199**.

2 As to the constitution and proceedings of disciplinary committees see PARAS **186, 188**; and see the British Wool Marketing Scheme (Approval) Order 1950, SI 1950/1326, Schedule para 81(2).

3 British Wool Marketing Scheme (Approval) Order 1950, SI 1950/1326, Schedule para 81(1)(a).

4 British Wool Marketing Scheme (Approval) Order 1950, SI 1950/1326, Schedule para 81(1)(b).

5 See the Agricultural Marketing Act 1958 s 9(2); and PARA **186**.

(3) GRANTS FOR MARKETING

201. Schemes for the payment of grants.

The Secretary of State and the Welsh Ministers[1] may, by a scheme made with the approval of the Treasury[2], make provision for the payment by the Secretary of State or the Welsh Ministers (as the case may be) of grants towards expenditure which has been, or is to be, incurred in carrying out proposals for the organisation, promotion, encouragement, development, co-ordination or facilitation of the marketing in Great Britain or elsewhere of:

(1)   the produce of agriculture[3] (including horticulture)[4];

(2)　　　the produce of fish farming[5];

(3)　　　the produce of an activity specified for these purposes by order made by the Secretary of State or the Welsh Ministers[6];

(4)　　　anything derived from produce falling within any of heads (1) to (3) above[7].

Without prejudice to the generality of these provisions, any such scheme may:

(a)　　　provide for the payment of grant by reference to proposals which have been approved by the Secretary of State or the Welsh Ministers after submission to and recommendation by such person as may be specified in the scheme[8];

(b)　　　authorise the approval of proposals to be varied or withdrawn with the written consent of the person making the proposals[9];

(c)　　　authorise the reduction or withholding of grant where assistance in respect of expenditure for which the grant is made is given under any other enactment[10];

(d)　　　confer a discretion on the Secretary of State or the Welsh Ministers as to the payment of grant, as to the manner and timing of payment of grant, and as to the amount of grant[11];

(e)　　　make the payment of grant subject to such conditions as may be specified in or determined under the scheme[12];

(f)　　　provide for functions in connection with the administration of the scheme to be carried out, subject to such conditions as may be specified in the scheme, by such person as may be so specified[13];

(g)　　　provide for any discretion conferred by or under the scheme to be exercisable in such circumstances and by reference to such matters as may be specified in or determined under the scheme[14];

(h)　　　contain such supplementary and consequential provision as the Secretary of State thinks or the Welsh Ministers think fit[15]; and

(i)　　　make different provision for different cases (including different provision for different areas)[16].

Two schemes have been made under these provisions: the Marketing Development Scheme[17] and the Food Industry Development Scheme[18].

It is an offence knowingly or recklessly to make a statement which is false or misleading in a material respect for the purpose of obtaining a payment under such a scheme[19].

1　　As to the Secretary of State and the Welsh Ministers see PARA 390.
2　　As to the Treasury see CONSTITUTIONAL AND ADMINISTRATIVE LAW vol 20 (2014) PARA 263 et seq. As to the schemes which have been made see PARAS 202–203.
3　　As to the meaning of 'agriculture' see PARA 10.
4　　Agriculture Act 1993 s 50(1), (2)(a).
5　　Agriculture Act 1993 s 50(2)(b). 'Fish farming' means the breeding, rearing or cultivating of fish (including shellfish) whether or not for the purpose of producing food for human consumption; and 'shellfish' includes crustaceans and molluscs of any kind: s 50(9).
6　　Agriculture Act 1993 s 50(2)(c). The Marketing Development Scheme (Specification of Activities) Order 1994, SI 1994/1404, and the Food Industry Development Scheme (Specification of Activities) Order 1997, SI 1997/2674, have specified activities for the purposes of the schemes having effect under these provisions: see PARAS 202–203.
7　　Agriculture Act 1993 s 50(2)(d).
8　　Agriculture Act 1993 s 50(3)(a).
9　　Agriculture Act 1993 s 50(3)(b).
10　Agriculture Act 1993 s 50(3)(c).
11　Agriculture Act 1993 s 50(3)(d).
12　Agriculture Act 1993 s 50(3)(e).
13　Agriculture Act 1993 s 50(3)(f).

14 Agriculture Act 1993 s 50(3)(g).
15 Agriculture Act 1993 s 50(3)(h). Where a scheme provides for functions under the scheme to be carried out by any body created by a statutory provision, the Secretary of State and the Welsh Ministers may, after consultation with the body, by regulations modify or add to its constitution or powers for the purpose of enabling it to carry them out: s 50(7). At the date at which this volume states the law no such regulations had been made.
16 Agriculture Act 1993 s 50(3)(i).
17 See the Marketing Development Scheme 1994, SI 1994/1403; the Marketing Development Scheme (Specification of Activities) Order 1994, SI 1994/1404; and PARA 202.
18 See the Food Industry Development Scheme 1997, SI 1997/2673; and PARA 203.
19 Agriculture Act 1993 s 51. Any person who commits such an offence is liable on summary conviction to a fine not exceeding level 5 on the standard scale or to imprisonment for a term not exceeding six months or to both: s 51. As to the standard scale and the powers of magistrates' courts to issue fines on summary conviction see SENTENCING vol 92 (2015) PARA 176. Notwithstanding anything in any other enactment, proceedings for an offence under Pt III (ss 50–53) must be commenced within the period of six months from the date on which evidence sufficient in the opinion of the prosecutor to warrant the proceedings came to his knowledge (s 52(1)), although no such proceedings may be commenced by virtue of these provisions more than three years after the commission of the offence (s 52(2)). For these purposes a certificate signed by or on behalf of the prosecutor and stating the date on which evidence sufficient in his opinion to warrant the proceedings came to his knowledge is conclusive evidence of that fact (s 52(3)), and a certificate stating that matter and purporting to be so signed is deemed to be so signed unless the contrary is proved (s 52(4)).
        Where a body corporate is guilty of an offence under the Agriculture Act 1993, and that offence is proved to have been committed with the consent or connivance of, or to be attributable to any neglect on the part of any director (which in relation to a body corporate whose affairs are managed by its members, means a member of the body corporate: s 61(2)), manager, secretary or other similar officer of the body corporate, or any person who was purporting to act in any such capacity, he, as well as the body corporate, is guilty of the offence and is liable to be proceeded against and punished accordingly: s 61(1).

202. The Marketing Development Scheme.

The Marketing Development Scheme, which in practice is now operative only in relation to Wales[1], enables the Secretary of State and the Welsh Ministers[2] to pay to any eligible person a grant towards expenditure incurred in carrying out a proposal for the organisation, promotion, encouragement, development, co-ordination or facilitation of the marketing in Great Britain or elsewhere of:

(1)   the produce of agriculture (including horticulture)[3];
(2)   the produce of the shooting and harvesting of game in the wild[4];
(3)   the produce of the repeated harvesting of short rotation coppice above ground level at intervals of less than ten years[5]; and
(4)   anything derived from produce falling within any of heads (1) to (3) above[6].

Subject to budgetary limits[7], a person is eligible to be considered for the payment of a grant under the scheme if he is able to demonstrate to the satisfaction of the Secretary of State or the Welsh Ministers that the purpose of the proposal in respect of which the grant is claimed is to achieve, or assist in the achievement of, a significant marketing or commercial development[8] and (unless the person in question is a trade association or industry body) that the business to which the proposal relates is likely to command a significant share of the market at which that proposal is targeted[9]. No person is eligible to be considered for the payment of a grant under the scheme unless he declares:

(a)   that the proposal for which the grant is to be made would not be carried out but for the grant[10];
(b)   that no assistance is to be given under any other enactment[11] in respect of expenditure for which the grant is to be made[12];

(c)   that his overall commercial viability is not dependent upon receipt of the grant[13]; and

(d)   (where he is a food processor or manufacturer) that the turnover of his business in the year in which the application for the grant is made is not likely to exceed £100 million[14].

Payments may represent no more than 50 per cent of the expenditure (other than value added tax) incurred[15], may relate only to items specified pursuant to the scheme[16], may not exceed £150,000[17] and may be subject to the satisfactory completion of feasibility studies or the submission of some other justification[18]. The carrying out of any proposal funded under the scheme may not be commenced without the written consent of the Secretary of State or the Welsh Ministers[19], who may also permit the recipient of a grant under the scheme to vary or withdraw the proposal to which the grant relates[20]. Provision is also made in connection with the making and determination of applications[21], the manner and timing of payments[22], record-keeping[23], and for the cessation of funding on the satisfactory completion of the relevant proposals[24].

1   Applications for the payment of a grant under the Marketing Development Scheme received on or after 5 November 1996 from applicants whose principal place of business, as respects the grant for which they would have been eligible, is in England, may not be accepted: Marketing Development (Limitation) Scheme 1996, SI 1996/2629.
2   As to the Secretary of State and the Welsh Ministers see PARA 390.
3   Marketing Development Scheme 1994, SI 1994/1403, art 2(a).
4   Marketing Development Scheme 1994, SI 1994/1403, art 2(b); Marketing Development Scheme (Specification of Activities) Order 1994, SI 1994/1404, art 2(1)(a) (art 2(1) amended by SI 1997/2674). As to the meaning of 'game' see the Poaching Prevention Act 1862 s 1; and ANIMALS vol 2 (2017) PARA 14 (definition applied by the Marketing Development Scheme (Specification of Activities) Order 1994, SI 1994/1404, art 2(2)(a)).
5   Marketing Development Scheme (Specification of Activities) Order 1994, SI 1994/1404, art 2(1)(b). 'Short rotation coppice' means a perennial crop of tree species which has been planted at high density: art 2(2)(b).
6   Marketing Development Scheme 1994, SI 1994/1403, art 2(c).
7   Where by reason of the number of grants already made under the Marketing Development Scheme the Secretary of State is or the Welsh Ministers are at any time of the opinion that the financial resources which he or they would otherwise make available under it should for a period be restricted he or they may decide that no further applications for grants under the scheme be accepted until a time subsequently specified by him or them: Marketing Development Scheme 1994, SI 1994/1403, art 12(1). Such a decision or specification must be published by notice in the London or Edinburgh Gazette, as appropriate: art 12(2).
8   Marketing Development Scheme 1994, SI 1994/1403, art 3(1).
9   Marketing Development Scheme 1994, SI 1994/1403, art 3(2).
10 Marketing Development Scheme 1994, SI 1994/1403, art 3(3)(a).
11 Ie any enactment other than the Agriculture Act 1993 s 50 (see PARA 201).
12 Marketing Development Scheme 1994, SI 1994/1403, art 3(3)(b).
13 Marketing Development Scheme 1994, SI 1994/1403, art 3(3)(c).
14 Marketing Development Scheme 1994, SI 1994/1403, art 3(3)(d).
15 Marketing Development Scheme 1994, SI 1994/1403, art 2.
16 Marketing Development Scheme 1994, SI 1994/1403, art 2. The items eligible for the payment of grants under the scheme are specified in Sch 1. In certain circumstances feasibility studies, market research or training must have been satisfactorily completed before payments can be made: art 6(1).
17 Marketing Development Scheme 1994, SI 1994/1403, art 5.
18 Marketing Development Scheme 1994, SI 1994/1403, art 4(2)–(4), Sch 2.
19 Marketing Development Scheme 1994, SI 1994/1403, art 10.
20 Marketing Development Scheme 1994, SI 1994/1403, art 11(1). Proposals may be varied or withdrawn only on written notice of such variation or withdrawal being given to the Secretary of State or the Welsh Ministers by the recipient (art 11(1)), and where a proposal is withdrawn in accordance with this provision the Secretary of State and the Welsh Ministers may on demand recover any part of a grant already paid with reference to the proposal (art 11(2)). Schemes may

also provide that if at any time after the approval of proposals under a scheme (and whether before or after the proposals have been fully carried out) it appears to the Secretary of State or the Welsh Ministers either that any condition imposed under the scheme in relation to the proposals has not been complied with or that in connection with the submission of the proposals the person submitting them gave information on any matter which was false or misleading in a material respect, the Secretary of State or the Welsh Ministers may on demand recover any grant or any part of a grant paid with reference to the proposals, and may revoke the approval in whole or in part (Agriculture Act 1993 s 50(5)), although this is subject to the proviso that the Secretary of State or the Welsh Ministers may not make such a demand or so revoke an approval unless he has or they have given at least 30 days' written notice of the reasons for the proposed action to any person to whom any payment by way of a grant in relation to the proposals would be payable, or from whom any such payment would be recoverable (s 50(6)). However neither the Marketing Development Scheme nor the Food Industry Development Scheme (see PARA 203) makes such provision.

21 Marketing Development Scheme 1994, SI 1994/1403, art 4(1), (5)–(7).
22 Marketing Development Scheme 1994, SI 1994/1403, arts 6(2), (3), 7.
23 Marketing Development Scheme 1994, SI 1994/1403, art 9.
24 Marketing Development Scheme 1994, SI 1994/1403, art 8.

203. The Food Industry Development Scheme.

The Food Industry Development Scheme enables the Secretary of State and the Welsh Ministers[1] to pay to any eligible person[2] a grant towards expenditure incurred in carrying out a proposal[3] for the organisation, promotion, encouragement, development, co-ordination or facilitation of the marketing in Great Britain or elsewhere of:

(1)   the produce of agriculture (including horticulture)[4];
(2)   the produce of fish farming[5];
(3)   the produce of the shooting and harvesting of game in the wild[6];
(4)   the produce of the repeated harvesting of short rotation coppice above ground level at intervals of less than ten years[7];
(5)   the produce of the catching of fish[8]; and
(6)   anything derived from produce falling within any of heads (1) to (5) above[9].

Applications may be made by associations[10] or partnerships, and from time to time the Secretary of State and the Welsh Ministers may indicate that they will also accept applications from individual persons or bodies corporate[11]. In order to be considered for the payment of a grant under the scheme an applicant must demonstrate to the satisfaction of the Secretary of State or the Welsh Ministers that the purpose of the application is to improve business performance or increase business activity within the food industry[12], although no application is eligible to be considered for the payment of a grant under the scheme unless the applicant declares that the application would not be carried out but for the grant[13] and that no assistance is to be given under any other enactment[14] in respect of expenditure for which the grant is to be made[15].

Payments may be made only in respect of expenditure on eligible items[16], and may represent any sum up to the specified percentage of such expenditure[17]. The carrying out of any proposal funded under the scheme may not be commenced without the written consent of the Secretary of State or the Welsh Ministers[18], who may also permit the recipient of a grant under the scheme to vary or withdraw the proposal to which the grant relates[19]. Provision is also made in connection with the making and determination of applications[20], record-keeping[21], reporting[22] and inspections[23].

1   As to the Secretary of State and the Welsh Ministers see PARA 390. Any discretion under the Food Industry Development Scheme exercisable by the Scottish or Welsh Ministers as to the payment of grant, as to the manner and timing of payment of grant and as to the amount of grant may be

exercised by the Secretary of State as their delegate and their respective functions in connection with the administration of the scheme may be carried out by the Secretary of State: Food Industry Development Scheme 1997, SI 1997/2673, art 3 (enacted pursuant to the Agriculture Act 1993 s 50(4), which enables such a scheme, in relation to any discretion thereunder, to include provision for delegation).

2   For these purposes, where the person referred to as satisfying the conditions specified in the text and notes 3–9 is a partnership, the expenditure of each partner is regarded as included in partnership expenditure: Food Industry Development Scheme 1997, SI 1997/2673, art 4(2). 'Partnership' means a group of people or businesses who have come together to carry out the objectives of an application and does not necessarily mean a legally constituted partnership ('partners' being construed accordingly); and 'applicant' means the person who has made an application for grant under these provisions ('application' being construed accordingly): art 2.

3   'Proposal' means an application which has been approved for payment of grant under these provisions by the Secretary of State or the Welsh Ministers: Food Industry Development Scheme 1997, SI 1997/2673, art 2.

4   Food Industry Development Scheme 1997, SI 1997/2673, art 4(1)(a). See *R (on the application of Speciality Produce Ltd) v Secretary of State for the Environment, Food and Rural Affairs* [2009] EWHC 1245 (Admin), [2009] All ER (D) 42 (Jun).

5   Food Industry Development Scheme 1997, SI 1997/2673, art 4(1)(b).

6   Food Industry Development Scheme 1997, SI 1997/2673, art 4(1)(c); Food Industry Development Scheme (Specification of Activities) Order 1997, SI 1997/2674, art 2(1)(a). As to the meaning of 'game' see the Poaching Prevention Act 1862 s 1; and ANIMALS vol 2 (2017) PARA 14 (definition applied by the Food Industry Development Scheme (Specification of Activities) Order 1997, SI 1997/2674, art 2(2)(a)).

7   Food Industry Development Scheme (Specification of Activities) Order 1997, SI 1997/2674, art 2(1)(b). 'Short rotation coppice' means a perennial crop of tree species which has been planted at high density: art 2(2)(b).

8   Food Industry Development Scheme (Specification of Activities) Order 1997, SI 1997/2674, art 2(1)(c). 'Fish' includes shellfish as defined in the Agriculture Act 1993 s 50(9) (see PARA 201 note 5): Food Industry Development Scheme (Specification of Activities) Order 1997, SI 1997/2674, art 2(2)(c).

9   Food Industry Development Scheme 1997, SI 1997/2673, art 4(1)(d).

10   'Association' means trade association and any other association of bodies which have grouped together for the purpose of making an application: Food Industry Development Scheme 1997, SI 1997/2673, art 2.

11   Food Industry Development Scheme 1997, SI 1997/2673, art 5(1). The Secretary of State and the Welsh Ministers must, from time to time, invite applications for grant under the scheme, such applications to be submitted by such deadlines as he or they may decide: art 6(2). An invitation by the Secretary of State or the Welsh Ministers for applications for the payment of a grant under the scheme may be restricted to such class or classes of person as the Secretary of State or the Welsh Ministers may determine: art 6(2A) (added by SI 2001/3339).

12   Food Industry Development Scheme 1997, SI 1997/2673, art 5(2). If the Secretary of State has or the Welsh Ministers have restricted applications pursuant to art 6(2A) (see note 11), the applicant must also demonstrate to the satisfaction of the Secretary of State or the Welsh Ministers that he falls within any class or classes to which the Secretary of State has or the Welsh Ministers have so restricted applications: art 5(2) (amended by SI 2001/3339).

13   Food Industry Development Scheme 1997, SI 1997/2673, art 5(3)(a).

14   Ie any enactment other than the Agriculture Act 1993 s 50 (see PARA 201) or any instrument of the European Economic Community: Food Industry Development Scheme 1997, SI 1997/2673, art 5(3)(b).

15   Food Industry Development Scheme 1997, SI 1997/2673, art 5(3)(b).

16   Food Industry Development Scheme 1997, SI 1997/2673, art 4(1). The items expenditure on which is eligible for payments of grant under the scheme (which include salaries, national insurance, pension and healthcare costs, depreciation on new equipment, other specified overheads and value added tax which cannot be reclaimed) are set out in art 8, Sch 2. Where contributions to expenditure on proposal items referred to in art 8 are made by a person who is not the applicant or a partner of the applicant and no charge has been or is to be made for those contributions, those contributions are regarded as items expenditure on which is eligible for payment of grant under the scheme: art 9.

17   Food Industry Development Scheme 1997, SI 1997/2673, art 4(1). In general the 'specified percentage', in relation to expenditure incurred on eligible items, means 50% (art 4(3)(a)); however where non-applicant contributions under art 9 (see note 16) have been made, the specified

percentage is whichever is the lower of such percentage as is equal to the sum of 50% of the expenditure so incurred plus 50% of the expenditure on those contributions (art 4(3)(b)(i)) or 100% of the expenditure so incurred (art 4(3)(b)(ii)).

18 Food Industry Development Scheme 1997, SI 1997/2673, art 12.
19 Food Industry Development Scheme 1997, SI 1997/2673, art 13(1). Proposals may be varied or withdrawn only on written notice of such variation or withdrawal being given to the Secretary of State or the Welsh Ministers by the recipient (art 13(1)), and where a proposal is withdrawn in accordance with this provision the Secretary of State and the Welsh Ministers may on demand recover any part of a grant already paid with reference to the proposal (art 13(2)).
20 Food Industry Development Scheme 1997, SI 1997/2673, arts 6(1), (3)–(6), 7, 10, Sch 1.
21 Food Industry Development Scheme 1997, SI 1997/2673, art 11.
22 Food Industry Development Scheme 1997, SI 1997/2673, art 14.
23 Food Industry Development Scheme 1997, SI 1997/2673, art 15.

(4) SPECIAL MARKETING PROVISIONS AS TO EGGS AND CHICKS

204. Eggs for hatching and chicks.
Provision is made for the enforcement and execution of directly applicable EU marketing standards relating to eggs for hatching and farmyard poultry chicks[1]. A person who contravenes or fails to comply with certain EU provisions that relate to eggs for hatching and chicks[2] is guilty of an offence[3].

The Secretary of State or, in relation to Wales, the Welsh Ministers are designated as the competent agency responsible for the registration of establishments for the production of eggs for hatching intended for the production of grandparent stock, parent stock or utility chicks ('pedigree breeding establishments'), establishments for the production of eggs for hatching intended for the production of utility chicks ('other breeding establishments') and establishments for incubating eggs, hatching and supplying chicks ('hatcheries')[4].

Eggs for hatching may be marked with any abstract black mark, except for a spot, instead of being marked with the distinguishing number of the producer establishment[5] if the following conditions are complied with:

(1)   the mark is indelible, clearly visible and at least 10 mm^2 in area: and
(2)   the marking of the eggs is carried out prior to insertion into the incubator, either at the producer establishment or at a hatchery[6].

1   The Eggs and Chicks (England) Regulations 2009, SI 2009/2163 Pt 2 (regs 4–7) and the Eggs and Chicks (Wales) Regulations 2010, SI 2010/1671 Pt 2 (regs 4–7) apply to eggs for hatching and chicks to which Council Regulation (EC) 1234/2007 (OJ L299, 16.11.2007, p 1) establishing a common organisation of agricultural markets and on specific provisions for certain agricultural products (the 'Single CMO Regulation') Annex XIV Part C point l(1) (but not establishments and hatcheries of the type mentioned in Annex XIV Part C point 1(2)) and Commission Regulation (EC) 617/2008 (OJ L168, 28.6.2008, p 5) laying down detailed rules for implementing Regulation (EC) 1234/2007 as regards marketing standards for eggs for hatching and farmyard poultry chicks, apply: Eggs and Chicks (England) Regulations 2009, SI 2009/2163, regs 3(1), 4; Eggs and Chicks (Wales) Regulations 2010, SI 2010/1671, regs 3(1), 4. Most definitions within those regulations are contained within the relevant EU provisions: see the Eggs and Chicks (England) Regulations 2009, SI 2009/2163, reg 3; and the Eggs and Chicks (Wales) Regulations 2010, SI 2010/1671, reg 3.
2   Ie the provisions mentioned in the Eggs and Chicks (England) Regulations 2009, SI 2009/2163, Sch 1 (amended by SI 2013/3235) or, in relation to Wales, the Eggs and Chicks (Wales) Regulations 2010, SI 2010/1671, Sch 1 (amended by SI 2013/3270).
3   Eggs and Chicks (England) Regulations 2009, SI 2009/2163, reg 5; Eggs and Chicks (Wales) Regulations 2010, SI 2010/1671, reg 5 (both amended by SI 2011/1043). A person guilty of an offence under the Eggs and Chicks (England) Regulations 2009, SI 2009/2163, regs 5, 9, 16, 20(3), (4), (6), (11) or (12), 22(3), (7) or (8), 24(4) or 26 or, in relation to Wales, the Eggs and Chicks (Wales) Regulations 2010, SI 2010/1671, regs 5, 9, 16, 20(3), (4), (6), (11) or (12), 22(3),

(7) or (8), 24(4) or 26, is liable on summary conviction to a fine not exceeding level 5 on the standard scale: Eggs and Chicks (England) Regulations 2009, SI 2009/2163, reg 27; Eggs and Chicks (Wales) Regulations 2010, SI 2010/1671, reg 27. Payment of the penalty must be made to the person mentioned in the penalty notice by sending it by post or such other method as may be mentioned in the notice (but must not be made by cash): Eggs and Chicks (England) Regulations 2009, SI 2009/2163, reg 34; Eggs and Chicks (Wales) Regulations 2010, SI 2010/1671, reg 34. As to the amount of the penalty see the Eggs and Chicks (England) Regulations 2009, SI 2009/2163, reg 32 and the Eggs and Chicks (Wales) Regulations 2010, SI 2010/1671, reg 32. As enforcement see the Eggs and Chicks (England) Regulations 2009, SI 2009/2163, reg 17 (amended by SI 2012/2897) and the Eggs and Chicks (Wales) Regulations 2010, SI 2010/1671, reg 17. As to the standard scale and the powers of magistrates' courts to issue fines on summary conviction see SENTENCING vol 92 (2015) PARA 176.

4   See the Eggs and Chicks (England) Regulations 2009, SI 2009/2163, reg 6; and the Eggs and Chicks (Wales) Regulations 2010, SI 2010/1671, reg 6.
5   Ie as required by Commission Regulation (EC) 617/2008 (OJ L168, 28.6.2008, p 5) art 3(2).
6   See the Eggs and Chicks (England) Regulations 2009, SI 2009/2163, reg 7; and the Eggs and Chicks (Wales) Regulations 2010, SI 2010/1671, reg 7.

205. Eggs in shells for consumption.

Provision is made for the enforcement and execution of directly applicable EU marketing standards relating to eggs in shell for consumption[1]. A person who contravenes or fails to comply with certain EU provisions that relate to eggs in shell for consumption[2] is guilty of an offence[3].

The Secretary of State or, in relation to Wales, the Welsh Ministers are designated as the competent agency responsible for authorising packing centres to grade eggs[4].

Derogation from EU requirements relating to the marking of eggs is permitted in certain circumstances[5].

Particular provision is made for the enforcement of directly applicable EU controls[6] for Salmonella serotypes with public health significance in relation to the marketing and use of eggs in shell for human consumption[7].

1   The Eggs and Chicks (England) Regulations 2009, SI 2009/2163 Pt 3 (regs 8–14) and the Eggs and Chicks (Wales) Regulations 2010, SI 2010/1671 Pt 3 (regs 8–14) apply to eggs to which European Parliament and Council Regulation of the European Parliament and of the Council (EU) 1308/2013 (OJ L347, 27.6.2014, p 261) establishing a common organisation of the markets in agricultural products and Commission Regulation (EC) 589/2008 (OJ L163, 24.6.2008, p 6) laying down detailed rules for implementing Council Regulation (EC) 1234/2007 as regards marketing standards for eggs, apply: Eggs and Chicks (England) Regulations 2009, SI 2009/2163, regs 3(1), 8(1); Eggs and Chicks (Wales) Regulations 2010, SI 2010/1671, regs 3(1), 8(2) (all amended by SI 2013/3270). This is subject to the exceptions contained in the Eggs and Chicks (England) Regulations 2009, SI 2009/2163, reg 8(2) and Eggs and Chicks (Wales) Regulations 2010, SI 2010/1671, reg 8(2) (both amended by SI 2013/3270). Most definitions within those regulations are contained within the relevant EU provisions: see the Eggs and Chicks (England) Regulations 2009, SI 2009/2163, reg 3; and the Eggs and Chicks (Wales) Regulations 2010, SI 2010/1671, reg 3.
2   Ie the provisions mentioned in the Eggs and Chicks (England) Regulations 2009, SI 2009/2163, Sch 2 (amended by SI 2013/3235) or, in relation to Wales, the Eggs and Chicks (Wales) Regulations 2010, SI 2010/1671, Sch 2 (amended by SI 2013/3270).
3   Eggs and Chicks (England) Regulations 2009, SI 2009/2163, reg 9; Eggs and Chicks (Wales) Regulations 2010, SI 2010/1671, reg 9 (both amended by SI 2011/1043). As to the penalty on conviction see PARA 204 note 3.
4   See the Eggs and Chicks (England) Regulations 2009, SI 2009/2163, reg 10; Eggs and Chicks (Wales) Regulations 2010, SI 2010/1671, reg 10.
5   See the Eggs and Chicks (England) Regulations 2009, SI 2009/2163, regs 11–14 (reg 11 amended by SI 2013/3235); Eggs and Chicks (Wales) Regulations 2010, SI 2010/1671, regs 11–14 (reg 11 amended by SI 2013/3270).
6   Ie the provisions mentioned in the Eggs and Chicks (England) Regulations 2009, SI 2009/2163, Sch 3 (amended by SI 2013/3235) or, in relation to Wales, the Eggs and Chicks (Wales) Regulations 2010, SI 2010/1671, Sch 3 (amended by SI 2013/3270).

7   See the Eggs and Chicks (England) Regulations 2009, SI 2009/2163, regs 15, 16 (reg 16 amended by SI 2011/1043); Eggs and Chicks (Wales) Regulations 2010, SI 2010/1671, regs 15, 16 (reg 16 amended by SI 2011/1043). These provisions apply to eggs to which European Parliament and Council Regulation (EC) 2160/2003 (OJ L325, 12.12.2002, p 1) on the control of salmonella and other specified food-borne zoonotic agents, applies as read with the exception in art 1(3).

(5) MARKETING OF HOPS

206. EU regulation of the marketing of hops.

Since the abolition of the Hops Marketing Scheme[1], the marketing of hops in and from the United Kingdom[2] has been governed by a number of EU regulations concerned with the common organisation of the market in hops[3], the certification of hops[4], and the importation of hops from non-member countries[5]. These regulations are referred to as the 'EU provisions'[6]. Provision has been made controlling the sale and certification of hops[7], the use of imported hops in the manufacture of hop products[8], the certification, sealing and marking of hops and hop products[9], the monitoring of hop processing[10], the submission of brewers' and processors' declarations[11] and record-keeping[12].

1   The Hops Marketing Scheme 1932 was set out and approved by the Hops Marketing Scheme (Approval) Order 1932, SR & O 1932/505 (now revoked), which also established a Hops Marketing Board to make provision for the administration of the scheme. The scheme was revoked on 1 April 1982 (see the Hops Marketing Act 1982 s 1(1)(a) (repealed) and the Hops Marketing Scheme (Revocation) (Appointed Day) Order 1982, SI 1982/463 (lapsed)), and the board accordingly wound up on 23 August 1982 (see the Hops Marketing Act 1982 s 4 (repealed); and the Hops Marketing Board (Dissolution) Order 1982, SI 1982/1120 (lapsed)).
2   As to the meaning of 'United Kingdom' see PARA 1 note 1.
3   See now Council Regulation (EC) 1952/2005 (OJ L314, 30.11.2005, p 1) concerning the common organisation of the market in hops.
4   See Commission Regulation (EC) 1850/2006 (OJ L355, 15.12.2006, p 72) laying down detailed rules for the certification of hops and hop products.
5   See Commission Regulation (EC) 3076/78 (OJ L367, 28.12.78, p 17) on the importation of hops from non-member countries.
6   Hops Certification Regulations 1979, SI 1979/1095, reg 1(2) (amended by SI 1991/2198 and SI 2011/1043).
7   See PARA 207.
8   See PARA 211.
9   See PARA 209.
10   See PARA 210.
11   See PARA 212.
12   See PARA 208.

207. Sale of hops.

It is an offence[1] for any person without reasonable excuse:

(1)   to sell any harvested hops[2] required to be certified[3] before being marketed, or any hop products[4] so required, unless they have been certified[5];

(2)   to sell or expose for sale any certified hops or certified hop products otherwise than in packages which are marked and sealed in accordance with the WU provisions[6]; or

(3)   to sell any imported hop cones[7] or hop products unless the required attestation has been issued in respect thereof[8].

1   The offence is punishable on summary conviction by a fine not exceeding level 5 on the standard scale: Hops Certification Regulations 1979, SI 1979/1095, reg 3(2) (amended by SI 1991/2198). As to the standard scale and the powers of magistrates' courts to issue fines on summary

conviction see SENTENCING vol 92 (2015) PARA 176. Where an offence is committed, there is a defence of due diligence: see the Hops Certification Regulations 1979, SI 1979/1095, reg 10. Provision is also made as to the commission of offences by bodies corporate: see reg 11. As to inspections to ensure compliance with these provisions see reg 5.

2   As to the meaning of 'hops' see Council Regulation (EC) 1952/2005 (OJ L314, 30.11.2005, p 1) concerning the common organisation of the market in hops, art 2(a); definition applied by the Hops Certification Regulations 1979, SI 1979/1095, reg 1(2).

3   'Certification' means certification under the EU provisions (defined in the Hops Certification Regulations 1979, SI 1979/1095, reg 1(2) (amended by SI 1991/2198)); and cognate expressions are to be construed accordingly: see the Hops Certification Regulations 1979, SI 1979/1095, reg 1(2); and PARA 206. As to the certification of hops and hop products see PARA 209.

4   'Hop products' means those products prepared or derived from hops which are mentioned in Council Regulation (EC) 1952/2005 (OJ L314, 30.11.2005, p 1) art 1: Hops Certification Regulations 1979, SI 1979/1095, reg 1(2).

5   Hops Certification Regulations 1979, SI 1979/1095, reg 3(1)(a), (2) (reg 3(1)(a), (b) amended by SI 2011/1043).

6   Hops Certification Regulations 1979, SI 1979/1095, reg 3(1)(b) (as amended: see note 5). As to the sealing and marking of hops and hop products see PARA 209.

7   Ie any hop cones or hop products imported from a third country and, in the case of imported hop cones, falling within combined nomenclature code 1210 10: Hops Certification Regulations 1979, SI 1979/1095, reg 3(1)(c), (d).

8   Hops Certification Regulations 1979, SI 1979/1095, reg 3(1)(c), (d) (reg 3(1)(c) substituted by SI 1991/2198).

208.   Keeping of records.

The Secretary of State and the Welsh Ministers[1] may, by notice[2] given to any person engaged, whether as principal or agent, in the production, grading, processing, packing or sale of any hops[3] or hop products[4] (not being hops or hop products exempt from certification[5]), require that person to keep such records of any of those activities as may be specified in the notice; and that person is required to comply with those requirements[6]. Every person required to keep records must retain them for three years from the end of the calendar year to which they relate, and produce them on demand to any authorised officer of the Secretary of State or the Welsh Ministers who presents his credentials[7]. Contravention of any of these provisions without reasonable excuse is an offence[8].

1   As to the Secretary of State and the Welsh Ministers see PARA 390.

2   Provision is made for the giving of notices: see the Hops Certification Regulations 1979, SI 1979/1095, reg 12.

3   As to the meaning of 'hops' see Council Regulation (EC) 1952/2005 (OJ L314, 30.11.2005, p 1) concerning the common organisation of the market in hops, art 2(a); definition applied by the Hops Certification Regulations 1979, SI 1979/1095, reg 1(2).

4   As to the meaning of 'hop products' see PARA 207 note 4.

5   As to the meaning of 'certification' see PARA 207 note 3.

6   Hops Certification Regulations 1979, SI 1979/1095, reg 8(1). As to inspections to ensure compliance see reg 5.

7   Hops Certification Regulations 1979, SI 1979/1095, reg 8(2).

8   Hops Certification Regulations 1979, SI 1979/1095, reg 8(3). The offence is punishable on summary conviction by a fine not exceeding level 4 on the standard scale: reg 8(3) (amended by SI 1991/2198). As to the standard scale and the powers of magistrates' courts to issue fines on summary conviction see SENTENCING vol 92 (2015) PARA 176. Where an offence is committed, there is a defence of due diligence: see the Hops Certification Regulations 1979, SI 1979/1095, reg 10. It is also an offence to make a false entry in a record: see PARA 209. As to the commission of offences by bodies corporate see reg 11.

209.   Certification, sealing and marking.

Where, under the EU provisions[1], hops[2] or hop products[3] are required to be certified[4] in the United Kingdom[5], the certification must be carried out in accordance with those provisions by a certifying officer[6], and no document purporting to be a certificate will be valid unless it is issued by a certifying officer[7].

It is an offence[8] for any person:

(1)	without due authority, and with intent to deceive, to remove, alter, conceal or deface any certificate[9], or any prescribed[10] seal or mark, lawfully applied to, accompanying or relating to any hops or hop products[11], or to apply to any hops or hop products any certificate, prescribed seal or mark[12];

(2)	with intent to deceive to apply to any hops or hop products any document, seal or mark so closely resembling a certificate or a prescribed seal or mark as to be likely to deceive[13];

(3)	knowingly to make a false entry in any declaration, certificate, book, account or record which is required[14] to be made, issued, kept or produced, or with intent to deceive to make use of any such entry knowing the entry to be false[15].

1	As to the EU provisions see PARA 206.
2	As to the meaning of 'hops' see Council Regulation (EC) 1952/2005 (OJ L314, 30.11.2005, p 1) concerning the common organisation of the market in hops, art 2(a); definition applied by the Hops Certification Regulations 1979, SI 1979/1095, reg 1(2).
3	As to the meaning of 'hop products' see PARA 207 note 4.
4	As to the meanings of 'certified' and 'certificate' see PARA 207 note 3.
5	As to the meaning of 'United Kingdom' see PARA 1 note 1.
6	'Certifying officer' means a person for the time being authorised by the Secretary of State or the Welsh Ministers to certify hops and hop products: Hops Certification Regulations 1979, SI 1979/1095, reg 1(2). As to the Secretary of State and the Welsh Ministers see PARA 390.
7	Hops Certification Regulations 1979, SI 1979/1095, reg 2 (amended by SI 2011/1043).
8	The offence is punishable on summary conviction by a fine not exceeding level 5 on the standard scale: Hops Certification Regulations 1979, SI 1979/1095, reg 9(1) (amended by SI 1991/2198). As to the standard scale and the powers of magistrates' courts to issue fines on summary conviction see SENTENCING vol 92 (2015) PARA 176. Where an offence is committed, there is a defence of due diligence: see the Hops Certification Regulations 1979, SI 1979/1095, reg 10. As to the commission of offences by bodies corporate see reg 11. As to inspections to ensure compliance with these provisions see reg 5.
9	See note 4. Note that for the purposes of the Hops Certification Regulations 1979, SI 1979/1095, reg 9 (see the text and notes 10–15), 'certificate' includes an attestation of equivalence provided for in Council Regulation (EC) 1952/2005 (OJ L314, 30.11.2005, p 1) concerning the common organisation of the market in hops, or a control attestation referred to in Commission Regulation (EC) 3076/78 (OJ L367, 28.12.78, p 17) on the importation of hops from non-member countries, art 4: Hops Certification Regulations 1979, SI 1979/1095, reg 9(2) (added by SI 1991/2198).
10	'Prescribed' means prescribed by the EU provisions: Hops Certification Regulations 1979, SI 1979/1095, reg 1(2).
11	Hops Certification Regulations 1979, SI 1979/1095, reg 9(1)(a).
12	Hops Certification Regulations 1979, SI 1979/1095, reg 9(1)(b).
13	Hops Certification Regulations 1979, SI 1979/1095, reg 9(1)(c).
14	Ie required by any provision of the EU provisions or of the Hops Certification Regulations 1979, SI 1979/1095. As to the keeping of records see PARA 208.
15	Hops Certification Regulations 1979, SI 1979/1095, reg 9(1)(d) (amended by SI 2011/1043).

## 210.	Monitoring of hop processing.

The EU provisions[1] require that the processing of hops for the production of hop products is carried out under the constant supervision of officials designated by member states[2], and pursuant to this requirement further require that the operators of hop-processing plants provide those officials with all information related to the technical layout of the processing plant[3]. Failure to provide such information, or intentionally obstructing an inspector[4] or a certifying officer[5] when seeking such information, is an offence[6].

1   As to the EU provisions see PARA 206.
2   Ie the officials referred to in Commission Regulation (EC) 1850/2006 (OJ L355, 15.12.2006, p 72) laying down detailed rules for the certification of hops and hop products.
3   Commission Regulation (EC) 1850/2006 (OJ L355, 15.12.2006, p 72) art 12.1.
4   As to inspections see the Hops Certification Regulations 1979, SI 1979/1095, reg 5.
5   As to the meaning of 'certifying officer' see PARA 209 note 6.
6   Hops Certification Regulations 1979, SI 1979/1095, reg 6A (added by SI 1991/2198). The offence is punishable on summary conviction by a fine not exceeding level 3 on the standard scale: Hops Certification Regulations 1979, SI 1979/1095, reg 6A (as so added). As to the standard scale and the powers of magistrates' courts to issue fines on summary conviction see SENTENCING vol 92 (2015) PARA 176. Where an offence is committed, there is a defence of due diligence: see reg 10. As to the commission of offences by bodies corporate see reg 11.

211.   Use of imported hops in manufacture of hop products.

Except in relation to hops[1] harvested on land owned by a brewery and used by that brewery in the natural or processed state[2], it is an offence[3] for any person without reasonable excuse to use for the manufacture of hop products[4] any hops imported from a third country unless an attestation of equivalence[5] has been issued in respect thereof[6].

1   As to the meaning of 'hops' see Council Regulation (EC) 1952/2005 (OJ L314, 30.11.2005, p 1) concerning the common organisation of the market in hops, art 2(a); definition applied by the Hops Certification Regulations 1979, SI 1979/1095, reg 1(2).
2   Ie except as provided for in Commission Regulation (EC) 1850/2006 (OJ L355, 15.12.2006, p 72) laying down detailed rules for the certification of hops and hop products, art 1(3)(a).
3   The offence is punishable on summary conviction by a fine not exceeding level 5 on the standard scale: Hops Certification Regulations 1979, SI 1979/1095, reg 3(2) (amended by SI 1991/2198). As to the standard scale and the powers of magistrates' courts to issue fines on summary conviction see SENTENCING vol 92 (2015) PARA 176. Where an offence is committed, there is a defence of due diligence: see the Hops Certification Regulations 1979, SI 1979/1095, reg 10. As to the commission of offences by bodies corporate see reg 11.
4   As to the meaning of 'hop products' see PARA 207 note 4.
5   Ie the attestation of equivalence provided for in Council Regulation (EC) 1952/2005 (OJ L314, 30.11.2005, p 1) concerning the common organisation of the market in hops.
6   Hops Certification Regulations 1979, SI 1979/1095, reg 3(1)(e), (2). As to inspections to ensure compliance with these provisions see reg 5.

212.   Brewers' declarations.

A brewer is required to declare specified particulars of hops harvested on his land and used by him[1] and to forward such declarations either to the Secretary of State or the Welsh Ministers[2] or to such other person as the Secretary of State or the Welsh Ministers may by notice[3] to the brewer from time to time direct[4]. Failure without reasonable excuse to comply with these requirements is an offence[5].

1   See Commission Regulation (EC) 1850/2006 (OJ L355, 15.12.2006, p 72) laying down detailed rules for the certification of hops and hop products, art 20.
2   As to the Secretary of State and the Welsh Ministers see PARA 390.
3   Provision is made for the giving of notices: see the Hops Certification Regulations 1979, SI 1979/1095, reg 12.
4   Hops Certification Regulations 1979, SI 1979/1095, reg 7(1). Brewers' declarations must be forwarded not later than 31 October in each year: reg 7(1). As to inspections to ensure compliance with these provisions see reg 5.
5   The offence is punishable on summary conviction by a fine not exceeding level 2 on the standard scale: Hops Certification Regulations 1979, SI 1979/1095, reg 7(3) (amended by SI 1991/2198). As to the standard scale and the powers of magistrates' courts to issue fines on summary conviction see SENTENCING vol 92 (2015) PARA 176. Where an offence is committed, there is

a defence of due diligence: see the Hops Certification Regulations 1979, SI 1979/1095, reg 10. As to the commission of offences by bodies corporate see reg 11.

(6) ECOLABELLING

213. The EU ecolabel award scheme.

An EU ecolabel award scheme has been established[1]. It is a voluntary scheme that applies to goods or services which are supplied for distribution, consumption or use on the EU market whether in return for payment or free of charge[2]. Under the scheme a producer, manufacturer, importer, service provider, wholesaler or retailer, may apply to use an EU Ecolabel[3].

The scheme also makes provision for the establishment and administration of a European Union Ecolabelling Board[4].

1 See European Parliament and Council Regulation (EC) 66/2010 (OJ L27, 30.1.2010, p 1) on the EU Ecolabel, art 1. Member states are required to take appropriate legal or administrative measures in cases of non-compliance with the Community Eco-Labelling Regulation: see art 18. The Community eco-label award scheme was originally established under Council Regulation (EC) 880/92 (OJ L99, 11.4.92, p 1) (repealed and replaced by Council Regulation (EC) 1980/2000 (OJ L237, 21.9.2000, p 1) (see art 19)).
2 See European Parliament and Council Regulation (EC) 66/2010 (OJ L27, 30.1.2010, p 1) on the EU Ecolabel, art 2(1).
3 See European Parliament and Council Regulation (EC) 66/2010 (OJ L27, 30.1.2010, p 1) on the EU Ecolabel, arts 3(2), 9.
4 See European Parliament and Council Regulation (EC) 66/2010 (OJ L27, 30.1.2010, p 1) on the EU Ecolabel, art 5.

9. HORTICULTURE AND HORTICULTURAL MARKETING

(1) HORTICULTURE GENERALLY

214. Horticulture and agriculture.

Horticulture is included in the definition of 'agriculture' for the purposes of the principal legislation governing agricultural operations[1], and horticultural products are included in the definition of 'agricultural products' for the purposes of the legislation relating to agricultural marketing[2]. Provisions relevant to horticulture are therefore considered in many other parts of this title and only the legislation specific to horticulture, and matters such as plant breeders' rights[3] and biotechnological inventions[4], which are mainly of interest to horticulturalists, are dealt with in this part. There are, for example, special provisions concerning the grading and transport of horticultural produce[5] and provisions relating to the sale of horticultural produce[6].

1   See PARA 10.
2   See the Agricultural Marketing Act 1958 s 52(1); and PARA 171 note 1. For special provisions concerning the sale of horticultural produce see PARAS 215–217.
3   See PARAS 239–291.
4   See PARAS 265–280.
5   See the Marketing of Fresh Horticultural Produce Regulations 2009, SI 2009/1361; the Marketing of Fresh Horticultural Produce (Wales) Regulations 2009, SI 2009/1551; and PARAS 218–228. For these purposes 'horticultural produce' means fruit and vegetables listed in European Parliament and Council Regulation (EU) 1308/2013 (OJ L347, 20.12.2013, p 671) establishing a common organisation of the markets in agricultural products, Annex I Part IX to which EU marketing rules apply: Marketing of Fresh Horticultural Produce Regulations 2009, SI 2009/1361, reg 2(2) (definition amended by SI 2011/1043, SI 2013/3235); Marketing of Fresh Horticultural Produce (Wales) Regulations 2009, SI 2009/1551, reg 2(2) (definition amended by SI 2011/2486, SI 2013/3270). 'EU marketing rules' means the general marketing standard and the specific marketing standards covering fresh fruit and vegetables listed in European Parliament and Council Regulation (EU) 1308/2013 Annex I Part IX and includes the rules relating to those standards contained Commission Implementing Regulation (EU) 543/2011 (OJ L157, 15.6.2011, p 1), arts 74, 75 and 76 and Title II: Marketing of Fresh Horticultural Produce Regulations 2009, SI 2009/1361, reg 2(2) (definition amended by SI 2011/1043, SI 2011/2587, SI 2013/3235);Marketing of Fresh Horticultural Produce (Wales) Regulations 2009, SI 2009/1551, reg 2(2) (definition amended by SI 2011/2486, SI 2013/3270).
   Provision is also made for the grading and marketing of fresh horticultural produce by the Agriculture and Horticulture Act 1964 Pt III (ss 11–24) (see PARA 229 et seq). For these purposes 'fresh horticultural produce' means:
   (1)   fruit, vegetables, herbs, nuts, and edible fungi, whether freshly gathered or stored or taken from store, but not including maincrop potatoes or hops or any dried, frozen, bottled, canned or preserved produce;
   (2)   cut flowers and decorative foliage;
   (3)   pot plants, bedding plants and herbaceous plants;
   (4)   shrubs and flowering trees;
   (5)   fruit trees, fruit bushes and fruit plants; and
   (6)   bulbs, corms and tubers: s 24.
   However, the Agriculture and Horticulture Act 1964 does not apply to horticultural produce: see the Marketing of Fresh Horticultural Produce Regulations 2009, SI 2009/1361, reg 22(a) and the Marketing of Fresh Horticultural Produce (Wales) Regulations 2009, SI 2009/1551, reg 22(a). Nor does it apply to bananas: see the Quality Standards for Green Bananas (England and Wales) Regulations 2012, SI 2012/947, reg 22(a)). As to the meanings of 'general marketing standard' and 'specific marketing standard' see PARA 218 notes 2, 3.
   The Horticultural Produce Act 1986 confers powers on authorised officers in relation to the movement of horticultural produce but the Act has been excluded from applying to horticultural produce (Marketing of Fresh Horticultural Produce Regulations 2009, SI 2009/1361, reg 22(a);

Marketing of Fresh Horticultural Produce (Wales) Regulations 2009, SI 2009/1551, reg 22(a)) and bananas (Quality Standards for Green Bananas (England and Wales) Regulations 2012, SI 2012/947, reg 22(a)).
6 See PARAS 215–217.

(2) SALE OF HORTICULTURAL PRODUCE

215. Duty to keep and deliver particulars of sale.

Where in the case of any horticultural produce[1] consigned for sale on commission[2] the salesman makes a charge by way of commission or otherwise, he must enter in a book kept by him for the purpose the names of the owner or consignor of the produce[3] and every purchaser, and the price paid or agreed to be paid by each purchaser[4]. Provided the owner, consignor or agent has sent to the salesman before the sale an advice note specifying the nature and description of the packages consigned and the contents thereof[5], the salesman must as soon as practicable after the sale send by post or deliver to the owner, consignor or agent an account containing:

(1) the actual price paid or agreed to be paid, and, where there is a variation in price, the number, weight, or quantity sold, or agreed to be sold, at each price[6];

(2) the commission or other charge made by him for selling the produce, with details of any charges made for services in connection with the sale[7]; and

(3) the amounts, if any, paid or payable by him on behalf of the owner or consignor in connection with the sale, with details thereof[8].

If any of the produce is bought by the salesman or by any person on his behalf, the fact must be stated in the account, although this does not render legal any transaction which is otherwise illegal[9].

1 'Horticultural produce' means vegetables, fruit, flowers and plants: Horticultural Produce (Sales on Commission) Act 1926 s 3(1).
2 Produce consigned for sale is deemed to have been consigned for sale on commission unless at or before the sale of the produce the salesman has received from the owner or consignor or his agent a written direction to the contrary (Horticultural Produce (Sales on Commission) Act 1926 s 3(2)(a)) or the owner, consignor or agent and the salesman have entered into a written agreement to the contrary (s 3(2)(b)). Any such agreement may apply either to a particular consignment or generally to all such consignments as may be specified in the agreement: s 3(2).
3 Where the owner or consignor of any horticultural produce has appointed a person to act as his agent for these purposes, anything authorised or required to be done to or by the owner or consignor by the Horticultural Produce (Sales on Commission) Act 1926 may be done to or by such agent: s 3(3).
4 Horticultural Produce (Sales on Commission) Act 1926 s 1(1). As to the penalty for failure to comply with any of the requirements of s 1 see PARA 216. As to the inspection of records and books see PARA 217.
5 If such an advice note has not been sent the salesman is not obliged to comply with the requirements of the Horticultural Produce (Sales on Commission) Act 1926 s 1(1)(a)–(c) (see the text and notes 6–8): s 1(4).
6 Horticultural Produce (Sales on Commission) Act 1926 s 1(1)(a).
7 Horticultural Produce (Sales on Commission) Act 1926 s 1(1)(b).
8 Horticultural Produce (Sales on Commission) Act 1926 s 1(1)(c).
9 Horticultural Produce (Sales on Commission) Act 1926 s 1(2). As to the general rule precluding an agent from buying his principal's property see AGENCY.

216. Penalties for breach of duty.

A person who fails to record any sale of horticultural produce[1] consigned for sale on commission[2], or who fails to send or deliver an account or sends an account not containing the required particulars[3], or who makes an entry or sends or delivers an account false in any material particular, commits an offence[4]. The defendant will, however, be discharged if he proves to the satisfaction of the court that the offence was due to a bona fide mistake or accident, in spite of all reasonable precautions being taken and all due diligence exercised by the defendant to prevent the occurrence of the offence, or if the offence was due to the action of some person over whom he had no control[5].

1　As to the meaning of 'horticultural produce' see PARA 215 note 1.
2　As to the meaning of 'consigned for sale on commission' see PARA 215 note 2. For the duty to record sales see PARA 215.
3　For the duty to send and deliver accounts of sales and the particulars required to be contained in those accounts see PARA 215.
4　Horticultural Produce (Sales on Commission) Act 1926 s 1(3). Punishment for the offence on summary conviction is a fine not exceeding level 3 on the standard scale: s 1(3) (amended by virtue of the Criminal Justice Act 1982 ss 38, 46). As to the standard scale and the powers of magistrates' courts to issue fines on summary conviction see SENTENCING vol 92 (2015) PARA 176.
5　Horticultural Produce (Sales on Commission) Act 1926 s 1(3).

217. Inspection of records and books.

Where an account has been delivered to the owner or consignor of horticultural produce[1] (or his agent[2]) following the sale of horticultural produce consigned for sale on commission[3], the owner or consignor may within one month, by notice in writing, require the salesman to produce any records, books or documents in his possession, so far as they relate to the sale[4], for inspection by an accountant nominated by the owner or consignor, being an accountant possessing such qualifications as may be prescribed by the Secretary of State[5]. A salesman who refuses or fails to produce for inspection, or destroys or obliterates any such records, books, or documents, or obstructs the accountant in his inspection, commits an offence[6].

1　As to the meaning of 'horticultural produce' see PARA 215 note 1.
2　For the powers and duties of agents see PARA 215.
3　As to the meaning of 'consigned for sale on commission' see PARA 215 note 2. For the duty to send and deliver accounts of sales and the particulars required to be contained in those accounts see PARA 215.
4　For the duty to record sales see PARA 215.
5　Horticultural Produce (Sales on Commission) Act 1926 s 2 (amended by the Horticulture Act 1960 s 20). As to the Secretary of State see PARA 390. The power to prescribe qualifications for these purposes has not been transferred, in so far as it is exercisable in relation to Wales, to the Welsh Ministers. See generally PARA 390. For the prescribed qualifications see the Horticultural Produce (Accountants' Qualification) Instrument 1965, SI 1965/1353 (prescribing for these purposes membership of the Institute of Chartered Accountants in England and Wales, the Institute of Chartered Accountants of Scotland, the Association of Certified and Corporate Accountants, and the Institute of Chartered Accountants in Ireland). As to the Secretary of State and the Welsh Ministers see PARA 390.
6　Horticultural Produce (Sales on Commission) Act 1926 s 2 (amended by virtue of the Criminal Justice Act 1982 ss 38, 46). Punishment for the offence on summary conviction is a fine not exceeding level 2 on the standard scale: Horticultural Produce (Sales on Commission) Act 1926 s 2 (as so amended). As to the standard scale and the powers of magistrates' courts to issue fines on summary conviction see SENTENCING vol 92 (2015) PARA 176.

(3) GRADING AND TRANSPORT OF HORTICULTURAL PRODUCE

(i) Marketing Standards

218. Requirement to comply with marketing standards.

A person is guilty of an offence if they display, offer for sale, deliver or market in any other manner, horticultural produce[1] in contravention of or which is not compliant with:

(1)   the general marketing standard[2], if applicable; or

(2)   any specific marketing standard[3] applying to that horticultural produce[4].

1 As to the meaning of 'horticultural produce' see PARA **214** note 5.

2 'General marketing standard' means the requirements of European Parliament and Council Regulation (EU) 1308/2013 (OJ L347, 20.12.2013, p 671) establishing a common organisation of the markets in agricultural products as detailed in Commission Implementing Regulation (EU) 543/2011 (OJ L157, 15.6.2011, p 1), art 3(1), Annex I Part A: Marketing of Fresh Horticultural Produce Regulations 2009, SI 2009/1361, reg 2(2) (definition amended by SI 2011/2587); Marketing of Fresh Horticultural Produce (Wales) Regulations 2009, SI 2009/1551, reg 2(2) (definition amended by SI 2011/2486, SI 2013/3270).

3 'Specific marketing standards' means the marketing standards provided for under European Parliament and Council Regulation (EU) 1308/2013 (OJ L347, 20.12.2013, p 671) establishing a common organisation of the markets in agricultural products, art 75(1)(b) as detailed in Commission Implementing Regulation (EU) 543/2011 (OJ L157, 15.6.2011, p 1), art 3(2), Annex I Part B and 'specific marketing standard' means one of those specific marketing standards: Marketing of Fresh Horticultural Produce Regulations 2009, SI 2009/1361, reg 2(2) (definition amended by SI 2011/2587, SI 2013/3235); Marketing of Fresh Horticultural Produce (Wales) Regulations 2009, SI 2009/1551, reg 2(2) (definition amended by SI 2011/2486; SI 2013/3270).

4 Marketing of Fresh Horticultural Produce Regulations 2009, SI 2009/1361, reg 4(1); Marketing of Fresh Horticultural Produce (Wales) Regulations 2009, SI 2009/1551, reg 4(1). A person guilty of an offence is liable on summary conviction to a fine not exceeding level 5 on the standard scale: Marketing of Fresh Horticultural Produce Regulations 2009, SI 2009/1361, reg 20; Marketing of Fresh Horticultural Produce (Wales) Regulations 2009, SI 2009/1551, reg 20. As to derogation from the offence mentioned in the text see PARA **219**. As to defences see PARA **99**. As to review of the Marketing of Fresh Horticultural Produce Regulations 2009, SI 2009/1361 by the Secretary of State: see reg 23 (added by SI 2011/2587). As to the standard scale and the powers of magistrates' courts to issue fines on summary conviction see SENTENCING vol 92 (2015) PARA 176.

219. Derogation from specific marketing standards.

Horticultural produce[1] to which a specific marketing standard[2] applies is not required to comply with that specific marketing standard if that horticultural produce complies with the general marketing standard[3] and if it is:

(1)   presented for retail sale to consumers for their personal use;

(2)   labelled 'product intended for processing' or with any other equivalent wording; and

(3)   not intended for industrial processing[4].

1 As to the meaning of 'horticultural produce' see PARA **214** note 5.

2 As to the meaning of 'specific marketing standard' see PARA **218** note 3.

3 As to the meaning of 'general marketing standard' see PARA **218** note 2.

4 Marketing of Fresh Horticultural Produce Regulations 2009, SI 2009/1361, reg 5; Marketing of Fresh Horticultural Produce (Wales) Regulations 2009, SI 2009/1551, reg 5.

220. Offences relating to EU marketing rules.

A person is guilty of an offence if he fails to comply with certain EU provisions[1] that relate to marketing of fruit and vegetables[2].

Where:

(1)   an authorised officer[3] has inspected horticultural produce[4] and found it not to be compliant with EU marketing rules[5]; and

(2)   the person in charge of that horticultural produce has given an undertaking, or has been responsible for the giving of an undertaking in relation to that horticultural produce,

it is an offence for that person to act in breach of the undertaking or to cause or permit their agent or employee to act in breach of the undertaking[6].

A person is guilty of an offence if, in purporting to provide the information particulars required by EU marketing rules for horticultural produce, they give an inaccurate or false description of that horticultural produce on a label affixed to, or in a notice or document accompanying, that horticultural produce[7].

A person, other than an authorised officer, is guilty of an offence if they affix, or cause or permit to be affixed, a re-graded label, an out-graded label or a labelling defect label to the container[8] of horticultural produce, or to the horticultural produce itself, or to any notice or document which is required by EU marketing rules to accompany that horticultural produce[9].

A person, other than an authorised officer, is guilty of an offence if they remove, conceal, deface or alter, or cause or permit to be removed, concealed, defaced or altered:

(a)   any notice or document which is required by EU marketing rules to accompany horticultural produce or any label required by EU marketing rules to be affixed to that horticultural produce or to its container;

(b)   a re-graded label, an out-graded label or a labelling defect label which has been applied by an authorised officer in the execution of these Regulations to the horticultural produce or to its container;

(c)   any demarcation tape or other material used by an authorised officer[10] to identify horticultural produce or a specific lot of horticultural produce which is found not to be compliant with EU marketing rules[11].

A person is guilty of an offence if they export or import any consignment of horticultural produce to or from any place outside the European Union without a document, label or notice required by EU marketing rules to accompany that horticultural produce[12].

1   Ie any provision of Commission Implementing Regulation (EU) 543/2011 (OJ L157, 15.6.2011, p 1), mentioned in the Marketing of Fresh Horticultural Produce Regulations 2009, SI 2009/1361, Schedule (substituted by SI 2011/2587) or, in relation to Wales, the Marketing of Fresh Horticultural Produce (Wales) Regulations 2009, SI 2009/1551, Schedule (Schedule substituted by SI 2011/2486).

2   See the Marketing of Fresh Horticultural Produce Regulations 2009, SI 2009/1361, reg 4(3) (amended by SI 2011/2587); and the Marketing of Fresh Horticultural Produce (Wales) Regulations 2009, SI 2009/1551, reg 4(3 (amended by SI 2011/2486). A person guilty of an offence is liable on summary conviction to a fine not exceeding level 5 on the standard scale: Marketing of Fresh Horticultural Produce Regulations 2009, SI 2009/1361, reg 20; Marketing of Fresh Horticultural Produce (Wales) Regulations 2009, SI 2009/1551, reg 20. As to defences see PARA 99. As to the standard scale and the powers of magistrates' courts to issue fines on summary conviction see SENTENCING vol 92 (2015) PARA 176.

3   The Secretary of State and, in relation to Wales, the Welsh Ministers, have power to appoint officers ('authorised officers') for the purposes of the enforcement of the Marketing of Fresh Horticultural Produce Regulations 2009, SI 2009/1361 and the Marketing of Fresh Horticultural Produce (Wales) Regulations 2009, SI 2009/1551: Marketing of Fresh Horticultural Produce

Regulations 2009, SI 2009/1361, reg 3(5); Marketing of Fresh Horticultural Produce (Wales) Regulations 2009, SI 2009/1551, reg 3(3). As to the Secretary of State and the Welsh Ministers see PARA 390.

4   As to the meaning of 'horticultural produce' see PARA 214 note 5.

5   As to the meaning of 'EU marketing rules' see PARA 214 note 5.

6   Marketing of Fresh Horticultural Produce Regulations 2009, SI 2009/1361, reg 4(4) (amended by SI 2011/1043); Marketing of Fresh Horticultural Produce (Wales) Regulations 2009, SI 2009/1551, reg 4(4) (amended by SI 2011/2486).

7   Marketing of Fresh Horticultural Produce Regulations 2009, SI 2009/1361, reg 4(5) (amended by SI 2011/1043); Marketing of Fresh Horticultural Produce (Wales) Regulations 2009, SI 2009/1551, reg 4(5) (amended by SI 2011/2486). 'Label' includes any device for conveying information by written characters or other symbols, and any characters or symbols stamped or otherwise placed directly on to any horticultural produce or container, and references to the affixing of a label are construed accordingly: Marketing of Fresh Horticultural Produce Regulations 2009, SI 2009/1361, reg 2(2); Marketing of Fresh Horticultural Produce (Wales) Regulations 2009, SI 2009/1551, reg 2(2).

8   'Container' includes any basket, pail, tray, package or receptacle of any kind, whether open or closed: Marketing of Fresh Horticultural Produce Regulations 2009, SI 2009/1361, reg 2(2); Marketing of Fresh Horticultural Produce (Wales) Regulations 2009, SI 2009/1551, reg 2(2).

9   Marketing of Fresh Horticultural Produce Regulations 2009, SI 2009/1361, reg 4(6) (amended by SI 2011/1043); Marketing of Fresh Horticultural Produce (Wales) Regulations 2009, SI 2009/1551, reg 4(6) (amended by SI 2011/2486).

10 Ie in accordance with the Marketing of Fresh Horticultural Produce Regulations 2009, SI 2009/1361, reg 8(1)(f) or the Marketing of Fresh Horticultural Produce (Wales) Regulations 2009, SI 2009/1551, reg 8(1)(f) (see PARA 221).

11 Marketing of Fresh Horticultural Produce Regulations 2009, SI 2009/1361, reg 4(7) (amended by SI 2011/1043); Marketing of Fresh Horticultural Produce (Wales) Regulations 2009, SI 2009/1551, reg 4(7) (amended by SI 2011/2486).

12 Marketing of Fresh Horticultural Produce Regulations 2009, SI 2009/1361, reg 4(8) (amended by SI 2011/1043); Marketing of Fresh Horticultural Produce (Wales) Regulations 2009, SI 2009/1551, reg 4(8) (amended by SI 2011/2486).

221. Powers of authorised officers.

Provision is made for authorised officers to have a power[1] to enter any premises[2] for the purposes of enforcing provisions[3] relating to EU marketing rules[4]. An authorised officer who has lawfully entered premises for enforcing such provisions may for those purposes:

(1)   require any person to provide such assistance, information or facilities as the authorised officer may reasonably require[5];

(2)   make any enquiries, observe any activity or process, and take photographs[6];

(3)   inspect and search the premises[7];

(4)   inspect any machinery or equipment, and any other article on the premises[8];

(5)   inspect and take samples of any horticultural produce found on the premises[9];

(6)   identify, with demarcation tape or other material, horticultural produce or a specific lot of horticultural produce which is found not to be compliant with EU marketing rules[10];

(7)   inspect, seize and detain any container used in connection with horticultural produce[11];

(8)   have access to, inspect and copy any label, notice, document or record (in whatever form they are held), remove them to enable them to be copied or require copies to be made[12];

(9)   detach, or give permission to be detached, any re-graded label, out-graded label, labelling defect label or stop notice label when the reasons for their being affixed no longer apply[13];

(10)   have access to, inspect and check the data on, and operation of, any computer and any associated apparatus or material that is or has been in use in connection with a label, notice, document or record mentioned in these provisions, including data relating to deleted files and activity logs; and for this purpose may require any person having charge of, or otherwise concerned with the operation of the computer, apparatus or material to afford such assistance (including the provision of passwords) as may reasonably be required and, where these items are kept by means of a computer, may require them to be produced in a form in which they may be taken away[14];

(11)   seize any computers and associated equipment for the purpose of copying any data, but only if that authorised officer has a reasonable suspicion that an offence under these relevant provisions has been committed, and provided they are returned as soon as practicable[15];

(12)   seize and detain any items in head (8) if that authorised officer has reason to believe that they may be required as evidence in proceedings under these provisions[16].

Where an authorised officer takes a bulk sample of horticultural produce from a specific lot[17] in accordance with and finds that horticultural produce not to be compliant with the EU marketing rules[18], the power to affix:

(a)   a re-graded label[19];
(b)   an out-graded label[20]
(c)   a labelling defect label[21];
(d)   a stop notice label under[22],

may be exercised in relation to all or any of the horticultural produce or containers of horticultural produce within that lot in the same way as in relation to the bulk sample taken[23].

1   As to the appointment of authorised officers see PARA 220 note 3. A person is guilty of an offence if they:

(1)   without reasonable excuse, proof of which lies on that person, obstruct an authorised officer acting for the purposes of the enforcement of the Marketing of Fresh Horticultural Produce Regulations 2009, SI 2009/1361 or, in relation to Wales, the Marketing of Fresh Horticultural Produce (Wales) Regulations 2009, SI 2009/1551, or a person accompanying such an authorised officer under the Marketing of Fresh Horticultural Produce Regulations 2009, SI 2009/1361, reg 7(3)(a) or, in relation to Wales, the Marketing of Fresh Horticultural Produce (Wales) Regulations 2009, SI 2009/1551, reg 7(3)(a);

(2)   without reasonable excuse, proof of which lies on that person, fail to give an authorised officer acting for the purposes of the enforcement of the Marketing of Fresh Horticultural Produce Regulations 2009, SI 2009/1361 or, in relation to Wales, the Marketing of Fresh Horticultural Produce (Wales) Regulations 2009, SI 2009/1551 any assistance or information or to provide any record or facilities that they may reasonably require;

(3)   without reasonable excuse, proof of which lies on that person, fail to make any request for inspection when so required by EU marketing rules or fail to give any notice or information required by EU marketing rules: Marketing of Fresh Horticultural Produce Regulations 2009, SI 2009/1361, reg 16(1) (amended by SI 2011/1043); Marketing of Fresh Horticultural Produce (Wales) Regulations 2009, SI 2009/1551, reg 16(1) (amended by SI 2011/2486).

A person who without reasonable excuse, proof of which lies on that person, supplies to an authorised officer acting for the purposes of the enforcement of the Marketing of Fresh Horticultural Produce Regulations 2009, SI 2009/1361 or, in relation to Wales, the Marketing of Fresh Horticultural Produce (Wales) Regulations 2009, SI 2009/1551 any information knowing it to be false or misleading is guilty of an offence: Marketing of Fresh Horticultural Produce Regulations 2009, SI 2009/1361, reg 16(2); Marketing of Fresh Horticultural Produce (Wales) Regulations 2009, SI 2009/1551, reg 16(2). A person guilty of such an offence is liable on summary conviction to a fine not exceeding level 5 on the standard scale: Marketing of Fresh Horticultural Produce Regulations 2009, SI 2009/1361; reg 20; Marketing of Fresh Horticultural Produce (Wales) Regulations 2009, SI 2009/1551, reg 20. Where the commission by a person ('A') of an offence under these provisions was due to an act or default of another person ('B'), B is guilty of an offence: Marketing of Fresh Horticultural Produce Regulations 2009, SI 2009/1361; reg 17(1); Marketing of Fresh Horticultural Produce (Wales) Regulations 2009, SI 2009/1551, reg 17(1). B may be charged with and convicted of the offence whether or not proceedings are taken against A: Marketing of Fresh Horticultural Produce Regulations 2009, SI 2009/1361; reg 17(2); Marketing of Fresh Horticultural Produce (Wales) Regulations 2009, SI 2009/1551, reg 17(2). As to offences committed by bodies corporate see the Marketing of Fresh Horticultural Produce Regulations 2009, SI 2009/1361, reg 19 or, in relation to Wales, the Marketing of Fresh Horticultural Produce (Wales) Regulations 2009, SI 2009/1551, reg 19. As to the meaning of 'EU marketing rules' see PARA **214** note 5. As to the standard scale and the powers of magistrates' courts to issue fines on summary conviction see SENTENCING vol 92 (2015) PARA **176**.

2   'Premises' includes any place, vehicle or trailer, stall, vessel, container, moveable structure, aircraft, or hovercraft: Marketing of Fresh Horticultural Produce Regulations 2009, SI 2009/1361, reg 2(2); Marketing of Fresh Horticultural Produce (Wales) Regulations 2009, SI 2009/1551, reg 2(2). The powers under the Marketing of Fresh Horticultural Produce Regulations 2009, SI 2009/1361, Pt 3 (regs 7–11) and Pt 4 (regs 12–15) or the Marketing of Fresh Horticultural Produce (Wales) Regulations 2009, SI 2009/1551, Pt 3 (regs 7–11) and Pt 4 (regs 12–15) may not be exercised on premises, or part of any premises, used only as a dwelling-house: Marketing of Fresh Horticultural Produce Regulations 2009, SI 2009/1361, reg 6; Marketing of Fresh Horticultural Produce (Wales) Regulations 2009, SI 2009/1551, reg 6.

3   Ie the Marketing of Fresh Horticultural Produce Regulations 2009, SI 2009/1361 or, in relation to Wales, the Marketing of Fresh Horticultural Produce (Wales) Regulations 2009, SI 2009/1551.

4   Marketing of Fresh Horticultural Produce Regulations 2009, SI 2009/1361, reg 7; Marketing of Fresh Horticultural Produce (Wales) Regulations 2009, SI 2009/1551, reg 7. As to the meaning of 'EU marketing rules' see PARA **214** note 5.

5   Marketing of Fresh Horticultural Produce Regulations 2009, SI 2009/1361, reg 8(1)(a); Marketing of Fresh Horticultural Produce (Wales) Regulations 2009, SI 2009/1551, reg 8(1)(a).

6   Marketing of Fresh Horticultural Produce Regulations 2009, SI 2009/1361, reg 8(1)(b); Marketing of Fresh Horticultural Produce (Wales) Regulations 2009, SI 2009/1551, reg 8(1)(b).

7   Marketing of Fresh Horticultural Produce Regulations 2009, SI 2009/1361, reg 8(1)(c); Marketing of Fresh Horticultural Produce (Wales) Regulations 2009, SI 2009/1551, reg 8(1)(c).

8   Marketing of Fresh Horticultural Produce Regulations 2009, SI 2009/1361, reg 8(1)(d); Marketing of Fresh Horticultural Produce (Wales) Regulations 2009, SI 2009/1551, reg 8(1)(d).

9   Marketing of Fresh Horticultural Produce Regulations 2009, SI 2009/1361, reg 8(1)(e); Marketing of Fresh Horticultural Produce (Wales) Regulations 2009, SI 2009/1551, reg 8(1)(e). As to the meaning of 'horticultural produce' see PARA **214** note 5.

10   Marketing of Fresh Horticultural Produce Regulations 2009, SI 2009/1361, reg 8(1)(f) (amended by SI 2011/1043); Marketing of Fresh Horticultural Produce (Wales) Regulations 2009, SI 2009/1551, reg 8(1)(f) (amended by SI 2011/2486). As to the meaning of 'EU marketing rules' see PARA **214** note 5.

11   Marketing of Fresh Horticultural Produce Regulations 2009, SI 2009/1361, reg 8(1)(g); Marketing of Fresh Horticultural Produce (Wales) Regulations 2009, SI 2009/1551, reg 8(1)(g). As to the meaning of 'container' see PARA **220** note 8. An authorised officer must, as soon as is reasonably practicable, provide to the person appearing to be responsible for any items that that authorised officer seizes and detains a written receipt identifying those items and, as soon as is reasonably practicable after deciding that those items are no longer required, return them, apart from those to be used as evidence in court proceedings: Marketing of Fresh Horticultural Produce Regulations 2009, SI 2009/1361, reg 8(3); Marketing of Fresh Horticultural Produce (Wales) Regulations 2009, SI 2009/1551, reg 8(3). Where an authorised officer has seized and detained items for use in evidence in court proceedings and it is subsequently decided that no court proceedings are to be brought or that those items are no longer needed as evidence in court proceedings, or the court proceedings are completed and no order in relation to those items has been made by the court, an authorised officer must return the items as soon as is reasonably practicable: Marketing of Fresh Horticultural Produce Regulations 2009, SI 2009/1361, reg 8(4); Marketing of Fresh Horticultural Produce (Wales) Regulations 2009, SI 2009/1551, reg 8(4).

12   Marketing of Fresh Horticultural Produce Regulations 2009, SI 2009/1361, reg 8(1)(h); Marketing of Fresh Horticultural Produce (Wales) Regulations 2009, SI 2009/1551, reg 8(1)(h).

13 Marketing of Fresh Horticultural Produce Regulations 2009, SI 2009/1361, reg 8(1)(i); Marketing of Fresh Horticultural Produce (Wales) Regulations 2009, SI 2009/1551, reg 8(1)(i). As to the meaning of 'label' see PARA 220 note 7.

14 Marketing of Fresh Horticultural Produce Regulations 2009, SI 2009/1361, reg 8(1)(j); Marketing of Fresh Horticultural Produce (Wales) Regulations 2009, SI 2009/1551, reg 8(1)(j).

15 Marketing of Fresh Horticultural Produce Regulations 2009, SI 2009/1361, reg 8(1)(k); Marketing of Fresh Horticultural Produce (Wales) Regulations 2009, SI 2009/1551, reg 8(1)(k).

16 Marketing of Fresh Horticultural Produce Regulations 2009, SI 2009/1361, reg 8(1)(l); Marketing of Fresh Horticultural Produce (Wales) Regulations 2009, SI 2009/1551, reg 8(1)(l).

17 Ie in accordance with Commission Implementing Regulation (EU) 543/2011 (OJ L157, 15.6.2011, p 1) Annex V.

18 See note 4.

19 Ie a label under the Marketing of Fresh Horticultural Produce Regulations 2009, SI 2009/1361, reg 9, or in relation to Wales, the Marketing of Fresh Horticultural Produce (Wales) Regulations 2009, SI 2009/1551, reg 9 (see PARA 222).

20 Ie a label under the Marketing of Fresh Horticultural Produce Regulations 2009, SI 2009/1361, reg 10, or in relation to Wales, the Marketing of Fresh Horticultural Produce (Wales) Regulations 2009, SI 2009/1551, reg 10 (see PARA 223).

21 Ie a label under the Marketing of Fresh Horticultural Produce Regulations 2009, SI 2009/1361, reg 11, or in relation to Wales, the Marketing of Fresh Horticultural Produce (Wales) Regulations 2009, SI 2009/1551, reg 11 (see PARA 224).

22 Ie label under the Marketing of Fresh Horticultural Produce Regulations 2009, SI 2009/1361, reg 13(1), or in relation to Wales, the Marketing of Fresh Horticultural Produce (Wales) Regulations 2009, SI 2009/1551, reg 13(1) (see PARA 226).

23 Marketing of Fresh Horticultural Produce Regulations 2009, SI 2009/1361, reg 8(2); Marketing of Fresh Horticultural Produce (Wales) Regulations 2009, SI 2009/1551, reg 8(2).

222. Powers to affix a re-graded label.

Where an authorised officer[1], who has lawfully entered premises[2] for the purposes of the enforcement of EU marketing provisions relating to fresh fruit and vegetables[3], finds horticultural produce[4] subject to a specific marketing standard[5] which has affixed to it a label[6] or is accompanied by a notice or a document required by EU marketing rules[7], or is in a container[8] to which such a label is affixed or which is accompanied by such a notice or document indicating in either case that that horticultural produce is of a particular class under the relevant specific marketing standard but which the authorised officer has reasonable cause to believe to be of an inferior class under that specific marketing standard, the authorised officer may amend or cancel the label, notice or document and may affix to the horticultural produce, or, as the case may be, to the notice or container, a label indicating that fact (a 're-graded label')[9].

1 As to the appointment of authorised officers see PARA 220 note 3.

2 As the meaning of 'premises' see PARA 98 note 1.

3 Ie for the purposes of the enforcement of the Marketing of Fresh Horticultural Produce Regulations 2009, SI 2009/1361 or, in relation to Wales, the Marketing of Fresh Horticultural Produce (Wales) Regulations 2009, SI 2009/1551.

4 As to the meaning of 'horticultural produce' see PARA 214 note 5.

5 As to the meaning of 'specific marketing standard' see PARA 218 note 3.

6 As to the meaning of 'label' see PARA 220 note 7.

7 As to the meaning of 'EU marketing rules' see PARA 214 note 5.

8 As to the meaning of 'container' see PARA 220 note 8.

9 Marketing of Fresh Horticultural Produce Regulations 2009, SI 2009/1361, reg 9(1) (amended by SI 2011/1043); Marketing of Fresh Horticultural Produce (Wales) Regulations 2009, SI 2009/1551, reg 9(1) (amended by SI 2011/2486). As to the information to be contained on the re-graded label see the Marketing of Fresh Horticultural Produce Regulations 2009, SI 2009/1361, reg 9(2); and the Marketing of Fresh Horticultural Produce (Wales) Regulations 2009, SI 2009/1551, reg 9(2).

223. Powers to affix an out-graded label.

Where an authorised officer[1], who has lawfully entered premises[2] for the purpose of enforcing EU marketing provisions relating to fresh fruit and vegetables[3], finds any horticultural produce[4] which either has affixed to it a label[5] or is accompanied by a notice or a document required by EU marketing rules[6], or is in a container[7] to which such a label is affixed or which is accompanied by such a notice or document, indicating in either case that one of the situations set out as follows applies, an authorised officer may amend or cancel the label, notice or document and may affix to the horticultural produce, or, as the case may be, to the notice or container, a label indicating that fact (an 'out-graded label')[8].

Situation 1 is where the label, notice or document indicates that horticultural produce is of a class marketable under the specific marketing standard[9] applicable to it but the authorised officer has reasonable cause to believe that the horticultural produce does not comply with any class of that specific marketing standard but only complies with the general marketing standard[10].

Situation 2 is where the label, notice or document indicates that horticultural produce is of a class marketable under the specific marketing standard applicable to it but the authorised officer has reasonable cause to believe that the horticultural produce is not of a standard marketable under EU marketing rules[11].

Situation 3 is where the label, notice or document indicates that horticultural produce complies with the general marketing standard but the authorised officer has reasonable cause to believe that the horticultural produce is not of a standard marketable under EU marketing rules[12].

1   As to the appointment of authorised officers see PARA 220 note 3.
2   As the meaning of 'premises' see PARA 98 note 1.
3   Ie for the purposes of the enforcement of the Marketing of Fresh Horticultural Produce Regulations 2009, SI 2009/1361 or, in relation to Wales, the Marketing of Fresh Horticultural Produce (Wales) Regulations 2009, SI 2009/1551.
4   As to the meaning of 'horticultural produce' see PARA 214 note 5.
5   As to the meaning of 'label' see PARA 220 note 7.
6   As to the meaning of 'EU marketing rules' see PARA 214 note 5.
7   As to the meaning of 'container' see PARA 220 note 8.
8   Marketing of Fresh Horticultural Produce Regulations 2009, SI 2009/1361, reg 10(1) (reg 10(1), (3), (4) amended by SI 2011/1043); Marketing of Fresh Horticultural Produce (Wales) Regulations 2009, SI 2009/1551, reg 10(1) (reg 10(1), (3), (4) amended by SI 2011/2486). As to the information to be contained on the out-graded label see the Marketing of Fresh Horticultural Produce Regulations 2009, SI 2009/1361, reg 10(5); and the Marketing of Fresh Horticultural Produce (Wales) Regulations 2009, SI 2009/1551, reg 10(5).
9   As to the meaning of 'specific marketing standard' see PARA 218 note 3.
10   Marketing of Fresh Horticultural Produce Regulations 2009, SI 2009/1361, reg 10(2); Marketing of Fresh Horticultural Produce (Wales) Regulations 2009, SI 2009/1551, reg 10(2). As to the meaning of 'general marketing standard' see PARA 218 note 2.
11   Marketing of Fresh Horticultural Produce Regulations 2009, SI 2009/1361, reg 10(3); Marketing of Fresh Horticultural Produce (Wales) Regulations 2009, SI 2009/1551, reg 10(3) (both as amended: see note 8).
12   Marketing of Fresh Horticultural Produce Regulations 2009, SI 2009/1361, reg 10(4); Marketing of Fresh Horticultural Produce (Wales) Regulations 2009, SI 2009/1551, reg 10(4) (both as amended: see note 8).

224. Powers to affix a labelling defect label.

Where an authorised officer[1], who has lawfully entered premises[2] for the purposes of the enforcement of EU marketing provisions relating to fresh fruit and vegetables[3], finds any horticultural produce[4], or container[5] holding horticultural produce, which:

(1)   does not have a label[6] required by the EU marketing rules[7] affixed to it[8]; or

(2)   is not accompanied by a notice or document required by the EU marketing rules[9]; or

(3)   has a label required by the EU marketing rules affixed to it, or to its container, but the label appears to the authorised officer to be incorrect (other than in relation to a particular class under the specific marketing standard[10] applying to that horticultural produce, if applicable), or to have been altered or defaced[11]; or

(4)   is accompanied by a notice or document required by the EU marketing rules but which appears to the authorised officer to be incorrect (other than in relation to a particular class under the specific marketing standard applying to that horticultural produce, if applicable), or to have been altered or defaced with the result that it is incorrect[12],

the authorised officer may, as appropriate, amend or cancel the label, notice or document and may affix to the horticultural produce, or, as the case may be, to the container, a label indicating that fact (a 'labelling defect' label)[13].

1   As to the appointment of authorised officers see PARA 220 note 3.
2   As the meaning of 'premises' see PARA 98 note 1.
3   Ie for the purposes of the enforcement of the Marketing of Fresh Horticultural Produce Regulations 2009, SI 2009/1361 or, in relation to Wales, the Marketing of Fresh Horticultural Produce (Wales) Regulations 2009, SI 2009/1551.
4   As to the meaning of 'horticultural produce' see PARA 214 note 5.
5   As to the meaning of 'container' see PARA 220 note 8.
6   As to the meaning of 'label' see PARA 220 note 7.
7   As to the meaning of 'EU marketing rules' see PARA 214 note 5.
8   Marketing of Fresh Horticultural Produce Regulations 2009, SI 2009/1361, reg 11(1)(a) (reg 11(1)(a)–(d) amended by SI 2011/1043); Marketing of Fresh Horticultural Produce (Wales) Regulations 2009, SI 2009/1551, reg 11(1)(a) (reg 11(1)(a)–(d) amended by SI 2011/2486). As to the information to be contained on the out-graded label see the Marketing of Fresh Horticultural Produce Regulations 2009, SI 2009/1361, reg 10(5); and the Marketing of Fresh Horticultural Produce (Wales) Regulations 2009, SI 2009/1551, reg 10(5).
9   Marketing of Fresh Horticultural Produce Regulations 2009, SI 2009/1361, reg 11(1)(b) (as amended: see note 8); Marketing of Fresh Horticultural Produce (Wales) Regulations 2009, SI 2009/1551, reg 11(1)(b) (as amended: see note 8).
10 As to the meaning of 'specific marketing standard' see PARA 218 note 3.
11 Marketing of Fresh Horticultural Produce Regulations 2009, SI 2009/1361, reg 11(1)(c) (as amended: see note 8); Marketing of Fresh Horticultural Produce (Wales) Regulations 2009, SI 2009/1551, reg 11(1)(c) (as amended: see note 8).
12 Marketing of Fresh Horticultural Produce Regulations 2009, SI 2009/1361, reg 11(1)(d) (as amended: see note 8); Marketing of Fresh Horticultural Produce (Wales) Regulations 2009, SI 2009/1551, reg 11(1)(d) (as amended: see note 8).
13 Marketing of Fresh Horticultural Produce Regulations 2009, SI 2009/1361, reg 11(1) (as amended: see note 8); Marketing of Fresh Horticultural Produce (Wales) Regulations 2009, SI 2009/1551, reg 11(1). As to the information to be shown on the labelling defect label see the Marketing of Fresh Horticultural Produce Regulations 2009, SI 2009/1361, reg 11(2); and the Marketing of Fresh Horticultural Produce (Wales) Regulations 2009, SI 2009/1551, reg 11(2).

225.   Powers to control the movement of horticultural produce.
An authorised officer[1] may, by written notice (a 'stop notice')[2], prohibit the movement of any horticultural produce if the authorised officer reasonably suspects that an offence under provisions relating to the marketing of fresh fruit and vegetables[3] is being committed in respect of that horticultural produce[4].

The person on whom the stop notice is served[5], or the owner of the horticultural produce or an agent or employee acting on behalf of the owner, may request a review[6].

The request must be made in a specified manner[7] as soon as reasonably practicable, and in any event within a specified time limit[8] as is applicable[9].

The Secretary of State or, in relation to Wales, the Welsh Ministers[10], must maintain arrangements for the conduct of a review by an authorised officer unconnected with the original decision to determine whether there were valid grounds for serving the stop notice[11].

The authorised officer conducting the review may cancel the notice or confirm it, with or without modification[12].

1   As to the appointment of authorised officers see PARA 220 note 3.
2   The written notice must be served on the person appearing to the authorised officer to be in charge of the horticultural produce concerned: Marketing of Fresh Horticultural Produce Regulations 2009, SI 2009/1361, reg 12(2); Marketing of Fresh Horticultural Produce (Wales) Regulations 2009, SI 2009/1551, reg 12(2). As to the information to be contained in the notices see the Marketing of Fresh Horticultural Produce Regulations 2009, SI 2009/1361, reg 12(2)(a)–(h) (reg 12(2)(e) amended by SI 2011/1043); and, in relation to Wales, the Marketing of Fresh Horticultural Produce (Wales) Regulations 2009, SI 2009/1551, reg 12(2)(a)–(h) (reg 12(2)(e) amended by SI 2011/2486). As to the meaning of 'horticultural produce' see PARA 214 note 5.
3   Ie an offence under the Marketing of Fresh Horticultural Produce Regulations 2009, SI 2009/1361 or, in relation to Wales, the Marketing of Fresh Horticultural Produce (Wales) Regulations 2009, SI 2009/1551. As to the commission of an offence due to the fault of another person see PARA 98 note 1.
4   Marketing of Fresh Horticultural Produce Regulations 2009, SI 2009/1361, reg 12(1); Marketing of Fresh Horticultural Produce (Wales) Regulations 2009, SI 2009/1551, reg 12(1).
5   Where the person on whom the notice is served is not the owner, or an agent or employee acting on behalf of the owner, the authorised officer must use best endeavours to identify such a person and bring the contents of the stop notice to that person's attention within 48 hours from service of the notice: Marketing of Fresh Horticultural Produce Regulations 2009, SI 2009/1361, reg 12(6); Marketing of Fresh Horticultural Produce (Wales) Regulations 2009, SI 2009/1551, reg 12(6).
6   Marketing of Fresh Horticultural Produce Regulations 2009, SI 2009/1361, reg 12(3); Marketing of Fresh Horticultural Produce (Wales) Regulations 2009, SI 2009/1551, reg 12(3).
7   A request for a review must be exercised by informing an authorised officer either in person, or by telephone to be confirmed in writing as soon as reasonably practicable, or by email or fax at the contact details indicated in the stop notice: Marketing of Fresh Horticultural Produce Regulations 2009, SI 2009/1361, reg 12(8); Marketing of Fresh Horticultural Produce (Wales) Regulations 2009, SI 2009/1551, reg 12(8).
8   The time limit for a person on whom the stop notice was served is 48 hours from service of the stop notice: Marketing of Fresh Horticultural Produce Regulations 2009, SI 2009/1361, reg 12(5); Marketing of Fresh Horticultural Produce (Wales) Regulations 2009, SI 2009/1551, reg 12(5). The time limit for a person referred to in the Marketing of Fresh Horticultural Produce Regulations 2009, SI 2009/1361, reg 12(6) or in relation to Wales, the Marketing of Fresh Horticultural Produce (Wales) Regulations 2009, SI 2009/1551, reg 12(6) is within 48 hours of the contents of the stop notice coming to that person's attention or within 96 hours from the time of service of the notice whichever is the sooner: Marketing of Fresh Horticultural Produce Regulations 2009, SI 2009/1361, reg 12(7); Marketing of Fresh Horticultural Produce (Wales) Regulations 2009, SI 2009/1551, reg 12(7).
9   Marketing of Fresh Horticultural Produce Regulations 2009, SI 2009/1361, reg 12(4); Marketing of Fresh Horticultural Produce (Wales) Regulations 2009, SI 2009/1551, reg 12(4).
10 As to the Secretary of State and the Welsh Ministers see PARA 390.
11 Marketing of Fresh Horticultural Produce Regulations 2009, SI 2009/1361, reg 12(9); Marketing of Fresh Horticultural Produce (Wales) Regulations 2009, SI 2009/1551, reg 12(9). The authorised officer must complete the review as soon as reasonably practicable and in any event within 48 hours of the request, and notify the person who requested it, and, if different, the person on whom the notice was served and any other person in possession of the horticultural produce, of the outcome, as soon as reasonably practicable: Marketing of Fresh Horticultural Produce Regulations 2009, SI 2009/1361, reg 12(11); Marketing of Fresh Horticultural Produce (Wales) Regulations 2009, SI 2009/1551, reg 12(11).
12 Marketing of Fresh Horticultural Produce Regulations 2009, SI 2009/1361, reg 12(10); Marketing of Fresh Horticultural Produce (Wales) Regulations 2009, SI 2009/1551, reg 12(10).

226. Powers to affix a stop notice label.

An authorised officer[1] may affix to any controlled horticultural produce[2], or to any container[3] in which the controlled horticultural produce is packed, a label[4] warning of the exercise[5] of a 'stop notice label'[6].

A person, other than an authorised officer, is guilty of an offence if they remove or cause or permit to be removed from that controlled horticultural produce or its container a stop notice label affixed by an authorised officer under the above provsions[7].

1 As to the appointment of authorised officers see PARA 220 note 3.
2 'Controlled' in relation to horticultural produce, means that the power conferred by the Marketing of Fresh Horticultural Produce Regulations 2009, SI 2009/1361, reg 12(1) or, in relation to Wales, the Marketing of Fresh Horticultural Produce (Wales) Regulations 2009, SI 2009/1551, reg 12(1) (stop notice: see PARA 226) has been exercised in relation to it and that the stop notice is for the time being in force: Marketing of Fresh Horticultural Produce Regulations 2009, SI 2009/1361, reg 2(2); Marketing of Fresh Horticultural Produce (Wales) Regulations 2009, SI 2009/1551, reg 2(2). As to the meaning of 'horticultural produce' see PARA 214 note 5.
3 As to the meaning of 'container' see PARA 220 note 8.
4 As to the meaning of 'label' see PARA 220 note 7.
5 Ie the exercise of the power in the Marketing of Fresh Horticultural Produce Regulations 2009, SI 2009/1361, reg 12(1) or the Marketing of Fresh Horticultural Produce (Wales) Regulations 2009, SI 2009/1551, reg 12(1) (see PARA 226).
6 Marketing of Fresh Horticultural Produce Regulations 2009, SI 2009/1361, reg 13(1); Marketing of Fresh Horticultural Produce (Wales) Regulations 2009, SI 2009/1551, reg 13(1). As to the information to be shown on the stop notice label see the Marketing of Fresh Horticultural Produce Regulations 2009, SI 2009/1361, reg 13(2) or, in relation to Wales, the Marketing of Fresh Horticultural Produce (Wales) Regulations 2009, SI 2009/1551, reg 13(2).
7 Marketing of Fresh Horticultural Produce Regulations 2009, SI 2009/1361, reg 15(2); Marketing of Fresh Horticultural Produce (Wales) Regulations 2009, SI 2009/1551, reg 15(2). A person guilty of such an offence under is liable on summary conviction to a fine not exceeding level 5 on the standard scale: Marketing of Fresh Horticultural Produce Regulations 2009, SI 2009/1361, reg 20; Marketing of Fresh Horticultural Produce (Wales) Regulations 2009, SI 2009/1551, reg 20. As to the commission of an offence due to the fault of another person see PARA 98 note 1. As to the standard scale and the powers of magistrates' courts to issue fines on summary conviction see SENTENCING vol 92 (2015) PARA 176.

227. Consent to move controlled horticultural produce.

An authorised officer[1] may, at any time, give written consent[3] to the movement of controlled horticultural produce[2] and to the lifting of the stop notice[3]. An authorised officer must, upon request, give written consent to the movement of controlled horticultural produce and to the lifting of the stop notice if the following circumstances apply[4].

The circumstances are where:

(1)	the authorised officer is satisfied that no offence under provisions relating to the marketing of fresh fruit and vegetables[5] would be committed in respect of the horticultural produce if it were sold in circumstances in which EU marketing rules[6] apply[7]; or

(2)	the authorised officer, or another authorised officer, has been given a written undertaking that the horticultural produce will be sold or disposed of in a specified manner and the authorised officer is satisfied that if the horticultural produce is sold or disposed of in that manner no offence under provisions relating to the marketing of fresh fruit and vegetables[8] will be committed in respect of it and the authorised officer has no reason to doubt that the terms of the undertaking will be met[9].

An authorised officer must, upon request, give written consent to the movement of controlled horticultural produce if the following circumstances apply[10].

The circumstances are where:

(a)   the authorised officer, or another authorised officer, has been given a written undertaking to the effect that:

    (i)   the horticultural produce will be moved to a place approved by an authorised officer;

    (ii)   at the approved place the steps required to ensure that the horticultural produce may be sold in circumstances in which EU marketing rules apply without an offence under these provisions being committed in respect of it will be taken;

    (iii) the horticultural produce will not be moved from that place without the written consent of an authorised officer[11]; and

(b)   the authorised officer has no reason to doubt that the terms of the undertaking will be met[12].

A person is guilty of an offence if they move controlled horticultural produce or a container with controlled horticultural produce in it, or cause or permit them to be moved without the written consent of an authorised officer[13]. A person is guilty of an offence if they fail to comply with the undertaking given under the above provisions[14].

1   As to the appointment of authorised officers see PARA 220 note 3.
3   A consent given by an authorised officer under the Marketing of Fresh Horticultural Produce Regulations 2009, SI 2009/1361 or, in relation to Wales, the Marketing of Fresh Horticultural Produce (Wales) Regulations 2009, SI 2009/1551 must specify the horticultural produce to which it relates and, where the consent is given under the Marketing of Fresh Horticultural Produce Regulations 2009, SI 2009/1361, reg 14(4) or, in relation to Wales, the Marketing of Fresh Horticultural Produce (Wales) Regulations 2009, SI 2009/1551, reg 14(4), state that the horticultural produce continues to be controlled: Marketing of Fresh Horticultural Produce Regulations 2009, SI 2009/1361, reg 14(6); Marketing of Fresh Horticultural Produce (Wales) Regulations 2009, SI 2009/1551, reg 14(6).
2   As to the meaning of 'controlled' see PARA 226 note 2. As to the meaning of 'horticultural produce' see PARA 214 note 5.
4   Marketing of Fresh Horticultural Produce Regulations 2009, SI 2009/1361, reg 14(2); Marketing of Fresh Horticultural Produce (Wales) Regulations 2009, SI 2009/1551, reg 14(2).
5   Ie under the Marketing of Fresh Horticultural Produce Regulations 2009, SI 2009/1361 or, in relation to Wales, the Marketing of Fresh Horticultural Produce (Wales) Regulations 2009, SI 2009/1551.
6   As to the meaning of 'EU marketing rules' see PARA 214 note 5.
7   Marketing of Fresh Horticultural Produce Regulations 2009, SI 2009/1361, reg 14(3)(a) (amended by SI 2011/1043); Marketing of Fresh Horticultural Produce (Wales) Regulations 2009, SI 2009/1551, reg 14(3)(a) (amended by SI 2011/2486).
8   See note 5.
9   Marketing of Fresh Horticultural Produce Regulations 2009, SI 2009/1361, reg 14(3)(b); Marketing of Fresh Horticultural Produce (Wales) Regulations 2009, SI 2009/1551, reg 14(3)(b).
10   Marketing of Fresh Horticultural Produce Regulations 2009, SI 2009/1361, reg 14(4); Marketing of Fresh Horticultural Produce (Wales) Regulations 2009, SI 2009/1551, reg 14(4).
11   Marketing of Fresh Horticultural Produce Regulations 2009, SI 2009/1361, reg 14(5)(a) (amended by SI 2011/1043); Marketing of Fresh Horticultural Produce (Wales) Regulations 2009, SI 2009/1551, reg 14(5)(a) (amended by SI 2011/2486).
12   Marketing of Fresh Horticultural Produce Regulations 2009, SI 2009/1361, reg 14(5)(b); Marketing of Fresh Horticultural Produce (Wales) Regulations 2009, SI 2009/1551, reg 14(5)(b).
13   Marketing of Fresh Horticultural Produce Regulations 2009, SI 2009/1361, reg 15(1); Marketing of Fresh Horticultural Produce (Wales) Regulations 2009, SI 2009/1551, reg 15(1). A person guilty of such an offence under is liable on summary conviction to a fine not exceeding level 5 on the standard scale: Marketing of Fresh Horticultural Produce Regulations 2009, SI 2009/1361, reg 20; Marketing of Fresh Horticultural Produce (Wales) Regulations 2009, SI 2009/1551, reg

20. As to the commission of an offence due to the fault of another person see PARA 98 note 1. As to the standard scale and the powers of magistrates' courts to issue fines on summary conviction see SENTENCING vol 92 (2015) PARA 176.

14 Marketing of Fresh Horticultural Produce Regulations 2009, SI 2009/1361, reg 15(3); Marketing of Fresh Horticultural Produce (Wales) Regulations 2009, SI 2009/1551, reg 15(3). A person guilty of such an offence under is liable on summary conviction to a fine not exceeding level 5 on the standard scale: Marketing of Fresh Horticultural Produce Regulations 2009, SI 2009/1361, reg 20; Marketing of Fresh Horticultural Produce (Wales) Regulations 2009, SI 2009/1551, reg 20.

228. Defences.

It is a defence for a person charged ('A') with an offence under provisions relating to the marketing of fresh fruit and vegetables[1], to prove that their actions were carried out with lawful authority or that they took all reasonable precautions and exercised all due diligence to avoid committing the offence[2].

Where A wishes to rely on this defence, he must serve on the prosecutor a written notice of that fact[3].

Where the defence involves an allegation that the commission of the offence was due to the act or default of another person, A is not, without leave of the court, entitled to rely on that defence unless A has served on the prosecutor a written notice[4] giving such information identifying or assisting in the identification of that person as was then in A's possession[5].

1 Ie for the purposes of the enforcement of the Marketing of Fresh Horticultural Produce Regulations 2009, SI 2009/1361, except for the offences in reg 16 or, in relation to Wales, the Marketing of Fresh Horticultural Produce (Wales) Regulations 2009, SI 2009/1551, except for the offences in reg 16.

2 Marketing of Fresh Horticultural Produce Regulations 2009, SI 2009/1361, reg 18(1); Marketing of Fresh Horticultural Produce (Wales) Regulations 2009, SI 2009/1551, reg 18(1).

3 Marketing of Fresh Horticultural Produce Regulations 2009, SI 2009/1361, reg 18(2); Marketing of Fresh Horticultural Produce (Wales) Regulations 2009, SI 2009/1551, reg 18(2). The notice must be served at least 7 clear days before the hearing and, where A has previously appeared before a court in connection with the alleged offence, within one month of A's first such appearance: Marketing of Fresh Horticultural Produce Regulations 2009, SI 2009/1361, reg 18(4); Marketing of Fresh Horticultural Produce (Wales) Regulations 2009, SI 2009/1551, reg 18(4).

4 See note 3.

5 Marketing of Fresh Horticultural Produce Regulations 2009, SI 2009/1361, reg 18(3); Marketing of Fresh Horticultural Produce (Wales) Regulations 2009, SI 2009/1551, reg 18(3).

(ii) Grading and Labelling under the Agriculture and Horticulture Act 1964

229. Application of the Agriculture and Horticulture Act 1964.

The Secretary of State and the Welsh Ministers[1] may by regulations[2] designate and define grades of quality for any description of fresh horticultural produce[3] (other than produce of a description which is subject to Community grading rules[4]) and may prescribe for each grade the form of a label[5] indicating that the produce falls within that grade[6]. Produce of a description in relation to which grades of quality are so designated and defined is known for these purposes[7] as 'regulated produce'[8]. Such regulations may provide that labels recognised by the law of any country outside Great Britain[9] as indicating a quality not inferior to that of a prescribed grade[10] are to be treated as if they were in the form prescribed for that grade[11].

Fresh horticultural produce which is subject to Community grading rules[12] is excluded from the scope of the powers of the Secretary of State and the Welsh Ministers to designate and define grades of quality and to prescribe forms of labelling[13]. The powers of the Secretary of State and the Welsh Ministers in relation to such produce are accordingly limited to making additional provision as to the form of any label required for the purpose of Community grading rules or as to the inclusion in any such label of additional particulars (not affecting the grading of the produce)[14] and providing for the modified application of all or any of the statutory provisions concerning the grading of fresh horticultural produce[15].

1   As to the Secretary of State and the Welsh Ministers see PARA 390.

2   Before making any regulations or orders under the Agriculture and Horticulture Act 1964 the Secretary of State and the Welsh Ministers must consult with such organisations as appear to be representative of affected interests: Agriculture and Horticulture Act 1964 s 23(1). However, this does not apply to regulations which apply, or to an order which applies, only in relation to England: s 23(1A) (added by the Deregulation Act 2015 Sch 22 para 3).

3   As to the meaning of 'fresh horticultural produce' and the disapplication of the Agriculture and Horticulture Act 1964 from applying to horticultural products and bananas see PARA 214 note 5.

4   See text and notes 12–15.

5   'Label' includes any device for conveying information by written characters or other symbols, and any characters or symbols stamped or otherwise placed directly on to any produce or container; and 'container' includes any basket, pail, tray, package or receptacle of any kind, whether open or closed: Agriculture and Horticulture Act 1964 s 24. References to the affixing of a label are to be construed accordingly: s 24.

6   Agriculture and Horticulture Act 1964 s 11(1). A scheme under the Agricultural Marketing Act 1958 (see PARA 171) cannot, notwithstanding anything in s 7 (see PARA 174), empower the board administering the scheme to grade, or regulate the grading of, any produce to which regulations under the Agriculture and Horticulture Act 1964 s 11(1) apply, otherwise than in conformity with those regulations: s 22(3)(a). A description or mark applied in pursuance of the Agriculture and Horticulture Act 1964 is not a 'trade description' for the purposes of the Trade Descriptions Act 1968: see s 2(4)(d); and CONSUMER PROTECTION vol 21 (2016) PARA 443.

7   Ie for the purposes of the Agriculture and Horticulture Act 1964 Pt III (ss 11–24) (see PARA 229 et seq).

8   Agriculture and Horticulture Act 1964 ss 12(1), 24.

9   As to the meaning of 'Great Britain' see PARA 1 note 1.

10   Ie, in relation to regulated produce of any description, a grade of quality designated and defined in relation to produce of that description under the Agriculture and Horticulture Act 1964 s 11(1) (see the text and notes 1–6): s 24.

11   Agriculture and Horticulture Act 1964 s 11(2).

12   'Community grading rules' means any directly applicable EU provisions establishing standards of quality for fresh horticultural produce: Agriculture and Horticulture Act 1964 s 24 (amended by the European Communities Act 1972 Sch 4 para 4(1); SI 2011/1043). For these purposes 'Community grading rules' is not limited to such EU provisions as were in existence before the European Communities Act 1972 (which added the Agriculture and Horticulture Act 1964 s 11(3): see note 14) came into force, but rather includes all subsequent relevant provisions (see *Department for Environment, Food and Rural Affairs v ASDA Stores Ltd* [2003] UKHL 71, [2004] 1 All ER 268, [2004] 1 WLR 105). The Agricultural and Horticulture Act 1964 is excluded from applying to horticultural products and bananas: see PARA 214 note 5. As to provision for grading and movement of horticultural produce see the Marketing of Fresh Horticultural Produce Regulations 2009, SI 2009/1361; the Marketing of Fresh Horticultural Produce (Wales) Regulations 2009, SI 2009/1551; and PARAS 218–228.

13   See the Agriculture and Horticulture Act 1964 s 11(3) (added by the European Communities Act 1972 Sch 4 para 4(1)(a)). A scheme under the Agricultural Marketing Act 1958 (see PARA 171) cannot, notwithstanding anything in s 7 (see PARA 174), empower the board administering the scheme to grade, or regulate the grading of, any produce to which Community grading rules apply, otherwise than in conformity with those rules: Agriculture and Horticulture Act 1964 s 22(3)(a) (amended by the European Communities Act 1972 Sch 4 para 4(1)(b)).

14   Agriculture and Horticulture Act 1964 s 11(3)(a).

15   Agriculture and Horticulture Act 1964 s 11(3)(b) (as added: see note 14). The statutory provisions mentioned in the text are considered in PARA 231 et seq. A description or mark applied in

pursuance of Community grading rules is not a 'trade description' for the purposes of the Trade Descriptions Act 1968: see s 2(4)(d); and CONSUMER PROTECTION vol 21 (2016) PARA 443.

230. Duties as to grading of produce.

No person may sell any regulated produce[1] unless:

(1)   the produce falls within a prescribed grade[2], and is packed in a container[3] to which is affixed a label[4] in the form prescribed for that or any lower grade[5] or, if not packed in a container, has affixed to it such a label[6];

(2)   the sale is by retail[7];

(3)   the produce is to be transported outside the United Kingdom[8] by, or to the order of, the buyer[9];

(4)   the produce is to be used by the buyer in manufacturing or producing any commodity for sale or other disposal by him[10];

(5)   the sale is a direct sale[11] by the producer to a person who gives undertakings as to compliance with the grading regulations[12]; or

(6)   the sale is a direct sale by the producer where the produce is, or is to be, delivered at premises, or at any stall or vehicle from which it is to be sold by retail[13].

1   As to the meaning of 'regulated produce' see PARA 229.
2   As to the meaning of 'prescribed grade' see PARA 229 note 10.
3   As to the meaning of 'container' see PARA 229 note 5.
4   As to the meaning of 'label', and as to the affixing of a label, see PARA 229 note 5.
5   As to the making of regulations prescribing grades see PARA 229.
6   Agriculture and Horticulture Act 1964 s 12(1).
7   Agriculture and Horticulture Act 1964 s 12(2)(a).
8   As to the meaning of 'United Kingdom' see PARA 1 note 1.
9   Agriculture and Horticulture Act 1964 s 12(2)(b).
10   Agriculture and Horticulture Act 1964 s 12(2)(c).
11   Ie a sale where negotiations on behalf of the vendor are not conducted by any agent other than his servant: Agriculture and Horticulture Act 1964 s 12(4).
12   Agriculture and Horticulture Act 1964 s 12(2)(d). The undertakings required to be given are:
    (1)   that before any future sale of any of the produce, not being either a sale in which the produce is to be transported outside the United Kingdom by, or to the order of, the buyer, or a sale in which the produce is to be used by the buyer in manufacturing or producing any commodity for sale or other disposal by him, the produce will be sorted into the prescribed grades and produce the quality of which is inferior to that required for the lowest prescribed grade will be separated from other produce (s 12(2)(d)(i)); and
    (2)   that on any sale by him of any of the produce falling within a prescribed grade, not being either a sale in which the produce is to be transported outside the United Kingdom by, or to the order of, the buyer, or a sale in which the produce is to be used by the buyer in manufacturing or producing any commodity for sale or other disposal by him, the produce will be packed in a container to which is affixed a label in the form prescribed for that or any lower grade or, if not packed in a container, will have affixed to it such a label (s 12(2)(d)(ii)).
    Failure to comply with any such undertaking is an offence: s 14(3). A person who commits such an offence is liable on summary conviction to a fine not exceeding level 5 on the standard scale: s 20(2) (amended by virtue of the Criminal Justice Act 1982 ss 37, 38, 46). Until a day to be appointed a person who commits an offence under the Agriculture and Horticulture Act 1964 s 14(3) is, in addition or as an alternative to the specified fine, liable to imprisonment for a term not exceeding three months (s 20(2)); as from that day, the option of imprisonment (either as an additional or alternative punishment) is removed (s 20(2) (as so amended; prospectively amended by the Criminal Justice Act 2003 s 332, Sch 37 Pt 9)). At the date at which this volume states the law no such day had been appointed. As to the standard scale and the powers of magistrates' courts to issue fines on summary conviction see SENTENCING vol 92 (2015) PARA 176.
    Where the commission by any person of an offence under the Agriculture and Horticulture Act 1964 s 14(3) was due to an act or default of another person occurring in Great Britain, then, whether proceedings are taken against the first-mentioned person or not, that other person may be

charged with and convicted of the offence, and is on conviction liable to the same punishment as that to which the first-mentioned person is, on conviction, liable: s 16. In proceedings for an offence in respect of any produce under the Agriculture and Horticulture Act 1964 s 14(3) it is a defence for the person charged to prove that the commission of the offence was due to the act or default of some other person, or to a mistake, or to an accident or some other cause beyond his control (s 18(a)) and that he took all reasonable precautions and exercised all due diligence to avoid the commission of the offence in respect of that produce by himself or any person under his control (s 18(b)). Provision is also made as to the commission of offences by corporations: see s 19; and PARA 238. As to the meaning of 'Great Britain' see PARA 1 note 1.
13 Agriculture and Horticulture Act 1964 s 12(1), (2)(e). This provision may be omitted by order of the Secretary of State or the Welsh Ministers if he thinks or they think fit, and any such order may be subsequently varied or revoked: s 12(3). At the date at which this volume states the law no order had been made under this provision.

231. Offences in connection with grading.

A person is guilty of an offence if he sells any regulated produce[1] in contravention of the statutory provisions governing the sale of such produce[2] or, with intent to sell any such produce in circumstances such that the sale would contravene the statutory provisions governing the sale of such produce, he:

(1)   offers or exposes produce for sale[3]; or

(2)   not being the producer thereof, has produce in his possession for sale[4]; or

(3)   being the producer thereof, consigns produce for sale[5].

A person is guilty of an offence if, on behalf of the owner of any regulated produce:

(a)   he carries out a sale of the produce in circumstances such that the sale contravenes the statutory provisions governing the sale of such produce[6]; or

(b)   with intent to carry out a sale of the produce in such circumstances, he offers or exposes it for sale or has it in his possession for sale[7].

A person is guilty of an offence if:

(i)   he wilfully represents, whether by affixing an incorrect label to the container[8] of any regulated produce or in any other manner, that regulated produce the quality of which is inferior to that required for a prescribed grade falls within that grade[9]; or

(ii)   without lawful authority affixes[10] to the container of any regulated produce, or to the produce itself, a label in a form prescribed for the purposes of the statutory regrading powers[11]; or

(iii)   where under the statutory regrading powers[12] a label has been affixed to the container of any regulated produce, or to the produce itself, he, with intent to deceive, removes, alters, defaces or conceals the label[13].

A person guilty of an offence[14] under any of these provisions is liable on summary conviction to a fine[15]. Provision is also made for statutory defences[16], the bringing of proceedings[17], and as to the commission of offences by corporations[18].

1   As to the meaning of 'regulated produce' see PARA 229.
2   Ie in contravention of the Agriculture and Horticulture Act 1964 s 12; and PARA 230.
3   Agriculture and Horticulture Act 1964 s 14(1)(a).
4   Agriculture and Horticulture Act 1964 s 14(1)(b).
5   Agriculture and Horticulture Act 1964 s 14(1)(c).
6   Agriculture and Horticulture Act 1964 s 14(2)(a). For the statutory provisions governing the sale of regulated produce see the Agriculture and Horticulture Act 1964 s 12; and PARA 230.
7   Agriculture and Horticulture Act 1964 s 14(2)(b).
8   As to the meaning of 'container' see PARA 229 note 5.
9   Agriculture and Horticulture Act 1964 s 14(4)(a).
10 As to the meaning of 'label', and as to the affixing of a label, see PARA 229 note 5.

11   Ie for the purposes of the Agriculture and Horticulture Act 1964 s 13(2) (see PARA **233**). These
     provisions also apply for the purposes of any corresponding provision of an enactment of the
     Parliament of Northern Ireland for the time being in force: s 14(4)(b).
12   Ie under the Agriculture and Horticulture Act 1964 s 13(2) or any such corresponding provision
     (see PARA **233**).
13   Agriculture and Horticulture Act 1964 s 14(4)(c).
14   Where the commission by any person of an offence under the Agriculture and Horticulture Act
     1964 s 14(1) or (2) was due to an act or default of another person occurring in Great Britain, then,
     whether proceedings are taken against the first-mentioned person or not, that other person may
     be charged with and convicted of the offence, and is on conviction liable to the same punishment
     as that to which the first-mentioned person is, on conviction, liable: s 16.
15   Agriculture and Horticulture Act 1964 s 20(2). The fine must not exceed level 5 on the standard
     scale: s 20(2) (amended by virtue of the Criminal Justice Act 1982 ss 37, 39, 46). Until a day to
     be appointed a person who commits an offence under the Agriculture and Horticulture Act 1964
     s 14(2) is, in addition or as an alternative to the specified fine, liable to imprisonment for a term
     not exceeding three months (s 20(2) (as so amended)); as from that day, the option of
     imprisonment (either as an additional or alternative punishment) is removed (s 20(2) (as so
     amended; prospectively amended by the Criminal Justice Act 2003 s 332, Sch 37 Pt 9)). At the date
     at which this volume states the law no such day had been appointed. As to the standard scale and
     the powers of magistrates' courts to issue fines on summary conviction see SENTENCING vol 92
     (2015) PARA 176.
16   See PARA **232**.
17   Proceedings in England and Wales for an offence under any of the provisions of the Agriculture
     and Horticulture Act 1964 Pt III (ss 11–20) may be instituted only by or with the consent of the
     Secretary of State or the Welsh Ministers or with the consent of the Attorney General: see s 20(3)
     (amended by the Horticultural Produce Act 1986 s 7(2)). As to the Attorney General see
     CONSTITUTIONAL AND ADMINISTRATIVE LAW vol 20 (2014) PARA 273 et seq. As to the Secretary
     of State and the Welsh Ministers see PARA **390**.
18   See PARA **238**.

232.   Defences in proceedings for unlawful sale of regulated produce.

Where in proceedings for an offence involving the sale of any regulated produce[1] it would have been a defence for the person charged to prove that the produce in question conformed to a prescribed grade[2], it is a defence for him to prove:

(1)   that he bought or took delivery of the produce as being of a quality
       falling within that grade, and with a written warranty[3] to that effect[4];

(2)   that at the time of the commission of the offence he had no reason to
       believe the statement contained in the warranty to be inaccurate, that he
       then did believe in its accuracy, and that he had taken such steps, if any,
       as were reasonably practicable to check its accuracy[5]; and

(3)   that he took all reasonable steps to ensure that the quality of the
       produce was the same at the time of the commission of the offence as
       when it left the possession of the person by whom the warranty was
       given[6].

A person intending to set up the defence of warranty must give notice to the prosecutor and the person alleged to have given the warranty[7], and the latter is entitled to appear and give evidence[8]. It is an offence for an accused person wilfully to attribute a warranty to goods not in fact covered by it[9].

In proceedings for an offence in respect of the unlawful sale or marketing of regulated produce[10] it is also a defence for the person charged to prove that the commission of the offence was due to the act or default of some other person, or to a mistake, or to an accident or some other cause beyond his control[11] and that he took all reasonable precautions and exercised all due diligence to avoid the commission of the offence in respect of that produce by himself or any person under his control[12].

1   Ie an offence under the Agriculture and Horticulture Act 1964 s 14(1) or s 14(2): see PARA 231.For the statutory provisions governing the sale of regulated produce see the Agriculture and Horticulture Act 1964 s 12; and PARA 230. As to the meaning of 'regulated produce' see PARA 229.
2   As to the meaning of 'prescribed grade' see PARA 229 note 10.
3   A grade designation entered in an invoice relating to any product or indicated by a label affixed to the produce or its container is deemed to be a written warranty that the produce conforms to the grade indicated by that designation: Agriculture and Horticulture Act 1964 s 17(6). As to the meaning of 'label', and as to the affixing of a label, see PARA 229 note 5. As to the meaning of 'container' see PARA 229 note 5.
4   Agriculture and Horticulture Act 1964 s 17(1)(a). Where the proceedings are in respect of an offence committed by a person charged in the course of his employment, it is a defence for him to prove:
    (1)   that if his employer had been charged the employer would have had a defence under the Agriculture and Horticulture Act 1964 s 17(1) in respect of a warranty (s 17(2)(a)); and
    (2)   that at the time of the commission of the offence the person charged had no reason to believe the statement contained in the warranty to be inaccurate (s 17(2)(b)).
5   Agriculture and Horticulture Act 1964 s 17(1)(b). See note 4.
6   Agriculture and Horticulture Act 1964 s 17(1)(c).
7   Agriculture and Horticulture Act 1964 s 17(3). Not later than three days before the hearing the person charged must send to the prosecutor a copy of the warranty with a notice stating that he intends to rely on it and specifying the name and address of the person by whom it is alleged to have been given, and send to the last-mentioned person a notice giving the date and place of the hearing and stating that he intends to rely on the warranty: s 17(3).
8   Agriculture and Horticulture Act 1964 s 17(4).
9   Agriculture and Horticulture Act 1964 s 17(5). A person who commits such an offence is liable on summary conviction to a fine not exceeding level 5 on the standard scale: s 20(2) (amended by virtue of the Criminal Justice Act 1982 ss 37, 38, 46). Until a day to be appointed a person who commits an offence under the Agriculture and Horticulture Act 1964 s 17(5) is, in addition or as an alternative to the specified fine, liable to imprisonment for a term not exceeding three months (s 20(2)); as from that day, the option of imprisonment (either as an additional or alternative punishment) is removed (s 20(2) (as so amended; prospectively amended by the Criminal Justice Act 2003 s 332, Sch 37 Pt 9)). At the date at which this volume states the law no such day had been appointed. As to the standard scale and the powers of magistrates' courts to issue fines on summary conviction see SENTENCING vol 92 (2015) PARA 176.
10 Ie an offence under the Agriculture and Horticulture Act 1964 s 14(1) or s 14(2): see PARA 231.
11 Agriculture and Horticulture Act 1964 s 18(a).
12 Agriculture and Horticulture Act 1964 s 18(b).

233.   Authorised officers' powers of entry and regrading.

The Secretary of State and the Welsh Ministers[1] may authorise a person[2]:
(1)   to enter, at any reasonable time, any premises[3] which he has, or they have, reasonable cause to believe to be premises where regulated produce[4] is grown for sale, graded or packed, or on which regulated produce intended for sale otherwise than by retail is to be found[5]; and
(2)   to inspect and take samples of any regulated produce found on the premises and to seize and detain any label[6] (together with any container[7] to which the label is affixed) used in connection with such produce[8].

An authorised officer may exercise these powers only on producing, if required, documentary authority[9].

Where in the exercise of these powers an authorised officer finds on any premises any regulated produce which has affixed to it a label in the form prescribed for any prescribed grade[10], or which is in a container to which such a label is affixed, but which he has reasonable cause to believe to be of a quality inferior to the quality required for that grade, he may, in such manner as may be prescribed by regulations[11], cancel that label and affix to the produce or, as the case may be, the container a label, in such form as may be so prescribed, indicating what appears to him to be the correct grade or, where it appears to him that the quality of the produce is inferior to that required for the lowest prescribed grade, indicating that fact[12]. Where an authorised officer inspects any produce which he is entitled to inspect under these provisions he may prohibit its movement if he is satisfied that a grading offence[13] is being committed in respect of it[14].

Provision is made for punishing the obstruction of authorised officers[15].

1   As to the Secretary of State and the Welsh Ministers see PARA 390.
2   Such a person is known as an 'authorised officer': Agriculture and Horticulture Act 1964 s 13(1).
3   For these purposes 'premises' includes a stall or vehicle, although a person is not authorised to stop any vehicle on a highway: see the Agriculture and Horticulture Act 1964 s 13(7). There is no power to enter a building used only as a private dwelling house: Agriculture and Horticulture Act 1964 s 13(1)(a).
      As to the applicability of the Agriculture and Horticulture Act 1964 Pt III (ss 11–24) (see PARAS 229–232) to produce generally see PARA 229.
4   As to the meaning of 'regulated produce' see PARA 229.
5   Agriculture and Horticulture Act 1964 s 13(1)(a).
      An authorised officer entering any premises by virtue of s 13 may take with him such other persons and such equipment as may appear to him necessary (Agriculture and Horticulture Act 1964 s 13(4)), and on leaving any premises which he has entered by virtue of s 13, being premises which are unoccupied or the occupier of which is temporarily absent, must leave them as effectively secured against unauthorised entry as he found them (s 13(5)). If any authorised officer or other person who enters any work-place by virtue of these provisions discloses to any person any information obtained by him in the work-place with regard to any manufacturing process or trade secret, he is, unless the disclosure was made in the performance of his duty, guilty of an offence: s 13(6). As to offences see PARA 231.
      If a justice of the peace, on sworn information in writing, is satisfied:
      (1)   that an authorised officer has been refused admission to any premises which he has a right to enter under these provisions, or that such a refusal is apprehended, and that notice of the intention to apply for a warrant has been given to the occupier; or
      (2)   that an application for admission to the premises, or the giving of such a notice, would defeat the object of the entry, or that the premises are unoccupied or the occupier temporarily absent,
      he may by warrant under his hand, which continues in force for a period of one month, give authority to an authorised officer to enter the premises by force if need be: s 13(3).
6   As to the meaning of 'label', and as to the affixing of a label, see PARA 229 note 5.
7   As to the meaning of 'container' see PARA 229 note 4.
8   Agriculture and Horticulture Act 1964 s 13(1)(b).
9   Agriculture and Horticulture Act 1964 s 13(1).
10 As to the designation of grades and the prescription of forms of labels see PARA 229.
11 Ie regulations made by the Secretary of State or the Welsh Ministers. At the date at which this volume states the law no regulations had been made for this purpose.
12 Agriculture and Horticulture Act 1964 s 13(2). Unlawful affixing of such a label is an offence: see PARA 231.
13 Ie an offence under the Agriculture and Horticulture Act 1964 s 14(1) or s 14(2) (see PARA 231): Horticultural Produce Act 1986 s 6.
14 See the Horticultural Produce Act 1986 s 1(1); and PARA 234.
15 See PARA 237.

234. Prohibition of movement of produce.

An authorised officer[1] may prohibit the movement of any produce in respect of which, on inspection[2], he is satisfied that a grading offence[3] is being committed[4]. Where an officer exercises this power he must, without delay, give to the person who appears to be in charge of the produce written notice specifying the produce and prohibiting movement of it without the written consent of an authorised officer[5]. An authorised officer may attach labels to produce the movement of which has been so prohibited[6].

Provision is made for punishing the obstruction of authorised officers acting in pursuance of these powers[7].

1   For these purposes 'authorised officer' means a person who is an authorised officer for the purposes of the Agriculture and Horticulture Act 1964 Pt III (ss 11–24) (see PARAS 229–231): Horticultural Produce Act 1986 s 6. As to such officers and their powers of inspection and regrading see PARA 233.

2   Ie on inspecting any produce which he is entitled to inspect under the Agriculture and Horticulture Act 1964 s 13: see PARA 233.

3   As to the meaning of 'grading offence' see PARA 233 note 5.

4   Horticultural Produce Act 1986 s 1(1). As to the disapplication of this Act to horticultural produce and bananas see PARA 214 note 5.

5   Horticultural Produce Act 1986 s 1(2). As to the giving of written consent to the movement of controlled produce see PARA 235. If the person in charge does not appear to be the owner of the produce or his agent or employee, the officer must use his best endeavours to bring the contents of the notice to the owner's, agent's or employee's attention as soon as practicable: s 1(3).

6   Horticultural Produce Act 1986 s 1(4). It is an offence to remove or cause the removal of such a label: see s 4(2); and PARA 236.

7   See PARA 237.

235. Movement of controlled produce by consent.

An authorised officer[1] must, on request, give written consent[2] to the movement of controlled produce if:

(1)   he is satisfied that no grading offence[3] would be committed if the produce were sold in circumstances in which grading rules[4] apply[5];

(2)   he or another authorised officer has been given a written undertaking, and is satisfied, that the produce will be disposed of in a specified manner which will not constitute a grading offence[6]; or

(3)   he or another authorised officer has been given a written undertaking stating, and is satisfied, that the produce will be moved to an approved place[7], that the necessary steps will be taken there to ensure that the produce may be sold in circumstances governed by the grading rules without involving the commission of a grading offence, and that the produce will not be further moved without written consent[8].

The circumstances in which an authorised officer is required to give written consent to the movement of controlled produce may be changed by order of the Secretary of State or the Welsh Ministers[9].

An authorised officer may at any time give written consent, without being requested so to do, to the movement of controlled produce[10].

It is an offence to move controlled produce without an officer's consent[11].

1   As to the meaning of 'authorised officer' see PARA 234 note 1.

2   A consent given by an authorised officer must specify the produce to which it relates (Horticultural Produce Act 1986 s 2(4)(a)) and, if given under s 2(3) (see the text and notes 7–8), must state that the produce continues to be controlled (s 2(4)(b)). 'Controlled', in relation to produce, means that the power conferred by s 1(1) (see PARA 234) has been exercised in relation to it and that no consent to its movement has been given under s 2(1) or s 2(2) (see the text and notes 3–6): s 6.

3   As to the meaning of 'grading offence' see PARA 233 note 5.

4   Ie the rules enforced under the Agriculture and Horticulture Act 1964 Pt III (ss 11–24) (see PARAS 229–231): Horticultural Produce Act 1986 s 6.

5   Horticultural Produce Act 1986 s 2(1), (2)(a). As to the disapplication of this Act to horticultural produce and bananas see PARA 214 note 5.

6   Horticultural Produce Act 1986 s 2(2)(b). Consent may only be given if the officer is satisfied that the produce will be disposed of in the specified manner and that no grading offence will be

committed, and he has no reason to doubt that the terms of the undertaking will be met: s 2(2)(b). Failure to comply with an undertaking given under s 2 is an offence: see s 4(3); and PARA 236.
7   Ie a place approved by an authorised officer: Horticultural Produce Act 1986 s 2(3)(a)(i).
8   Horticultural Produce Act 1986 s 2(3). Failure to comply with an undertaking given under s 2 is an offence: see s 4(3); and PARA 236.
9   The Secretary of State and the Welsh Ministers may by order make such amendments of the Horticultural Produce Act 1986 as they think fit for the purpose of changing the circumstances in which an authorised officer is required to give written consent to the movement of produce: s 3(1), (4). Before making any such order, the Secretary of State or the Welsh Ministers must consult such organisations as appear to him or them to represent interests likely to be affected by the order but this does not apply to an order which makes amendments that apply only in relation to England: s 3(2), (2A) (s 3(2A) added by the Deregulation Act 2015 Sch 22 para 8). At the date at which this volume states the law no such order had been made. As to the Secretary of State and the Welsh Ministers see PARA 390.
10   Horticultural Produce Act 1986 s 2(1).
11   See the Horticultural Produce Act 1986 s 4(1); and PARA 236.

236.   Offences in connection with the movement of controlled produce.

Any person who fails to comply with an undertaking given by him for the purpose of obtaining a consent to the movement of controlled[1] produce[2] is guilty of an offence[3], although it is a defence for a person charged with this offence to prove that he took all reasonable precautions and exercised all due diligence to avoid the commission of such an offence[4].

It is an offence for any person who knows produce to be controlled:
(1)   knowingly to move the produce, or cause it to be moved, without the written consent of an authorised officer[5]; and
(2)   knowingly to remove or cause to be removed from such produce a label warning that the power to prohibit the movement of the produce[6] has been exercised[7],
although it is a defence for a person charged with this offence to prove that there was a reasonable excuse for the act or omission in respect of which he is charged[8].

It is a defence for a person charged with any of these offences to prove that, when the power to prohibit the movement of the produce was exercised, no grading offence[9] was being committed in respect of the produce concerned[10].

A person found guilty of any of these offences is liable on summary conviction to a fine[11].

Provision is made as to the bringing of proceedings[12] and the commission of offences by corporations[13].

1   As to the meaning of 'controlled' see PARA 235 note 2.
2   Ie a consent under the Horticultural Produce Act 1986 s 2: see PARA 235.
3   Horticultural Produce Act 1986 s 4(3). As to the disapplication of this Act to horticultural produce and bananas see PARA 214 note 5.
4   Horticultural Produce Act 1986 s 4(4)(c).
5   Horticultural Produce Act 1986 s 4(1). As to the meaning of 'authorised officer' see PARA 234 note 1. As to the giving of consent by authorised officers to the movement of controlled produce see PARA 235.
6   Ie the power under the Horticultural Produce Act 1986 s 1: see PARA 234.
7   Horticultural Produce Act 1986 s 4(2).
8   Horticultural Produce Act 1986 s 4(4)(b).
9   As to the meaning of 'grading offence' see PARA 233 note 5.
10   Horticultural Produce Act 1986 s 4(4)(a).
11   Horticultural Produce Act 1986 s 4(5). The fine may not exceed level 5 on the standard scale: s 4(5). As to the standard scale and the powers of magistrates' courts to issue fines on summary conviction see SENTENCING vol 92 (2015) PARA 176.
12   Proceedings in England and Wales for offences under the Horticultural Produce Act 1986 may be instituted only by or with the consent of the Secretary of State or the Welsh Ministers or with the

consent of the Attorney General: see the Agriculture and Horticulture Act 1964 s 20(3) (amended by the Horticultural Produce Act 1986 s 7(2)); the Horticultural Produce Act 1986 s 5(c). As to the Attorney General see CONSTITUTIONAL AND ADMINISTRATIVE LAW vol 20 (2014) PARA 273 et seq. As to the Secretary of State and the Welsh Ministers see PARA 390.

13   See PARA 238.

237.   Obstruction of authorised officers.

A person is guilty of an offence if:

(1)   he wilfully obstructs an authorised officer[1] acting in the execution of his powers of inspection and grading[2] or his powers in connection with the control of the movement of regulated produce[3];

(2)   he fails, without reasonable cause, to give to any authorised officer so acting any assistance or information which the officer may reasonably require of him for the purposes of the performance by the officer of his functions in connection with inspection and grading[4] or the movement of regulated produce[5];

(3)   in giving to an authorised officer any such information as is referred to above, he gives any information which he knows to be false[6]; or

(4)   he fails to make any request for inspection or give any notice or information required by Community grading rules[7].

A person guilty of an offence under any of these provisions is liable on summary conviction to a fine[8].

Provision is made as to the bringing of proceedings[9] and the commission of offences by corporations[10].

1   As to the meaning of 'authorised officer' see PARAS 233 note 2, 234 note 1. For the powers of officers see generally PARA 233 et seq.
2   Ie under the Agriculture and Horticulture Act 1964 Pt III (ss 11–24) (see PARAS 229–231).
3   Ie under the Horticultural Produce Act 1986: see PARAS 234–236: Agriculture and Horticulture Act 1964 s 15(1)(a); Horticultural Produce Act 1986 s 5(a). As to the applicability of the Agriculture and Horticulture Act 1964 Pt III to produce generally see PARA 229.
4   Ie under the Agriculture and Horticulture Act 1964 Pt III.
5   Ie under the Horticultural Produce Act 1986: Agriculture and Horticulture Act 1964 s 15(1)(b). This provision is not to be construed as requiring anyone to answer any question or give any information if to do so might incriminate him: Agriculture and Horticulture Act 1964 s 15(3). It is thought that the word 'incriminate' is to be understood in the same sense as in the common law doctrine of privilege against self-incrimination (as to which see CIVIL PROCEDURE vol 12 (2015) PARAS 646, 801).
6   Agriculture and Horticulture Act 1964 s 15(2).
7   Agriculture and Horticulture Act 1964 s 15(1)(c).
8   Agriculture and Horticulture Act 1964 s 20(1), (2). The fine for an offence under any of heads (1), (2), (4) in the text must not exceed level 3 on the standard scale: s 20(1) (s 20(1), (2) amended by virtue of the Criminal Justice Act 1982 ss 37, 39, 46). The fine for the offence under head (3) in the text must not exceed level 5 on the standard scale: Agriculture and Horticulture Act 1964 s 20(2) (as so amended). Until a day to be appointed a person who commits the offence under head (3) is, in addition or as an alternative to the specified fine, liable to imprisonment for a term not exceeding three months (s 20(2) (as so amended)); as from that day, the option of imprisonment (either as an additional or alternative punishment) is removed (s 20(2) (as so amended; prospectively amended by the Criminal Justice Act 2003 s 332, Sch 37 Pt 9)). At the date at which this volume states the law no such day had been appointed. As to the standard scale and the powers of magistrates' courts to issue fines on summary conviction see SENTENCING vol 92 (2015) PARA 176.
9   Proceedings in England or Wales for an offence under the Agriculture and Horticulture Act 1964 s 15 and the Horticultural Produce Act 1986 s 5(a) may be instituted only by or with the consent of the Secretary of State or the Welsh Ministers or with the consent of the Attorney General: Agriculture and Horticulture Act 1964 s 20(3) (amended by the Horticultural Produce Act 1986

s 7(2)); Horticultural Produce Act 1986 s 5(c). As to the Attorney General see CONSTITUTIONAL
AND ADMINISTRATIVE LAW vol 20 (2014) PARA 273 et seq. As to the Secretary of State and the
Welsh Ministers see PARA 390.
10 See PARA 238.

238. Offences by corporations.
Where an offence under any of the statutory provisions governing the grading
and sale of regulated produce[1] or the movement of such produce[2] which has been
committed by a body corporate is proved to have been committed with the
consent or connivance of, or to be attributable to any neglect on the part of, any
director[3], manager, secretary or other similar officer of the body corporate, or any
person who was purporting to act in any such capacity, he as well as the body
corporate is deemed to be guilty of that offence and is liable to be proceeded
against and punished accordingly[4].

1   Ie the Agriculture and Horticulture Act 1964 Pt III (ss 11–24): see PARAS 229–231.
2   Ie the Horticultural Produce Act 1986: see PARAS 234–236.
3   For these purposes 'director', in relation to any board established under the Agricultural
    Marketing Act 1958 (see PARA 171 et seq) or any body corporate established by or under any
    enactment for the purpose of carrying on under national ownership any industry or part of an
    industry or undertaking, being a body corporate whose affairs are managed by the members
    thereof, means a member of that board or body corporate: Agriculture and Horticulture Act 1964
    s 19(2); Horticultural Produce Act 1986 s 5(b).
4   Agriculture and Horticulture Act 1964 s 19(1) (amended by the Horticultural Produce Act 1986
    s 7(2)).

(4) PLANT BREEDERS' RIGHTS AND BIOTECHNOLOGICAL
INVENTIONS

(i) Plant Breeders' Rights

A. NATURE AND SCOPE

239. Rights under statute.
Plant breeders' rights may subsist in varieties[1] of all plant genera and species[2],
and are granted under statute[3]. The holder of rights[4] is entitled to prevent any
person without the holder's authority[5] from doing any of these acts as regards the
propagating material of the protected variety[6]:
(1)   production or reproduction (multiplication)[7];
(2)   conditioning for the purpose of propagation[8];
(3)   offering for sale[9];
(4)   selling or other marketing[10];
(5)   exporting[11];
(6)   importing[12];
(7)   stocking for any of these purposes[13]; and
(8)   any other act prescribed[14] for these purposes[15].
Rights also apply as respects harvested material[16] obtained through the
unauthorised use of propagating material of the protected variety[17], any product
of a prescribed description which is made directly from such harvested material[18],
and any variety which is dependent[19] on the protected variety[20] (unless the
existence of the dependent variety was common knowledge[21] immediately before

8 May 1998[22]). They do not, however, apply for the purposes of certain non-commercial activities, for breeding purposes, or in relation to farm saved seed[23].

Plant breeders' rights are assignable like other kinds of proprietary rights, but rights over protected varieties[24] and rights over dependent varieties[25] may not be assigned separately[26].

1 'Variety' means a plant grouping within a single botanical taxon of the lowest known rank, which grouping, irrespective of whether the conditions for the grant of plant breeders' rights (see PARA 243 et seq) are met, can be:
   (1)   defined by the expression of the characteristics resulting from a given genotype or combination of genotypes;
   (2)   distinguished from any other plant grouping by the expression of at least one of those characteristics; and
   (3)   considered as a unit with regard to its suitability for being propagated unchanged: Plant Varieties Act 1997 ss 1(3), 38(1).
2 Plant Varieties Act 1997 s 1(2).
3 Plant Varieties Act 1997 s 1(1). The statute under which plant breeders' rights are granted is the Plant Varieties Act 1997. The Act enables the implementation in the United Kingdom of the International Convention for the Protection of New Varieties of Plants (Paris, 2 December 1961; Cmnd 9152), replacing the former provision made in this regard (ie the Plant Varieties and Seeds Act 1964 Pt I (ss 1–15) (repealed)) following the adoption of Council Regulation (EC) 2100/94 (OJ L227, 01.09.99, p 1) on Community plant variety rights, the provisions of which are closely followed by the Plant Varieties Act 1997. As to the meaning of 'United Kingdom' see PARA 1 note 1.
4 References to the holder of plant breeders' rights include, where the context allows, references to his predecessors in title or his successors in title: Plant Varieties Act 1997 s 38(2).
5 The holder of plant breeders' rights may give authority for these purposes with or without conditions or limitations: Plant Varieties Act 1997 s 6(2).
6 'Protected variety' means the variety which was the basis of the application for the grant of the rights: Plant Varieties Act 1997 s 38(1). As to applications for grants of rights see PARA 243 et seq.
7 Plant Varieties Act 1997 s 6(1)(a).
8 Plant Varieties Act 1997 s 6(1)(b).
9 Plant Varieties Act 1997 s 6(1)(c).
10 Plant Varieties Act 1997 s 6(1)(d).
11 Plant Varieties Act 1997 s 6(1)(e).
12 Plant Varieties Act 1997 s 6(1)(f).
13 Plant Varieties Act 1997 s 6(1)(g).
14 Ie prescribed by regulations made by the ministers (in general, the Secretary of State and the Welsh Ministers: see PARA 390) acting jointly: Plant Varieties Act 1997 s 6(6)(a).
15 Plant Varieties Act 1997 s 6(1)(h). At the date at which this volume states the law no additional act had been prescribed.
16 For these purposes references to harvested material include entire plants and parts of plants: Plant Varieties Act 1997 s 6(6)(b).
17 Plant Varieties Act 1997 s 6(3). The rights holder cannot, however, exercise his rights in respect of the harvested material if he has had a reasonable opportunity before the harvested material is obtained to exercise his rights in relation to the unauthorised use of the propagating material: s 6(3).
18 Plant Varieties Act 1997 s 6(4). At the date at which this volume states the law no description of a product had been prescribed for these purposes. The rights holder cannot, however, exercise his rights in respect of such product if, before the product was made, any act mentioned in s 6(1) (see the text and notes 5–15) was done as respects the harvested material from which the product was made and the rights holder either authorised the act or had a reasonable opportunity to exercise his rights in relation to the doing of the act: s 6(4), (5).
19 For these purposes one variety is 'dependent' on another if either its nature is such that repeated production of the variety is not possible without repeated use of the other variety or it is essentially derived from the other variety and the other variety is not itself essentially derived from a third variety: Plant Varieties Act 1997 s 7(2).
    A variety is deemed to be essentially derived from another variety if: (1) it is predominantly derived from the initial variety, or a variety that is itself predominantly derived from the initial variety, while retaining the expression of the essential characteristics resulting from the genotype

or combination of genotypes of the initial variety (s 7(3)(a)); (2) it is clearly distinguishable from the initial variety by one or more characteristics which are capable of a precise description (s 7(3)(b)); and (3) except for the differences which result from the act of derivation (eg by the selection of a natural or induced mutant, a somaclonal variant, or a variant individual from plants of the initial variety, by backcrossing, or by transformation by genetic engineering: s 7(4)) it conforms to the initial variety in the expression of the essential characteristics that result from the genotype or combination of genotypes of the initial variety (s 7(3)(c)).

20   Plant Varieties Act 1997 s 7(1).
21   The existence of a variety is taken to be a matter of common knowledge if it is, or has been, the subject of a plant variety right under any jurisdiction, or it is, or has been, entered in an official register of plant varieties under any jurisdiction, or it is the subject of an application which subsequently leads to its falling within either of these categories: Plant Varieties Act 1997 s 38(3). Otherwise, common knowledge may be established for these purposes by reference, for example, to plant varieties already in cultivation or exploited for commercial purposes, plant varieties included in a recognised commercial or botanical reference collection, or plant varieties of which there are precise descriptions in any publication: s 38(4).
22   Plant Varieties Act 1997 s 7(5). 8 May 1998 is the date on which the Plant Varieties Act 1997 was brought into force: see the Plant Varieties Act 1997 (Commencement) Order 1998, SI 1998/1028.
23   See PARAS 240–241.
24   Ie rights under the Plant Varieties Act 1997 s 6 (see the text and notes 5–18).
25   Ie rights under the Plant Varieties Act 1997 s 7 (see the text and notes 19–22).
26   Plant Varieties Act 1997 s 12.

240.   General exemptions.

Plant breeders' rights[1] do not extend to any act done for private and non-commercial purposes[2], for experimental purposes[3], or for the purpose of breeding another variety[4]. Rights also do not apply to any act concerning material[5] of a variety if the material has been sold or otherwise marketed in the United Kingdom by, or with the consent of, the holder of the rights[6], or is derived from material which has been so sold or otherwise marketed[7], although this exemption will not apply where the act involves either further propagation of the variety[8] or the export of material which enables propagation of the variety to a non-qualifying country[9] otherwise than for the purposes of final consumption[10].

1   As to the nature and scope of plant breeders' rights see PARA 239.
2   Plant Varieties Act 1997 s 8(a).
3   Plant Varieties Act 1997 s 8(b).
4   Plant Varieties Act 1997 s 8(c). As to the meaning of 'variety' see PARA 239 note 1.
5   For these purposes 'material', in relation to a variety, means any kind of propagating material of the variety and harvested material (including any product made directly from such material) of the variety, including entire plants and parts of plants: Plant Varieties Act 1997 s 10(4).
6   Plant Varieties Act 1997 s 10(1)(a). As to the meaning of 'United Kingdom' see PARA 1 note 1.
7   Plant Varieties Act 1997 s 10(1)(b).
8   Plant Varieties Act 1997 s 10(2)(a).
9   A non-qualifying country is one which does not provide for the protection of varieties of the genus or species to which the variety belongs: Plant Varieties Act 1997 s 10(3).
10 Plant Varieties Act 1997 s 10(2)(b).

241.   Exemption for farm saved seed.

Plant breeders' rights[1] do not extend to the use by farmers of specified varieties[2] of material[3] for propagating purposes[4]. A farmer can benefit from this exemption only where he uses on his own holding[5] material which is the product of the harvest which he has obtained by planting on his own holding propagating material of either the protected variety[6] or a variety which is essentially derived from the protected variety[7]. If a farmer's use of material is excepted from plant breeders' rights by these provisions he is nevertheless required, unless he is a small farmer[8], to pay equitable remuneration[9], at the time of the use, to the rights holder[10].

Regulations make provision as to the information to be supplied for the purposes of this exemption and for restricting the movement of farm saved seed[11].

1   As to the nature and scope of plant breeders' rights see PARA 239.
2   As to the meaning of 'variety' see PARA 239 note 1.
3   The varieties in relation to which this exemption applies are set out in the Plant Breeders' Rights (Farm Saved Seed) (Specification of Species and Groups) Order 1998, SI 1998/1025.
4   Plant Varieties Act 1997 s 9(1), (2). The Secretary of State and the Welsh Ministers may by order amend s 9 as they think fit for the purpose of securing that it corresponds with the provisions for the time being of the law relating to Community plant variety rights (ie Council Regulation (EC) 2100/94 (OJ L227, 01.09.99, p 1) on Community plant variety rights (see PARA 239 note 3)) about farm saved seed: Plant Varieties Act 1997 s 9(12). At the date at which this volume states the law no such order had been made. As to the Secretary of State and the Welsh Ministers see PARA 390.
5   References to a farmer's own holding are to any land which he actually exploits for plant growing, whether as his property or otherwise managed under his own responsibility and on his own account: Plant Varieties Act 1997 s 9(11).
6   Plant Varieties Act 1997 s 9(1)(a). As to the meaning of 'protected variety' see PARA 239 note 6.
7   Plant Varieties Act 1997 s 9(1)(b). As to when a variety is deemed to be essentially derived from another variety see PARA 239 note 19; definition applied by s 9(9).
8   Plant Varieties Act 1997 s 9(4). For these purposes a 'small farmer' is a farmer who is considered to be a small farmer for the purposes of Council Regulation (EC) 2100/94 (OJ L227, 01.09.99, p 1) art 14(3): Plant Varieties Act 1997 s 9(4). See Case C-56/11 *Raiffeisen-Waren-Zentrale Rhein-Main eG v Saatgut-Treuhandverwaltungs GmbH* [2012] All ER (D) 336 (Nov), ECJ.
9   The remuneration payable must be sensibly lower (within the meaning of Council Regulation (EC) 2100/94 (OJ L227, 01.09.99, p 1) art 14(3)) than the amount charged for the production of propagating material of the same variety in the same area with the holder's authority: Plant Varieties Act 1997 s 9(3), (10). For the power of the rights holder to authorise the use of material see PARA 239.
10 Plant Varieties Act 1997 s 9(3).
11 The Secretary of State and the Welsh Ministers may by regulations:
    (1)   make provision, including provision imposing obligations of confidentiality, enabling holders of plant breeders' rights to require farmers or seed processors, and farmers or seed processors to require holders of plant breeders' rights, to supply such information as may be specified, being information the supply of which the ministers consider necessary for these purposes (Plant Varieties Act 1997 s 9(7)(a), (8))
    (2)   make provision restricting the circumstances in which the product of a harvest of a variety which is subject to plant breeders' rights may be moved, for the purpose of being processed for planting, from the holding on which it was obtained (s 9(7)(b)); and
    (3)   make provision for the purpose of enabling the ministers to monitor the operation of s 9 or regulations thereunder (s 9(7)(c)).
    The Plant Breeders' Rights (Farm Saved Seed) (Specified Information) Regulations 1998, SI 1998/1026, have been made in pursuance of this power. These regulations make provision as to the information to be supplied by farmers, seed processors and holders of plant breeders' rights (regs 3–6, 8–10) and prohibit the movement of farm saved seed from the holding on which it was obtained without the rights holder's permission (reg 7).

242.   Restrictive trade agreements and plant breeders' rights.

The grant of an exclusive licence of plant breeders' rights[1] is not in itself incompatible with the provisions of the Treaty on the Functioning of the European Union (the 'TFEU') prohibiting agreements between undertakings which have the effect of preventing, restricting or distorting competition[2] where such exclusivity promotes the dissemination of a new technology and competition in the Community between the new product and similar existing products[3], although an exclusive licence or assignment with absolute territorial protection results in the artificial maintenance of separate national markets and is therefore contrary to the Treaty[4]. A clause prohibiting a licensee for the propagation of basic seeds from selling, transferring or exporting them does not come within the prohibition to the extent that such clause enables a breeder to reserve propagation for the propagation establishments chosen by him[5].

1   As to the nature and scope of plant breeders' rights see PARA 239.
2   The Treaty on the Functioning of the European Union (Rome, 25 March 1957; TS 1 (1973); Cmnd 5179) art 105. The TFEU was formerly known as the Treaty Establishing the European Community (often abbreviated to TEC and also known as the 'EC Treaty' or the Treaty of Rome) and was renamed by the Treaty of Lisbon Amending the Treaty Establishing the European Union and the Treaty Establishing the European Community (Lisbon, 13 December 2007, ECS 13 (2007); Cm 7294) (often referred to as the 'Lisbon Treaty'), which came into force on 1 December 2009: see EUROPEAN UNION vol 47A (2014) PARA 6.
3   See Case 258/78 *LC Nungesser KG and Kurt Eisele v EC Commission* [1982] ECR 2015, [1983] 1 CMLR 278, ECJ.
4   Case 258/78 *LC Nungesser KG and Kurt Eisele v EC Commission* [1982] ECR 2015, [1983] 1 CMLR 278, ECJ.
5   Case 27/87 *Louis Erauw-Jacquery Sprl v La Hesbignonne Société Co-opérative* [1988] ECR 1919, [1988] 4 CMLR 576, ECJ.

B. APPLICATION AND GRANT

243.   Grant of rights by Controller of Plant Variety Rights.
Plant breeders' rights[1] are granted by the Controller of Plant Variety Rights[2], to whom applications for the granting of rights should be made[3]. The person entitled to the grant of plant breeders' rights in respect of a variety[4] is the person who breeds it, or discovers[5] and develops it, or his successor in title[6], although if a person breeds a variety, or discovers and develops it, in the course of his employment, then, subject to agreement to the contrary, his employer, or his employer's successor in title, is the person entitled to the grant of plant breeders' rights in respect of it[7].

The Controller must grant plant breeders' rights in respect of a variety where he is satisfied that the variety to which the application relates is distinct[8], uniform[9], stable[10], and new[11] (that is, a 'qualifying variety'[12]) and that the person by whom the application is made is the person entitled to the grant of plant breeders' rights in respect of the variety to which it relates[13].

The Controller's decision as to whether to allow or refuse an application for the grant of plant breeders' rights, and any decision preliminary to the determination as to the conditions which must be satisfied in connection with such an application[14], are subject to appeal to the Plant Varieties and Seeds Tribunal[15] and accordingly may not be made until the opportunity to make representations on the matter has been afforded to interested parties[16]. The giving of false information in connection with an application for the grant of plant breeders' rights is an offence[17].

1   As to the nature and scope of plant breeders' rights see PARA 239.
2   Plant Varieties Act 1997 s 3(1). The Controller of Plant Variety Rights grants rights through the Plant Variety Rights Office constituted in accordance with s 2, Sch 1 (see PARAS 281–284). As to the Controller's powers with respect to dealing with applications see PARA 282.
3   Every application made under the relevant legislation must be made in writing, signed by the applicant and delivered to the Controller: Plant Breeders' Rights Regulations 1998, SI 1998/1027, reg 3. Provision is made for the avoidance of repeated applications: see reg 4. Applications, and proposed decisions as to whether they are to be allowed or refused, must be notified in the gazette by the Controller, and specified persons may make representations in connection with them (regs 5–8, Sch 1 Pt A, Pt B(2)); and withdrawals of applications must be similarly notified (reg 5, Sch 1 Pt C(1)). 'Gazette' means the gazette published under the Plant Varieties and Seeds Act 1964 s 34 (see PARA 17): Plant Varieties Act 1997 s 38(1). As to regulations governing the Controller's functions see PARA 282. The Controller may by notice require an applicant for the grant of plant breeders' rights to provide him, within such time as may be specified in the notice, with such

information, documents, plant or other material, facilities or test or trial results relevant to the carrying out of his function under the Plant Varieties Act 1997 s 3(1) (see the text and notes 1–2) as may be so specified (s 3(2)); and failure to comply with any such notice above within the period specified in the notice is a ground for refusing the application (s 3(3)).

If an application for plant breeders' rights is granted, the rights holder is entitled to reasonable compensation for anything done during the application period (ie the period beginning with the day on which details of the application for the grant of the rights are published in the gazette and ending with the grant of the rights) which, if done after the grant of the rights, would constitute an infringement of them: s 5.

4   As to the meaning of 'variety' see PARA 239 note 1.
5   For the purposes of the Plant Varieties Act 1997 s 4, Sch 2 (see PARAS 244–249), references to the discovery of a variety are to the discovery of a variety, whether growing in the wild or occurring as a genetic variant, whether artificially induced or not: s 4(6).
6   Plant Varieties Act 1997 s 4(3). Where two or more persons independently breed, discover or develop a variety, rights are granted to the first of those persons to apply for them: see s 4(5), Sch 2 para 5; and PARA 248. References to an applicant for the grant of plant breeders' rights include, where the context allows, references to his predecessors in title or his successors in title: s 38(2).
7   Plant Varieties Act 1997 s 4(4).
8   See the Plant Varieties Act 1997 s 3(1), 4(2)(a); and PARA 244.
9   See the Plant Varieties Act 1997 s 4(2)(b); and PARA 245.
10 See the Plant Varieties Act 1997 s 4(2)(c); and PARA 246.
11 See the Plant Varieties Act 1997 s 4(2)(d); and PARA 247.
12 See the Plant Varieties Act 1997 s 4(1)(a).
13 Plant Varieties Act 1997 s 4(1)(b). Proposed decisions preliminary to the determination of an application for the grant of plant breeders' rights as to the conditions laid down in s 4 (see the text and notes 8–12; and PARAS 244–247) must be notified in the gazette, and specified persons may make representations: see the Plant Breeders' Rights Regulations 1998, SI 1998/1027, regs 5, 7, 8, Sch 1 Pt B(1).
    Rights may be declared null and void if it is established that the protected variety is neither distinct, uniform, stable nor new or that the person to whom the rights were granted was not the person entitled to those rights (see PARA 251), and may be terminated if the Controller is satisfied that the protected variety has ceased to be uniform or stable (see PARA 252).
14 Ie the conditions laid down in the Plant Varieties Act 1997 s 4 (see the text and notes 4–13; and PARAS 244–247).
15 Plant Varieties Act 1997 s 26(1)(a), (b). As to the tribunal and appeals thereto see PARA 285 et seq.
16 See the Plant Varieties Act 1997 s 24; and PARA 282. As to the making of representations for these purposes see notes 3, 13.
17 Plant Varieties Act 1997 s 31(1). The offence is punishable on summary conviction by a fine not exceeding level 3 on the standard scale, and is committed by any person (whether the applicant or a person giving information on his behalf) who, in connection with the application, either knowingly or recklessly gives information which is false in a material particular: s 31(1), (2)(a), (b). As to the standard scale and the powers of magistrates' courts to issue fines on summary conviction see SENTENCING vol 92 (2015) PARA 176.
    Without prejudice to any jurisdiction otherwise exercisable, proceedings for an offence under Pt I (ss 1–41) may be taken against a person before the appropriate court in the United Kingdom having jurisdiction in the place where that person is for the time being: s 37. As to the meaning of 'United Kingdom' see PARA 1 note 1.
    Where an offence under Pt I committed by a body corporate is proved to have been committed with the consent or connivance of, or to be attributable to any neglect on the part of, any director, manager, secretary or other similar officer of the body corporate, or any person who was purporting to act in any such capacity, he, as well as the body corporate, is guilty of the offence and liable to be proceeded against and punished accordingly: s 36(1).

244.   Requirement of distinctiveness.

The Controller of Plant Variety Rights[1] may not grant plant breeders' rights[2] in respect of a variety[3] unless he is satisfied that the variety to which the application relates is, amongst other characteristics[4], distinct[5]. A variety is distinct for these purposes if it is clearly distinguishable by one or more characteristics which are capable of a precise description from any other variety whose existence is a matter of common knowledge[6] at the time of the application[7].

Any decision of the Controller as to these conditions is subject to appeal to the Plant Varieties and Seeds Tribunal[8].

1   As to the Controller of Plant Variety Rights see PARAS 243 note 2, 281–284.
2   For the power of the Controller to grant plant breeders' rights see PARA 243. As to the nature and scope of such rights see PARAS 239–242.
3   As to the meaning of 'variety' see PARA 239 note 1.
4   The variety is also required to be uniform, stable and new: see the Plant Varieties Act 1997 ss 3(1), 4(1)(a), (2)(b)–(d); and PARAS 245–247.
5   See the Plant Varieties Act 1997 ss 3(1), 4(1)(a), (2)(a); and PARA 243.
6   As to when something is a matter of common knowledge see PARA 239 note 21.
7   Plant Varieties Act 1997 Sch 2 para 1. Where an application for plant breeders' rights under Pt I (ss 1–41) is made in respect of a variety for which the applicant has made an earlier rights application under EU law, the law of an international organisation, or the law of a foreign country or state, the application under Pt I may under certain circumstances be deemed to have been made on the date of such earlier application: see Sch 2 para 6; and PARA 249.
8   Plant Varieties Act 1997 s 26(1)(b). As to the tribunal and appeals thereto see PARA 285 et seq.

245. Requirement of uniformity.

The Controller of Plant Variety Rights[1] may not grant plant breeders' rights[2] in respect of a variety[3] unless he is satisfied that the variety to which the application relates is, amongst other characteristics[4], uniform[5]. A variety is uniform for these purposes if, subject to the variation that may be expected from the particular features of its propagation, it is sufficiently uniform in those characteristics which are included in the examination for distinctness[6].

Any decision of the Controller as to these conditions is subject to appeal to the Plant Varieties and Seeds Tribunal[7].

1   As to the Controller of Plant Variety Rights see PARAS 243 note 2, 281–284.
2   For the power of the Controller to grant plant breeders' rights see PARA 243. As to the nature and scope of such rights see PARAS 239–242.
3   As to the meaning of 'variety' see PARA 239 note 1.
4   The variety is also required to be distinct, stable and new: see the Plant Varieties Act 1997 ss 3(1), 4(1)(a), (2)(a), (c), (d); and PARAS 244, 246–247.
5   See the Plant Varieties Act 1997 ss 3(1), 4(1)(a), (2)(b); and PARA 243.
6   Plant Varieties Act 1997 Sch 2 para 2. As to the examination for distinctness see PARA 244. A variety is 'sufficiently uniform' if it is as uniform as a capable breeder skilled in the art can reasonably be expected to achieve: *Zephyr Spring Barley* [1967] FSR 576; *Moulin Winter Wheat* [1985] FSR 283 (decided under the corresponding provisions of the Plant Varieties and Seeds Act 1964 Sch 2 Pt II para 4 (repealed)).
7   Plant Varieties Act 1997 s 26(1)(b). As to the tribunal and appeals thereto see PARA 285 et seq.

246. Requirement of stability.

The Controller of Plant Variety Rights[1] may not grant plant breeders' rights[2] in respect of a variety[3] unless he is satisfied that the variety to which the application relates is, amongst other characteristics[4], stable[5]. A variety is stable if those characteristics which are included in the examination for distinctness[6], as well as any others used for the variety description, remain unchanged after repeated propagation or, in the case of a particular cycle of propagation, at the end of each such cycle[7].

Any decision of the Controller as to these conditions is subject to appeal to the Plant Varieties and Seeds Tribunal[8].

1   As to the Controller of Plant Variety Rights see PARAS 243 note 2, 281–284.

2   For the power of the Controller to grant plant breeders' rights see PARA 243. As to the nature and
     scope of such rights see PARAS 239–242.
3   As to the meaning of 'variety' see PARA 239 note 1.
4   The variety is also required to be distinct, uniform and new: see the Plant Varieties Act 1997
     ss 3(1), 4(1)(a), (2)(a), (b), (d); and PARAS 244–245, 1183.
5   See the Plant Varieties Act 1997 ss 3(1), 4(1)(a), (2)(c); and PARA 243.
6   As to the examination for distinctness see PARA 244.
7   Plant Varieties Act 1997 Sch 2 para 3.
8   Plant Varieties Act 1997 s 26(1)(b). As to the tribunal and appeals thereto see PARA 285 et seq.

247.   Requirement of novelty.

The Controller of Plant Variety Rights[1] may not grant plant breeders' rights[2] in respect of a variety[3] unless he is satisfied that the variety to which the application relates is, amongst other characteristics[4], new[5]. A variety is new if no sale or other disposal of propagating or harvested material of the variety for the purposes of exploiting the variety[6] has, with the consent of the applicant, taken place:

(1)   in the United Kingdom, earlier than one year before the date of the application[7]; and

(2)   elsewhere than in the United Kingdom, earlier than four years, or, in the case of trees or vines, six years, before the date of the application[8].

For these purposes there is disregarded:

(a)   any sale or other disposal of a stock of material of the variety to a person who at the time of the sale or other disposal is, or who subsequently becomes, the person entitled to the grant of plant breeders' rights in respect of the variety[9];

(b)   any sale or other disposal of propagating material of the variety to a person as part of arrangements concerned with testing or developing the applicant's stock[10];

(c)   any sale or other disposal to the applicant, by a person who uses propagating material of the variety under any such arrangements[11], of the material produced directly or indirectly from the use[12];

(d)   any sale or other disposal of material of the variety, other than propagating material, produced in the course of breeding, increasing the applicant's stock, or carrying out tests or trials, of the variety which does not involve identifying the variety from which the material is produced[13]; and

(e)   any disposal of material of the variety, otherwise than by way of sale, at an exhibition or for the purposes of display at an exhibition[14].

Any decision of the Controller as to these conditions is subject to appeal to the Plant Varieties and Seeds Tribunal[15].

1   As to the Controller of Plant Variety Rights see PARAS 243 note 2, 281–284.
2   For the power of the Controller to grant plant breeders' rights see PARA 243. As to the nature and
     scope of such rights see PARAS 239–242.
3   As to the meaning of 'variety' see PARA 239 note 1.
4   The variety is also required to be distinct, uniform and stable: see the Plant Varieties Act 1997
     ss 3(1), 4(1)(a), (2)(a)–(c); and PARAS 244–246.
5   See the Plant Varieties Act 1997 ss 3(1), 4(1)(a), (2)(d); and PARA 243.
6   For these purposes any sale or other disposal of propagating or harvested material of a variety for
     the purposes of exploiting the variety is, if the variety is related to another variety, treated as being
     also a sale or other disposal of propagating or harvested material of the other variety for the
     purposes of exploiting that variety: Plant Varieties Act 1997 Sch 2 para 4(10). For these purposes
     a variety is related to another if its nature is such that repeated production of the variety is not
     possible without repeated use of the other variety: Sch 2 para 4(11).

7   Plant Varieties Act 1997 Sch 2 para 4(1), (2). As to the meaning of 'United Kingdom' see PARA
    1 note 1. Where an application for plant breeders' rights under Pt I (ss 1–41) is made in respect
    of a variety for which the applicant has made an earlier rights application under EU law, the law
    of an international organisation, or the law of a foreign country or state, the application under Pt
    I may under certain circumstances be deemed to have been made on the date of such earlier
    application: see Sch 2 para 6; and PARA 249.
8   Plant Varieties Act 1997 Sch 2 para 4(1), (3).
9   Plant Varieties Act 1997 Sch 2 para 4(4), (5).
10 Plant Varieties Act 1997 Sch 2 para 4(6)(a). The reference in the text to arrangements concerned
    with testing or developing the applicant's stock is a reference to arrangements under which a
    person uses propagating material of the variety under the applicant's control for the purpose of
    increasing the applicant's stock, or of carrying out tests or trials, and the whole of the material
    produced, directly or indirectly, from the material becomes or remains the property of the
    applicant: Sch 2 para 4(7). Such arrangements are known as 'qualifying arrangements': Sch 2 para
    4(7).
11 Ie under qualifying arrangements: see note 10.
12 Plant Varieties Act 1997 Sch 2 para 4(6)(b).
13 Plant Varieties Act 1997 Sch 2 para 4(8).
14 Plant Varieties Act 1997 Sch 2 para 4(9).
15 Plant Varieties Act 1997 s 26(1)(b). As to the tribunal and appeals thereto see PARA 285 et seq.

248. Granting of rights where there is more than one applicant.

If a variety[1] is bred, or discovered and developed, by two or more persons
independently, the first of those persons, and any successor in title of theirs, to
apply for the grant of plant breeders' rights[2] in respect of it is the person entitled
to the grant[3]. As between persons making applications for the grant of plant
breeders' rights in respect of the same variety on the same date, the one who was
first in a position to make an application for the grant of rights in respect of that
variety, or who would have been first in that position if the statutory provisions
governing the granting of rights[4] had always been in force, is the person entitled
to the grant[5].

1   As to the meaning of 'variety' see PARA 239 note 1.
2   For the power of the Controller of Plant Variety Rights to grant plant breeders' rights see PARA
    243. As to the nature and scope of such rights see PARAS 239–242. As to the Controller see PARAS
    243 note 2, 281–284. As to the Controller's powers with respect to dealing with applications see
    PARA 282.
3   Plant Varieties Act 1997 Sch 2 para 5(1). Where an application for plant breeders' rights under
    Pt I (ss 1–41) is made in respect of a variety for which the applicant has made an earlier rights
    application under EU law, the law of an international organisation, or the law of a foreign country
    or state, the application under Pt I may under certain circumstances be deemed to have been made
    on the date of such earlier application: see Sch 2 para 6; and PARA 249.
4   Ie the Plant Varieties Act 1997 Pt I.
5   Plant Varieties Act 1997 Sch 2 para 5(2).

249. Timing of the application.

Where an application for plant breeders' rights[1] under the domestic legislation[2]
is made in respect of a variety[3] for which the applicant has made an earlier rights
application (a 'parallel application'[4]) under EC law[5], the law of an international
organisation[6], or the law of a foreign country or state[7], the domestic application
is deemed to have been made on the date of the parallel application[8]. An applicant
may take advantage of this provision only if:

(1)   the parallel application was made in the 12 months immediately
        preceding the domestic application[9];
(2)   the applicant has not duly made such a parallel application earlier than
        12 months before the domestic application[10];

(3)   the domestic application includes a claim to priority[11] by reference to the parallel application[12];

(4)   the parallel application by reference to which priority is claimed has not been withdrawn or refused when the domestic application is made[13]; and

(5)   within three months from the date of the domestic application, the applicant submits to the Controller of Plant Variety Rights a copy of the documents constituting the parallel application, certified as a true copy by the authority to whom it is made[14].

Any priority which an application enjoys by virtue of these provisions is forfeited if the requirements set out above are not met within a specified period[15].

1   For the power of the Controller of Plant Variety Rights to grant plant breeders' rights see PARA 243. As to the nature and scope of such rights see PARAS 239–242. As to the Controller see PARAS 243 note 2, 281–284. As to the Controller's powers with respect to dealing with applications see PARA 282.

2   Ie the Plant Varieties Act 1997 Pt I (ss 1–41).

3   As to the meaning of 'variety' see PARA 239 note 1.

4   A 'parallel application' is an application for the grant of plant variety rights in respect of the variety to which the application under the Plant Varieties Act 1997 Pt I relates: Sch 2 para 6(9)(b). If more than one parallel application has been made, the references in Sch 2 para 6(4)–(7) (see the text and notes 8–14) to the parallel application are to be construed as references to the earlier, or earliest, of the applications: Sch 2 para 6(8).

5   Plant Varieties Act 1997 Sch 2 para 6(1), (2)(a).

6   Plant Varieties Act 1997 Sch 2 para 6(2)(b). To qualify for these purposes the intergovernmental organisation in question must be, and must have been at the time of the application, a member of the Union as defined by the International Convention for the Protection of New Varieties of Plants (Paris, 2 December 1961; Cmnd 9152) art 1(xi): Plant Varieties Act 1997 Sch 2 para 6(9)(a).

7   Plant Varieties Act 1997 Sch 2 para 6(2)(b), (c). To qualify for these purposes the country in question must be either a state, which is, and was at the time of the application, a member of the Union as defined by the International Convention for the Protection of New Varieties of Plants (Paris, 2 December 1961; Cmnd 9152) art 1(xi), or any country or territory which is, and was at the time of the application, designated for these purposes of this provision by order made by the Secretary of State or the Welsh Ministers: Plant Varieties Act 1997 Sch 2 para 6(2)(b), (c). At the date at which this volume states the law no such order had been made. As to the Secretary of State and the Welsh Ministers see PARA 390.

8   Plant Varieties Act 1997 Sch 2 para 6(7). These provisions are of particular significance in connection with the requirements that a variety in respect of which an application for rights is made must be shown to be distinct (see PARA 244) and new (see PARA 247), and for the purposes of the provisions assigning priority as between applicants for rights in respect of the same variety (see PARA 248): Sch 2 para 6(1).

9   Plant Varieties Act 1997 Sch 2 para 6(2).

10   Plant Varieties Act 1997 Sch 2 para 6(3).

11   Ie under the Plant Varieties Act 1997 Sch 2 para 6.

12   Plant Varieties Act 1997 Sch 2 para 6(4).

13   Plant Varieties Act 1997 Sch 2 para 6(5).

14   Plant Varieties Act 1997 Sch 2 para 6(6).

15   See the Plant Varieties Act 1997 Sch 2 para 7, which provides that any priority which an application for the grant of plant breeders' rights enjoys by virtue of Sch 2 para 6 is forfeited if the applicant does not, before the end of the period of two years beginning with the day after the last day on which the applicant could have claimed priority under Sch 2 para 6 for his application (or, if the application by reference to which the application enjoys priority is withdrawn or refused before the applicant has satisfied all the requirements which are to be satisfied by an applicant before plant breeders' rights can be granted to him, such period as the Controller may specify), satisfy all the requirements which are to be satisfied by an applicant before plant breeders' rights can be granted to him.

C. DURATION, TERMINATION AND SUSPENSION

250. Period for which rights are exercisable.

A grant of plant breeders' rights[1] has effect for 25 years from the date of the grant[2], except in the case of potatoes, trees and vines, where it has effect for 30 years from that date[3]; the Secretary of State and the Welsh Ministers[4] may, however, by regulations substitute alternative periods not exceeding 30 years for general purposes or 35 years for the purposes of potatoes, trees and vines[5].

The period for which a grant of plant breeders' rights has effect is not affected by the fact that it becomes impossible to invoke the rights[6].

1 For the power of the Controller of Plant Variety Rights to grant plant breeders' rights see PARA 243. As to the nature and scope of such rights see PARAS 239–242. As to the Controller see PARAS 243 note 2, 281–284.
2 Plant Varieties Act 1997 s 11(1)(b).
3 Plant Varieties Act 1997 s 11(1)(a).
4 As to the Secretary of State and the Welsh Ministers see PARA 390.
5 Plant Varieties Act 1997 s 11(2). At the date at which this volume states the law no such regulations had been made.
6 Plant Varieties Act 1997 s 11(3). The reference in the text to its becoming impossible to invoke plant breeders' rights is a reference to its becoming impossible either because of Council Regulation (EC) 2100/94 (OJ L227, 01.09.99, p 1) on Community plant variety rights, art 92(2) (effect of subsequent grant of Community plant variety right) or because of suspension under the Plant Varieties Act 1997 s 23 (see PARA 264): s 11(3).

251. Circumstances in which rights may be declared null and void.

The Controller of Plant Variety Rights[1] must declare the grant of plant breeders' rights[2] null and void if it is established that:

(1)   the protected variety[3] was neither distinct nor new[4] when the rights were granted[5];

(2)   in a case where the grant of the rights was essentially based upon information and documents furnished by the applicant, the protected variety was neither uniform nor stable[6] when the rights were granted[7]; or

(3)   the person to whom the rights were granted was not the person entitled to the grant of the rights and the rights have not subsequently been transferred to him, or his successor in title[8].

Where a grant of rights is declared null and void under these provisions, it is deemed never to have had effect[9].

A decision of the Controller under any of these provisions is subject to appeal to the Plant Varieties and Seeds Tribunal[10] and accordingly may not be made until the opportunity to make representations on the matter has been afforded to interested parties[11].

The giving of false information in connection with an application for a declaration of rights as null and void is an offence[12].

1 As to the Controller of Plant Variety Rights see PARAS 243 note 2, 281–284.
2 For the power of the Controller to grant plant breeders' rights see PARA 243. As to the nature and scope of such rights see PARAS 239–242.
3 As to the meaning of 'protected variety' see PARA 239 note 6. As to the meaning of 'variety' see PARA 239 note 1.
4 Ie that the variety did not meet the criterion specified in the Plant Varieties Act 1997 s 4(2)(a) or s 4(2)(d) (see PARAS 243–244, 247): s 21(1)(a).
5 Plant Varieties Act 1997 s 21(1)(a). Proposed decisions under s 21(1) must be notified in the gazette by the Controller, and specified persons may make representations in connection with

them: see the Plant Breeders' Rights Regulations 1998, SI 1998/1027, regs 5, 7, 8, Sch 1 Pt B(6). As to the gazette see PARA 17. As to regulations governing the Controller's functions see PARA 282.

6   Ie the variety did not meet the criterion specified in the Plant Varieties Act 1997 s 4(2)(b) or s 4(2)(c) (see PARAS 243, 245–246): s 21(1)(b).

7   Plant Varieties Act 1997 s 21(1)(b). As to the notification of decisions and the making of representations see note 5.

8   Plant Varieties Act 1997 s 21(1)(c). As to the notification of decisions and the making of representations see note 5. If, because of Sch 2 para 6 (see PARA 249), priority is established for an application for the grant of plant breeders' rights after such rights have been granted in pursuance of an application against which priority is established, s 21(1)(c) only applies to the grant if the Controller decides that the application for which priority is established should be granted: s 21(2).

9   Plant Varieties Act 1997 s 21(3).

10   Plant Varieties Act 1997 s 26(1)(d). As to the tribunal and appeals thereto see PARA 285 et seq.

11   See the Plant Varieties Act 1997 s 24; and PARA 282. As to the making of representations for these purposes see note 5.

12   Plant Varieties Act 1997 s 31(1). The offence is punishable on summary conviction by a fine not exceeding level 3 on the standard scale, and is committed by any person (whether the applicant or a person giving information on his behalf) who, in connection with the application, either knowingly or recklessly gives information which is false in a material particular: s 31(1), (2)(a), (b). As to the standard scale and the powers of magistrates' courts to issue fines on summary conviction see SENTENCING vol 92 (2015) PARA 176. As to jurisdiction, and the commission of offences by bodies corporate, see PARA 243 note 17.

252. Termination of rights.

The Controller of Plant Variety Rights[1] may terminate the period for which a grant of plant breeders' rights[2] has effect[3] if he is satisfied that the protected variety[4] is no longer uniform or stable[5], or it appears to him that the rights holder is no longer in a position to produce to the Controller propagating material capable of producing the protected variety[6], or he is satisfied that the rights holder has failed to comply with a request aimed at establishing whether he is in such a position[7], or he is satisfied, on application by the rights holder, that the rights may properly be surrendered[8].

A decision of the Controller under any of these provisions is subject to appeal to the Plant Varieties and Seeds Tribunal[9] and accordingly may not be made until the opportunity to make representations on the matter has been afforded to interested parties[10].

The giving of false information in connection with an application for the termination of rights is an offence[11].

1   As to the Controller of Plant Variety Rights see PARAS 243 note 2, 281–284.

2   For the power of the Controller to grant plant breeders' rights see PARA 243. As to the nature and scope of such rights see PARAS 239–242.

3   As to the period for which rights are exercisable see PARA 250.

4   As to the meaning of 'protected variety' see PARA 239 note 6. As to the meaning of 'variety' see PARA 239 note 1.

5   Plant Varieties Act 1997 s 22(1)(a). The reference in the text to the protected variety being no longer uniform or stable is a reference to that variety no longer meeting the criterion specified in s 4(2)(b) or s 4(2)(c) (see PARAS 243, 245–246): s 22(1)(a). If the Controller is satisfied, not only that the protected variety no longer meets the criterion specified in s 4(2)(b) or s 4(2)(c), but also that it ceased to do so at some earlier date, he may make the termination retrospective to that date: s 22(3).

6   Plant Varieties Act 1997 s 22(1)(b). The reference in the text to the rights holder being no longer in a position to produce propagating material capable of producing the protected variety is a reference to him being no longer in a position to provide the Controller with the propagating material mentioned in s 16(1) (see PARA 283): s 22(1)(b). Proposed decisions under s 22(1) must be notified in the gazette by the Controller, and specified persons may make representations in

connection with them: Plant Breeders' Rights Regulations 1998, SI 1998/1027, regs 5, 7, 8, Sch 1 Pt B(7). As to the gazette see PARA 17. As to regulations governing the Controller's functions see PARA 282.

7   Plant Varieties Act 1997 s 22(1)(c). The reference in the text to the rights holder failing to comply with a request aimed at establishing whether he is in a position to provide the Controller with the propagating material mentioned in s 16(1) is a reference to failure to comply with a request under s 16(2) (see PARA 283): s 22(1)(c). As to the notification of termination decisions and the making of representations thereon see note 6.

8   Plant Varieties Act 1997 s 22(1)(d). Proposed decisions as to termination under s 22(1)(d) must be notified in the gazette by the Controller, and specified persons may make representations in connection with them: s 22(2)(a), (b); Plant Breeders' Rights Regulations 1998, SI 1998/1027, regs 5, 7, 8, Sch 1 Pt B(8). The termination of rights following an application to surrender must also be notified in the gazette: Sch 1 Pt C(3).

9   Plant Varieties Act 1997 s 26(1)(d), (e). As to the tribunal and appeals thereto see PARA 285 et seq.

10   See the Plant Varieties Act 1997 s 24; and PARA 282.

11   Plant Varieties Act 1997 s 31(1). The offence is punishable on summary conviction by a fine not exceeding level 3 on the standard scale, and is committed by any person (whether the applicant or a person giving information on his behalf) who, in connection with the application, either knowingly or recklessly gives information which is false in a material particular: s 31(2)(a), (b). As to the standard scale and the powers of magistrates' courts to issue fines on summary conviction see SENTENCING vol 92 (2015) PARA 176. As to jurisdiction, and the commission of offences by bodies corporate, see PARA 243 note 17.

253. Suspension of rights.

The Controller of Plant Variety Rights[1] may suspend the exercise of any plant breeders' rights[2] if he is satisfied that the rights holder is in breach of any obligation imposed on him by a licence for the exploitation of those rights[3].

1   As to the Controller of Plant Variety Rights see PARAS 243 note 2, 281–284.

2   For the power of the Controller to grant plant breeders' rights see PARA 243. As to the nature and scope of such rights see PARAS 239–242.

3   See the Plant Varieties Act 1997 s 23; and PARA 264. As to the issue of licences for the exploitation of plant breeders' rights see s 17; and PARA 261.

D. REGISTRATION AND NAMING OF PROTECTED VARIETIES

254. Selection and registration of names for plant varieties.

The Secretary of State and the Welsh Ministers[1] may by regulations[2] make provision:

(1)   for the selection of names[3] for varieties[4] which are the subject of applications for the grant of plant breeders' rights[5];

(2)   about change of name in relation to varieties in respect of which plant breeders' rights have been granted[6]; and

(3)   for the keeping of a register of the names of varieties in respect of which plant breeders' rights have been granted[7].

Regulations so made require the Controller of Plant Variety Rights to keep a register of the names of plant varieties in respect of which plant breeders' rights[8] have been granted[9], and to keep records of plant varieties for which applications for grants of rights are under consideration[10] and for which rights have been granted[11]. The Controller must publish notice of all entries made in the register, including alterations, corrections and erasures[12], in the gazette[13] and in such other manner as appears to the Controller to be convenient for the publication of these to all concerned[14]. Provision is made for the register and the records to be open to inspection by the public[15].

The ministers may by regulations confer a right of appeal to the Plant Varieties and Seeds Tribunal against any decision of the Controller under these provisions[16].

1   As to the Secretary of State and the Welsh Ministers see PARA 390.
2   The regulations having effect for these purposes are the Plant Breeders' Rights (Naming and Fees) Regulations 2006, SI 2006/648. Regulations may, in particular:
    (1)   make provision enabling the Controller of Plant Variety Rights to require an applicant for the grant of plant breeders' rights to select a name for the variety to which the application relates (Plant Varieties Act 1997 s 18(2)(a));
    (2)   make provision enabling the Controller to require the holder of plant breeders' rights to select a different name for the protected variety (s 18(2)(b));
    (3)   prescribe classes of variety for the purposes of the regulations (s 18(2)(c));
    (4)   prescribe grounds on which the registration of a proposed name may be refused (s 18(2)(d));
    (5)   prescribe the circumstances in which representations may be made regarding any decision as to the name to be registered in respect of any variety (s 18(2)(e));
    (6)   make provision enabling the Controller either to refuse an application for the grant of plant breeders' rights, or to terminate the period for which a grant of plant breeders' rights has effect, if the applicant or holder fails to comply with a requirement imposed under the regulations (s 18(2)(f));
    (7)   make provision for the publication or service of notices of decisions which the Controller proposes to take (s 18(2)(g)); and
    (8)   prescribe the times at which, and the circumstances in which, the register may be inspected by members of the public (s 18(2)(h)).
    As to the Controller see PARAS 243 note 2, 281–284.
3   'Name' includes any designation: Plant Varieties Act 1997 s 38(1).
4   As to the meaning of 'variety' see PARA 239 note 1. For these purposes the variety in respect of which plant breeders' rights are granted is the protected variety: Plant Varieties Act 1997 s 18(4). As to the meaning of 'protected variety' see PARA 239 note 6.
5   Plant Varieties Act 1997 s 18(1)(a). For the power of the Controller to grant plant breeders' rights see PARA 243. As to the nature and scope of such rights see PARAS 239–242.
6   Plant Varieties Act 1997 s 18(1)(b).
7   Plant Varieties Act 1997 s 18(1)(c).
8   Ie rights which may be granted under the Plant Varieties Act 1997 Pt I (ss 1–41): Plant Breeders' Rights Regulations 1998, SI 1998/1027, reg 2(1).
9   Plant Breeders' Rights Regulations 1998, SI 1998/1027, reg 12(1).
10 Plant Breeders' Rights Regulations 1998, SI 1998/1027, reg 12(2)(a). These records must record:
    (1)   the date on which the application was received (reg 12(3)(a));
    (2)   the date on which details of the application were published in the gazette (reg 12(3)(b));
    (3)   the name and address of the applicant (reg 12(3)(c));'
    (4)   the description of the characteristics of the plant variety provided by the applicant (reg 12(3)(d))
    (5)   the reference number allocated to the plant variety by the Controller when the application was published in the gazette (reg 12(3)(e));
    (6)   the names of the plant variety as published from time to time in the gazette (reg 12(3)(f)); and
    (7)   such other particulars as appear to the Controller to be desirable (reg 12(3)(g)).
    As to publication of notices in the gazette see PARA 17. Any person whose name and address are entered on the plant varieties records and who has changed his name or address must apply to the Controller for amendment of the plant varieties records accordingly: reg 12(6).
11 Plant Breeders' Rights Regulations 1998, SI 1998/1027, reg 12(2)(b). These records must record:
    (1)   the name and address of the rights holder (reg 12(4)(a));
    (2)   a description of the characteristics of the plant variety (reg 12(4)(b));
    (3)   the names of the plant variety as published from time to time in the gazette (reg 12(4)(c));
    (4)   the date upon which and the period (including any extended period) for which rights in the plant variety were granted, and the date upon which such rights expired or were otherwise terminated or were declared null and void, as the case may be (reg 12(4)(d));
    (5)   the information recorded against the variety pursuant to reg 12(2)(a) (see the text and note 10) prior to the grant of rights (reg 12(4)(e)); and
    (6)   such other particulars as appear to the Controller to be desirable (reg 12(4)(f)).

Any person who has become a holder of rights in succession to another person may apply to the Controller to be entered in the records and upon being satisfied that such person is so entitled the Controller must amend the records accordingly: reg 12(5). As to amendments to the records see note 12.

12 The Controller may, without prejudice to any other powers vested in him, either upon the application of any person or without such an application, rectify any error or omission in the register or the plant varieties records: Plant Breeders' Rights Regulations 1998, SI 1998/1027, reg 12(7). Before rectifying the register or the records the Controller must (unless he considers that the correction is so trifling that it is not necessary for him to do so) give notice of his proposal to do so to the rights holder in the plant variety in respect of which the register or records are proposed to be corrected, must advertise his proposal in the gazette, and must invite written observations to be made within a specified period in regard to the proposal; and he must not make the correction until he has considered any observations so made to him: reg 12(8).

13 Plant Varieties Act 1997 s 18(3)(a). It is no defence in civil or criminal proceedings to show that at any time a person did not know of an entry in the register under s 18 if before that time notice of that entry has been published in the gazette: Plant Varieties and Seeds Act 1964 s 34(2) (amended by the European Communities Act 1972 Sch 3 Pt III; and the Plant Varieties Act 1997 s 51(1)(b)).

14 Plant Varieties Act 1997 s 18(3)(b).

15 See PARA 284.

16 Plant Varieties Act 1997 s 26(2)(b). At the date at which this volume states the law no such regulations had been made. As to the tribunal and appeals thereto see PARA 285 et seq.

255. Use of registered name.

Where a name[1] is registered[2] in respect of a variety[3] a person may not use any other name in selling, offering for sale or otherwise marketing propagating material of that variety[4], although this does not preclude the use of any trade mark or trade name[5] if that mark or name and the registered name are juxtaposed[6], and the registered name is easily recognisable[7].

If any person uses the registered name[8] of a protected variety[9] in offering for sale, selling or otherwise marketing material of a different variety within the same class[10], the use of the name is a wrong actionable in proceedings by the rights holder[11]; and this also applies to the use of a name so nearly resembling the registered name as to be likely to deceive or cause confusion[12]. In any such proceedings it is a defence to a claim for damages to prove that the defendant took all reasonable precautions against committing the wrong and had not, when using the name, any reason to suspect that it was wrongful[13].

1 As to the meaning of 'name' see PARA 254 note 3.

2 Ie under the Plant Varieties Act 1997 s 18 (see PARA 254). References to names registered under s 18 include names accepted pursuant to the Plant Breeders' Rights (Naming and Fees) Regulations 2006, SI 2006/648: reg 5(3).

3 As to the meaning of 'variety' see PARA 239 note 1. These provisions have effect in relation to any variety from the date on which plant breeders' rights in respect of that variety are granted, and continue to apply after the period for which the grant of those rights has effect: Plant Varieties Act 1997 s 19(2). For the power of the Controller of Plant Variety Rights to grant plant breeders' rights see PARA 243. As to the Controller see PARAS 243 note 2, 281–284. As to the nature and scope of such rights see PARAS 239–242.

4 Plant Varieties Act 1997 s 19(1). A person who contravenes s 19(1) is liable on summary conviction to a fine not exceeding level 3 on the standard scale: s 19(4). In any proceedings for an offence under s 19(4), it is a defence to prove that the accused took all reasonable precautions against committing the offence and had not at the time of the offence any reason to suspect that he was committing an offence: s 19(5). As to the standard scale and the powers of magistrates' courts to issue fines on summary conviction see SENTENCING vol 92 (2015) PARA 176. As to jurisdiction, and the commission of offences by bodies corporate, see PARA 243 note 17.

5 Ie any trade mark or trade name whether registered under the Trade Marks Act 1994 or not: Plant Varieties Act 1997 s 19(3). As to registration under the Trade Marks Act 1994 see TRADE MARKS AND TRADE NAMES vol 97A (2014) PARAS 4, 19 et seq.

6 Plant Varieties Act 1997 s 19(3)(a).

7 Plant Varieties Act 1997 s 19(3)(b). A description or mark applied in pursuance of the Plant Varieties Act 1997 is not a 'trade description' for the purposes of the Trade Descriptions Act 1968: see s 2(4)(h); and CONSUMER PROTECTION vol 21 (2016) PARAS 442, 443.

8 'Registered name', in relation to a protected variety, means the name registered in respect of it under the Plant Varieties Act 1997 s 18 (see PARA 254): s 20(4). See note 2.

9 As to the meaning of 'protected variety' see PARA 239 note 6.

10 'Class' means a class prescribed for the purposes of regulations under the Plant Varieties Act 1997 s 18(1) (see PARA 254): s 20(4).

11 Plant Varieties Act 1997 s 20(1). As to the holder of plant breeders' rights see PARA 239 note 4. The Crown is not immune from suit in this regard: if any servant or agent of the Crown makes himself liable to civil proceedings under s 20, and the infringement or wrong is committed with the authority of the Crown, civil proceedings in respect of the infringement or wrong lie against the Crown (Plant Varieties Act 1997 s 39(1)); however, except as so provided, no proceedings lie against the Crown by virtue of the Crown Proceedings Act 1947 (see CROWN AND CROWN PROCEEDINGS vol 29 (2014) PARA 93 et seq) in respect of any wrong under the Plant Varieties Act 1997 s 20 (s 39(2)). Section 39 has effect as if contained in the Crown Proceedings Act 1947 Pt I (ss 1–12): Plant Varieties Act 1997 s 39(3).

12 Plant Varieties Act 1997 s 20(2).

13 Plant Varieties Act 1997 s 20(3).

E. PROTECTION OF EXISTING RIGHTS

256. Plant breeders' rights granted under previous legislation.

Plant breeders' rights were formerly granted in respect of plant varieties of such species or groups as were prescribed by a scheme[1] made under the Plant Varieties and Seeds Act 1964[2]. Such of those rights as were exercisable on 8 May 1998[3] continue to have effect and are subject to the new statutory provisions for the protection of plant variety rights[4] to the same extent[5] as are rights granted pursuant to those provisions[6].

1 Schemes were made, following consultation, by statutory instrument: see the Plant Varieties and Seeds Act 1964 s 1(5), (6) (repealed). See note 6.

2 Plant Varieties and Seeds Act 1964 s 1(1) (repealed).

3 Ie the date on which the substantive provisions of the Plant Varieties Act 1997 were brought into force: see the Plant Varieties Act 1997 (Commencement) Order 1998, SI 1998/1028.

4 Ie the Plant Varieties Act 1997 Pt I (ss 1–41).

5 Except that the Plant Varieties Act 1997 s 5 (see PARA 243 note 3) does not apply to existing rights and s 11 (see PARA 250) applies to existing rights only if its effect is to extend the period for which the rights are exercisable: s 40(2), (3).

6 Plant Varieties Act 1997 s 40(1), (4). The following schemes, prescribing the plant varieties to which they refer, continue to have effect subject to the provisions of Pt I:
   (1)   Plant Breeders' Rights (Apples and Pears) Scheme 1966, SI 1966/1226;
   (2)   Plant Breeders' Rights (Cactaceae) Scheme 1985, SI 1985/1095;
   (3)   Plant Breeders' Rights (Carnations) Scheme 1968, SI 1968/624;
   (4)   Plant Breeders' Rights (Cereals) Scheme 1980, SI 1980/321;
   (5)   Plant Breeders' Rights (Cherries and Cherry Rootstocks) Scheme 1977, SI 1977/143;
   (6)   Plant Breeders' Rights (Red Clover and White Clover) Scheme 1977, SI 1977/142;
   (7)   Plant Breeders' Rights (Compositae) Scheme 1985, SI 1985/1093;
   (8)   Plant Breeders' Rights (Conifers and Taxads) Scheme 1969, SI 1969/1025;
   (9)   Plant Breeders' Rights (Cymbidiums) Scheme 1971, SI 1971/1092;
   (10)   Plant Breeders' Rights (Elatior Begonias) Scheme 1982, SI 1982/1096;
   (11)   Plant Breeders' Rights (Fenugreek) Scheme 1978, SI 1978/301;
   (12)   Plant Breeders' Rights (Festulolium) Scheme 1990, SI 1990/1593;
   (13)   Plant Breeders' Rights (Fodder Kale and Swedes) Scheme 1982, SI 1982/1097;
   (14)   Plant Breeders' Rights (Herbaceous Perennials) Scheme 1995, SI 1995/526;
   (15)   Plant Breeders' Rights (Hops) Scheme 1977, SI 1977/144;
   (16)   Plant Breeders' Rights (Lilies) Scheme 1977, SI 1977/145;
   (17)   Plant Breeders' Rights (Lucerne) Scheme 1968, SI 1968/257;
   (18)   Plant Breeders' Rights (Lupins) Scheme 1978, SI 1978/302;
   (19)   Plant Breeders' Rights (Narcissi, Freesias and Gladioli) Scheme 1969, SI 1969/1026;

(20)   Plant Breeders' Rights (Nerine) Scheme 1985, SI 1985/1097;
(21)   Plant Breeders' Rights (Oil and Fibre Plants) Scheme 1980, SI 1980/318;
(22)   Plant Breeders' Rights (Miscellaneous Ornamental Plants) Scheme 1995, SI 1995/527;
(23)   Plant Breeders' Rights (Pelargoniums) Scheme 1972, SI 1972/85;
(24)   Plant Breeders' Rights (Perennial Delphiniums) Scheme 1966, SI 1966/643;
(25)   Plant Breeders' Rights (Plums and Damsons) Scheme 1968, SI 1968/620;
(26)   Plant Breeders' Rights (Poinsettias) Scheme 1985, SI 1985/1094;
(27)   Plant Breeders' Rights (Potatoes) Scheme 1965, SI 1965/724;
(28)   Plant Breeders' Rights (Quince Rootstock) Scheme 1993, SI 1993/2781;
(29)   Plant Breeders' Rights (Red Fescue (including Chewings Fescue)) Scheme 1978, SI 1978/305;
(30)   Plant Breeders' Rights (Rhododendrons) Scheme 1968, SI 1968/623;
(31)   Plant Breeders' Rights (Rhubarb) Scheme 1966, SI 1966/644;
(32)   Plant Breeders' Rights (Roses) Scheme 1965, SI 1965/725;
(33)   Plant Breeders' Rights (Ryegrass) Scheme 1968, SI 1968/258;
(34)   Plant Breeders' Rights (Sainfoin and Birdsfoot Trefoil) Scheme 1993, SI 1993/2779;
(35)   Plant Breeders' Rights (Saintpaulia) Scheme 1982, SI 1982/1100;
(36)   Plant Breeders' Rights (Soft Fruits) Scheme 1980, SI 1980/331;
(37)   Plant Breeders' Rights (Streptocarpus) Scheme 1972, SI 1972/86;
(38)   Plant Breeders' Rights (Sweet Peas) Scheme 1995, SI 1995/529;
(39)   Plant Breeders' Rights (Timothy, Cocksfoot, Tall Fescue and Meadow Fescue) Scheme 1977, SI 1977/147;
(40)   Plant Breeders' Rights (Tomatoes) Scheme 1993, SI 1993/2777;
(41)   Plant Breeders' Rights (Trees, Shrubs and Woody Climbers) Scheme 1993, SI 1993/2776;
(42)   Plant Breeders' Rights (Vegetables) (including Field Beans and Field Peas) Scheme 1980, SI 1980/319;
(43)   Plant Breeders' Rights (Velvet bent, Red top, Creeping bent and Brown top) Scheme 1978, SI 1978/307; and
(44)   Plant Breeders' Rights (Wood Meadow-Grass, Swamp Meadow-Grass, Smooth Stalked Meadow-Grass and Rough Stalked Meadow-Grass) Scheme 1978, SI 1978/308.

F. INFRINGEMENT AND ENFORCEMENT

257.   False representations as to rights.

Any person who, in relation to any variety[1], falsely represents that he is entitled to exercise plant breeders' rights[2], or any rights derived from such rights, knowing that the representation is false, or makes such a representation recklessly, is guilty of an offence[3]. It is immaterial for these purposes whether or not the variety to which the representation relates is the subject of plant breeders' rights[4].

1   As to the meaning of 'variety' see PARA 239 note 1.
2   As to the nature and scope of plant breeders' rights see PARAS 239–242.
3   Plant Varieties Act 1997 s 32(1). A person who is guilty of an offence under this provision is liable on summary conviction to a fine not exceeding level 3 on the standard scale: s 32(1). As to the standard scale and the powers of magistrates' courts to issue fines on summary conviction see SENTENCING vol 92 (2015) PARA 176. As to jurisdiction, and the commission of offences by bodies corporate, see PARA 243 note 17.
4   Plant Varieties Act 1997 s 32(2).

258.   Infringement of rights actionable.

Plant breeders' rights[1] are actionable at the suit of the rights holder[2]. The Crown is not immune from suit in this regard[3]. In any proceedings for the infringement of plant breeders' rights, all such relief by way of damages, injunction, interdict, account or otherwise is available as is available in any corresponding proceedings in respect of infringements of other proprietary rights[4].

1   As to the nature and scope of plant breeders' rights see PARAS 239–242.
2   Plant Varieties Act 1997 s 13(1). As to the holder of plant breeders' rights see PARA 239 note 4.

3   If any servant or agent of the Crown infringes any plant breeders' rights and the infringement is
     committed with the authority of the Crown, civil proceedings in respect of the infringement lie
     against the Crown (Plant Varieties Act 1997 s 39(1)); however, except as so provided, no
     proceedings lie against the Crown by virtue of the Crown Proceedings Act 1947 (see CROWN AND
     CROWN PROCEEDINGS vol 29 (2014) PARA 93 et seq) in respect of the infringement of plant
     breeders' rights (Plant Varieties Act 1997 s 39(2)). Section 39 has effect as if contained in the
     Crown Proceedings Act 1947 Pt I (ss 1–12): Plant Varieties Act 1997 s 39(3).
4   Plant Varieties Act 1997 s 13(2).

259. Enforcement of rights in respect of harvested material.

Holders of plant breeders' rights[1] in respect of harvested material are enabled,
for the purpose of protecting their rights, to issue notices known as 'information
notices' to persons who trade in the protected varieties[2]. An information notice
must be in the prescribed form[3] and must:

(1)   specify the material to which it relates[4];
(2)   contain, in relation to that material, a request for the supply of
       prescribed information[5]; and
(3)   contain such other particulars as may be prescribed[6].

Failure to comply with an information notice gives rise to a presumption, in any
proceedings relating to the infringement of the rights holder's rights[7], that the use
of the material in question is unauthorised[8].

Similar provision is made in respect of products made directly from harvested
material[9].

1   As to the holder of plant breeders' rights see PARA 239 note 4.
2   See the Plant Varieties Act 1997 s 14(1), (2)(a).
3   Plant Varieties Act 1997 s 14(4)(a). For the prescribed form see the Plant Breeders' Rights
     (Information Notices) Regulations 1998, SI 1998/1024, reg 3(1)(a), Schedule. The Plant Breeders'
     Rights (Information Notices) Regulations 1998, SI 1998/1024, Schedule, is modified in its
     application to plant breeders' rights granted under Council Regulation (EC) 2100/94 (OJ L227,
     01.09.99, p 1) on Community plant variety rights: see the Plant Breeders' Rights (Information
     Notices) (Extension to European Community Plant Variety Rights) Regulations 1998,
     SI 1998/1023, reg 2(1), (2)(b).
4   Plant Varieties Act 1997 s 14(4)(b). The notice must specify the registered name and species of the
     variety: Plant Breeders' Rights (Information Notices) Regulations 1998, SI 1998/1024, reg
     3(1)(b), (2)(a), (b).
5   Plant Varieties Act 1997 s 14(4)(c); Plant Breeders' Rights (Information Notices) Regulations
     1998, SI 1998/1024, reg 3(1)(c). The information which may be requested is:
     (1)   the name and address of the recipient of the information notice (reg 3(3)(a));
     (2)   the name and address of the person from whom the recipient acquired possession of the
            material specified in the notice (reg 3(3)(b));
     (3)   the date on which the recipient acquired possession of the material specified in the notice
            (reg 3(3)(c)); and
     (4)   the size of the consignment of which the specified material formed part (reg 3(3)(d)). No
            other information may be requested: Plant Varieties Act 1997 s 14(4)(c).
     If the holder of plant breeders' rights obtains information pursuant to an information notice, he
     owes an obligation of confidence in respect of the information (excepting such as would restrict the
     disclosure of information for the purposes of, or in connection with: (a) establishing whether plant
     breeders' rights have been infringed; or (b) any proceedings for the infringement of plant breeders'
     rights) to the person who supplied it: s 34.
6   Plant Varieties Act 1997 s 14(4)(d); Plant Breeders' Rights (Information Notices) Regulations
     1998, SI 1998/1024, reg 3(1)(b). The additional particulars are:
     (1)   the date on which plant breeders' rights were granted in the variety (reg 3(2)(c));
     (2)   confirmation that the rights were granted under the Plant Varieties Act 1997 (Plant
            Breeders' Rights (Information Notices) Regulations 1998, SI 1998/1024, reg 3(2)(d));
     (3)   the name and address of the rights holder (reg 3(2)(e));
     (4)   the name and address of the agent of the rights holder, if one has been appointed (reg
            3(2)(f)); and
     (5)   the date on which the information notice was served (reg 3(2)(g)).

Regulation 3(2)(d) is modified in its application to plant breeders' rights granted under Council Regulation (EC) 2100/94 (OJ L227, 01.09.99, p 1) on Community plant variety rights: Plant Breeders' Rights (Information Notices) (Extension to European Community Plant Variety Rights) Regulations 1998, SI 1998/1023, reg 2(1), (2)(a).

7   See PARA 258.
8   See PARA 260.
9   Holders of plant breeders' rights in respect of products made directly from harvested material are enabled to issue information notices, in the prescribed form:
      (1)   specifying the product to which they relate;
      (2)   containing, in relation to that product, a request for the supply of prescribed, but no other, information; and
      (3)   containing such other particulars as may be prescribed: see the Plant Varieties Act 1997 s 15(1), (2)(a), (5), (6); and PARA 260.
    However, at the date at which this volume states the law no regulations had been made prescribing the form or content of such notices.

260. Presumptions in proceedings relating to harvested material or to products made from harvested material.

If, in any proceedings for the infringement of plant breeders' rights[1] as respects harvested material or any product made directly therefrom, the rights holder[2] proves that any of the material or product to which the proceedings relate has been the subject of an information notice[3] which has not been complied with[4], it is presumed as regards that material or product:

(1)   that the material, or the harvested material from which the product was made, was obtained through unauthorised use of propagating material[5];

(2)   that the rights holder did not have a reasonable opportunity before the material or harvested material was obtained to exercise his rights in relation to the unauthorised use of the propagating material[6]; and

(3)   (in proceedings relating to products made directly from harvested material only) that no relevant act[7] was done, before the product was made, as respects the harvested material from which it was made[8].

These presumptions apply unless the contrary is proved or the defendant shows that he had a reasonable excuse for not supplying the information[9].

1   As to the nature and scope of plant breeders' rights see PARAS 239–242. As to such proceedings see PARA 258.
2   As to the holder of plant breeders' rights see PARA 239 note 4.
3   Ie a notice given to the defendant by or on behalf of the rights holder requesting information as to the acquisition and use of the material or product: see the Plant Varieties Act 1997 ss 14(2)(a), (4), (5), 15(2)(a), (5), (6); and PARA 259.
4   Ie the defendant has not, within the prescribed time after the service of the notice, supplied the holder with the information about it requested in the notice: Plant Varieties Act 1997 ss 14(2)(b), 15(2)(b). The prescribed time for the purposes of proceedings relating to harvested material is 21 days: see the Plant Breeders' Rights (Information Notices) Regulations 1998, SI 1998/1024, reg 4. At the date at which this volume states the law no regulations had been made prescribing a time for the purposes of proceedings relating to products made directly from harvested material.
5   Plant Varieties Act 1997 ss 14(1), (2), (3)(a), 15(1), (2), (3)(a).
6   Plant Varieties Act 1997 ss 14(3)(b), 15(3)(b).
7   A 'relevant act' is:
      (1)   production or reproduction (multiplication);
      (2)   conditioning for the purpose of propagation;
      (3)   offering for sale;
      (4)   selling or other marketing;
      (5)   exporting;
      (6)   importing;
      (7)   stocking for any of these purposes; and
      (8)   any other act prescribed for these purposes (Plant Varieties Act 1997 ss 6(1)(a)–(h), 15(4)),

provided it is either done with the authority of the holder (s 15(4)(a)) or is an act in relation to the doing of which the holder has a reasonable opportunity to exercise his rights (s 15(4)(b)).

At the date at which this volume states the law no additional act had been prescribed.

8   Plant Varieties Act 1997 s 15(3)(c).
9   Plant Varieties Act 1997 ss 14(2), 15(2).

G. COMPULSORY LICENSING

261. Compulsory licensing of plant breeders' rights.
Where a person has applied to the holder of plant breeders' rights[1] for a licence to exploit those rights and the Controller of Plant Variety Rights[2] is satisfied, on an application, that the rights holder has either unreasonably refused to grant a licence or has imposed or put forward unreasonable terms in granting, or offering to grant, a licence, the Controller may grant to the applicant in the form of a licence any such rights as might have been granted by the holder[3]. A decision of the Controller to allow or refuse an application for such a licence is subject to appeal to the Plant Varieties and Seeds Tribunal[4] and accordingly may not be made until the opportunity to make representations on the matter has been afforded to interested parties[5].

A licence so granted will not be an exclusive licence[6], and may be granted only if the Controller is satisfied:

(1)   that it is necessary to grant a compulsory licence for the purpose of securing that the variety[7] to which the application relates is available to the public at reasonable prices, is widely distributed or is maintained in quality[8];

(2)   that the applicant is financially and otherwise in a position to exploit in a competent and businesslike manner the rights to be conferred on him[9]; and

(3)   that the applicant intends so to exploit those rights[10].

An application for a compulsory licence may be granted whether or not the relevant rights holder has granted licences to the applicant or any other person[11]. Any agreement purporting to bind any person not to apply for a compulsory licence is void[12].

The giving of false information in connection with an application for a licence is an offence[13].

1   As to the nature and scope of such rights see PARAS **239–242**.
2   As to the Controller of Plant Variety Rights see PARAS **243** note 2, 281–284.
3   Plant Varieties Act 1997 s 17(1). As to the terms of a compulsory licence see PARA **263**. Receipt of an application under s 17(1) must be notified by the Controller in the gazette, and specified persons may make representations: see the Plant Breeders' Rights Regulations 1998, SI 1998/1027, regs 5, 7, 8, Sch 1 Pt B(3). As to the gazette see PARA **17**. As to regulations governing the Controller's functions see PARA **282**.
4   Plant Varieties Act 1997 s 26(1)(c). As to the tribunal and appeals thereto see PARA **285** et seq.
5   See the Plant Varieties Act 1997 s 24; and PARA **282**. As to the making of representations for these purposes see note 3.
6   Plant Varieties Act 1997 s 17(3).
7   As to the meaning of 'variety' see PARA **239** note 1.
8   Plant Varieties Act 1997 s 17(2)(a).
9   Plant Varieties Act 1997 s 17(2)(b).
10   Plant Varieties Act 1997 s 17(2)(c).
11   Plant Varieties Act 1997 s 17(6).
12   Plant Varieties Act 1997 s 17(7).
13   Plant Varieties Act 1997 s 31(1). The offence is punishable on summary conviction by a fine not exceeding level 3 on the standard scale, and is committed by any person (whether the applicant or a person giving information on his behalf) who, in connection with the application, either

knowingly or recklessly gives information which is false in a material particular: s 31(1), (2)(a), (b). As to the standard scale and the powers of magistrates' courts to issue fines on summary conviction see SENTENCING vol 92 (2015) PARA 176. As to jurisdiction, and the commission of offences by bodies corporate, see PARA 243 note 17.

262.   Right to make representations to Controller.

Where the holder of plant breeders' rights[1] to which an application for the grant of a compulsory licence[2] relates is, or includes, or is represented by, a society or other organisation which has as its main object, or one of its main objects, the negotiation or granting of licences to exercise plant breeders' rights, either as the holder of the rights or as agent for holders, that organisation or person is entitled to be heard, and to make representations, in connection with the application[3]. If any such organisation or person applies to the Controller of Plant Variety Rights[4] for an opportunity of making representations concerning such an application[5], and the Controller is satisfied:

(1)   that the organisation or person has a substantial interest in the application[6];

(2)   that the application involves issues which may affect other such applicants[7]; and

(3)   where the application to make representations is made by an organisation, that the organisation is reasonably representative of the class of persons which it claims to represent[8],

he must afford to the organisation or person by whom the application is made an opportunity of making representations to him and of being heard by him or by a person appointed by him for the purpose[9].

A decision of the Controller to make representations for these purposes is subject to appeal to the Plant Varieties and Seeds Tribunal[10] and accordingly may not be made until the opportunity to make representations on the matter has been afforded to interested parties[11].

The giving of false information in connection with an application for the opportunity of making representations is an offence[12].

1   As to the nature and scope of such rights see PARAS 239–242.
2   Ie an application for the grant of a licence under the Plant Varieties Act 1997 s 17 (see PARA 261).
3   See the Plant Varieties Act 1997 s 25(1)–(3).
4   As to the Controller of Plant Variety Rights see PARAS 243 note 2, 281–284.
5   Proposed decisions to refuse such applications must be notified in the gazette by the Controller, and specified persons may make representations in connection with them: see the Plant Breeders' Rights Regulations 1998, SI 1998/1027, regs 5, 7, 8, Sch 1 Pt B(4). As to the gazette see PARA 17. As to regulations governing the Controller's functions see PARA 282.
6   Plant Varieties Act 1997 s 25(4)(a).
7   Plant Varieties Act 1997 s 25(4)(b).
8   Plant Varieties Act 1997 s 25(4)(c).
9   Plant Varieties Act 1997 s 25(3). The rights conferred by s 25 are in addition to any rights which may be conferred under s 24 (see PARA 282): s 25(5).
10 See the Plant Breeders' Rights Regulations 1998, SI 1998/1027, reg 11.
11 See the Plant Varieties Act 1997 s 24; and PARA 282. As to the making of representations for these purposes see note 5.
12 Plant Varieties Act 1997 s 31(1). The offence is punishable on summary conviction by a fine not exceeding level 3 on the standard scale, and is committed by any person (whether the applicant or a person giving information on his behalf) who, in connection with the application, either knowingly or recklessly gives information which is false in a material particular: s 31(1), (2)(a), (b). As to the standard scale and the powers of magistrates' courts to issue fines on summary conviction see SENTENCING vol 92 (2015) PARA 176. As to jurisdiction, and the commission of offences by bodies corporate, see PARA 243 note 17.

263. Content and effect of compulsory licences.

A compulsory licence for the exploitation of plant breeders' rights[1] may be on such terms as the Controller of Plant Variety Rights[2] thinks fit, and may in particular include terms as to the remuneration payable to the rights holder[3] and obliging the rights holder to make propagating material available to the licensee[4]. In deciding on what terms to grant a compulsory licence the Controller must have regard to the desirability of securing that the variety[5] to which the application relates is available to the public at reasonable prices[6], is widely distributed[7] and is maintained in quality[8]. Note that these factors correspond to some of those in relation to which the Controller must be satisfied in order to grant the licence[9]. The Controller must also have regard to the desirability of securing that there is reasonable remuneration for the rights holder[10].

If a compulsory licence is granted with regard to a variety of a species or group, in relation to which a period is specified for these purposes by regulations made by the Secretary of State and the Welsh Ministers[11], and the grant takes place before a period of that length has passed since the date of grant of the rights to which the licence relates, the licence will not have effect until a period of that length has passed since that date[12].

The Controller may, at any time, on the application of any person, extend, limit or in any other respect vary a compulsory licence, or revoke it[13]. A decision of the Controller to allow or refuse such an application is subject to appeal to the Plant Varieties and Seeds Tribunal[14] and accordingly may not be made until the opportunity to make representations on the matter has been afforded to interested parties[15]. The giving of false information in connection with an application for the variation of a licence is an offence[16].

1 As to the granting of compulsory licences see PARA 261. As to the nature and scope of plant breeders' rights see PARAS 239–242.
2 As to the Controller of Plant Variety Rights see PARAS 243 note 2, 281–284.
3 Plant Varieties Act 1997 s 17(4)(a).
4 Plant Varieties Act 1997 s 17(4)(b).
5 As to the meaning of 'variety' see PARA 239 note 1.
6 Plant Varieties Act 1997 s 17(5)(a)(i).
7 Plant Varieties Act 1997 s 17(5)(a)(ii).
8 Plant Varieties Act 1997 s 17(5)(a)(iii).
9 See the Plant Varieties Act 1997 s 17(2)(a); and PARA 261.
10 Plant Varieties Act 1997 s 17(5)(b).
11 As to the Secretary of State and the Welsh Ministers see PARA 390.
12 Plant Varieties Act 1997 s 17(8). The specified period is two years: see the Plant Breeders' Rights Regulations 1998, SI 1998/1027, reg 10.
13 Plant Varieties Act 1997 s 17(9). Receipt of an application under s 17(9) must be notified by the Controller in the gazette, and specified persons may make representations: see the Plant Breeders' Rights Regulations 1998, SI 1998/1027, regs 5, 7, 8, Sch 1 Pt B(3). As to the gazette see PARA 17. As to regulations governing the Controller's functions see PARA 282.
14 Plant Varieties Act 1997 s 26(1)(b). As to the tribunal and appeals thereto see PARA 285 et seq.
15 See the Plant Varieties Act 1997 s 24; and PARA 282. As to the making of representations for these purposes see note 13.
16 Plant Varieties Act 1997 s 31(1). The offence is punishable on summary conviction by a fine not exceeding level 3 on the standard scale, and is committed by any person (whether the applicant or a person giving information on his behalf) who, in connection with the application for variation, either knowingly or recklessly gives information which is false in a material particular: s 31(1), (2)(a), (b). As to the standard scale and the powers of magistrates' courts to issue fines on summary conviction see SENTENCING vol 92 (2015) PARA 176. As to jurisdiction, and the commission of offences by bodies corporate, see PARA 243 note 17.

264. Breach of licence obligations.

The Controller of Plant Variety Rights[1] may suspend the exercise of any plant breeders' rights[2] if he is satisfied that the rights holder[3] is in breach of any obligation imposed on him by the licence[4], and may terminate such a suspension only if, on application by the rights holder concerned, he is satisfied that the holder is no longer in breach of the obligation whose breach led to the suspension[5]. A decision of the Controller to allow or refuse an application for the suspension of rights or the termination of such a suspension is subject to appeal to the Plant Varieties and Seeds Tribunal[6] and accordingly may not be made until the opportunity to make representations on the matter has been afforded to interested parties[7]. The giving of false information in connection with an application for the suspension of rights is an offence[8].

1   As to the Controller of Plant Variety Rights see PARAS 243 note 2, 281–284.
2   For the power of the Controller to grant plant breeders' rights see PARA 243. As to the nature and scope of such rights see PARAS 239–242.
3   Ie the holder of a licence for the exploitation of plant breeders' rights under the Plant Varieties Act 1997 s 17 (see PARAS 261–263).
4   Plant Varieties Act 1997 s 23(1). This is without prejudice to the remedies available to the licence holder by the taking of proceedings in any court: s 23(3). Proposed decisions to allow or refuse applications under s 23(1) or s 23(2) (see the text and note 5) must be notified in the gazette by the Controller, and specified persons may make representations in connection with them: see the Plant Breeders' Rights Regulations 1998, SI 1998/1027, regs 5, 7, 8, Sch 1 Pt B(5). As to the gazette see PARA 17. As to regulations governing the Controller's functions see PARA 282.
5   Plant Varieties Act 1997 s 23(2). As to the notification of decisions and the making of representations see note 4.
6   Plant Varieties Act 1997 s 26(1)(f). As to the tribunal and appeals thereto see PARA 285 et seq.
7   See the Plant Varieties Act 1997 s 24; and PARA 282. As to the making of representations for these purposes see note 4.
8   Plant Varieties Act 1997 s 31(1). The offence is punishable on summary conviction by a fine not exceeding level 3 on the standard scale, and is committed by any person (whether the applicant or a person giving information on his behalf) who, in connection with the application, either knowingly or recklessly gives information which is false in a material particular: s 31(1), (2)(a), (b). As to the standard scale and the powers of magistrates' courts to issue fines on summary conviction see SENTENCING vol 92 (2015) PARA 176. As to jurisdiction, and the commission of offences by bodies corporate, see PARA 243 note 17.

(ii) Biotechnological Inventions

A. PROTECTION OF BIOTECHNOLOGICAL INVENTIONS

265. Directive on the Protection of Biotechnological Inventions.

The European Directive on the legal protection of biotechnological inventions[1] requires member states to protect biotechnological inventions under national patent law and, if necessary, to adjust their national patent law to take account of its provisions[2]. Pursuant to the Directive inventions which are new, which involve an inventive step and which are susceptible of industrial application are patentable even if they concern a product consisting of or containing biological material[3] or a process by means of which biological material is produced, processed or used[4]. The Directive has been fully implemented in United Kingdom law: the provisions concerned with the patenting of biotechnological inventions generally[5] and the deposit, access and re-deposit of biological material[6] have been implemented in the legislation relating to patents[7], while the provisions requiring the introduction of a system of compulsory cross licensing[8] have been implemented by the introduction of two new systems of compulsory licensing (supplementing the existing provisions for the compulsory licensing of plant breeders' rights[9]), one concerning compulsory patent licences[10] and the other concerning compulsory plant variety licences[11].

1   Ie Council Directive (EC) 98/44 (OJ L213, 30.7.98, p 13) on the legal protection of biotechnological inventions.

2   See Council Directive (EC) 98/44 (OJ L213, 30.7.98, p 13) art 1.1.

3   'Biological material' means any material containing genetic information and capable of reproducing itself or being reproduced in a biological system: Council Directive (EC) 98/44 (OJ L213, 30.7.98, p 13) art 2.1(a).

4   Council Directive (EC) 98/44 (OJ L213, 30.7.98, p 13) art 3.1. Biological material which is isolated from its natural environment or produced by means of a technical process may be the subject of an invention even if it previously occurred in nature: art 3.2. Plant and animal varieties, and essentially biological processes for the production of plants or animals, are not, however, patentable, although inventions which concern plants or animals will be patentable if the technical feasibility of the invention is not confined to a particular plant or animal variety: arts 4.1, 4.2. Inventions are also considered unpatentable where their commercial exploitation would be contrary to public order or morality; however, exploitation is not deemed to be so contrary merely because it is prohibited by law or regulation: art 6.1.

5   Ie Council Directive (EC) 98/44 (OJ L213, 30.7.98, p 13) arts 1–11.

6   Ie Council Directive (EC) 98/44 (OJ L213, 30.7.98, p 13) arts 13, 14.

7   Council Directive (EC) 98/44 (OJ L213, 30.7.98, p 13) arts 1–11 were implemented by the Patents Regulations 2000, SI 2000/2037 (amending the Patents Act 1977 ss 1, 60, 130, and adding ss 76A, 125A, Schs A1, A2); Council Directive (EC) 98/44 (OJ L213, 30.7.98, p 13) arts 13, 14 were implemented by the Patents (Amendment) Rules 2001, SI 2001/1412 (amending the Patents Rules 1995, SI 1995/2093 (now the Patents Rules 2007, SI 2007/3291)): see PATENTS AND REGISTERED DESIGNS.

8   Ie Council Directive (EC) 98/44 (OJ L213, 30.7.98, p 13) art 12.

9   As to the existing provisions for the compulsory licensing of plant breeders' rights see PARAS 261–264.

10   See the Patents and Plant Variety Rights (Compulsory Licensing) Regulations 2002, SI 2002/247, Pt II (regs 3–10); and PARAS 266–271, 279.

11   See the Patents and Plant Variety Rights (Compulsory Licensing) Regulations 2002, SI 2002/247, Pt III (regs 11–16); and PARAS 272–278, 280.

B. COMPULSORY PATENT LICENCES

266.   Applications for compulsory patent licences.

Pursuant to the European Directive on the legal protection of biotechnological inventions[1], it is provided that where a person cannot exploit plant breeders' rights[2] or a Community plant variety right[3] in a new variety[4] without infringing a prior patent, he may apply to the Comptroller General of Patents[5] for a licence under the patent[6]. Applications must be made in accordance with rules established for this purpose[7] and be accompanied by particulars which seek to demonstrate that:

(1)   the applicant cannot acquire or exploit plant breeders' rights or a Community plant variety right without infringing a prior patent[8];

(2)   the applicant has applied unsuccessfully to the proprietor of the prior patent concerned for a licence to use that patent to acquire or exploit plant breeders' rights or a Community plant variety right[9]; and

(3)   the new plant variety, in which the applicant wishes to acquire or exploit the plant breeders' rights or Community plant variety right, constitutes significant technical progress of considerable economic interest in relation to the invention protected by the patent[10].

1   Ie Council Directive (EC) 98/44 (OJ L213, 30.7.98, p 13) on the legal protection of biotechnological inventions: see PARA 265.

2   For the purposes of the Patents and Plant Variety Rights (Compulsory Licensing) Regulations
    2002, SI 2002/247, 'plant breeders' rights' means rights granted by the Controller of Plant Variety
    Rights under the Plant Varieties Act 1997 s 3 (see PARA 243) and existing rights as defined by s
    40(4) (see PARA 256): Patents and Plant Variety Rights (Compulsory Licensing) Regulations
    2002, SI 2002/247, reg 2(1).
3   'Community plant variety right' means a right granted by the Community Plant Variety Office
    under Council Regulation (EC) 2100/94 (OJ L227, 1.9.99, p 1) on Community plant variety
    rights: Patents and Plant Variety Rights (Compulsory Licensing) Regulations 2002, SI 2002/247,
    reg 2(1).
4   'New plant variety' means the plant variety produced, or to be produced as the case may be, by
    using an invention protected by a patent: Patents and Plant Variety Rights (Compulsory Licensing)
    Regulations 2002, SI 2002/247, reg 2(1). As to the meaning of 'plant variety' see the Patents Act
    1977 Sch A2 para 11; and PATENTS AND REGISTERED DESIGNS vol 79 (2014) PARA 433 (definition
    applied by the Patents and Plant Variety Rights (Compulsory Licensing) Regulations 2002,
    SI 2002/247, reg 2(1)). 'Patent' means a patent under the Patents Act 1977: s 130(1); Patents and
    Plant Variety Rights (Compulsory Licensing) Regulations 2002, SI 2002/247, reg 2(1).
5   Ie the Comptroller General of Patents, Designs and Trade Marks appointed under the Patents and
    Designs Act 1907 s 63(1): Patents and Plant Variety Rights (Compulsory Licensing) Regulations
    2002, SI 2002/247, reg 2(1). See PATENTS AND REGISTERED DESIGNS vol 79 (2014) PARA 575.
6   Patents and Plant Variety Rights (Compulsory Licensing) Regulations 2002, SI 2002/247, reg
    3(1); Council Directive (EC) 98/44 (OJ L213, 30.7.98, p 13) on the legal protection of
    biotechnological inventions, art 12.1. As to proceedings before the Comptroller General see PARA
    279. Note, however, that although an application for a compulsory patent licence is additional to
    any application an applicant may make for a compulsory licence under the Patents Act 1977 s 48
    (see PATENTS AND REGISTERED DESIGNS vol 79 (2014) PARA 394), the provisions of ss 48, 48A,
    48B, 49, 50, 52 (see PATENTS AND REGISTERED DESIGNS vol 79 (2014) PARA 394 et seq) do not
    extend and apply to, and are not taken to make corresponding provision in respect of, compulsory
    patent licences and cross licences ordered to be granted under the Patents and Plant Variety Rights
    (Compulsory Licensing) Regulations 2002, SI 2002/247: reg 26(2). As to cross licences see PARA
    269.
        If and so far as any agreement purports to bind any person not to apply for a licence under reg
    3(1), it is void: reg 3(3).
7   Patents and Plant Variety Rights (Compulsory Licensing) Regulations 2002, SI 2002/247, reg
    3(1). The power of the Secretary of State to make rules under the Patents Act 1977 s 123 (see
    PATENTS AND REGISTERED DESIGNS vol 79 (2014) PARA 574) is extended so as to permit him to
    make rules regulating the business of the Patent Office in respect of: (1) applications for the grant
    of licences under the Patents and Plant Variety Rights (Compulsory Licensing) Regulations 2002,
    SI 2002/247, regs 3(1), 15(1); (2) applications under regs 8, 16(4) for variation and under regs 9,
    16(5) for revocation of compulsory patent licences and cross licences; (3) proceedings before the
    Controllers or the Comptroller General of Patents as the case may be in relation to such
    applications; (4) fees; and (5) other matters related to or arising under the Patents and Plant
    Variety Rights (Compulsory Licensing) Regulations 2002, SI 2002/247: reg 20. The Patents Act
    1977 s 124 (see PATENTS AND REGISTERED DESIGNS vol 79 (2014) PARA 574) applies accordingly:
    Patents and Plant Variety Rights (Compulsory Licensing) Regulations 2002, SI 2002/247, reg 20.
    Note that the Patent Office is now operating under the name the 'UK Intellectual Property Office':
    see the UK Intellectual Property Office Name Change Fact Sheet. At the date at which this volume
    states the law the Secretary of State had not exercised the above powers, and unless and until such
    time as he does, 'rules' means the Patents Rules 2007, SI 2007/3291, in respect of:
    (a)   applications for the grant and revocation of compulsory licences under the Patents Act
          1977 s 48(1) including forms (see PATENTS AND REGISTERED DESIGNS vol 79 (2014)
          PARA 394);
    (b)   proceedings before the Comptroller General of Patents in relation to the grant of such
          applications and the revocation of compulsory licences granted under s 48(1); and
    (c)   other matters provided for in the Patents Rules 2007, SI 2007/3291, related to
          applications and proceedings in respect of such compulsory licences,
    extended and applied to, and taken to make corresponding provision in respect of, applications for
    the grant of licences under the Patents and Plant Variety Rights (Compulsory Licensing)
    Regulations 2002, SI 2002/247, reg 3(1), proceedings before the Controllers in relation to the
    grant of such applications, the variation or revocation of compulsory patent licences and cross

licences under regs 7(2), (3), 15(3), and other matters related to or arising under those regulations: regs 2(1), 22(1) (reg 2(1) amended by SI 2007/3293). The Patents Rules 2007, SI 2007/3291 have effect for these purposes with appropriate modifications: Patents and Plant Variety Rights (Compulsory Licensing) Regulations 2002, SI 2002/247, reg 22(2). 'Controllers' means the Controller of Plant Variety Rights (see PARAS 281–284) and the Comptroller General of Patents acting jointly in accordance with the provisions of the Patents and Plant Variety Rights (Compulsory Licensing) Regulations 2002, SI 2002/247: reg 2(1). As to the Secretary of State see PARA 390.

8 Patents and Plant Variety Rights (Compulsory Licensing) Regulations 2002, SI 2002/247, reg 3(2)(a); Council Directive (EC) 98/44 (OJ L213, 30.7.98, p 13) art 12.1.

9 Patents and Plant Variety Rights (Compulsory Licensing) Regulations 2002, SI 2002/247, reg 3(2)(b); Council Directive (EC) 98/44 (OJ L213, 30.7.98, p 13) art 12.3(a).

10 Patents and Plant Variety Rights (Compulsory Licensing) Regulations 2002, SI 2002/247, reg 3(2)(c); Council Directive (EC) 98/44 (OJ L213, 30.7.98, p 13) art 12.3(b).

267. Consideration of applications and grant of licences.

On receipt by the Comptroller General of Patents[1] of an application for a patent licence[2], and payment of the prescribed fee[3], the Controllers[4] must consider and process the application[5]. The proprietor of the patent[6] concerned or any other person wishing to oppose such an application may give to the Comptroller General of Patents notice of opposition[7], which the Controllers, in deciding whether to grant an application, must consider and process[8]. Where, having considered the application, the Controllers are satisfied as to the matters sought to be demonstrated in it[9], they must order the grant to the applicant[10] of a licence to use the invention protected by the prior patent[11].

1 As to the meaning of 'Comptroller General of Patents' see PARA 266 note 5.

2 Ie an application under the Patents and Plant Variety Rights (Compulsory Licensing) Regulations 2002, SI 2002/247, reg 3(1): see PARA 266.

3 Unless and until the Secretary of State exercises his powers to make rules under the Patents Act 1977 s 123 as extended by the Patents and Plant Variety Rights (Compulsory Licensing) Regulations 2002, SI 2002/247, reg 20 and prescribes a fee (see PARA 266 note 7), 'prescribed fee' means the fee payable under the Patents (Fees) Rules 2007, SI 2007/3292, in respect of making an application for the grant of compulsory licences under the Patents Act 1977 s 48(1) including forms (see PATENTS AND REGISTERED DESIGNS vol 79 (2014) PARA 394), and giving a notice of opposition to an application made under s 48, those rules being extended and applied to, and taken to make corresponding provision in respect of, an application for a licence under the Patents and Plant Variety Rights (Compulsory Licensing) Regulations 2002, SI 2002/247, reg 3(1) or reg 15(1), and giving a notice of opposition under reg 5(1): regs 2(1), 24. Applications for patent licences are required to be accompanied by the prescribed fee: reg 3(1).

4 As to the meaning of 'Controllers' see PARA 266 note 7.

5 Patents and Plant Variety Rights (Compulsory Licensing) Regulations 2002, SI 2002/247, reg 4. The Controllers are required to consider and process the application in accordance with rules: reg 4. As to the rules see PARA 266 note 7. As to proceedings see PARA 279. For the right of appeal from the decisions of the Controller and of the Comptroller General of Patents see PARA 271.

6 As to the meaning of 'patent' see PARA 266 note 4.

7 Patents and Plant Variety Rights (Compulsory Licensing) Regulations 2002, SI 2002/247, reg 5(1). Notices must be given in accordance with rules, and the person giving the notice must pay the prescribed fee: reg 5(1).

8 Patents and Plant Variety Rights (Compulsory Licensing) Regulations 2002, SI 2002/247, reg 5(2). Opposition must be considered and processed in accordance with rules: reg 5(2).

9 As to the matters sought to be demonstrated in an application for a patent licence see PARA 266.

10 Where the applicant is a government department the Controllers must order the grant to any person specified in the application: Patents and Plant Variety Rights (Compulsory Licensing) Regulations 2002, SI 2002/247, reg 6.

11 Patents and Plant Variety Rights (Compulsory Licensing) Regulations 2002, SI 2002/247, reg 6. As to the scope of licences and the conditions under which they must be granted see PARA 268.

268. Scope and conditions of patent licences.

Compulsory patent licences[1] may be granted only in so far as they are necessary for the exploitation of the new plant variety[2] in connection with which the application was made[3]. Licences must not be exclusive[4], must entitle the proprietor of the patent concerned to an appropriate royalty[5], and must entitle the proprietor of the patent concerned to a cross licence on reasonable terms to use the new plant variety[6], and may in addition be granted on such other terms as the Controllers think fit[7].

1 'Compulsory patent licence' means a licence ordered to be granted by the Controllers under the Patents and Plant Variety Rights (Compulsory Licensing) Regulations 2002, SI 2002/247, reg 6 (see PARA 267): reg 2(1). As to the meaning of 'Controllers' see PARA 266 note 7. For the right of appeal from the decisions of the Controllers see PARA 271.
2 As to the meaning of 'new plant variety' see PARA 266 note 4.
3 Patents and Plant Variety Rights (Compulsory Licensing) Regulations 2002, SI 2002/247, reg 6; Council Directive (EC) 98/44 (OJ L213, 30.7.98, p 13) on the legal protection of biotechnological inventions, art 12.1. As to proceedings see PARA 279. As to the directive see PARA 265.
4 Patents and Plant Variety Rights (Compulsory Licensing) Regulations 2002, SI 2002/247, reg 7(1)(a); Council Directive (EC) 98/44 (OJ L213, 30.7.98, p 13) art 12.1.
5 Patents and Plant Variety Rights (Compulsory Licensing) Regulations 2002, SI 2002/247, reg 7(1)(b); Council Directive (EC) 98/44 (OJ L213, 30.7.98, p 13) art 12.1.
6 Patents and Plant Variety Rights (Compulsory Licensing) Regulations 2002, SI 2002/247, reg 7(1)(c); Council Directive (EC) 98/44 (OJ L213, 30.7.98, p 13) art 12.1. As to cross licences PARA 1205.
7 Patents and Plant Variety Rights (Compulsory Licensing) Regulations 2002, SI 2002/247, reg 6.

269. Cross licences.

Where the Controllers[1] order the grant of a compulsory patent licence[2] to a person who has been granted, or has yet to acquire, plant breeders' rights[3] in a new plant variety[4], the proprietor of the patent[5] concerned may request a cross licence on reasonable terms of the plant breeders' rights to use the new plant variety in respect of which the compulsory patent licence has been granted[6]. On such a request, the Controllers must order the grant of such a cross licence to that proprietor[7]. Where the Controllers order the grant of a compulsory patent licence to a person who has been granted a Community plant variety right[8] in the new variety, and the proprietor of the patent so wishes, the compulsory patent licence must be subject to the grant to the proprietor of the patent concerned of a cross licence of the Community plant variety right on reasonable terms to use in the United Kingdom[9] the new variety in respect of which the compulsory patent licence has been granted[10].

1 As to the meaning of 'Controllers' see PARA 266 note 7.
2 As to the meaning of 'compulsory patent licence' see PARA 268 note 1.
3 As to the meaning of 'plant breeders' rights' see PARA 266 note 2.
4 As to the meaning of 'new plant variety' see PARA 266 note 4.
5 As to the meaning of 'patent' see PARA 266 note 4.
6 Patents and Plant Variety Rights (Compulsory Licensing) Regulations 2002, SI 2002/247, reg 7(1)(c), (2), (3); Council Directive (EC) 98/44 (OJ L213, 30.7.98, p 13) on the legal protection of biotechnological inventions, art 12.1. As to proceedings see PARA 279. Note, however, that although an application for a compulsory patent licence (see PARA 266) is additional to any application an applicant may make for a compulsory licence under the Patents Act 1977 s 48 (see PATENTS AND REGISTERED DESIGNS vol 79 (2014) PARAS 394, 395), the provisions of ss 48, 48A, 48B, 49, 50, 52 (see PATENTS AND REGISTERED DESIGNS vol 79 (2014) PARA 394 et seq) do not extend and apply to, and are not taken to make corresponding provision in respect of, compulsory patent licences and cross licences ordered to be granted under the Patents and Plant Variety Rights (Compulsory Licensing) Regulations 2002, SI 2002/247: reg 26(2). For the right of appeal from the decisions of the Controllers see PARA 271. As to the directive see PARA 265.

7 Patents and Plant Variety Rights (Compulsory Licensing) Regulations 2002, SI 2002/247, reg 7(2), (3). Where the proprietor of the patent is a government department, the cross licence may be granted to any person specified in the request: reg 7(2), (3). Where the compulsory patent licence is granted to a person who has yet to acquire plant breeders' rights in the new plant variety, the cross licence comes into effect on the grant to the holder of the compulsory patent licence of plant breeders' rights in the new plant variety: reg 7(3).

8 As to the meaning of 'Community plant variety right' see PARA 266 note 3.

9 Ie England, Wales, Scotland and Northern Ireland: Patents and Plant Variety Rights (Compulsory Licensing) Regulations 2002, SI 2002/247, reg 2(1).

10 Patents and Plant Variety Rights (Compulsory Licensing) Regulations 2002, SI 2002/247, reg 7(4). Where the Controllers order the grant of a compulsory patent licence to a person who has yet to acquire a Community plant variety right in the new plant variety, the order for grant must, if the proprietor of the patent wishes, include a condition that, on the grant of the Community plant variety right to such person in the new variety in respect of which the compulsory patent licence has been granted, the proprietor of the patent concerned must be granted a cross licence on reasonable terms to use in the United Kingdom the new plant variety in respect of which the compulsory patent licence has been granted: reg 7(5). Where the proprietor of the patent is a government department, the cross licence may be granted to any person specified in the request: reg 7(4), (5).

270. Variation and revocation of compulsory plant licences and cross licences.

The Controllers[1] may extend, limit or in any other respect vary both a compulsory patent licence[2] and a cross licence granted in respect of a compulsory patent licence granted to a person who has been granted plant breeders' rights[3] in respect of a new plant variety[4]. The amendment may be made either to the order for the grant of such a licence or to the licence itself[5]. The Controllers are also entitled to revoke an order for the grant of such a licence, and to terminate the licence so granted, if they are satisfied that the circumstances which led to the order for its grant have ceased to exist or are unlikely to recur[6]. Any party[7] may apply for variation or revocation at any time[8].

1 As to the meaning of 'Controllers' see PARA 266 note 7.

2 As to the meaning of 'compulsory patent licence' see PARA 268 note 1.

3 As to the meaning of 'plant breeders' rights' see PARA 266 note 2.

4 Patents and Plant Variety Rights (Compulsory Licensing) Regulations 2002, SI 2002/247, reg 8(1). As to the meaning of 'new plant variety' see PARA 266 note 4. The cross licence referred to in the text is a cross licence granted under reg 7(2) or reg 7(3) (see PARA 269): reg 8(1). As to proceedings see PARA 279. For the right of appeal from the decisions of the Controllers and of the Comptroller General of Patents see PARA 271.

5 Patents and Plant Variety Rights (Compulsory Licensing) Regulations 2002, SI 2002/247, reg 8(1).

6 Patents and Plant Variety Rights (Compulsory Licensing) Regulations 2002, SI 2002/247, reg 9(2). Any revocation or termination may be subject to such terms and conditions as the Controllers think necessary for the protection of the legitimate interests of the holder of the compulsory patent licence or the cross licence ordered to be granted under reg 7(2) or reg 7(3): reg 9(2).

7 'Party' means the proprietor of the patent concerned or the applicant, as the case may be, in an application under the Patents and Plant Variety Rights (Compulsory Licensing) Regulations 2002, SI 2002/247, reg 3(1) (see PARA 266) or their respective successors in title: reg 10.

8 Patents and Plant Variety Rights (Compulsory Licensing) Regulations 2002, SI 2002/247, regs 8(1), 9(1). Applications for variation or revocation are made to the Comptroller General of Patents (see PARA 266 note 5), and are required to be made, and considered and processed by the Controllers, in accordance with rules: regs 8(1), (2), 9(1), (2). As to the rules see PARA 266 note 7.

271. Appeals.

An appeal lies from a decision of the Controllers[1] or the Comptroller General of Patents[2] under the provisions concerning compulsory patent licences[3], and an appeal may be brought to the court[4] from a decision of the Controllers relating to a compulsory patent licence[5] or a cross licence ordered to be granted in respect of a compulsory patent licence granted to a person who has been granted plant breeders' rights[6] in respect of a new plant variety[7].

1   As to the meaning of 'Controllers' see PARA 266 note 7.
2   As to the meaning of 'Comptroller General of Patents' see PARA 266 note 5.
3   Patents and Plant Variety Rights (Compulsory Licensing) Regulations 2002, SI 2002/247, reg 17(1). The provisions concerning compulsory patent licences are the provisions of Pt II (regs 3–10): see PARAS 266–270.
4   Ie the Patents Court of the High Court: Patents and Plant Variety Rights (Compulsory Licensing) Regulations 2002, SI 2002/247, reg 2(1).
5   As to the meaning of 'compulsory patent licence' see PARA 268 note 1.
6   As to the meaning of 'plant breeders' rights' see PARA 266 note 2.
7   Patents and Plant Variety Rights (Compulsory Licensing) Regulations 2002, SI 2002/247, reg 17(2). As to the meaning of 'new plant variety' see PARA 266 note 4. The cross licence referred to in the text is a cross licence granted under reg 7(2) or reg 7(3) (see PARA 269): reg 17(2).

C. COMPULSORY PLANT VARIETY LICENCES

272. Applications for compulsory plant variety licences.
Pursuant to the European Directive on the legal protection of biotechnological inventions[1], it is provided that where a proprietor of a patent[2] for a biotechnological invention[3] cannot exploit a biotechnological invention protected by the patent without infringing prior plant breeders' rights[4], he may apply to the Controller of Plant Variety Rights[5] for a licence[6].

Applications must be made in accordance with the Plant Breeders' regulations[7] and be accompanied by particulars which seek to demonstrate that:

(1)   the proprietor of the patent for a biotechnological invention cannot exploit the biotechnological invention protected by the patent without infringing prior plant breeders' rights[8];

(2)   the proprietor of the patent has unsuccessfully applied to the holder of the prior plant breeders' rights for a licence[9]; and

(3)   the biotechnological invention protected by the patent constitutes significant technical progress of considerable economic interest in relation to the plant variety[10] protected by the prior plant breeders' rights[11].

1   Ie Council Directive (EC) 98/44 (OJ L213, 30.7.98, p 13) on the legal protection of biotechnological inventions: see PARA 265.
2   As to the meaning of 'patent' see PARA 266 note 4.
3   'Biotechnological invention' means an invention which concerns a product consisting of or containing biological material or a process by means of which biological material is produced, processed or used: Patents Act 1977 s 130 (amended by SI 2000/2037); Patents and Plant Variety Rights (Compulsory Licensing) Regulations 2002, SI 2002/247, reg 2(1). 'Biological material' means any material containing genetic information and capable of reproducing itself or being reproduced in a biological system: Patents Act 1977 s 130 (as so amended).
4   As to the meaning of 'plant breeders' rights' see PARA 266 note 2.
5   Ie the officer appointed under the Plant Varieties Act 1997 s 2(1) (see PARA 281): Patents and Plant Variety Rights (Compulsory Licensing) Regulations 2002, SI 2002/247, reg 2(1).
6   Patents and Plant Variety Rights (Compulsory Licensing) Regulations 2002, SI 2002/247, reg 11(1); Council Directive (EC) 98/44 (OJ L213, 30.7.98, p 13) art 12.2. As to proceedings see PARA 280. Note, however, that although an application for a compulsory plant variety licence is additional to any application an applicant may make for a compulsory licence under the Plant Varieties Act 1997 s 17 (see PARAS 261, 263), the provisions of ss 17, 23 (see PARAS 261, 263–264) do not extend and apply to, and are not taken to make corresponding provision in

respect of, compulsory plant variety licences and cross licences under the Patents and Plant Variety Rights (Compulsory Licensing) Regulations 2002, SI 2002/247: reg 27(2). As to cross licences see PARA 275.

If and so far as any agreement purports to bind any person not to apply for a licence under reg 11(1), it is void: reg 11(3).

7 Patents and Plant Variety Rights (Compulsory Licensing) Regulations 2002, SI 2002/247, reg 11(1). The power of the Secretary of State and the Welsh Ministers to make regulations under the Plant Varieties Act 1997 ss 24, 26(2)(a), 28, 29, 44, 48(1) (see PARAS 243 et seq, 282) is extended so as to permit them to make regulations in respect of:

 (1) applications for the grant of licences under the Patents and Plant Variety Rights (Compulsory Licensing) Regulations 2002, SI 2002/247, reg 11(1);
 (2) applications under reg 16(1) for variation and under reg 16(2) for revocation of compulsory plant variety licences and cross licences;
 (3) proceedings before the Controllers in relation to such applications;
 (4) appeals from the decisions of the Controllers in relation to such applications;
 (5) fees; and
 (6) other matters related to or arising under the Patents and Plant Variety Rights (Compulsory Licensing) Regulations 2002, SI 2002/247: reg 21.

The Patents Act 1977 s 48(2)–(5) (see PATENTS AND REGISTERED DESIGNS vol 79 (2014) PARAS 394–395) applies accordingly: Plant Variety Rights (Compulsory Licensing) Regulations 2002, SI 2002/247, reg 21. At the date at which this volume states the law the Secretary of State and the Welsh Ministers had not exercised these powers, and unless and until such time as they do, the 'Breeders' regulations' means the Plant Breeders' Rights Regulations 1998, SI 1998/1027, in respect of:

 (a) applications for the grant, variation and revocation of compulsory licences under the Plant Varieties Act 1997 s 17(1) (see PARA 261);
 (b) proceedings before the Controller of Plant Variety Rights in relation to the grant of such applications and the variation or revocation of compulsory licences granted under s 17(1);
 (c) appeals to the Plant Varieties Tribunal (see PARAS 285–291); and
 (d) other matters provided for in the Plant Breeders' Rights Regulations 1998, SI 1998/1027, related to applications and proceedings in respect of such compulsory licences,

extended and applied to, and taken to make corresponding provision in respect of, applications under the Patents and Plant Variety Rights (Compulsory Licensing) Regulations 2002, SI 2002/247, reg 11(1), proceedings before the Controllers in relation to such applications, the variation or revocation of compulsory plant variety licences and cross licences granted under reg 14(2), appeals to the tribunal, and other matters related to or arising under those regulations: regs 2(1), 23(1). The Plant Breeders' Rights Regulations 1998, SI 1998/1027, have effect for these purposes as if a reference therein to the Comptroller General of Patents were to the Controllers and with any other necessary modifications: Patents and Plant Variety Rights (Compulsory Licensing) Regulations 2002, SI 2002/247, reg 22(2). As to the meaning of 'Controllers' see PARA 266 note 7. As to the Secretary of State and the Welsh Ministers see PARA 390. The Plant Breeders' Rights Regulations 1998, SI 1998/1027, reg 10 (see PARA 263) does not extend and apply to and should not be taken to make corresponding provision in the Patents and Plant Variety Rights (Compulsory Licensing) Regulations 2002, SI 2002/247: reg 23(3).

8 Patents and Plant Variety Rights (Compulsory Licensing) Regulations 2002, SI 2002/247, reg 11(2)(a); Council Directive (EC) 98/44 (OJ L213, 30.7.98, p 13) art 12.1.
9 Patents and Plant Variety Rights (Compulsory Licensing) Regulations 2002, SI 2002/247, reg 11(2)(b); Council Directive (EC) 98/44 (OJ L213, 30.7.98, p 13) art 12.3(a).
10 As to the meaning of 'plant variety' see PARA 266 note 4.
11 Patents and Plant Variety Rights (Compulsory Licensing) Regulations 2002, SI 2002/247, reg 11(2)(c); Council Directive (EC) 98/44 (OJ L213, 30.7.98, p 13) art 12.3(b).

273. Consideration of applications and grant of licences.

On receipt by the Controller of Plant Variety Rights[1] of an application for a plant variety licence[2], and payment of the appropriate plant breeder's fee[3], the Controllers[4] must consider and process the application[5], and where having considered the application the Controllers are satisfied as to the matters sought to be demonstrated in it[6], they must grant to the proprietor of the patent[7] for the biotechnological invention[8] a licence to use the plant variety[9] protected by prior plant breeders' rights[10].

1 As to the Controller of Plant Variety Rights see PARAS 272 note 5, 281–284.
2 Ie an application under the Patents and Plant Variety Rights (Compulsory Licensing) Regulations 2002, SI 2002/247, reg 11(1): see PARA 272.
3 Applications for plant variety licences are required to be accompanied by the plant breeder's fee: Patents and Plant Variety Rights (Compulsory Licensing) Regulations 2002, SI 2002/247, reg 11(1). As to the plant breeder's fee see (by virtue of regs 2(1), 25) the Plant Breeders' Rights (Naming and Fees) Regulations 2006, SI 2006/648.
4 As to the meaning of 'Controllers' see PARA 266 note 7.
5 Patents and Plant Variety Rights (Compulsory Licensing) Regulations 2002, SI 2002/247, reg 12(1). The Controllers are required to consider and process the application in accordance with the Breeders' regulations (Patents and Plant Variety Rights (Compulsory Licensing) Regulations 2002, SI 2002/247, reg 12(1)) and may also, in proceedings before them in relation to an application under reg 11(1), give such directions as they think fit with regard to the subsequent procedure (reg 12(2)). Any person entitled under the Breeders' regulations to make written or oral representations on an application under the Patents and Plant Variety Rights (Compulsory Licensing) Regulations 2002, SI 2002/247, reg 11(1) must do so in accordance with the Breeders' regulations and must pay the appropriate plant breeder's fee: Patents and Plant Variety Rights (Compulsory Licensing) Regulations 2002, SI 2002/247, reg 12(3). As to the Breeders' regulations see PARA 272 note 7. For the right of appeal see PARA 278.
6 As to the matters to be demonstrated in an application for a plant variety licence see PARA 272.
7 As to the meaning of 'patent' see PARA 266 note 4.
8 As to the meaning of 'biotechnological invention' see PARA 272 note 3. Where the proprietor is a government department the Controllers must order the grant to any person specified in the application: Patents and Plant Variety Rights (Compulsory Licensing) Regulations 2002, SI 2002/247, reg 13.
9 As to the meaning of 'plant variety' see PARA 266 note 4.
10 Patents and Plant Variety Rights (Compulsory Licensing) Regulations 2002, SI 2002/247, reg 13. As to the meaning of 'plant breeders' rights' see PARA 266 note 2. As to the scope of licences and the conditions under which they must be granted see PARA 274. As to proceedings see PARA 280.

274. Scope and conditions of plant variety licences.

Compulsory plant variety licences[1] must not be exclusive[2], must entitle the holder of the plant breeders' rights[3] concerned to an appropriate royalty[4], and must entitle the holder of the plant breeders' rights concerned to a cross licence on reasonable terms to use the biotechnological invention[5] protected by the patent[6], and may in addition be granted on such other terms as the Controllers think fit[7].

1 'Compulsory plant variety licence' means a licence granted by the Controllers under the Patents and Plant Variety Rights (Compulsory Licensing) Regulations 2002, SI 2002/247, reg 13 (see PARA 273): reg 2(1). As to the meaning of 'Controllers' see PARA 266 note 7. For the right of appeal see PARA 278.
2 Patents and Plant Variety Rights (Compulsory Licensing) Regulations 2002, SI 2002/247, reg 14(1)(a); Council Directive (EC) 98/44 (OJ L213, 30.7.98, p 13) on the legal protection of biotechnological inventions, art 12.1. As to the directive see PARA 265.
3 As to the meaning of 'plant breeders' rights' see PARA 266 note 2.
4 Patents and Plant Variety Rights (Compulsory Licensing) Regulations 2002, SI 2002/247, reg 14(1)(b); Council Directive (EC) 98/44 (OJ L213, 30.7.98, p 13) art 12.1.
5 As to the meaning of 'biotechnological invention' see PARA 272 note 3.
6 Patents and Plant Variety Rights (Compulsory Licensing) Regulations 2002, SI 2002/247, reg 14(1)(c); Council Directive (EC) 98/44 (OJ L213, 30.7.98, p 13) art 12.1. As to the meaning of 'patent' see PARA 266 note 4. As to cross licences see PARA 275.
7 Patents and Plant Variety Rights (Compulsory Licensing) Regulations 2002, SI 2002/247, reg 13. As to proceedings see PARA 280.

275.   Cross licences granted by Controllers.

Where the Controllers[1] grant a compulsory plant variety licence[2] to a proprietor of a patent[3] for a biotechnological invention[4], the holder of the plant breeders' rights[5] concerned may request a cross licence on reasonable terms to use the biotechnological invention protected by the patent[6]. On such a request, the Controllers must grant such a cross licence to the holder of plant breeders' rights[7].

1   As to the meaning of 'Controllers' see PARA 266 note 7.
2   As to the meaning of 'compulsory plant variety licence' see PARA 274 note 1.
3   As to the meaning of 'patent' see PARA 266 note 4.
4   As to the meaning of 'biotechnological invention' see PARA 272 note 3.
5   As to the meaning of 'plant breeders' rights' see PARA 266 note 2.
6   Patents and Plant Variety Rights (Compulsory Licensing) Regulations 2002, SI 2002/247, reg 14(1)(c), (2); Council Directive (EC) 98/44 (OJ L213, 30.7.98, p 13) on the legal protection of biotechnological inventions, art 12.2. As to proceedings see PARA 280. Note, however, that although an application for a compulsory plant variety licence is additional to any application an applicant may make for a compulsory licence under the Plant Varieties Act 1997 s 17, the provisions of ss 17, 23 (see PARAS 261, 263–264) do not extend and apply to, and are not taken to make corresponding provision in respect of, compulsory plant variety licences and cross licences under the Patents and Plant Variety Rights (Compulsory Licensing) Regulations 2002, SI 2002/247: reg 27(2). For the right of appeal see PARA 278. As to the directive see PARA 265.
7   Patents and Plant Variety Rights (Compulsory Licensing) Regulations 2002, SI 2002/247, reg 14(2). Where the holder of plant breeders' rights is a government department, the cross licence may be granted to any person specified in the request: reg 14(2).

276.   Cross licences granted by Community Plant Variety Office.

Where the Community Plant Variety Office has granted[1] a compulsory exploitation right in respect of a Community plant variety right[2] to a proprietor of a biotechnological invention[3] protected by a patent[4], who could not otherwise exploit in the United Kingdom[5] the biotechnological invention protected by the patent without infringing a Community plant variety right, then the holder of the Community plant variety right concerned may apply to the Comptroller General of Patents[6] for a cross licence of the biotechnological invention protected by the patent[7]. On receipt of such an application and payment of the prescribed fee[8], the Comptroller General must consider and process the application[9]. Where the holder of the Community plant variety right concerned has paid the prescribed fee and demonstrated in his application to the satisfaction of the Comptroller General that he has a Community plant variety right and the Community Plant Variety Office has granted[10] a compulsory exploitation right in respect of it which allows a proprietor of a patent for a biotechnological invention to exploit in the United Kingdom the biotechnological invention protected by the patent, the Comptroller General must order the grant of a cross licence on reasonable terms to the holder of the Community plant variety right concerned to use the biotechnological invention protected by the patent in the United Kingdom[11].

1   Ie on the grounds specified in Council Directive (EC) 98/44 (OJ L213, 30.7.98, p 13) on the legal protection of biotechnological inventions, art 12.3 (ie that the applicant has applied unsuccessfully to the holder of the plant variety right to obtain a contractual licence and the biotechnological invention constitutes significant technical progress of considerable economic interest compared with the invention claimed in the protected plant variety) and under Council Regulation (EC) 2100/94 (OJ L227, 1.9.99, p 1) on Community plant variety rights, art 29 (granting of compulsory exploitation rights on public interest grounds): Patents and Plant Variety Rights (Compulsory Licensing) Regulations 2002, SI 2002/247, reg 15(1)(a), (b). As to the directive see PARA 265.
2   As to the meaning of 'Community plant variety right' see PARA 266 note 3.
3   As to the meaning of 'biotechnological invention' see PARA 272 note 3.
4   As to the meaning of 'patent' see PARA 266 note 4.

5   As to the meaning of 'United Kingdom' see PARA 1 note 1.
6   As to the meaning of 'Comptroller General of Patents' see PARA 266 note 5.
7   Patents and Plant Variety Rights (Compulsory Licensing) Regulations 2002, SI 2002/247, reg
    15(1). Applications must be made in accordance with rules: reg 15(1). As to the rules see PARA
    266 note 7. As to proceedings see PARA 279.
8   Applications under the Patents and Plant Variety Rights (Compulsory Licensing) Regulations
    2002, SI 2002/247, reg 15(1) are required to be accompanied by the prescribed fee: reg 15(1). As
    to the prescribed fee see PARA 267 note 3.
9   Patents and Plant Variety Rights (Compulsory Licensing) Regulations 2002, SI 2002/247, reg
    15(2). Applications must be considered and processed in accordance with rules: reg 15(2). As to
    the rules see PARA 266 note 7.
10 Ie under Council Regulation (EC) 2100/94 (OJ L227, 1.9.99, p 1) art 29 (see note 1).
11 Patents and Plant Variety Rights (Compulsory Licensing) Regulations 2002, SI 2002/247, reg
    15(3). Where the holder of the Community plant variety right is a government department, the
    cross licence may be granted to any person specified in the application: reg 15(3). For the right of
    appeal see PARA 278.

277. Variation and revocation of compulsory plant variety licences and cross licences.

The Controllers[1] may extend, limit or in any other respect vary both a compulsory plant variety licence[2] and a cross licence granted to the holder of plant variety rights in respect of a compulsory plant variety licence granted to a proprietor of a patent[3] for a biotechnological invention[4]. The Controllers are also entitled to revoke the grant of a compulsory plant variety licence and a cross licence if they are satisfied that the circumstances which led to the grant of the licence or the cross licence have ceased to exist or are unlikely to recur[5]. Any person may apply for variation or revocation at any time[6].

The Comptroller General of Patents[7] may extend, limit or in any other respect vary an order for the grant of a cross licence to the holder of a Community plant variety right[8] to use a biotechnological invention protected by a patent[9]. The amendment may be made either to the order for the grant of such a licence or to the licence itself[10]. The Comptroller General is also entitled to revoke an order for grant of such a licence, and to terminate the licence so granted, if he is satisfied that the circumstances which led to the order for grant have ceased to exist or are unlikely to recur[11]. Any party[12] may apply for variation or revocation at any time[13].

1   As to the meaning of 'Controllers' see PARA 266 note 7.
2   As to the meaning of 'compulsory plant variety licence' see PARA 274 note 1.
3   As to the meaning of 'patent' see PARA 266 note 4.
4   Patents and Plant Variety Rights (Compulsory Licensing) Regulations 2002, SI 2002/247, reg
    16(1). The cross licence referred to in the text is a cross licence granted under reg 14(2) (see PARA
    275): reg 16(1). As to the meaning of 'biotechnological invention' see PARA 272 note 3. For the
    right of appeal see PARA 278.
5   Patents and Plant Variety Rights (Compulsory Licensing) Regulations 2002, SI 2002/247, reg
    16(3). Any revocation or termination may be subject to such terms and conditions as the
    Controllers think necessary for the protection of the legitimate interests of the holder of the
    compulsory plant variety licence or the cross licence: reg 16(3).
6   Patents and Plant Variety Rights (Compulsory Licensing) Regulations 2002, SI 2002/247, reg
    16(1), (2). Applications for variation or revocation are made to the Comptroller General of
    Patents (see PARA 266 note 5), and are required to be made, and considered and processed by the
    Controllers, in accordance with the Breeders' regulations: reg 16(1)–(3). As to the Breeders'
    regulations see PARA 272 note 7. As to proceedings see PARAS 279–280. Applicants must pay the
    appropriate plant breeder's fee: reg 16(1)–(3).
7   As to the meaning of 'Comptroller General of Patents' see PARA 266 note 5.
8   As to the meaning of 'Community plant variety right' see PARA 266 note 3.

9   Patents and Plant Variety Rights (Compulsory Licensing) Regulations 2002, SI 2002/247, reg 16(4). The cross licence referred to in the text is a cross licence granted under reg 15(3) (see PARA 276): reg 16(4). For the right of appeal see PARA 278.

10   Patents and Plant Variety Rights (Compulsory Licensing) Regulations 2002, SI 2002/247, reg 16(4).

11   Patents and Plant Variety Rights (Compulsory Licensing) Regulations 2002, SI 2002/247, reg 16(5), (6). Any revocation or termination may be subject to such terms and conditions as the Comptroller General of Patents thinks necessary for the protection of the legitimate interests of the holder of the cross licence: reg 16(6).

12   'Party' means the proprietor of the patent concerned or the applicant, as the case may be, in an application under the Patents and Plant Variety Rights (Compulsory Licensing) Regulations 2002, SI 2002/247, reg 15(1) (see PARA 276) or their respective successors in title: reg 16(7).

13   Patents and Plant Variety Rights (Compulsory Licensing) Regulations 2002, SI 2002/247, reg 16(4), (5). Applications for variation or revocation are made to the Comptroller General of Patents and are required to be made, and considered and processed by the Comptroller General, in accordance with rules: reg 16(4)–(6). As to the rules see PARA 266 note 7.

278. Appeals.

An appeal lies from a decision of the Controllers[1] or Comptroller General of Patents[2] under the provisions concerning compulsory plant variety licences[3], and an appeal may be brought to the court[4] from a decision of the Comptroller General relating to a cross licence ordered to be granted to the holder of a Community plant variety right[5] to use a biotechnological invention[6] protected by a patent[7].

Where a decision of the Controllers relates to a compulsory plant variety licence or cross licence of a patent for a biotechnological invention[8], an appeal may be brought to the Plant Varieties and Seeds Tribunal[9] as if the decision of the Controllers were one made in connection with compulsory licences under the Plant Varieties Act 1997[10] by the Controller of Plant Variety Rights[11].

1   As to the meaning of 'Controllers' see PARA 266 note 7.
2   As to the meaning of 'Comptroller General of Patents' see PARA 266 note 5.
3   Patents and Plant Variety Rights (Compulsory Licensing) Regulations 2002, SI 2002/247, reg 17(1). As to the meaning of 'compulsory plant variety licence' see PARA 274 note 1. The provisions concerning compulsory plant variety licences are the provisions of Pt III (regs 11–16): see PARAS 272–277.
4   As to the meaning of 'court' see PARA 271 note 4.
5   As to the meaning of 'Community plant variety right' see PARA 266 note 3.
6   As to the meaning of 'biotechnological invention' see PARA 272 note 3.
7   Patents and Plant Variety Rights (Compulsory Licensing) Regulations 2002, SI 2002/247, reg 17(2). The cross licence referred to in the text is a cross licence granted under reg 15(3) (see PARA 276): reg 17(2). As to the meaning of 'patent' see PARA 266 note 4. As to proceedings see PARA 280.
8   Ie a cross licence granted under the Patents and Plant Variety Rights (Compulsory Licensing) Regulations 2002, SI 2002/247, reg 14(2) (see PARA 275): reg 17(3).
9   Ie the tribunal referred to in the Plant Varieties Act 1997 s 42 (see PARA 285): Patents and Plant Variety Rights (Compulsory Licensing) Regulations 2002, SI 2002/247, reg 2(1). Appeals to the tribunal under reg 17(3) are governed by the provisions of the Plant Varieties Act 1997 Pt II (ss 42–46) (see PARA 285 et seq) and the Breeders' regulations: Patents and Plant Variety Rights (Compulsory Licensing) Regulations 2002, SI 2002/247, reg 19(1). As to the Breeders' regulations see PARA 272 note 7. The provisions of the Plant Varieties Act 1997 Sch 3 (see PARA 285) apply to appeals under the Patents and Plant Variety Rights (Compulsory Licensing) Regulations 2002, SI 2002/247, reg 17(3) with the modifications specified in the notes thereto: reg 19(2).
10   Ie made under the Plant Varieties Act 1997 s 17 (see PARAS 261, 263), and referred to in s 26(1)(c) (see PARA 286): Patents and Plant Variety Rights (Compulsory Licensing) Regulations 2002, SI 2002/247, reg 17(3). The Plant Varieties Act 1997 s 45 (see PARA 291) applies accordingly: Patents and Plant Variety Rights (Compulsory Licensing) Regulations 2002, SI 2002/247, reg 17(3).

11   Patents and Plant Variety Rights (Compulsory Licensing) Regulations 2002, SI 2002/247, reg
     17(3). As to the Controller of Plant Variety Rights see PARAS 272 note 5, 281–284.

D. PROCEDURAL PROVISIONS

279. Proceedings concerning compulsory patent licences and cross licences.

The provisions of the Patents Act 1977 concerned with proceedings before the
Comptroller General of Patents[1], decisions of the Comptroller General including
orders for grant of compulsory licences[2], legal proceedings in respect of appeals
from the Comptroller General[3], and other matters, as and to the extent they relate
to compulsory licences[4], extend and apply to, and are taken to make
corresponding provision in the United Kingdom[5] in respect of the following:

(1)   proceedings before the Controllers[6];

(2)   decisions of the Controllers including orders for the grant, variation and
       revocation of compulsory patent licences[7] and cross licences[8] (including
       cross licences of patents granted by the Community Plant Variety
       Office[9]);

(3)   legal proceedings in respect of appeals from the Controllers' decisions[10];
       and

(4)   other matters related to compulsory patent licences and cross licences[11]
       arising under the relevant regulations[12].

1   As to the meaning of 'Comptroller General of Patents' see PARA 266 note 5.
2   As to the grant of compulsory licences under the Patents Act 1977 see ss 48–50; and PATENTS AND
    REGISTERED DESIGNS vol 79 (2014) PARA 394 et seq.
3   As to legal proceedings in respect of appeals from the Comptroller General under the Patents Act
    1977 see ss 97–108; and PATENTS AND REGISTERED DESIGNS vol 79 (2014) PARAS 621–622.
4   Ie compulsory licences under the Patents Act 1977 s 48(1). See the Patents and Plant Variety
    Rights (Compulsory Licensing) Regulations 2002, SI 2002/247, reg 26(1); and PATENTS AND
    REGISTERED DESIGNS vol 79 (2014) PARA 394.
5   As to the meaning of 'United Kingdom' see PARA 1 note 1.
6   As to the meaning of 'Controllers' see PARA 266 note 7. For these purposes, the provisions of the
    Patents Act 1977 have effect as if a reference to the Comptroller General were a reference to the
    Controllers, other than in relation to applications under the Patents and Plant Variety Rights
    (Compulsory Licensing) Regulations 2002, SI 2002/247, regs 15(1), 16(3), (4) (see PARAS
    276–277), and with any other necessary modifications: reg 26(3).
7   As to the meaning of 'compulsory patent licence' see PARA 268 note 1.
8   Ie cross licences ordered to be granted under the Patents and Plant Variety Rights (Compulsory
    Licensing) Regulations 2002, SI 2002/247, reg 7(2), (3) (see PARA 269).
9   Ie cross licences ordered to be granted under the Patents and Plant Variety Rights (Compulsory
    Licensing) Regulations 2002, SI 2002/247, reg 15(3) (see PARA 276).
10 See PARA 271.
11 See notes 8, 9.
12 Patents and Plant Variety Rights (Compulsory Licensing) Regulations 2002, SI 2002/247, reg
    26(1). The 'relevant regulations' are the Patents and Plant Variety Rights (Compulsory Licensing)
    Regulations 2002, SI 2002/247. The application of the provisions of the Patents Act 1977 in
    respect of proceedings concerning compulsory patent licences and cross licences is, however,
    restricted: see PARAS 266 note 6, 269 note 6.

280. Proceedings concerning compulsory plant variety licences and cross licences.

The provisions of the Plant Varieties Act 1997 in respect of proceedings before
the Controller of Plant Variety Rights[1], decisions of the Controller in relation to
compulsory licences[2], appeals from the Controller to the Plant Varieties and Seeds
Tribunal[3], appeals from the Tribunal[4], and other matters, as and to the extent they
relate to compulsory licences[5], extend and apply to, and are taken to make

corresponding provision in respect of, proceedings before the Controllers[6], decisions of the Controllers including the grant, variation and revocation of compulsory plant variety licences[7] and cross licences[8], appeals from the Controllers[9] and other matters related to compulsory plant variety licences and cross licences[10] arising under the relevant regulations[11].

1 As to the Controller of Plant Variety Rights see PARAS 281–284. As to proceedings before the Controller see the Plant Varieties Act 1997 ss 24–26; and PARAS 262, 286.
2 As to compulsory licensing of rights under the Plant Varieties Act 1997 see PARAS 261–264.
3 See PARA 286.
4 See PARA 291.
5 Ie compulsory licences under the Plant Varieties Act 1997 s 17(1). See the Patents and Plant Variety Rights (Compulsory Licensing) Regulations 2002, SI 2002/247, reg 27(1); and PARA 261.
6 As to the meaning of 'Controllers' see PARA 266 note 7. For these purposes, the provisions of the Plant Varieties Act 1997 have effect as if a reference to the Controller of Plant Variety Rights were a reference to the Controllers, and with any other necessary modifications: Patents and Plant Variety Rights (Compulsory Licensing) Regulations 2002, SI 2002/247, reg 27(3).
7 As to the meaning of 'compulsory plant variety licence' see PARA 274 note 1. As to the grant, variation and revocation of compulsory plant variety licences see PARAS 272–278.
8 Ie cross licences ordered to be granted under the Patents and Plant Variety Rights (Compulsory Licensing) Regulations 2002, SI 2002/247, reg 14(2) (see PARA 275).
9 See PARA 278.
10 See note 8.
11 Patents and Plant Variety Rights (Compulsory Licensing) Regulations 2002, SI 2002/247, reg 27(1). The 'relevant regulations' are the Patents and Plant Variety Rights (Compulsory Licensing) Regulations 2002, SI 2002/247. The application of the provisions of the Plant Varieties Act 1997 in respect of proceedings concerning compulsory plant variety licence and cross licences is, however, restricted: see PARAS 272 note 6, 275 note 6.

(iii) The Controller of Plant Variety Rights and the Plant Variety Rights Office

281. Establishment and continuation of office.

The Controller of Plant Variety Rights is an officer appointed by the Secretary of State and the Welsh Ministers[1] who has immediate control of the Plant Variety Rights Office[2]. In the exercise of his functions the Controller acts under the general direction of the ministers except in relation to the taking of a decision where an appeal lies from his decision to the Plant Varieties and Seeds Tribunal[3].The manner in which the Controller is to discharge his functions is the subject of regulations[4].

1 As to the Secretary of State and the Welsh Ministers see PARA 390.
2 Plant Varieties Act 1997 s 2(1). The Plant Variety Rights Office, headed by the Controller, was originally established under the Plant Varieties and Seeds Act 1964 s 11 (repealed). A deputy controller and other officers and servants may be appointed at the discretion of the Secretary of State and the Welsh Ministers (Plant Varieties Act 1997 Sch 1 para 1), although outside officers may also be employed where necessary (see PARA 283). Any act or thing directed to be done by or to the Controller may be done by or to any officer authorised by the Secretary of State and the Welsh Ministers (Sch 1 para 3), and prima facie evidence of any document issued by the Controller may be given in legal proceedings by the production of a copy or extract certified by an authorised officer (Sch 1 paras 4, 5). There must be paid to the Controller and any other officers or servants appointed under Sch 1 para 1 such remuneration and allowances as the Secretary of State and the Welsh Ministers may with the consent of the Minister for the Civil Service determine: Sch 1 para 2.
    The Controller, through the Plant Variety Rights Office, also has power to carry out such functions as may be entrusted to the Office by the Community Plant Variety Office in accordance with Council Regulation (EC) 2100/94 (OJ L227, 1.9.99, p 1) on Community plant variety rights, arts 30(4), 55(1) (under which the Community Office is empowered to entrust national offices with specified administrative functions and with certain functions relating to technical examinations

pursuant to the grant of Community plant variety rights): see the Plant Variety Rights Office (Extension of Functions) Regulations 1995, SI 1995/2655.
3   Plant Varieties Act 1997 s 27. As to appeals to the tribunal see PARA 286 et seq.
4   See PARA 282.

282. Regulations concerning functions of Controller.

The Secretary of State and the Welsh Ministers[1] may by regulations make such provision as they think fit as respects the manner in which the Controller of Plant Variety Rights[2] is to discharge his functions[3], in particular as respects applications for the grant of plant breeders' rights[4] and other applications to the Controller[5]. Such regulations may, in particular:

(1)   make provision for restricting the making of repeated applications on the same subject[6];

(2)   prescribe the circumstances in which representations may be made regarding any decision on an application or in connection with the charging of fees[7];

(3)   make provision as to the keeping of registers and records by the Controller and their rectification, and prescribe the circumstances in which they may be inspected by members of the public[8];

(4)   make provision for the publication or service of notices of application, and of the Controller's decisions[9]; and

(5)   prescribe the manner of dealing with objections to applications[10].

The Secretary of State and the Welsh Ministers may also make regulations as respects the charging of fees by the Controller, including periodical fees payable by persons holding plant breeders' rights[11]. Such regulations may authorise the Controller:

(a)   in the case of a failure to pay any fees payable in connection with any application to him[12], to refuse the application[13]; and

(b)   in the case of a failure by a holder of plant breeders' rights to pay any fees payable in connection with those rights, to terminate the period for which the grant of those rights has effect[14],

and may provide for the restoration of the application or the rights if the failure to pay fees is made good[15].

The Secretary of State and the Welsh Ministers may also by regulations confer a right of appeal to the Plant Varieties and Seeds Tribunal against any decision of the Controller under regulations made under these provisions[16].

1   As to the Secretary of State and the Welsh Ministers see PARA 390.
2   As to the Controller of Plant Variety Rights see PARA 281.
3   Ie his functions under the Plant Varieties Act 1997 Pt I (ss 1–41).
4   As to applications for the grant of plant breeders' rights see PARAS 243–249.
5   Plant Varieties Act 1997 s 28(1).
6   Plant Varieties Act 1997 s 28(2)(a). Regulations provide that if an application appears to the Controller to be a repeated application (ie an application in similar circumstances on the same subject made within 12 months of the making of a previous application upon which the Controller has taken a decision) made without reasonable cause, the Controller may refuse to entertain such application: Plant Breeders' Rights Regulations 1998, SI 1998/1027, reg 4.
7   Plant Varieties Act 1997 s 28(2)(b). This should be read in conjunction with s 24, which empowers the Secretary of State and the Welsh Ministers by regulations to make provision for any decision of the Controller against which an appeal lies to the Plant Varieties and Seeds Tribunal (see PARA 286) to be made only after an opportunity of making representations to him, and of being heard by him or by a person appointed by him for the purpose, has been afforded both to the person entitled to appeal to the tribunal against that decision and to persons of such other descriptions as may be prescribed by the regulations. As to the provision that has been made see the Plant Breeders' Rights Regulations 1998, SI 1998/1027, regs 6–8, Sch 1 Pts A, B. As to representations with respect to the granting of plant breeders' rights and concerning proposed determinations as

to conditions see PARA 243 notes 3, 13; as to representations with respect to proposed decisions to declare a grant of plant breeders' rights null and void see PARA 251 note 5; as to representations with respect to proposed terminations of rights see PARA 252 notes 6, 8; as to representations with respect to applications for compulsory licences see PARA 261 note 3; as to representations with respect to proposed decisions to refuse applications for an opportunity of making representations concerning applications for the grant of compulsory licences see PARA 262 note 5; as to representations with respect to the extension, limitation, variation or revocation of compulsory licences see PARA 263 note 13; and as to representations with respect to proposed decisions to allow or refuse applications for the suspension, or the termination of suspension, of plant breeders' rights see PARA 264 note 4.

8   Plant Varieties Act 1997 s 28(2)(c). For the provision which has been made in this regard see the Plant Breeders' Rights Regulations 1998, SI 1998/1027, reg 12; and PARA 254.

9   Plant Varieties Act 1997 s 28(2)(d). Provision with regard to publication is made by the Plant Breeders' Rights Regulations 1998, SI 1998/1027, reg 5, Sch 1 Pts A–C. As to notification of proposed decisions with respect to the granting of plant breeders' rights, and of withdrawals of applications for such rights see PARA 243 note 3; as to notification of proposed decisions preliminary to the determination of an application for the grant of plant breeders' rights as to conditions see PARA 243 note 13; as to notification of proposed decisions to declare a grant of plant breeders' rights null and void see PARA 251 note 5; as to notification of proposed terminations of rights and of terminations following applications to surrender see PARA 252 notes 5, 8; as to notification of applications for compulsory licences see PARA 261 note 3; as to notification of proposed decisions to refuse applications for an opportunity of making representations concerning applications for the grant of compulsory licences see PARA 262 note 5; as to notification of applications for the extension, limitation, variation or revocation of compulsory licences see PARA 263 note 13; as to notification of proposed decisions to allow or refuse applications for the suspension, or the termination of suspension, of plant breeders' rights see PARA 264 note 4. Provision with regard to the service of documents is made by regs 14, 16–20.

10 Plant Varieties Act 1997 s 28(2)(e). At the date at which this volume states the law no provision had been made in this regard.

11 Plant Varieties Act 1997 s 29(1). Provision for the charging of fees is made by the Plant Breeders' Rights (Naming and Fees) Regulations 2006, SI 2006/648.

12 Ie any application under the Plant Varieties Act 1997 Pt I.

13 Plant Varieties Act 1997 s 29(2)(a).

14 Plant Varieties Act 1997 s 29(2)(b).

15 Plant Varieties Act 1997 s 29(2).

16 Plant Varieties Act 1997 s 26(2)(b). At the date at which this volume states the law no such regulations had been made. As to the tribunal and appeals thereto see PARA 285 et seq.

283. Tests and trials.

The Controller of Plant Variety Rights[1] may, in carrying out the tests and trials which he considers expedient for these purposes[2] and in assessing the results thereof (whether carried out by him or not), use the services of persons other than his officers and servants[3]. The Controller may also establish and maintain reference collections of plant material[4] or, by means of grants of such amounts as he may determine, defray or contribute towards the expenses incurred by any other person in maintaining any such collection[5].

The holder of any plant breeders' rights must ensure that, throughout the period for which the grant of the rights has effect, he is in a position to produce to the Controller propagating material which is capable of producing the protected variety[6], and must give to the Controller, within such time as he may specify, all such information and facilities as he may request for the purpose of satisfying himself that he is fulfilling this duty[7]. The giving of false information in pursuance of such a request is an offence[8].

Provision is made for the results of tests and trials to be open to inspection by the public[9].

1   As to the Controller of Plant Variety Rights see PARA 281.

2   Ie for the purposes of the Plant Varieties Act 1997 Pt I (ss 1–41).
3   Plant Varieties Act 1997 s 30. As to the appointment of the officers and servants of the Controller
     see PARA 281 note 2.
4   Plant Varieties Act 1997 s 35(1).
5   Plant Varieties Act 1997 s 35(2).
6   Plant Varieties Act 1997 s 16(1). As to the meaning of 'variety' see PARA 239 note 1; and as to
     the meaning of 'protected variety' see PARA 239 note 6.
7   Plant Varieties Act 1997 s 16(2). The facilities to be given under this provision include facilities
     for the inspection by or on behalf of the Controller of the measures taken for the preservation of
     the protected variety: s 16(3).
8   Plant Varieties Act 1997 s 31(1), (2)(c). The offence is punishable on summary conviction by a fine
     not exceeding level 3 on the standard scale, and is committed by any person who, pursuant to such
     a request, either knowingly or recklessly gives information which is false in a material particular:
     s 31(1), (2)(c). As to the standard scale and the powers of magistrates' courts to issue fines on
     summary conviction see SENTENCING vol 92 (2015) PARA 176. As to jurisdiction, and the
     commission of offences by bodies corporate, see PARA 243 note 17.
9   See PARA 284.

284.   Inspection of reports and records.

The register of the names of plant varieties and the plant varieties records[1], and
any report received by the Controller of Plant Variety Rights of the result of any
tests or trials which have been carried out in respect of a plant variety which is the
subject of an application for a grant of plant breeders' rights and which may be
relevant to his decision, are available for inspection by any member of the public
at the Plant Variety Rights Office[2]. This is, however, subject to the proviso that the
details of the hereditary sources of a hybrid must not be available for inspection
unless the rights holder has consented[3].

1   For the duty of the Controller of Plant Variety Rights to keep a register of the names of plant
     varieties in respect of which plant breeders' rights have been granted, and to keep records of plant
     varieties for which applications for grants of rights are under consideration and for which rights
     have been granted, see PARA 254. As to the Controller see PARAS 281–283.
2   Plant Breeders' Rights Regulations 1998, SI 1998/1027, regs 12(9), 13(1).
3   Plant Breeders' Rights Regulations 1998, SI 1998/1027, regs 12(9), 13(1), (2).

(iv)   The Plant Varieties and Seeds Tribunal

285.   The tribunal.

The Plant Varieties and Seeds Tribunal[1] has been established to hear appeals
against decisions of the Controller of Plant Variety Rights[2] and to hear and
determine any matter agreed to be referred to the tribunal by any arbitration
agreement relating to the infringement of plant breeders' rights or to matters
which include the infringement of plant breeders' rights[3].

The tribunal consists of a chairman[4], who must have a seven year general
qualification[5], and members selected from panels which are drawn up and revised
from time to time by the Secretary of State and the Welsh Ministers[6]. One panel
consists of persons who have wide general knowledge in the field of agriculture,
of horticulture or of forestry[7], and the other of persons who have specialised
knowledge of particular species or groups of plants or of the seeds industry[8]. A
further panel has been established for the purposes of hearings concerning
biotechnological inventions[9].

The jurisdiction of the tribunal is exercised by three members consisting of the
chairman and two members selected from the panels[10]. Decisions may be given on
a majority vote[11]. If, after the commencement of a hearing, one of the members
becomes incapable of continuing to hear the proceedings for any reason, the

proceedings may, with the consent of all parties, be continued before the remaining two members and heard and determined accordingly[12], but if the two members differ in opinion the case must, on the application of any party, be re-argued and determined by the tribunal as ordinarily constituted[13]. A decision of the tribunal may not be questioned on the ground that a member was not validly appointed or selected[14].

The tribunal may order any party to pay to any other party either a specified sum in respect of his costs or the assessed amount of his costs[15].

1　The tribunal was established under the Plant Varieties and Seeds Act 1964 s 10, Sch 4 (repealed) and continues in effect by virtue of the Plant Varieties Act 1997 s 42(1).

2　As to the Controller of Plant Variety Rights see PARAS 281–284. As to the decisions of the Controller from which appeals to the tribunal lie see PARA 286.

3　Plant Varieties Act 1997 s 43(1). For these purposes 'arbitration agreement' has the same meaning as in the Arbitration Act 1996 Pt I (ss 1–82) (see ss 5(1), 6; and ARBITRATION vol 2 (2017) PARA 513): Plant Varieties Act 1997 s 43(4). As to arbitration agreements see ARBITRATION vol 2 (2017) PARA 513 et seq. The fees payable to the tribunal for acting under an arbitration agreement are to be determined by the tribunal: s 43(2).

4　Plant Varieties Act 1997 Sch 3 para 2. As to the appointment, and termination of appointment, of the chairman see Sch 3 para 5 (Sch 3 paras 4(1), (2), 5(5), 7(2), 16 amended, and Sch 3 para 5(5A) added, by the Constitutional Reform Act 2005 s 15(1), Sch 4 para 269). The chairman is disqualified for membership of the House of Commons: see the House of Commons Disqualification Act 1975 s 1(1)(f), Sch 1 Pt III; and PARLIAMENT vol 78 (2010) PARA 908. A deputy chairman may be appointed in the case of the temporary absence or inability to act of the chairman: Plant Varieties Act 1997 Sch 3 para 6.

5　Ie within the meaning of the Courts and Legal Services Act 1990 s 71: see LEGAL PROFESSIONS vol 65 (2015) PARA 540.

6　Plant Varieties Act 1997 Sch 3 para 7(1). As to the Secretary of State and the Welsh Ministers see PARA 390. The power to revise the panels includes power to terminate membership, and is to that extent subject to the Tribunals and Inquiries Act 1992 s 7 (see CONSTITUTIONAL AND ADMINISTRATIVE LAW vol 20 (2014) PARA 619): Plant Varieties Act 1997 Sch 3 para 7(2) (as amended: see note 4). General recommendations as to appointment of members may be made by the Council on Tribunals: see the Tribunals and Inquiries Act 1992 Sch 1 para 36(b); and CONSTITUTIONAL AND ADMINISTRATIVE LAW vol 20 (2014) PARA 619. As to the remuneration of members of the tribunal and the appointment and remuneration of officers and servants see the Plant Varieties Act 1997 Sch 3 paras 14, 15(2).

7　Plant Varieties Act 1997 Sch 3 para 7(1)(a).

8　Plant Varieties Act 1997 Sch 3 para 7(1)(b).

9　The Secretary of State is required to draw up and from time to time revise a panel of persons who have specialised knowledge of biotechnological inventions: Patents and Plant Variety Rights (Compulsory Licensing) Regulations 2002, SI 2002/247, reg 18. As to the functions of this panel see note 10.

10　Ie, generally, the relevant chairman (Plant Varieties Act 1997 Sch 3 para 1(a)), a member of the panel constituted under Sch 3 para 7(1)(a) (see the text and note 7) (Sch 3 para 1(b)) and a member of the panel constituted under Sch 3 para 7(1)(b) (see the text and note 8) (Sch 3 para 1(c)); however, where the tribunal is hearing an appeal under the Patents and Plant Variety Rights (Compulsory Licensing) Regulations 2002, SI 2002/247, reg 17(3) (see PARA 278), instead of a member of the panel constituted under the Plant Varieties Act 1997 Sch 3 para 7(1)(a), there is a member of the panel of persons drawn up and revised by the Secretary of State pursuant to the Patents and Plant Variety Rights (Compulsory Licensing) Regulations 2002, SI 2002/247, reg 18 (see note 9) (reg 19(2)(a)).

　　The Secretary of State and the Welsh Ministers may either select a member or members to deal with a particular case or class or group of cases, or may select for a class or group of cases members from amongst whom members to deal with any particular case are selected, the selection from amongst those members of a member or members to deal with the particular case then to be made either by the ministers, or, if they so direct, by the relevant chairman: Plant Varieties Act 1997 Sch 3 para 8(1). Where the tribunal is hearing an appeal under the Patents and Plant Variety Rights (Compulsory Licensing) Regulations 2002, SI 2002/247, reg 17(3) (see PARA 278), the panels

referred to in the Plant Varieties Act 1997 Sch 3 para 8(1) are treated as including the panel constituted under the Patents and Plant Variety Rights (Compulsory Licensing) Regulations 2002, SI 2002/247, reg 18 (see note 9): reg 19(2)(b).
11 Plant Varieties Act 1997 Sch 3 para 10(1).
12 Plant Varieties Act 1997 Sch 3 para 10(2).
13 Plant Varieties Act 1997 Sch 3 para 10(3).
14 Plant Varieties Act 1997 Sch 3 para 10(4).
15 Plant Varieties Act 1997 Sch 3 para 11(1). As to the award of costs on withdrawal of an appeal see the Plant Varieties and Seeds Tribunal Rules 1974, SI 1974/1136, r 8(3).

286. Jurisdiction to hear appeals against decisions of Controller of Plant Variety Rights.

An appeal lies to the Plant Varieties and Seeds Tribunal[1] against various decisions of the Controller of Plant Variety Rights[2], namely:

(1)   a decision to allow or refuse an application for the grant of plant breeders' rights[3];

(2)   any decision preliminary to the determination of such an application as to the conditions which must be satisfied in connection with the application[4];

(3)   a decision to allow or refuse an application for a compulsory licence[5];

(4)   a decision to allow or refuse an application for the extension, limitation, variation or revocation of a compulsory licence[6];

(5)   a decision to refuse an application for an opportunity to make representations in connection with applications for compulsory licences[7];

(6)   any decision relating to the declaration of plant breeders' rights as null and void[8];

(7)   any decision in connection with the termination of plant breeders' rights[9]; and

(8)   any decision to allow or refuse an application for the suspension of plant breeders' rights or the termination of such a suspension[10].

The Secretary of State and the Welsh Ministers may additionally, by regulations, confer a right of appeal to the tribunal against any decision of the Controller under the regulations concerning the selection and registration of plant variety names[11] or the regulations concerning the functions of the Controller (including the charging of fees)[12].

1   As to the tribunal see PARA 285.
2   As to the Controller of Plant Variety Rights see PARAS 281–284.
3   Plant Varieties Act 1997 s 26(1)(a). As to the granting and refusal of applications see PARA 243.
4   Plant Varieties Act 1997 s 26(1)(b). As to the conditions which must be satisfied in connection with applications for the grant of plant breeders' rights see s 4; and PARAS 243–247.
5   Plant Varieties Act 1997 s 26(1)(c). For the power of the Controller to allow or refuse an application for a compulsory licence see s 17(1); and PARA 261.
6   Plant Varieties Act 1997 s 26(1)(c). As to applications for the extension, limitation or variation of compulsory licences see s 17(9); and PARA 263.
7   Plant Breeders' Rights Regulations 1998, SI 1998/1027, reg 11. As to the making of applications to make representations in connection with applications for compulsory licences see the Plant Varieties Act 1997 s 25(3)(a); and PARA 262. This power has been conferred pursuant to s 26(2)(a), which provides that the Secretary of State and the Welsh Ministers may by regulations confer a right of appeal to the tribunal against a decision of the Controller to refuse an application under s 25(3)(a). As to the Secretary of State and the Welsh Ministers see PARA 390.
8   Plant Varieties Act 1997 s 26(1)(d). As to the making of decisions relating to the declaration of plant breeders' rights as null and void see s 21; and PARA 251.
9   Plant Varieties Act 1997 s 26(1)(d), (e). As to the making of decisions in connection with the termination of plant variety rights see s 22(1)(a)–(d); and PARA 252.

10 Plant Varieties Act 1997 s 26(1)(f). As to the making of decisions in connection with the suspension of plant variety rights see s 23(1), (2); and PARA 264.
11 Ie the Plant Breeders' Rights Regulations 1998, SI 1998/1027, reg 12 (made under the Plant Varieties Act 1997 s 18): see PARA 254. At the date at which this volume states the law no such regulations had been made.
12 Plant Varieties Act 1997 s 26(2)(b). The regulations mentioned in the text are the Plant Breeders' Rights Regulations 1998, SI 1998/1027, made under the Plant Varieties Act 1997 s 28 or s 29 (see PARA 282) or the Plant Breeders' Rights (Naming and Fees) Regulations 2006, SI 2006/648.

287. Bringing the appeal.

The procedure on appeals from decisions of the Controller of Plant Variety Rights[1] to the Plant Varieties and Seeds Tribunal[2] is governed by rules[3] and regulations[4]. Where an appeal is brought, the operation of the decision in question is suspended pending the final determination of the appeal[5].

The appeal is to be instituted by giving a notice of appeal in the prescribed form[6] which is to be accompanied by all documents referred to therein[7]. Provision is made for the Controller to furnish information and particulars to the secretary of the tribunal, who is to give notice to the appellant and to persons entitled to appear and be heard on the appeal[8]. Persons intending to appear must give due notice to the secretary[9]. The appellant and any person who has given notice of intention to appear may, on serving notice on the secretary, inspect any document and any plants or plant material supplied or made available by the Controller or by any party to the appeal and is entitled, on payment of the prescribed fee[10], to be supplied with copies of such documents[11].

1 As to the Controller of Plant Variety Rights see PARAS 281–284.
2 As to the tribunal and its jurisdiction to hear appeals see PARAS 285–286.
3 See the Plant Varieties and Seeds Tribunal Rules 1974, SI 1974/1136 (originally made under the Plant Varieties and Seeds Act 1964 s 10, Sch 4 para 9 (repealed); but now having effect under the Plant Varieties Act 1997 Sch 3 para 13). The Plant Varieties Act 1997 Sch 3 para 13 provides that such rules may in particular make provisions as to:
    (1)   the circumstances in which the tribunal need not sit, or is not to sit, in public;
    (2)   the form of any decision of the tribunal;
    (3)   the time within which any proceedings are to be instituted;
    (4)   the evidence which may be required or admitted in any proceedings;
    (5)   the examination of the parties, and of witnesses, on oath or affirmation in any proceedings; and
    (6)   the procedure for securing the attendance of witnesses and the production of documents in any proceedings: Sch 3 para 13(1).
4 See the Plant Breeders' Rights Regulations 1998, SI 1998/1027, reg 9 (made pursuant to the Plant Varieties Act 1997 s 44).
5 Plant Breeders' Rights Regulations 1998, SI 1998/1027, reg 9(3) (made pursuant to the Plant Varieties Act 1997 s 44(c), which empowers the Secretary of State and the Welsh Ministers by regulations to make provision for suspending, or authorising or requiring the suspension of, the operation of a decision pending final determination of an appeal against it). The Controller must publish in the gazette a notice of any suspension of the operation of his decision in accordance therewith: Plant Breeders' Rights Regulations 1998, SI 1998/1027, reg 9(4) (made pursuant to the Plant Varieties Act 1997 s 44(d), which empowers the Secretary of State and the Welsh Ministers by regulations to make provision for the publication of notices or the taking of other steps for securing that the persons affected by the suspension of the operation of a decision appealed against will be informed of its suspension). As to the gazette see PARA 17. As to the Secretary of State and the Welsh Ministers see PARA 390.
6 Ie the Plant Varieties and Seeds Tribunal Rules 1974, SI 1974/1136, Sch 1 Form 1. The Controller must publish in the gazette a notice of the appeal: Plant Breeders' Rights Regulations 1998, SI 1998/1027, reg 9(4) (made pursuant to the Plant Varieties Act 1997 s 44(d): see note 5).
7 Plant Varieties and Seeds Tribunal Rules 1974, SI 1974/1136, r 3.
8 Plant Varieties and Seeds Tribunal Rules 1974, SI 1974/1136, r 4, Sch 1 Forms 2, 3 (Form 3 amended by SI 2002/3198). As to who may be heard see PARA 290.

9   Plant Varieties and Seeds Tribunal Rules 1974, SI 1974/1136, r 5(1), Sch 1 Form 4 (Form 4
     amended by SI 2002/3198). The Controller must also notify the secretary if he intends to appear:
     Plant Varieties and Seeds Tribunal Rules 1974, SI 1974/1136, r 5(2).
10   See the Plant Varieties and Seeds Tribunal Rules 1974, SI 1974/1136, r 23, Sch 2 (Sch 2 amended
     by SI 2002/3198).
11   Plant Varieties and Seeds Tribunal Rules 1974, SI 1974/1136, r 6(1), Sch 1 Form 5 (Form 5
     amended by SI 2002/3198). The Controller has similar rights of inspection and to be supplied with
     copies: Plant Varieties and Seeds Tribunal Rules 1974, SI 1974/1136, r 6(2).

288. Withdrawing an appeal.

An appellant who wishes to withdraw his appeal may do so by serving notice
on the secretary before the hearing, and an appellant who without good cause fails
to attend the hearing[1] is to be deemed to have withdrawn his appeal[2]. The
Controller of Plant Variety Rights must publish in the gazette[3] a notice of any
withdrawal of the appeal[4].

1   For provisions as to attendance see PARA 290.
2   Plant Varieties and Seeds Tribunal Rules 1974, SI 1974/1136, r 8(1), (2). As to the award of costs
    on withdrawal of an appeal see r 8(3). The procedure on appeals from decisions of the Controller
    of Plant Variety Rights to the Plant Varieties and Seeds Tribunal is governed by rules and
    regulations: see PARA 287 notes 3, 5. As to the Controller of Plant Variety Rights see PARAS
    281–284.
3   As to the gazette see PARA 17.
4   Plant Breeders' Rights Regulations 1998, SI 1998/1027, reg 9(4) (made pursuant to the Plant
    Varieties Act 1997 s 44(d), which empowers the Secretary of State and the Welsh Ministers by
    regulations to make provision for, inter alia, the publication of notices). As to the Secretary of
    State and the Welsh Ministers see PARA 390.

289. Hearing the appeal.

Where an appeal is to be heard by the Plant Varieties and Seeds Tribunal, and
members of the tribunal to hear the appeal have been selected from the panels[1],
the chairman must fix a date, time and place for the hearing[2]. The secretary to the
tribunal must serve not less than 28 days' notice of the hearing on the appellant,
the Controller of Plant Variety Rights[3] and every person who has given notice of
intention to appear[4]. The hearing is to take place in such part of the United
Kingdom[5] as may be determined by the chairman[6], who is to have regard to the
convenience of the persons concerned and their witnesses, the convenience of the
members of the tribunal and, if he proposes to appear, the convenience of the
Controller, to the situation of any land or premises to be viewed and to the other
circumstances of the case, including the wishes of and expense to the persons
concerned[7].
The tribunal is to sit in public unless it appears that there are exceptional
reasons making it desirable that the hearing or any part of it should take place in
private[8].

1   See PARA 285. As to the tribunal and its jurisdiction to hear appeals see PARAS 285–286.
2   Plant Varieties and Seeds Tribunal Rules 1974, SI 1974/1136, r 7(1).
3   As to the Controller of Plant Variety Rights see PARAS 281–284.
4   Plant Varieties and Seeds Tribunal Rules 1974, SI 1974/1136, r 7(1). As to the hearing of appeals
    together see r 7(2); and as to alteration of the date, time or place of the hearing see r 7(3). The
    procedure on appeals from decisions of the Controller to the Plant Varieties and Seeds Tribunal
    is governed by rules and regulations: see PARA 287 notes 3, 5.
5   As to the meaning of 'United Kingdom' see PARA 1 note 1.
6   Plant Breeders' Rights Regulations 1998, SI 1998/1027, reg 9(1) (made pursuant to the Plant
    Varieties Act 1997 s 44(a), which empowers the Secretary of State and the Welsh Ministers by
    regulations to make provision for determining in which part of the United Kingdom an appeal is
    to be heard). See also Sch 3 para 9, which provides that the tribunal may sit in any place in the
    United Kingdom. As to the Secretary of State and the Welsh Ministers see PARA 390.

7   See the Plant Breeders' Rights Regulations 1998, SI 1998/1027, regs 8(2), 9(1); and note 5.
8   Plant Varieties and Seeds Tribunal Rules 1974, SI 1974/1136, r 10(1).

290. Attendance and procedure.

The persons concerned, or persons appointed by them for the purpose of the proceedings in respect of which the decision was given, are entitled to appear and be heard as a party to any appeal to the Plant Varieties and Seeds Tribunal against the decision of the Controller of Plant Variety Rights[1]. The Controller, the appellant and any other person entitled to appear may do so in person, by counsel or solicitor, or by a representative appointed in writing[2]. The appellant, or, if more than one, such of them as the tribunal directs, begins and the other parties are heard in such order as the tribunal determines[3]. Every party appearing may give evidence and call witnesses and is entitled to cross-examine and re-examine witnesses[4], and the tribunal may itself call witnesses[5]. The tribunal may also consider any representations submitted to the Controller and any written evidence or other documents given or supplied in the course of the proceedings before him, and may inspect any plants or plant material made available by the Controller or by any person entitled to appear[6].

Further rules deal with adjournments[7], the service of documents[8], the extension of the time for compliance with any requirement of the rules[9], interim applications[10], the effect of failure to comply with the rules[11], and the fees payable thereunder[12].

1   Plant Breeders' Rights Regulations 1998, SI 1998/1027, reg 9(2) (made pursuant to the Plant Varieties Act 1997 s 44(b), which empowers the Secretary of State and the Welsh Ministers by regulations to make provision authorising persons other than the person by whom an appeal is made and the authority whose decision is appealed against to appear and be heard as parties to the appeal). The procedure on appeals from decisions of the Controller of Plant Variety Rights to the Plant Varieties and Seeds Tribunal is governed by rules and regulations. As to the tribunal and its jurisdiction to hear appeals see PARAS 285–286. As to the Controller see PARAS 281–284. As to the Secretary of State and the Welsh Ministers see PARA 390.
2   Plant Varieties and Seeds Tribunal Rules 1974, SI 1974/1136, r 11(1).
3   Plant Varieties and Seeds Tribunal Rules 1974, SI 1974/1136, r 11(2). Subject to the rules and any direction of the chairman, the procedure at the hearing is to be as the tribunal directs: r 11(3).
4   Plant Varieties and Seeds Tribunal Rules 1974, SI 1974/1136, r 12(1). The tribunal may, however, refuse to hear any witness who has not been named in the notice of appeal or in a notice of intention to appear and it may also refuse to consider any documents or inspect plants or plant material not submitted with or sufficiently described in any such notice: r 12(4). The tribunal may require any witness to give evidence on oath or affirmation to be administered by the chairman: r 12(5). It is not bound to reject evidence that would be inadmissible in a court of law: r 12(6).
    The attendance of witnesses, with or without documents, may be secured by notice served by the secretary, and the appellant, any person who has given notice of intention to appear and the Controller may apply for the issue of such a notice: r 9, Sch 1 Forms 6, 7.
5   Plant Varieties and Seeds Tribunal Rules 1974, SI 1974/1136, r 12(3). A witness called by the tribunal may, after giving evidence, be cross-examined by any party: r 12(3).
6   Plant Varieties and Seeds Tribunal Rules 1974, SI 1974/1136, r 12(2).
7   Plant Varieties and Seeds Tribunal Rules 1974, SI 1974/1136, r 13.
8   Plant Varieties and Seeds Tribunal Rules 1974, SI 1974/1136, r 19.
9   Plant Varieties and Seeds Tribunal Rules 1974, SI 1974/1136, r 20.
10   Plant Varieties and Seeds Tribunal Rules 1974, SI 1974/1136, r 21.
11   Plant Varieties and Seeds Tribunal Rules 1974, SI 1974/1136, r 22.
12   Plant Varieties and Seeds Tribunal Rules 1974, SI 1974/1136, r 23, Sch 2 (Sch 2 amended by SI 2002/3198).

291. Decisions, enforcement and further appeals.

The decision of the Plant Varieties and Seeds Tribunal is to be given in writing, together with a statement of its reasons[1]. Decisions must be notified in the gazette[2], and a copy of the decision and reasons is to be served on the appellant, the Controller of Plant Variety Rights, and on every person who was entitled to appear[3]. The Controller must take such steps as may be necessary to give effect to any decision given on the final determination of an appeal and such other steps as he would be required[4] to take if such decision were his own[5].

On questions of law an appeal lies from the tribunal to the High Court and thence to the Court of Appeal[6], but otherwise the decisions of the tribunal are final and conclusive[7].

1   Plant Varieties and Seeds Tribunal Rules 1974, SI 1974/1136, r 14(1). The procedure on appeals from decisions of the Controller of Plant Variety Rights to the Plant Varieties and Seeds Tribunal is governed by rules and regulations: see PARA 287 notes 3, 5. As to the tribunal and its jurisdiction to hear appeals see PARAS 285–286. As to the Controller see PARAS 281–284. The chairman may correct any clerical mistake in the written record of the decision: r 14(2). Rule 14(1) would appear to render inapplicable the Tribunals and Inquiries Act 1992 s 10(1), under which reasons for the decisions of the tribunal need to be given only if requested (see, in particular, Sch 1 para 36(b); and JUDICIAL REVIEW vol 61 (2010) PARA 646). Any statement of reasons is to form part of the decision and is to be incorporated in the record: see the Tribunals and Inquiries Act 1992 s 10(6); and JUDICIAL REVIEW vol 61 (2010) PARA 646.
2   Plant Breeders' Rights Regulations 1998, SI 1998/1027, reg 5, Sch 1 Pt C(2). As to the gazette see PARA 17.
3   Plant Varieties and Seeds Tribunal Rules 1974, SI 1974/1136, r 14(3).
4   Ie by the Plant Breeders' Rights Regulations 1998, SI 1998/1027.
5   Plant Breeders' Rights Regulations 1998, SI 1998/1027, reg 9(5).
6   Plant Varieties Act 1997 s 45(1) (applying the Tribunals and Inquiries Act 1992 s 11).
7   Plant Varieties Act 1997 s 45(2).

10. EMPLOYMENT IN AGRICULTURE

(1) TERMS AND CONDITIONS OF EMPLOYMENT OF AGRICULTURAL WORKERS

(i) Terms and Conditions in England

292. Employment protection, wages and safety.

Agricultural workers benefit from the same legal protection regarding their employment as all other employees: thus such matters as employment contracts[1], employee representation and industrial relations[2], discipline and grievance procedures[3], dismissal and redundancy[4], discrimination generally[5], health and safety at work[6], occupational and personal pensions[7], and social security[8] are dealt with in the agricultural sector in the same manner as elsewhere.

Agricultural workers in England employed after 1 October 2013[9] are entitled to receive at least the national minimum wage and other statutory minimum terms of employment[10].

1   See EMPLOYMENT vol 39 (2014) PARA 1 et seq.
2   See EMPLOYMENT vol 41 (2014) PARA 891 et seq.
3   See EMPLOYMENT vol 40 (2014) PARA 698 et seq.
4   See EMPLOYMENT vol 41 (2014) PARA 722 et seq.
5   See DISCRIMINATION vol 33 (2013) PARA 1 et seq.
6   See PARA 303 et seq; and HEALTH AND SAFETY AT WORK vol 52 (2014) PARA 314.
7   See PERSONAL AND OCCUPATIONAL PENSIONS vol 80 (2013) PARA 201 et seq.
8   See WELFARE BENEFITS AND STATE PENSIONS vol 104 (2014) PARA 1 et seq.
9   Agricultural workers employed in England before 1 October 2013 were subject to measures specifically applicable to agricultural employment which included the fixing of rates of pay and holiday entitlements: see the Agricultural Wages Act 1948 ss 1, 3 (repealed); and the Agricultural Wages (England and Wales) Order 2012 ('the 2012 Order'). Savings provisions provide for rights accrued and liabilities incurred, and the validity of anything done under the 2012 Order and for the continued application of the enforcement provisions of the Agriculture Wages Act 1948 (see PARA 298 et seq) on and after 1 October 2013 (the date on which the repeal of those provisions came into force) in relation to a worker employed before that date: see the Enterprise and Regulatory Reform Act 2013 (Commencement No 1, Transitional Provisions and Savings) Order 2013, SI 2013/1455, arts 3, 4 (both amended by SI 2013/2271).
10 See EMPLOYMENT vol 39 (2014) PARAS 113, 169 et seq.

(ii) Terms and Conditions in Wales

293. Agricultural Advisory Panel for Wales.

The Welsh Ministers[1] must by order establish the Agricultural Advisory Panel for Wales[2] to:
(1)   promote careers in agriculture[3];
(2)   prepare agricultural wages orders[4] in draft, consulting on such orders and submitting them to the Welsh Ministers for approval;
(3)   advise the Welsh Ministers on such other matters relating to the agricultural sector in Wales as the Welsh Ministers may require; and
(4)   carry out such other functions as the Welsh Ministers may specify in the order[5].

1   As to the Welsh Ministers see PARA 390.

2   See the Agricultural Advisory Panel for Wales (Establishment) Order 2016, SI 2016/255. The
     Panel is to consist of a member to chair the Panel and at least three, but not more than ten, other
     members: Agricultural Section (Wales) Act 2014 s 2(3). In exercising any functions in relation to
     the membership of the Panel, the Welsh Ministers must seek to ensure that the membership
     includes persons with the skills and expertise necessary to enable the Panel to perform its functions
     efficiently and effectively, and adequately reflects the interests of all parts of the agricultural sector:
     s 2(4). The Welsh Ministers may by order, after consulting such persons as they consider
     appropriate, make provision about the constitution and proceedings of the Panel, the appointment
     of members to the Panel, about the general powers of the Panel, adding, amending or removing
     functions of the Panel: s 2(5), (6). The Welsh Ministers may make orders for the purposes of, or
     in connection with giving full effect to any provision made by or under s 16. The powers of the
     Welsh Ministers to make orders and regulations must be exercised by statutory instrument: s 17.
3   As to the meaning of 'agriculture' see PARA 10.
4   As to the agricultural wages orders see PARA 294.
5   Agricultural Sector (Wales) Act 2014 s 2(1), (2). The Welsh Ministers must, as soon as practicable
     after 30 July 2019 (ie after the period of three years beginning with date on which the Agricultural
     Sector (Wales) Act 2014) comes into force, lay before the National Assembly for Wales a report
     on the operation and effect of the 2014 Act during that period, and publish that report: ss 13, 19.
     The Agricultural Sector (Wales) Act 2014 ceases to have effect on 30 July 2020 (ie four years after
     it came into force) unless, before that day but after 30 July 2019, the Welsh Ministers provide for
     its continuation: s 14(1), (2), (4). The Welsh Ministers may by order make such provision
     (including provision modifying, amending or repealing any enactment) as may be necessary or
     expedient in consequence of the Agricultural Sector (Wales) Act 2014 ceasing to have effect: s
     14(3).

294. Agricultural wages orders.

An agricultural wages order is an order making provision about the minimum
rates of remuneration and other terms and conditions of employment for
agricultural workers[1], but may not include any provision about the pensions[2].
An agricultural wages order may, in particular, include provision:

(1)   specifying the minimum rates of remuneration to be paid to agricultural
       workers (including rates for periods when such workers are absent in
       consequence of sickness or injury);

(2)   about any benefits or advantages which, for the purposes of a minimum
       rate of remuneration, may be reckoned as remuneration in lieu of
       payment in cash;

(3)   requiring employers of agricultural workers to allow such workers to
       take such holidays and other leave as may be specified in the order[3].

An agricultural wages order may specify different rates and make different
provision for different descriptions of agricultural workers, but may not specify a
minimum rate which is less than the national minimum wage[4].

After receiving a draft agricultural wages order from the Agricultural Advisory
Panel for Wales[5] the Welsh Ministers[6] may approve and make the order or refer
it back to the Panel for further consideration and resubmission[7].

1   'Agricultural worker' means a person employed in agriculture in Wales, whether or not the whole
     of the work undertaken by virtue of that employment is undertaken in Wales: Agricultural Sector
     (Wales) Act 2014 s 18.
2   Agricultural Sector (Wales) Act 2014 s 3(1), (4). The Agricultural Wages (Wales) Order 2017,
     SI 2017/1058 (as made by the Welsh Ministers in exercise of their powers under the Agricultural
     Sector (Wales) Act 2014 ss 3, 4(1)), provides for agricultural workers to be employed subject to
     the terms and conditions set out in the order and the different categories of agricultural worker.
3   Agricultural Sector (Wales) Act 2014 s 3(2).
4   Agricultural Sector (Wales) Act 2014 s 3(3), (5). 'The national minimum wage' means the single
     hourly rate for the time being in force by virtue of regulations under the National Minimum Wage
     Act 1998 s 1(3) (see EMPLOYMENT VOL 39 (2014) PARA 199): s 10(1). Certain persons do not

qualify for the national minimum wage, or qualify for the national minimum wage at a reduced rate: s 10(2)–(5). As to the making of orders and regulations under the Agricultural Sector (Wales) Act 2014 see PARA 293.

5   As to the Agricultural Advisory Panel for Wales see PARA 293. Before the Panel is established, the Welsh Ministers may, of their own initiative, after consulting such persons or bodies they consider are likely to have an interest, make agricultural wages orders: s 4(2), (3).

6   As to the Welsh Ministers see PARA 390. The Welsh Ministers may, by regulations, make further provision about agricultural wages orders including, in particular, provision about the form and content of an order and about the procedure to be followed and consultation to be carried out in relation to an order: Agricultural Sector (Wales) Act 2014 s 4(4).

7   Agricultural Sector (Wales) Act 2014 s 4(1). As to orders made under s 4(1) see note 2.

295. Enforcement of minimum wages and holiday entitlement.

It is an offence for an employer[1] of an agricultural worker[2] to fail to allow the worker to take the holidays specified in an agricultural wages order[3].

An employer who willfully neglects to pay the agricultural worker the minimum wage may be guilty of an offence and liable to a penalty[4].

1   Where an offence under the Agricultural Sector (Wales) Act 2014 is committed by a body corporate, if the offence is proved to have been committed with the consent or connivance of, or to be attributable to any neglect on the part of any director, manager or secretary of the body corporate (or any similar officer of the body), or any person who was purporting to act in any such capacity, that person is also guilty of the offence and liable to be proceeded against and punished accordingly: s 15.

2   As to the meaning of 'agricultural worker' see PARA 294 note 1.

3   Agricultural Sector (Wales) Act 2014 s 6(1). A person guilty of an offence under this section is liable on summary conviction to a fine not exceeding level 3 on the standard scale: s 6(2). In any proceedings against a person under s 6 it is for the person to prove that the agricultural worker was allowed to take the holidays to which the worker was entitled: s 6(3). As to entitlement to annual leave see the Agricultural Wages (Wales) Order 2017, SI 2017/1058, arts 29–35. However, see also art 36 which permits payment in lieu of annual leave. A person guilty of such an offence is liable on summary conviction to a fine not exceeding level 3 on the standard scale: Agricultural Sector (Wales) Act 2014 s 6(2). In any proceedings against a person under s 6 it is for the person to prove that the agricultural worker was allowed to take the holidays to which the worker was entitled: s 6(3). The Welsh Ministers may appoint officers to act in Wales for the purposes of the Agricultural Sector (Wales) Act 2014: s 8(1). An officer must, on request, produce some duly authenticated document showing his authority to act, and if it appears to an officer that, when acting for the purposes of the 2014 Act, any person with whom the officer is dealing is unaware that the officer is so acting, the officer must inform the person of that fact: s 8(2), (3). Information that has been obtained by an officer acting for the purposes of the 2014 Act may be supplied to the Welsh Ministers and, where it relates to an identifiable agricultural worker, may be supplied to that worker: s 9(1). As to the standard scale and the powers of magistrates' courts to issue fines on summary conviction see SENTENCING vol 92 (2015) PARA 176.

4   Subject to certain modifications, the enforcement provisions of the National Minimum Wage Act 1998 have effect for the purposes of the Agricultural Sector (Wales) Act 2014 as they have effect for the purposes of the 1998 Act: Agricultural Sector (Wales) Act 2014 Agricultural Sector (Wales) Act 2014 s 5(1), (3)–(8). The enforcement provisions are the National Minimum Wage Act 1998 ss 10 and 11 (records) (see EMPLOYMENT vol 39 (2014) PARAS 227–228), s 14 (powers of officers) (see EMPLOYMENT vol 39 (2014) PARA 238), s 17(1), (2), (4)–(6) (entitlement of worker to additional remuneration) (see EMPLOYMENT vol 39 (2014) PARA 242), s 19 (notices of underpayment: arrears) (see EMPLOYMENT vol 39 (2014) PARA 243), s 19C (except for s 19C(1)(c), (6), (8) (so far as relating to appeals under s 19(1)(c)) (notices of underpayment: appeals) (see EMPLOYMENT vol 39 (2014) PARA 245), s 19D (non-compliance with notice of underpayment: recovery of arrears) (see EMPLOYMENT vol 39 (2014) PARA 246), s 19F (except for s 19F(2)(a), (4)) (withdrawal of notice of underpayment) (see EMPLOYMENT vol 39 (2014) PARA 247), s 19G (replacement notice of underpayment) (see EMPLOYMENT vol 39 (2014) PARA 248), s 19H (except for s 19H(4), (5)) (effect of replacement notice of underpayment) (see EMPLOYMENT vol 39 (2014) PARA 248), ss 23 and 24 (right not to suffer detriment) (see EMPLOYMENT vol 39 (2014) PARA 249), s 28 (evidence: reversal of burden of proof in civil

proceedings) (see EMPLOYMENT vol 39 (2014) PARA 250), ss 31 and 33 (offences) (see EMPLOYMENT vol 39 (2014) PARAS 251–253), s 48 (application of the National Minimum Wage Act 1998 to superior employers) (see EMPLOYMENT vol 39 (2014) PARA 170), and s 49 (restriction on contracting out) (see EMPLOYMENT vol 39 (2014) PARA 173): Agricultural Sector (Wales) Act 2014 s 5(2).

296. Benefits and advantages in lieu of wages.

Until a day to be appointed the following provisions have effect in relation to Wales[1].

If an agricultural wages committee[2] is satisfied, on an application in that behalf made by a worker employed in agriculture in its county or by his employer[3], that the value determined for the purposes of these provisions, for a house or part of a house occupied as a separate dwelling by the worker does not correspond with its true value, it may, within any limits imposed by order, direct that its value be reckoned at the amount specified by the committee in the direction[4].

1   The Agricultural Wages Act 1948 s 7(3) is repealed by the Enterprise and Regulatory Reform Act 2013 Sch 20 para 2 by order made under s 103(3). At the date at which this volume states the law no order had been made in relation to Wales. The repeal of the Agricultural Wages Act 1948 s 7(3) is in force in relation to England however, s 7(3) continues in force in relation to England on and after 1 October 2013 but only in relation to the employment of a worker employed in agriculture before that date if it continues after 30 September 2013: see the Enterprise and Regulatory Reform Act 2013 (Commencement No 1, Transitional Provisions and Savings) Order 2013, SI 2013/1455, art 4(4), Sch 3 para 4 (art 4(4) substituted by SI 2013/2271). 'Worker' includes a boy, woman and girl: Agricultural Wages Act 1948 s 17(1). 'Employment' means employment under a contract of service or apprenticeship, and the expressions 'employed' and 'employer' are construed accordingly: Agricultural Wages Act 1948 s 17(1). As to the meaning of 'agriculture' see PARA 10.
2   Every agricultural wages committee for an area in England has been abolished (Enterprise and Regulatory Reform Act 2013 s 72(2)) but such committees are still established for each county, or combination of two or more counties, in Wales: see the Agricultural Wages Act 1948 s 2(1); and the Agricultural Wages Committees (Areas) Order 1974, SI 1974/515, art 3 (both amended by the Enterprise and Regulatory Reform Act 2013 Sch 20 para 2). As to the constitution and proceedings of agricultural wages committees see the Agricultural Wages Act 1948 Sch 3; and the Agricultural Wages Committees Regulations 1949, SI 1949/1885. It is possible for two or more committees to unite so as to form one committee (see s 2(1)(b), (5)), and conversely for a committee for a combination of counties to be dissolved (s 2(2), (5)). There is also power to establish a committee for the combination of all the counties in Wales instead of separate committees for counties or combinations of counties: see s 2(1)(c) (added by the Government of Wales Act 1998 s 149). A combination of counties for which a single committee is established is deemed to be one county: Agricultural Wages Act 1948 s 2(3). As to the power to combine or dissolve the Committees: see s 2(1), (2). The functions of an agricultural wages committee for an area in Wales may be transferred to another body by the Welsh Ministers: Government of Wales Act 1998 Sch 4 para 2. At the date at which this volume states the law this power had not been exercised. 'County' means a county established by or under the Local Government Act 1972: see the Agricultural Wages Act 1948 s 17(1) (amended by SI 1974/514). As to the counties so established see LOCAL GOVERNMENT vol 69 (2009) PARA 22 et seq.
      Compensation is payable to persons who attend before a committee or sub-committee as parties or witnesses: See the Agricultural Wages Act 1948 s 9(2) (repealed in relation to England and prospectively repealed in relation to Wales by the Enterprise and Regulatory Reform Act 2013 Sch 20 para 2).
      As to the power to make regulations providing for further functions of agricultural wages committees: see the Agriculture (Miscellaneous Provisions) Act 1968 s 46(1), (2) (repealed in relation to England and prospectively repealed in relation to Wales by the Enterprise and Regulatory Reform Act 2013 Sch 20 para 2). Pursuant to these powers provision has been made for committees to issue craft certificates (and carry out related functions) where the Board has made an order fixing minimum rates of wages for workers of a special class defined wholly or partly by reference to the issuing of such certificates to members of that class: see the Agricultural Wages Committee (Wages Structure) Regulations 1971, SI 1971/844 (revoked in relation to England and prospectively revoked in relation to Wales by the Enterprise and Regulatory Reform Act 2013 Sch 20 para 2).

The Children's Commissioner for Wales may review the effect on children of the exercise or proposed exercise in relation to Wales of any functions of an agricultural wages committee for an area wholly in, or consisting of, Wales: see the Care Standards Act 2000 s 72B(1)(b), Sch 2A para 11; and CHILDREN AND YOUNG PERSONS vol 9 (2017) PARA 189.

In any legal proceedings the production of a document purporting to be a copy of a resolution or order passed or made by an agricultural wages committee and to be certified by the chairman or secretary of the committee to be a true copy is sufficient evidence of the order or resolution and, in the case of an order, that any notices required to be given in relation thereto have been duly given, and no proof is required of the handwriting or official position of the person certifying the truth of the copy: Agricultural Wages Act 1948 s 15 (repealed in relation to England and prospectively repealed in relation to Wales by the Enterprise and Regulatory Reform Act 2013 Sch 20 para 2). Notwithstanding the repeal of the Agricultural Wages Act 1948 s 15 in relation to England, s 15 continues in force in relation to England on and after 16th December 2013 but only in relation to the employment of a worker employed in agriculture before 1st October 2013 which continues after 15th December 2013: Enterprise and Regulatory Reform Act 2013 (Commencement No 4 and Saving Provision) Order 2013, SI 2013/2979, art 4.

3   Notice of any such application must be given to the other party, so as to enable him to make representations to the committee: Agricultural Wages Committees Regulations 1949, SI 1949/1885, reg 16(c) (revoked in relation to England and as from a day to be appointed in relation to Wales by the Enterprise and Regulatory Reform Act 2013 Sch 20 para 2).
4   See the Agricultural Wages Act 1948 s 7(3).

297.   Records, agricultural enforcement officers and information.

The Welsh Ministers[1] may, by regulations[2], make provision requiring employers of agricultural workers[2] to keep, in such form and manner as may be specified, such records as may be specified, and to preserve those records for such period as may be specified[3].

1   As to the Welsh Ministers see PARA 390.
2   As to the making of regulations under the Agricultural Sector (Wales) Act 2014 see PARA 293. At the date at which this volume states the law no such regulations had been made.
3   Agricultural Sector (Wales) Act 2014 s 7.

298.   Agreements in contravention.

Until a day to be appointed, the following provisions apply in relation to Wales[1].

The following agreements are void:

(1)   any provision in any agreement (whether the contract of a worker employed in agriculture or not) to the extent it purports to exclude or limit the operation of any provision of the Agricultural Wages Act 1948 or to preclude a person from bringing proceedings under that Act before an employment tribunal[2];

(2)   any agreement as to holidays that is inconsistent with a direction of the Agricultural Wages Board[3] in that regard, or for abstaining from exercising the right to holidays conferred by such a direction[4]; and

(3)   any term or condition of a contract of employment that is inconsistent with a term or condition fixed by an order of the Board, or any agreement for abstaining from enforcing a term or condition[5].

The Agricultural Wages Act 1948 does not, however, affect the operation of agreements or customs for the payment of wages above the minimum rate, or of agreements or customs as to holidays or other terms or conditions of the contract of employment, that are not inconsistent with the Board's directions[6].

1   The Agricultural Wages Act 1948 ss 3A, 11, Sch 1 para 8 are repealed by the Enterprise and Regulatory Reform Act 2013 Sch 20 para 2 by order made under s 103(3). At the date at which this volume states the law no order had been made in relation to Wales. The repeal of the Agricultural Wages Act 1948 s 11 is in force in relation to England however, s 3A continues in force in relation to England on and after 1 October 2013 but only in relation to the employment

of a worker employed in agriculture before that date if it continues after 30 September 2013: see the Enterprise and Regulatory Reform Act 2013 (Commencement No 1, Transitional Provisions and Savings) Order 2013, SI 2013/1455, art 4(4), Sch 3 para 1 (art 4(4) substituted by SI 2013/2271). 'Worker' includes a boy, woman and girl: Agricultural Wages Act 1948 s 17(1). 'Employment' means employment under a contract of service or apprenticeship, and the expressions 'employed' and 'employer' are construed accordingly: Agricultural Wages Act 1948 s 17(1). As to the meaning of 'agriculture' see PARA 10.

2 National Minimum Wage Act 1998 s 49(1) (modified by the Agricultural Wages Act 1948 s 3A(1), (2)(h), (3)(a), (b) (s 3A added by the National Minimum Wage Act 1998 Sch 2 para 3)). See EMPLOYMENT vol 39 (2014) PARA 173.

3 The Agricultural Wages Board has now been abolished: see the Enterprise and Regulatory Reform Act 2013 s 72(1). However, provision is still in place, in relation to Wales, for members of the Agricultural Wages Board to be reimbursed for expenses and time: see the Agricultural Wages Act 1948 Sch 1 para 8 (repealed in relation to England and prospectively repealed in relation to Wales: see note 1). As to annual reports relating to proceedings under the Agricultural Wages Act 1948 and the proceedings of the Agricultural Wages Board and of agricultural wages committees see the Agricultural Wages Act 1948 ss 13, 14 (repealed in relation to England and prospectively repealed in relation to Wales, by the Enterprise and Regulatory Reform Act 2013 Sch 20 para 2).

4 Agricultural Wages Act 1948 s 11(1)(b).

5 Agricultural Wages Act 1948 s 11(1)(c) (added by the Employment Protection Act 1975 Sch 9 Pt II para 3(1)).

6 Agricultural Wages Act 1948 s 11(2) (amended by the Employment Protection Act 1975 Sch 9 Pt II para 3(2)).

299. Enforcement of minimum wage entitlement and protection from dismissal.

Until a day to be appointed, the following provisions apply in relation to Wales[1].

If a worker employed in agriculture who is entitled to the minimum rate applicable for such workers[2] is remunerated for any pay reference period[3] by his employer[4] at a rate which is less than that rate, the worker is to be taken to be entitled under his contract to be paid, as additional remuneration in respect of that period, the difference between the remuneration received by him as a worker employed in agriculture for the pay reference period from his employer and the amount which he would have received as a worker employed in agriculture for that period had he been remunerated by the employer at the minimum rate[5].

An employee[6] who is dismissed[7] is to be regarded as unfairly dismissed[8] if the reason (or, if more than one, the principal reason) for the dismissal is that he is, or will or might become, entitled to be paid the minimum rate[9] or a particular minimum rate[10].

The statutory provisions concerned, in connection with the national minimum wage, with the keeping of records[11], the powers of officers[12], enforcement[13], the right not to suffer detriment[14], the burden of proof[15], offences[16], and superior employers[17] have effect, with appropriate modifications, for the purposes of protecting agricultural workers' entitlement to be paid the minimum rate[18]. The powers conferred under these provisions take precedence over any similar powers conferred on investigating officers[19] for the purpose of investigating complaints and otherwise securing the proper observation of the Agricultural Wages Act 1948[20].

1 The Agricultural Wages Act 1948 ss 3A, 12 are repealed by the Enterprise and Regulatory Reform Act 2013 Sch 20 para 2 by order made under s 103(3). At the date at which this volume states the law no order had been made in relation to Wales. In relation to England, the provisions continue in force on and after 1 October 2013 but only in relation to the employment of a worker employed in agriculture before that date if it continues after 30 September 2013: see the Enterprise and Regulatory Reform Act 2013 (Commencement No 1, Transitional Provisions and Savings) Order 2013, SI 2013/1455, art 4(4), Sch 3 paras 1, 6 (art 4(4) substituted by SI 2013/2271). As to the

meaning of 'worker' see PARA **298** note 1. As to the meaning of 'employed' see PARA **298** note 1. As to the meaning of 'agriculture' see PARA **10**.

2   Ie the minimum rate applicable under the Agricultural Wages Act 1948: see s 3 (now repealed).

3   As to pay reference periods see the National Minimum Wage Act 1998 ss 1(4), 55(1); and EMPLOYMENT vol 39 (2014) PARA 202.

4   As to the employer for these purposes see the National Minimum Wage Act 1998 ss 48, 54(4); and EMPLOYMENT vol 39 (2014) PARA 170.

5   National Minimum Wage Act 1998 s 17(1), (2) (modified by the Agricultural Wages Act 1948 s 3A(1), (2)(c), (3)(b)–(e), (3A) (s 3A added by the National Minimum Wage Act 1998 Sch 2 para 3; Agricultural Wages Act 1948 s 3A(2)(c) amended by the Employment Relations Act 2004 s 46(5)(a); Agricultural Wages Act 1948 s 3A(3A) added by SI 1999/712)). No amount is recoverable both under or by virtue of the National Minimum Wage Act 1998 in its application for the purposes of the Agricultural Wages Act 1948 and the Agricultural Sector (Wales) Act 2014, and under or by virtue of the National Minimum Wage Act 1998 in its application otherwise than for those purposes, in respect of the same work: see the Agricultural Wages Act 1948 s 17A(2)(a) (s 17A added by the National Minimum Wage Act 1998 Sch 2 para 10); and the National Minimum Wage Act 1998 s 46(2)). See EMPLOYMENT vol 39 (2014) PARA 253.

6   As to the meaning of 'employee' for these purposes see the Employment Rights Act 1996 s 230(1); and EMPLOYMENT vol 39 (2014) PARA 2.

7   As to what constitutes dismissal see the Employment Rights Act 1996 s 95; and EMPLOYMENT vol 41 (2014) PARA 762.

8   Ie for the purposes of the Employment Rights Act 1996 Pt X (ss 94–134A): see EMPLOYMENT vol 41 (2014) PARA 755 et seq.

9   Ie the minimum rate applicable under the Agricultural Wages Act 1948: see s 3 (now repealed).

10 Employment Rights Act 1996 s 104A(1)(c) (s 104A added by the National Minimum Wage Act 1998 s 25(1); Employment Rights Act 1996 s 104A(1)(c) modified by the Agricultural Wages Act 1948 s 3A(5) (as added: see note 7)).

11 Ie the National Minimum Wage Act 1998 ss 9–11: see EMPLOYMENT vol 39 (2014) PARAS 226–228.

12 Ie the National Minimum Wage Act 1998 s 14: see EMPLOYMENT vol 39 (2014) PARA 238.

13 Ie the National Minimum Wage Act 1998 s 17 (as modified: see the text and notes 5–8) (see EMPLOYMENT vol 39 (2014) PARA 242), and ss 19–22, 22A–22F (see EMPLOYMENT vol 39 (2014) PARAS 243–248).

14 Ie the National Minimum Wage Act 1998 ss 23, 24: see EMPLOYMENT vol 39 (2014) PARA 249.

15 Ie the National Minimum Wage Act 1998 s 28: see EMPLOYMENT vol 39 (2014) PARA 250.

16 Ie the National Minimum Wage Act 1998 ss 31–33: see EMPLOYMENT vol 39 (2014) PARAS 251–253. A mechanism exists to prevent a person being prosecuted twice for the same conduct (ie once under the National Minimum Wage Act 1998 in its application for the purposes of the Agricultural Wages Act 1948 and again under the National Minimum Wage Act 1998 in its application otherwise than for those purposes): see the Agricultural Wages Act 1948 s 17A(2)(a) (as added: see note 7); and the National Minimum Wage Act 1998 s 46(1). See EMPLOYMENT vol 39 (2014) PARA 253.

17 Ie the National Minimum Wage Act 1998 s 48: see EMPLOYMENT vol 39 (2014) PARA 170.

18 See the Agricultural Wages Act 1948 s 3A(1)–(3), (3A), (4) (s 3A and s 3A(3A) as added, and s 3A(2)(c) as amended (see note 7); s 3A(2) amended by SI 1999/712).

19 As to the appointment and powers of investigating officers see PARA **301**.

20 See the Agricultural Wages Act 1948 s 12(8), (9) (added by the National Minimum Wage Act 1998 Sch 2 para 7(3)). See PARA **301**. The National Minimum Wage Act 1998 and the Agricultural Wages Act 1948 (and relevant subordinate legislation) do not otherwise affect one another's operation: see the Agricultural Wages Act 1948 s 17A(1) (as added: see note 7); and the National Minimum Wage Act 1998 s 46(3). See EMPLOYMENT vol 39 (2014) PARA 253.

300.   Offences concerning holidays orders and payments to persons under instruction.

Until a day to be appointed, the following provisions apply in relation to Wales[1].

An employer who fails to allow a worker the holidays fixed under an agricultural wages order[2] commits an offence[3].

An employer who receives directly or indirectly from a worker who is an apprentice or learner employed in agriculture[4] a payment by way of premium, unless it is made in pursuance of an agreement approved by the appropriate agricultural wages committee[5], commits an offence[6]. Whether there is a conviction or not, the court must order the employer to repay any sum found to have been received by way of premium in contravention of this provision[7].

Where an offence in relation to the taking of holidays or to the receipt of premiums, for which an employer is liable to a fine, has in fact been committed by some agent of the employer or other person, that agent or other person is liable to proceedings as if he were the employer and on conviction to the same punishment as that to which the employer is liable[8]; but, where an employer proves that he has used due diligence to secure compliance with the relevant statutory provisions, and that the offence was in fact committed by the agent or other person without his knowledge, consent or connivance, he is on the conviction of the agent or other person exempt from conviction[9].

1   The Agricultural Wages Act 1948 ss 4, 6(1)–(7), 10, 12 are repealed by the Enterprise and Regulatory Reform Act 2013 Sch 20 para 2 by order made under s 103(3). At the date at which this volume states the law no order had been made in relation to Wales. In relation to England, s 10 is repealed but ss 4, 6(1)–(7), 12 continue in force on and after 1 October 2013 but only in relation to the employment of a worker employed in agriculture before that date if it continues after 30 September 2013: see the Enterprise and Regulatory Reform Act 2013 (Commencement No 1, Transitional Provisions and Savings) Order 2013, SI 2013/1455, art 4(4), Sch 3 paras 2, 3, 6 (art 4(4) substituted by SI 2013/2271). As to the meaning of 'worker' see PARA 298 note 1. As to the meaning of 'employed' and 'employer' see PARA 298 note 1. As to the meaning of 'agriculture' see PARA 10.

2   The last agricultural wages order made under the Agricultural Wages Act 1948 was the Agricultural Wages (England and Wales) Order 2012 ('the 2012 Order'): see PARA 292. As to agricultural wages orders made by the Agricultural Advisory Panel for Wales: see the Agricultural Sector (Wales) Act 2014; and PARA 294.

3   Agricultural Wages Act 1948 s 4(1)(c) (s 4(1)(c), (3) amended by the National Minimum Wage Act 1998 Sch 2 para 4(1)(a)(ii), (c), Sch 3). Such a person is liable to a fine not exceeding level 3 on the standard scale: Agricultural Wages Act 1948 s 4(1) (as so amended). In any proceedings against a person under this provision it lies with the person being proceeded against to prove that he has allowed the holidays fixed by the order: s 4(3) (as so amended). As to the standard scale and the powers of magistrates' courts to issue fines on summary conviction see SENTENCING vol 92 (2015) PARA 176.

4   As to the meaning of 'agriculture' see PARA 10.

5   As to agricultural wages committees see PARA 296.

6   Agricultural Wages Act 1948 s 6(5). Such a person is liable on summary conviction for each offence to a fine not exceeding level 3 on the standard scale: see s 6(6) amended by the Criminal Justice Act 1982 ss 38, 46).

7   Agricultural Wages Act 1948 s 6(6). Where it appears to an investigating officer that a sum is due from an employer to a worker on account of the receipt of a premium in contravention of the Act, the officer may institute, on behalf of or in the name of the worker, civil proceedings before any competent court of jurisdiction for the recovery of the sum in question: s 12(5)(b) (amended by the Employment Protection Act 1975 Sch 18). The officer may also institute civil proceedings in respect of the failure to comply with a term or condition of employment fixed by the Agricultural Wages Board: Agricultural Wages Act 1948 s 12(5A) (s 12(5A), (5B) added by the Employment Protection Act 1975 Sch 9 Pt II para 4). If the officer is not a party to the proceedings the court has the same power to make an order for the payment of costs by the officer as if he were a party: Agricultural Wages Act 1948 s 12(5B) (as so added). These powers to institute proceedings are not in derogation of the worker's right to proceed independently: ss 6(7), 12(6) (s 12(6) substituted by the Employment Protection Act 1975 Sch 9 Pt II para 4). Proceedings must be commenced within six years of the date of the underpayment: *Gutsell v Reeve* [1936] 1 KB 272, CA. As to the

appointment, powers etc of officers see PARA 301 et seq. The Agricultural Wages Board has now been abolished see the Enterprise and Regulatory Reform Act 2013 s 72(1).
8   Agricultural Wages Act 1948 s 10(1).
9   Agricultural Wages Act 1948 s 10(2).

301. Appointment, powers and duties of agricultural wages officers.

Until a day to be appointed, the following provisions apply in relation to Wales[1].

Officers may be appointed[2] for the purpose of investigating complaints and otherwise securing the proper observation of the Agricultural Wages Act 1948[3].

Provided there are no corresponding or similar powers under the National Minimum Wage Act 1998 exercisable for that purpose[4], such an officer may:

(1)   require the production of, and inspect and take copies of, wages sheets or other records of wages paid to workers employed in agriculture or of any records of terms and conditions of employment of such workers[5];

(2)   enter any premises or place for the purpose of such inspection or for the enforcement of the Act[6];

(3)   require any worker, or the employer, or any agent of the employer, to give any information which it is in his power to give with respect to the employment of the worker or the wages paid to him[7]; and

(4)   take proceedings in respect of offences, and prosecute or conduct before a court of summary jurisdiction any proceedings arising under the Act[8].

Officers so acting may be required to prove their authority so to do[9].

It is an offence to hinder or obstruct an officer in the exercise of these powers (other than that relating to the taking of proceedings)[10].

Agricultural wages officers are also empowered to supply information for the purposes of the national minimum wage legislation[11].

1   The Agricultural Wages Act 1948 ss 11A, 12 are repealed by the Enterprise and Regulatory Reform Act 2013 Sch 20 para 2 by order made under s 103(3). At the date at which this volume states the law no order had been made in relation to Wales. In relation to England, the Agricultural Wages Act 1948 ss 11A, 12 continue in force on and after 1 October 2013 but only in relation to the employment of a worker employed in agriculture before that date if it continues after 30 September 2013: see the Enterprise and Regulatory Reform Act 2013 (Commencement No 1, Transitional Provisions and Savings) Order 2013, SI 2013/1455, art 4(4), Sch 3 paras 5, 6 (art 4(4) substituted by SI 2013/2271). As to the meaning of 'worker' see PARA 298 note 1. As to the meaning of 'employed' see PARA 298 note 1. As to the meaning of 'agriculture' see PARA 10. See also note 3.

2   The Secretary of State appoints officers to act for England and the Welsh Ministers appoint officers to act for Wales: Agricultural Wages Act 1948 s 11A(1)(a), (2)(a) (s 11A added by the Employment Relations Act 2004 s 47). Instead of or in addition to appointing any officers under the Agricultural Wages Act 1948 s 11A, the Secretary of State and the Welsh Ministers may arrange with any Minister of the Crown or government department, or any body performing functions on behalf of the Crown, that officers of that minister, department or body must act in England or, as the case may be, Wales, for these purposes: s 11A(1)(b), (2)(b) (as so added).

      Officers were formerly appointed under s 12(1) (repealed), and any such appointment which was in force immediately before 6 April 2005 (ie the date on which the Employment Relations Act 2004 s 47 was brought into force: see the Employment Relations Act 2004 (Commencement No 3 and Transitional Provisions) Order 2005, SI 2005/872) will, without prejudice to the generality of the Interpretation Act 1978 s 17(2)(b) (see STATUTES AND LEGISLATIVE PROCESS vol 96 (2012) PARAS 1702, 1709), have effect on and after that date as if made under the Agricultural Wages Act 1948 s 11A: Employment Relations Act 2004 s 47(3).

3   Agricultural Wages Act 1948 s 11A(1) (as added: see note 1).

4   The powers conferred by the Agricultural Wages Act 1948 s 12(3), (4) (see the text and notes 5–11) are not exercisable in any case where corresponding or similar powers conferred by any of the enforcement provisions of the National Minimum Wage Act 1998 (ie ss 9–11 (records: see EMPLOYMENT vol 39 (2014) PARAS 226–228), s 14 (powers of officers: see EMPLOYMENT vol

39 (2014) PARA 238), ss 17, 19–22 (enforcement of right to national minimum wage: see EMPLOYMENT vol 39 (2014) PARAS 242–248), ss 23, 24 (right not to suffer detriment: see EMPLOYMENT vol 39 (2014) PARA 249), s 28 (reversal of burden of proof in civil proceedings: see EMPLOYMENT vol 39 (2014) PARA 250), ss 31–33 (offences: see EMPLOYMENT vol 39 (2014) PARAS 251–253), s 48 (superior employers: see EMPLOYMENT vol 39 (2014) PARA 170) and s 49 (restriction on contracting out: see EMPLOYMENT vol 39 (2014) PARA 173)), as they have effect for the purposes of the Agricultural Wages Act 1948, are exercisable by virtue of s 3A (see PARA 299): s 12(8), (9) (added by the National Minimum Wage Act 1998 Sch 2 para 7(3)).

5   Agricultural Wages Act 1948 s 12(3)(a) (s 12(3), (4) amended by the Employment Relations Act 2004 s 47; and the Agricultural Wages Act 1948 s 12(3)(a) amended by the Employment Protection Act 1975 Sch 9 Pt II para 4). Reasonable notice must be given: Agricultural Wages Act 1948 s 12(3)(a) (as so amended).

6   Agricultural Wages Act 1948 s 12(3)(b) (s 12(3) as amended: see note 5). Entry is permitted at all reasonable times, but in the case of a dwelling house reasonable notice must be given: s 12(3)(b).

7   Agricultural Wages Act 1948 s 12(3)(c) (s 12(3) as amended: see note 5).

8   Agricultural Wages Act 1948 s 12(4) (as amended: see note 5). The power to take, prosecute and conduct proceedings exists notwithstanding that the officer is neither a barrister nor a solicitor, and may be exercised only in pursuance of a direction of the Secretary of State or the Welsh Ministers: s 12(4) (as so amended). As to the circumstances in which proceedings may be instituted for the recovery of money due from an employer to a worker see PARA 300.

9   When acting for the purposes of the Agricultural Wages Act 1948, an officer must, if so required, produce some duly authenticated document showing his authority so to act: s 11A(3) (as added: see note 1). If it appears to an officer that any person with whom he is dealing while acting for these purposes does not know that he is an officer so acting, the officer must identify himself as such to that person: s 11A(4) (as so added).

10 Any person who hinders or molests an officer acting in the exercise of his powers under the Agricultural Wages Act 1948 s 12(3) (see the text and notes 3–9), or refuses to produce any document or give any information which an officer lawfully requires him to produce or give, is liable on summary conviction to a fine not exceeding level 3 on the standard scale: s 12(7)(a), (b) (amended by the Employment Protection Act 1975 Sch 9 Pt II para 5; and the Criminal Justice Act 1982 ss 37, 38, 46). Any person who produces or causes to be produced or knowingly allows to be produced to an officer any wages sheet, record or other document which is false in any material particular, knowing the document to be false, or furnishes to an officer any information knowing it to be false, is liable on summary conviction to a fine not exceeding level 5 on the standard scale: Agricultural Wages Act 1948 s 12(7)(c), (d) (amended by the Employment Protection Act 1975 Sch 9 Pt II para 5; and the Criminal Justice Act 1982 ss 37, 38, 46). Until a day to be appointed a person who commits an offence under the Agricultural Wages Act 1948 s 12(7) is, in addition or as an alternative to the specified fine, liable to imprisonment for a term not exceeding three months (s 12(7) (as so amended)); as from that day, the option of imprisonment (either as an additional or alternative punishment) is removed (s 12(7) (as so amended; prospectively amended by the Criminal Justice Act 2003 s 332, Sch 37 Pt 9)). At the date at which this volume states the law no such day had been appointed. As to the standard scale and the powers of magistrates' courts to issue fines on summary conviction see SENTENCING vol 92 (2015) PARA 176.

11 Ie for the purposes of the National Minimum Wage Act 1998: see s 16; and EMPLOYMENT vol 39 (2014) PARA 239 et seq. As to the supply of information obtained by national minimum wage officers see PARA 302.

302. Supply of information obtained by national minimum wage officers.

Until a day to be appointed, the following provisions apply in relation to Wales[1].

Information which has been obtained by national minimum wage officers[2], other than information relating to a failure to allow holidays[3] or to any terms and conditions of employment fixed by an agricultural wages order[4], may, with the authority of the Secretary of State[5], be supplied to the Secretary of State or the Welsh Ministers for use for any purpose relating to the Agricultural Wages Act 1948[6]. The recipient of such information may not supply it to any other person or body unless it could lawfully be supplied to that person or body[7] or the recipient supplies it for the purposes of any civil or criminal proceedings relating to the Agricultural Wages Act 1948, and even in these circumstances the recipient may not supply it without the authority of the Secretary of State[8]. The circumstances in which information may be supplied or used are not otherwise limited[9].

There is a similar power under which agricultural wages officers[10] may disclose information for the purposes of the national minimum wage legislation[11].

1   The Agricultural Wages Act 1948 s 15A is repealed by the Enterprise and Regulatory Reform Act 2013 Sch 20 para 2 by order made under s 103(3). At the date at which this volume states the law no order had been made in relation to Wales. In relation to England, the Agricultural Wages Act 1948 s 15A continues in force on and after 1 October 2013 but only in relation to the employment of a worker employed in agriculture before that date if it continues after 30 September 2013: see the Enterprise and Regulatory Reform Act 2013 (Commencement No 1, Transitional Provisions and Savings) Order 2013, SI 2013/1455, art 4(4), Sch 3 para 8 (art 4(4) substituted by SI 2013/2271). As to the meaning of 'worker' see PARA 298 note 1. As to the meaning of 'employed' see PARA 298 note 1. As to the meaning of 'agriculture' see PARA 10. See also note 3.
2   Ie officers acting for the purposes of the National Minimum Wage Act 1998: Agricultural Wages Act 1948 s 15A(1) (s 15A added by the National Minimum Wage Act 1998 Sch 2 para 8). See the National Minimum Wage Act 1998 ss 13–15; and EMPLOYMENT vol 39 (2014) PARAS 237–239.
3   Ie holidays directed to be allowed to an agricultural worker under the Agricultural Wages Act 1948 s 3 (repealed).
4   Ie any terms and conditions of employment fixed by such an agricultural wages order by virtue of the Agricultural Wages Act 1948 s 3(1)(c) (repealed). The last agricultural wages order made under the Agricultural Wages Act 1948 was the Agricultural Wages (England and Wales) Order 2012 ('the 2012 Order'): see PARA 292. As to agricultural wages orders made by the Agricultural Advisory Panel for Wales: see the Agricultural Sector (Wales) Act 2014; and PARA 294.
5   The power to authorise the supply of information under the Agricultural Wages Act 1948 s 15A has not been transferred, in so far as it is exercisable in relation to Wales, to the Welsh Ministers: see PARA 390.
6   Agricultural Wages Act 1948 s 15A(1)–(3), (6) (as added: see note 1). Nothing in s 15A prevents a disclosure in accordance with the National Minimum Wage Act 1998 s 16A (see EMPLOYMENT vol 39 (2014) PARA 240): Agricultural Wages Act 1948 s 15A(5A) (s 15A as added (see note 1); s 15A(5A) added by the Employment Relations Act 2004 Sch 1 para 1).
7   Ie under the Agricultural Wages Act 1948 s 15A(3).
8   Agricultural Wages Act 1948 s 15A(4) (as added: see note 1).
9   Agricultural Wages Act 1948 s 15A(5) (as added: see note 1).
10 As to agricultural wages officers and their powers and duties see PARA 301.
11 See the National Minimum Wage Act 1998 ss 16, 16A; and EMPLOYMENT vol 39 (2014) PARA 240.

(2) SAFETY, HEALTH AND TRAINING OF AGRICULTURAL WORKERS

303. Health and safety regulations.

Provision for health and safety in agricultural operations is contained in the Health and Safety at Work etc Act 1974 and the various schemes made thereunder[1]. Most of those schemes apply to particular specified industries but of those that are generally applicable, the Workplace (Health, Safety and Welfare) Regulations 1992[2] and the Provision and Use of Work Equipment Regulations 1998[3] are of particular significance to agriculture. These regulations make provision in connection with:

(1)   the use of the workplace by disabled persons[4];
(2)   the maintenance, cleaning and inspection of the workplace, its equipment and its systems[5];

(3)   the stability and solidity of the workplace (including the conditions of the floors and traffic routes)[6];

(4)   ventilation and temperature[7];

(5)   lighting[8];

(6)   room dimensions, space and overcrowding[9];

(7)   falls or falling objects[10];

(8)   windows, transparent or translucent doors, gates and walls, skylights and ventilators[11];

(9)   escalators and moving walkways[12];

(10)   sanitary conveniences and washing facilities[13];

(11)   drinking water[14];

(12)   accommodation for clothing and changing facilities[15];

(13)   facilities for rest and for meals[16];

(14)   the suitability of work equipment[17];

(15)   specific risks[18];

(16)   information and instructions[19];

(17)   training[20];

(18)   dangerous parts of machinery[21];

(19)   protection against specified hazards[22];

(20)   controls and control systems (including stop and emergency stop controls)[23];

(21)   isolation from sources of energy[24];

(22)   stability of work equipment[25];

(23)   markings and warnings[26];

(24)   the operation of mobile work equipment[27]; and

(25)   power presses[28].

Health and safety regulations also make provision in connection with:

(a)   first aid[29];

(b)   electricity at work[30];

(c)   noise[31];

(d)   manual handling[32];

(e)   working at height[33];

(f)   safety signs and signals[34];

(g)   the management of health and safety generally[35]; and

(h)   the control of substances hazardous to health[36].

Provision specifically relating to agricultural operations is made for the prevention of accidents to children[37].

1   As to the Health and Safety at Work etc Act 1974 and the regulations made thereunder see HEALTH AND SAFETY AT WORK vol 52 (2014) PARA 302 et seq; and as to the making of those regulations see HEALTH AND SAFETY AT WORK vol 52 (2014) PARA 320. Provision for securing the safety and health of agricultural employees was formerly made by the Agriculture (Safety, Health and Welfare Provisions) Act 1956 ss 1–6 (repealed) and a series of regulations specific to agricultural operations made or having effect under that Act (ie the Agriculture (Ladders) Regulations 1957, SI 1957/1385, the Agriculture (Power Take-off) Regulations 1957, SI 1957/1386, the Agriculture (Safeguarding of Workplaces) Regulations 1959, SI 1959/428, the Agriculture (Stationary Machinery) Regulations 1959, SI 1959/1216, the Agriculture (Threshers and Balers) Regulations 1960, SI 1960/1199, and the Agriculture (Field Machinery) Regulations 1962, SI 1962/1472 (all of which have now been revoked), and the Agriculture (Tractor Cabs) Regulations 1974, SI 1974/2034 (amended by SI 1990/1075), which remain in force by virtue of the Agriculture (Safety, Health and Welfare Provisions) Act 1956 (Repeals and Modifications) Regulations 1975, SI 1975/46, reg 3, Sch 1 (see HEALTH AND SAFETY AT WORK vol 53 (2014) PARA 699).

2   The Workplace (Health, Safety and Welfare) Regulations 1992, SI 1992/3004, were made under the Health and Safety at Work etc Act 1974 s 15(1), (2), (3)(a), (5)(b) (see HEALTH AND SAFETY AT WORK vol 52 (2014) PARAS 388, 389). As to the application and requirements of the Workplace (Health, Safety and Welfare) Regulations 1992, SI 1992/3004, see regs 3, 4; and HEALTH AND SAFETY AT WORK vol 52 (2014) PARAS 420, 421.

3   The Provision and Use of Work Equipment Regulations 1998, SI 1998/2306, were made under the Health and Safety at Work etc Act 1974 ss 15(1), (2), (3)(a), (5), (6)(a), 49 (see HEALTH AND SAFETY AT WORK vol 52 (2014) PARAS 388, 389). As to the application of the Provision and Use of Work Equipment Regulations 1998, SI 1998/2306, see reg 3; and HEALTH AND SAFETY AT WORK vol 52 (2014) PARA 445.

4   See the Workplace (Health, Safety and Welfare) Regulations 1992, SI 1992/3004, reg 25A; and HEALTH AND SAFETY AT WORK vol 52 (2014) PARA 422.

5   See the Workplace (Health, Safety and Welfare) Regulations 1992, SI 1992/3004, regs 5, 9, 16; the Provision and Use of Work Equipment Regulations 1998, SI 1998/2306, regs 5, 6, 22; and HEALTH AND SAFETY AT WORK vol 52 (2014) PARAS 423, 428, 434, 447.

6   See the Workplace (Health, Safety and Welfare) Regulations 1992, SI 1992/3004, regs 4A, 12, 17; and HEALTH AND SAFETY AT WORK vol 52 (2014) PARAS 424, 431, 435.

7   See the Workplace (Health, Safety and Welfare) Regulations 1992, SI 1992/3004, regs 6, 7; the Provision and Use of Work Equipment Regulations 1998, SI 1998/2306, reg 13; and HEALTH AND SAFETY AT WORK vol 52 (2014) PARAS 425, 426, 453.

8   See the Workplace (Health, Safety and Welfare) Regulations 1992, SI 1992/3004, reg 8; the Provision and Use of Work Equipment Regulations 1998, SI 1998/2306, reg 21; and HEALTH AND SAFETY AT WORK vol 52 (2014) PARAS 427, 457.

9   See the Workplace (Health, Safety and Welfare) Regulations 1992, SI 1992/3004, reg 10; and HEALTH AND SAFETY AT WORK vol 52 (2014) PARA 429.

10 See the Workplace (Health, Safety and Welfare) Regulations 1992, SI 1992/3004, reg 13; and HEALTH AND SAFETY AT WORK vol 52 (2014) PARA 432.

11 See the Workplace (Health, Safety and Welfare) Regulations 1992, SI 1992/3004, regs 14–16, 18; and HEALTH AND SAFETY AT WORK vol 52 (2014) PARAS 433, 434, 436.

12 See the Workplace (Health, Safety and Welfare) Regulations 1992, SI 1992/3004, reg 19; and HEALTH AND SAFETY AT WORK vol 52 (2014) PARA 437.

13 See the Workplace (Health, Safety and Welfare) Regulations 1992, SI 1992/3004, regs 20, 21; and HEALTH AND SAFETY AT WORK vol 52 (2014) PARAS 438, 439.

14 See the Workplace (Health, Safety and Welfare) Regulations 1992, SI 1992/3004, reg 22; and HEALTH AND SAFETY AT WORK vol 52 (2014) PARA 440.

15 See the Workplace (Health, Safety and Welfare) Regulations 1992, SI 1992/3004, regs 23, 24; and HEALTH AND SAFETY AT WORK vol 52 (2014) PARA 441.

16 See the Workplace (Health, Safety and Welfare) Regulations 1992, SI 1992/3004, reg 25; and HEALTH AND SAFETY AT WORK vol 52 (2014) PARA 442.

17 See the Provision and Use of Work Equipment Regulations 1998, SI 1998/2306, reg 4; and HEALTH AND SAFETY AT WORK vol 52 (2014) PARA 446. Provision is also made for the application of a number of statutory instruments giving effect to Community directives concerning the safety of products: see reg 10; and HEALTH AND SAFETY AT WORK vol 52 (2014) PARA 446.

18 See the Provision and Use of Work Equipment Regulations 1998, SI 1998/2306, reg 7; and HEALTH AND SAFETY AT WORK vol 52 (2014) PARA 448.

19 See the Provision and Use of Work Equipment Regulations 1998, SI 1998/2306, reg 8; and HEALTH AND SAFETY AT WORK vol 52 (2014) PARA 449.

20 See the Provision and Use of Work Equipment Regulations 1998, SI 1998/2306, reg 9; and HEALTH AND SAFETY AT WORK vol 52 (2014) PARA 450.

21 See the Provision and Use of Work Equipment Regulations 1998, SI 1998/2306, reg 11; and HEALTH AND SAFETY AT WORK vol 52 (2014) PARA 451.

22 See the Provision and Use of Work Equipment Regulations 1998, SI 1998/2306, reg 12; and HEALTH AND SAFETY AT WORK vol 52 (2014) PARA 452.

23 See the Provision and Use of Work Equipment Regulations 1998, SI 1998/2306, regs 14–18; and HEALTH AND SAFETY AT WORK vol 52 (2014) PARA 454.

24 See the Provision and Use of Work Equipment Regulations 1998, SI 1998/2306, reg 19; and HEALTH AND SAFETY AT WORK vol 52 (2014) PARA 455.

25 See the Provision and Use of Work Equipment Regulations 1998, SI 1998/2306, reg 20; and HEALTH AND SAFETY AT WORK vol 52 (2014) PARA 456.

26 See the Provision and Use of Work Equipment Regulations 1998, SI 1998/2306, reg 23, 24; and HEALTH AND SAFETY AT WORK vol 52 (2014) PARA 458.

27 See the Provision and Use of Work Equipment Regulations 1998, SI 1998/2306, reg 25–30; and HEALTH AND SAFETY AT WORK vol 52 (2014) PARAS 459–462. See also the Agriculture (Tractor Cabs) Regulations 1974, SI 1974/2034; the Prevention of Accidents to Children in Agriculture Regulations 1998, SI 1998/3262; and HEALTH AND SAFETY AT WORK vol 53 (2014) PARAS 699, 700.

28 See the Provision and Use of Work Equipment Regulations 1998, SI 1998/2306, regs 31–35; and HEALTH AND SAFETY AT WORK vol 52 (2014) PARAS 463–466.

29 See the Health and Safety (First Aid) Regulations 1981, SI 1981/917; and HEALTH AND SAFETY AT WORK vol 52 (2014) PARA 408.

30 See the Electricity at Work Regulations 1989, SI 1989/635; and HEALTH AND SAFETY AT WORK vol 53 (2014) PARAS 568–571.

31 See the Control of Noise at Work Regulations 2005, SI 2005/1643; and HEALTH AND SAFETY AT WORK vol 53 (2014) PARAS 574–581.

32 See the Manual Handling Operations Regulations 1992, SI 1992/2793; and HEALTH AND SAFETY AT WORK vol 53 (2014) PARA 545.

33 See the Work at Height Regulations 2005, SI 2005/735; and HEALTH AND SAFETY AT WORK vol 53 (2014) PARA 546 et seq.

34 See the Health and Safety (Safety Signs and Signals) Regulations 1996, SI 1996/341; and HEALTH AND SAFETY AT WORK vol 52 (2014) PARA 409.

35 See the Management of Health and Safety at Work Regulations 1999, SI 1999/3242; and HEALTH AND SAFETY AT WORK vol 52 (2014) PARA 392 et seq.

36 See the Control of Substances Hazardous to Health Regulations 2002, SI 2002/2677; and HEALTH AND SAFETY AT WORK vol 53 (2014) PARA 582 et seq.

37 See the Prevention of Accidents to Children in Agriculture Regulations 1998, SI 1998/3262; and HEALTH AND SAFETY AT WORK vol 53 (2014) PARA 700.

304. Compliance with health and safety regulations.

It is an offence, punishable by a fine, to contravene any of the health and safety regulations[1], although it is generally a defence for a person charged with a contravention of any of the regulations to prove that he used all due diligence to secure compliance[2]. A breach of the regulations will not give rise to civil liability except in so far as the regulations provide[3]. These provisions bind the Crown[4].

1 See the Agriculture (Safety, Health and Welfare Provisions) Act 1956 s 1(6); the Health and Safety at Work etc Act 1974 s 33(1)(c), (3); and HEALTH AND SAFETY AT WORK vol 52 (2014) PARAS 314, 388. As to the health and safety regulations see PARA 303. Note that the offence under the Agriculture (Safety, Health and Welfare Provisions) Act 1956 s 1(6) now applies only in connection with a contravention of the Agriculture (Tractor Cabs) Regulations 1974, SI 1974/2034 (see PARA 303 note 1). Third parties and bodies corporate may also be liable for contravention of the Health and Safety at Work etc Act 1974: see ss 36, 37; and HEALTH AND SAFETY AT WORK vol 53 (2014) PARAS 811, 812.

2 See the Agriculture (Safety, Health and Welfare Provisions) Act 1956 s 16. See also the relevant provisions of the regulations noted to PARA 1246. As to the defence of 'all due diligence' see *Tesco Supermarkets Ltd v Nattrass* [1972] AC 153, [1971] 2 All ER 127, HL.

3 See the Health and Safety at Work etc Act 1974 s 47(2), (2A); and HEALTH AND SAFETY AT WORK vol 52 (2014) PARAS 380, 384.

4 See the Agriculture (Safety, Health and Welfare Provisions) Act 1956 s 22; the Health and Safety at Work etc Act 1974 s 48; and HEALTH AND SAFETY AT WORK vol 52 (2014) PARAS 304, 314.

305. Notification, recording and investigation of accidents.

Subject to certain exceptions[1], all injuries, diseases and dangerous occurrences are required to be notified to the Health and Safety Executive[2]. Records must also be kept of events or diseases which are so notified[3].

An inquest into a death which may have been caused by an accident occurring in the course of agricultural operations must be adjourned unless a representative of the Executive is present to watch the proceedings, and the Executive must be given at least four days' notice of the time and place of the adjourned inquest[4].

The Executive may appoint as inspectors persons having suitable qualifications as it thinks necessary for carrying into effect the relevant statutory provisions within its field of responsibility[5]. Inspectors are granted powers for the purpose of carrying into effect the relevant statutory provisions[6], and obstruction of an inspector is an offence[7].

1 The exceptions are generally concerned with deaths or injuries arising out of medical treatment (see the Reporting of Injuries, Diseases and Dangerous Occurrences Regulations 1995, SI 1995/3163, reg 10; and HEALTH AND SAFETY AT WORK vol 52 (2014) PARA 363) and those on premises which are or are on an authorised defence site or a new nuclear build site (see the Health and Safety (Enforcing Authority) Regulations 1998, SI 1998/494, reg 4A).
2 See the Health and Safety (Enforcing Authority) Regulations 1998, SI 1998/494, reg 4; and HEALTH AND SAFETY AT WORK vol 52 (2014) PARA 335. The Health and Safety Executive is the enforcing authority for all agricultural activities and any activity at an agricultural show which involves the handling of livestock or the working of agricultural equipment: Sch 2 para 7. For these purposes 'agricultural activities' includes horticulture, fruit growing, seed growing, dairy farming, livestock breeding and keeping, including the management of livestock up to the point of slaughter or export from Great Britain, forestry, the use of land as grazing land, market gardens and nursery grounds and the preparation of land for agricultural use but does not include such activities at a garden centre or other shop; 'livestock breeding and keeping' does not include activities the main purpose of which is entertainment; and 'livestock' means any creature kept for the production of food, wool, skins or fur or for the purpose of any agricultural activity: reg 2(1). As to the Health and Safety Executive generally see HEALTH AND SAFETY AT WORK vol 52 (2014) PARA 326 et seq. As to the meaning of 'Great Britain' see PARA 1 note 1.
3 See the Reporting of Injuries, Diseases and Dangerous Occurrences Regulations 2013, SI 2013/1471, reg 12; and HEALTH AND SAFETY AT WORK vol 52 (2014) PARA 375.
4 See the Agriculture (Safety, Health and Welfare Provisions) Act 1956 s 9(1); and HEALTH AND SAFETY AT WORK vol 53 (2014) PARA 701. If the inquest relates to the death of only one person, and the coroner has informed an inspector of the Health and Safety Executive of the time and place of the inquest not less than 24 hours before it is held, the coroner is not bound to adjourn it: see s 9(1)(b); and HEALTH AND SAFETY AT WORK vol 53 (2014) PARA 701.
5 See the Health and Safety at Work etc Act 1974 s 19; and HEALTH AND SAFETY AT WORK vol 52 (2014) PARA 338.
6 See the Health and Safety at Work etc Act 1974 s 20, where the powers are listed; and HEALTH AND SAFETY AT WORK vol 52 (2014) PARA 339.
7 See the Health and Safety at Work etc Act 1974 s 33(1)(h); and HEALTH AND SAFETY AT WORK vol 52 (2014) PARA 339.

306. Employment of children.

Local authority byelaws[1] may authorise the employment[2], on an occasional basis by their parents or guardians, of children aged 13 in light agricultural or horticultural work[3]. This provision is an exception to the general rule prohibiting the employment of children under the age of 14[4]. Byelaws[5] may also authorise the employment of children for not more than one hour before the commencement of school hours on any day on which they are required to attend school[6]. There are additional general restrictions on the hours which children may work[7], and no child may be employed on any work other than light work[8]. Contravention of these provisions is punishable by a fine, although there is a statutory defence of due diligence available to the employer[9].

1　As to the local authorities for these purposes, and the confirmation of byelaws, see the Children and Young Persons Act 1933 ss 27, 96; and CHILDREN AND YOUNG PERSONS vol 10 (2017) PARA 703. As from a day to be appointed the power of local authorities in this regard is transferred to the Secretary of State (or the Welsh Ministers), who may make regulations for these purposes: see s 18(1), (2) (prospectively amended by the Employment of Children Act 1973 s 1(3), Sch 1 para 1). At the date at which this volume states the law no such day had been appointed. As to the Secretary of State and the Welsh Ministers see PARA 390.

2　A child (ie a person who is not over compulsory school age) who assists in a trade or occupation carried on for profit is deemed to be employed notwithstanding that he receives no reward for his labour: Children and Young Persons Act 1933 s 30(1) (renumbered, and definition added, by the Employment Act 1989 Sch 3 Pt III para 8). 'Compulsory school age' is to be construed in accordance with the Education Act 1996 (see s 8; and EDUCATION vol 35 (2015) PARA 19): Children and Young Persons Act 1933 s 30(1) (as so renumbered).

3　See the Children and Young Persons Act 1933 s 18(2)(a)(i), (ia); and CHILDREN AND YOUNG PERSONS vol 10 (2017) PARA 703.

4　See the Children and Young Persons Act 1933 s 18(1)(a); and CHILDREN AND YOUNG PERSONS vol 10 (2017) PARA 702.

5　Or, as from a day to be appointed, regulations: see note 1.

6　See the Children and Young Persons Act 1933 s 18(2)(a)(ii); and CHILDREN AND YOUNG PERSONS vol 10 (2017) PARA 703.

7　See the Children and Young Persons Act 1933 s 18(1)(b)–(j); and CHILDREN AND YOUNG PERSONS vol 10 (2017) PARA 702.

8　See the Children and Young Persons Act 1933 s 18(1)(aa); and CHILDREN AND YOUNG PERSONS vol 10 (2017) PARA 702. 'Light work' means work which, on account of the inherent nature of the tasks which it involves and the particular conditions under which it is performed, is not likely to be harmful to the safety, health or development of children and is not such as to be harmful to their attendance at school or to their participation in work experience in accordance with the Education Act 1996 s 560 (see CHILDREN AND YOUNG PERSONS vol 10 (2017) PARA 700) or their capacity to benefit from the instruction received or experience gained: Children and Young Persons Act 1933 s 18(2A) (added by SI 1998/276).

9　See the Children and Young Persons Act 1933 s 21; and CHILDREN AND YOUNG PERSONS vol 10 (2017) PARAS 704–705.

307. Training in agriculture.

ATB-Landbase, a company limited by guarantee, was established for agricultural training purposes[1], and the Agricultural Training Board[2] was accordingly wound up[3], and its assets transferred to ATB-Landbase[4] (now Lantra), which is required to apply those assets for charitable purposes related to or in connection with training for employment[5].

The Secretary of State[6] may also make provision for the training in agricultural occupations of persons (whether employed or not) who are above the upper limit of the compulsory school age[7], which may include the payment of expenses, the provision of residential accommodation and other facilities or services[8].

1　See the Agricultural Training Board (Revocation) Order 1994, SI 1994/555 (lapsed).

2　The Agricultural Training Board was established (as the Agricultural, Horticultural and Forestry Industrial Training Board) by the Industrial Training (Agricultural, Horticultural and Forestry) Board Order 1966, SI 1966/969 (revoked) (made under the Industrial Training Act 1964 s 1(1) (repealed)), and, having been renamed the Agricultural Training Board by the Employment and Training Act 1973 s 6(3) (repealed), was continued under the Agricultural Training Board Act 1982. See note 3.

3   See the Agricultural Training Board (Revocation) Order 1994, SI 1994/555, art 2(1) (lapsed). The Agricultural Training Board Acts 1982, 1985 and 1987 were accordingly all repealed by the Statute Law (Repeals) Act 2004.
4   See the Agricultural Training Board (Revocation) Order 1994, SI 1994/555, arts 2, 4 (lapsed).
5   Agricultural Training Board (Revocation) Order 1994, SI 1994/555, art 2(4) (lapsed).
6   As to the Secretary of State see PARA 390. Note that the functions of the Secretary of State in this regard have not been transferred, in so far as they are exercisable in relation to Wales, to the Welsh Ministers.
7   As to the compulsory school age and its upper limit see the Education Act 1996 s 8; and EDUCATION vol 35 (2015) PARA 19.
8   Agriculture (Miscellaneous Provisions) Act 1949 s 8 (amended by the Employment and Training Act 1973 Sch 4).

308. Grants for proficiency testing.

The Secretary of State and the Welsh Ministers[1] may, with the approval of the Treasury[2], make payments by way of grant to any body of persons the activities of which include the taking of measures for some or all of:

(1)   devising, formulating and promoting proficiency tests in crafts related to agriculture[3] in England and Wales, formulating standards for those tests, and revising those tests and standards from time to time[4];

(2)   co-ordinating the activities of bodies carrying out such proficiency tests in England or Wales, and monitoring the methods and standards of such bodies in carrying out those tests[5]; and

(3)   making and maintaining arrangements for obtaining and evaluating data about the use and results of such proficiency tests in England and Wales[6].

Such grants may be paid for use in or towards meeting expenditure incurred or to be incurred by the body for or in connection with any of the above purposes[7]. Payments may be conditional[8] and sums paid out may in certain circumstances be recovered[9].

1   As to the Secretary of State and the Welsh Ministers see PARA 390.
2   As to the Treasury see CONSTITUTIONAL AND ADMINISTRATIVE LAW vol 20 (2014) PARA 263 et seq.
3   For these purposes 'agriculture' includes horticulture and forestry: Agriculture (Miscellaneous Provisions) Act 1976 s 4(5).
4   Agriculture (Miscellaneous Provisions) Act 1976 s 4(1)(a), (2).
5   Agriculture (Miscellaneous Provisions) Act 1976 s 4(1)(b).
6   Agriculture (Miscellaneous Provisions) Act 1976 s 4(1)(c) (amended by the Enterprise and Regulatory Reform Act 2013 Sch 20 para 2).
7   Agriculture (Miscellaneous Provisions) Act 1976 s 4(2).
8   See the Agriculture (Miscellaneous Provisions) Act 1976 s 4(3) (a payment under s 4 may be made on such conditions as the Secretary of State thinks or the Welsh Ministers think fit to impose, including conditions for restricting the purposes for which it can be used).
9   The Secretary of State and the Welsh Ministers may on demand recover an amount equal to any payment under the Agriculture (Miscellaneous Provisions) Act 1976 s 4, or an appropriate part of it, as the case may be, if it appears to him or them that the payment or any part of it has not been used for the purpose for which it was made (s 4(4)(a)) or that, as regards the payment or any part of it, any condition on which the payment was made has not been complied with in a material respect (s 4(4)(b)).

(3) REGULATION OF THE ACTIVITIES OF GANGMASTERS

(i) Scope of Regulation

309. Regulation of activities of gangmasters.

The activities of persons who supply workers[1] to carry out certain kinds of agricultural and fisheries work ('gangmasters') are regulated by statute[2]. The work to which the legislation applies is agricultural work[3], the gathering of shellfish[4], and the processing or packaging of any produce derived from agricultural work[5] or shellfish, fish or products derived therefrom[6]; and the Secretary of State[7] may also by regulations make provision excluding work of a prescribed[8] description from being work to which the legislation applies[9] or including work of a prescribed description[10], as being work to which it applies[11]. To fall within the legislation's ambit, the work in question must be carried out either in the United Kingdom[12], on any portion of the shore or bed of the sea, or of an estuary or tidal river, adjacent to the United Kingdom, whether above or below (or partly above and partly below) the low water mark[13], or in UK coastal waters[14]. The legislation establishes a Gangmasters and Labour Abuse Authority[15] to oversee a system of licensing for gangmasters[16], and makes it an offence to act as a gangmaster[17] without a licence[18] or to enter into arrangements with unlicensed gangmasters[19].

1 'Worker' means an individual who does work to which the Gangmasters (Licensing) Act 2004 applies: s 26(1). A person is not prevented from being a worker for these purposes by reason of the fact that he has no right to be, or to work, in the United Kingdom: s 26(2). As to the meaning of 'United Kingdom' see PARA 1 note 1.

2 See the Gangmasters (Licensing) Act 2004; and PARA 310 et seq.

3 Gangmasters (Licensing) Act 2004 s 3(1)(a). For these purposes 'agricultural work' means work in agriculture (s 3(2)). As to the meaning of 'agriculture' see PARA 10.

4 Gangmasters (Licensing) Act 2004 s 3(1)(b). 'Shellfish' means crustaceans and molluscs of any kind, and includes any part of a shellfish and any (or any part of any) brood, ware, halfware or spat of shellfish, and any spawn of shellfish, and the shell, or any part of the shell, of a shellfish: s 3(4).

5 Gangmasters (Licensing) Act 2004 s 3(1)(c)(i).

6 Gangmasters (Licensing) Act 2004 s 3(1)(c)(ii).

7 As to the Secretary of State see PARA 390.

8 Unless otherwise indicated, 'prescribed' means prescribed by regulations made by the Secretary of State: Gangmasters (Licensing) Act 2004 s 25(1).

9 Gangmasters (Licensing) Act 2004 s 3(5)(a). The Secretary of State must consult the Authority and the Director of Labour Market Enforcement before making regulations under s 3(5): s 3(6) (added by the Immigration Act 2016 Sch 3 para 17(b)).

10 Such regulations may provide for the application of the Gangmasters (Licensing) Act 2004 s 4(5), (6) (which provides for the circumstances when a person acts as a gangmaster for the purposes of the legislation: see PARA 310) in relation to work to which the Gangmasters (Licensing) Act 2004 applies by virtue of the regulations: s 4(7). At the date at which this volume states the law no such regulations had been made.

11 Gangmasters (Licensing) Act 2004 s 3(5)(b) (amended by the Immigration Act 2016 Sch 3 para 17(a)).

12 Gangmasters (Licensing) Act 2004 s 5(1)(a).

13 Gangmasters (Licensing) Act 2004 s 5(1)(b).

14 Gangmasters (Licensing) Act 2004 s 5(1)(c). For these purposes 'UK coastal waters' means waters adjacent to the United Kingdom to a distance of six miles (ie six international nautical miles of 1,852 metres each) measured from the baselines from which the breadth of the territorial sea is measured: s 5(2).

15 As to the Gangmasters and Labour Abuse Authority see PARA 320.

16 See PARA 324 et seq.

17 As to 'acting as a gangmaster' see PARA 310.

18 See PARA 311.
19 See PARA 312.

310.   Acting as a gangmaster.

A person acts as a gangmaster[1] if he:
(1)   supplies a worker[2] to do applicable work[3] for another person[4];
(2)   uses[5] a worker to do applicable work in connection with services provided by him to another person[6];
(3)   for the purposes of a business carried on by him, uses a worker to harvest or otherwise gather agricultural produce[7], to process or package agricultural produce so harvested or gathered[8], or to gather shellfish[9], so far as such work is applicable work.

It is unlawful to act as a gangmaster without a licence[10] or to enter into arrangements with unlicensed gangmasters[11]. These provisions[12] apply wherever a person acts as a gangmaster, whether in the United Kingdom[13] or elsewhere, in relation to applicable work[14].

1   As to the meaning of 'gangmaster' see PARA 309.
2   As to the meaning of 'worker' see PARA 309 note 1.
3   Ie work to which the Gangmasters (Licensing) Act 2004 applies (as to which see PARA 309).
4   Gangmasters (Licensing) Act 2004 s 4(1), (2). For these purposes, it does not matter whether:
    (1)   the worker works under a contract with the gangmaster or is supplied to him by another person (s 4(3)(a));
    (2)   the worker is supplied directly under arrangements between the gangmaster and the other person or indirectly under arrangements involving one or more intermediaries (s 4(3)(b));
    (3)   the gangmaster supplies the worker himself or procures that the worker is supplied (s 4(3)(c));
    (4)   the work is done under the control of the gangmaster, the other person or an intermediary (s 4(3)(d)); or
    (5)   the work done for the other person is for the purposes of a business carried on by him or in connection with services provided by him to another person (s 4(3)(e)).
5   For the purposes of the Gangmasters (Licensing) Act 2004 s 4(4), (5), a gangmaster is treated as 'using' a worker to do applicable work if he makes arrangements under which the worker does the work whether the worker works for the gangmaster (or for another) or on his own account, and whether or not he works under a contract (with the gangmaster or another): s 4(6). The Secretary of State may by regulations extend the scope of s 4(5), (6): see PARA 309. As to the Secretary of State see PARA 390.
6   Gangmasters (Licensing) Act 2004 s 4(4).
7   Ie to harvest or otherwise gather agricultural produce following either a sale, an assignment or a lease of produce to the gangmaster, or the making of any other agreement with him, where the sale, assignment, lease or other agreement was entered into for the purpose of enabling the harvesting or gathering to take place: Gangmasters (Licensing) Act 2004 s 4(5)(a). 'Agricultural produce' means any produce derived from agriculture: s 4(5). As to the meaning of 'agriculture' see PARA 10. See also note 5.
8   Gangmasters (Licensing) Act 2004 s 4(5)(c). See also note 5.
9   Gangmasters (Licensing) Act 2004 s 4(5)(b). As to the meaning of 'shellfish' see PARA 309 note 4. See also note 5.
10 See PARA 311. As to the licensing of gangmasters PARA 1262 et seq.
11 See PARA 312.
12 Ie the Gangmasters (Licensing) Act 2004.
13 As to the meaning of 'United Kingdom' see PARA 1 note 1.
14 Gangmasters (Licensing) Act 2004 s 5(3).

(ii) Unlawful Operations

311. Acting as a gangmaster other than under the authority of a licence.

A person may not in general[1] act as a gangmaster[2] except under the authority of a licence granted by the Gangmasters and Labour Abuse Authority[3]. A person commits an offence if he either acts as a gangmaster in contravention of this requirement[4] or has in his possession or under his control false[5] or improperly obtained[6] documentation with the intention of inducing another person to believe that he or another person acting as a gangmaster in contravention of the licensing requirements[7] is acting under the authority of a licence[8]. These offences may be dealt with either summarily or on indictment[9].

1   The Secretary of State may by regulations specify circumstances in which a licence is not required: Gangmasters (Licensing) Act 2004 s 6(2). As to the Secretary of State see PARA 390. For the circumstances in which a licence is not required see the Gangmasters Licensing (Exclusion) Regulations 2013, SI 2013/2216; and PARA 313.

2   As to the meaning of 'gangmaster' see PARA 309. As to the meaning of 'acting as a gangmaster' see PARA 310.

3   Gangmasters (Licensing) Act 2004 ss 1(2)(a), 6(1), 7(1). As to the Gangmasters and Labour Abuse Authority see PARA 320. Licences may be granted to individuals, bodies corporate, unincorporated associations, and partnerships: see ss 20(1), 21(1), 22(1); and PARA 320 et seq. For enforcement officers' powers of entry to enforce these requirements see PARA 316. The legislation governing the activities of employment agencies (ie the Employment Agencies Act 1973: see TRADE AND INDUSTRY vol 97 (2015) PARA 974 et seq) does not apply to an employment agency or an employment business (as to the meaning of which see s 13(1); and TRADE AND INDUSTRY vol 97 (2015) PARA 974) in so far as it consists of activities for which a licence is required under these provisions: Gangmasters (Licensing) Act 2004 s 27. However, in framing licence conditions dealing with the recruitment or supply of workers, the Gangmasters and Labour Abuse Authority (see PARA 320) must ensure that, where a gangmaster would be an employment agency or employment business within the meaning of the Employment Agencies Act 1973 if this exclusion were not in force, the licence conditions include provisions imposing on the licensee, or (as appropriate) other specified persons, requirements corresponding to those which would apply under the Employment Agencies Act 1973 if the exclusion were not in force in so far as the requirements appear to the authority to be appropriate in the circumstances: Gangmasters (Licensing Authority) Regulations 2015, SI 2015/805, reg 8(3).

4   Gangmasters (Licensing) Act 2004 s 12(1). As to powers of arrest see PARA 315. For this purpose, a person acting as a gangmaster does not contravene s 6 by reason only of the fact that he breaches a condition of the licence which authorises him to so act: s 12(1). A person who enters into an arrangement with an unlicensed gangmaster also commits an offence: see PARA 312. As to conditions in licences see PARA 324. As to the commission of offences by bodies corporate, unincorporated associations, and partnerships see PARA 318.

5   A document is false only if it is false within the meaning of the Forgery and Counterfeiting Act 1981 Pt I (ss 1–13) (see s 9(1); and CRIMINAL LAW vol 25 (2016) PARA 404), and references to the making of a false document include references to the modification of a document so that it becomes false: Gangmasters (Licensing) Act 2004 s 12(5)(a).

6   A document is improperly obtained if false information was provided, in or in connection with the application for its issue or an application for its modification, to the person who issued it or (as the case may be) to a person entitled to modify it: Gangmasters (Licensing) Act 2004 s 12(5)(b).

7   Ie in contravention of the Gangmasters (Licensing) Act 2004 s 6 (see the text and notes 1–3).

8   Gangmasters (Licensing) Act 2004 s 12(2). The offence is committed if a person has in his possession or under his control a 'relevant document' (ie either a licence or any document issued by the Gangmasters and Labour Abuse Authority in connection with a licence) that is false and that he knows or believes to be false, that was improperly obtained and that he knows or believes to have been improperly obtained, or that relates to someone else, and he has the requisite intention of inducing another person to believe that he or another person acting as a gangmaster in contravention of s 6 (see the text and notes 1–3) is acting under the authority of a licence: s 12(2), (6).

9   Until a day is appointed for the coming into force of the Criminal Justice Act 2003 s 154(1) (general limit on magistrates' courts' power to impose imprisonment) a person guilty of an offence under the Gangmasters (Licensing) Act 2004 s 12(1) or (2) (see the text and notes 4–8) is liable on summary conviction to imprisonment for a term not exceeding six months, or to a fine not exceeding the statutory maximum, or to both (s 12(3)(a)) or on conviction on indictment to imprisonment for a term not exceeding ten years, or to a fine, or to both (s 12(4)); as from that day the maximum term of imprisonment on summary conviction is 12 months (unless the offence was committed before that day, in which case the maximum remains six months) (s 12(3)). At the date at which this volume states the law no such day had been appointed. As to the statutory maximum see PARA 58 note 1.

312. Entering into arrangements with unlicensed gangmasters.

A person commits an offence if he enters into arrangements under which a gangmaster[1] supplies him with workers[2] or services and the gangmaster in supplying those workers or services contravenes the statutory licensing requirements for persons acting as gangmasters[3]. The offence is dealt with summarily[4]. It is a defence for a person charged with this offence to prove that he took all reasonable steps[5] to satisfy himself that the gangmaster was acting under the authority of a valid licence[6] and that he did not know, and had no reasonable grounds for suspecting, that the gangmaster was not the holder of a valid licence[7].

1   As to the meaning of 'gangmaster' see PARA 309.
2   As to the meaning of 'worker' see PARA 309 note 1.
3   Gangmasters (Licensing) Act 2004 s 13(1). For the statutory licensing requirements for persons acting as gangmasters see PARA 320 et seq. For the circumstances in which a licence is not required see PARA 313. As to the meaning of 'acting as a gangmaster' see PARA 310. As to the commission of offence by bodies corporate, unincorporated associations, and partnerships see PARA 318.
4   Until a day is appointed for the coming into force of the Criminal Justice Act 2003 s 154(1) (general limit on magistrates' courts' power to impose imprisonment) a person guilty of an offence under the Gangmasters (Licensing) Act 2004 s 13(1) is liable on summary conviction to imprisonment for a term not exceeding six months, or to a fine not exceeding the statutory maximum, or to both (s 13(4)(a)); as from that day the maximum term of imprisonment on summary conviction is 51 weeks (unless the offence was committed before that day, in which case the maximum remains six months) (s 13(4)). At the date at which this volume states the law no such day had been appointed. As to the statutory maximum see PARA 58 note 1.
5   The Secretary of State may by regulations make provision as to what constitutes 'reasonable steps' for these purposes: Gangmasters (Licensing) Act 2004 s 13(3). At the date at which this volume states the law no such regulations had been made. As to the Secretary of State see PARA 390.
6   Gangmasters (Licensing) Act 2004 s 13(2)(a).
7   Gangmasters (Licensing) Act 2004 s 13(2)(b).

313. Circumstances in which a licence is not required.

A person does not require a licence[1] to act as a gangmaster[2] in the following circumstances[3]:

    (1)   the supply of a worker[4] to process or pack produce[5], the worker is supplied to a catering establishment[6], a shop or other retail establishment, a wholesale market, a wholesale establishment[7] or a distribution warehouse[8];

    (2)   the supply of a worker to process or pack a product which includes a derivative of produce but where the product concerned is not a food product, pet food product or a product which is primarily an agricultural, fish or shellfish product[9];

    (3)   the supply of a worker for agricultural work by a farmer (A)[10] to another farmer (B) where:

        (a)   the supply is to do work on a farm which is the subject of a share farming agreement[11] between the two farmers;

(b)   the total hours the worker works for B are not more than thirty per cent of the total hours the worker worked for A in the twelve months immediately preceding the commencement of the period of work undertaken for B;

(c)   the worker has been supplied to A by a person (C) who acts as a gangmaster in making that supply, and the supply by A is made with C's agreement to the nature of the work to be undertaken for B and is a one-off arrangement of less than two weeks[12];

(4)   the use of a worker for agricultural work by a farmer (A) to provide a service to another farmer (B) where the service provided involves a one-off arrangement of less than four weeks and:

(a)   the total hours the worker works delivering services to B are not more than thirty per cent of the total hours the worker worked for A in the twelve months immediately preceding the commencement of the delivery of services to B; or

(b)   the worker has been supplied to A by a person (C) who acts as a gangmaster in making that supply, and the use of the worker to deliver services by A is made with C's agreement to the nature of the services to be provided to B[13];

(5)   the supply of a worker by a farmer to a person (A) to operate machinery supplied by A for the purpose of undertaking agricultural work for that farmer[14];

(6)   the supply of a worker by a sole operator in the Seasonal Agricultural Workers Scheme[15] to another Seasonal Agricultural Workers Scheme operator[16];

(7)   the use of a worker for agricultural work by a person (A) to provide a service to a farmer where the service involves the use of machinery owned or hired by A and the worker is employed by A to operate or to support the operation of that machinery[17];

(8)   the use of a worker for agricultural work by a person (A) to provide a service to a farmer where A enters into an arrangement with another person (B) to deliver the service, the service involves the use of machinery owned or hired by B and the worker is employed by B to operate or to support the operation of that machinery[18];

(9)   the use of a worker by a person (A) to provide a food and drink processing and packaging service where A is the worker's employer, A owns, hires or leases any equipment, tools or machinery used by the worker which are necessary to carry out the service and A owns or leases the premises where the work is carried out[19];

(10)   the use of a worker to harvest crops by a person who has transferred title to the land on which the crops are grown, but has retained title to the crops[20];

(11)   the supply of a licensed person[21] for the purpose of killing an animal[22];

(12)   the supply of a worker by an educational establishment to undertake agricultural work solely in furtherance of education or training provided to the worker by that establishment leading to an agricultural qualification[23];

(13)   the supply of an apprentice by an Apprentice Training Agency recognised the Skills Funding Agency or the Welsh Government or registered with the National Apprenticeship Service or Welsh Government as an Apprentice Training Agency in development[24];

(14)   the supply by a person (A) to a farmer of a worker to undertake agricultural work in which that worker is specialised[25];

(15)   the use of a worker for agricultural work by a person (A) to provide a service where the worker is a member of A's family[26];

(16)   the use of a worker by a land agent where the land agent is a member of the Royal Institute of Chartered Surveyors, the land agent is contracted to manage the land on which the workers will be employed and the use of that worker is incidental to the fulfillment of the land agent's contract to manage that land[27];

(17)   the use of a worker by a farmer to plant, raise, care for or harvest crops of animals with are the property of a third party, managed by the farmer under the terms of a written agreement and grown or kept on land owned or occupied by the farmer[28];

(18)   the supply of volunteers to undertake conservation work[29];

(19)   the use of a worker by A for forestry work where A uses the worker to do work in connection with services provided by A to another person[30];

(20)   the use of a worker by a member of the Royal College of Veterinary Surgeons, or an incorporated veterinary practice, to carry out work incidental to the supply of veterinary services[31];

(21)   the use by a worker by a supplier of vaccines to perform vaccinations[32];

(22)   the use of a worker to determine the sex of chickens and other poultry[33];

(23)   the supply of a worker by a person authorised to carry out functions of, or under contract to provide services to, the Secretary of State for Work and Pensions in connection with employment related support designed to assist the worker to obtain or remain in work or be able to do so[34];

(24)   the use of a worker either to dive with the aid of breathing apparatus to gather shellfish from the sea bed or to operate a net, dredge or other machinery used to gather shellfish from the sea bed, other than a hand net or hand-held rake, where the worker is using the net, dredge or other machinery on board a fishing vessel which is operating at sea[35];

(25)   the use by shellfish cultivators with an exclusive right to cultivate shellfish on an area of the seabed of a worker to gather shellfish from the shore for cultivation or to gather shellfish cultivated on the areas to which they have exclusive access[36];

(26)   the use of a worker by the owner or operator of a shellfish hatchery to gather shellfish[37].

1   Ie under the Gangmasters (Licensing) Act 2004 s 6(1) (see PARA 311).
2   As to the meaning of 'gangmaster' see PARA 309. As to the meaning of 'acting as a gangmaster' see PARA 310.
3   Gangmasters Licensing (Exclusion) Regulations 2013, SI 2013/2216, reg 2.
4   As to the meaning of 'worker' see PARA 309 note 1.
5   'Produce' means produce derived from agricultural work, shellfish, fish or products derived from shellfish or fish: Gangmasters Licensing (Exclusion) Regulations 2013, SI 2013/2216, Schedule para 3.
6   'Catering establishment' means:
    (1)   a restaurant, canteen, club, public house, school kitchen, prison kitchen, hospital kitchen or similar establishment (including a vehicle or a fixed or mobile stall) where food is cooked or made ready for consumption without further preparation and food is prepared for service to the consumer; and
    (2)   other premises used solely for the purpose of cooking or making food ready for consumption, without further preparation, after delivery to the consumer: Gangmasters Licensing (Exclusion) Regulations 2013, SI 2013/2216, Schedule para 3.

7   'Wholesale establishment' means a facility operated solely for the purpose of selling produce for the purposes of resale or to a catering establishment, and includes a cash and carry warehouse but excludes a food processing or packaging facility: Gangmasters Licensing (Exclusion) Regulations 2013, SI 2013/2216, Schedule para 3.

8   Gangmasters Licensing (Exclusion) Regulations 2013, SI 2013/2216, Schedule para 1. 'Distribution warehouse' means premises where produce is received prior to onward distribution to a wholesale or retail establishment and:
    (1)   there is no change in the ownership of the produce concerned between receipt and onward distribution;
    (2)   the wholesale or retail establishment to which delivery is made is excluded under Schedule para 1; and
    (3)   the premises are owned by the same company that owns the retail or wholesale establishment to which the produce is delivered: Schedule para 3.

9   Gangmasters Licensing (Exclusion) Regulations 2013, SI 2013/2216, Schedule para 2.

10   'Farmer' means a person who occupies land which the person uses for agriculture or is an employed by a person with title to land to manage the use of that land for agriculture: Gangmasters Licensing (Exclusion) Regulations 2013, SI 2013/2216, Schedule para 25.

11   For these purposes 'share farming agreement' means an agreement entered into between two or more persons to share the net receipts of either their separate business assets or services for carrying out specified farming operations, as divided between them and paid to the businesses in agreed proportions: Gangmasters Licensing (Exclusion) Regulations 2013, SI 2013/2216, Schedule para 4(2).

12   Gangmasters Licensing (Exclusion) Regulations 2013, SI 2013/2216, Schedule para 4(1).

13   Gangmasters Licensing (Exclusion) Regulations 2013, SI 2013/2216, Schedule para 5.

14   Gangmasters Licensing (Exclusion) Regulations 2013, SI 2013/2216, Schedule para 6.

15   'Seasonal Agricultural Workers Scheme' means a scheme operated by the Home Office, which allows farmers and growers in the United Kingdom to recruit overseas workers to undertake work that is both seasonal and agricultural: Gangmasters Licensing (Exclusion) Regulations 2013, SI 2013/2216, Schedule para 7(2).

16   Gangmasters Licensing (Exclusion) Regulations 2013, SI 2013/2216, Schedule para 7(1).

17   Gangmasters Licensing (Exclusion) Regulations 2013, SI 2013/2216, Schedule para 8.

18   Gangmasters Licensing (Exclusion) Regulations 2013, SI 2013/2216, Schedule para 9.

19   Gangmasters Licensing (Exclusion) Regulations 2013, SI 2013/2216, Schedule para 10.

20   Gangmasters Licensing (Exclusion) Regulations 2013, SI 2013/2216, Schedule para 11.

21   Ie where the worker has a certificate of competence or licence to kill animals under the Welfare of Animals at the Time of Killing (England) Regulations 2015, SI 2015/1782 or the Welfare of Animals at the Time of Killing (Wales) Regulations 2014, SI 2014/951 (see FOOD AND DRINK vol 51 (2013) PARA 946).

22   Gangmasters Licensing (Exclusion) Regulations 2013, SI 2013/2216, Schedule para 12 (substituted by SI 2015/1782).

23   Gangmasters Licensing (Exclusion) Regulations 2013, SI 2013/2216, Schedule para 13. The agricultural qualification mentioned in the text is, in relation to England, a qualification to which the Apprenticeships, Skills, Children and Learning Act 2009, Pt 7 applies or, in relation to Wales, is a qualification within the meaning of the Qualifications Wales Act 2015 s 56 (see EDUCATION vol 36 (2015) PARA 934): Gangmasters Licensing (Exclusion) Regulations 2013, SI 2013/2216, Schedule para 13 (amended by SI 2016/236).

24   Gangmasters Licensing (Exclusion) Regulations 2013, SI 2013/2216, Schedule para 14.

25   Gangmasters Licensing (Exclusion) Regulations 2013, SI 2013/2216, Schedule para 15. This exclusion applies where:
    (1)   the worker holds a specific qualification at or above National Vocational Qualification Level 2 or Scottish National Vocational Qualification Level 2, or an equivalent qualification, which is relevant and necessary to ensure the worker can effectively discharge the responsibilities that the worker will be required to undertake; and
    (2)   the farmer employs the worker following the worker's supply by A; and
    (3)   no more than four such workers are supplied to the farmer by A at any one time: Schedule para 15(a)–(c).

26   Gangmasters Licensing (Exclusion) Regulations 2013, SI 2013/2216, Schedule para 16(1). For these purposes the members of A's family are:
    (1)   A's spouse or civil partner;
    (2)   any other person (whether of a different sex or the same sex) with whom A lives as partner in an enduring family relationship;
    (3)   any child, step-child, parent, grandchild, grandparent, brother or sister of A; and

   (4)   any child or step-child of a person within head (3) (and who is not a child or stepchild of A) who lives with A and has not attained the age of 18: Schedule para 16(2).

27 Gangmasters Licensing (Exclusion) Regulations 2013, SI 2013/2216, Schedule para 17.
28 Gangmasters Licensing (Exclusion) Regulations 2013, SI 2013/2216, Schedule para 18.
29 Gangmasters Licensing (Exclusion) Regulations 2013, SI 2013/2216, Schedule para 19.
30 Gangmasters Licensing (Exclusion) Regulations 2013, SI 2013/2216, Schedule para 20.
31 Gangmasters Licensing (Exclusion) Regulations 2013, SI 2013/2216, Schedule para 21.
32 Gangmasters Licensing (Exclusion) Regulations 2013, SI 2013/2216, Schedule para 22.
33 Gangmasters Licensing (Exclusion) Regulations 2013, SI 2013/2216, Schedule para 23.
34 Gangmasters Licensing (Exclusion) Regulations 2013, SI 2013/2216, Schedule para 24.
35 Gangmasters Licensing (Exclusion) Regulations 2013, SI 2013/2216, Schedule para 26(1).
36 Gangmasters Licensing (Exclusion) Regulations 2013, SI 2013/2216, Schedule para 26(2).
37 Gangmasters Licensing (Exclusion) Regulations 2013, SI 2013/2216, Schedule para 26(3).

314. Appointment of enforcement officers.

The Secretary of State[1] may appoint officers ('enforcement officers'[2]) to enforce the prohibition of unlicensed activities by gangmasters[3] and to take action in circumstances in which it appears that the offence of entering into arrangements with gangmasters[4] has been, is being, or may be committed[5], and may also, either instead of or in addition to making such appointments, make arrangements with a relevant authority[6] for officers of that authority to be enforcement officers[7].

A person who either intentionally obstructs an enforcement officer who is acting in the exercise of his statutory functions[8], without reasonable cause fails to comply with any requirement made of him by such an officer who is so acting[9], or in giving any information which is required of him by an enforcement officer makes a statement which is false in a material particular[10], commits an offence[11].

An enforcement officer must, if so required, produce some duly authenticated document showing his authority to act[12].

1 As to the Secretary of State see PARA 390.
2 For the powers and duties of enforcement officers see PARA 315 et seq.
3 Gangmasters (Licensing) Act 2004 s 15(1)(a). As to the prohibition of unlicensed activities by gangmasters see s 6; and PARA 311. As to the meaning of 'gangmaster' see PARA 309.
4 Ie an offence under the Gangmasters (Licensing) Act 2004 s 13 (see PARA 312).
5 Gangmasters (Licensing) Act 2004 s 15(1)(b).
6 Ie the Gangmasters and Labour Abuse Authority, any Minister of the Crown or government department, the Welsh Ministers, the Scottish Ministers, and any body performing functions on behalf of the Crown: Gangmasters (Licensing) Act 2004 s 15(3)(a)–(e). As to the Gangmasters and Labour Abuse Authority see PARA 320.
7 Gangmasters (Licensing) Act 2004 s 15(2). As from a day to be appointed s 15 does not prevent the Secretary of State from making arrangements for ensuring that functions relating to the institution or conduct of proceedings in England and Wales for an offence under this Act are carried out by the Director of Public Prosecutions and, accordingly, the terms of appointments under s 15(1), or arrangements under a 15(2), may include provision, or be modified so as to include provision, for enforcement officers not to carry out such functions at any time when they are being carried out by the Director: s 15(7) (added by the Deregulation Act 2015 s 92). At the date at which this volume states the law no such day had been appointed.
8 Gangmasters (Licensing) Act 2004 s 18(1)(a). An enforcement officer's statutory functions are his functions under the Gangmasters (Licensing) Act 2004 or functions conferred by virtue of the Police and Criminal Evidence Act 1984 s 114B (application of that Act to Authority officers): see PARAS 315–317.
9 Gangmasters (Licensing) Act 2004 s 18(1)(b) (amended by the Immigration Act 2016 s 12(2)).
10 Gangmasters (Licensing) Act 2004 s 18(2).
11 Until a day is appointed for the coming into force of the Criminal Justice Act 2003 s 281(5) (alteration of penalties for summary offences) a person guilty of an offence under the Gangmasters (Licensing) Act 2004 s 18(1) or (2) (see the text and notes 8–10) is liable on summary conviction to imprisonment for a term not exceeding six months, or to a fine not exceeding the statutory maximum, or to both (s 18(3)(a)); as from that day the maximum term of imprisonment on summary conviction is 51 weeks (unless the offence was committed before that day, in which case

the maximum remains six months) (s 18(3)). At the date at which this volume states the law no such day had been appointed. As to the statutory maximum see PARA 58 note 1. As to the commission of offences by bodies corporate, unincorporated associations and partnerships see PARA 318.

12   Gangmasters (Licensing) Act 2004 s 15(5). If it appears to an enforcement officer that any person with whom he is dealing while acting for the purposes of the Gangmasters (Licensing) Act 2004 does not know that he is an officer so acting, the officer must identify himself as such to that person: s 15(6). Section 15(5), (6) do not apply to an enforcement officer who is acting for the purposes of the Gangmasters (Licensing) Act 2004 in relation to England and Wales if the officer is a labour abuse prevention officer within the meaning of the Police and Criminal Evidence Act 1984 s 114B (PACE powers for labour abuse prevention officers: see EMPLOYMENT vol 41A (2014) PARA 1532B): Gangmasters (Licensing) Act 2004 s 15(6A) (added by the Immigration Act 2016 Sch 3 para 20).

315.   Powers of arrest.

An enforcement officer[1] who has reasonable grounds for suspecting that either of the offences involving the unlicensed activities of gangmasters[2], or any relevant inchoate offence[3], has been committed, may arrest without warrant any person whom he has reasonable grounds for suspecting to be guilty of the offence[4]. He may also arrest without warrant anyone who is about, or anyone whom he has reasonable grounds for suspecting to be about, to commit such an offence or relevant inchoate offence[5]. These powers are in addition to existing statutory powers of arrest[6].

1   As to the appointment of enforcement officers and their authority and powers generally see PARA 314. The Gangmasters (Licensing) Act 2004 s 14(1), (2) does not apply to an enforcement officer who is acting for the purposes of the Gangmasters (Licensing) Act 2004 in relation to England and Wales if the officer is a labour abuse prevention officer within the meaning of the Police and Criminal Evidence Act 1984 s 114B (see EMPLOYMENT law vol 41A (2014) PARA 1532B): Gangmasters (Licensing) Act 2004 s 14(2A) (added by the Immigration Act 2016 Sch 3 para 19.
2   Ie any offence under the Gangmasters (Licensing) Act 2004 s 12(1) or (2) (see PARA 311). As to the meaning of 'gangmaster' see PARA 309. As to the meaning of 'acting as a gangmaster' see PARA 310.
3   Ie conspiring or attempting to commit an offence involving the unlicensed activities of gangmasters (Gangmasters (Licensing) Act 2004 s 14(1)(b), (c)) or inciting, aiding, abetting, counselling or procuring the commission of any such offence (s 14(1)(d)).
4   Gangmasters (Licensing) Act 2004 s 14(1)(a), (2)(a).
5   Gangmasters (Licensing) Act 2004 s 14(2)(b)(i), (ii).
6   Gangmasters (Licensing) Act 2004 s 14(1) (amended by the Serious Organised Crime and Police Act 2005 s 111, Sch 7 para 62(a)). The existing statutory powers of arrest are those set out in the Police and Criminal Evidence Act 1984 s 24A (see POLICE AND INVESTIGATORY POWERS vol 84A (2013) PARA 488): Gangmasters (Licensing) Act 2004 s 14(1) (as so amended).

316.   Powers of entry.

An enforcement officer[1] may be empowered to enter premises[2] for the purpose of ascertaining whether there has been any contravention of the statutory prohibitions on the unlicensed activities of gangmasters[3]. Entry may be effected only by warrant, which a justice of the peace may issue if he is satisfied by written information on oath that there are reasonable grounds for entering the premises for the stated purpose[4] and that the warrant is otherwise necessary in order to secure entry or to achieve that purpose[5]. Entry may, where necessary, be achieved by the use of reasonable force[6].

An enforcement officer entering any premises by virtue of these provisions may take with him such other persons and such other equipment as he considers necessary[7], may carry out on those premises such inspections and examinations as he considers necessary for the purpose of ascertaining whether there has been any contravention of the statutory prohibitions of unlicensed activities by gangmasters[8], and may take possession of any book, document, data, record (in whatever form it is held) or product which is on the premises and retain it for as long as he considers necessary for that purpose[9]. On leaving the premises the officer must, if the premises are unoccupied or the occupier is temporarily absent, leave the premises as effectively secured against trespassers as he found them[10].

1   As to the appointment of enforcement officers and their authority and powers generally see PARA 314. The Gangmasters (Licensing) Act 2004 s 17 does not apply to an enforcement officer who is acting for the purposes of the Gangmasters (Licensing) Act 2004 in relation to England and Wales if the officer is a labour abuse prevention officer within the meaning of the Police and Criminal Evidence Act 1984 s 114B (see EMPLOYMENT law vol 41A (2014) PARA 1532B): Gangmasters (Licensing) Act 2004 s 17(A1) (added by the Immigration Act 2016 Sch 3 para 22).
2   Ie any premises which the officer has reasonable cause to believe to be premises at which a person acting as a gangmaster, or a person supplied with workers or services by a person acting as a gangmaster, carries on business, and premises which such a person uses in connection with his business: Gangmasters (Licensing) Act 2004 s 16(6). Such premises are referred to as 'relevant premises': s 16(6). 'Premises' includes any place and, in particular, includes any vehicle, vessel, aircraft or hovercraft, and any tent or movable structure: s 16(6). As to the meaning of 'gangmaster' see PARA 309. As to the meaning of 'acting as a gangmaster' see PARA 310. As to the meaning of 'worker' see PARA 309 note 1. Powers of entry are also conferred pursuant to enforcement officers' power to request and obtain information: see PARA 317.
3   Gangmasters (Licensing) Act 2004 s 17(1). For the statutory prohibitions of unlicensed activities by gangmasters see s 6; and PARA 311.
4   Gangmasters (Licensing) Act 2004 s 17(1).
5   Thus before issuing a warrant the justice must be satisfied either:
    (1)   that admission to the premises has been refused, or that a refusal is expected, and (in either case) that notice of the intention to apply for a warrant has been given to the occupier (Gangmasters (Licensing) Act 2004 s 17(1)(a));
    (2)   that an application for admission, or the giving of such a notice, would defeat the object of the entry (s 17(1)(b));
    (3)   that the case is one of extreme urgency (s 17(1)(c)); or
    (4)   that the premises are unoccupied or the occupier is temporarily absent (s 17(1)(d)).
6   Gangmasters (Licensing) Act 2004 s 17(1).
7   Gangmasters (Licensing) Act 2004 s 17(2)(a).
8   Gangmasters (Licensing) Act 2004 s 17(2)(b).
9   Gangmasters (Licensing) Act 2004 s 17(2)(c). Where by virtue of s 17(2)(c) an enforcement officer takes possession of any item, he must leave on the premises from which the item was removed a statement giving particulars of what he has taken and stating that he has taken possession of it: s 17(4).
10 Gangmasters (Licensing) Act 2004 s 17(3).

317.   Power to request, obtain and supply information.

An enforcement officer[1] may, for the performance of his duties:

(1)   require the production by a relevant person[2] of any records required to be kept[3], to inspect and examine those records, to remove those records from the premises[4] where they are kept and to copy any material part of them[5];

(2)   require a relevant person to furnish to him (either alone or in the presence of any other person, as the officer thinks fit) an explanation of any such records[6]; and

(3)   require a relevant person to furnish to him (either alone or in the presence of any other person, as the officer thinks fit) any additional information known to the relevant person which might reasonably be needed in order to establish whether any provision of the Gangmasters (Licensing) Act 2004, or any condition of any licence granted under it[7], is being complied with[8].

Officers are also empowered at all reasonable times to enter any relevant premises[9] in order to exercise any power conferred on the officer by virtue of these provisions[10].

These powers are also enjoyed by compliance officers in pursuance of their statutory functions, and references to an 'officer' should be read accordingly[11].

Notwithstanding any restriction on the disclosure of information imposed by any enactment[12] or rule of law[13], and without limiting the circumstances in which information may otherwise be used or supplied[14], information held by any person for the purposes of, or for any purpose connected with, the exercise of functions under the Gangmasters (Licensing) Act 2004 and information held by any officer by virtue of his investigative functions in connection with labour market enforcement undertakings and orders[15]:

(a)　　may be supplied to any person for use for the purpose of, or for any purpose connected with, the exercise of functions under the Gangmasters (Licensing) Act 2004[16];

(b)　　may be supplied to any person by whom, or by whose officers, labour market enforcement functions are exercisable for the purposes of, or for any purpose connected with, the exercise of such functions[17]; and

(c)　　may be supplied to any person having functions in relation to:

(i)　　the enforcement of any other enactment applying to the operations of a person acting as a gangmaster;

(ii)　　the enforcement of any other enactment in connection with accommodation, meals or facilities provided to workers, or the conditions in which they work; or

(iii)　　offences committed by workers in connection with or by reason of their doing work to which the Gangmasters (Licensing) Act 2004 applies,

for use for the purposes of, or for any purpose connected with, those functions[18].

Similarly, information which is held by any person for the purposes of, or for any purposes connected with, such functions as are mentioned in head (2) or (3) above may be supplied to any person having functions under the Gangmasters (Licensing) Act 2004 for the purposes of, or for any purpose connected with, the exercise of those functions[19].

1　　As to the appointment of enforcement officers and their authority and powers generally see PARA 314. The Gangmasters (Licensing) Act 2004 s 16 does not apply to an enforcement officer who is acting for the purposes of the Gangmasters (Licensing) Act 2004 in relation to England and Wales if the officer is a labour abuse prevention officer within the meaning of the Police and Criminal Evidence Act 1984 s 114B (see EMPLOYMENT law vol 41A (2014) PARA 1532B): Gangmasters (Licensing) Act 2004 s 16(A1) (added by the Immigration Act 2016 Sch 3 para 21).

2　　For these purposes 'relevant person' means any person whom an officer acting for the purposes of the Gangmasters (Licensing) Act 2004 has reasonable cause to believe to be either a person acting as a gangmaster, a person supplied with workers or services by a person acting as a gangmaster, or an employee or agent of any such person: s 16(5). As to the meaning of 'gangmaster' see PARA 309. As to the meaning of 'acting as a gangmaster' see PARA 310. As to the meaning of 'worker' see PARA 309 note 1.

3　　Ie required to be kept by virtue of the Gangmasters (Licensing) Act 2004: s 16(1)(a).

4　　As to the meaning of 'premises' see PARA 316 note 2.

5　　Gangmasters (Licensing) Act 2004 s 16(1)(a). This power includes the power, on reasonable written notice, to require a relevant person to produce any such records to an officer at such time and place as may be specified in the notice (s 16(2)(a)) and, in relation to records which are kept by means of a computer, the power to require the records to be produced in a form in which they are legible and can be taken away (s 16(3)). A person authorised by virtue of s 16(1)(a) to inspect any records is entitled to have access to, and to check the operation of, any computer and any associated apparatus or material which is or has been in use in connection with the records in question: s 16(4).

6   Gangmasters (Licensing) Act 2004 s 16(1)(b). This power includes the power, on reasonable written notice, to require a relevant person to attend before an officer at such time and place as may be specified in the notice to furnish any such explanation or additional information as is mentioned in s 16(1)(b): s 16(2)(b).

7   As to the granting of licences see PARA 320 et seq.

8   Gangmasters (Licensing) Act 2004 s 16(1)(c). This power includes the power, on reasonable written notice, to require a relevant person to attend before an officer at such time and place as may be specified in the notice to furnish any such explanation or additional information as is mentioned in s 16(1)(c): s 16(2)(b).

9   As to the meaning of 'relevant premises' see PARA 316 note 2.

10 Gangmasters (Licensing) Act 2004 s 16(1)(d).

11 As to the appointment of compliance officers and their functions, authority and powers see PARA 354.

12 'Enactment' means an Act of Parliament, an Act of the Scottish Parliament or any Northern Ireland legislation or any instrument made under or having effect by virtue of an Act of Parliament, an Act of the Scottish Parliament or any Northern Ireland legislation: Gangmasters (Licensing) Act 2004 s 19(5).

13 Gangmasters (Licensing) Act 2004 s 19(4)(a).

14 Gangmasters (Licensing) Act 2004 s 19(4)(b).

15 Gangmasters (Licensing) Act 2004 s 19(1A) (s 19(1A), (1B) added by the Immigration Act 2016 Sch 3 para 23(3)). Information mentioned in the text is information held by virtue of the Immigration Act 2016 s 26(3). As to the meaning of 'labour market enforcement functions' see the Immigration Act 2016 s 3; and IMMIGRATION AND ASYLUM (definition applied by the Gangmasters (Licensing) Act 2004 s 19(1B) (as so added)).

16 Gangmasters (Licensing) Act 2004 s 19(1)(a) (s 19(1) amended s 19(1)(a) substituted and s 19(1)(aa) added by the Immigration Act 2016 Sch 3 para 23(2)).

17 Gangmasters (Licensing) Act 2004 s 19(1)(aa) (as added: see note 16).

18 Gangmasters (Licensing) Act 2004 s 19(1)(b).

19 Gangmasters (Licensing) Act 2004 s 19(2) (amended by the Immigration Act 2016 Sch 3 para 23(4)(a)). Information supplied under this provision by or on behalf of the Commissioners of Inland Revenue or the Commissioners of Customs and Excise must not be supplied by the recipient to any other person without the consent of the Commissioners concerned: Gangmasters (Licensing) Act 2004 s 19(3).

318. Commission of offences by bodies corporate, unincorporated associations and partnerships.

If an offence[1] committed by a body corporate, an unincorporated association or a partnership[2] is shown either to have been committed with the consent or connivance of an officer[3] of the body or association or a partner[4] of the partnership, or to be attributable to any neglect on the part of the officer or partner, that officer or partner, as well as the body, association or partnership, is guilty of the offence and liable to be proceeded against and punished accordingly[5].

Proceedings for an offence alleged to have been committed by an unincorporated association or partnership may be brought against the association or partnership in the name of the association or partnership[6], and for the purposes of such proceedings, rules of court relating to the service of documents have effect as if the association or partnership were a body corporate[7] and the statutory provisions dealing with the procedure on charges of offences against corporations[8] apply as they apply in relation to a body corporate[9].

A fine imposed on an unincorporated association or a partnership on its conviction of an offence must be paid out of the funds of the association or partnership[10].

1   Ie under the Gangmasters (Licensing) Act 2004.

2   These provisions apply in the case of a partnership which is regarded as a legal person under the law of the country or territory under which it is formed. For the applicable requirements in the case of a partnership which is not regarded as a legal person under the law of the country or territory under which it is formed see note 5.

3   Ie, in relation to a body corporate, any director, manager, secretary or other similar officer of the body corporate (Gangmasters (Licensing) Act 2004 s 20(4)(a)) or, in relation to an unincorporated association, any officer of the association or any member of its governing body (s 21(7)(a)) or, in either case, any person purporting to act in any such capacity (ss 20(4)(b), 21(7)(b)).

4   For these purposes 'partner' includes a person purporting to act as a partner: Gangmasters (Licensing) Act 2004 s 22(9).

5   Gangmasters (Licensing) Act 2004 ss 20(3), 21(6), 22(8). If the affairs of a body corporate are managed by its members, this provision applies in relation to the acts and defaults of a member in connection with his functions of management as if he were a director of the body: s 20(5). In connection with a partnership which is not regarded as a legal person under the law of the country or territory under which it is formed, it is alternatively provided that if an offence committed by a partner is shown either to have been committed with the consent or connivance of another partner, or to be attributable to any neglect on the part of another partner, that other partner, as well as the first-mentioned partner, is guilty of the offence and liable to be proceeded against and punished accordingly: s 22(3).

6   Gangmasters (Licensing) Act 2004 ss 21(3), 22(5).

7   Gangmasters (Licensing) Act 2004 ss 21(4)(a), 22(6)(a).

8   Ie the Criminal Justice Act 1925 s 33 and the Magistrates' Courts Act 1980 Sch 3: see MAGISTRATES vol 71 (2013) PARA 513.

9   Gangmasters (Licensing) Act 2004 ss 21(4)(b), 22(6)(b).

10   Gangmasters (Licensing) Act 2004 ss 21(5), 22(7).

319.   Proceeds of crime.

Offences involving the unlicensed activities of gangmasters[1] are 'lifestyle offences' for the purposes of the legislation providing for the confiscation of the proceeds of crime[2], and the proceeds of such an offence are accordingly liable to be made the subject of a confiscation order on the conviction of any person for the offence[3].

1   Ie an offence under the Gangmasters (Licensing) Act 2004 s 12(1) or (2) (see PARA 311). As to the meaning of 'gangmaster' see PARA 309. As to the meaning of 'acting as a gangmaster' see PARA 310.

2   See the Proceeds of Crime Act 2002 Sch 2 para 9A (Sch 2 para 9A added by the Gangmasters (Licensing) Act 2004 s 14(4)). See also SENTENCING vol 92 (2015) PARA 230. The legislation providing for the confiscation of the proceeds of crime is the Proceeds of Crime Act 2002 Pt 2 (ss 6–91) (see SENTENCING vol 92 (2015) PARA 189 et seq).

3   See the Proceeds of Crime Act 2002 Pt II (ss 6–91); and SENTENCING vol 92 (2015) PARA 189 et seq.

(iii)   Licensing of Operations

A. LICENSING OF ACTIVITIES OF GANGMASTERS

320.   The Gangmasters and Labour Abuse Authority.

The body known as the Gangmasters Licensing Authority is to continue to exist and is to be known as the Gangmasters and Labour Abuse Authority ('the Authority')[1]. It is a body corporate[2] possessing a number of functions concerning the licensing and regulation of gangmasters[3]. The Authority is required to submit an annual report and accounts[4].

1   Gangmasters (Licensing) Act 2004 s 1(1) (substituted by the Immigration Act 2016 Sch 3 para 15(b)); Immigration Act 2016 s 10(1).

2   Gangmasters (Licensing Authority) Regulations 2015, SI 2015/805, reg 2(1). These regulations are made pursuant to the Gangmasters (Licensing) Act 2004 s 1(5), which empowers the Secretary

of State by regulations to make provision for the status and constitution of the Authority, the appointment of its members, the payment of remuneration and allowances to its members, and such other matters in connection with its establishment and operation as he thinks fit. As to the Secretary of State see PARA 390. As to the constitution of the Gangmasters and Labour Abuse Authority see the Gangmasters (Licensing Authority) Regulations 2015, SI 2015/805. In any enactment passed before 12 July 2016 (ie the day on which the Immigration Act 2016 s 10) came into force, and in any instrument or other document made before that day, references to the Gangmasters Licensing Authority are to be read, in relation to any time on or after that day, as references to the Gangmasters and Labour Abuse Authority: see s 10(2).

3   As to the functions of the Authority and the licensing of gangmasters see PARA 321 et seq.
4   See the Gangmasters (Licensing) Act 2004 s 23; and the Gangmasters (Licensing Authority) Regulations 2015, SI 2015/805, regs 9, 10. The Secretary of State may make payments to the Authority of such amounts, at such times and on such conditions (if any) as he considers appropriate (Gangmasters (Licensing) Act 2004 s 24(1)) and the Authority must (unless the Secretary of State directs otherwise) pay to the Secretary of State all sums received by it in the course of, or in connection with, the carrying out of its functions (s 24(2)).

321. Functions of the Authority.

The functions of the Gangmasters and Labour Abuse Authority[1] are:

(1)   to carry out the functions relating to the licensing of gangmasters[2] that are conferred on it by the Gangmasters (Licensing) Act 2004[3];

(2)   to ensure the carrying out of such inspections as it considers necessary of persons holding licences under that Act[4];

(3)   to keep under review generally the activities of persons acting as gangmasters[5];

(4)   to supply information held by it to specified persons in accordance with the statutory provisions[6];

(5)   to keep under review the operation of the Act[7]; and

(6)   to perform such other functions as may be prescribed in regulations made by the Secretary of State[8].

The Authority may do anything that it considers is calculated to facilitate, or is incidental or conducive to, the carrying out of any of its functions[9]; in carrying out its functions it must, however, comply with any general or specific directions given to it in writing by the Secretary of State[10] and have regard to certain principles regarding the exploitation of workers[11].

The Secretary of State may be regulations confer other functions on the Gangmasters and Labour Abuse Authority in relation to the labour market[12].

1   As to the establishment, constitution and status of the Authority see PARA 320. When carrying out functions during a year to which a labour market enforcement strategy approved under the Immigration Act 2016 s 2 relates, the Authority and its officers must carry out those functions in accordance with the strategy: Gangmasters (Licensing) Act 2004 s 1(3A) (added by the Immigration Act 2016 Sch 3 para 15(c)).
2   As to the meaning of 'gangmaster' see PARA 309.
3   Gangmasters (Licensing) Act 2004 s 1(1), (2)(a). As to the functions relating to licensing see PARA 324 et seq.
4   Gangmasters (Licensing) Act 2004 s 1(2)(b).
5   Gangmasters (Licensing) Act 2004 s 1(2)(c). As to the meaning of 'acting as a gangmaster' see PARA 310.
6   Gangmasters (Licensing) Act 2004 s 1(2)(d).
7   Gangmasters (Licensing) Act 2004 s 1(2)(e).
8   Gangmasters (Licensing) Act 2004 s 1(2)(f). As to the Secretary of State see PARA 390. At the date at which this volume states the law no such regulations had been made. The Authority may also be required by the Secretary of State to appoint enforcement officers (see s 15(3)(a); and PARA 314), and the Secretary of State may delegate specified ministerial functions to the Authority (see the Natural Environment and Rural Communities Act 2006 Pt 8 Ch 1 (ss 78–86); and OPEN SPACES AND COUNTRYSIDE vol 78 (2010) PARA 520). See in particular Sch 7 para 13.
9   Gangmasters (Licensing) Act 2004 s 1(3).

10 Gangmasters (Licensing) Act 2004 s 2(1). Before giving any such directions the Secretary of State must consult the Authority and the Director of Labour Market Enforcement: s 2(2) (amended by the Immigration Act 2016 Sch 3 para 16). The Authority must provide the Secretary of State with such information about its activities as he may request: Gangmasters (Licensing) Act 2004 s 2(3).

11 For the purposes of the exercise of its functions under the Gangmasters (Licensing) Act 2004 ss 1, 7, 8, 9 and rules made under s 8 (see the text and notes 1–9; and PARA 324 et seq), in determining the criteria for assessing the fitness of an applicant for a licence or of a specified person, and the conditions of a licence and any modification of those conditions, the Authority must have regard to the principle that a person should be authorised to act as a gangmaster only if and in so far as his conduct, and the conduct of the specified person, complies with requirements as to the avoidance of any exploitation of workers as respects their recruitment, use or supply and with any obligations imposed by or under any enactment in so far as they relate to, or affect the conduct of, the licence holder or specified person as persons authorised to undertake certain activities: Gangmasters (Licensing Authority) Regulations 2015, SI 2015/805, reg 8(1), (2). For these purposes 'specified person' means any person proposed to be named or otherwise specified in the licence by virtue of the Gangmasters (Licensing) Act 2004 s 7(3)(b) (see PARA 324): Gangmasters (Licensing Authority) Regulations 2015, SI 2015/805, reg 8(5). As to conditions attaching to licences see PARA 328 et seq.

12 Immigration Act 2016 s 11(2).

322. Information gateways.

A specified person[1] may disclose information to the Gangmasters and Labour Abuse Authority (the 'Authority')[2] or a relevant officer[3] if the disclosure is made for the purposes of the exercise of any function of the Authority or the officer under the Modern Slavery Act 2015[4].

Information obtained by the Authority or a relevant officer in connection with the exercise of any function of the Authority or the officer under the Modern Slavery Act 2015 may be used by the Authority or the officer in connection with the exercise of any other such function of the Authority or the officer[5].

The Authority or a relevant officer may disclose to a specified person information obtained in connection with the exercise of any function of the Authority or the officer under the Modern Slavery Act 2015 if the disclosure is made for the purposes of the exercise of any function of the specified person[6].

A disclosure of information which is authorised by this provision does not breach:

(1)   an obligation of confidence owed by the person making the disclosure; or

(2)   any other restriction on the disclosure of information (however imposed)[7].

1   The following are specified persons for the purposes of the Modern Slavery Act 2015 s 54A:
    (1)   the Secretary of State;
    (2)   a person by whom, or by whose officers, labour market enforcement functions (within the meaning given by the Immigration Act 2016 s 3 (see EMPLOYMENT vol 41A (2014) PARA 1532A)) are exercisable;
    (3)   a chief officer of police for a police area in England and Wales;
    (4)   the chief constable of the British Transport Police Force;
    (5)   an immigration officer;
    (6)   a county council in England or Wales;
    (7)   a county borough council in Wales; a district council in England;
    (8)   a London borough council; the Greater London Authority;
    (9)   the Common Council of the City of London;
    (10)   the Council of the Isles of Scilly;
    (11)   a National Health Service trust established under the National Health Service Act 2006 s 25 or the National Health Service (Wales) Act 2006 s 18;
    (12)   an NHS foundation trust within the meaning given by the National Health Service Act 2006 s 30 (see HEALTH SERVICES vol 54 (2017) PARA 244);

(13)   a Local Health Board established under the National Health Service (Wales) Act 2006 s 11 (see HEALTH SERVICES vol 54 (2017) PARA 98); and
(14)   the Independent Anti-slavery Commissioner: Modern Slavery Act 2015 Sch 4A (added by the Immigration Act 2016 Sch 3 para 35).
The Secretary of State may by regulations amend the Modern Slavery Act 2015 Sch 4A: s 54A(8) (added by the Immigration Act 2016 Sch 3 para 30).

2   As to the establishment, constitution and status of the Authority see PARA 320.
3   For these purposes, 'relevant officer' means an officer of the Authority who is acting for the purposes of the Modern Slavery Act 2015 Pt 1 or 2 (ss 1–34) (see ss 11A, 30A): s 54A(9) (as added: see note 1).
4   Modern Slavery Act 2015 s 54A(1), (7) (as added: see note 1).
5   Modern Slavery Act 2015 s 54A(2) (as added: see note 1).
6   Modern Slavery Act 2015 s 54A(3) (as added: see note 1).
7   Modern Slavery Act 2015 s 54A(4) (as added: see note 1). But nothing in this provision authorises the making of a disclosure which contravenes the Data Protection Act 1998, or is prohibited by the Regulation of Investigatory Powers Act 2000 Pt 1 (ss 1–25) (see POLICE AND INVESTIGATORY POWERS vol 84A (2013) PARA 657 et seq): Modern Slavery Act 2015 s 54A(5) (as so added). This provision does not limit the circumstances in which information may be disclosed apart from this provision: s 54A(6) (as so added).

323.   Requests for assistance.

The Gangmasters and Labour Abuse Authority[1] may request any of the following to provide assistance to the Authority or any of its officers:
(1)   a chief officer of police for a police area in England and Wales;
(2)   the Director General of the National Crime Agency;
(3)   a person appointed as an immigration officer[2];
(4)   any other person prescribed or of a prescribed[3] description[4].
The Authority may make such a request only if it considers that the assistance would facilitate the exercise of any function by the Authority or any of its officers[5].

Any of the following persons may request the Authority to provide assistance to the person:
(a)   a chief officer of police for a police area in England and Wales;
(b)   a person appointed as an immigration officer[6];
(c)   any other person prescribed or of a prescribed description[7].
A person may make such a request only if the person considers that the assistance would facilitate the exercise by the person of any function[8].

A request under the above provisions must set out what assistance is being requested and explain how the assistance would facilitate the exercise of the function[9].

1   As to the establishment, constitution and status of the Authority see PARA 320.
2   Ie appointed under the Immigration Act 1971 Sch 2 para 1 (see IMMIGRATION AND ASYLUM).
3   Ie prescribed by regulations made by the Secretary of State: Gangmasters (Licensing) Act 2004 s 25(1). Regulations under this section must not make provision which would be within the legislative competence of the Scottish Parliament if contained in an Act of that Parliament, within the legislative competence of the National Assembly for Wales if contained in an Act of that Assembly, or within the legislative competence of the Northern Ireland Assembly if contained in an Act of that Assembly made without the consent of the Secretary of State: s s 22A(7) (s 22A added by the Immigration Act 2016 s 13(2)).
4   Gangmasters (Licensing) Act 2004 s 22A(1) (as added: see note 3). A person who receives a request under s 22A must respond to it in writing within a reasonable period: s 22A(7) (as so added).
5   Gangmasters (Licensing) Act 2004 s 22A(2) (as added: see note 3).
6   See note 2.
7   Gangmasters (Licensing) Act 2004 s 22A(3) (as added: see note 3).
8   Gangmasters (Licensing) Act 2004 s 22A(4) (as added: see note 3).
9   Gangmasters (Licensing) Act 2004 s 22A(5) (as added: see note 3).

324. Licensing of gangmasters.

The Gangmasters and Labour Abuse Authority [1] is empowered to grant gangmaster licences at its discretion[2] and subject to such conditions as it considers appropriate[3]. Licences may be granted to individuals, bodies corporate[4], unincorporated associations[5] and partnerships[6], and may authorise activities both by the holder of the licence[7] and by persons employed or engaged by the holder of the licence who are named or otherwise specified in the licence[8]. An application for a licence must be made on the form provided by the Authority and contain such information as the Authority requires for the purposes of determining the application[9]. The form must be signed by the individual responsible for the day-to-day management of a business (the 'principal authority') of the applicant[10] and be accompanied by the appropriate fee[11].

For the purposes of determining the application, the Authority may require the applicant:

(1)   to permit an inspection[12] of the applicant's business by the Authority or any person acting on its behalf; and

(2)   to supply or make available to the Authority or any person acting on its behalf any document or information[13].

1   As to the establishment, constitution and status of the Authority see PARA 320.
2   Gangmasters (Licensing) Act 2004 s 7(1).
3   Gangmasters (Licensing) Act 2004 s 7(5). As to conditions attaching to licences see PARA 328 et seq. In carrying out its licensing functions the Authority is required to have regard to certain principles regarding the exploitation of workers: see PARA 321 note 11.
4   Gangmasters (Licensing) Act 2004 s 20(1); and see note 7.
5   Gangmasters (Licensing) Act 2004 s 21(1); and see note 7.
6   Gangmasters (Licensing) Act 2004 s 22(1); and see note 7. Where a partnership is not regarded as a legal person under the law of the country or territory under which it is formed, the grant of a licence to the partnership in the firm name continues to have effect notwithstanding a change of partners, so long as at least one of the persons who was a partner before the change remains a partner after it (s 22(2)(a)), and has effect as the grant of a licence to those partners named in the licence (s 22(2)(b)).
7   Gangmasters (Licensing) Act 2004 s 7(3)(a). A licence granted to a body corporate or an unincorporated association authorises activities carried on by the body or association through such persons representing, or acting on behalf of, the body or association as are named or otherwise specified in the licence (ss 7(4), 20(2), 21(2)); and a licence granted to a partnership that is regarded as a legal person under the law of the country or territory under which it is formed authorises activities carried on by the partnership through those partners named in the licence (s 22(4)).
8   Gangmasters (Licensing) Act 2004 s 7(3)(b).
9   Gangmasters (Licensing Conditions) Rules 2009, SI 2009/307, r 3(1).
     The Gangmasters (Licensing Conditions) Rules 2009, SI 2009/307, are made pursuant to the Gangmasters (Licensing) Act 2004 s 8, which provides that the Gangmasters and Labour Abuse Authority may with the approval of the Secretary of State make such rules as it thinks fit in connection with the licensing of persons acting as gangmasters (s 8(1) (amended by the Immigration Act 2016 Sch 3 para 18(a))) and that such rules may, in particular:
     (1)   prescribe the form and contents of applications for licences and other documents to be filed in connection with applications (Gangmasters (Licensing) Act 2044 s 8(2)(a), (4));
     (2)   regulate the procedure to be followed in connection with applications and authorise the rectification of procedural irregularities (s 8(2)(b));
     (3)   prescribe time limits for doing anything required to be done in connection with an application and provide for the extension of any period so prescribed (s 8(2)(c));
     (4)   prescribe the requirements which must be met before a licence is granted (s 8(2)(d));
     (5)   provide for the manner in which the meeting of those requirements is to be verified (s 8(2)(e));
     (6)   allow for the grant of licences on a provisional basis before it is determined whether the requirements for the grant of a licence are met and for the withdrawal of such licences (if appropriate) if it appears that those requirements are not met (s 8(2)(f));
     (7)   prescribe the form of licences and the information to be contained in them (s 8(2)(g));

(8)   require the payment of such fees as may be prescribed or determined in accordance with the rules (s 8(2)(h));
(9)   provide that licences are to be granted subject to conditions requiring the licence holder to produce, in prescribed circumstances, evidence in a prescribed form of his being licensed and to comply with any prescribed requirements relating to the recruitment, use and supply of workers (s 8(i)).

Where the Authority has made provision in rules under s 8(2)(f) (see head (6)) for a licence to be granted on a provisional basis, it must assume in relation to any application for such a licence that the applicant or a specified person is a fit person to be granted the licence or specified in the licence as the case may be unless, on the basis of information held or obtained, it has reasonable grounds to believe otherwise: Gangmasters (Licensing Authority) Regulations 2015, SI 2015/805, reg 8(4). As to the Secretary of State see PARA 390.

As to the meaning of 'gangmaster' see PARA 309. As to the meaning of 'acting as a gangmaster' see PARA 310. As to the meaning of 'worker' see PARA 309 note 1.

10   Gangmasters (Licensing Conditions) Rules 2009, SI 2009/307, r 3(2). 'Business' includes a sole trader, a company, an unincorporated association and a partnership; r 2(1).
12   For the purposes of head (1) in the text 'inspection' includes conducting interviews with such persons as the Authority considers appropriate: Gangmasters (Licensing Conditions) Rules 2009, SI 2009/307, r 3(4).
13   Gangmasters (Licensing Conditions) Rules 2009, SI 2009/307, r 3(3). All fees are payable to the Authority: r 6(1). As to the fee payable see r 6, Table.

325.   Expiration and renewal of licences.

A gangmaster's licence expires if the licence holder's[1] registered number (if it is a company), Unique Tax Reference or Value Added Tax number change[2]. A licence may be renewed before it expires[3].

1   'Licence holder' means the business granted a licence: Gangmasters (Licensing Conditions) Rules 2009, SI 2009/307, r 2(1). As to the meaning of 'business' see PARA 324 note 10.
2   Gangmasters (Licensing Conditions) Rules 2009, SI 2009/307, r 5.
3   Gangmasters (Licensing Conditions) Rules 2009, SI 2009/307, r 3(5). As to the power of the Authority to revoke the licence see PARA 326.

326.   Modification, revocation and transfer of licences.

The Gangmasters and Labour Abuse Authority [1] may by notice in writing to the licensee modify[2] or revoke any licence granted to him (including any of the conditions of that licence)[3] either with the consent of the licensee[4] or where it appears to the Authority that a condition of the licence or any statutory requirement[5] has not been complied with[6]. A licence may also be transferred with the written consent of the Authority and in such other cases as may be determined by the Authority[7].

There is a right of appeal against a decision of the Authority to refuse consent to the transfer of a licence or to modify or revoke a licence[8].

1   As to the establishment, constitution and status of the Authority see PARA 320.
2   The modifications that may be made include one suspending the effect of the licence for such period as the Authority may determine: Gangmasters (Licensing) Act 2004 s 9(2). In carrying out its licensing functions the Authority is required to have regard to certain principles regarding the exploitation of workers: see PARA 321 note 11.
3   As to conditions attaching to licences see PARA 328 et seq.
4   Gangmasters (Licensing) Act 2004 s 9(1)(a).
5   Ie any requirement of the Gangmasters (Licensing) Act 2004.
6   Gangmasters (Licensing) Act 2004 s 9(1)(b).
7   Gangmasters (Licensing) Act 2004 s 9(3).
8   See the Gangmasters (Appeals) Regulations 2006, SI 2006/662, reg 5(1)(c), (d); and PARAS 346–352.

327. Register of licensed persons.

The Gangmasters and Labour Abuse Authority [1] is required to establish and maintain a register of persons licensed under the legislation relating to the licensing of gangmasters[2]. The register must contain such particulars as the Authority may determine of every person who for the time being holds a licence or whose activities are authorised by a licence (whether or not they are named in the licence)[3]. The Authority must ensure that appropriate arrangements are in force for allowing members of the public to inspect the contents of the registe[4].

1   As to the establishment, constitution and status of the Authority see PARA 320.
2   Gangmasters (Licensing) Act 2004 s 11(1).
3   Gangmasters (Licensing) Act 2004 s 11(2).
4   Gangmasters (Licensing) Act 2004 s 11(3).

B. CONDITIONS OF OPERATIONS UNDER LICENCES

328. Gangmaster licence conditions.

The Gangmasters and Labour Abuse Authority (the 'Authority')[1] may grant a gangmaster's licence[2] if it thinks fit[3], and a licence must describe the activities authorised by it[4]. A licence is granted subject to certain conditions[5] and the Authority can also impose such additional conditions as it thinks fit[6].

There is a right of appeal against any decision of the Authority as to the conditions to which the grant of a licence is subject[7].

Contravention of or failure to comply with any of these provisions on the part of a licence holder[8] is actionable if it causes damage[9].

1   As to the establishment, constitution and status of the Authority see PARA 320. As to the licensing of gangmasters by the Authority see PARA 324. As to the enforcement of compliance with licensing requirements see PARA 354. As to the meaning of 'gangmaster' see PARA 309.
2   As to applications for a gangmaster's licence see PARA 324.
3   Gangmasters (Licensing) Act 2004 s 7(1).
4   Gangmasters (Licensing) Act 2004 s 7(2).
5   See the Gangmasters (Licensing Conditions) Rules 2009, SI 2009/307, r 4(1), Schedule; and PARAS 329–345. As to the appointment of enforcement officers and their authority and powers generally see PARA 314.
6   See the Gangmasters (Licensing Conditions) Rules 2009, SI 2009/307, r 4.
7   See PARAS 346–352.
8   As to the meaning of 'licence holder' see PARA 325 note 1.
9   See PARA 353. As to the provision of information see PARA 355. As to the enforcement of compliance with licensing requirements see PARA 354.

329. Obligation to act in a fit and proper manner.

The licence holder[1], the principal authority[2] and any person named or otherwise specified in the licence must at all times act in a fit and proper manner[3].

1   As to the meaning of 'licence holder' see PARA 325 note 1. As to licensing conditions generally see PARA 328.
2   As to the meaning of 'principal authority' see PARA 324.
3   Gangmasters (Licensing Conditions) Rules 2009, SI 2009/307, Schedule, para 4(1). If the licence holder or any person named or otherwise specified in the licence is a body corporate, an unincorporated association or partnership:
    (1)   every director, manager, secretary or other similar officer of the body corporate;
    (2)   every officer of the association or any member of its governing body; and
    (3)   every partner,
including any person purporting to act in any such capacity, must at all times act in a fit and proper manner: Schedule para 4(2).

330. Obligation to provide information.

The licence holder[1] must notify the Gangmasters and Labour Abuse Authority (the 'Authority')[2] within 20 working days[3] of commencing an activity authorised by the licence[4]. The licence holder must notify the Authority within 20 working days if there are significant changes to details submitted with his application, including any changes to the persons named or the positions otherwise specified in the licence[5]. The licence holder must notify the Authority as soon as reasonably practicable if he knows or suspects that the holder's licence has been used by someone not authorised to act on behalf of that holder[6]. The licence holder must, on request, provide details of the holder's licence to any constable, enforcement officer or compliance officer[7].

1   As to the meaning of 'licence holder' see PARA 325 note 1. As to licensing conditions generally see PARA 328.
2   As to the establishment, constitution and status of the Authority see PARA 320. As to the licensing of gangmasters by the Authority see PARA 324. As to the enforcement of compliance with licensing requirements see PARA 354. As to the meaning of 'gangmaster' see PARA 309.
3   As to the giving of notifications see PARA 355. 'Working day' means a day other than a Saturday or a Sunday, Christmas Day or Good Friday, or a date which is a bank holiday under or by virtue of the Banking and Financial Dealings Act 1971 (see TIME vol 97 (2015) PARA 321): Gangmasters (Licensing Conditions) Rules 2009, SI 2009/307, r 2(1).
4   Gangmasters (Licensing Conditions) Rules 2009, SI 2009/307, Schedule, para 5(1).
5   Gangmasters (Licensing Conditions) Rules 2009, SI 2009/307, Schedule, para 5(2).
6   Gangmasters (Licensing Conditions) Rules 2009, SI 2009/307, Schedule, para 5(3).
7   Gangmasters (Licensing Conditions) Rules 2009, SI 2009/307, Schedule, para 5(4).

331. Inspection of the business.

The licence holder[1] must permit the Gangmasters and Labour Abuse Authority (the 'Authority')[2] to inspect the business at any reasonable time[3].

1   As to the meaning of 'licence holder' see PARA 325 note 1. As to licensing conditions generally see PARA 328.
2   As to the establishment, constitution and status of the Authority see PARA 320. As to the licensing of gangmasters by the Authority see PARA 324. As to the enforcement of compliance with licensing requirements see PARA 354. As to the meaning of 'gangmaster' see PARA 309.
3   Gangmasters (Licensing Conditions) Rules 2009, SI 2009/307, Schedule, para 6.

332. Prohibition on charging fees.

A licence holder[1] may not charge a fee to a worker[2] for any work-finding service[3].

1   As to the meaning of 'licence holder' see PARA 325 note 1. As to licensing conditions generally see PARA 328.
2   As to the meaning of 'worker' see PARA 309 note 1.
3   Gangmasters (Licensing Conditions) Rules 2009, SI 2009/307, Schedule para 7. For these purposes 'work-finding services' means services (whether by the provision of information or otherwise) provided by a licence holder:
    (1)   to a person for the purpose of finding that person employment or seeking to find that person employment;
    (2)   to an employee of the licence holder for the purpose of finding or seeking to find another person, with a view to the employee acting for and under the control of that other person;
    (3)   to a person ('B') for the purpose of finding or seeking to find another person ('C'), with a view to B becoming employed by the licence holder and acting for and under the control of C: Schedule para 3.
As to the meaning of 'employee' see the Employment Rights Act 1996 s 230(1); and EMPLOYMENT vol 39 (2014) PARA 2 (definition applied by the Gangmasters (Licensing Conditions) Rules 2009, SI 2009/307, Schedule, para 2).

333. Prohibition on requiring workers to use additional services.

The licence holder[1] must not make the provision of work-finding services[2] conditional upon the worker[3]:

(1)   using other services or hiring or purchasing goods provided by the licence holder or any person with whom the licence holder is connected; or

(2)   giving or not withdrawing consent to the disclosure of information relating to the worker[4].

1   As to the meaning of 'licence holder' see PARA 325 note 1. As to licensing conditions generally see PARA 328. As to the enforcement of compliance with licensing requirements see PARA 354. Contravention of or failure to comply with these provisions on the part of a licence holder is actionable if it causes damage: see PARA 353.
2   As to the meaning of 'work finding services' see PARA 332 note 3.
3   As to the meaning of 'worker' see PARA 309 note 1.
4   Gangmasters (Licensing Conditions) Rules 2009, SI 2009/307, Schedule para 8(1). Where a worker uses services for which the Gangmasters (Licensing Conditions) Rules 2009, SI 2009/307 do not prohibit the charging of a fee, a licence holder providing or making provision for such services must ensure that the worker is able to cancel or withdraw from those services at any time without incurring any detriment or penalty, subject to the worker giving to the provider of those services notice of five working days or, for services relating to the provision of living accommodation, notice of ten working days: Schedule para 8(2).

334. Restriction on taking detrimental action against workers who work elsewhere.

The licence holder[1] must not subject or threaten to subject a worker[2] to any detriment[3] on the ground that the worker has:

(1)   terminated or given notice to terminate any contract between the worker and the licence holder; or

(2)   taken up or proposes to take up employment with any other person[4].

The licence holder must not require the worker to notify the licence holder, or any person with whom the holder is connected[5], of the identity of any future employer[6].

1   As to the meaning of 'licence holder' see PARA 325 note 1. As to licensing conditions generally see PARA 328. As to the enforcement of compliance with licensing requirements see PARA 354. Contravention of or failure to comply with these provisions on the part of a licence holder is actionable if it causes damage: see PARA 353.
2   As to the meaning of 'worker' see PARA 309 note 1.
3   For these purposes 'detriment' does not include:
    (1)   the loss of any benefits to which the worker might have become entitled had the worker not terminated the contract;
    (2)   the recovery of losses incurred by the licence holder as a result of the failure of the worker to perform agreed work; or
    (3)   a requirement in a contract with the licence holder for the worker to give a reasonable period of notice to terminate the contract: Gangmasters (Licensing Conditions) Rules 2009, SI 2009/307, Schedule para 9(3).
4   Gangmasters (Licensing Conditions) Rules 2009, SI 2009/307, Schedule para 9(1).
5   For these purposes a person ('A') is considered to be connected with:
    (1)   the members of A's family;
    (2)   any individual who employs A or A's employee;
    (3)   any person who is in partnership with A;
    (4)   any company of which A is an officer and any company connected with that company;
    (5)   in the case of a company:
        (a)   any person who is an officer of that company;
        (b)   any subsidiary or holding company both as defined in the Companies Act 2006 s 1159, of that company and any person who is an officer or an employee of any such subsidiary or holding company; and
        (c)   any company of which the same person or persons have control; and

(6)   in the case of a trustee of a trust, a beneficiary of the trust and any person to whom the terms of the trust confer a power that may be exercised for that person's benefit: Gangmasters (Licensing Conditions) Rules 2009, SI 2009/307, Schedule para 1(1).

In Schedule para 1(1), the members of A's family are:
(i)   A's spouse or civil partner;
(ii)   any other person (whether of a different sex or the same sex) with whom A lives as partner in an enduring family relationship;
(iii)   any child, step-child, parent, grandchild, grandparent, brother, sister, cousin, uncle or aunt of A;
(iv)   any child or step-child of a person within head (ii) (and who is not a child or step-child of A) who lives with A and has not attained the age of 18: Schedule para 1(2).

6   Gangmasters (Licensing Conditions) Rules 2009, SI 2009/307, Schedule para 9(2).

335. Restriction on providing workers in industrial disputes.

A licence holder[1] must not introduce or supply a worker[2] to a labour user[3] to perform either:

(1)   the duties normally performed by a worker who is taking part in a strike or other industrial action (the 'first worker')[4]; or

(2)   the duties normally performed by any other worker employed by the labour user and who is assigned by the labour user to perform the duties normally performed by the first worker[5],

unless in either case the licence holder does not know, and had no reasonable grounds for knowing, that the first worker is taking part in a strike or other industrial action[6].

Where a labour user pays any money pursuant to a contractual term which is unenforceable by virtue of these provisions[7] the labour user is entitled to recover that money[8].

1   As to the meaning of 'licence holder' see PARA 325 note 1. As to licensing conditions generally see PARA 328. As to the enforcement of compliance with licensing requirements see PARA 354. Contravention of or failure to comply with these provisions on the part of a licence holder is actionable if it causes damage: see PARA 353.
2   As to the meaning of 'worker' see PARA 309 note 1.
3   'Labour user' means a person to whom workers or services are supplied: Gangmasters (Licensing Conditions) Rules 2009, SI 2009/307, r 2(1).
4   Gangmasters (Licensing Conditions) Rules 2009, SI 2009/307, Schedule para 10(1)(a). This restriction does not, however, apply if, in relation to the first worker, the strike or other industrial action is an unofficial strike or other unofficial industrial action for the purposes of the Trade Union and Labour Relations (Consolidation) Act 1992 s 237 (see EMPLOYMENT vol 41A (2014) PARA 1350): Gangmasters (Licensing Conditions) Rules 2009, SI 2009/307, Schedule para 10(2)(b).
5   Gangmasters (Licensing Conditions) Rules 2009, SI 2009/307, Schedule para 10(1). See note 4.
6   Gangmasters (Licensing Conditions) Rules 2009, SI 2009/307, Schedule para 10(2)(a).
7   Ie by virtue of the Gangmasters (Licensing Conditions) Rules 2009, SI 2009/307, Schedule para 10 (see the text and notes 1–6).
8   Gangmasters (Licensing Conditions) Rules 2009, SI 2009/307, r 8(2).

336. Restriction on paying workers' remuneration.

The licence holder[1] must not in respect of a worker[2] whom the holder has introduced or supplied to a labour user who has then employed the worker:

(1)   pay or make arrangements to pay to the worker the worker's remuneration arising from the employment with the labour user, or

(2)   introduce or refer the labour user to any person with whom the licence holder is connected with a view to that person paying, or making arrangements to pay the remuneration to the worker[3].

1   As to the meaning of 'licence holder' see PARA 325 note 1. As to licensing conditions generally see PARA 328. As to the enforcement of compliance with licensing requirements see PARA 354.

Contravention of or failure to comply with these provisions on the part of a licence holder is actionable if it causes damage: see PARA 353.

2   As to the meaning of 'worker' see PARA 309 note 1.

3   Gangmasters (Licensing Conditions) Rules 2009, SI 2009/307, Schedule para 11(1). However, this does not apply where the labour user and the licence holder are connected: Schedule para 11(2).

337. Restriction on charges to labour users.

Any term of a contract between a licence holder[1] and a labour user[2] which is contingent on a worker[3] taking up employment with the labour user or working for the labour user pursuant to being supplied by another licence holder is in general unenforceable by the licence holder in relation to that worker, unless the contract provides that instead of a transfer fee[4] the labour user may by notice to the licence holder elect for a hire period of such length as is specified in the contract during which the worker will be supplied to the labour user:

(1)   in a case where there has been no supply, on the terms specified in the contract; or

(2)   in any other case, on terms no less favourable to the labour user than those which applied immediately before the licence holder received the notice[5].

Such a term is also unenforceable where the licence holder does not supply the worker to the labour user, in accordance with the contract, for the duration of the hire period[6] unless the licence holder is in no way at fault[7].

Any term of a contract between a licence holder and a labour user which is contingent on a worker:

(a)   taking up employment with the labour user or any other person to whom the labour user has introduced the worker; or

(b)   working for the labour user pursuant to being supplied by another licence holder[8],

is unenforceable by the licence holder in relation to the event concerned where the worker takes up such employment or begins working pursuant to being supplied by another licence holder, as the case may be, after the end of the 'relevant period'[9].

A licence holder must not seek to enforce against the labour user, or otherwise seek to give effect to, any term of a contract which is unenforceable by virtue of these provisions[10] or otherwise directly or indirectly request a payment to which by virtue of these provisions the licence holder is not entitled[11]. However, where any term of a contract is prohibited or made unenforceable under these provisions[12] the contract continues to bind the parties if it is capable of continuing in existence without that term[13].

1   As to the meaning of 'licence holder' see PARA 325 note 1. As to licensing conditions generally see PARA 328. As to the enforcement of compliance with licensing requirements see PARA 354. Contravention of or failure to comply with these provisions on the part of a licence holder is actionable if it causes damage: see PARA 353.

2   As to the meaning of 'labour user' see PARA 335 note 3.

3   As to the meaning of 'worker' see PARA 309 note 1.

4   A 'transfer fee' is any payment in connection with the worker taking up employment with the labour user or in connection with the worker working for the labour user pursuant to being supplied by another licence holder: Gangmasters (Licensing Conditions) Rules 2009, SI 2009/307, Schedule para 12(2).

5   Gangmasters (Licensing Conditions) Rules 2009, SI 2009/307, Schedule para 12(1).

6   Ie the hire period referred to in the Gangmaster (Licensing Conditions) Rules 2009, SI 2009/307, Schedule para 12(1).

7   Gangmasters (Licensing Conditions) Rules 2009, SI 2009/307, Schedule para 12(3).

8   Gangmasters (Licensing Conditions) Rules 2009, SI 2009/307, Schedule para 12(4)(a), (b).
9   Gangmasters (Licensing Conditions) Rules 2009, SI 2009/307, Schedule para 12(4). 'Relevant period' means the period of:
    (1)   eight weeks starting on the day after the day on which the worker last worked for the labour user pursuant to being supplied by the licence holder; or
    (2)   14 weeks starting on the first day on which the worker worked for the labour user pursuant to the supply of that worker to that labour user by the licence holder (Schedule para 12(5)).

In determining for these purposes the first day on which the worker worked for the labour user pursuant to the supply of that worker to that labour user by the licence holder, no account may be taken of any supply that occurred prior to a period of more than 42 days during which that worker did not work for that labour user pursuant to being supplied by that licence holder: Schedule para 12(6).

10   Ie which is unenforceable by virtue of the Gangmasters (Licensing Conditions) Rules 2009, SI 2009/307, Schedule para 12(1), (3) or (4).
11   Gangmasters (Licensing Conditions) Rules 2009, SI 2009/307, Schedule para 12(7).
12   Ie under the Gangmasters (Licensing Conditions) Rules 2009, SI 2009/307.
13   Gangmasters (Licensing Conditions) Rules 2009, SI 2009/307, r 8(1).

338. Prohibition on withholding payment to workers.

A licence holder[1] may not withhold or threaten to withhold the whole or any part of any payment due to the worker[2] in respect of any work done by the worker on grounds of:

    (1)   non-receipt of payment from the labour user[3];
    (2)   the worker's failure to prove that he has worked during a particular period of time[4];
    (3)   the worker not having worked during any period other than that to which the payment relates[5]; or
    (4)   any matter within the control of the licence holder[6].

1   As to the meaning of 'licence holder' see PARA 325 note 1. As to licensing conditions generally see PARA 328. As to the enforcement of compliance with licensing requirements see PARA 354. Contravention of or failure to comply with these provisions on the part of a licence holder is actionable if it causes damage: see PARA 353.
2   As to the meaning of 'worker' see PARA 309 note 1. Where any term of a contract is prohibited or made unenforceable under the Gangmasters (Licensing Conditions) Rules 2009, SI 2009/307, the contract continues to bind the parties if it is capable of continuing in existence without that term: r 8(1).
3   Gangmasters (Licensing Conditions) Rules 2009, SI 2009/307, Schedule para 13(a). As to the meaning of 'labour user' see PARA 335 note 3.
4   Gangmasters (Licensing Conditions) Rules 2009, SI 2009/307, Schedule para 13(b). This provision does not prevent the licence holder from satisfying himself by other means that the worker worked for the particular period in question: Schedule para 13(b).
5   Gangmasters (Licensing Conditions) Rules 2009, SI 2009/307, Schedule para 13(c).
6   Gangmasters (Licensing Conditions) Rules 2009, SI 2009/307, Schedule para 13(d).

339. Requirement to agree terms with workers and labour users.

Before supplying a worker[1] to a labour user[2], a licence holder[3] must agree the terms which will apply between the licence holder and the worker, including:

    (1)   the type of work the licence holder will find or seek to find for the worker[4];
    (2)   whether the worker is or will be supplied by the licence holder under a contract of service or a contract for services, and in either case, the terms and conditions which will apply[5];
    (3)   an undertaking that the licence holder will pay the worker in respect of work done by him, whether or not the licence holder is paid by the labour user in respect of that work[6];

(4)   the length of notice of termination which the worker is obliged to give the licence holder, and entitled to receive from him, in respect of any particular assignment[7];

(5)   either the rate of remuneration payable or the minimum rate of remuneration[8] the licence holder reasonably expects to achieve for the worker[9];

(6)   details of the intervals at which remuneration will be paid[10]; and

(7)   details of any entitlement to annual holidays and to payment in respect of such holidays[11].

A licence holder must record all the terms, where possible in one document, and give the worker the written terms before the holder provides any services to the worker[12].

A licence holder may not make the continued provision of any services by him to a worker conditional on the agreement by the worker to any variation[13].

Before first providing services (other than the provision of information in the form of a publication) to a labour user, a licence holder must agree the terms which will apply between the licence holder and labour user, including details of:

(a)   any fee which may be payable by the labour user to the licence holder[14]; and

(b)   the procedure to be followed if a worker introduced or supplied to the labour user proves unsatisfactory[15].

The licence holder must record the terms in a single document and send a copy to the labour user as soon as reasonably practicable[16].

1   As to the meaning of 'worker' see PARA 309 note 1.
2   As to the meaning of 'labour user' see PARA 335 note 3.
3   As to the meaning of 'licence holder' see PARA 325 note 1. As to licensing conditions generally see PARA 328. As to the enforcement of compliance with licensing requirements see PARA 354. Contravention of or failure to comply with these provisions on the part of a licence holder is actionable if it causes damage: see PARA 353.
4   Gangmasters (Licensing Conditions) Rules 2009, SI 2009/307, Schedule para 15(1), (2)(a).
5   Gangmasters (Licensing Conditions) Rules 2009, SI 2009/307, Schedule para 15(2)(b).
6   Gangmasters (Licensing Conditions) Rules 2009, SI 2009/307, Schedule para 15(2)(c).
7   Gangmasters (Licensing Conditions) Rules 2009, SI 2009/307, Schedule para 15(2)(d). As to giving notice see PARA 355.
8   As to the national minimum wage see EMPLOYMENT vol 39 (2014) PARA 199.
9   Gangmasters (Licensing Conditions) Rules 2009, SI 2009/307, Schedule para 15(2)(e).
10 Gangmasters (Licensing Conditions) Rules 2009, SI 2009/307, Schedule para 15(2)(f).
11 Gangmasters (Licensing Conditions) Rules 2009, SI 2009/307, Schedule para 15(2)(g). Those terms may only be varied by written agreement, a copy of which must be provided to the worker as soon as possible and in any event no later than the end of the fifth working day following the day the variation was agreed: Schedule para 15(4).
12 Gangmasters (Licensing Conditions) Rules 2009, SI 2009/307, Schedule para 15(3). However, this does not apply if the worker has been given a written statement of particulars of employment in accordance with the Employment Rights Act 1996 Pt 1 (ss 1–12) (see EMPLOYMENT vol 39 (2014) PARAS 118–127): Gangmasters (Licensing Conditions) Rules 2009, SI 2009/307, Schedule para 15(5).
13 Gangmasters (Licensing Conditions) Rules 2009, SI 2009/307, Schedule para 15(6).
14 Gangmasters (Licensing Conditions) Rules 2009, SI 2009/307, Schedule para 16(1), (2)(a). The agreed term must include an agreement on the amount or method of calculation of the fee (Schedule para 16(2)(a)(i)) and the circumstances, if any, in which refunds or rebates are payable to the labour user, the scale of such refunds or rebates and, if no refunds or rebates are payable, a statement to that effect (Schedule para 16(2)(a)(ii)).
15 Gangmasters (Licensing Conditions) Rules 2009, SI 2009/307, Schedule para 16(2)(b).
16 Gangmasters (Licensing Conditions) Rules 2009, SI 2009/307, Schedule para 16(3). As to sending documents see PARA 355. If the licence holder and the labour user agree to any variation in the

terms set out in such a document, the licence holder must provide a document containing details and the date of the variation as soon as is reasonably practicable: Schedule para 16(4).

340. Information to be obtained from and provided to labour users and workers.

On the first occasion that a licence holder[1] offers to provide or arrange the provision of a service to a worker[2], the holder must give notice to the worker stating:

(1)   whether that service is a work-finding service[3] (for which the licence holder is prohibited from charging a fee)[4]; and

(2)   whether any other services or goods which may be provided by the licence holder or any other person are services or goods for which the holder or other person providing them will or may charge a fee, together with details of any such fee including:

    (a)   the amount or method of calculation of the fee[5];

    (b)   the identity of the person to whom the fee is or will be payable[6];

    (c)   a description of the services or goods to which the fee relates and a statement of the worker's right to cancel or withdraw from the service and the notice period required[7]; and

    (d)   the circumstances in which refunds or rebates are payable to the worker, the scale of such refunds or rebates, and if no refunds or rebates are payable, a statement to that effect[8].

Where a licence holder offers any gift, or makes an offer of any benefit to a worker, in order to induce the worker to engage the licence holder to provide the worker with services, the holder must notify the worker of the terms on which the gift or benefit is offered before the offer is open for acceptance by the worker[9].

1   As to the meaning of 'licence holder' see PARA 325 note 1. As to licensing conditions generally see PARA 328. As to the enforcement of compliance with licensing requirements see PARA 354. Contravention of or failure to comply with these provisions on the part of a licence holder is actionable if it causes damage: see PARA 353.

2   As to the meaning of 'worker' see PARA 309 note 1.

3   As to the meaning of 'work finding services' see PARA 332 note 3.

4   Gangmasters (Licensing Conditions) Rules 2009, SI 2009/307, Schedule para 14(1)(a). As to the prohibition on charging for work finding services see PARA 333.

5   Gangmasters (Licensing Conditions) Rules 2009, SI 2009/307, Schedule para 14(1)(b)(i).

6   Gangmasters (Licensing Conditions) Rules 2009, SI 2009/307, Schedule para 14(1)(b)(ii).

7   Gangmasters (Licensing Conditions) Rules 2009, SI 2009/307, Schedule para 14(1)(b)(iii).

8   Gangmasters (Licensing Conditions) Rules 2009, SI 2009/307, Schedule para 14(1)(b)(iv). Schedule para 14(1) only applies where one or more services or goods referred to in Schedule para 14(1)(b) for which the worker will or may be charged a fee may be provided to the worker: Schedule para 14(2). A licence holder must give a further notice to a worker stating the matters referred to in Schedule para 14(1)(b) where, subsequent to the first occasion that it offers to provide or arrange the provision of a service to the worker, the licence holder or the person providing to the worker any services or goods referred to in Schedule para 14(1)(b), introduces or varies any fees in relation to any services or goods referred to in Schedule para 14(1)(b): Schedule para 14(3).

9   Gangmasters (Licensing Conditions) Rules 2009, SI 2009/307, Schedule para 14(4).

341. Information to be obtained from and provided to labour users and workers.

A licence holder[1] may not supply a worker[2] to a labour user[3] unless he has obtained the following information[4]:

(1)   the identity of the labour user and, if applicable, the nature of the labour user's business[5];

(2)   the date on which the labour user requires a worker to commence work and the duration, or likely duration, of the work[6];

(3)   the position which the labour user seeks to fill, including the type of work a worker in that position would be required to do, the location at which and the hours during which he would be required to work[7];

(4)   any risks to health or safety known to the licence holder or labour user and the steps the licence holder or labour user has taken to prevent or control such risks[8];

(5)   the experience, training, qualifications and any authorisation which the licence holder or labour user considers are necessary, or which are required by law or by any professional body, for a worker to possess in order to work in the position[9]; and

(6)   any expenses payable by or to the worker[10].

A licence holder must ensure that at the same time as he offers a worker a position with a labour user he gives to the worker (orally or otherwise) all information[11] he has been provided with pursuant to these requirements[12] and if a rate of remuneration has not been agreed with the labour user he informs the worker (orally or otherwise)[13] of the rate of remuneration he will pay him to work in that position[14].

A licence holder may not supply a worker to a labour user unless he has obtained confirmation:

(a)   of the identity of the worker[15];

(b)   that the worker has the experience, training, qualifications and any authorisation which the licence holder or labour user considers are necessary, or which are required by law or by any professional body, to work in the position which the labour user seeks to fill[16]; and

(c)   that the worker is willing to work in the position which the labour user seeks to fill[17].

A licence holder must ensure that at the same time as he supplies or proposes to supply a particular worker to a labour user he gives to the labour user the information about the worker obtained pursuant to these requirements[18] and informs the worker whether he will be supplied under a contract of service or a contract for services[19].

1   As to the meaning of 'licence holder' see PARA 325 note 1. As to licensing conditions generally see PARA 328. As to the enforcement of compliance with licensing requirements see PARA 354. Contravention of or failure to comply with these provisions on the part of a licence holder is actionable if it causes damage: see PARA 353.

2   As to the meaning of 'worker' see PARA 309 note 1.

3   As to the meaning of 'labour user' see PARA 335 note 3.

4   As to the provision of information see PARA 355.

5   Gangmasters (Licensing Conditions) Rules 2009, SI 2009/307, Schedule para 17(a).

6   Gangmasters (Licensing Conditions) Rules 2009, SI 2009/307, Schedule para 17(b).

7   Gangmasters (Licensing Conditions) Rules 2009, SI 2009/307, Schedule para 17(c).

8   Gangmasters (Licensing Conditions) Rules 2009, SI 2009/307, Schedule para 17(d).

9   Gangmasters (Licensing Conditions) Rules 2009, SI 2009/307, Schedule para 17(e).

10 Gangmasters (Licensing Conditions) Rules 2009, SI 2009/307, Schedule para 17(f).

11 Where any of the information is given orally, the licence holder must afterwards provide it in writing as soon as possible and in any event within three working days: Gangmasters (Licensing Conditions) Rules 2009, SI 2009/307, Schedule para 20(3).

12 Gangmasters (Licensing Conditions) Rules 2009, SI 2009/307, Schedule para 20(2)(a). The requirements referred to in the text are the requirements of Schedule para 17 (see the text and notes 1–10).

13 See note 11.

14 Gangmasters (Licensing Conditions) Rules 2009, SI 2009/307, Schedule para 20(2)(b). See note 12.
15 Gangmasters (Licensing Conditions) Rules 2009, SI 2009/307, Schedule para 18(a).
16 Gangmasters (Licensing Conditions) Rules 2009, SI 2009/307, Schedule para 18(b).
17 Gangmasters (Licensing Conditions) Rules 2009, SI 2009/307, Schedule para 18(c).
18 Gangmasters (Licensing Conditions) Rules 2009, SI 2009/307, Schedule para 20(1)(a). The requirements referred to in the text are the requirements of Schedule para 18 (see the text and notes 15–17).

This does not apply where the worker has performed the same type of work with the labour user during the previous five working days (Schedule para 20(4)(a)) and the information required is the same as the information which the worker and labour user have already received (Schedule para 20(4)(b)).

Subject to Schedule para 20(4) and (6), where a licence holder intends to introduce or supply a worker to a labour user for an assignment of five consecutive working days' duration or less:

(1) Schedule para 20(1)(a) may be satisfied by the holder giving to the labour user (orally or otherwise) the name of the worker to be supplied and a written confirmation by the holder that the holder has complied with Schedule para 18; and

(2) Schedule para 20(1)(b) may be satisfied, where the holder has previously provided the worker with the information referred to under that provision and that information remains unchanged, by the employment business giving to the worker in writing the information referred to in Schedule para 17(a) and (b): Schedule para 20(5).

Where, after it has started, an assignment to which Schedule para 20(5) applies is extended beyond a duration of five working days, the information referred to in Schedule para 20(1) which has not already been provided must be provided in writing by the end of the eighth working day of the assignment, or by the end of the assignment if sooner: Schedule para 20(6).

19 Gangmasters (Licensing Conditions) Rules 2009, SI 2009/307, Schedule para 20(1)(b). See note 18.

342. Steps to be taken for the protection of the labour user and worker.

Where a licence holder[1] receives or obtains information which gives him reasonable grounds to believe that a worker[2] is unsuitable for the position with a labour user[3] for which the worker is being supplied[4] or which does not give such reasonable grounds but otherwise indicates that the worker may be unsuitable for that position, the holder must without delay[5] inform the labour user and any intermediaries of that information[6] and end the supply of that worker to the labour user[7].

Before any work is commenced, a licence holder must ensure that he has taken all such steps as are reasonably practicable to ensure that the worker and the labour user are each aware of any requirements imposed by law, or by any professional body, which must be satisfied[8] and that he has made all reasonably practicable inquiries[9] to ensure that it would not be detrimental to the interests of the worker or the labour user for the worker to work for the labour user in the position which the labour user seeks to fill[10].

1 As to the meaning of 'licence holder' see PARA 325 note 1. As to licensing conditions generally see PARA 328. As to the enforcement of compliance with licensing requirements see PARA 354. Contravention of or failure to comply with these provisions on the part of a licence holder is actionable if it causes damage: see PARA 353.
2 As to the meaning of 'worker' see PARA 309 note 1.
3 As to the meaning of 'labour user' see PARA 335 note 3. As to the provision of information see PARA 355. As to the making of inquiries and the receipt of answers see PARA 355. Nothing in the Gangmasters (Licensing Conditions) Rules 2009, SI 2009/307, Schedule para 19 authorises the making of a disclosure in contravention of the Data Protection Act 1998: Gangmasters (Licensing Conditions) Rules 2009, SI 2009/307, Schedule para 19(9).
4 Gangmasters (Licensing Conditions) Rules 2009, SI 2009/307, Schedule para 19(3)(a). The licence holder must also end the supply of that worker to the labour user: Schedule para 19(4).
5 'Without delay' means on the same day, or where not reasonably practicable, the next working day: Gangmasters (Licensing Conditions) Rules 2009, SI 2009/307, Schedule para 19(8). As to the meaning of 'working day' see PARA 151 note 6.

6   Gangmasters (Licensing Conditions) Rules 2009, SI 2009/307, Schedule para 19(3)(b). The
    licence holder must also make such further enquiries as are reasonably practicable as to the
    suitability of the worker for the position concerned: Schedule para 19(5). The licence holder must
    inform the labour user and any intermediaries about those enquiries and any further information
    obtained: Schedule para 19(6). Where information resulting from those enquiries gives the licence
    holder reasonable grounds to believe that the worker is unsuitable for the position concerned, the
    holder must without delay inform the labour user and any intermediaries of that information and
    end the supply of that worker to the labour user: Schedule para 19(7).
7   Gangmasters (Licensing Conditions) Rules 2009, SI 2009/307, Schedule para 19(4).
8   Gangmasters (Licensing Conditions) Rules 2009, SI 2009/307, Schedule para 19(1)(a). This
    without prejudice to any of the licence holder's duties under any enactment or rule of law in
    relation to health and safety at work: Schedule para 19(2).
9   As to the making of inquiries see PARA 355.
10 Gangmasters (Licensing Conditions) Rules 2009, SI 2009/307, Schedule para 19(1)(b).

343. Protection of shellfish gatherers.

The licence holder[1] must ensure that for each individual group of workers[2]
gathering shellfish[3] there is a competent supervisor[4], who must:

(1)   be named on the licence[5];
(2)   accompany the workers at all times to the work area[6];
(3)   be familiar with the use of any equipment or procedures used when
        gathering shellfish or accessing the work area[7]; and
(4)   be able to communicate directly with every one of the group of
        workers[8].

The licence holder or the supervisor must also notify[9] the Maritime and
Coastguard Agency Rescue Co-ordination Centre of:

(a)   the licence holder's licence number[10];
(b)   contact details for the licence holder or supervisor[11];
(c)   the number of workers in the group[12];
(d)   where the work area is[13]; and
(e)   the times the group is going out and returning from the work area[14].

If a fisheries permit or licence is required to gather shellfish the licence holder must
ensure that workers comply with the provisions of that permit or licence[15].

1   As to the meaning of 'licence holder' see PARA 325 note 1. As to licensing conditions generally see
    PARA 328. As to the enforcement of compliance with licensing requirements see PARA 354.
    Contravention of or failure to comply with these provisions on the part of a licence holder is
    actionable if it causes damage: see PARA 353.
2   As to the meaning of 'worker' see PARA 309 note 1.
3   Gangmasters (Licensing Conditions) Rules 2009, SI 2009/307, Schedule para 26(1).
4   Gangmasters (Licensing Conditions) Rules 2009, SI 2009/307, Schedule para 26(2).
5   Gangmasters (Licensing Conditions) Rules 2009, SI 2009/307, Schedule para 26(3).
6   Gangmasters (Licensing Conditions) Rules 2009, SI 2009/307, Schedule para 26(4)(a). 'Work
    area' means the place where the shellfish are gathered: Schedule para 26(6).
7   Gangmasters (Licensing Conditions) Rules 2009, SI 2009/307, Schedule para 26(4)(b).
8   Gangmasters (Licensing Conditions) Rules 2009, SI 2009/307, Schedule para 26(4)(c).
9   As to the giving of notifications see PARA 355.
10 Gangmasters (Licensing Conditions) Rules 2009, SI 2009/307, Schedule para 26(5)(a).
11 Gangmasters (Licensing Conditions) Rules 2009, SI 2009/307, Schedule para 26(5)(b).
12 Gangmasters (Licensing Conditions) Rules 2009, SI 2009/307, Schedule para 26(5)(c).
13 Gangmasters (Licensing Conditions) Rules 2009, SI 2009/307, Schedule para 26(5)(d).
14 Gangmasters (Licensing Conditions) Rules 2009, SI 2009/307, Schedule para 26(5)(e).
15 Gangmasters (Licensing Conditions) Rules 2009, SI 2009/307, Schedule para 26(7).

344. Travel expenses and living away from home.

A licence holder[1] may not arrange for a worker[2] to take up a position[3] if, in
order to take up that position, the worker must occupy accommodation other
than his home, unless:

(1) suitable accommodation will be available for the worker and details have been provided to the worker, including the terms on which it is offered and any cost[4]; and

(2) suitable arrangements have been made for the worker to travel to such accommodation[5].

Where a worker is to be supplied to a labour user other than as the labour user's employee, or is under the age of 18,[6] and the licence holder, labour user or any intermediary has arranged free travel or payment of fares for the worker's journey to the place of work[7], the licence holder must, if the work does not start or upon it ending, arrange free travel for the worker's return journey, pay his return fare or obtain an undertaking from the labour user or any intermediary to arrange free travel or pay the return fare[8].

If a worker is loaned money by the licence holder, the labour user or any intermediary to meet travel or other expenses in order to take up a position, he must be provided with details in writing of the amount loaned and repayment terms[9] and may not be asked to repay a greater sum than the amount loaned[10].

1 As to the meaning of 'licence holder' see PARA 325 note 1. As to licensing conditions generally see PARA 328. As to the enforcement of compliance with licensing requirements see PARA 354. Contravention of or failure to comply with these provisions on the part of a licence holder is actionable if it causes damage: see PARA 353.
2 As to the meaning of 'worker' see PARA 309 note 1.
3 Ie a position other than as a labour user's employee (within the meaning of the Employment Rights Act 1996 s 230(1): see EMPLOYMENT vol 39 (2014) PARA 2): Gangmasters (Licensing Conditions) Rules 2009, SI 2009/307, Schedule para 1(2). As to the meaning of 'labour user' see PARA 335 note 3.
4 Gangmasters (Licensing Conditions) Rules 2009, SI 2009/307, Schedule para 21(1), (2)(a).
5 Gangmasters (Licensing Conditions) Rules 2009, SI 2009/307, Schedule para 21(2)(b).
6 Gangmasters (Licensing Conditions) Rules 2009, SI 2009/307, Schedule para 21(3)(a). As to the meaning of 'employee' see the Employment Rights Act 1996 s 230(1); and note 3.
7 Gangmasters (Licensing Conditions) Rules 2009, SI 2009/307, Schedule para 21(3)(b).
8 Gangmasters (Licensing Conditions) Rules 2009, SI 2009/307, Schedule para 21(3). If a labour user or intermediary does not comply with an undertaking so given the licence holder must either arrange free travel for the return journey of the worker or pay his fare: Schedule para 21(5). The licence holder must give notice to the worker setting out the details of the free travel or payment of fares including any conditions on which the same are offered: Schedule para 21(4). As to giving notice see PARA 355.
9 Gangmasters (Licensing Conditions) Rules 2009, SI 2009/307, Schedule para 21(7)(a).
10 Gangmasters (Licensing Conditions) Rules 2009, SI 2009/307, Schedule para 21(7)(b).

345. Keeping of records and confidentiality.

Every licence holder[1] must record, as soon as reasonably practicable, the following details in relation to every application received from a worker[2]:

(1) the date terms are agreed between the licence holder and the worker[3];

(2) the worker's name, address and, if under 22, date of birth[4];

(3) any terms which apply or will apply between the licence holder and the worker, and any document recording any variation[5];

(4) any relevant details of the worker's training, experience or qualifications and any authorisation to undertake particular work (and copies of any documentary evidence of the same obtained by the licence holder)[6];

(5) details of any requirements specified by the worker in relation to taking up employment[7];

(6) the names of labour users[8] or sub-contractors to whom the worker is supplied[9];

(7)   details of any resulting engagement and the date from which it takes effect[10];

(8)   the date the contract was terminated (where applicable)[11]; and

(9)   details of any inquiries made[12] about the worker and the position concerned, with copies of all relevant documents and dates they were received or sent[13].

Every licence holder must record, as soon as reasonably practicable, the following details relating to labour users:

(a)   the date terms are agreed between the licence holder and the labour user[14];

(b)   the labour user's name and address, and location of the place of work if different[15];

(c)   details of any sub-contractors[16];

(d)   details of the position the labour user seeks to fill[17];

(e)   the duration or likely duration of the work[18];

(f)   any experience, training, ability, qualifications or authorisation required by the licence holder or labour user by law, or by any professional body, and any other conditions attaching to the position the labour user seeks to fill[19];

(g)   the terms offered in respect of the position the labour user seeks to fill[20];

(h)   a copy of the terms between the licence holder and the labour user, and any document recording any variation[21];

(i)   the names of workers supplied[22];

(j)   details of inquiries[23] about the labour user and the position he seeks to fill, with copies of all relevant documents and dates of their receipt[24];

(k)   the details of each resulting engagement and date from which it takes effect[25]; and

(l)   dates of requests by the licence holder for fees or other payment from the labour user and of receipt of such fees or other payments, and copies of statements or invoices[26].

Every licence holder must record, as soon as reasonably practicable, the names of any other licence holders whose services he uses, and details of inquiries made to ascertain that the other licence holder is licensed[27]. A licence holder who has assigned or sub-contracted any of its obligations under any contract or arrangement with a worker or labour user to another licence holder must ensure that the terms upon which those obligations are assigned or sub-contracted are recorded, where possible in a single document[28].

A licence holder must keep all records for at least one year from creation or, where they have been supplied by another person, from last supply[29]. If the records are kept other than at premises a licence holder uses for or in connection with the carrying on of its business[30], the licence holder must ensure that they are readily accessible and capable of being delivered to the licence holder's premises in the United Kingdom[31] or to the Gangmasters and Labour Abuse Authority[32] within two working days[33].

1   As to the meaning of 'licence holder' see PARA 325 note 1. As to licensing conditions generally see PARA 328. As to the enforcement of compliance with licensing requirements see PARA 354. Contravention of or failure to comply with these provisions on the part of a licence holder is actionable if it causes damage: see PARA 353.

2   As to the meaning of 'worker' see PARA 309 note 1.

3   Gangmasters (Licensing Conditions) Rules 2009, SI 2009/307, Schedule para 22(a).

4   Gangmasters (Licensing Conditions) Rules 2009, SI 2009/307, Schedule para 22(b).

5   Gangmasters (Licensing Conditions) Rules 2009, SI 2009/307, Schedule para 22(c).

6   Gangmasters (Licensing Conditions) Rules 2009, SI 2009/307, Schedule para 22(d).
7   Gangmasters (Licensing Conditions) Rules 2009, SI 2009/307, Schedule para 22(e).
8   As to the meaning of 'labour user' see PARA 335 note 3.
9   Gangmasters (Licensing Conditions) Rules 2009, SI 2009/307, Schedule para 22(f).
10 Gangmasters (Licensing Conditions) Rules 2009, SI 2009/307, Schedule para 22(g).
11 Gangmasters (Licensing Conditions) Rules 2009, SI 2009/307, Schedule para 22(h).
12 Ie under the Gangmasters (Licensing Conditions) Rules 2009, SI 2009/307, Schedule paras 18, 19
    (see PARAS 341–342). As to the making of inquiries see PARA 355.
13 Gangmasters (Licensing Conditions) Rules 2009, SI 2009/307, Schedule para 22(i).
14 Gangmasters (Licensing Conditions) Rules 2009, SI 2009/307, Schedule para 23(a).
15 Gangmasters (Licensing Conditions) Rules 2009, SI 2009/307, Schedule para 23(b).
16 Gangmasters (Licensing Conditions) Rules 2009, SI 2009/307, Schedule para 23(c).
17 Gangmasters (Licensing Conditions) Rules 2009, SI 2009/307, Schedule para 23(d).
18 Gangmasters (Licensing Conditions) Rules 2009, SI 2009/307, Schedule para 23(e).
19 Gangmasters (Licensing Conditions) Rules 2009, SI 2009/307, Schedule para 23(f).
20 Gangmasters (Licensing Conditions) Rules 2009, SI 2009/307, Schedule para 23(g).
21 Gangmasters (Licensing Conditions) Rules 2009, SI 2009/307, Schedule para 23(h).
22 Gangmasters (Licensing Conditions) Rules 2009, SI 2009/307, Schedule para 23(i).
23 Ie under the Gangmasters (Licensing Conditions) Rules 2009, SI 2009/307, Schedule paras 17, 19
    (see PARAS 341–342).
24 Gangmasters (Licensing Conditions) Rules 2009, SI 2009/307, Schedule para 23(j).
25 Gangmasters (Licensing Conditions) Rules 2009, SI 2009/307, Schedule para 23(k).
26 Gangmasters (Licensing Conditions) Rules 2009, SI 2009/307, Schedule para 23(l).
27 Gangmasters (Licensing Conditions) Rules 2009, SI 2009/307, Schedule para 24(1).
28 Gangmasters (Licensing Conditions) Rules 2009, SI 2009/307, Schedule para 24(2).
29 Gangmasters (Licensing Conditions) Rules 2009, SI 2009/307, Schedule para 25(1).
30 As to the meaning of 'business' see PARA 324 note 10.
31 As to the meaning of 'United Kingdom' see PARA 1 note 1.
32 As to the establishment, constitution and status of the Authority see PARA 320.
33 Gangmasters (Licensing Conditions) Rules 2009, SI 2009/307, Schedule para 25(2). As to the
    meaning of 'working day' see PARA 330 note 3.

C. APPEALS

346. Appeals against licensing decisions.

The Secretary of State[1] must appoint a person (an 'appointed person') from members of the panel of Employment Tribunal chairmen[2] to hear and determine appeals concerning the licensing of gangmasters[3] and must ensure that arrangements are made for the provision of a secretariat to administer the appeals process and provide administrative assistance to appointed persons[4].

1   As to the Secretary of State see PARA 390.
2   As to the panel of Employment Tribunal chairmen see EMPLOYMENT vol 41A (2014)
    PARA 1401.
3   Gangmasters (Appeals) Regulations 2006, SI 2006/662, reg 3(1). The appeals referred to in the
    text are those brought under the regulations (reg 3(1)): see PARA 347 et seq. The regulations are
    made under the Gangmasters (Licensing) Act 2004 s 10, which empowers the Secretary of State
    by regulations to make provision for an appeal against any decision of the Gangmasters and
    Labour Abuse Authority to refuse an application for a licence (s 10(1)(a)), as to the conditions to
    which the grant of the licence is subject (s 10(1)(b)), to refuse consent to the transfer of a licence
    (s 10(1)(c)), or to modify or revoke a licence (s 10(1)(d)). See PARA 347. The regulations must
    make provision for and in connection with the appointment of a person to hear and determine
    such appeals (including provision for the payment of remuneration and allowances to such a
    person) (s 10(2)(a)) and as to the procedure to be followed in connection with an appeal (s
    10(2)(b)). As to the establishment, constitution and status of the Authority see PARA 320.
        The overriding objective of the regulations is to enable the appointed person to deal with
    appeals justly: Gangmasters (Appeals) Regulations 2006, SI 2006/662, reg 2(1). This includes, so
    far as practicable, ensuring that the parties are on an equal footing (reg 2(2)(a)), dealing with the
    appeal in ways which are proportionate to the complexity or importance of the issues (reg 2(2)(b)),
    and ensuring it is dealt with expeditiously and fairly (reg 2(2)(c)). The appointed person must seek

to give effect to the overriding objective when he exercises powers given to him by the regulations (reg 2(3)(a)) and interprets any provision (reg 2(3)(b)). The parties must assist the appointed person to further the overriding objective: reg 2(4).

Any irregularity resulting from a failure to comply with any provision of the Gangmasters (Appeals) Regulations 2006, SI 2006/662, does not of itself render the proceedings void: reg 24(1). At any stage in the proceedings the appointed person may, on his own initiative or on the application of either party, give such directions as he considers necessary or desirable to further the conduct of the appeal and may direct either party to provide any further particulars or documents which may reasonably be required: reg 14(1). The secretariat must send a copy of any application and documents submitted to the other party: reg 14(2).

Anything required to be sent under the Gangmasters (Appeals) Regulations 2006, SI 2006/662, may be delivered personally (reg 25(1)(a)) or sent by post, fax or e-mail (reg 25(1)(b)). A person's postal address for these purposes is the address stated in his notice of appeal or (in the case of the Gangmasters and Labour Abuse Authority) its reply, or such other address as may be subsequently notified to the secretariat: reg 25(2). Any document or information required by the Gangmasters (Appeals) Regulations 2006, SI 2006/662, to be sent to, or provided by, an appointed person may be sent to, or provided on his behalf by, the secretariat: reg 4(2).

4   Gangmasters (Appeals) Regulations 2006, SI 2006/662, reg 4(1). The Secretary of State may pay such remuneration and allowances to appointed persons as he may determine: reg 3(2).

347. Bringing an appeal.
An appeal may be brought by a person against a decision of the Gangmasters and Labour Abuse Authority[1]:

(1)   to refuse his application for a licence[2];

(2)   as to the conditions to which the grant of the licence to that person is subject[3];

(3)   to refuse consent to the transfer of a licence granted to that person[4]; or

(4)   to modify or revoke a licence granted to that person[5].

In order for an appeal to be valid, a notice of appeal[6] must be received by the secretariat[7]:

(a)   not later than twenty working days[8] after the date of the decision document[9]; or

(b)   in the case of a decision with immediate effect[10], not later than ten working days after the date of the decision document[11].

The appellant may amend his appeal, or any part of it, with the consent of the appointed person at any time before the hearing of the appeal[12] and may withdraw his appeal at any time before it is determined[13], while the Authority may notify the secretariat at any time before the appeal is determined that it no longer wishes to uphold a disputed decision[14].

1   As to the establishment, constitution and status of the Authority see PARA 320.
2   Gangmasters (Appeals) Regulations 2006, SI 2006/662, reg 5(1)(a). 'Licence' means a licence granted by the Authority under the Gangmasters (Licensing) Act 2004 s 7(1) (see PARA 324) authorising a person to act as a gangmaster: Gangmasters (Appeals) Regulations 2006, SI 2006/662, reg 1(2). An appeal may be brought in respect of a full licence or a provisional licence: reg 5(2). As to the meaning of 'gangmaster' see PARA 309. As to the meaning of 'acting as a gangmaster' see PARA 310. As to applications for a licence see PARA 320; and as to applications for the renewal of a licence see PARA 325.
3   Gangmasters (Appeals) Regulations 2006, SI 2006/662, reg 5(1)(b). As to licensing conditions see PARAS 328–345.
4   Gangmasters (Appeals) Regulations 2006, SI 2006/662, reg 5(1)(c). As to transfers see PARA 326.
5   Gangmasters (Appeals) Regulations 2006, SI 2006/662, reg 5(1)(d). As to modifications and revocations see PARA 326. Other than in the case of an appeal against a decision with immediate effect (reg 5(4)), a licence which is the subject of an appeal against modification or revocation continues to have effect according to its original terms and conditions until such date as determined by the appointed person (reg 5(3)). As to the appointed person see PARA 346.

6   A notice of appeal must be in writing and must state the name and address of the appellant and, if different, an address to which he requires notices and documents relating to the appeal to be sent (Gangmasters (Appeals) Regulations 2006, SI 2006/662, reg 6(2)(a)) and the grounds of the appeal (reg 6(2)(b)).

7   As to the secretariat see PARA 346.

8   'Working day' means a day other than a Saturday or a Sunday, Christmas Day or Good Friday, or a date which is a bank holiday under or by virtue of the Banking and Financial Dealings Act 1971 (see TIME vol 97 (2015) PARA 321): Gangmasters (Appeals) Regulations 2006, SI 2006/662, reg 1(2).

    An appointed person may, on the application of either party or on his own initiative, extend the time for doing any act appointed by or under the Gangmasters (Appeals) Regulations 2006, SI 2006/662, where he considers there are reasonable grounds to do so, and may do so whether or not the time so appointed has expired: reg 13(1). Such an application must be made by presenting to the secretariat a notice stating the name of the appellant (reg 13(2)(a)), the nature and date of the disputed decision which is the subject of appeal (reg 13(2)(b)) and the grounds of the application (reg 13(2)(c)). The secretariat must notify each of the parties of any extension of time so granted: reg 13(3). 'Disputed decision' means the decision of the Authority in relation to which the appellant appeals: reg 1(2).

9   Gangmasters (Appeals) Regulations 2006, SI 2006/662, reg 6(1)(a). 'Decision document' means the letter, notice or other communication by which the appellant is informed of a decision of the Authority: reg 1(2).

10   'Decision with immediate effect' means a decision of the Authority to revoke or suspend a licence, where the period between the date of the decision document and the date on which a decision comes into effect is five working days or less: Gangmasters (Appeals) Regulations 2006, SI 2006/662, reg 1(2).

11   Gangmasters (Appeals) Regulations 2006, SI 2006/662, reg 6(1)(b).

12   Gangmasters (Appeals) Regulations 2006, SI 2006/662, reg 8(1). The secretariat must send to the Authority a copy of any documentation received from the appellant under reg 8: reg 8(4). As to the means of delivery see PARA 346 note 3.

13   Gangmasters (Appeals) Regulations 2006, SI 2006/662, reg 8(2). Where the appellant withdraws his appeal, he may not submit a subsequent appeal on the same grounds in relation to the same disputed decision: reg 8(3). Upon the withdrawal of an appeal against revocation of a licence or modification of a licence or its conditions, the secretariat must notify the parties that the appeal has been withdrawn and the disputed decision takes effect on the later of: (1) the date specified in the original decision document as the date when the disputed decision was to take effect (reg 5(5)(a)); and (2) the sixth working day after the date of the document sent by the secretariat to the parties notifying them of the withdrawal (reg 5(5)(b)).

14   Gangmasters (Appeals) Regulations 2006, SI 2006/662, reg 9(2). If the Authority notifies the secretariat that it no longer wishes to uphold the disputed decision, the appointed person must uphold the appeal: reg 9(2).

348. Acknowledgement, notification and reply.

On receipt of a notice of appeal[1] the secretariat[2] must send[3] to the appellant an acknowledgement of receipt of the notice[4] and must at the same time send a copy of the notice to the Gangmasters and Labour Abuse Authority[5]. The Authority must then send to the secretariat a reply to the notice of appeal[6] stating, inter alia, whether it seeks to uphold the disputed decision[7] and, if so, it's reply to each of the grounds of appeal supplied by the appellant[8], upon receipt of which the secretariat must send a statement informing the parties that if either party wants the appeal to be determined without an oral hearing[9] it must notify the secretariat as soon as possible[10]. The Authority may amend its reply, or any part of it, with the consent of the appointed person at any time before the hearing of the appeal[11] and may amend or withdraw any documentation submitted in support of the reply at any time with the consent of the appointed person[12].

1   As to the giving of notices of appeal see PARA 347.

2   As to the secretariat see PARA 346.

3   As to the means of delivery see PARA 346 note 3.

4   Gangmasters (Appeals) Regulations 2006, SI 2006/662, reg 7(1). The acknowledgement must specify a date by which the appellant must supply any additional documentation he seeks to rely on for the purposes of the appeal: reg 7(1).

5   Gangmasters (Appeals) Regulations 2006, SI 2006/662, reg 7(2). The secretariat must also send any accompanying documentation, or additional documentation to the Authority: reg 7(2). As to the establishment, constitution and status of the Authority see PARA 320.

6   Gangmasters (Appeals) Regulations 2006, SI 2006/662, reg 9(1). The reply must be sent so that it is received no later than the end of the period of 20 working days beginning with the date on which the copy of the notice of appeal is received by the Authority (or as extended under reg 13: see PARA 347 note 8): reg 9(1). If the Authority fails to send a reply within the time specified in reg 9(1) or by a new date set by the appointed person under reg 13 it may not take any further part in the proceedings unless the appointed person so directs: reg 9(3). As to the meaning of 'working day' see PARA 347 note 8.

7   Gangmasters (Appeals) Regulations 2006, SI 2006/662, regs 9(2), 10(b). As to the meaning of 'disputed decision' see PARA 347 note 8. If in its reply the Authority notifies the secretariat that it no longer wishes to uphold the disputed decision, the appointed person must uphold the appeal: reg 9(2).

8   Gangmasters (Appeals) Regulations 2006, SI 2006/662, reg 10(c). The Authority's reply must also state an address to which it requires notices and documentation relating to the appeal to be sent: reg 10(a).

9   As to the circumstances in which an appeal may be determined without an oral hearing see PARA 349. As to where an oral hearing is to be held see PARA 350.

10 Gangmasters (Appeals) Regulations 2006, SI 2006/662, reg 11(c). Upon receipt of the Authority's reply the secretariat must also send an acknowledgement of receipt to the Authority specifying a date by which the Authority must supply any additional documentation it seeks to rely on for the purposes of the appeal (reg 11(a)) and a copy of the reply and any accompanying documentation to the appellant (reg 11(b)).

11 Gangmasters (Appeals) Regulations 2006, SI 2006/662, reg 12(1). The secretariat must send to the appellant a copy of any documentation received from the Authority under reg 12: reg 12(3).

12 Gangmasters (Appeals) Regulations 2006, SI 2006/662, reg 12(2). See note 10.

349. Deciding the appeal without an oral hearing.

If both parties agree[1], and the appointed person[2] considers it appropriate[3], an appeal against a licensing decision[4] is to be determined without an oral hearing but otherwise must generally be determined with an oral hearing[5].

If the appellant agrees that the case can be determined without an oral hearing[6], the Gangmasters and Labour Abuse Authority has not[7] sent its reply[8], and the appointed person does not consider that there are reasonable grounds for an oral hearing[9], then the secretariat[10] must notify the parties that the appointed person will determine the appeal without an oral hearing[11].

Before determining an appeal without an oral hearing, the appointed person must[12] consider any written representations from the parties[13].

1   Gangmasters (Appeals) Regulations 2006, SI 2006/662, reg 15(1)(a).
2   As to the appointed person see PARA 346.
3   Gangmasters (Appeals) Regulations 2006, SI 2006/662, reg 15(1)(b).
4   As to the bringing of appeals see PARA 347.
5   Gangmasters (Appeals) Regulations 2006, SI 2006/662, reg 15(1). As to where an oral hearing is to be held see PARA 350.
6   Gangmasters (Appeals) Regulations 2006, SI 2006/662, reg 15(2)(a).
7   Ie before the date specified in the Gangmasters (Appeals) Regulations 2006, SI 2006/662, reg 9(1) (see PARA 348) (or as extended under reg 13: see PARA 347 note 8).
8   Gangmasters (Appeals) Regulations 2006, SI 2006/662, reg 15(2)(b). As to the Authority's reply under reg 9(1) see PARA 348. As to the establishment, constitution and status of the Authority see PARA 320.
9   Gangmasters (Appeals) Regulations 2006, SI 2006/662, reg 15(2)(c).
10 As to the secretariat see PARA 346.
11 Gangmasters (Appeals) Regulations 2006, SI 2006/662, reg 15(2).

12 Ie unless the Gangmasters (Appeals) Regulations 2006, SI 2006/662, reg 9(3) (see PARA 348) applies in the case of the Authority: reg 15(3).
13 Gangmasters (Appeals) Regulations 2006, SI 2006/662, reg 15(3).

350. Fixing a date and time for an oral hearing.

Where an oral hearing is to be held[1], the secretariat[2] must fix a date for the hearing within 20 working days of the date of receiving the Gangmasters and Labour Abuse Authority's reply[3] to the notice of appeal[4]. The date must be not less than 15 working days after the date on which the hearing notice[5] is sent to the parties[6]. The appointed person[7] may change the place, date or time of the hearing if he considers it appropriate[8].

An appeal against a decision with immediate effect[9] must be heard and determined not later than 35 working days after the date on which the notice of appeal is received by the secretariat, unless the appointed person decides in the interests of justice that such expedited procedure[10] should not apply[11].

1 As to the circumstances in which an oral hearing need not be held see PARA 349. As to the hearing itself see PARA 351.
2 As to the secretariat see PARA 346.
3 Ie within 20 working days of the date of receiving the Authority's reply within the period specified by the Gangmasters (Appeals) Regulations 2006, SI 2006/662, reg 9(1) (see PARA 348). As to the meaning of 'working day', and as to extensions of time limits, see PARA 347 note 8. As to the establishment, constitution and status of the Authority see PARA 320.
4 Gangmasters (Appeals) Regulations 2006, SI 2006/662, reg 16(1). The secretariat must send to the parties a notice: (1) stating the time and place of the hearing of the appeal (reg 16(2)(a)); (2) giving guidance regarding the procedure to be followed at the hearing (reg 16(2)(b)); (3) stating the consequences under reg 19(5) (see PARA 351) of not attending the hearing (reg 16(2)(c)); and (4) giving guidance regarding the right to submit written representations if that party elects not to attend or be represented at the hearing pursuant to reg 17(1)(a) (see PARA 351) (reg 16(2)(d)). If the Authority fails to send a reply within the period specified in reg 9(1) (see PARA 348) and an extension of time is not granted under reg 13 (see PARA 347 note 8), the secretariat must fix a date for the hearing within 20 working days of the end of the period specified in reg 9(1): reg 16(3). As to the means of delivery see PARA 346 note 3.
5 Ie the notice referred to in the Gangmasters (Appeals) Regulations 2006, SI 2006/662, reg 16(2) (see note 4).
6 Gangmasters (Appeals) Regulations 2006, SI 2006/662, reg 16(4).
7 As to the appointed person see PARA 346.
8 Gangmasters (Appeals) Regulations 2006, SI 2006/662, reg 18(1). If he does so, the secretariat must notify the parties immediately of the change: reg 18(2). Any altered hearing date must not be before the date notified under reg 16 (see the text and notes 1–6) unless both parties agree: reg 18(3).
9 As to the meaning of 'decision with immediate effect' see PARA 347 note 10.
10 Ie the procedure set out in the Gangmasters (Appeals) Regulations 2006, SI 2006/662, reg 20 (see PARA 351).
11 Gangmasters (Appeals) Regulations 2006, SI 2006/662, reg 20(1).

351. The hearing.

Not less than ten working days[1] before the date fixed for an oral hearing[2], both parties must inform the secretariat[3] whether they intend to appear and, whether or not they intend to appear in person, whether they will be represented[4]; and not later than five working days prior to the oral hearing either party may submit written representations to the appointed person[5].

Unless the expedited procedure for appeals against decisions with immediate effect applies[6], the appointed person may give directions to the parties concerning the procedure to be followed at the hearing of the appeal[7], which must be in public unless the appointed person determines that it is appropriate, fair and reasonable for it, or any part of it, to be held in private[8]. The parties may each appear at the hearing and may be assisted by any person[9]; they also may each be represented by any person whether or not they appear at the hearing[10] and may give evidence, call witnesses, question any witnesses and make submissions on the evidence and issues in the appeal[11]. The appointed person may adjourn the hearing where he considers there are reasonable grounds to do so[12]. If the expedited procedure for appeals against decisions with immediate effect applies, the appointed person must determine the applicable procedure and time limits for the appeal[13] and may vary the procedure so determined at any time if he considers there are reasonable grounds to do so[14].

Where any irregularity resulting from a failure to comply with any provision of the regulations governing appeals[15] comes to the attention of the appointed person prior to finally determining the appeal, he may give such directions as he thinks appropriate to overcome any prejudice caused to a party by the irregularity[16].

1 As to the meaning of 'working day', and as to extensions of time limits, see PARA 347 note 8.
2 As to fixing the date for an oral hearing see PARA 350.
3 As to the secretariat see PARA 346.
4 Gangmasters (Appeals) Regulations 2006, SI 2006/662, reg 17(1)(a). If appearing or being represented, parties must also specify which, if any, witnesses they intend to call and enclose a signed witness statement for each witness containing the evidence the witness intends to give at the oral hearing: reg 17(1)(b). The secretariat must send a copy of any representations or witness statements received under reg 17 to the other party: reg 17(3). As to the means of delivery see PARA 346 note 3. If either party elects to appear at the hearing but fails without reasonable excuse to appear, the appointed person may proceed to hear the appeal and, provided he has considered any representations made by the absent party, determine it in the absence of that party: reg 19(5). As to the appointed person see PARA 346.
5 Gangmasters (Appeals) Regulations 2006, SI 2006/662, reg 17(2). This applies whether or not the party in question has elected to appear or be represented unless reg 9(3) (see PARA 348) applies in the case of the Gangmasters and Labour Abuse Authority: reg 17(2). As to the establishment, constitution and status of the Authority see PARA 320. The secretariat must send a copy of any representations or witness statements received under reg 17 to the other party: reg 17(3).
6 As to the meaning of 'decision with immediate effect' see PARA 347 note 10. As to when the expedited procedure applies see PARA 350.
7 Gangmasters (Appeals) Regulations 2006, SI 2006/662, reg 19(1).
8 Gangmasters (Appeals) Regulations 2006, SI 2006/662, reg 19(2).
9 Gangmasters (Appeals) Regulations 2006, SI 2006/662, reg 19(3).
10 Gangmasters (Appeals) Regulations 2006, SI 2006/662, reg 19(4).
11 Gangmasters (Appeals) Regulations 2006, SI 2006/662, reg 19(6). The appointed person may give directions at the hearing concerning the exercise of the rights specified in reg 19(6) where he considers that the directions are in the interests of justice: reg 19(7).
12 Gangmasters (Appeals) Regulations 2006, SI 2006/662, reg 19(8). The appointed person must send to the parties, not later than three working days after the date on which the hearing is adjourned, a notice informing them of the place, date and time of the adjourned hearing: reg 19(9).
13 Gangmasters (Appeals) Regulations 2006, SI 2006/662, reg 20(2). The appointed person must promptly notify each party of the applicable procedure to be followed and of any subsequent variation: reg 20(4).
14 Gangmasters (Appeals) Regulations 2006, SI 2006/662, reg 20(3). See note 13.
15 Ie the Gangmasters (Appeals) Regulations 2006, SI 2006/662.
16 Gangmasters (Appeals) Regulations 2006, SI 2006/662, reg 24(2). Such an irregularity does not of itself render the proceedings void: reg 24(1).

352. Determining the appeal and recording the decision.

The appointed person[1] must allow or dismiss the appeal[2]. His decision may be given orally at the end of the hearing or reserved[3], is binding on the parties[4], and must be recorded in a document, along with the reasons for it, as soon as possible[5].

The secretariat[6] must keep a register containing a copy of all decisions and statements of reasons issued by the appointed person[7].

1   As to the appointed person see PARA 346.
2   Gangmasters (Appeals) Regulations 2006, SI 2006/662, reg 21(1).
3   Gangmasters (Appeals) Regulations 2006, SI 2006/662, reg 22(1)(a).
4   Gangmasters (Appeals) Regulations 2006, SI 2006/662, reg 21(2).
5   Gangmasters (Appeals) Regulations 2006, SI 2006/662, reg 22(1)(b). The record of decision and the reasons for the decision are a matter of public record: reg 22(3). The decision must be signed and dated by the appointed person: reg 22(1)(c). The statement of reasons may be in summary form, and the document must also record the date from which the decision is to take effect: reg 22(1)(b). The appointed person must send to the parties a copy of a statement of the reasons for his decision, specifying the date from which the decision is to take effect: reg 22(2). As to the means of delivery see PARA 346 note 3.
6   As to the secretariat see PARA 346.
7   Gangmasters (Appeals) Regulations 2006, SI 2006/662, reg 23(1), (2). The register or any part of it may be kept by means of a computer (reg 23(3)) and must be open to inspection by any person without charge at all reasonable hours (reg 23(1)).

D. LIABILITY AND COMPLIANCE

353. Civil liability for contravention of legislation.

Contravention by a licence holder[1] of, or failure of a licence holder to comply with, any of the statutory provisions relating to the licensing of gangmasters[2] is actionable in so far as it causes damage[3]. This is without prejudice to any right of action or any defence which exists or may be available apart from the provisions of the Gangmasters (Licensing) Act 2004 and those provisions[4].

1   As to the meaning of 'licence holder' see PARA 325 note 1.
2   The statutory provisions relating to the Gangmasters (Licensing Conditions) Rules 2009, SI 2009/307 including the conditions in the Schedule (see PARA 320 et seq): r 7(1).
3   Gangmasters (Licensing Conditions) Rules 2009, SI 2009/307, r 7(1). 'Damage' includes the death of, or injury to, any person (including any disease and any impairment of that person's physical or mental condition): r 7(3).
4   Gangmasters (Licensing Conditions) Rules 2009, SI 2009/307, r 7(2).

354. Appointment and powers of compliance officers.

The Gangmasters and Labour Abuse Authority[1] may appoint officers ('compliance officers') to act for the purposes of verifying, from time to time or in such circumstances as the Authority may determine, compliance by a licence holder with the conditions of his licence[2]. Compliance officers have the same powers to request, obtain and supply information for these purposes as do enforcement officers[3] in pursuance of their statutory functions[4].

A person who:

(1)   intentionally obstructs a compliance officer who is acting in the exercise of his statutory functions[5];

(2)   without reasonable cause fails to comply with any requirement made of him by such an officer who is so acting[6]; or

(3)   in giving any information which is required of him by a compliance officer, makes a statement which is false in a material particular[7],

commits an offence[8].

A compliance officer must, if so required, produce some duly authenticated document showing his authority to act[9].

1   As to the establishment, constitution and status of the Authority see PARA 320.
2   Gangmasters (Licensing) Act 2004 s 15(4). As to the licensing of gangmasters see PARA 324 et seq; and as to conditions in licences see PARA 328 et seq.

3   As to the appointment of enforcement officers and their authority and powers generally see PARA
     314.
4   See the Gangmasters (Licensing) Act 2004 s 16; and PARA 317.
5   Gangmasters (Licensing) Act 2004 s 18(1)(a) (amended by the Immigration Act 2016 s 12(2)). A
     compliance officer's statutory functions are his functions under the Gangmasters (Licensing) Act
     2004 or functions conferred by virtue of the Police and Criminal Evidence Act 1984 s 114B. See
     also the Gangmasters (Licensing) Act 2004 s 16(6A), (7); and PARA 317.
6   Gangmasters (Licensing) Act 2004 s 18(1)(b).
7   Gangmasters (Licensing) Act 2004 s 18(2).
8   Until a day is appointed for the coming into force of the Criminal Justice Act 2003 s 281(5)
     (alteration of penalties for summary offences) a person guilty of an offence under the Gangmasters
     (Licensing) Act 2004 s 18(1) or (2) (see the text and notes 5–7) is liable on summary conviction
     to imprisonment for a term not exceeding six months, or to a fine not exceeding the statutory
     maximum, or to both (s 18(3)(a)); as from that day the maximum term of imprisonment on
     summary conviction is 51 weeks (unless the offence was committed before that day, in which case
     the maximum remains six months) (s 18(3)). At the date at which this volume states the law no
     such day had been appointed. As to the statutory maximum see PARA 58 note 1. As to the
     commission of offences by bodies corporate, unincorporated associations and partnerships see
     PARA 318.
9   Gangmasters (Licensing) Act 2004 s 15(5). If it appears to a compliance officer that any person
     with whom he is dealing while acting for the purposes of the Gangmasters (Licensing) Act 2004
     does not know that he is an officer so acting, the officer must identify himself as such to that
     person: s 15(6).

355. Communications requirements.

Any notification, notice or document (including a record) required to be given,
sent or made under the rules governing the licensing of gangmasters[1] must be in
writing[2].

Any notification, notice or document required or authorised by the rules
governing the licensing of gangmasters[3] to be given or sent to any person ('the
recipient') may be given or sent:
  (1)   by delivering it to the recipient[4];
  (2)   by leaving it at the recipient's last known address[5];
  (3)   by sending it by post to the recipient at that address[6]; or
  (4)   by transmitting it by means of an electronic communication, providing
          that the following conditions are met[7]:
          (a)   the recipient has stated a willingness to receive the document by
                 means of an electronic communication[8];
          (b)   the statement has not been withdrawn[9]; and
          (c)   the document was transmitted to an electronic address specified
                 by the recipient[10].

1   The rules governing the licensing of gangmasters are the Gangmasters (Licensing Conditions)
     Rules 2009, SI 2009/307 (see PARA 324 et seq).
2   Gangmasters (Licensing Conditions) Rules 2009, SI 2009/307, r 9(1).
3   See note 1.
4   Gangmasters (Licensing Conditions) Rules 2009, SI 2009/307, r 9(2)(a).
5   Gangmasters (Licensing Conditions) Rules 2009, SI 2009/307, r 9(2)(b).
6   Gangmasters (Licensing Conditions) Rules 2009, SI 2009/307, r 9(2)(c).
7   Gangmasters (Licensing Conditions) Rules 2009, SI 2009/307, r 9(2)(d).
8   Gangmasters (Licensing Conditions) Rules 2009, SI 2009/307, r 9(3)(a).
9   Gangmasters (Licensing Conditions) Rules 2009, SI 2009/307, r 9(3)(b). A statement may be:
     (1)   limited to documents of a specified description;
     (2)   require a document to be in a specified electronic form;
     (3)   modified or withdrawn:
            (a)   in a case where the statement was made by being published, by publishing the
                   modification or withdrawal in the same or in a similar manner;
            (b)   in any other case, by giving a notice to the person to whom the statement was
                   made: r 9(4).

For these purposes 'electronic address' includes any number or address used for the purposes of receiving electronic communications, 'electronic communication' means an electronic communication within the meaning of the Electronic Communications Act 2000, and 'specified' means specified in a statement made for the purposes of r 9(2)(a): r 9(5).

10　Gangmasters (Licensing Conditions) Rules 2009, SI 2009/307, r 9(3)(c).

(4) ACCOMMODATION FOR AGRICULTURAL WORKERS

356. Tied cottages and agricultural accommodation.

Persons employed in agriculture who occupy accommodation tied to or otherwise connected with their employment enjoy the benefit of statutory provisions concerned with security of tenure and protection from eviction[1], rehousing[2], fitness for habitation[3], and the obtaining of information about housing accommodation[4]. Provision is also made for the establishment of agricultural dwelling house advisory committees in Wales[5] to advise housing authorities and occupiers of agricultural dwellings in cases where an authority has been asked to provide suitable alternative accommodation for a person whose dwelling house is subject to a protected agricultural occupancy, a statutory tenancy or an assured agricultural occupancy, but whose house is required for a person to be employed in agriculture[5].

1　See the Rent (Agriculture) Act 1976 Pts I–III (ss 1–26) (see LANDLORD AND TENANT vol 64 (2016) PARA 1699 et seq); and the Housing Act 1988 ss 24, 25 (see LANDLORD AND TENANT vol 64 (2016) PARAS 1747–1750). The Protection from Eviction Act 1977 s 4 also provides statutory protection for the very limited class of agricultural workers who occupy premises under the terms of their employment as persons employed in agriculture but are not statutory tenants under the Rent (Agriculture) Act 1976 (ie licensees of certain bodies, such as local authorities, which are not covered by the Rent (Agriculture) Act 1976 but which provide tied accommodation): see LANDLORD AND TENANT vol 64 (2016) PARAS 1759–1760.

2　See the Rent (Agriculture) Act 1976 ss 27–28; and LANDLORD AND TENANT vol 64 (2016) PARAS 1752–1753.

3　See the Landlord and Tenant Act 1985 ss 8–10; and LANDLORD AND TENANT vol 62 (2016) PARA 311. For general provisions as to fitness for habitation see LANDLORD AND TENANT vol 62 (2016) PARAS 308–313.

4　See the Rent (Agriculture) Act 1976 Pt V (ss 30–31); and LANDLORD AND TENANT vol 64 (2016) PARAS 1755–1756.

5　There is to be an agricultural dwelling-house advisory committee in each area of an agricultural wages committee established under the Agricultural Wages Act 1948 (see PARA 296). Every agricultural dwelling-house advisory committee for an area in England is abolished: see the Enterprise and Regulatory Reform Act 2013 s 72(3).

357. Accommodation for temporary workers.

Local authorities[1] may make byelaws for securing the decent lodging and accommodation of hop-pickers and other persons engaged temporarily in picking, gathering or lifting fruit, flowers, bulbs, roots or vegetables within their district[2].

1　Ie, for these purposes, district and London borough councils and the Common Council of the City of London and, in Wales, county and county borough councils: Public Health Act 1936 ss 1(2), 343(1) (s 1 substituted by the Local Government Act 1972 Sch 14 para 1; and amended by the Local Government (Wales) Act 1994 Sch 9 para 3(1), (2)). As to the districts in England and their councils see LOCAL GOVERNMENT vol 69 (2009) PARA 22 et seq. As to the London boroughs and their councils see LONDON GOVERNMENT vol 71 (2013) PARAS 5, 14–15, 20 et seq. As to the Common Council of the City of London see LONDON GOVERNMENT vol 71 (2013) PARA 34 et seq. As to local authorities in Wales see LOCAL GOVERNMENT vol 69 (2009) PARAS 22–23, 37 et seq.

2   Public Health Act 1936 s 270.

11. CONTROL OF AGRICULTURAL POLLUTION

(1) APPLICATION OF ENVIRONMENTAL PROTECTION LEGISLATION TO AGRICULTURE

358. Introduction.

A number of specific statutory provisions have been enacted for the purpose of restricting or reducing the polluting effect of agricultural operations[1]. Particular provision is made for:

(1)   controlling statutory nuisances arising from the emission of smoke, fumes or gases from agricultural premises[2];

(2)   prohibiting the unlicensed burning of heather, rough grass, bracken, gorse or vaccinium[3];

(3)   prohibiting and restricting the burning of crop residues on agricultural land[4];

(4)   offences involving the lighting of fires which endanger the users of highways[5];

(5)   the setting of emissions limits for tractor engines[6];

(6)   preventing the pollution of controlled waters and carrying out anti-pollution works in respect of such waters[7];

(7)   the designation and protection of nitrate vulnerable zones[8];

(8)   restricting the production, marketing and use of persistent organic pollutants[9]; and

(9)   controlling the manufacture and use of pesticides, plant protection products, fertilisers, feeding stuffs and sludge[10].

1   See PARAS 361–372.

2   See the Environmental Protection Act 1990 Pt III (ss 79–84); the Clean Air Act 1993; PARA 361 note 1; and ENVIRONMENTAL QUALITY AND PUBLIC HEALTH vol 45 (2010) PARA 207 et seq; NUISANCE vol 78 (2010) PARA 155 et seq.

3   See the Hill Farming Act 1946 s 20; the Heather and Grass etc Burning (England) Regulations 2007, SI 2007/2003; the Heather and Grass etc Burning (Wales) Regulations 2008, SI 2008/1081; and PARAS 362–365.

4   See the Environmental Protection Act 1990 s 152; the Crop Residues (Burning) Regulations 1993, SI 1993/1366; and PARA 366 note 2, 6.

5   See the Highways Act 1980 s 161A; PARA 367; and HIGHWAYS, STREETS AND BRIDGES vol 55 (2012) PARA 384.

6   See the Agricultural or Forestry Tractors (Emission of Gaseous and Particulate Pollutants) Regulations 2002, SI 2002/1891; and PARA 368 note 1.

7   See the Water Resources Act 1991 ss 85–92, 97, 161, 161A–161D; Water Resources (Control of Pollution) (Silage, Slurry and Agricultural Fuel Oil) (England) Regulations 2010, SI 2010/639; the Water Resources (Control of Pollution) (Silage, Slurry and Agricultural Fuel Oil) (Wales) Regulations 2010, SI 2010/1493; PARA 369 note 5; and ENVIRONMENTAL QUALITY AND PUBLIC HEALTH vol 45 (2010) PARA 288 et seq.

8   See the Water Resources Act 1991 ss 94–96, Sch 12; the Nitrate Pollution Regulations 2015, SI 2015/668; PARA 370; and ENVIRONMENTAL QUALITY AND PUBLIC HEALTH vol 45 (2010) PARA 316.

9   See Council Regulation (EC) 850/2004 (OJ L229, 30.04.2004, p 5) on persistent organic pollutants; and the Persistent Organic Pollutants Regulations 2007, SI 2007/3106.

10 See the Food and Environment Protection Act 1985 ss 16–19, Sch 2; the Sludge (Use in Agriculture) Regulations 1989, SI 1989/1263; the Plant Protection Products Regulations 2011, SI 2011/2131.

359. Integrated pollution prevention and control.

A European regulatory system for integrated pollution prevention and control has been established, requiring member states to take appropriate measures to prevent environmental impacts from industrial emissions[1]. The system is applicable to a range of industrial activities and also to specified slaughterhouses, food and milk processing operations, installations for the intensive rearing of poultry and pigs, and installations for the disposal or recycling of animal carcasses and animal waste[2]. Integrated pollution and control was implemented in England and Wales by statute[3], under which the Secretary of State and the Welsh Ministers[4] were empowered to prescribe processes for which authorisations were required and descriptions of substances whose release into the environment were subject to control[5] and to establish emission limits and quality objectives[6]. These provisions have been replaced by a new statutory regime for integrated pollution prevention and control (IPPC), implementing the European regulatory system and further regulating and controlling polluting activities[7]. IPPC applies to a wider range of processes and activities including (in addition to a number of industrial, refining and extraction processes) the production of chemical fertilisers, plant health products and biocides, the storage of chemicals, waste management and recovery, animal slaughtering and food and milk processing operations, and the intensive rearing of poultry and pigs[8].

Certain agricultural activities, such as intensive farming, are regulated activities and are required to have an environmental permit[9]. A person who operates a regulated facility except under and to the extent authorised by an environmental permit, commits an offence[10]. It is also an offence for a person to fail to comply with or to contravene an environmental permit condition[11].

1   See European Parliament and Council Directive (EU) 2010/75 (OJ L334, 17.12.2010, p 17) on industrial emissions (integrated pollution and control); and ENVIRONMENTAL QUALITY AND PUBLIC HEALTH vol 45 (2010) PARA 6.
2   See European Parliament and Council Directive (EU) 2010/75 (OJ L334, 17.12.2010, p 17) Annex I; and ENVIRONMENTAL QUALITY AND PUBLIC HEALTH.
3   See the Environmental Protection Act 1990 Pt I (ss 1–28); and ENVIRONMENTAL QUALITY AND PUBLIC HEALTH vol 45 (2010) PARA 159 et seq.
4   As to the Secretary of State and the Welsh Ministers, and their powers, for these purposes see ENVIRONMENTAL QUALITY AND PUBLIC HEALTH vol 45 (2010) PARAS 58–59.
5   See the Environmental Protection Act 1990 ss 2, 3; and ENVIRONMENTAL QUALITY AND PUBLIC HEALTH vol 45 (2010) PARA 159.
6   See the Environmental Protection Act 1990 s 4; the Greenhouse Gas Emissions Trading Scheme Regulations 2012, SI 2012/3038; and ENVIRONMENTAL QUALITY AND PUBLIC HEALTH vol 45 (2010) PARAS 160, 260.
7   See the Pollution Prevention and Control Act 1999 (which repeals the Environmental Protection Act 1990 Pt I: see the Pollution Prevention and Control Act 1999 s 6(2), Sch 3); the Environmental Permitting (England and Wales) Regulations 2016, SI 2016/1154; and ENVIRONMENTAL QUALITY AND PUBLIC HEALTH.
8   See European Parliament and Council Directive (EU) 2010/75 (OJ L334, 17.12.2010, p 17); and ENVIRONMENTAL QUALITY AND PUBLIC HEALTH.
9   See the Environmental Permitting (England and Wales) Regulations 2016, SI 2016/1154, reg 8, Sch 1; and ENVIRONMENTAL QUALITY AND PUBLIC HEALTH.
10 See the Environmental Permitting (England and Wales) Regulations 2016, SI 2016/1154, reg 12(1)(a), 38(1); and ENVIRONMENTAL QUALITY AND PUBLIC HEALTH. A person found guilty of an offence under s 38(1) or (2) is liable on summary conviction to a fine or imprisonment for a term not exceeding 12 months, or to both and on conviction on indictment to a fine or imprisonment for a term not exceeding 5 years, or to both (reg 39(1)) unless the offence is in respect of a flood risk activity in which case he is liable on summary conviction to a fine or imprisonment for a term

not exceeding 12 months or to both or on conviction on indictment to a fine or imprisonment for a term not exceeding 2 years or both (reg 39(2)).

11 See the Environmental Permitting (England and Wales) Regulations 2016, SI 2016/1154, reg 39(2); and ENVIRONMENTAL QUALITY AND PUBLIC HEALTH. See note 1.

360. Assessments of environmental impacts.

Pursuant to the EU Directive on Environmental Impact Assessment[1] and the powers of the Secretary of State and the Welsh Ministers[2] to legislate in relation to the requirement for an assessment of the impact on the environment of projects likely to have significant effects on the environment and the conservation of natural habitats and of wild flora and fauna[3], provision has been made for the regulation of projects for the restructuring of rural land holdings and projects to increase the productivity for agriculture of uncultivated land[4]. Those provisions put structures in place for the pre-screening of such projects; require the submission of environmental statements, detailing the likely environmental effects of the proposed projects; and provide that pre-screened projects may be carried out only with the consent of, and subject to conditions imposed by, the Secretary of State or the Welsh Ministers[5].

1 See European Parliament and Council Directive (EU) 2011/92 (OJ L26, 28.01.2012, p 1) on the assessment of the effects of certain public and private projects on the environment.
2 As to the Secretary of State and the Welsh Ministers see PARA 390.
3 See the Environmental Impact Assessment (Agriculture) (England) (No 2) Regulations 2006, SI 2006/2522, preamble; and the Environmental Impact Assessment (Agriculture) (Wales) Regulations 2017, SI 2017/565, preamble.
4 See the Environmental Impact Assessment (Agriculture) (England) (No 2) Regulations 2006, SI 2006/2522; the Environmental Impact Assessment (Agriculture) (Wales) Regulations 2017, SI 2017/565; and AGRICULTURAL LAND AND ALLOTMENTS vol 1 (2017) PARAS 622–626.
5 See AGRICULTURAL LAND AND ALLOTMENTS vol 1 (2017) PARAS 622–626.

(2) STATUTORY NUISANCES AND CLEAN AIR

361. Statutory nuisances arising from agricultural operations.

Smoke, fumes or gases emitted from premises[1] so as to be prejudicial to health or a nuisance are statutory nuisances for the purposes of the Environmental Protection Act 1990[2] and are actionable both by local authorities[3], who are empowered to serve abatement notices[4] and to take civil proceedings in the High Court[5], and by aggrieved individuals, who may complain to a magistrates' court[6]. Local authorities are also required to cause their areas to be inspected from time to time in order to detect any statutory nuisances which ought to be dealt with under these provisions and to take appropriate steps for investigating complaints concerning statutory nuisances[7].

The provisions of the Clean Air Act 1993, which regulate the omission of smoke from chimneys, may also be relevant in the context of agricultural operations[8].

1 For the purposes of the Environmental Protection Act 1990 Pt III (ss 79–84) (see NUISANCE vol 78 (2010) PARA 155 et seq) 'premises' includes, inter alia, land: see s 79(7); and NUISANCE vol 78 (2010) PARA 160.
2 Environmental Protection Act 1990 s 79(1)(b), (c). The text refers to statutory nuisances for the purposes of Pt III (see NUISANCE vol 78 (2010) PARA 155 et seq).
3 As to local authorities for public health and environmental purposes see ENVIRONMENTAL QUALITY AND PUBLIC HEALTH vol 45 (2010) PARA 99; and as to local authorities generally see LOCAL GOVERNMENT vol 69 (2009) PARA 22 et seq.

4   See the Environmental Protection Act 1990 ss 80, 81; and NUISANCE vol 78 (2010) PARA 199
     et seq. Failure to comply with an abatement notice is an offence: see s 80(4); and NUISANCE vol 78
     (2010) PARA 203.
5   See the Environmental Protection Act 1990 s 81(5); and NUISANCE vol 78 (2010) PARA 205.
6   See the Environmental Protection Act 1990 s 82; and NUISANCE vol 78 (2010) PARAS 210–211.
     The court may order the abatement of the nuisance or prohibit its recurrence or may impose a fine:
     see s 82(2); and NUISANCE vol 78 (2010) PARA 211.
7   See the Environmental Protection Act 1990 s 79(1); and NUISANCE vol 78 (2010) PARAS 156,
     162 et seq.
8   See the Clean Air Act 1993; and ENVIRONMENTAL QUALITY AND PUBLIC HEALTH vol 45 (2010)
     PARA 207 et seq.

362. Burning of heather and rough grass.

The burning of heather, rough grass, bracken, gorse or vaccinium[1] is
prohibited, except under licence[2] issued by Natural England[3] or the Welsh
Ministers[4] (as applicable):

(1)   in relation to land in England, which is within an upland area, the
       period from 1 October in one year to 15 April in the following year,
       both dates inclusive[5];

(2)   in relation to land in Wales, which is within an upland area, the period
       from 1 October in one year to 31 March in the following year, both
       dates inclusive[6];

(3)   in relation to land in England, which is not within an upland area[7],
       between 1 April and 30 October inclusive[8]; and

(4)   in relation to land in Wales, which is not within an upland area[9],
       between 31 March and 16 April and between 30 September and 1
       November[10].

In addition, at no time of the year may any person commence to burn any such
vegetation between sunset and sunrise[11]. There are also further restrictions as to
the extents of areas on which permitted burning may take place[12].

Contravention of any of these provisions is an offence[13]. Natural England and
the Welsh Ministers are also empowered to issue 'burning notices' in respect of
contraventions[14].

1   Ie 'specified vegetation' for the purposes of the Heather and Grass etc Burning (England)
     Regulations 2007, SI 2007/2003 (see reg 2) and the Heather and Grass etc Burning (Wales)
     Regulations 2008, SI 2008/1081 (see reg 2).
2   As to the issue of licences see PARAS 363–364.
3   As to Natural England see the Natural Environment and Rural Communities Act 2006 Pt 1 Ch
     1 (ss 1–16); and OPEN SPACES AND COUNTRYSIDE vol 78 (2010) PARA 523.
4   As to the Welsh Ministers see PARA 390.
5   Heather and Grass etc Burning (England) Regulations 2007, SI 2007/2003, regs 2, 6(1)(a). These
     regulations and the Heather and Grass etc Burning (Wales) Regulations 2008, SI 2008/1081, reg
     6(1)(a) are made under the Hill Farming Act 1946 s 20(1) (amended by the Hill Farming Act 1985
     s 1; and SI 1955/554), under which the Secretary of State and the Welsh Ministers are empowered
     by regulations to make provision for regulating or prohibiting the burning of heather, grass,
     bracken, gorse and vaccinium on land in England or Wales, and it is provided that any such
     regulations may be made so as to extend to the whole of England and Wales or to any specified
     area therein, may regulate or prohibit the burning of heather, grass, bracken, gorse and vaccinium
     at all times or during such period as may be specified in the regulations, and may contain different
     provisions with respect to land in different parts of England and Wales and to different periods.
     Breach of the Heather and Grass etc Burning (England) Regulations 2007, SI 2007/2003, regs 2,
     6(1)(a) constitutes a non-compliance with the standards for good agricultural and environment
     conditions: see the Common Agricultural Policy (Control and Enforcement, Cross-Compliance,
     Scrutiny of Transactions and Appeals) Regulations 2014, SI 2014/3263, Sch 2 para 2; and PARA
     3. In relation to Wales, provision, closely corresponding to these provisions is also made pursuant

to the implementation of the Common Agricultural Policy: see the Common Agricultural Policy (Integrated Administration and Control System and Enforcement and Cross Compliance) (Wales) Regulations 2014, SI 2014/3223, Sch 1 para 9; and PARA 3 note 2.

These provisions do not apply to land cultivated as private gardens or allotment gardens: see the Heather and Grass etc Burning (England) Regulations 2007, SI 2007/2003, reg 3; and the Heather and Grass etc Burning (Wales) Regulations 2008, SI 2008/1081, reg 3. As to allotment gardens see AGRICULTURAL LAND AND ALLOTMENTS vol 1 (2017) PARA 424 note 11. Additionally, the Heather and Grass etc Burning (England) Regulations 2007, SI 2007/2003, regs 6(1)(b)–(e), 8, 9 and the Heather and Grass etc Burning (Wales) Regulations 2008, SI 2008/1081, regs 5(2)(c), 6–8 do not apply to the burning of relevant vegetation carried out by or under authority on railway land (see the Heather and Grass etc Burning (England) Regulations 2007, SI 2007/2003, reg 4; and the Heather and Grass etc Burning (Wales) Regulations 2008, SI 2008/1081, reg 4).

6   Heather and Grass etc Burning (Wales) Regulations 2008, SI 2008/1081, regs 2, 6(1)(a).
7   'Upland areas' in England are identified for these purposes by reference to departmental maps: see the Heather and Grass etc Burning (England) Regulations 2007, SI 2007/2003, reg 2.
8   Heather and Grass etc Burning (England) Regulations 2007, SI 2007/2003, regs 2, 6(1)(a).
9   'Upland areas' in Wales are identified for these purposes by reference to departmental maps: see the Heather and Grass etc Burning (Wales) Regulations 2008, SI 2008/1081, reg 2(1).
10   Heather and Grass etc Burning (Wales) Regulations 2008, SI 2008/1081, regs 2, 6(1)(a).
11   Heather and Grass etc Burning (England) Regulations 2007, SI 2007/2003, reg 5(1); Heather and Grass etc Burning (Wales) Regulations 2008, SI 2008/1081, reg 5(1).
12   A person must not, except under and in accordance with a licence issued by Natural England or, in relation to Wales, the Welsh Ministers:
  (1)   burn, in a burning season (ie the dates between which unlicensed burning is permissible: see the text and notes 5–7), a single area, or two or more areas within 5 metres of each other with a combined area, of more than 0.5 hectares of specified vegetation which has a slope of more than 45 degrees or where more than half of that area is covered by exposed rock or scree (Heather and Grass etc Burning (England) Regulations 2007, SI 2007/2003, reg 6(1)(b); Health and Grass etc Burning (Wales) Regulations 2008, SI 2008/1081, reg 6(1)(b));
  (2)   burn, in a single burn, an area of more than 10 hectares of specified vegetation (Heather and Grass etc Burning (England) Regulations 2007, SI 2007/2003, reg 6(1)(c); Health and Grass etc Burning (Wales) Regulations 2008, SI 2008/1081, reg 6(1)(c));
  (3)   burn, in a burning season, specified vegetation in a manner which exposes a single area, or two or more areas within 5 metres of each other with a combined area, of more than 0.5 hectares of bare soil or an area of bare soil which extends more than 25 metres along the bank of a watercourse and is more than a metre wide at all points (for a continuous stretch of more than 25 metres), measured from the edge of the bank of the watercourse (Heather and Grass etc Burning (England) Regulations 2007, SI 2007/2003, reg 6(1)(d); Health and Grass etc Burning (Wales) Regulations 2008, SI 2008/1081, reg 6(1)(d)); or
  (4)   in connection with the burning of specified vegetation, leave soil smouldering for more than 48 hours (Heather and Grass etc Burning (England) Regulations 2007, SI 2007/2003, reg 6(1)(e); Health and Grass etc Burning (Wales) Regulations 2008, SI 2008/1081, reg 6(1)(e)).
  For these purposes 'area of bare soil' means an area of soil of which no more than 2% is covered by vegetation or plant litter; and 'watercourse' means any natural or artificial channel through which water flows, whether some or all of the time, including rivers, streams, ditches, grips, drains, cuts, culverts, dykes and sluices, but excluding mains and other pipes burning of specified vegetation, leave soil smouldering for more than 48 hours (Heather and Grass etc Burning (England) Regulations 2007, SI 2007/2003, reg 6(2); Health and Grass etc Burning (Wales) Regulations 2008, SI 2008/1081, reg 6(2)).
13   See the Hill Farming Act 1946 s 20(2) (amended by virtue of the Criminal Justice Act 1982 s 46), which provides that contravention of any of the provisions of the Heather and Grass etc Burning (England) Regulations 2007, SI 2007/2003, or the Heather and Grass etc Burning (Wales) Regulations 2008, SI 2008/1081, is punishable on summary conviction by a fine not exceeding level 3 on the standard scale. As to the standard scale and the powers of magistrates' courts to issue fines on summary conviction see SENTENCING vol 92 (2015) PARA 176.
14   If Natural England or the Welsh Ministers believe that specified vegetation has been burnt in contravention of the Heather and Grass etc Burning (England) Regulations 2007, SI 2007/2003 or the Heather and Grass etc Burning (Wales) Regulations 2008, SI 2008/1081, it may serve a notice (a 'burning notice') on the occupier of the land concerned requiring him to notify them, in the manner specified in the burning notice, of any proposed burning of any specified vegetation on

any land occupied by him from the date it is served: Heather and Grass etc Burning (England) Regulations 2007, SI 2007/2003, reg 8(1); Heather and Grass etc Burning (Wales) Regulations 2008, SI 2008/1081, reg 8(1). A burning notice may not apply for more than two years from the date the notice is served: Heather and Grass etc Burning (England) Regulations 2007, SI 2007/2003, reg 8(2); Heather and Grass etc Burning (Wales) Regulations 2008, SI 2008/1081, reg 8(2). A person may, within 28 days of the date of the service of a burning notice on him, make representations against the notice to a person appointed for the purpose by the Secretary of State or the Welsh Ministers, as appropriate: Heather and Grass etc Burning (England) Regulations 2007, SI 2007/2003, reg 9(1), (2); Heather and Grass etc Burning (Wales) Regulations 2008, SI 2008/1081, reg 9(1), (2). The appointed person must consider the representations and report in writing to the Secretary of State or the Welsh Ministers, as appropriate, who must give written notice of his final determination and the reasons for it: Heather and Grass etc Burning (England) Regulations 2007, SI 2007/2003, reg 9(3), (4); Heather and Grass etc Burning (Wales) Regulations 2008, SI 2008/1081, reg 9(3), (4). Where a person makes representations against a burning notice, the burning notice has effect until it is revoked by the Secretary of State or withdrawn by Natural England, or revoked or withdrawn by the Welsh Ministers, or its period expires: Heather and Grass etc Burning (England) Regulations 2007, SI 2007/2003, reg 9(5); Heather and Grass etc Burning (Wales) Regulations 2008, SI 2008/1081, reg 9(5). As to the Secretary of State and the Welsh Ministers see PARA 390.

363. Application for licences to burn heather and rough grass.

A person may apply to Natural England[1], or in relation to Wales, the Welsh Ministers, for a licence permitting him to burn heather, rough grass, bracken, gorse or vaccinium[2] outside the burning season[3] or in a manner otherwise prohibited[4].

1　As to Natural England see the Natural Environment and Rural Communities Act 2006 Pt 1 Ch 1 (ss 1–16); and OPEN SPACES AND COUNTRYSIDE vol 78 (2010) PARA 523. As to the Welsh Ministers see PARA 390.

2　Ie 'specified vegetation': see PARA 362 note 1.

3　As to the burning season see PARA 362.

4　Heather and Grass etc Burning (England) Regulations 2007, SI 2007/2003, reg 7(1); Heather and Grass etc Burning (Wales) Regulations 2008, SI 2008/1081, reg 7(1). For the other prohibitions on burning see PARA 362. Any such application must be made in a manner specified by Natural England, or the Welsh Ministers, and must be made not less than 28 days before the date (or the first date if more than one) on which the applicant proposes to burn, and:

    (1)　in the case of a burn (or burns) intended to take place during a burning season, not before the end of the preceding burning season (Heather and Grass etc Burning (England) Regulations 2007, SI 2007/2003, reg 7(2)(a); Heather and Grass etc Burning (Wales) Regulations 2008, SI 2008/1081, reg 7(2)(a)); or

    (2)　in the case of a burn (or burns) intended to take place outside a burning season, not more than 56 days before the date (or the last date if more than one) on which the applicant proposes to burn (Heather and Grass etc Burning (England) Regulations 2007, SI 2007/2003, reg 7(2)(b); Heather and Grass etc Burning (Wales) Regulations 2008, SI 2008/1081, reg 7(2)(b)).

364. Grant or refusal of licences to burn heather and rough grass.

Except in the case of land forming part of an operational railway, Natural England or the Welsh Ministers (as appropriate)[1] may grant a licence for burning heather, rough grass, bracken, gorse or vaccinium[2] outside the burning season[3] only[4] if it is satisfied that the proposed burning is necessary or expedient for the conservation, enhancement or management of the natural environment for the benefit of present and future generations or the safety of any person[5]. Where the land forms part of an operational railway in England or railway land in Wales, Natural England and the Welsh Ministers may grant a licence only if satisfied that the proposed burning is necessary or expedient for good maintenance of the land or for the purpose of pest control[6].

If Natural England or the Welsh Ministers (as appropriate) propose not to issue a licence[7], to issue a licence in respect of part only of the land to which the application relates[8], or to issue a licence subject to any conditions[9], they must notify the applicant in writing of the proposed decision and of the reasons for it[10].

1   As to Natural England see the Natural Environment and Rural Communities Act 2006 Pt 1 Ch 1 (ss 1–16); and OPEN SPACES AND COUNTRYSIDE vol 78 (2010) PARA 523. As to the Welsh Ministers see PARA 390.
2   Ie 'specified vegetation': see PARA 362 note 1.
3   As to the burning season see PARA 362.
4   As to the requirement for a licence and the making of applications see PARAS 362–363.
5   Heather and Grass etc Burning (England) Regulations 2007, SI 2007/2003, reg 7(3)(b); Heather and Grass etc Burning (Wales) Regulations 2008, SI 2008/1081, reg 7(3)(b).
6   Heather and Grass etc Burning (England) Regulations 2007, SI 2007/2003, reg 7(3)(a); Heather and Grass etc Burning (Wales) Regulations 2008, SI 2008/1081, reg 7(3)(a).
7   Heather and Grass etc Burning (England) Regulations 2007, SI 2007/2003, reg 7(4)(a); Heather and Grass etc Burning (Wales) Regulations 2008, SI 2008/1081, reg 7(4)(a).
8   Heather and Grass etc Burning (England) Regulations 2007, SI 2007/2003, reg 7(4)(b); Heather and Grass etc Burning (Wales) Regulations 2008, SI 2008/1081, reg 7(4)(b).
9   Heather and Grass etc Burning (England) Regulations 2007, SI 2007/2003, reg 7(4)(c); Heather and Grass etc Burning (Wales) Regulations 2008, SI 2008/1081, reg 7(4)(c).
10 Heather and Grass etc Burning (England) Regulations 2007, SI 2007/2003, reg 7(4); Heather and Grass etc Burning (Wales) Regulations 2008, SI 2008/1081, reg 7(4).

365. Regulation of permitted burning.

A person may not at any time burn any heather, rough grass, bracken, gorse or vaccinium[1] on any land[2] unless:

(1)   there are where the burning is taking place sufficient persons and equipment to control and regulate the burning during the entire period of the operation[3]; and

(2)   he takes, before commencing burning and during the entire period of the operation, all reasonable precautions to prevent injury or damage to any adjacent land, or to any person or thing whatsoever on that land[4].

In Wales, it is additionally provided that a person may not at any time burn any heather, rough grass, bracken, gorse or vaccinium on any land unless he has prepared a burning plan and is proposing to burn in accordance with provisions of that plan[5]. Further, in relation to Wales, a person may not at any time burn any heather, rough grass, bracken, gorse or vaccinium on any land unless he has not less than 24 hours and not more than 72 hours before commencing burning on any land, given notice in writing of the date or dates, time and place at which, and the extent of the area on which it is the intention to burn to any other person who has an interest in that land either as owner or occupier, and except in the case of any burning carried out on railway land, to any other person whom is known, or could with reasonable diligence have been discovered, to be in charge of any land adjacent to that on which the burning is to take place[6].

Contravention of these provisions is an offence in respect of which Natural England is, and the Welsh Ministers are, empowered to issue a 'burning notice'[7].

1   Ie 'specified vegetation': see PARA 362.
2   Ie including under licence (see PARA 362 et seq).
3   Heather and Grass etc Burning (England) Regulations 2007, SI 2007/2003, reg 5(2)(a); Heather and Grass etc Burning (Wales) Regulations 2008, SI 2008/1081, reg 5(2)(b).
4   Heather and Grass etc Burning (England) Regulations 2007, SI 2007/2003, reg 5(2)(b); Heather and Grass etc Burning (Wales) Regulations 2008, SI 2008/1081, reg 5(2)(c).
5   Heather and Grass etc Burning (Wales) Regulations 2008, SI 2008/1081, reg 5(2)(a).
6   Heather and Grass etc Burning (Wales) Regulations 2008, SI 2008/1081, reg 5(2)(d).

7   See the Hill Farming Act 1946 s 20(2); the Heather and Grass etc Burning (England) Regulations 2007, SI 2007/2003, regs 8, 9; Heather and Grass etc Burning (Wales) Regulations 2008, SI 2008/1081, reg 8, 9; and PARA 362 notes 5, 13.

366. Burning of crop residues.

The Secretary of State and the Welsh Ministers[1] may by regulations prohibit or restrict the burning of crop residues[2] on agricultural land[3] by persons engaged in agriculture[4], and may by the same or other regulations provide exemptions from any prohibition or restriction so imposed[5]. Pursuant to these powers regulations have been made prohibiting the burning on agricultural land, by any person engaged in agriculture, of any crop residue[6] of a specified kind[7] unless the burning is for the purposes of education or research[8], disease control or the elimination of plant pests[9], or the disposal of straw stack remains or broken bales[10], and providing that even such burning as is allowed under these provisions[11] may be undertaken only in accordance with a number of specified restrictions and requirements as to: the time of burning; the area of residue to be burned; the existence and use of fire-breaks[12]; the proximity of the residue to other areas of burning, trees and hedgerows, combustible material, buildings, utility installations, roads and railways; the giving of notice of burning; the qualifications and skills of the persons undertaking the burning; the availability of extinguishing equipment and materials; and the disposal of ashes[13].

Pursuant to the enactment of these provisions, all local authority byelaws dealing with the burning of crop residues on agricultural land[14] have been repealed[15].

1   As to the Secretary of State and the Welsh Ministers see PARA 390.
2   For these purposes 'crop residue' means straw or stubble or any other crop residue: Environmental Protection Act 1990 s 152(5). See also note 6.
3   As to the meaning of 'agricultural land' see PARA 10.
4   As to the meaning of 'agriculture' see PARA 10.
5   Environmental Protection Act 1990 s 152(1), (5). The power to make regulations includes power:
       (1)   to make different provision for different areas or circumstances (s 152(3)(a));
       (2)   where burning of a crop residue is restricted, to impose requirements to be complied with before or after the burning (s 152(3)(b));
       (3)   to create offences subject to the limitation that no offence may be made punishable otherwise than on summary conviction and the fine prescribed for the offence may not exceed level 5 on the standard scale (s 152(3)(c)); and
       (4)   to make such incidental, supplemental and transitional provision as the Secretary of State considers or the Welsh Ministers consider appropriate (s 152(3)(d)).
    As to the standard scale and the powers of magistrates' courts to issue fines on summary conviction see SENTENCING vol 92 (2015) PARA 176. For general provisions as to regulations and orders under the Environmental Protection Act 1990 see ENVIRONMENTAL QUALITY AND PUBLIC HEALTH vol 45 (2010) PARA 61. Regulations providing an exemption from any prohibition or restriction may make the exemption applicable:
       (a)   in all, or only in specified, areas (s 152(2)(a));
       (b)   to all, or only to specified, crop residues (s 152(2)(b)); or
       (c)   in all, or only in specified, circumstances (s 152(2)(c)).
6   For these purposes 'crop residue' means straw or stubble or any other crop residue remaining on the land after harvesting of the crop grown thereon: Crop Residues (Burning) Regulations 1993, SI 1993/1366, reg 2(1).
7   The specified crop residues are: cereal straw; cereal stubble; and residues of oil-seed rape and field beans or peas harvested dry: Crop Residues (Burning) Regulations 1993, SI 1993/1366, reg 4, Sch 1. A person who contravenes reg 4 or reg 5 is guilty of an offence and is liable on summary conviction to a fine not exceeding level 5 on the standard scale: reg 6. For general provisions as to the commission of offences under the Environmental Protection Act 1990 see ENVIRONMENTAL QUALITY AND PUBLIC HEALTH vol 45 (2010) PARAS 145–146.
8   Crop Residues (Burning) Regulations 1993, SI 1993/1366, reg 4(a).

9   Crop Residues (Burning) Regulations 1993, SI 1993/1366, reg 4(b).
10 Crop Residues (Burning) Regulations 1993, SI 1993/1366, reg 4(c).
11 Ie the burning of the residues referred to in note 7 to which an exemption specified in the text and
    notes 8–9 applies, and the burning of any linseed residues: Crop Residues (Burning) Regulations
    1993, SI 1993/1366, reg 5(a), (b).
12 'Fire-break' means an area of ground of which the surface consists wholly or mainly of substances
    other than combustible material: Crop Residues (Burning) Regulations 1993, SI 1993/1366, reg
    2(1).
13 See the Crop Residues (Burning) Regulations 1993, SI 1993/1366, reg 5, Sch 2. See note 7.
14 Ie all relevant byelaws made for the suppression of nuisances under the Local Government Act
    1972 s 235(1) (see LOCAL GOVERNMENT vol 69 (2009) PARA 555).
15 See the Burning of Crop Residues (Repeal of Byelaws) Order 1992, SI 1992/693 (made under the
    Environmental Protection Act 1990 s 152(4), which enables the making of orders repealing any
    byelaws of local authorities dealing with the burning of crop residues on agricultural land where
    it appears appropriate to do so in consequence of any regulations made under s 152(1)–(3) (see
    the text and notes 1–5)).

367. Fires affecting highways.

A person who lights a fire on any land not forming part of a highway which
consists of or comprises a carriageway or directs or permits a fire to be lit on any
such land is guilty of an offence if in consequence thereof a user of any highway
which consists of or comprises a carriageway is injured, interrupted or endangered
by, or by smoke from, that fire or any other fire caused by that fire[1], unless he can
prove that at the time the fire was lit he was satisfied on reasonable grounds that
it was unlikely that users of any such highway would be so injured, interrupted or
endangered and that he either did all he reasonably could to prevent users of any
such highway from being so injured, interrupted or endangered or had a
reasonable excuse for not doing so[2].

1   See the Highways Act 1980 s 161A(1); and HIGHWAYS, STREETS AND BRIDGES vol 55 (2012)
    PARA 384.
2   See the Highways Act 1980 s 161A(2); and HIGHWAYS, STREETS AND BRIDGES vol 55 (2012)
    PARA 384.

368. Emissions from tractor engines.

No person may enter into service for the first time[1]:

(1)   any relevant tractor engine[2] (other than a replacement engine[3]) that does
        not comply with the determined limit values[4] for the category[5] to which
        it belongs[6];

(2)   any replacement engine that does not comply with the limit values for
        the category to which the engine it replaces belonged[7]; or

(3)   any agricultural or forestry tractor fitted with a relevant engine unless
        either the engine complies with the limit values for the category to which
        it would have belonged if it had been manufactured and entered into
        service on the day the tractor was entered into service for the first time;
        or certain conditions apply[8].

These provisions are enforceable by the Secretary of State[9], who may also, on the
application of the manufacturer of an end of series engine[10] and subject to
specified restrictions, designate that engine as an exempted engine[11].

1   These provisions apply in respect of the entering of engines into service on or after a specified date
    (the 'relevant date'), depending on the category of engine in question, ranging from 30 June 2001
    to 30 September 2016: see the Agricultural or Forestry Tractors (Emission of Gaseous and
    Particulate Pollutants) Regulations 2002, SI 2002/1891, regs 2, 4(4), Sch 1 (reg 2 amended, and
    regs 3, 4 substituted by SI 2006/2393, Agricultural or Forestry Tractors (Emission of Gaseous and
    Particulate Pollutants) Regulations 2002, SI 2002/1891,reg 4(3) substituted and 4(3A), (3B)
    added and Sch 1 substituted by SI 2013/3171). The regulations implement Council Directive (EC)

2000/25 (OJ L173, 12.07.2000, p 1) on action to be taken against the emission of gaseous and particulate pollutants by engines intended to power agricultural or forestry tractors, arts 4.3–4.5 which have been repealed and replaced by European Parliament and Council Regulation (EU) 167/2013 (OJ L60, 2.3.2013, p 1–51) on the approval and market surveillance of agricultural and forestry vehicles.

2   Ie any tractor engine (whether or not for the time being installed in a tractor) which falls within a category specified in the Agricultural or Forestry Tractors (Emission of Gaseous and Particulate Pollutants) Regulations 2002, SI 2002/1891, Sch 1 (see note 1) unless it is an engine which is installed or intended to be installed in an agricultural or forestry tractor for export to a state which is not a member state (reg 3(a) (as substituted: see note 1)), an exempted engine (reg 3(b) (as so substituted)) or an engine which has, at any time in the past, been placed on the market under a flexibility scheme (reg 3(c) (as so substituted)). 'Tractor engine' means any internal combustion engine operating on the compression ignition principle which is intended to power an agricultural or forestry tractor and 'engine' is to be construed accordingly; and 'agricultural or forestry tractor' and 'tractor' mean any motor vehicle, fitted with wheels on at least two axles or with caterpillar tracks, where the main function of the vehicle lies in its tractive power and it is specifically designed to tow, push, carry or power certain tools, machinery or trailers intended for agricultural or forestry use: reg 2 (as amended: see note 1). 'Exempted engine' means an end of series engine (see note 10) designated in accordance with reg 5 (see the text and notes 10–11); 'flexibility scheme' means a scheme, in accordance with Council Directive (EC) 2000/25 (OJ L173, 12.07.2000, p 1) art 3a, Annex IV (replaced: see note 1, for the placing on the market of tractor engines or tractors which has been approved by the UK type approval authority under the provisions of Sch 3 and which consists of the exemption procedure permitting the placing on the market and entry into service of a limited number of such engines, or tractors fitted with engines, approved in accordance with the requirements of the emission limits stage immediately preceding the one which would otherwise be applicable, or a flexibility scheme authorised by any other approval authority in accordance with Council Directive (EC) 2000/25 (OJ L173, 12.07.2000, p 1) art 3a, Annex IV and 'placing on the market' means the action of making an engine or tractor available for the first time on the market, for payment or free of charge, with a view to distribution or use in a member state (and, in particular, when a tractor engine is supplied by an engine manufacturer to a tractor manufacturer, it is considered to be placed on the market; and when a tractor is placed on the market, its engine is considered to be placed on the market): Agricultural or Forestry Tractors (Emission of Gaseous and Particulate Pollutants) Regulations 2002, SI 2002/1891, reg 2 (definition 'flexibility scheme' substituted by SI 2013/3171). As to type approval certificates generally see ROAD TRAFFIC vol 89 (2011) PARAS 503–518.

3   'Replacement engine' means a newly built relevant engine (ie a tractor engine to which these provisions apply by virtue of the Agricultural or Forestry Tractors (Emission of Gaseous and Particulate Pollutants) Regulations 2002, SI 2002/1891, reg 3 (see note 2)) which replaces an engine in a machine, which has been supplied for this purpose only, and to which a label bearing the text 'REPLACEMENT ENGINE' is affixed or where the owner's manual in relation to the engine in question contains the text 'REPLACEMENT ENGINE': reg 2 (as amended: see note 1).

4   The applicable limit values are determined in accordance with the Agricultural or Forestry Tractors (Emission of Gaseous and Particulate Pollutants) Regulations 2002, SI 2002/1891, reg 2, Sch 1 (see note 1).

5   The categories are specified by the Agricultural or Forestry Tractors (Emission of Gaseous and Particulate Pollutants) Regulations 2002, SI 2002/1891, reg 2, Sch 1 (see note 1).

6   Agricultural or Forestry Tractors (Emission of Gaseous and Particulate Pollutants) Regulations 2002, SI 2002/1891, reg 4(1) (as substituted: see note 1).

7   Agricultural or Forestry Tractors (Emission of Gaseous and Particulate Pollutants) Regulations 2002, SI 2002/1891, reg 4(2) (as substituted: see note 1).

8   Agricultural or Forestry Tractors (Emission of Gaseous and Particulate Pollutants) Regulations 2002, SI 2002/1891, reg 4(3) (as substituted: see note 1). As to the conditions see reg 4(3A), (3B) (as so substituted).

9   Agricultural or Forestry Tractors (Emission of Gaseous and Particulate Pollutants) Regulations 2002, SI 2002/1891, regs 2, 6(1). As to the Secretary of State see PARA 390. Proceedings for an offence under these provisions are instituted by the Secretary of State: reg 6(2)(a). For further provision with regard to offences, enforcement and other matters see reg 6(3), Sch 2.

10 Ie a tractor engine, whether or not installed in a tractor, which has not been entered into service for the first time, is stored within the territory of any member state; and either was manufactured to conform with an EC type approval certificate granted on the basis of compliance with EC type approval requirements which did not include the requirements which are currently in force in accordance with Council Directive (EC) 2000/25 (OJ L173, 12.07.2000, p 1) or was not

manufactured to comply with any EC type approval certificate: Agricultural or Forestry Tractors (Emission of Gaseous and Particulate Pollutants) Regulations 2002, SI 2002/1891, reg 2.

11   Agricultural or Forestry Tractors (Emission of Gaseous and Particulate Pollutants) Regulations 2002, SI 2002/1891, reg 5(1). The manufacturer must before the relevant date submit an application to the Secretary of State which specifies the engines to which the application relates (reg 5(2)(a)), any relevant technical or economic issues (reg 5(2)(b)), and the total number of tractor engines placed on the market by that manufacturer during the period of 12 months expiring on the previous calendar year (reg 5(2)(c)).

The Secretary of State may not designate an engine for these purposes if a period of 12 months has elapsed since the relevant date for that engine (reg 5(3)(a)) or the number of engines so designated by him during the current calendar year exceeds, or would exceed, 10% of the number of tractor engines placed on the market by the manufacturer making the application during the immediately preceding calendar year (reg 5(3)(b)).

The Secretary of State must, within one month of designating an engine for these purposes, send to the competent authorities of the other member states particulars of, and reasons for, the exemption granted to the manufacturer: reg 5(4). The Secretary of State must at the end of each calendar year (ie the period of 12 months expiring on 31 December) send to the European Commission a list of designations made under the Agricultural or Forestry Tractors (Emission of Gaseous and Particulate Pollutants) Regulations 2002, SI 2002/1891 during the year, specifying the technical or economic reasons on which each designation is based: reg 5(5).

(3) PROTECTION OF SOIL AND WATERS

369. Pollution of waters arising from agricultural operations.

A person who knowingly permits a water discharge activity[1] or groundwater activity[2], except under and to the extent authorised by an environmental permit, commits an offence[3].

Provision is made empowering the Environment Agency or, in relation to Wales, the Natural Resources Body for Wales[7] to carry out or require the carrying out of anti-pollution works in respect of controlled waters, if necessary at the polluter's expense[4]; empowering the Secretary of State to require persons in possession of poisonous, noxious or polluting matter to take precautions against the pollution of controlled waters by such matter[5]; and for the establishment of codes of good agricultural practice for the protection of controlled waters from pollution[6].

1   Several activities fall within the definition of 'water discharge activity' but for the purposes of agricultural activities, the follow are of relevance:
    (1)   the discharge or entry to inland freshwaters, coastal waters or relevant territorial waters of any poisonous, noxious or polluting matter, waste matter or trade effluent or sewage effluent (Environmental Permitting (England and Wales) Regulations 2016, SI 2016/1154, Sch 21, para 3(1)(a));
    (2)   the discharge from land through a pipe into the sea outside the seaward limits of relevant territorial waters of any trade effluent or sewage effluent (Sch 21 para 3(1)(b));
    (3)   the cutting or uprooting of a substantial amount of vegetation in any inland freshwaters or so near to any such waters that it falls into them, where it is not reasonable to take steps to remove the vegetation from these waters (Sch 21 para 3(1)(d)).
For the full definition of 'water discharge activity' see ENVIRONMENTAL QUALITY AND PUBLIC HEALTH.

2   Several activities fall within the definition of 'groundwater activity' but for the purposes of agricultural activities, the follow are of relevance:
    (1)   the discharge of a pollutant that results in the direct input of that pollutant to groundwater;
    (2)   the discharge of a pollutant in circumstances that might lead to an indirect input of that pollutant to groundwater;
    (3)   any other discharge that might lead to the direct or indirect input of a pollutant to groundwater;

(4)   an activity in respect of which the appropriate notice has been served and has taken effect;

(5)   an activity that might lead to a discharge mentioned in head (1), (2) or (3) where that activity is carried on as part of the operation of a regulated facility of another class: Environmental Permitting (England and Wales) Regulations 2016, SI 2016/1154, Sch 22 para 3(1).

For the full definition of 'groundwater activity' see ENVIRONMENTAL QUALITY AND PUBLIC HEALTH.

3   See the Environmental Permitting (England and Wales) Regulations 2016, SI 2016/1154, reg 12(1)(b), 38(1); and ENVIRONMENTAL QUALITY AND PUBLIC HEALTH. A person found guilty of an offence under s 38(1) or (2) is liable on summary conviction to a fine or imprisonment for a term not exceeding 12 months, or to both and on conviction on indictment to a fine or imprisonment for a term not exceeding 5 years, or to both (reg 39(1)) unless the offence is in respect of a flood risk activity in which case he is liable on summary conviction to a fine or imprisonment for a term not exceeding 12 months or to both or on conviction on indictment to a fine or imprisonment for a term not exceeding 2 years or both (reg 39(2)).

4   See the Water Resources Act 1991 ss 161, 161A–161D; and ENVIRONMENTAL QUALITY AND PUBLIC HEALTH vol 45 (2010) PARAS 321–328. 'Controlled waters' are, broadly, any relevant territorial waters, coastal waters, inland freshwaters or groundwaters: see the Water Resources Act 1991 s 104(1); and ENVIRONMENTAL QUALITY AND PUBLIC HEALTH vol 45 (2010) PARA 289.

5   See the Water Resources Act 1991 s 92; the Water Resources (Control of Pollution) (Silage, Slurry and Agricultural Fuel Oil) (England) Regulations 2010, SI 2010/639; the Water Resources (Control of Pollution) (Silage, Slurry and Agricultural Fuel Oil) (Wales) Regulations 2010, SI 2010/1493; and ENVIRONMENTAL QUALITY AND PUBLIC HEALTH vol 46 (2010) PARAS 711, 713.

6   See the Water Resources Act 1991 s 97; and ENVIRONMENTAL QUALITY AND PUBLIC HEALTH vol 45 (2010) PARA 320.

370. Nitrate vulnerable zones.

Provision is made, for the purpose of reducing water pollution caused or induced by nitrates from agricultural sources, for the designation of nitrate vulnerable zones[1].

The occupier of a holding[2] within a nitrate free zone has a duty to ensure that the amount of nitrogen in livestock manure applied to the holding, whether directly by an animal or by spreading[3], and the amount of nitrogen in organic manure spread on any given hectare of land on the holding, does not exceed set amounts[4].

Before spreading nitrogen fertiliser, the occupier must make certain calculations regarding the amount of nitrogen in the soil and the optimum amount to be spread and produce a plan for the spreading of nitrogen fertiliser that growing season (a 'fertilisation plan')[5]. An occupier of a holding who spreads organic manure must produce and maintain a 'risk map' providing certain details[6].

1   See the Nitrate Pollution Regulations 2015, SI 2015/668, regs 3–5A; and ENVIRONMENTAL QUALITY AND PUBLIC HEALTH.

2   'Holding' (except in the phrase 'relevant holding', as to which see the Nitrate Pollution Prevention Regulations 2015, SI 2015/668, reg 5(5)) means all the land located within a nitrate vulnerable zone and its associated buildings which are at the disposal of the occupier and which are used for the growing of crops in soil or rearing of livestock for agricultural purposes: reg 2(1).

3   'Spreading', in relation to land, includes applying to the surface of the land, injecting into the land or mixing with the surface layers of the land, but does not include the direct deposit of excreta on to land by animals: Nitrate Pollution Prevention Regulations 2015, SI 2015/668, reg 2(1).

4   See the Nitrate Pollution Prevention Regulations 2015, SI 2015/668, regs 7, 8; and ENVIRONMENTAL QUALITY AND PUBLIC HEALTH.

5   See the Nitrate Pollution Prevention Regulations 2015, SI 2015/668, reg 10; and ENVIRONMENTAL QUALITY AND PUBLIC HEALTH.

6   See the Nitrate Pollution Prevention Regulations 2015, SI 2015/668, reg 15; and ENVIRONMENTAL QUALITY AND PUBLIC HEALTH.

371. Storage of organic manure and slurry.

Provision is made, for the storage of nitrogen fertiliser in the form of organic manure or bedding contaminated with organic manure[1] and for the method by which slurry must be separated into solid and liquid fractions[2]. An occupier of a holding must provide sufficient storage for slurry and poultry manure produced on the holding[3].

1   See the Nitrate Pollution Regulations 2015, SI 2-15/668, reg 23; and ENVIRONMENTAL QUALITY AND PUBLIC HEALTH.
2   See the Nitrate Pollution Regulations 2015, SI 2-15/668, reg 24; and ENVIRONMENTAL QUALITY AND PUBLIC HEALTH.
3   See the Nitrate Pollution Regulations 2015, SI 2-15/668, reg 25; and ENVIRONMENTAL QUALITY AND PUBLIC HEALTH. Provision is made for the calculation of the storage capacity: see the Nitrate Pollution Regulations 2015, SI 2-15/668, reg 25, Sch 1; and ENVIRONMENTAL QUALITY AND PUBLIC HEALTH.

372. Manufacture and use of pesticides, plant protection products, fertilisers, feeding stuffs and sludge.

With a view, partly, to safeguarding the environment[1], the manufacture and use of pesticides is regulated by the Secretary of State and the Welsh Ministers[2]. Provision is made for the preparation and issue of codes of practice for the purpose of providing practical guidance as to the use of pesticides[3]. The use of plant protection products is also regulated, partly for the purpose of protecting the environment[4], and provision is made for controlling the composition and content of fertilisers and feedings stuffs[6]. Regulations are also in force for the purpose of protecting the environment where sewage sludge is used on agricultural land, requiring the sludge and the soil on which it is to be used to be tested at regular intervals[7] and restricting the grazing of animals and the growth and harvesting of crops on soil to which sludge is applied[8] and the production and sale of crops grown on sludge disposal sites[9]. These regulations also require sludge producers not to supply sludge unless they are satisfied that the regulations are being complied with[10].

1   See the Food and Environment Protection Act 1985 s 16(1)(a)(ii).
2   See the Food and Environment Protection Act 1985 ss 16, 18, 19, Sch 2; the Control of Pesticides Regulations 1986, SI 1986/1510; the Plant Protection Products Regulations 2011, SI 2011/2131; and PARAS 130–131, 138–140. As to the Secretary of State and the Welsh Ministers see PARA 390. Contravention of these regulations is an offence: see the Food and Environment Protection Act 1985 s 16(12); and PARA 131.
3   See the Food and Environment Protection Act 1985 s 17; and PARA 141.
4   See the Plant Protection Products Regulations 2011, SI 2011/2131; and PARAS 132–137.
6   See PARA 37 et seq.
7   See the Sludge (Use in Agriculture) Regulations 1989, SI 1989/1263, Schs 1, 2; and PARAS 67–68.
8   See the Sludge (Use in Agriculture) Regulations 1989, SI 1989/1263, regs 3, 4; and PARAS 63–64.
9   See the Sludge (Use in Agriculture) Regulations 1989, SI 1989/1263, reg 8(1), (3), (4), Sch 2 para 5; and PARA 66.
10 See the Sludge (Use in Agriculture) Regulations 1989, SI 1989/1263, reg 3(1); and PARA 65.

(4) CODE OF GOOD AGRICULTURAL PRACTICE

373. The Water, Soil and Air Code.

The Department for Environment, Food and Rural Affairs publishes a Code of Good Agricultural Practice for farmers, growers and land managers as a practical guide to help them protect the environment in which they operate[1]. The Code discusses the sources of pollution and impact it has and sets out what to do if any surface water or groundwater is at risk of becoming polluted or becomes polluted, along with the requirement to have an accident and emergency plan in place[2],

The Code has been given statutory effect[3].

1　See the Code of Good Agricultural Practice for the Protection of Water, Soil and Air (2009), summary.
2　See the Code of Good Agricultural Practice for the Protection of Water, Soil and Air (2009), 1.1, 1.4, 1.5.
3　See the Water (Prevention of Pollution) (Code of Good Agricultural Practice) (England) Order 2009, SI 2009/46 and the Water (Prevention of Pollution) (Code of Good Agricultural Practice) (Wales) Order 2011, SI 2011/1012 (both made under the Water Resources Act 1991 s 97(1)); and ENVIRONMENTAL QUALITY AND PUBLIC HEALTH vol 45 (2010) PARA 320.

12. LEVIES ON CATTLE, SHEEP AND PIGS

(1) LEVY UNDER THE RED MEAT INDUSTRY (WALES) ACT 2010

374. Welsh Ministers power to impose a levy.
The Welsh Ministers may impose a levy or levies[1] for the purpose of meeting expenditure incurred, or to be incurred, in:

(1)   furthering any of the objectives[2] of the Red Meat Industry (Wales) Measure 2010;

(2)   carrying out other functions[3] relevant to the red meat industry; and

(3)   otherwise providing services relevant to the red meat industry[4].

Levy paid by persons in respect of activities in the cattle sector[5], the sheep sector[6] or the pig sector[7] may not be used for the purpose of meeting expenditure incurred, or to be incurred, specifically in relation to a different sector[8].

The Welsh Ministers may impose a levy:

(a)   on slaughterers[9] if (and only if) slaughterers have been designated, by order made by the Welsh Ministers, as liable to levy under the Red Meat Industry (Wales) Measure 2010; and

(b)   on exporters[10] if (and only if) exporters have been designated, by order made by the Welsh Ministers, as liable to levy under the Red Meat Industry (Wales) Measure 2010[11],

and slaughterers and exporters have been so designated as liable to levy[12].

The Welsh Ministers may impose a levy on persons who carry out a primary activity if (and only if) that primary activity[13] has been designated, by order made by the Welsh Ministers, as liable to levy under the Red Meat Industry (Wales) Measure 2010[14].

The Welsh Ministers may impose a levy on persons who carry out a secondary activity if (and only if) that secondary activity[15] has been designated, by order made by the Welsh Ministers, as liable to levy under the Red Meat Industry (Wales) Measure 2010[16].

1   Ie in accordance with the Red Meat Industry (Wales) Measure 2010 s 4. As to the exercise of powers conferred on the Welsh Ministers see PARA 167. As to the Welsh Ministers see PARA 390.
2   As to the objectives of the Red Meat Industry (Wales) Measure 2010 see PARA 166.
3   As to functions under the Red Meat Industry (Wales) Measure 2010 see PARA 167.
4   Red Meat Industry (Wales) Measure 2010 s 4(1).
5   In the Red Meat Industry (Wales) Measure 2010 'cattle sector' means the red meat industry so far as it relates to cattle: s 1(2). As to the meaning of 'cattle' see PARA 375 note 3.
6   In the Red Meat Industry (Wales) Measure 2010 'sheep sector' means the red meat industry so far as it relates to sheep: s 1(2).
7   In the Red Meat Industry (Wales) Measure 2010 'pig sector' means the red meat industry so far as it relates to pigs s 1(2). As to the meaning of 'pigs' see PARA 375 note 3.
8   Red Meat Industry (Wales) Measure 2010 s 4(2).
9   'Slaughterer' means any person who has the control and management of a slaughterhouse: Red Meat Industry (Wales) Measure 2010 s 14.
10 'Exporter' means any person who exports cattle, sheep or pigs; and to 'export' means to transport cattle, sheep or pigs outside the United Kingdom: Red Meat Industry (Wales) Measure 2010s 14. For further provision as to orders see s 17; and PARA 167 note 6.
11 Red Meat Industry (Wales) Measure 2010 s 4(3).
12 See the Red Meat Industry (Designation of Slaughterers and Exporters) (Wales) Order 2012, SI 2012/247.
13 In the Red Meat Industry (Wales) Measure 2010 s 4 'primary activity' means breeding, keeping, processing, marketing or distributing cattle, sheep or pigs (but does not include slaughtering or exporting cattle, sheep or pigs): s 4(6).

14 Red Meat Industry (Wales) Measure 2010 s 4(4). At the date at which this volume states the law
    no order had been made under s 4(4).
15 In the Red Meat Industry (Wales) Measure 2010 s 4 'secondary activity' means an activity which:
    (1)   is carried out in connection with the red meat industry;
    (2)   is not slaughtering or exporting cattle, sheep or pigs; and
    (3)   is not a primary activity: s 4(6).
16 Red Meat Industry (Wales) Measure 2010 s 4(5). At the date at which this volume states the law
    no order had been made under s 4(5).

375. Calculating the levy and payment imposed on slaughterers or exporters.

A levy imposed on slaughterers[1] or exporters[2] for any period is calculated by
reference to the number of chargeable cattle, sheep or pigs[3]. The levy imposed on
a slaughterer or exporter is to be calculated in accordance with the following[4].

The levy is calculated by adding together the following separate components in
respect of each animal slaughtered or exported:
(1)   the production component[5]; and
(2)   the slaughter or export component[6].

The Welsh Ministers may determine the rate of the production component and the
slaughter or export component[7] which may involve different rates for different
cases (including different descriptions of slaughterer or exporter and different
descriptions of animal)[8].

In respect of levies imposed on slaughterers or exporters, the Welsh Ministers
may make regulations about procedures relating to the imposition of levies
(including notification to persons liable to pay a levy of the amount which they are
required to pay), and to payment and collection of levies[9].

1 As to the meaning of 'slaughters' see PARA 375 note 1.
2 As to the meaning of 'exporters' see PARA 375 note 2.
3 Red Meat Industry (Wales) Measure 2010 s 5(1). 'Chargeable cattle, sheep or pigs', in respect of
    any period for which levy is imposed:
    (1)   in relation to a slaughterer, means cattle, sheep or pigs slaughtered by the slaughterer in
           that period; and
    (2)   in relation to an exporter, means cattle, sheep or pigs exported by the exporter in that
           period: s 5(5).
    'Cattle' means bovine animals, including bison and buffalo and 'pigs' means porcine animals,
    including wild boar and other feral pigs: s 14.
        As to the exercise of powers conferred on the Welsh Ministers see PARA 167.
4 Ie in accordance with the Red Meat Industry (Wales) Measure 2010 Sch 2 Pt 1: Sch 2 para 1. The
    Welsh Ministers may by order amend Sch 2: s 5(4). For further provision as to orders see s 17; and
    PARA 167 note 6. As to the Welsh Ministers see PARA 390.
5 Red Meat Industry (Wales) Measure 2010 Sch 2 para 2(a). The maximum rate of production
    component per animals is £6.91 for cattle, £0.50 for calves, £1.00 for sheep and £1.67 for pigs:
    Sch 2 para 5 (substituted by SI 2011/2946). For these purposes a calf is an animal under six
    months old (in the case of an exported animal) or an animal with a dressed slaughter weight of
    less than 68 kg (in the case of a slaughtered animal); and 'cattle' does not include calves: Red Meat
    Industry (Wales) Measure 2010 Sch 2 para 4.
6 Red Meat Industry (Wales) Measure 2010 Sch 2 para 2(b). The maximum rate of slaughter or
    export per component per animal is £2.12 for cattle, £0.50 for calves, £0.32 for sheep and £0.40
    for pigs: Sch 2 para 6 (substituted by SI 2011/2946).
7 Red Meat Industry (Wales) Measure 2010 Sch 2 para 3(1).
8 See the Red Meat Industry (Wales) Measure 2010 Sch 2 para 3(2). The rates determined under
    Sch 2 para 3 may include a nil rate, but cannot exceed the maximum rates set out in Sch 2: Sch 2
    para 3(3). As to the rates see notes 5, 6.
9 Red Meat Industry (Wales) Measure 2010 s 5(3). Persons liable to pay a levy' means persons who
    have been designated, by order made by the Welsh Ministers, as liable to levy under the Red Meat
    Industry (Wales) Measure 2010, or persons carrying out a designated primary or designated
    secondary activity: s 14. At the date at which this volume states the law no such persons had been
    designated.

376. Power to make provision about levies imposed in respect of persons carrying out a designated primary activity or a designated secondary activity.

A levy imposed on persons carrying out a designated primary activity[1] or a designated secondary activity[2] for any period is calculated by reference to the number of chargeable cattle, sheep or pigs[3].

The Welsh Ministers may, by order[4], make further provision about levies imposed on persons carrying out a designated primary activity or a designated secondary activity, including, but not limited to, provision about:

(1) rates and components of a levy, and how levies are calculated;

(2) how levies are to be held and paid;

(3) offences for non-compliance[5];

(4) exceptions from levy payment in certain circumstances;

(5) procedures relating to the imposition (including notification to persons liable to pay a levy of the amount which they are required to pay) and payment and collection of levies[6].

1   As to the meaning of 'primary activity' and when such activity has been designated see PARA 376 note1.

2   As to the meaning of 'secondary activity' and when such activity has been designated see PARA 376 note 2.

3   Red Meat Industry (Wales) Measure 2010 s 6(1). In the Red Meat Industry (Wales) Measure 2010 'chargeable cattle, sheep or pigs', in relation to a person carrying out a designated primary or secondary activity and in respect of any period for which levy is imposed, means cattle, sheep or pigs in respect of which that activity is carried out in that period: s 6(4). As to the meanings of 'cattle' and 'pigs' see PARA 375 note 3.

4   As to the Welsh Ministers see PARA 390. At the date at which this volume states the law no order had been made under the Red Meat Industry (Wales) Measure 2010 s 6. As to the Welsh Ministers see PARA 390.

5   Where a body corporate is guilty of an offence under the Red Meat Industry (Wales) Measure 2010, and that offence is proved to have been committed with the consent or connivance of, or to have been attributable to any neglect on the part of, any director, manager, secretary or other similar officer of the body corporate; or any person purporting to act in any such capacity, that person is guilty of the offence as well as the body corporate, and is liable to be proceeded against and punished accordingly: Red Meat Industry (Wales) Measure 2010 s 12(1). For the purposes of s 12 'director' in relation to a body corporate whose affairs are managed by its members, means a member of the body corporate: s 12(2). Proceedings for an offence alleged to have been committed under the Red Meat Industry (Wales) Measure 2010 by an unincorporated body are to be brought in the name of that body (and not in that of any of its members) and, for the purposes of any such proceedings, any rules of court relating to the service of documents have effect as if that body were a corporation: s 12(3). Any fine imposed on an unincorporated body on its conviction of an offence under the Red Meat Industry (Wales) Measure 2010 is to be paid out of the funds of that body: s 12(4). If an unincorporated body is charged with an offence under the Red Meat Industry (Wales) Measure 2010, the Criminal Justice Act 1925 s 33 and the Magistrates' Courts Act 1980 Sch 3 (see MAGISTRATES vol 71 (2013) PARA 513) have effect as if a corporation had been charged: Red Meat Industry (Wales) Measure 2010 s 12(5). Where an offence under the Red Meat Industry (Wales) Measure 2010 committed by an unincorporated body (other than a partnership) is proved to have been committed with the consent or connivance of, or attributable to any neglect on the part of, any officer of the body or any member of its governing body, that person as well as the body is guilty of the offence and liable to be proceeded against and punished accordingly: s 12(6). Where an offence under the Red Meat Industry (Wales) Measure 2010 committed by a partnership is proved to have been committed with the consent or connivance of, or to be attributable to any neglect on the part of, a partner, that partner as well as the partnership is guilty of the offence and liable to be proceeded against and punished accordingly: s 12(7). Proceedings for an offence under the Red Meat Industry (Wales) Measure 2010 may be brought at any time within the period of six months beginning with the date on

which evidence sufficient in the opinion of the prosecutor to warrant the proceedings came to the prosecutor's knowledge but proceedings cannot be commenced more than two years after the date on which the offence was committed: s 13.

6   Red Meat Industry (Wales) Measure 2010 s 6(2). An order under s 6(2) may make any amendments to the Red Meat Industry (Wales) Measure 2010 as appear necessary or expedient to the Welsh Ministers in connection with any provisions made under s 6(2): s 6(3).

377. Returns and estimates.

The Welsh Ministers may give directions[1] requiring persons who are liable to pay a levy in respect of any period to submit a return relating to that period[2]. The return must contain:

(1)   the number of chargeable cattle, sheep or pigs[3] in respect of the period to which the return relates; and

(2)   such other details as may be directed by the Welsh Ministers[4].

The return must be submitted by such date, and in such manner and form, as may be specified in a direction given by the Welsh Ministers[5]. If any person liable to submit a return:

(a)   fails to submit the return by the date directed[6];

(b)   fails to include in the return an estimate of the number of chargeable cattle, sheep or pigs; or

(c)   includes in the return an estimate which in the opinion of the Welsh Ministers is unreasonably low,

the Welsh Ministers may estimate the number of animals that ought have been noted in the return[7] and notify the person liable to pay the levy in writing of that estimate[8].

If, having been notified of the estimate, the person liable to pay the levy fails to submit a return containing an estimate within 28 days of receiving the notification, that person must pay a levy on the number of animals estimated[9].

1   As to the Welsh Ministers see PARA 390. As to giving directions under the Red Meat Industry (Wales) Measure 2010 see PARA 168 note 4.
2   Red Meat Industry (Wales) Measure 2010 s 8(1).
3   As to the meanings of 'cattle' and 'pigs' see PARA 375 note 3.
4   Red Meat Industry (Wales) Measure 2010 s 8(2).
5   Red Meat Industry (Wales) Measure 2010 s 8(3).
6   A person who fails without reasonable excuse to submit a return in accordance with any direction is guilty of an offence and liable on summary conviction to a fine not exceeding level 5 on the standard scale: Red Meat Industry (Wales) Measure 2010 s 8(8). As to the standard scale and the powers of magistrates' courts to issue fines on summary conviction see SENTENCING vol 92 (2015) PARA 176. A person who provides false or misleading information relating to any requirements under the Red Meat Industry (Wales) Measure 2010 is guilty of an offence and liable on summary conviction to a fine not exceeding level 5 on the standard scale: s 8(9).
7   Red Meat Industry (Wales) Measure 2010 s 8(4).
8   Red Meat Industry (Wales) Measure 2010 s 8(5). The Welsh Ministers may determine that a higher rate of levy is payable where the number of animals is estimated by them under s 8, but that rate must not exceed any maximum levy rates provided under the Red Meat Industry (Wales) Measure 2010: s 8(7).
9   Red Meat Industry (Wales) Measure 2010 s 8(6).

378. Provision of information.

Persons liable to pay a levy under the Red Meat Industry (Wales) Measure 2010 must:

(1)   keep sufficient records to enable the Welsh Ministers[1] to establish how much levy is due; and

(2)   produce those records to an officer of the Welsh Ministers on demand[2].

1   As to the Welsh Ministers see PARA 390.
2   Red Meat Industry (Wales) Measure 2010 s 9(1). A person who fails to comply with s 9 is guilty
    of an offence and liable on summary conviction to a fine not exceeding level 5 on the standard
    scale: s 9(2). As to the standard scale and the powers of magistrates' courts to issue fines on
    summary conviction see SENTENCING vol 92 (2015) PARA 176.

379. Inspection and powers of entry.

The Welsh Ministers[1] may appoint a person (an 'appointed person') to
ascertain whether:

(1)   the information provided in any return is accurate[2];
(2)   the number of animals on which the levy has been based is accurate[3];
(3)   the levy due under the Red Meat Industry (Wales) Measure 2010 has
        been paid[4]; and
(4)   an offence under the Red Meat Industry (Wales) Measure 2010 is being
        or has been committed[5].

The general and specific conditions that need to be met before an inspector
(appointed person) may apply for a warrant to enter land or premises for the
purpose of enforcing the Red Meat Industry (Wales) Measure 2010 are set out[6].

1   As to the Welsh Ministers see PARA 390.
2   As to directions requiring returns see PARA 377.
3   As to estimated returns see PARA 377.
4   As to the power of the Welsh Ministers to impose a levy see PARA 374.
5   Red Meat Industry (Wales) Measure 2010 s 10.
6   Red Meat Industry (Wales) Measure 2010 s 11.

(2) LEVY UNDER THE PIG INDUSTRY ACT 1983

380. Pig industry levy under the Pig Industry Act 1983.

Any costs incurred by the Secretary of State or the Welsh Ministers[1] in
consequence of exercising any of their powers under the Animal Health Act 1981
in relation to Aujeszky's disease or in relation to pigs which are affected or
suspected of being affected with, or have been exposed to the infection of, that
disease, may be met from the proceeds of a pig industry levy[2]. The Agriculture and
Horticulture Board[3] may submit to the Secretary of State or the Welsh Ministers
a pig industry levy scheme:

(1)   for the imposition of charges for the purposes of meeting any costs
        incurred as mentioned above and compensating the owners of pigs in
        respect of losses incurred by them in consequence of action taken by the
        Secretary of State or the Welsh Ministers in relation to those pigs under
        the Animal Health Act 1981[4]; and
(2)   for the recovery of charges by the Board as specified in the scheme[5].

Subject to the following provisions, the proceeds of any levy imposed under a pig
industry levy scheme (the 'levy fund') may be applied solely for making payments
for levy purposes[6]. The Board may make arrangements for payments to be made
for levy purposes by any other person and may transfer sums collected under the
scheme to such person, who may receive expenses from the levy fund[7]. Any
expenses incurred by the Board:

(a)   in collecting charges under any pig industry levy scheme;
(b)   in making payments for levy purposes; or
(c)   for the purpose of arrangements[8],

may be met from the levy fund[9].

The Board may not make payments for levy purposes out of sums collected in pursuance of a pig industry levy scheme, or pay sums so collected to any person responsible in accordance with any arrangements[10], except in accordance with directions given by the Secretary of State or the Welsh Ministers[11]. Directions may be given requiring sums which are surplus to requirements[12] to be applied for such purposes or dealt with in such manner as may be specified[13].

1　As to the Secretary of State and the Welsh Ministers see PARA 390.
2　See the Pig Industry Levy Act 1983 s 1(2). The provisions of s 1 apply if the Secretary of State directs or the Welsh Ministers direct that the Animal Health Act 1981 s 32 (see ANIMALS vol 2 (2017) PARA 420) applies to Aujeszky's disease or if that disease is one to which s 32 applies on 1 March 1983: see the Pig Industry Levy Act 1983 s 1(1).
3　The Pig Industry Levy Act 1983 refers to the Meat and Livestock Commission but this Commission has been abolished and is not part of the Agriculture and Horticulture Development Board see PARA 380.
4　See the Pig Industry Levy Act 1983 s 1(3). As to the application of the Agriculture Act 1967 ss 13, 14 to the pig industry levy scheme see PARA 380 note 5.
5　See the Pig Industry Levy Act 1983 s 1(3).
6　See the Pig Industry Levy Act 1983 s 1(5).
7　Pig Industry Levy Act 1983 s 1(6), (7). Certain sums transferred by the Board for payment for levy purposes are held on trust for the Board: see s 3.
8　Ie under the Pig Industry Levy Act 1983 s 1(6) (see the text and note 7).
9　Pig Industry Levy Act 1983 s 1(8).
10　Ie under the Pig Industry Levy Act 1983 s 1(6) (see the text and note 7).
11　See the Pig Industry Levy Act 1983 s 2(1).
12　Ie not required for levy purposes or for meeting any expenses that may be met from the levy fund in accordance with the Pig Industry Levy Act 1983 s 1: see s 2(7).
13　See the Pig Industry Levy Act 1983 s 2(2). The purposes or manner must be connected with or beneficial to persons engaged in the pig industry or the pig products industry: s 2(3). 'Pig industry' means any part of the livestock industry that is concerned with pigs; and 'pig products industry' means any part of the livestock products industry that is concerned with pig products: s 2(8). As to the meanings of 'livestock industry' and 'livestock product industry' see PARA 380 note 13. See further s 2(4)–(6), (8).

(3) LEVIES UNDER THE AGRICULTURE AND HORTICULTURE DEVELOPMENT BOARD ORDER 2008

381.　Levy on cattle, sheep and pigs.

The Agriculture and Horticulture Development Board[1] must impose a levy to enable it to provide services for industries that include the beef and sheep industry in England, the milk industry in Great Britain and the pig industry in England[2].

The levies are to enable the Board to:

(1)　cover its costs in providing certain services[3];
(2)　meet its administrative expenses;
(3)　further a purpose of the Board[4]; and
(4)　establish a reserve fund[5].

A person who is the occupier of a slaughterhouse ('the slaughterer') must pay a levy on all cattle, sheep and pigs slaughtered[6]. Any person who exports live cattle, sheep or pigs ('an exporter') must pay a levy[7].

The levy is based on the number of animals slaughtered or exported[8] and consists of two parts, the producer levy and the slaughter or export levy[9].

The Agriculture and Horticulture Development Board may make provision for a reduction of the slaughter levy and export levy to cover the administrative costs of the slaughterer or exporter in administering the levy[10].

If a slaughterer or exporter buys an animal for slaughter or export, he must deduct the producer levy from the price he pays, and hold it on trust for the Board[11].

If a slaughterer slaughters an animal without buying it, he must charge the owner both the producer levy and the slaughter levy, and hold it on trust for the Board[12].

1   As to the establishment of the Agriculture and Horticulture Development Board see PARA 393.
2   See the Agriculture and Horticulture Development Board Order 2008, SI 2008/576, arts 2(1)(a), (d), (e), 6(1). As to the meanings of 'beef and sheep industry', 'milk industry' and 'pig industry' see PARA 395 note 25 respectively.
3   Ie any of the services specified in the Agriculture and Horticulture Development Board Order 2008, SI 2008/576, Sch 1 (see PARA 395).
4   Ie a purpose in the Agriculture and Horticulture Development Board Order 2008, SI 2008/576, art 3(2) (see PARA 393 note 2).
5   Agriculture and Horticulture Development Board Order 2008, SI 2008/576, art 6(3).
6   Agriculture and Horticulture Development Board Order 2008, SI 2008/576, Sch 3 para 3(1).
7   Agriculture and Horticulture Development Board Order 2008, SI 2008/576, Sch 3 para 3(2).
8   Agriculture and Horticulture Development Board Order 2008, SI 2008/576, Sch 3 para 3(3).
9   Agriculture and Horticulture Development Board Order 2008, SI 2008/576, Sch 3 para 3(4). The maximum rate of producer levy per head is £5.25 for cattle (except calves), £0.50 for calves, £1.075 for pigs and £0.60 for sheep: Sch 3 para 3(8), Table. The maximum rate of slaughterer levy and exporter levy is £1.75 for cattle (except calves), £0.50 for calves, £0.275 for pigs and £0.20 for sheep: Sch 3 para 3(8), Table. For these purposes a calf is an animal under six months old (in the case of an exported animal) or an animal with a dressed slaughter weight of less than 68 kg (in the case of slaughtered animal: Sch 3 para 3(8)(a).
10   Agriculture and Horticulture Development Board Order 2008, SI 2008/576, Sch 3 para 3(5).
11   Agriculture and Horticulture Development Board Order 2008, SI 2008/576, Sch 3 para 3(6).
12   Agriculture and Horticulture Development Board Order 2008, SI 2008/576, Sch 3 para 3(7).

382. Exceptions to the levy on cattle, sheep and pigs.

Levy is not payable for animals imported from another member state and slaughtered within three months in the case of cattle and two months in the case of pigs or sheep[1].

Levy is not payable if an animal is subject to compulsory slaughter or the entire carcase is declared unfit for human consumption by the official veterinarian[2].

1   Agriculture and Horticulture Development Board Order 2008, SI 2008/576, Sch 3 para 4(1).
2   Agriculture and Horticulture Development Board Order 2008, SI 2008/576, Sch 3 para 4(2).

383. Returns and payment of the levy by slaughterhouse occupier.

An occupier of a slaughterhouse must notify the Agriculture and Horticulture Development Board, by the end of each Wednesday, of the number of animals subject to levy slaughtered in the previous week up to the end of Sunday, broken down into types of animal[1].

If an occupier estimates that the total number of animals that will be slaughtered will be fewer than 25 each week, he may apply to the Board to be registered as a small operator; and if the Board agrees to so register him, he must notify the Board on or before the 15th day of each month of the number of animals subject to levy slaughtered in the previous month broken down into types of animal[2].

Failure to notify in accordance with the above provisions is an offence[3].

An occupier must pay the levy due for animals slaughtered in any month within 15 days from the end of that month[4].

1   Agriculture and Horticulture Development Board Order 2008, SI 2008/576, Sch 3 para 5(1).
2   Agriculture and Horticulture Development Board Order 2008, SI 2008/576, Sch 3 para 5(2).
3   Agriculture and Horticulture Development Board Order 2008, SI 2008/576, Sch 3 para 5(3). A person guilty of an offence under the Agriculture and Horticulture Development Board Order 2008, SI 2008/576 is liable on summary conviction to a fine not exceeding level 5 on the standard scale: art 16(1). Proceedings for an offence under the Agriculture and Horticulture Development Board Order 2008, SI 2008/576 may be brought within the period of 6 months beginning with the date on which evidence sufficient in the opinion of the prosecutor to warrant the proceedings came to his knowledge, provided that the commencement of such proceedings is not more than 2 years after the date on which the offence was committed: art 16(2). Where a body corporate is guilty of an offence under the Agriculture and Horticulture Development Board Order 2008, SI 2008/576, and that offence is proved to have been committed with the consent or connivance of, or to have been attributable to any neglect on the part of:
     (1)   any director, manager, secretary or other similar person of the body corporate; or
     (2)   any person who was purporting to act in any such capacity,
    that person is guilty of the offence as well as the body corporate: art 16(3).
        For the purposes of art 16 'director', in relation to a body corporate whose affairs are managed by its members, means a member of the body corporate: art 16(4). As to the standard scale and the powers of magistrates' courts to issue fines on summary conviction see SENTENCING vol 92 (2015) PARA 176.
4   Agriculture and Horticulture Development Board Order 2008, SI 2008/576, Sch 3 para 6.

384.   Returns and payment of the levy by exporters.

An exporter must notify the Agriculture and Horticulture Development Board[1], within 30 days of the end of the month, of the number of animals exported in the previous month, and failure to do so is an offence[2]. He must pay the levy on invoice[3].

1   As to the establishment of the Agriculture and Horticulture Development Board see PARA 393.
2   Agriculture and Horticulture Development Board Order 2008, SI 2008/576, Sch 3 para 7(1). A person guilty of such an offence is liable on summary conviction to a fine not exceeding level 5 on the standard scale: art 16(1). See further PARA 383 note 3. As to the standard scale and the powers of magistrates' courts to issue fines on summary conviction see SENTENCING vol 92 (2015) PARA 176.
3   Agriculture and Horticulture Development Board Order 2008, SI 2008/576, Sch 3 para 7(2).

385.   Enforcement.

A person appointed by the Agriculture and Horticulture Development Board[1] may, on producing a duly authenticated document showing his authority if required, enter any slaughterhouse at any reasonable hour to check any records to ensure that the correct levy has been paid[2]. It is an offence to obstruct any such person or to fail to produce records on demand[3].

1   As to the establishment of the Agriculture and Horticulture Development Board see PARA 393.
2   Agriculture and Horticulture Development Board Order 2008, SI 2008/576, Sch 3 para 8(1).
3   Agriculture and Horticulture Development Board Order 2008, SI 2008/576, Sch 3 para 8(2). A person guilty of such an offence is liable on summary conviction to a fine not exceeding level 5 on the standard scale: art 16(1). See further PARA 383 note 3. As to the standard scale and the powers of magistrates' courts to issue fines on summary conviction see SENTENCING vol 92 (2015) PARA 176.

386.   Levy on cereal and oilseed.

Any person who buys cereal or oilseed grown in the United Kingdom from the grower must pay a levy[1]. The levy is based on the weight bought[2].

In the case of cereal:
(1)   the levy consists of two parts, the grower levy and the buyer levy;

(2)   when he buys cereal the buyer must deduct the grower levy from the price he pays, and hold it on trust for the Agriculture and Horticulture Development Board[3];

(3)   he may then take five percent of the combined grower levy and buyer levy as commission; and

(4)   he must pay the remainder of the levy to the Agriculture and Horticulture Development Board[4].

In the case of oilseed the buyer must:

(a)   deduct all the levy from the price he pays the grower, and hold it on trust for the Agriculture and Horticulture Development Board; and

(b)   pay it to the Board[5].

If the buyer is the appropriate authority or outside the United Kingdom (or, in the case of a company, registered outside the United Kingdom), the grower must pay the levy to the Board himself, based on the weight sold[6].

Any person who by way of business carries out an industrial process to cereal grown in the United Kingdom must pay a levy to the Agriculture and Horticulture Development Board[7]. The levy is based on the weight of cereal to be processed[8].

1   Agriculture and Horticulture Development Board Order 2008, SI 2008/576, Sch 3 para 9(1). The maximum rate of levy is for a cereal grower, 60 pence per tonne, for a cereal buyer, 5 pence per tonne, for cereal processor (feeding stuffs) 6 pence per tonne, for a cereal processor (non-feeding stuffs) 12 pence per tonne and for oilseed (grower) 98 pence per tonne: Sch 3 para 11. The feeding stuff rate is payable in relation to cereal processed into animal feeding stuffs: Sch 3 para 11(a).

2   Agriculture and Horticulture Development Board Order 2008, SI 2008/576, Sch 3 para 9(2).

3   As to the establishment of the Agriculture and Horticulture Development Board see PARA 393. Any person liable to pay levy relating to cereal to the Agriculture and Horticulture Development Board must notify it of the amount of cereal bought, processed or sold on which levy is due in each three month period ending 31st December, 31st March, 30th June and 30th September: Sch 3 para 12(1). Any person who has bought less than 250 tonnes of cereal in any year ending 30th June, or processed less than 1,000 tonnes in any year, may instead notify once a year the amount bought in that year: Sch 3 para 12(2). Any person liable to pay levy relating to oilseed must notify the Board of the amount of oilseed bought in the six month period ending 31st December and 30th June each year: Sch 3 para 12(3). That person must notify within 28 days of the end of any period referred to in Sch 3 para 12(1), (2) or (3), and failure to so is an offence: Sch 3 para 12(5). If any person buys more than 1,000 tonnes of cereal grown in the United Kingdom in any year ending 30th June, he must in the following year make a written weekly return to the Agriculture and Horticulture Development Board in accordance with Sch 3 para 13, and failure to do so is an offence: Sch 3 para 13(1). Each return must show:

    (1)   the amount in tonnes of cereal grown in the United Kingdom and bought by him in the previous week (ending on Friday), broken down by type of cereal; and

    (2)   the prices paid: Sch 3 para 13(2).

The return must be submitted by the end of Thursday in the following week: Sch 3 para 12(3). The Board must publish the mean average price of each type of cereal on a weekly, monthly and annual basis: Sch 3 para 13(4). As to offences under the Agriculture and Horticulture Development Board Order 2008, SI 2008/576 PARA 383 note 3.

4   Agriculture and Horticulture Development Board Order 2008, SI 2008/576, Sch 3 para 9(3).

5   Agriculture and Horticulture Development Board Order 2008, SI 2008/576, Sch 3 para 9(4).

6   Agriculture and Horticulture Development Board Order 2008, SI 2008/576, Sch 3 para 9(5).

7   Agriculture and Horticulture Development Board Order 2008, SI 2008/576, Sch 3 para 10(1). Schedule 3 para 10 does not apply in relation to cereal processed by or for the person who grew them: Sch 3 para 10(3).

8   Agriculture and Horticulture Development Board Order 2008, SI 2008/576, Sch 3 para 10(2).

387. Levy on horticultural products.

Any person must pay a levy if he grows the following horticultural products:

(1)   all vegetables grown in the open and sold for human consumption, including watercress but excluding potatoes;

(2)   all soft fruit and orchard fruit, including nuts but excluding:

       (a)   varieties of apples certified as cider apples, and varieties of pears certified as perry pears, by the Agriculture and Horticulture Development Board;

       (b)   hops; and

       (c)   grapes;

  (3)   all flowers (whether cut or in pot), foliage, flower bulbs, corms, tubers and rhizomes;

  (4)   all hardy nursery stock including:

       (a)   fruit trees, bushes and canes, strawberries for runner production and other fruit stock for transplanting;

       (b)   roses (including stock for budding);

       (c)   shrubs and hedging plants;

       (d)   ornamental trees and trees for sale for amenity purposes;

       (e)   perennial herbaceous plants; and

       (f)   aquatic plants.

  (5)   all other nursery stock, seedlings and cuttings for propagation;

  (6)   all crops grown in glasshouses and other forms of protection including pot plants, bedding plants and plants being propagated for growing elsewhere;

  (7)   all species of herbs,

and he sells those products grown by him, or anything derived from such products grown by him and he has adjusted sales figures[1] from those products or derivatives in any year ending 31 March of £60,000 or more[2].

Any person must pay a levy if, in any year ending 31 March, he buys more than 700 litres of mushroom spawn or buys compost containing more than 700 litres of mushroom spawn[3].

On or before 30 June each year any person liable to pay a levy mentioned above must, using the form published by the Agriculture and Horticulture Development Board for the purpose, provide sufficient information to enable the Board to calculate the levy due for the year ending 31 March that year[4].

The information must be certified by an accountant unless the Board has notified the person that this is not necessary and for these purposes an accountant is a person who is a fully-qualified member of one of the bodies constituting the Consultative Committee of Accountancy Bodies (in the United Kingdom or Ireland) or who holds an equivalent qualification in another member state[5].

If the Agriculture and Horticulture Development Board believes on reasonable grounds that any person is liable to pay levy under these provisions, and that person has not submitted a return, the Board may serve a notice on that person requiring him, within a time specified in the notice, to provide sufficient information concerning any horticultural business operated by that person to enable the Board to assess whether levy is payable and, if it is payable, the amount[6].

1   As calculated in accordance with the Agriculture and Horticulture Development Board Order 2008, SI 2008/576, Sch 3 para 18. The levy is payable on invoice: Sch 3 para 20.

2   Agriculture and Horticulture Development Board Order 2008, SI 2008/576, Sch 3 para 14.

3   Agriculture and Horticulture Development Board Order 2008, SI 2008/576, Sch 3 para 15. As to the maximum levy for mushrooms see Sch 3 para 19.

4   Agriculture and Horticulture Development Board Order 2008, SI 2008/576, Sch 3 para 16(1). Failure to comply with Sch 3 para 16 is an offence: Sch 3 para 16(3).

5   Agriculture and Horticulture Development Board Order 2008, SI 2008/576, Sch 3 para 16(2).

6   Agriculture and Horticulture Development Board Order 2008, SI 2008/576, Sch 3 para 17(1). It is an offence to fail to comply with such a notice: Sch 3 para 17(2).

388.   Levies on milk.

A person who buys milk from a producer must pay a levy[1]. He must deduct the levy from the price paid to the producer[2].

A direct seller[3] of milk must pay a levy[4].

1   Agriculture and Horticulture Development Board Order 2008, SI 2008/576, Sch 3 para 21(1). The levy is based on volume and the maximum levy is 0.08 pence per litre: Sch 3 para 21(4). At the end of every month a buyer of milk must notify to the Agriculture and Horticulture Development Board the amount of milk bought that month, and failure to do so is an offence: Sch 3 para 22(1). As to offences under the Agriculture and Horticulture Development Board Order 2008, SI 2008/576 PARA 383 note 3.
2   Agriculture and Horticulture Development Board Order 2008, SI 2008/576, Sch 3 para 21(2).
3   'Direct seller' means a producer who sells milk products or packaged milk if the milk was produced on his own holding: Agriculture and Horticulture Development Board Order 2008, SI 2008/576, Sch 3 para 21(3).
4   Agriculture and Horticulture Development Board Order 2008, SI 2008/576, Sch 3 para 21(3). A direct seller of milk must notify to the Board by 14th May each year the amount of milk produced on his holding in the previous year ending 1st April, and failure to do so is an offence: Sch 3 para 22(2). As to offences under the Agriculture and Horticulture Development Board Order 2008, SI 2008/576 PARA 383 note 3.

389.   Levy on potatoes.

Any person who grows three hectares or more of potatoes in any calendar year must pay a levy based on area planted[1].

Any person who buys 1,000 or more tonnes of potatoes grown in Great Britain (excluding seed potatoes) in any year ending 30th June must pay a levy based on the weight of potatoes bought[2]. However, this does not apply to a person buying potatoes to sell by retail or a caterer, unless he buys directly from the grower[3].

Nor does it apply to a co-operative when it is buying potatoes from its members (but it does apply when it is buying potatoes from persons other than its members); and for these purposes a co-operative is a business carried on by a group of potato growers that stores, prepares for market or markets potatoes grown by its members[4].

1   Agriculture and Horticulture Development Board Order 2008, SI 2008/576, Sch 3 para 23(1). The maximum levy is £50 per hectare: Sch 3 para 23(2). A grower liable to pay a levy under these provisions must notify the Agriculture and Horticulture Development Board, by 1st June, using the form published by it for the purpose, of the area planted or intended to be planted that calendar year and of the identity of the fields planted; and failure to do so is an offence: Sch 3 para 25(1). A person who had not planted, and who did not intend to plant, potatoes before 1st June, but who subsequently plants them in that calendar year, must notify the Board of the details in Sch 3 para 25(1) within 30 days of planting, and failure to do so is an offence: Sch 3 para 25(2). He must pay the levy to the Board by 1st December following: Sch 3 para 25(3). As to the establishment of the Agriculture and Horticulture Development Board see PARA 393. As to offences under the Agriculture and Horticulture Development Board Order 2008, SI 2008/576 PARA 383 note 3.
2   Agriculture and Horticulture Development Board Order 2008, SI 2008/576, Sch 3 para 24(1). The maximum levy is £0.25 per tonne: Sch 3 para 24(4). A buyer liable to pay levy under these provisions must notify the Agriculture and Horticulture Development Board by the 28th day of each month using the form provided by it of the tonnage bought in the previous month, and failure to do so is an offence: Sch 3 para 26(1). He must pay the levy on invoice: Sch 3 para 26(2). As to offences under the Agriculture and Horticulture Development Board Order 2008, SI 2008/576 PARA 383 note 3.
3   Agriculture and Horticulture Development Board Order 2008, SI 2008/576, Sch 3 para 24(2).
4   Agriculture and Horticulture Development Board Order 2008, SI 2008/576, Sch 3 para 24(3).

13. ADMINISTRATION AND FINANCE

(1) THE SECRETARY OF STATE AND THE WELSH MINISTERS

390. Ministerial powers and functions in respect of agricultural production and marketing.

Powers and functions in respect of agricultural production and marketing in England and Wales are exercised primarily by the Secretary of State for Environment, Food and Rural Affairs[1] or, in Wales, by the Welsh Ministers[2].

In discharging any functions connected with agriculture[3] in relation to any land the Secretary of State and the Welsh Ministers must, so far as is consistent with the proper and efficient discharge of those functions, have regard to and endeavour to achieve a reasonable balance between:

(1)   the promotion and maintenance of a stable and efficient agricultural industry[4];

(2)   the economic and social interests of rural areas[5];

(3)   the conservation and enhancement of the natural beauty and amenity[6] of the countryside (including its flora and fauna and geological and physiographical features) and of any features of archaeological interest there[7]; and

(4)   the promotion of the enjoyment of the countryside by the public[8].

The Secretary of State is also empowered to give or arrange for the giving of financial assistance in respect of expenditure incurred or to be incurred in any matter related to or connected with a function of the Department for Environment, Food and Rural Affairs[9] and by agreement to delegate such functions to designated agricultural or conservation bodies in England[10], and to make grants, in such manner and subject to such conditions as he may determine, to bodies of persons in England and Wales whose object or main object is the organisation, promotion or development of co-operation in agriculture or horticulture (including any connected activities) or of co-operation in the marketing of agricultural or horticultural produce[11]. The Secretary of State and the Welsh Ministers are required to publish an annual report on such matters relevant to price support for agricultural produce as they consider appropriate and include in the report such account as they consider appropriate of developments in agricultural policy[12], so far as relevant to such matters[13].

1   The office of Secretary of State for Environment, Food and Rural Affairs was constituted by the Secretaries of State for Transport, Local Government and the Regions and for Environment, Food and Rural Affairs Order 2001, SI 2001/2568 (amended by SI 2002/2626), which also made provision for the transfer to the Department for Environment, Food and Rural Affairs of the functions of the former Minister of Agriculture, Fisheries and Food relating to agriculture and food production (see note 3) and the functions of the former Department of the Environment, Transport and the Regions relating to the environment, rural development, countryside, wildlife and sustainable development. As to transfer of functions generally see CONSTITUTIONAL AND ADMINISTRATIVE LAW vol 20 (2014) PARA 162.

      In any enactment, 'Secretary of State' means one of Her Majesty's principal Secretaries of State: see the Interpretation Act 1978 s 5, Sch 1. The office of Secretary of State is a unified office, and in law each Secretary of State is generally capable of performing the functions of all or any of them: see CONSTITUTIONAL AND ADMINISTRATIVE LAW vol 20 (2014) PARA 153. In practice, the agriculture functions of the Secretary of State are exercised by the Secretary of State for Environment, Food and Rural Affairs. As to government departments and ministerial responsibilities generally see CONSTITUTIONAL AND ADMINISTRATIVE LAW vol 20 (2014) PARA 234 et seq.

The Secretary of State is also empowered to give or arrange for the giving of financial assistance in respect of expenditure incurred or to be incurred in any matter related to or connected with a function of the Department for Environment, Food and Rural Affairs (see the Natural Environment and Rural Communities Act 2006 s 98; and OPEN SPACES AND COUNTRYSIDE vol 78 (2010) PARA 521) and by agreement to delegate such functions to designated agricultural or conservation bodies in England (see Pt 8 Ch 1 (ss 78–86); and OPEN SPACES AND COUNTRYSIDE vol 78 (2010) PARA 520).

2   Pursuant to the establishment of the Welsh Assembly Government under the Government of Wales Act 2006 Pt 2 (ss 45–92) (see CONSTITUTIONAL AND ADMINISTRATIVE LAW vol 20 (2014) PARA 375), statutory functions relating to agricultural production and marketing, including functions under subordinate legislation, so far as exercisable in relation to Wales are now almost exclusively the responsibility of Welsh Ministers.
3   As to the meanings of 'agriculture' and 'agricultural' see PARA 10.
4   Agriculture Act 1986 s 17(1)(a).
5   Agriculture Act 1986 s 17(1)(b).
6   As to the meaning of 'amenity' see *Re Ellis and Ruislip-Northwood UDC* [1920] 1 KB 343 at 370, CA; *Cartwright v Post Office* [1968] 2 All ER 646 at 648 (affd [1969] 2 QB 62, [1969] 1 All ER 421, CA). Note, however, that those cases were decided under planning legislation.
7   Agriculture Act 1986 s 17(1)(c).
8   Agriculture Act 1986 s 17(1)(d).
9   See the Natural Environment and Rural Communities Act 2006 s 98; and OPEN SPACES AND COUNTRYSIDE vol 78 (2010) PARA 521.
10   See the Natural Environment and Rural Communities Act 2006 Pt 8 Ch 1; and OPEN SPACES AND COUNTRYSIDE vol 78 (2010) PARA 520.
11   Agriculture (Miscellaneous Provisions) Act 1963 s 8.
12   For this purpose, 'agricultural policy' includes policy relating to agriculture and the environment: Agriculture Act 1993 s 58(2).
13   Agriculture Act 1993 s 58(1).

391. Provision of goods and services.

The Secretary of State and the Welsh Ministers[1] may make provision for the supply to any person of any goods or services[2] relating to:

(1)   the production and marketing of agricultural produce and other food[3];
(2)   the conservation and enhancement of the natural beauty and amenity[4] of the countryside[5]; or
(3)   any other agricultural activity or other enterprise of benefit to the rural economy[6].

Such provision includes, in particular, provision for:

(a)   the giving of information, advice, instruction and training[7];
(b)   the undertaking of research and development[8];
(c)   the examination or testing of any substance[9];
(d)   the supply of veterinary services and of goods required for veterinary purposes[10]; and
(e)   the performance of any service required in connection with the drainage of agricultural land[11].

Any services or goods thus provided may be provided free of charge or for such reasonable charge as the Secretary of State and the Welsh Ministers may determine[12].

1   As to the Secretary of State and the Welsh Ministers see PARA 390.
2   'Services' includes services to enable the owner or occupier of land to carry out work under the authorisation of an order under the Land Drainage Act 1991 s 29 (which is concerned with the restoration and improvement of ditches): see s 29(7); and WATER AND WATERWAYS vol 101 (2009) PARA 588. The provision which may be made hereunder includes provision for any services or

goods mentioned in the Agriculture Act 1986 s 1(1) to be supplied through any person with whom the Secretary of State or the Welsh Ministers may enter into a contract for the making of the supply (s 1(3)(a) (s 1(3) substituted by the Deregulation and Contracting Out Act 1994 Sch 16 para 14)) or through any organisation established by him or it for these purposes (Agriculture Act 1986 s 1(3)(b) (as so substituted)).

3   Agriculture Act 1986 s 1(1)(a). As to the meaning of 'agriculture' see PARA 10. As to the meaning of 'food' see the Food Safety Act 1990 s 1; and FOOD AND DRINK vol 51 (2013) PARA 608 (definition applied by the Agriculture Act 1986 s 1(6) (amended by the Food Safety Act 1990 Sch 3 para 35)).
4   As to the meaning of 'amenity' see PARA 390 note 6.
5   Agriculture Act 1986 s 1(1)(b). The conservation of the natural beauty of the countryside includes the conservation of flora and fauna and geological and physiographical features: s 1(5).
6   Agriculture Act 1986 s 1(1)(c).
7   Agriculture Act 1986 s 1(2)(a).
8   Agriculture Act 1986 s 1(2)(b).
9   Agriculture Act 1986 s 1(2)(c).
10 Agriculture Act 1986 s 1(2)(d).
11 Agriculture Act 1986 s 1(2)(e). As to the drainage of land see WATER AND WATERWAYS vol 101 (2009) PARA 573 et seq.
12 Agriculture Act 1986 s 1(4).

392. Powers of entry and inspection.

For the purpose of determining whether any of the powers conferred by the Agriculture Act 1947[1] are to be exercised in relation to land, or whether any direction given under any such power has been complied with, any person authorised to do so by the Secretary of State or the Welsh Ministers[2] has power at all reasonable times to enter on and inspect any land[3]. In the case of land which is used for residential purposes, 24 hours' notice must be given to the occupier[4]. In all other cases notice must be given to the occupier that it is proposed to enter during a specified period, not exceeding 14 days and beginning at least 24 hours after the giving of the notice, and the entry must take place during that period[5]. In the event of a power of entry being used to secure compliance with certain directions or requirements[6] the necessity as to notice of entry applies only on the first entry and not on subsequent occasions[7]. In all cases the authorised person may be required to produce documentary proof of his authority[8]. Any person who obstructs the exercise of these powers[9] is guilty of an offence[9].

1   The powers relevant to this title are the powers as to the control of pests and captive animals under the Agriculture Act 1947 ss 98–100 (see PARAS 116–119).
2   As to the Secretary of State and the Welsh Ministers see PARA 390.
3   Agriculture Act 1947 s 106(1).
4   Agriculture Act 1947 s 106(3). For these purposes, 'occupier' in relation to unoccupied land means the person entitled to occupy it: Pests Act 1954 s 1(13). As to the service of notices see PARA 116 note 4.
5   Agriculture Act 1947 s 106(4) (amended by the Agriculture Act 1958 Sch 2 Pt I).
6   The relevant directions or requirements are those under the Agriculture Act 1947 ss 100 (see PARAS 116–118).
7   Agriculture Act 1947 s 106(4) proviso. Where in such a case notice is served upon an occupier and he is not the person to whom the original direction was given, or on whom the original requirement was imposed, a like notice must also be served upon the other person: see s 106(5). Such notice may be served in the same manner as the notice giving the direction or requirement: s 106(6).
8   Agriculture Act 1947 s 106(2) (amended by the Agriculture Act 1970 Sch 5 Pt III).
9   Ie any person who, in any case for which no penalty is provided by the foregoing provisions of Agriculture Act 1947 or under the Tribunals, Courts and Enforcement Act 2007 s 25 (supplementary powers of the Upper Tribunal), obstructs the exercise of any such power as aforesaid or of any other power conferred by the Agriculture Act 1947 s 100(2).

(2) AGRICULTURE AND HORTICULTURE DEVELOPMENT BOARD

393. Establishment of the Agriculture and Horticulture Development Board.

A body called the Agriculture and Horticulture Development Board is established[1] with the purposes of:

(1)   increasing efficiency or productivity in the industry;

(2)   improving marketing in the industry;

(3)   improving or developing services that the industry provides or could provide to the community; and

(4)   improving the ways in which the industry contributes to sustainable development[2].

1   Agriculture and Horticulture Development Board Order 2008, SI 2008/576, art 3(1). As to the constitution of the Agriculture and Horticulture Development Board see Sch 2. As to the functions of the Board see PARA 395. Pursuant to their power under the Natural Environment and Rural Communities Act 2006 ss 91–93 which allowed for the Secretary of State and the Welsh Ministers to dissolve such bodies, the following bodies are dissolved and all property, right and liability of the dissolved bodies are transferred to the Agriculture and Horticulture Development Board in accordance with Sch 4 (provisions relating to the transfer):

    (1)   the British Potato Council;

    (2)   the Home-Grown Cereals Authority;

    (3)   the Horticultural Development Council;

    (4)   the Meat and Livestock Commission; and

    (5)   the Milk Development Council: art 17.

2   Agriculture and Horticulture Development Board Order 2008, SI 2008/576, art 3(2).

394. Acting through subsidiaries.

The Agriculture and Horticulture Development Board[1] may establish a subsidiary company for each of the following industries:

(1)   the beef and sheep industry in England[2];

(2)   the cereal and oilseed industries in the United Kingdom[3];

(3)   the horticulture industry in Great Britain[4];

(4)   the milk industry in Great Britain[5];

(5)   the pig industry in England[6]; and

(6)   the potato industry in Great Britain[7],

within the scope of the Agriculture and Horticulture Development Board Order 2008[8] and may establish such other subsidiary companies as may be conducive or incidental to its functions, and a reference to a subsidiary company in that Order is a reference to such a company[9].

1   As to the establishment and constitution of the Agriculture and Horticulture Development Board see PARA 393.

2   For these purposes 'beef and sheep industry' means all the activities comprised in the production, marketing and distribution of:

    (1)   cattle and sheep, including the carrying on of slaughterhouses and cattle and sheep auctions and markets;

    (2)   meat and meat products (other than milk and milk products) from cattle and sheep: Agriculture and Horticulture Development Board Order 2008, SI 2008/576, art 2(2).

3   For these purposes 'cereal and oilseed industries' means the industries comprising the activities of growers and persons trading as wholesale buyers or sellers of cereal or oilseed, or processing cereal, and:

    (1)   'cereal' means wheat (including durum wheat), barley, oats, rye, maize, triticale or any two or more of such cereals grown as one crop; and

    (2)   'oilseed' means rapeseed, linseed, soyabean or sunflowerseed or any two or more of such oilseeds grown as one crop: Agriculture and Horticulture Development Board Order 2008, SI 2008/576, art 2(2).

4   For these purposes 'horticulture industry' means the growing of the horticultural products listed in the Agriculture and Horticulture Development Board Order 2008, SI 2008/576, Sch 3, Part 4 by way of business: art 2(2).

5   For these purposes 'milk industry' means the industry comprising the activities of producers in producing cows' milk or milk products and selling them by way of business: Agriculture and Horticulture Development Board Order 2008, SI 2008/576, art 2(2).

6   For these purposes 'pig industry" means all the activities comprised in the production, marketing and distribution of pigs or pig products, including the carrying on of slaughterhouses and pig auctions and markets: Agriculture and Horticulture Development Board Order 2008, SI 2008/576, art 2(2).

7   For these purposes 'potato industry' means the activities of persons in growing, selling, buying or in any way dealing in potatoes, whether raw or processed, by way of business: Agriculture and Horticulture Development Board Order 2008, SI 2008/576, art 2(2).

8   Ie within the Agriculture and Horticulture Development Board Order 2008, SI 2008/576.

9   Agriculture and Horticulture Development Board Order 2008, SI 2008/576, art 5(1). As to the function of the Agriculture and Horticulture Development Board see PARA 395. The Board may delegate any of its functions to a subsidiary company, but may continue to carry out any function it has delegated: art 5(2). A subsidiary company must carry out the functions in Sch 1 (see PARA 395) that the Board delegates to it: art 5(3).

395. Functions of the Agriculture and Horticulture Development Board.

The functions of the Agriculture and Horticulture Development Board[1] are the provision of any of the following services[2]:

(1)   promoting or undertaking scientific research[3];

(2)   promoting or undertaking inquiry[4] as to materials and equipment and as to methods of production, management and labour utilisation[4];

(3)   promoting the production and marketing of standard products[5];

(4)   promoting the better definition of trade descriptions and consistency in the use of trade descriptions[6];

(5)   developing, promoting, marketing or operating standards relating to the quality of products or systems for the classification of products[7];

(6)   developing, reviewing or operating schemes for the certification of products or of operations connected with production or supply of products[8];

(7)   undertaking the certification of products, the registration of certification trade marks, and the functions of proprietors of such marks[9];

(8)   providing or promoting the provision of:

       (a)   training for persons engaged in or proposing to be engaged in the industry, and

       (b)   their education in subjects relevant to the industry[10];

(9)   promoting:

       (a)   the adoption of measures for securing safer and better working conditions; and

       (b)   the provision and improvement of amenities for persons employed[11];

(10)   promoting or undertaking inquiry as to measures for securing safer and better working conditions[12];

(11)   promoting or undertaking research for improving arrangements for marketing and distributing products[13];

(12)   promoting or undertaking research into matters relating to the consumption or use of goods and services supplied by the industry[14];

(13)   promoting arrangements for co-operative organisations, for supplying materials and equipment and for marketing and distributing products[15];

(14)   promoting the development of export trade, including promoting or undertaking arrangements for publicity overseas[16];

(15)   promoting or undertaking arrangements for better acquainting the public in the United Kingdom with the goods and services supplied by the industry and methods of using them[17];

(16)   promoting or undertaking the collection and formulation of statistics[18];

(17)   advising on any matters relating to the industry (other than remuneration or conditions of employment) as to which the appropriate authority may request the Board to advise, and undertaking inquiry for the purpose of enabling it to advise on such matters[19];

(18)   undertaking arrangements for making available information obtained, and for advising, on matters with which the Board is concerned in the exercise of any of its functions[20];

(19)   engaging in any form of collaboration or co-operation with other persons in performing any of their functions[21];

(20)   promoting or undertaking research into the incidence, prevention and cure of industrial diseases[22];

(21)   promoting or undertaking arrangements for encouraging the entry of persons into the industry[23].

The Agriculture and Horticulture Development Board must impose a levy[24] to enable it to provide services for the beef and sheep industry in England, the cereal and oilseed industries in the United Kingdom, the horticulture industry in Great Britain, the milk industry in Great Britain, the pig industry in England and the potato industry in Great Britain[25].

1   As to the establishment and constitution of the Agriculture and Horticulture Development Board: see PARA 393.

2   Agriculture and Horticulture Development Board Order 2008, SI 2008/576, art 3(3). The Agriculture and Horticulture Development Board must provide the appropriate authority with such information as it may require relating to its property or to the discharge or proposed discharge of its functions: art 14(1). The Board must also permit any person authorised by the appropriate authority to inspect and make copies of its accounts or other documents and it must provide such explanation of them as that person or the appropriate authority may require: art 14(2).

3   Agriculture and Horticulture Development Board Order 2008, SI 2008/576, Sch 1 para 1.

4   Agriculture and Horticulture Development Board Order 2008, SI 2008/576, Sch 1 para 2(1). Promoting or undertaking inquiry under head (2) in the text includes promoting or undertaking:
    (1)   the discovery and development of new materials, equipment and methods and improvements in those already in use;
    (2)   the assessment of the advantages of different alternatives; and
    (3)   the conduct of experimental establishments and of tests on a commercial scale: Sch 1 para 2(2).

5   Agriculture and Horticulture Development Board Order 2008, SI 2008/576, Sch 1 para 3.
6   Agriculture and Horticulture Development Board Order 2008, SI 2008/576, Sch 1 para 4.
7   Agriculture and Horticulture Development Board Order 2008, SI 2008/576, Sch 1 para 5.
8   Agriculture and Horticulture Development Board Order 2008, SI 2008/576, Sch 1 para 6.
9   Agriculture and Horticulture Development Board Order 2008, SI 2008/576, Sch 1 para 7.
10   Agriculture and Horticulture Development Board Order 2008, SI 2008/576, Sch 1 para 8.
11   Agriculture and Horticulture Development Board Order 2008, SI 2008/576, Sch 1 para 9(1).
12   Agriculture and Horticulture Development Board Order 2008, SI 2008/576, Sch 1 para 9(2).
13   Agriculture and Horticulture Development Board Order 2008, SI 2008/576, Sch 1 para 10.
14   Agriculture and Horticulture Development Board Order 2008, SI 2008/576, Sch 1 para 11.
15   Agriculture and Horticulture Development Board Order 2008, SI 2008/576, Sch 1 para 12.
16   Agriculture and Horticulture Development Board Order 2008, SI 2008/576, Sch 1 para 13.
17   Agriculture and Horticulture Development Board Order 2008, SI 2008/576, Sch 1 para 14.
18   Agriculture and Horticulture Development Board Order 2008, SI 2008/576, Sch 1 para 15.
19   Agriculture and Horticulture Development Board Order 2008, SI 2008/576, Sch 1 para 16.
20   Agriculture and Horticulture Development Board Order 2008, SI 2008/576, Sch 1 para 17.
21   Agriculture and Horticulture Development Board Order 2008, SI 2008/576, Sch 1 para 18.
22   Agriculture and Horticulture Development Board Order 2008, SI 2008/576, Sch 1 para 19.

23 Agriculture and Horticulture Development Board Order 2008, SI 2008/576, Sch 1 para 20.
24 Agriculture and Horticulture Development Board Order 2008, SI 2008/576, art 6(1). The levies
    are to enable the Board to cover its costs in providing any of the services specified in Sch 1, meet
    its administrative expenses, further a purpose in art 3(2) and establish a reserve fund: art 6(3). The
    figures are given in Sch 3 and exclude VAT: art 6(2). The rate of levy (and any higher rate for late
    payment of the levy) must be approved annually by the appropriate authority: art 6(3). The Board
    may delegate the collection of levy to a subsidiary company: art 6(4). Levy raised in relation to an
    industry may only be used in relation to that industry: art 6(6). As to the power to estimate the
    amount see art 7. As to the power to establish a reserve fund see art 9. As to the incidental powers
    of the Board see art 10.
25 Agriculture and Horticulture Development Board Order 2008, SI 2008/576, art 6(1). As to the
    meanings of 'beef and sheep industry', the 'cereal and oilseed industries', the 'horticulture
    industry', the 'milk industry', the 'pig industry' and the 'potato industry' see PARA 394 notes 2–7.
    The Agriculture and Horticulture Development Board, or any subsidiary company, may make
    such charges for any services in addition to the services referred to in article 6 as appear to the
    Board or subsidiary company to be reasonable: art 8.

396. Ballots.

The Agriculture and Horticulture Development Board[1] may hold a ballot at
any time on whether or not a levy should continue[2]. It must do so if directed by
the appropriate authority[3]. It must do so if it receives within a three month period
one or more requests for a ballot signed by at least five percentage of persons
entitled to vote in a ballot[4].

The Board must immediately inform the appropriate authority of the result of
a ballot, but the appropriate authority is not bound by the result[5].

1 As to the establishment and constitution of the Agriculture and Horticulture Development Board:
   see PARA 393.
2 Agriculture and Horticulture Development Board Order 2008, SI 2008/576, art 11(1).
3 Agriculture and Horticulture Development Board Order 2008, SI 2008/576, art 11(2). As to who
   can vote see art 12.
4 Agriculture and Horticulture Development Board Order 2008, SI 2008/576, art 11(3). The three
   month period is calculated from the first day of any month: art 11(4). The maximum frequency
   with which ballots for the same levy can be held at the request of persons entitled to vote is 5 years:
   art 11(5).
5 Agriculture and Horticulture Development Board Order 2008, SI 2008/576, art 11(7).

(3) AGRICULTURAL BOARDS

397. Power to establish and dissolve boards.

The Secretary of State and the Welsh Ministers[1] may by order[2] establish a body
for one or more of the purposes of:

(1)   increasing efficiency or productivity in an agricultural[3] or related
       industry[4];
(2)   improving marketing in an agricultural or related industry[5];
(3)   improving or developing services[6] that an agricultural or related
       industry provides or could provide to the community[7]; and
(4)   improving the ways in which an agricultural or related industry
       contributes to sustainable development[8].

Such an order must specify the purpose or purposes for which the board is
established[9] and the industry to which the order relates[10], and must assign
functions to the board[11] and specify the area or areas in relation to which those
functions are exercisable[12]. The Secretary of State and the Welsh Ministers may
make grants to a board[13].

The Secretary of State and the Welsh Ministers may also by order provide for the dissolution of a board so established[14].

1   Ie the 'appropriate authority' in England and Wales: see generally PARA 390.
2   An order establishing a board under these provisions may make provision as to its functions (see PARA 398) and constitution (see PARA 399).
3   As to the meaning of 'agricultural' see PARA 10.
4   Natural Environment and Rural Communities Act 2006 ss 87(1)(a), 88(1)(a). 'Related industry' means an industry which is concerned with the production, processing, manufacture, marketing or distribution of anything (including any creature alive or dead) produced in the course of agriculture (s 88(5)(a)) and any product which is derived to any substantial extent from anything so produced (s 88(5)(b)).
5   Natural Environment and Rural Communities Act 2006 s 88(1)(b).
6   'Services' includes environmental and educational services: Natural Environment and Rural Communities Act 2006 s 88(6).
7   Natural Environment and Rural Communities Act 2006 s 88(1)(c).
8   Natural Environment and Rural Communities Act 2006 s 88(1)(d).
9   Natural Environment and Rural Communities Act 2006 s 88(2)(a).
10 Natural Environment and Rural Communities Act 2006 s 88(2)(b). For these purposes it does not matter whether the specified industry is regarded for any other purpose as an industry, a group of industries or a sector or sectors of an industry: s 88(3).
11 See the Natural Environment and Rural Communities Act 2006 s 87(1)(b); and PARA 398.
12 Natural Environment and Rural Communities Act 2006 s 87(2). The areas which may be so specified are England or an area in England, Wales or an area in Wales, Scotland or an area in Scotland, Northern Ireland or an area in Northern Ireland, or any combination of any of these areas: s 87(3).
13 Natural Environment and Rural Communities Act 2006 s 94(1). Any grants so made are to be of such amounts, and may be made subject to such conditions, as the Secretary of State thinks or the Welsh Ministers think fit: s 94(1), (2).
14 Natural Environment and Rural Communities Act 2006 s 92(1). Such an order must provide for the revocation of the order under s 87 establishing the board (s 92(2)), for the transfer of any property, rights or liabilities of the board (s 93(1)(b), (2)) and, if the order provides for the dissolution of a board in relation to which provision has been made by virtue of Sch 10 para 5 (levies: see PARA 400), for the application of any surplus either for the purposes for which the board was established (s 93(3)(b), (4)(a)) or for connected purposes (s 93(4)(b)). 'Surplus' means an amount by which the assets of the existing levy body exceeds its liabilities and expenses: Natural Environment and Rural Communities Act 2006 s 93(5).

398. Functions of boards.

An order establishing an agricultural board[1] must assign to that board a function or functions[2], which may include:

(1)   promoting or undertaking scientific research[3];
(2)   promoting or undertaking inquiry[4] as to materials and equipment[5] and methods of production, management and labour utilisation[6];
(3)   promoting the production and marketing of standard products[7];
(4)   promoting the better definition of trade descriptions and consistency in the use of trade descriptions[8];
(5)   developing, promoting, marketing or operating standards relating to the quality of products[9] or systems for the classification of products[10];
(6)   developing, reviewing or operating schemes for the certification of products or of operations connected with production or supply of products[11];
(7)   undertaking the certification of products, the registration of certification trade marks, and the functions of proprietors of such marks[12];
(8)   providing or promoting the provision of training for persons engaged in or proposing to be engaged in the industry[13] and their education in subjects relevant to the industry[14];

(9)   promoting the adoption of measures for securing safer and better working conditions[15] and the provision and improvement of amenities for persons employed[16];

(10)   promoting or undertaking inquiry as to measures for securing safer and better working conditions[17];

(11)   promoting or undertaking research into the incidence, prevention and cure of industrial diseases[18];

(12)   promoting or undertaking arrangements for encouraging the entry of persons into the industry[19];

(13)   promoting or undertaking research for improving arrangements for marketing and distributing products[20];

(14)   promoting or undertaking research into matters relating to the consumption or use of goods and services supplied by the industry[21];

(15)   promoting arrangements for co-operative organisations[22], for supplying materials and equipment[23], and for marketing and distributing products[24];

(16)   promoting the development of export trade, including promoting or undertaking arrangements for publicity overseas[25];

(17)   promoting or undertaking arrangements for better acquainting the public in the United Kingdom with the goods and services[26] supplied by the industry and methods of using them[27];

(18)   promoting or undertaking the collection and formulation of statistics[28];

(19)   advising on any matters relating to the industry (other than remuneration or conditions of employment) as to which the Secretary of State and the Welsh Ministers[29] may request the board to advise, and undertaking inquiry for the purpose of enabling the board to advise on such matters[30];

(20)   undertaking arrangements for making available information obtained, and for advising, on matters with which the board is concerned in the exercise of any of its functions[31];

(21)   a function which is a more limited version of any of the above[32];

(22)   an existing function (that is, a function which, immediately before the commencement of the order, is a function of the existing levy bodies)[33];

(23)   a function which is a more limited version of an existing function[34];

(24)   a function which is a combination of two or more functions described in heads (1) to (20) above or existing functions[35]; or

(25)   any additional function, if it appears to the Secretary of State or the Welsh Ministers to be related or similar to, or connected with, any function being assigned by virtue of any of heads (1) to (24) above[36] or to be capable of being conveniently exercised in association with any function being so assigned[37].

The Secretary of State and the Welsh Ministers may give a board general or specific directions as to the exercise of its functions[38], with which the board must comply[39].

1   Ie a body established by order under the Natural Environment and Rural Communities Act 2006 s 87 (see PARA 397): s 87(4).

2   Natural Environment and Rural Communities Act 2006 s 87(1)(b).

3   Natural Environment and Rural Communities Act 2006 s 89(1)(a), Sch 9 para 1.

4   For this purpose 'promoting or undertaking inquiry' includes promoting or undertaking the discovery and development of new materials, equipment and methods (Natural Environment and Rural Communities Act 2006 Sch 9 para 2(2)(a)(i)) and improvements in those already in use

(Sch 9 para 2(2)(a)(ii)), the assessment of the advantages of different alternatives (Sch 9 para 2(2)(b)), and the conduct of experimental establishments and of tests on a commercial scale (Sch 9 para 2(2)(c)).

5   Natural Environment and Rural Communities Act 2006 Sch 9 para 2(1)(a).
6   Natural Environment and Rural Communities Act 2006 Sch 9 para 2(1)(b).
7   Natural Environment and Rural Communities Act 2006 Sch 9 para 3.
8   Natural Environment and Rural Communities Act 2006 Sch 9 para 4.
9   Natural Environment and Rural Communities Act 2006 Sch 9 para 5(a).
10 Natural Environment and Rural Communities Act 2006 Sch 9 para 5(b).
11 Natural Environment and Rural Communities Act 2006 Sch 9 para 6.
12 Natural Environment and Rural Communities Act 2006 Sch 9 para 7.
13 Natural Environment and Rural Communities Act 2006 Sch 9 para 8(a).
14 Natural Environment and Rural Communities Act 2006 Sch 9 para 8(b).
15 Natural Environment and Rural Communities Act 2006 Sch 9 para 9(1)(a).
16 Natural Environment and Rural Communities Act 2006 Sch 9 para 9(1)(b).
17 Natural Environment and Rural Communities Act 2006 Sch 9 para 9(2).
18 Natural Environment and Rural Communities Act 2006 Sch 9 para 10.
19 Natural Environment and Rural Communities Act 2006 Sch 9 para 11.
20 Natural Environment and Rural Communities Act 2006 Sch 9 para 12.
21 Natural Environment and Rural Communities Act 2006 Sch 9 para 13.
22 Natural Environment and Rural Communities Act 2006 Sch 9 para 14(a).
23 Natural Environment and Rural Communities Act 2006 Sch 9 para 14(b).
24 Natural Environment and Rural Communities Act 2006 Sch 9 para 14(c).
25 Natural Environment and Rural Communities Act 2006 Sch 9 para 15.
26 As to the meaning of 'services' see PARA 332 note 3.
27 Natural Environment and Rural Communities Act 2006 Sch 9 para 16.
28 Natural Environment and Rural Communities Act 2006 Sch 9 para 17.
29 As to the Secretary of State and the Welsh Ministers (ie the 'appropriate authority' in England and Wales) see generally PARA 390.
30 Natural Environment and Rural Communities Act 2006 Sch 9 para 18.
31 Natural Environment and Rural Communities Act 2006 Sch 9 para 19.
32 Natural Environment and Rural Communities Act 2006 s 89(1)(c).
33 Natural Environment and Rural Communities Act 2006 s 89(1)(b). As to the existing levy bodies, and for the power to dissolve any or all of them, see s 91.
34 Natural Environment and Rural Communities Act 2006 s 89(1)(c).
35 Natural Environment and Rural Communities Act 2006 s 89(1)(d).
36 Natural Environment and Rural Communities Act 2006 s 89(1)(e)(i).
37 Natural Environment and Rural Communities Act 2006 s 89(1)(e)(ii).
38 Natural Environment and Rural Communities Act 2006 s 95(1). The power to give directions includes power to vary or revoke the directions: s 95(3). The Secretary of State and the Welsh Ministers must publish any directions so given as soon as is reasonably practicable after giving the directions: s 95(2).
39 Natural Environment and Rural Communities Act 2006 s 95(4).

399.   Constitution of boards.

An agricultural board[1] is to be known by a name specified in the order establishing it[2]. A board is[3] a body corporate[4] and is not to be regarded as a servant or agent of the Crown[5] or as enjoying any status, privilege or immunity of the Crown[6], and its property is not to be regarded as property of, or held on behalf of, the Crown[7]. A board is to consist of a chairman appointed by the Secretary of State or the Welsh Ministers[8] and such other number of members as the Secretary of State or the Welsh Ministers may appoint[9]; and the Secretary of State or the Welsh Ministers may appoint one of the members to be deputy chairman[10].

The order establishing the board[11] may include provision:

(1)   as to qualification or disqualification for membership[12];
(2)   as to the term of office of members[13], and their removal from office[14];
(3)   as to the payment to the members of remuneration and allowances[15];
(4)   as to the payment of pensions, gratuities or allowances to or in respect of the members[16];

(5)   as to the appointment of employees, their remuneration and other terms of employment[17];

(6)   requiring the board to prepare and submit reports to persons specified in the order[18]; and

(7)   requiring any documents of a description specified in the order to be subject to administrative scrutiny[19],

and must include provision:

(a)   requiring the board to prepare and submit accounts to persons specified in the order[20]; and

(b)   requiring a statement of the accounts to be examined, certified and reported on by the Comptroller and Auditor General[21].

1   Ie a body established by order under the Natural Environment and Rural Communities Act 2006 s 87 (see PARA 397): s 87(4).

2   Natural Environment and Rural Communities Act 2006 s 87(5).

3   Ie by virtue of the Natural Environment and Rural Communities Act 2006 Sch 8.

4   Natural Environment and Rural Communities Act 2006 Sch 8 para 1.

5   Natural Environment and Rural Communities Act 2006 Sch 8 para 2(a).

6   Natural Environment and Rural Communities Act 2006 Sch 8 para 2(b).

7   Natural Environment and Rural Communities Act 2006 Sch 8 para 2.

8   Natural Environment and Rural Communities Act 2006 Sch 8 para 3(a). As to the Secretary of State and the Welsh Ministers (ie the 'appropriate authority' in England and Wales) see generally PARA 390.

9   Natural Environment and Rural Communities Act 2006 Sch 8 para 3(b).

10   Natural Environment and Rural Communities Act 2006 Sch 8 para 4.

11   Ie the order under the Natural Environment and Rural Communities Act 2006 s 87 (see PARA 397).

12   Natural Environment and Rural Communities Act 2006 Sch 8 para 5.

13   Natural Environment and Rural Communities Act 2006 Sch 8 para 6(a).

14   Natural Environment and Rural Communities Act 2006 Sch 8 para 6(b).

15   Natural Environment and Rural Communities Act 2006 Sch 8 para 7(a).

16   Natural Environment and Rural Communities Act 2006 Sch 8 para 7(b).

17   Natural Environment and Rural Communities Act 2006 Sch 8 para 8.

18   Natural Environment and Rural Communities Act 2006 Sch 8 para 9.

19   Natural Environment and Rural Communities Act 2006 Sch 8 para 11. This involves including provision requiring any documents of a description specified in the order to be laid before each House of Parliament (Sch 8 para 11(a)), the National Assembly for Wales (Sch 8 para 11(b)), the Scottish Parliament (Sch 8 para 11(c)) or the Northern Ireland Assembly (Sch 8 para 11(d)), as applicable. As to the laying of documents before Parliament see the Laying of Documents before Parliament (Interpretation) Act 1948; and STATUTES AND LEGISLATIVE PROCESS vol 96 (2012) PARAS 1048, 1052. As respects Wales see the Government of Wales Act 2006 s 162, Sch 11 para 36; and STATUTES AND LEGISLATIVE PROCESS vol 96 (2012) PARA 1035.

20   Natural Environment and Rural Communities Act 2006 Sch 8 para 10(a).

21   Natural Environment and Rural Communities Act 2006 Sch 8 para 10(b). As to the Comptroller and Auditor General see CONSTITUTIONAL AND ADMINISTRATIVE LAW vol 20 (2014) PARAS 494–496.

400. Powers of boards.

The order establishing an agricultural board[1] may include provision:

(1)   enabling the board to establish[2], and enabling or requiring it to carry out specified functions through[3], subsidiaries[4];

(2)   with respect to registration in a register kept by the board of persons carrying on business in a specified industry[5];

(3)   conferring power on the board to require persons carrying on business in a specified industry to supply to the board returns and other information[6];

(4)   conferring a power of entry on authorised officers[7] for the purpose of enabling them to carry out functions of the board[8];

(5)   conferring power on authorised officers to require persons of a specified description to provide information of a specified description[9] or to produce documents of a specified description[10];

(6)   enabling the board to hold inquiries[11];

(7)   enabling the board to establish and maintain a reserve fund for the purposes of its functions[12];

(8)   conferring on the board power to borrow money[13] and charge property[14];

(9)   for the imposition by the board of charges ('levies') on such persons as may be specified[15];

(10) enabling the board to do anything that appears to it to be conducive or incidental to the discharge of its functions[16];

(11) making the exercise of a specified function or description of functions conferred on the board subject to the approval of the Secretary of State or the Welsh Ministers[17] or to any other conditions[18]; and

(12) for the appointment of a Consumers' Committee which the board is required to consult in relation to specified matters[19].

An order may also provide that the board (or a subsidiary of the board) may make such charges for any services as appear to the board (or the subsidiary) to be reasonable[20].

1   Ie an order under the Natural Environment and Rural Communities Act 2006 s 87 (see PARA 397).

2   Natural Environment and Rural Communities Act 2006 Sch 10 para 1(1)(a).

3   Natural Environment and Rural Communities Act 2006 Sch 10 para 1(1)(b).

4   'Subsidiary' means a subsidiary as defined in the Companies Act 1985 s 736 (see COMPANIES vol 14 (2016) PARA 22): Natural Environment and Rural Communities Act 2006 Sch 10 para 1(2).

5   Natural Environment and Rural Communities Act 2006 Sch 10 para 2(1)(a). The order may include provision requiring the register to be made available (in accordance with the order) for inspection by the public (Sch 10 para 2(1)(b)) and under which any right to inspect the register is subject to the payment of a reasonable fee (Sch 10 para 2(1)(c)), and may also create offences in relation to failing to comply with a requirement relating to registration (Sch 10 para 9(1)(a)). If an order creates an offence by virtue of Sch 10 para 9(1), it must provide for the offence to be triable only summarily (Sch 10 para 9(2)(a)) and may not provide for the offence to be punishable with imprisonment (Sch 10 para 9(2)(b)); it may make provision enabling proceedings for an offence under the order to be brought within the period of six months beginning with the date on which evidence sufficient in the opinion of the prosecutor to warrant the proceedings came to his knowledge (Sch 10 para 9(3)(a)) but may not authorise the commencement of proceedings for such an offence more than two years after the date on which the offence was committed (Sch 10 para 9(3)(b)).

6   Natural Environment and Rural Communities Act 2006 Sch 10 para 2(2). An order may create offences in relation to providing false or misleading information to the board: Sch 10 para 9(1)(e). As to offences under Sch 10 para 9(1) generally see note 5.

7   'Authorised officer', in relation to a power, means a person authorised to exercise the power by, or on behalf of, the board to which the order under the Natural Environment and Rural Communities Act 2006 s 87 relates: Sch 10 para 3(4).

8   Natural Environment and Rural Communities Act 2006 Sch 10 para 3(1). An order may not, however, include provision conferring power to enter a dwelling: Sch 10 para 3(2). An order may create offences in relation to obstructing an authorised officer exercising a power of entry: Sch 10 para 9(1)(b). As to offences under Sch 10 para 9(1) generally see note 5.

9   Natural Environment and Rural Communities Act 2006 Sch 10 para 3(3)(a). An order may create offences in relation to failing to comply with a requirement to provide information (Sch 10 para 9(1)(c)) or providing false or misleading information to an authorised officer (Sch 10 para 9(1)(e)). As to offences under Sch 10 para 9(1) generally see note 5.

10 Natural Environment and Rural Communities Act 2006 Sch 10 para 3(3)(b). An order may create offences in relation to failing to comply with a requirement to produce documents: Sch 10 para 9(1)(c). As to offences under Sch 10 para 9(1) generally see note 5.

11 Natural Environment and Rural Communities Act 2006 Sch 10 para 3(5)(a). Pursuant to this an order may include provision enabling a board to require a person to attend to give evidence (Sch 10 para 3(5)(b)), and as to appeals against a requirement so imposed (Sch 10 para 3(5)(c)), and may create offences in relation to neglecting or failing to comply with a requirement to attend to give evidence (Sch 10 para 9(1)(d)). As to offences under Sch 10 para 9(1) generally see note 5.

12 Natural Environment and Rural Communities Act 2006 Sch 10 para 4(1). As to a board's functions see PARA 398. The order may also make provision with respect to powers of investment over a reserve fund or any other money of the board which is not immediately required for any other purpose: Sch 10 para 4(2).

13 Natural Environment and Rural Communities Act 2006 Sch 10 para 4(3)(a).

14 Natural Environment and Rural Communities Act 2006 Sch 10 para 4(3)(b).

15 Natural Environment and Rural Communities Act 2006 Sch 10 para 5(1)(a). The purpose or purposes for which any levies are imposed must be specified in the order: Sch 10 para 5(3). Provision may be made as to limits on the amounts of levies (Sch 10 para 5(1)(b)) and for the recovery of levies in such ways and through such channels as may be specified in the order (Sch 10 para 5(1)(c)); however, the order may not include any provision for the imposition by the board of levies except for the purpose of enabling a board to meet its expenses in the exercise of its functions (Sch 10 para 5(2)(a)), to meet its administrative expenses (Sch 10 para 5(2)(b)), to further a purpose or the purposes for which it is established (Sch 10 para 5(2)(c)), or to establish a reserve fund (Sch 10 para 5(2)(d)).

16 Natural Environment and Rural Communities Act 2006 Sch 10 para 7(1). The order may, in particular, provide that the board may enter into agreements (Sch 10 para 7(2)(a)), acquire or dispose of property (Sch 10 para 7(2)(b)), raise funds by means of voluntary contributions (whether or not the order also makes provision for the imposition of levies) (Sch 10 para 7(2)(c), (3)), or accept gifts (Sch 10 para 7(2)(d)).

17 Natural Environment and Rural Communities Act 2006 Sch 10 para 8(1)(a). As to the Secretary of State and the Welsh Ministers (ie the 'appropriate authority' in England and Wales) see generally PARA 390.

18 Natural Environment and Rural Communities Act 2006 Sch 10 para 8(1)(b). The provision that may be made by virtue of Sch 10 para 8(1)(b) includes, in particular, provision requiring the board to be satisfied, before a levy is either imposed or terminated, that the imposition or termination of the levy is desired by a substantial number of the persons who would be or are affected by the levy (Sch 10 para 8(2)(a)), provision requiring ballots to be conducted, in such circumstances as may be specified in the order, for the purpose of ascertaining the views of persons who would be or are affected by a levy (Sch 10 para 8(2)(b)), and provision requiring the board to consult a specified person or a description of persons before exercising a specified function or description of functions (Sch 10 para 8(2)(c)).

19 Natural Environment and Rural Communities Act 2006 Sch 10 para 8(3).

20 Natural Environment and Rural Communities Act 2006 Sch 10 para 6.

(4) ROYAL AGRICULTURAL SOCIETY AND ROYAL HORTICULTURAL SOCIETY

401. Royal Agricultural Society.

The Royal Agricultural Society of England was incorporated by charter in 1840[1]. By its most recent charter, granted in 1996, the society's objects are:

(1)   to promote and improve the science, technology, art and practice of agriculture, forestry, horticulture, kindred activities and the husbandry of livestock (including horses) and land;

(2)   to promote the application of improved methods and processes connected therewith by demonstration and other appropriate means;

(3) to promote agricultural and environmental education, research and development and experimental work by maintaining and conducting a learned society and by publications, grants and other means;

(4) to advance religion by the promotion of religious activities and values amongst rural communities in such ways as may from time to time be determined.

1 By supplemental charter of 1905, the method of holding general and other meetings, and of electing officers and members, was varied.

402. Royal Horticultural Society.

The Royal Horticultural Society was founded in 1804 (originally under the title 'The Horticultural Society of London') and was incorporated by royal charter in 1809[1]. The objects of the society are the encouragement and improvement of the science, art and practice of horticulture in all its branches[2]. The society holds shows, meetings and lectures. It has established an experimental garden, and maintains a library, conducts trials and investigations. It has instituted a series of examinations and qualifications in horticulture and offers a wide ranging advisory service to all gardeners. The society is governed by a president and a council of between 12 and 19 members.

1 Supplementary charters were granted in 1861 (when the society took its present name), 1899, 1928 and 1987.
2 See the preamble to the 1987 charter.

(5) COLLECTION OF AGRICULTURAL STATISTICS

403. Power to obtain statistics.

For the purpose of obtaining agricultural statistics the Secretary of State and the Welsh Ministers[1] may serve notices on owners and occupiers of land used for agriculture or which may be so used[2], requiring them to furnish such information as may be specified in the notices[3]. Notices may require information to be given relating to:

(1) the situation, area, description and extent of the land, the date when acquired and the date at which so much of it as is comprised in any agricultural unit[4] became so comprised, and the rates payable in respect of the land[5];

(2) any person who is an owner or occupier of the land or any part of it, and the terms on which, and arrangements under which, the land or any part of it is owned, occupied, managed or farmed by any person[6];

(3) the character and use of different parts of the land, the time at which any use of such parts was begun or will become fully effective, and their produce at any time during the period beginning one year before, and ending one year after, the time at which the information is required to be furnished[7];

(4) fixed and other equipment[8], livestock[9], and the stocks of agricultural produce and requisites held in respect of the land, and the provision and maintenance of such equipment, livestock and requisites and the provision of agricultural services for the benefit of the land[10];

(5)   the methods and operations used on the land, the marketing or other disposal of its produce, any payments received under any enactment in respect of such produce, and the provision of agricultural services otherwise than for the benefit of the land[11]; and

(6)   the number and description of persons employed on the land, or employed by the occupier in disposing of its produce, and the remuneration paid to, and hours worked by, persons so employed or such persons of different descriptions[12],

although no person may be required pursuant to these provisions to furnish any balance sheet or profit and loss account[13].

Information which could be required by notice to be furnished may also be required to be furnished by an oral demand by any person authorised by the Secretary of State or the Welsh Ministers in that behalf, after giving not less than 24 hours' notice and on producing, if so required, evidence of authority: such information may be required to be given within a reasonable time after the demand and may be given orally or in writing as the informant may elect[14].

1   As to the Secretary of State and the Welsh Ministers see PARA 390.
2   'Owner' means a person, other than a mortgagee not in possession, who is for the time being entitled to dispose of the fee simple of the land, and includes also a person holding, or entitled to the rents and profits of, the land under a lease or agreement (Agricultural Statistics Act 1979 s 6(1)); and for the purposes of s 1(1), (2) includes a person exercising, as servant or agent of the owner, functions of estate management in relation to the land (s 1(3)). As to the meanings of 'agriculture' and 'occupier' see PARA 10. For the purposes of s 1, the term 'occupier' includes persons responsible for the control and farming of the land as servants or agents of the occupier: s 1(3). 'Land' includes messuages, tenements and hereditaments, houses and buildings of any tenure: s 6(1).
    Any notice authorised by the Agricultural Statistics Act 1979 to be served on any person is duly served if it is delivered to him, or left at his proper address or sent to him by post in a registered letter (s 5(1)), and any such notice authorised to be served on an incorporated company or body is duly served if served on the secretary or clerk of the company or body (s 5(2)). For these purposes the 'proper address' of any person on whom any such notice is to be served, in the case of the secretary or clerk of any incorporated company or body, is that of the registered or principal office of the company or body, and in any other case is the last known address of the person in question: s 5(3). Where any such notice is to be served on a person as being the person having any interest in land, and it is not practicable after reasonable inquiry to ascertain his name or address, the notice may be served by addressing it to him by the description of the person having that interest in the land (naming it), and delivering the notice to some responsible person on the land or by affixing it, or a copy of it, to some conspicuous object on the land: s 5(4). Where any such notice is to be served on any person as being the owner of the land and the land is vested in the incumbent of a benefice of the Church of England, a copy must be served on the Diocesan Board of Finance for the diocese in which the land is situated (s 5(5) (amended by the Church of England (Miscellaneous Provisions) Measure 2006 Sch 5 para 19)). Without prejudice to these requirements, any notice under the Agricultural Statistics Act 1979 to be served on an occupier is deemed to be duly served if it is addressed to him by the description of 'the occupier' of the land in question and sent by post to, or delivered to some person on, the land: s 5(6).
3   Agricultural Statistics Act 1979 s 1(1).
4   As to the meaning of 'agricultural unit' see PARA 10 note 7.
5   Agricultural Statistics Act 1979 s 1(1)(a).
6   Agricultural Statistics Act 1979 s 1(1)(b) (substituted by the Agriculture (Amendment) Act 1984 s 2).
7   Agricultural Statistics Act 1979 s 1(1)(d).
8   As to the meaning of 'fixed equipment' see PARA 11 note 7; definition applied by the Agricultural Statistics Act 1979 s 6(2).
9   'Livestock' includes creatures kept for any purpose: Agricultural Statistics Act 1979 s 6(1).
10 Agricultural Statistics Act 1979 s 1(1)(e).
11 Agricultural Statistics Act 1979 s 1(1)(f).
12 Agricultural Statistics Act 1979 s 1(1)(g).

13 Agricultural Statistics Act 1979 s 1(4). This does not, however, prevent the requiring of information by reason only that it is or might be contained as an item in such a balance sheet or account: s 1(4).
14 Agricultural Statistics Act 1979 s 1(2).

404. Use and disclosure of information.

The Secretary of State and the Welsh Ministers[1] may use any information they obtain[2] in any manner they think necessary or expedient in connection with maintaining food supplies in the United Kingdom[3], but no such information relating to any particular land[4] or business may be disclosed without the written consent of the informant and of every owner or occupier[5] whose interests may be affected[6], except:

(1)   to the minister in charge of any government department, the Scottish Ministers, any authority acting under an enactment for regulating the marketing of any agricultural produce, or any person exercising functions on behalf of any such minister, the Scottish Ministers or authority for the purpose of the exercise of those functions[7];

(2)   to an authority having power under any enactment to give permission for the development of land, for the purpose of assisting that authority in the preparation of proposals relating to such development or in considering whether or not to give such permission[8];

(3)   if the disclosure is confined to situation, extent, number and kind of livestock[9], character of land, and name and address of owner and occupier, to any person to whom the Secretary of State considers or the Welsh Ministers consider that the disclosure is required in the public interest[10];

(4)   to any person for the purposes of any criminal proceedings[11] or for the purposes of any report of such proceedings[12];

(5)   to an institution of the European Communities[13];

(6)   to the Food Standards Agency[14] for purposes connected with the carrying out of any of its functions[15];

(7)   in connection with the use of information in any manner which the Secretary of State thinks or the Welsh Ministers think necessary or expedient in connection with the maintenance of the supply of food in the United Kingdom[16]; or

(8)   to the Statistics Board[17] for purposes connected with the carrying out of any of its functions, or by the Board to an approved researcher[18].

1   As to the Secretary of State and the Welsh Ministers see PARA 390.
2   Ie under the Agricultural Statistics Act 1979 s 1: see PARA 403.
3   As to the meaning of 'United Kingdom' see PARA 49 note 10.
4   As to the meaning of 'land' see PARA 403 note 2.
5   As to the meanings of 'owner' and 'occupier', see PARA 403 note 2.
6   Agricultural Statistics Act 1979 s 3(1).
7   Agricultural Statistics Act 1979 s 3(2)(a) (amended by SI 1999/1820). Information that may under these provisions be disclosed to a government department, the minister in charge of a government department or the Scottish Ministers may, in like manner, be disclosed in pursuance of an EU obligation to an EU institution: European Communities Act 1972 s 12 (amended by the Agricultural Statistics Act 1979 Sch 1 para 4; and SI 1999/1820).
8   Agricultural Statistics Act 1979 s 3(2)(b).
9   As to the meaning of 'livestock' see PARA 403 note 9.
10 Agricultural Statistics Act 1979 s 3(2)(c).
11 Ie under the Agricultural Statistics Act 1979 s 4 (see PARA 405).
12 Agricultural Statistics Act 1979 s 3(2)(d).

13 Agricultural Statistics Act 1979 s 3(2)(f). Such disclosure may be effected under the European Communities Act 1972 s 12.

14 As to the Food Standards Agency and its functions see FOOD AND DRINK vol 51 (2013) PARAS 634–653.

15 Agricultural Statistics Act 1979 s 3(2)(g) (added by the Food Standards Act 1999 Sch 5 para 5).

16 Agricultural Statistics Act 1979 s 3(2).

17 As to the Statistics Board see the Statistics and Registration Service Act 2007 Pt 1 (ss 1–67).

18 Agricultural Statistics Act 1979 s 3(2)(h) (added by the Statistics and Registration Service Act 2007 Sch 2 para 4). As to the meaning of 'approved researcher' see s 39(4)(i); definition applied by the Agricultural Statistics Act 1979 s 3(2)(h) (as so added).

405. Offences and penalties.

Failure to furnish any information required[1], without reasonable excuse, is punishable on summary conviction by a fine not exceeding level 3 on the standard scale[2]. Knowingly or recklessly furnishing any information that is false in any material particular, in purported compliance with a disclosure requirement[3], or publishing or disclosing any information in contravention of the prohibition against disclosure[4], is punishable on summary conviction by three months' imprisonment or a fine not exceeding the prescribed sum[5] or both such fine and imprisonment, or on conviction on indictment by two years' imprisonment or a fine or both such fine and imprisonment[6].

1 Ie under the Agricultural Statistics Act 1979 s 1: see PARA 403.

2 Agricultural Statistics Act 1979 s 4(1) (amended by virtue of the Criminal Justice Act 1982 ss 38, 46). As to the standard scale and the powers of magistrates' courts to issue fines on summary conviction see SENTENCING vol 92 (2015) PARA 176.

3 See note 1.

4 See PARA 404.

5 As to the prescribed sum see PARA 58 note 1.

6 Agricultural Statistics Act 1979 s 4(2).

(6) AGRICULTURAL CHARGES

406. Creation and nature of an agricultural charge.

A farmer[1] may, notwithstanding any provision in his contract of tenancy to the contrary[2], by instrument in writing[3] create in favour of a bank[4] an agricultural charge on all or any of his farming stock[5] and other agricultural assets[6] as security for sums on short term credit advanced to him or paid on his behalf under any guarantee by the bank, and interest, commission, and charges thereon[7].

An agricultural charge may be either a fixed charge or a floating charge, or both[8], and may be in such form and made upon such conditions as may be agreed, and sureties may be made parties thereto[9]. The amount secured by an agricultural charge may be either a specified amount, or a fluctuating amount advanced on current account not exceeding at any one time such amount, if any, as may be specified in the charge; and in the latter case the mere fact that the current account has ceased to be in debit does not redeem the charge[10].

1 For these purposes a 'farmer' is any person (not being an incorporated company or society) who, as tenant or owner of an agricultural holding, cultivates the holding for profit: Agricultural Credits Act 1928 s 5(7). As to the meanings of 'agriculture' and 'cultivation' see PARA 10. As to agricultural holdings see AGRICULTURAL LAND AND ALLOTMENTS vol 1 (2017) PARA 421 et seq.

2 Agricultural Credits Act 1928 s 13.

3 The instrument creating the charge is exempt from stamp duty: Agricultural Credits Act 1928 s 8(8).

4　By virtue of the Agricultural Credits Act 1928 s 5(7) (definition substituted by SI 2001/3649 and amended by the Financial Services Act 2012 Sch 18 Pt 2 para 28), 'bank' means:

　　(1)　the Bank of England (see FINANCIAL INSTITUTIONS vol 48 (2015) PARAS 97–111);

　　(2)　a person who has permission under the Financial Services and Markets Act 2000 Pt 4A (ss 55A–55Z4) to accept deposits (see FINANCIAL SERVICES REGULATION vol 50 (2016) PARAS 508–542); or

　　(3)　an EEA firm of the kind mentioned in Sch 3 para 5(b) which has permission under Sch 3 para 15 (as a result of qualifying for authorisation under Sch 3 para 12(1)) to accept deposits or other repayable funds from the public (see FINANCIAL SERVICES REGULATION vol 50 (2016) PARA 462).

　　Heads (2) and (3) of this definition must be read with s 22, any relevant order thereunder and Sch 2 (see FINANCIAL SERVICES REGULATION vol 50 (2016) PARAS 107–108): Agricultural Credits Act 1928 s 5(7A) (added by SI 2001/3649).

5　'Farming stock' means crops or horticultural produce, whether growing or severed from the land, and after severance whether subjected to any treatment or process of manufacture or not; livestock, including poultry and bees, and the produce and progeny thereof; any other agricultural or horticultural produce whether subjected to any treatment or process of manufacture or not; seeds and manures; agricultural vehicles, machinery, and other plant; agricultural tenant's fixtures and other agricultural fixtures which a tenant is by law authorised to remove: Agricultural Credits Act 1928 s 5(7).

6　'Other agricultural assets' means a tenant's right to compensation under the Agricultural Holdings Act 1986 (except s 60(2)(b) (see AGRICULTURAL LAND AND ALLOTMENTS vol 1 (2017) PARA 545) or s 62 (see AGRICULTURAL LAND AND ALLOTMENTS vol 1 (2017) PARA 551)) for improvements, damage by game, disturbance or otherwise, a tenant's right to compensation under the Agricultural Tenancies Act 1995 s 16 (see AGRICULTURAL LAND AND ALLOTMENTS vol 1 (2017) PARA 411) and any other tenant right (see AGRICULTURAL LAND AND ALLOTMENTS vol 1 (2017) PARA 528 et seq): Agricultural Credits Act 1928 s 5(7) (amended by the Agricultural Holdings Act 1986 Sch 14 para 16; and the Agricultural Tenancies Act 1995 Schedule para 7).

7　Agricultural Credits Act 1928 s 5(1). A bank which takes an assignment of farming stock and other agricultural assets does not become a 'tenant' within the meaning of the Agricultural Holdings Act 1986 s 96(1) (see AGRICULTURAL LAND AND ALLOTMENTS vol 1 (2017) PARA 423 note 5), and so has no right to proceed to arbitration under that Act: *Ecclesiastical Comrs for England v National Provincial Bank Ltd* [1935] 1 KB 566.

8　Agricultural Credits Act 1928 s 5(2).

9　Agricultural Credits Act 1928 s 5(6).

10　Agricultural Credits Act 1928 s 5(5).

407.　Fixed charges.

A fixed charge affects such of the farming stock[1] and other agricultural assets[2] belonging to the farmer[3] at the date of the charge as is specified in the charge, but may also include, in the case of livestock, any progeny born after the date of the charge[4], and any agricultural plant substituted for the plant specified in the charge[5].

A fixed charge confers on the bank[6] a right, upon the happening of any event specified in the charge as being an event authorising seizure of property subject to the charge, to take possession of such property[7], and where possession has been so taken, a right, after an interval of five clear days or such less time as may be allowed by the charge, to sell the property by auction or, if the charge so provides, by private treaty, and either for a lump sum payment or payment by instalments[8]. In the event of such power of sale being exercised, the bank is under an obligation to apply the proceeds of sale towards the discharge of the money and liabilities secured by the charge, and the costs of seizure and sale, and to pay the surplus, if any, of the proceeds to the farmer[9].

Whenever the farmer sells any of the property, or receives any money in respect of other agricultural assets comprised in the charge[10], or in the event of his receiving any money under a policy of insurance on any of the property charged, or paid as compensation under the Animal Health Act 1981[11] or under the Plant Health Act 1967[12], in respect of the destruction of any livestock or crops comprised in the charge[13], the fixed charge imposes on the farmer the obligation forthwith to pay to the bank the amount of the proceeds of the sale or the money so received, except to such extent as the charge otherwise provides or the bank otherwise allows, and the sum so paid must be applied, except so far as otherwise agreed, by the bank in or towards the discharge of the money and liabilities secured by the charge[14]. If any proceeds of sale are paid to a person other than the bank, the bank has no right to recover such proceeds from that person unless the bank proves that he knew that the proceeds were paid to him in breach of the obligation[15]. A farmer who, with intent to defraud, fails to comply with the obligations as to payment over to the bank of any money received by him[16], or removes from the holding any property subject to the charge[17], is guilty of an offence[18].

Subject to compliance with these obligations, a fixed charge does not prevent the farmer selling any of the property subject to the charge, and neither the purchaser nor, in the case of a sale by auction, the auctioneer is concerned to see that the obligations are complied with, notwithstanding that he may be aware of the existence of the charge[19].

1   As to the meaning of 'farming stock' see PARA 406 note 5.
2   As to the meaning of 'other agricultural assets' see PARA 406 note 6.
3   As to the meaning of 'farmer' see PARA 406 note 1.
4   Agricultural Credits Act 1928 s 5(3)(a).
5   Agricultural Credits Act 1928 s 5(3)(b).
6   As to the meaning of 'bank' see PARA 406 note 4.
7   Agricultural Credits Act 1928 s 6(1)(a).
8   Agricultural Credits Act 1928 s 6(1)(b).
9   Agricultural Credits Act 1928 s 6(1)(c).
10 Agricultural Credits Act 1928 s 6(2)(a).
11 The Agricultural Credits Act 1928 as enacted refers to the Diseases of Animals Acts 1894 to 1927; these were repealed and replaced by the Diseases of Animals Act 1950, which was itself repealed and replaced by the Animal Health Act 1981. See ANIMALS vol 2 (2017) PARA 374 et seq.
12 The Agricultural Credits Act 1928 as enacted refers to the Destructive Insects and Pests Acts 1877 to 1927, which were repealed and replaced by the Plant Health Act 1967; as to which see PARAS 111–115.
13 Agricultural Credits Act 1928 s 6(2)(b).
14 Agricultural Credits Act 1928 s 6(2).
15 Agricultural Credits Act 1928 s 6(4). Notice of the charge does not amount to such knowledge: s 6(4).
16 Agricultural Credits Act 1928 s 11(1)(a).
17 Agricultural Credits Act 1928 s 11(1)(b).
18 Agricultural Credits Act 1928 s 11(1) (read with the Criminal Law Act 1967 s 1). A person guilty of this offence is liable on summary conviction to imprisonment for a term not exceeding six months or a fine not exceeding the prescribed sum, or both, and on conviction on indictment to imprisonment for a term not exceeding three years: Agricultural Credits Act 1928 s 11(1) (read with the Criminal Justice Act 1948 s 1(1), (2); and the Magistrates' Courts Act 1980 ss 17, 32, Sch 1 para 20). As to the prescribed sum see PARA 58 note 1.
19 Agricultural Credits Act 1928 s 6(3).

408. Floating charges.

A floating charge affects the farming stock[1] and other agricultural assets[2] belonging to the farmer[3] from time to time, or the part of these mentioned in the charge[4]. The floating charge has the effect of a charge created by a duly registered debenture of a company[5]. However, the charge becomes a fixed charge upon the property comprised in the charge as existing at the date of its becoming a fixed charge upon:

(1) the making of a bankruptcy order against the farmer[6];
(2) the farmer's death[7];
(3) dissolution of partnership where the property charged is partnership property[8]; or
(4) written notice by the bank[9] on the happening of an event which under the charge confers on the bank the right to give such notice[10].

Whilst the charge remains a floating charge the farmer is subject to the same obligation as under a fixed charge to pay over to the bank money received by him[11], except where the amount received is expended in the purchase of farming stock which becomes subject to the charge[12].

1   As to the meaning of 'farming stock' see PARA 406 note 5.
2   As to the meaning of 'other agricultural assets' see PARA 406 note 6.
3   As to the meaning of 'farmer' see PARA 406 note 1.
4   Agricultural Credits Act 1928 s 5(4).
5   Agricultural Credits Act 1928 s 7(1). As to the registration of debentures see COMPANIES vol 15A (2016) PARA 1504 et seq.
6   Agricultural Credits Act 1928 s 7(1)(a)(i) (amended by the Insolvency Act 1985 s 235 (1), Sch 8 para 6). As to the making of bankruptcy orders see BANKRUPTCY AND INDIVIDUAL INSOLVENCY vol 5 (2013) PARA 198 et seq.
7   Agricultural Credits Act 1928 s 7(1)(a)(ii).
8   Agricultural Credits Act 1928 s 7(1)(a)(iii).
9   As to the meaning of 'bank' see PARA 406 note 4.
10 Agricultural Credits Act 1928 s 7(1)(a)(iv).
11 See the Agricultural Credits Act 1928 s 6(2); and PARA 407.
12 Agricultural Credits Act 1928 s 7(1)(b).

409.   Registration of charges.

An agricultural charge must be registered within seven clear days after execution[1], and, if not so registered, it is void as against persons other than the farmer[2]; but, on proof that omission to register within this period was accidental or due to inadvertence, the High Court may extend the time for registration[3].

Registration is effected by sending by post to the Land Registry a memorandum of the instrument of charge together with the prescribed particulars and fee[4]. The Land Registrar must enter the particulars in the register of agricultural charges which it is his duty to keep[5] and file the memorandum[6]. The register and memorandum are open to inspection on payment (except where the inspection is made by or on behalf of a bank[7]) of the prescribed fee[8], and copies may be made or furnished[9].

Registration may be proved by the production of a certified copy of the entry in the register[10], and special provisions apply to official searches in the agricultural charges register[11]. In favour of a purchaser or intending purchaser, as against persons interested under or in respect of an agricultural charge, the certificate of the registrar setting forth the result of an official search is conclusive according to its tenor, affirmatively or negatively, as the case may be[12].

Registration is deemed to constitute actual notice of the charge, and of the fact of registration, to all persons and for all purposes connected with the property comprised in the charge as from the date of registration, or other prescribed date[13], and so long as the registration continues in force[14]. Where, however, a charge in favour of a bank is expressly made for securing a current account or other further advances, the bank, in relation to the making of further advances under the charge, is not deemed to have notice of another charge by reason only of registration if it was not registered when the first charge was created or the last search by the bank was made, whichever last happened[15].

1 Sundays and other days when the registry is not open are excluded: Agricultural Credits Regulations 1928, SR & O 1928/667, reg 6(3). These regulations are made under the Agricultural Credits Act 1928 s 9(9) (amended by SI 2011/2436), under which regulations may be made by the Secretary of State prescribing anything which under s 9 is to be prescribed, subject as respects fees to the approval of the Treasury, and generally as to the keeping of the register and the filing of memoranda, the removal of entries from the register on proof of discharge, and the rectification of the register. As to the Treasury see CONSTITUTIONAL AND ADMINISTRATIVE LAW vol 20 (2014) PARA 263 et seq.

2 Agricultural Credits Act 1928 s 9(1). As to the meaning of 'farmer' see PARA 406 note 1.

3 Agricultural Credits Act 1928 s 9(1) proviso.

4 Agricultural Credits Act 1928 s 9(3). As to forms of application for registration, including the prescribed particulars, and for cancellation or rectification, and as to priority of applications, posting and official searches, see the Agricultural Credits Regulations 1928, SR & O 1928/667, regs 1–5, 6(1), (2), 7, 8, 10, Schedule. As to fees payable see the Agricultural Credits Fees Order 1985, SI 1985/372.

5 Agricultural Credits Act 1928 s 9(2). The Land Registrar must keep at the Land Registry a register of agricultural charges in such form as the Registrar may from time to time determine and containing the particulars prescribed by the Agricultural Credits Regulations 1928, SR & O 1928/667, reg 1.

6 Agricultural Credits Act 1928 s 9(3).

7 As to the meaning of 'bank' see PARA 406 note 4.

8 As to fees payable see the Agricultural Credits Fees Order 1985, SI 1985/372.

9 Agricultural Credits Act 1928 s 9(4), (5). As to the certification of copies see the Agricultural Credits Regulations 1928, SR & O 1928/667, reg 9.

10 Agricultural Credits Act 1928 s 9(6). A certified true copy is evidence in legal proceedings of the matters stated therein without proof of the signature or authority of the person signing it: s 9(6). As to the certification of copies see the Agricultural Credits Regulations 1928, SR & O 1928/667, reg 9.

11 Agricultural Credits Act 1928 s 9(7) (s 9(7) substituted, and Schedule added, by the Land Charges Act 1972 Sch 3 para 7). Searches are to be made by the Registrar upon a written requisition lodged with the prescribed fee at the Land Registry, or such office of the Land Registry as the Registrar may direct, whether in London or elsewhere: Agricultural Credits Act 1928 s 9(7), Schedule paras 1–3, 5 (as so added).

12 Agricultural Credits Act 1928 Schedule paras 3, 4 (as added: see note 11). A solicitor, trustee, personal representative, agent or other person in a fiduciary position is not answerable for any loss arising from error in a certificate obtained by him; and any officer, clerk or other person employed in the registry who commits, or is party or privy to, any act of fraud or collusion, or is wilfully negligent, in the making of or otherwise in relation to a certificate is guilty of an offence: Schedule paras 6, 7 (as so added). This offence is punishable on summary conviction with a fine not exceeding the prescribed sum or imprisonment for up to three months or both, and on conviction on indictment with imprisonment for up to two years: Schedule para 6 (as so added; and amended by virtue of the Magistrates' Courts Act 1980 s 32(2)). As to the prescribed sum see PARA 58 note 1.

13 At the date at which this volume states the law no such date had been prescribed.

14 Agricultural Credits Act 1928 s 9(8). Cf the Law of Property Act 1925 s 198; and EQUITABLE JURISDICTION vol 47 (2014) PARA 131; MORTGAGE vol 77 (2016) PARA 263; REAL PROPERTY AND REGISTRATION vol 87 (2017) PARAS 656–657.

15 Agricultural Credits Act 1928 s 9(8) proviso. Cf the Law of Property Act 1925 s 94(2); and MORTGAGE vol 77 (2016) PARA 267.

410. Charges on property of registered societies.

A debenture issued by a society registered under the Industrial and Provident Societies Act 1965[1], creating in favour of a bank[2] a floating charge on farming stock[3], may be registered as an agricultural charge, and the statutory provisions governing the registration of agricultural charges[4] are applicable[5]. Notice of every such registered charge must be signed by the secretary of the society and sent to the Financial Conduct Authority and registered there[6].

1 The Agricultural Credits Act 1928 s 14 refers to the Industrial and Provident Societies Acts 1893 to 1928, which were repealed and replaced by the Industrial and Provident Societies Act 1965: see ss 4, 77(3) which has been repealed and replaced by the Co-operative and Community Benefit Societies Act 2014; and FINANCIAL INSTITUTIONS vol 48 (2015) PARAS 883, 890 et seq.

2 As to the meaning of 'bank' see PARA 406 note 4.

3 As to the meaning of 'farming stock' see PARA 406 note 5.

4 Ie the Agricultural Credits Act 1928 s 9, Schedule (see PARA 409).

5 Agricultural Credits Act 1928 s 14(1). Charges so registered need not be recorded under the Co-operative and Community Benefit Societies Act 2014: see s 59(6); and FINANCIAL INSTITUTIONS vol 48 (2015) PARA 942.

6 See the Agricultural Credits Act 1928 s 14(1) (read with the Co-operative and Community Benefit Societies Act 2014 s 59; and FINANCIAL INSTITUTIONS vol 48 (2015) PARA 942. The Agricultural Credits Act 1928 s 14 refers to the Friendly Societies Act 1896, which was repealed and replaced by the Friendly Societies Act 1974: see Sch 10 para 2; and FINANCIAL INSTITUTIONS vol 48 (2015) PARA 662.

411. Supplemental provisions as to agricultural charges.

Neither an agricultural charge, nor a registered debenture issued by an agricultural society, is a bill of sale within the Bills of Sale Acts 1878 and 1882[1]. Charges in relation to one another have priority in accordance with the times at which they are respectively registered[2].

When an agricultural charge creating a floating charge has been made and remains in force, an agricultural charge purporting to create a fixed charge on, or a bill of sale comprising, any of the property comprised in the floating charge is void as respects such property[3].

When a farmer[4] made bankrupt has within three months of the making of the bankruptcy application or presentation of the bankruptcy petition created a charge in favour of a bank[5] operating to secure any sum owing prior to the giving of the charge, the amount secured by the charge must be reduced by the amount of the prior debt, unless it is proved that he was solvent immediately after the execution of the charge, but without prejudice to the bank's right to enforce any other security or to claim payment thereof as an unsecured debt[6].

A charge is no protection against recovery proceedings for rent, taxes or rates[7].

If growing crops are included in a charge, the rights of the bank in respect of the crops have priority to those of a mortgagee under a mortgage made after 2 August 1928, whether in possession or not, and irrespective of the dates of the mortgage and charge[8].

Publication[9] of lists of charges or of the names of farmers who have created charges is forbidden[10].

1 Agricultural Credits Act 1928 ss 8(1), 14(1). As to the Bills of Sale Acts see FINANCIAL INSTRUMENTS AND TRANSACTIONS vol 49 (2015) PARA 413 et seq.

2 Agricultural Credits Act 1928 s 8(2).

3 Agricultural Credits Act 1928 s 8(3).

4 As to the meaning of 'farmer' see PARA 406 note 1.

5 As to the meaning of 'bank' see PARA 406 note 4.

6 Agricultural Credits Act 1928 s 8(5) (amended by SI 2016/481).

7 Agricultural Credits Act 1928 s 8(7). The recovery proceedings within the purview of this provision are distress for o the exercise of a power to use the procedure in the Tribunals, Courts and Enforcement Act 2007 Sch 12 (taking control of goods) to recover) rent, taxes or rates: Agricultural Credits Act 1928 s 8(7) (amended by the Tribunals, Courts and Enforcement Act 2007 Sch 13 para 23).

8 Agricultural Credits Act 1928 s 8(6).

9   For these purposes 'publication' means the issue of copies to the public, and 'publish' has a corresponding meaning; and without prejudice to the generality of this the confidential notification by an association representative of a particular trade to its members trading or carrying on business in the district in which property subject to an agricultural charge is situate of the creation of the charge is not deemed to be 'publication' for these purposes: Agricultural Credits Act 1928 s 10(4).

10 Agricultural Credits Act 1928 s 10(1). There is a penalty of a fine not exceeding level 2 on the standard scale on summary conviction for acting in contravention of this prohibition (s 10(2) (amended by virtue of the Criminal Justice Act 1982 s 46)), but no prosecution may be commenced without the consent of the Attorney General (s 10(3)) and no person other than a proprietor, editor, master printer or publisher is liable (s 10(2)). As to the standard scale and the powers of magistrates' courts to issue fines on summary conviction see SENTENCING vol 92 (2015) PARA 176.

(7) GRANTS FOR FARMERS

(i) Grants other than under the Common Agricultural Policy

412. Financial assistance outside the Common Agricultural Policy.
Although most of the legislation providing for the giving of financial assistance to farmers is made under the European Communities Act 1972 for the purpose of implementing the obligations of the United Kingdom under the Common Agricultural Policy[1], a number of statutory provisions remain in force which derive from the United Kingdom's own post-war policies of helping farmers to improve their efficiency, manage the land more effectively and improve the quality of the land with which they work[2]. Pursuant to these the Secretary of State and the Welsh Ministers[3] may provide grants for a wide variety of schemes in accordance with provisions of the Hill Farming Act 1946[4], the Agriculture Act 1967[5] or the Agriculture Act 1970[6].

1   See the European Communities Act 1972 s 2(2), Sch 2; and PARA 1 et seq.
2   See PARA 413 et seq.
3   As to the Secretary of State and the Welsh Ministers see PARA 390.
4   As to schemes made under the Hill Farming Act 1946 s 1 see PARAS 413–415.
5   Ie the Agriculture Act 1967 Pt II (ss 28–40) (see PARAS 416–422).
6   Ie the Agriculture Act 1970 Pt II (ss 28–33) (see PARAS 423–427).

(ii) Grants under the Hill Farming Acts 1946 to 1985

413. Improvement grants.
The Hill Farming Act and Livestock Rearing Acts 1946 to 1959[1] enabled the Minister of Agriculture, Fisheries and Food[2] to make grants known as 'improvement grants' in accordance with approved schemes for the rehabilitation of livestock rearing land[3]. The kind of improvement eligible for grant was set out in the Hill Farming Act 1946, and more improvements were added by the Livestock Rearing Act 1951[4]. The last day for submission of proposals for all such schemes was 5 November 1963[5]. The last day for receipt of claims for grant under schemes already approved was fixed as 5 November 1975[6].

Subject to certain special provisions, the improvements made under improvement schemes were treated in the same way as other improvements to agricultural holdings[7]. There are still a number of statutes which empower the

Secretary of State to make grants to farmers and local authorities in areas of hill farms[8].

1   Ie the Hill Farming Act 1946; the Livestock Rearing Act 1951; the Hill Farming Act 1954; the Hill Farming Act 1956; and the Agricultural Improvement Grants Act 1959: see the Agricultural Improvement Grants Act 1959 s 2(1) (repealed). All the schemes made under these provisions have lapsed, and although some powers remain under the Hill Farming Act 1946 and the Livestock Rearing Act 1951, compensatory allowances which can be paid to hill farmers are now paid under Countryside Stewardship (see PARA 8).

2   The functions of the former Minister of Agriculture, Fisheries and Food are now exercised by the Secretary of State and, where applicable, the Welsh Ministers: see PARA 390.

3   See the Hill Farming Act 1946 s 1(1); the Livestock Rearing Act 1951 s 1(2)(b); and the Hill Farming Act 1956 s 1(1) (all repealed).

4   See the Hill Farming Act 1946 s 1(3), (4), Sch 1 (amended by the Livestock Rearing Act 1951 ss 1(3), 5; the Agriculture Act 1970 Sch 5 Pt II; SI 1949/548; SI 1949/2169), providing that the applicable improvements are: erection, alteration, enlargement or reconditioning of farm buildings; erection, alteration, enlargement or reconditioning of farm houses; erection, improvement or reconditioning of cottages attached, or to be attached, to a farm; making or improvement of roads or bridges and of piers, jetties, or slips; making or improvement of watercourses, ponds or wells or of works for the application of water power or for the supply of water for agricultural or domestic purposes; execution of works for or in connection with the supply of electricity for agricultural or domestic purposes; provision or improvement of accommodation for the dipping or treatment of sheep or cattle; provision or improvement of pens and other equipment for use for or in connection with the sheltering, gathering, marking, dipping or treatment of sheep or cattle; construction or improvement of silos; making or removal of permanent fences; restoration or improvement of permanent fences; provision or improvement of grids designed or adapted to prevent the passage of sheep or cattle; drainage; reclaiming of waste land; establishment of shelter belts; liming of land; application to land of purchased artificial or other purchased manure; laying down of permanent pasture; reseeding and regeneration of grazings and other cultural operations; removal of bracken, whins, gorse, bushes, scrubs, stumps, roots, boulders or other like obstructions to cultivation; burning heather or grass or making muirburn; provision of machinery and implements; and pest destruction.

5   Hill Farming Act 1946 s 1(1) (repealed); Hill Farming Act 1956 s 1(1) (repealed).

6   See the Agriculture Act 1970 s 35 (repealed). While it was not essential that the improvements envisaged in the approved scheme should be completed by 5 November 1975 (s 35(2) (repealed)), all schemes stood revoked from the following day if they were uncompleted (s 35(3)(a) (repealed); Livestock Rearing Land Improvement Schemes (Terminal Date) Order 1971, SI 1971/832 (lapsed)).

7   See the Agricultural Holdings Act 1986 s 68(3), (4); and AGRICULTURAL LAND AND ALLOTMENTS vol 1 (2017) PARAS 533, 543.

8   Eg improvements to common land (see the Hill Farming Act 1946 s 12; the Agriculture Act 1970 s 30(3); and PARA 414).

414. Improvements on land subject to rights of common.

The Secretary of State and the Welsh Ministers[1] have power to make improvements on livestock rearing land[2] subject to rights of common of pasture[3] which they think it is expedient to rehabilitate, and may recover from the persons claiming such rights of common half of the cost of the work[4]. Before beginning the work the Secretary of State or the Welsh Ministers must publish, in the way he thinks or they think best adapted for informing the owner of the land and the persons with the right of common[5], a notice stating his or their intentions and inviting persons claiming such rights and willing to bear an apportioned part of half the cost to communicate with him or them, giving their names and addresses and the rights they claim to enjoy[6]. The notice must specify the improvements which the Secretary of State thinks or the Welsh Ministers think ought to be made, and the work required for making them, the land on which it is proposed to do the work, the estimated cost of the work and the period (which must not be less than 28 days) within which written objection by persons interested may be made[7]. If an objection is duly made no further steps may be taken, unless it is withdrawn or appears to the Secretary of State or the Welsh Ministers to be frivolous, or the Secretary of State is or the Welsh Ministers are satisfied that the objector's claim to a right of common is groundless, though a fresh notice may be published later[8]. If no objection of substance is made within the time limited, the Secretary of State or the Welsh Ministers must execute an instrument apportioning half the estimated cost, in such amounts as he thinks or they think just, amongst those who have furnished him or them with their names and addresses[9]. The Secretary of State or the Welsh Ministers must then serve each of those persons with a copy of that instrument, together with particulars of the way in which he has or they have arrived at the amounts, and afford them a period of not less than 28 days in which to object to the apportionment so far as they are individually affected[10]. If no objections to the apportionment are made within the time as stated, the Secretary of State or the Welsh Ministers may carry out the work[11], but if an objection is made he or they may revise the apportionment, and the provisions applicable to a new notice will apply to the revised one[12]. When the work is completed the Secretary of State and the Welsh Ministers may recover the amounts apportioned (or those amounts rateably abated where the work costs less than was estimated)[13]. The category of improvements to which this procedure applies may be further enlarged by regulations[14].

1   As to the Secretary of State and the Welsh Ministers see PARA 390.
2   'Livestock rearing land' is land in an area consisting predominantly of mountains, hills or heath, which is, or by improvement could be made, suitable for use for the breeding, rearing and maintenance of sheep or cattle, but not for the carrying on, to any material extent, of dairy farming, or for the production, to any material extent, of fat sheep or fat cattle, or for the production of crops in quantity materially greater than that necessary to feed the number of sheep or cattle capable of being maintained on the land: Hill Farming Act 1946 s 1(3) (amended by the Livestock Rearing Act 1951 s 1(2), (3)).
3   As to rights of common of pasture see COMMONS vol 13 (2017) PARAS 332–355.
4   Hill Farming Act 1946 s 12(1) (amended by the Livestock Rearing Act 1951 s 1(2)(b); and SI 1955/554). Where the work includes the making or restoration of permanent fences, persons occupying adjoining land may be called upon to make a contribution (Hill Farming Act 1946 s 12(8)), although nothing that such persons do in pursuance of these provisions is to amount to an admission on their part of an obligation to fence against animals (s 12(9)). Any sum recoverable under these provisions by the Secretary of State or the Welsh Ministers may be recovered as a debt due to the Crown or summarily as a civil debt, and a complaint made for the purposes of recovering any such sum summarily as a civil debt may be made at any time within 12 months from the time when the matter of the complaint arose: s 35.
5   This includes occupiers of adjoining land, where the work includes the making and restoration of permanent fences: Hill Farming Act 1946 s 12(8).
6   Hill Farming Act 1946 s 12(2).
7   Hill Farming Act 1946 s 12(2)(a).
8   Hill Farming Act 1946 s 12(3).
9   Hill Farming Act 1946 s 12(4).
10 Hill Farming Act 1946 s 12(4).
11 Hill Farming Act 1946 s 12(5). The work must not prevent or impede access to the land for a longer period than three years from its commencement (s 12(10)), and it may not be done on other land without the consent of all the persons interested in that other land (s 12(12)).
12 Hill Farming Act 1946 s 12(6).
13 Hill Farming Act 1946 s 12(7).
14 Under the Agriculture Act 1970 s 30(3), regulations may be made, with the approval of the Treasury, providing for the application with modifications of the Hill Farming Act 1946 s 12(1)–(12) to any of the matters eligible for grant under the Agriculture Act 1970 s 29 (see PARAS 423–427). As to the Treasury see CONSTITUTIONAL AND ADMINISTRATIVE LAW vol 20 (2014) PARA 263 et seq. At the date at which this volume states the law, no regulations had been made under these provisions. As to the meaning of 'improvement' for these purposes see PARA 413 note 4. Any amendment to the Hill Farming Act 1946 Sch 1 after publication of a notice under s 12(2) does not affect the continuation of the operations notified: s 12(11).

415. Inspections.

Authorised officers of the Secretary of State and the Welsh Ministers[1] have power to enter and inspect any land which they have reason to believe is used, or could be used, for livestock rearing purposes[2] or in connection therewith[3]. An officer may not demand entry as of right unless he has given 24 hours' notice of his intention to enter and must, if so required, produce written evidence of his authority[4]. Obstructing or impeding an officer is an offence[5].

1   Ie officers authorised in that behalf by general or special directions given by the Secretary of State or the Welsh Ministers: Hill Farming Act 1946 s 34(1) (amended by the Livestock Rearing Act 1951 s 1(2)(b); and the Agriculture (Miscellaneous Provisions) Act 1972 Sch 6). As to the Secretary of State and the Welsh Ministers see PARA 390. The Hill Farming Act 1946 s 34 applies in relation to land in England as if, for the purposes of an agreement under the Natural Environment and Rural Communities Act 2006 Pt 8 Ch 1 (ss 78–86) (agreements with designated bodies: see OPEN SPACES AND COUNTRYSIDE vol 78 (2010) PARA 520), references to an officer of the Secretary of State or the Welsh Ministers authorised by general or special directions given by him or them were references to a person authorised by the Secretary of State or the Welsh Ministers by general or special directions given by him or them: Hill Farming Act 1946 s 34(3) (added by the Natural Environment and Rural Communities Act 2006 Sch 11 Pt 1 para 3).
2   'Livestock rearing purposes' means the breeding, rearing and maintenance of sheep or cattle, and includes other activities carried on in connection therewith: Hill Farming Act 1946 s 1(3) (amended by the Livestock Rearing Act 1951 s 1(3)).
3   Hill Farming Act 1946 s 34(1) (as amended: see note 1).
4   Hill Farming Act 1946 s 34(1) (as amended: see note 1).
5   Hill Farming Act 1946 s 34(2) (amended by the Agriculture (Miscellaneous Provisions) Act 1972 Sch 6; and by virtue of the Criminal Justice Act 1982 ss 35, 46). This offence is punishable by a fine not exceeding level 2 on the standard scale: Hill Farming Act 1946 s 34(2) (as so amended). As to the standard scale and the powers of magistrates' courts to issue fines on summary conviction see SENTENCING vol 92 (2015) PARA 176.

(iii) Grants under the Agriculture Act 1967

416. Schemes.

The Secretary of State and the Welsh Ministers[1] may, in accordance with a scheme[2], make grants out of money provided by Parliament in connection with the carrying out of approved transactions in the nature of amalgamations and boundary adjustments[3]. The transactions which may be approved are:

(1)   transactions for securing that agricultural land[4] which is or forms part of an uncommercial unit[5], but which together with some other agricultural land could form an intermediate unit[6] or commercial unit, is owned and occupied with that other land or, if not so owned, occupied with that other land by a person who is to occupy any part of the resulting unit not owned by him as tenant[7];

(2)   transactions for securing that, where an intermediate unit or a commercial unit is not all in the same ownership, any part of it comes to be in the same ownership as the rest of that unit, or in the same ownership as some other part of that unit, but excluding transactions which bring into the same ownership and occupation two or more parts of the unit each of which could by itself form a commercial unit[8];

(3)   transactions for securing that, where the occupier of a commercial unit or intermediate unit is neither the owner nor a tenant for a term of years or from year to year[9], he comes to occupy the unit or the relevant parts of it as owner or as such a tenant[10]; and

(4)   transfers or exchanges of agricultural land (or estates or interests in agricultural land) for the purpose of giving more satisfactory boundaries to one or more agricultural units[11].

The transactions described under heads (1) to (3) above are known as 'amalgamations' and those in head (4) above are known as 'boundary adjustments'[12].

Schemes are to provide for the manner in which the amount of grant is to be determined, and may restrict the amalgamations and boundary adjustments to which they apply in any way[13].

The maximum duration of a scheme is seven years[14]. The most recent farm amalgamation scheme was made in 1973[15], and is now spent: applications for approval of amalgamations under the scheme had to be submitted before 16 December 1976[16]. No further scheme has been made.

1   As to the Secretary of State and the Welsh Ministers see PARA 390.
2   Schemes may contain provisions as to reduction or withholding of grants and incidental and supplemental provisions and may be revoked or varied: Agriculture Act 1967 s 35(f), (g) (s 35(f) amended by the Agriculture Act 1970 s 32(1), (5)).
3   Agriculture Act 1967 s 26(1) (amended by the Agriculture Act 1970 s 32(2); and the Agriculture (Miscellaneous Provisions) Act 1972 s 9(2)).
4   As to the meaning of 'agricultural land' see PARA 10.
5   A 'commercial unit' for the purposes of the Agriculture Act 1967 Pt II (ss 26–40) is an agricultural unit which in the opinion of the Secretary of State or the Welsh Ministers is capable, when farmed under reasonably skilled management, of providing full-time employment for an individual occupying it and for at least one other person (or full-time employment for an individual occupying it and employment for members of his family or other persons equivalent to full-time employment for one person) (s 40(2)(a)); and 'uncommercial unit' is to be construed by reference to this definition subject to the power of the Secretary of State and the Welsh Ministers to direct that a dwelling house or an area sufficient to provide a site for one dwelling house be excluded (s 40(3) (amended by the Agriculture (Miscellaneous Provisions) Act 1972 s 9(6))). 'Full-time employment' is to be defined by the scheme: Agriculture Act 1967 s 40(2). As to the meaning of 'agricultural unit' see PARA 10.
6   'Intermediate unit' means an agricultural unit which, in the opinion of the Secretary of State or the Welsh Ministers, is capable, when farmed under reasonably skilled management, of providing full-time employment for an individual occupying it: Agriculture Act 1967 s 40(2)(b).
7   Agriculture Act 1967 s 26(1)(a) (amended by the Agriculture Act 1970 s 32(2)(a); the Agricultural Holdings Act 1986 Sch 14 para 37; and SI 1973/1402). As to the meaning of 'tenant' see the Agricultural Holdings Act 1986 s 96(1); and AGRICULTURAL LAND AND ALLOTMENTS vol 1 (2017) PARA 423 note 5 (definition applied by the Agriculture Act 1967 s 26(1)(a) (as so amended)). The Secretary of State and the Welsh Ministers may make such assumptions as they consider reasonable as to the works and facilities to be carried out or provided for the benefit of the unit to be formed: s 26(1) (as so amended).
8   Agriculture Act 1967 s 26(1)(b).
9   See the definitions of 'tenant' and 'contract of tenancy' in the Agricultural Holdings Act 1986; and AGRICULTURAL LAND AND ALLOTMENTS vol 1 (2017) PARAS 423 note 5, 425.
10 Agriculture Act 1967 s 26(1)(bb) (added by the Agriculture (Miscellaneous Provisions) Act 1972 s 9(2)).
11 Agriculture Act 1967 s 26(1)(c).
12 Agriculture Act 1967 s 26(1) (amended by the Agriculture (Miscellaneous Provisions) Act 1972 s 9(2)).
13 Agriculture Act 1967 s 26(1), (2) (amended by the Agriculture (Miscellaneous Provisions) Act 1972 s 9(2)).
14 Agriculture Act 1967 s 26(9). The period may, however, be extended by further schemes: s 26(9).
15 Ie the Farm Amalgamation Scheme 1973, SI 1973/1404.
16 Farm Amalgamation Scheme 1973, SI 1973/1404, para 4(1) (amended by SI 1976/2125).

417. Approval, certification and conditions.

The approval[1] of an amalgamation[2] or boundary adjustment[3] in pursuance of a scheme[4] may be given before or after it has been carried out, may be conditional[5] and may be varied or withdrawn with the applicant's consent[6]. The Secretary of State and the Welsh Ministers may also, if they think fit, certify as eligible for a farm capital grant[7] any work or facility which they consider to be necessary or desirable as a consequence of an amalgamation or to be necessary in consequence of a boundary adjustment[8].

1 Ie approval by the Secretary of State or the Welsh Ministers: see PARA 416. As to the Secretary of State and the Welsh Ministers see PARA 390.
2 As to the meaning of 'amalgamation' see PARA 416.
3 As to the meaning of 'boundary adjustment' see PARA 416.
4 As to the power to make schemes see PARA 416.
5 The Secretary of State and the Welsh Ministers may impose such conditions as they think fit when they make a grant, including conditions requiring the recipient of the grant to make repayments in specified circumstances: Agriculture (Miscellaneous Provisions) Act 1972 s 10(4).
6 Agriculture Act 1967 s 26(6) (amended by the Agriculture Act 1970 s 32(1), (2); and the Agriculture (Miscellaneous Provisions) Act 1972 s 9(1), (2)).
7 Ie a grant under the Agriculture Act 1970 s 29 (see PARAS 423–427).
8 Agriculture Act 1967 s 26(6) (as amended: see note 6).

418. Relinquishment of uncommercial units.

The Secretary of State and the Welsh Ministers[1] may in accordance with a scheme[2] make a grant by way of lump sum or annuity[3] to an individual who relinquishes occupation[4] of an uncommercial unit[5], or part of such a unit, of agricultural land as part of an approved amalgamation[6], or arrangements for afforestation[7] or for reshaping agricultural units[8]. Grants may also be paid in pursuance of provisions of a scheme implementing, or arising out of or related to, an EU obligation[9]. Grants may be conditional and an individual may receive a grant in respect of only one uncommercial unit[10]. The scheme may impose requirements as to occupation[11], and there may be an income test[12]. The scheme may provide that, if the applicant, having either relinquished occupation of the unit or become obliged to relinquish it, dies before the application has been dealt with, the application may proceed and that the grant, if approved, is to be payable either by way of annuity for the benefit of the deceased's estate or spouse, or by way of a lump sum for the benefit of the deceased's estate[13]. Provision may also be made that on the death of a person in receipt of an annuity, a specified amount of grant may be payable to the deceased's surviving spouse[14].

1 As to the Secretary of State and the Welsh Ministers see PARA 390.
2 As to the power to make schemes see PARA 416. The maximum duration of schemes is seven years, subject to extension by subsequent schemes: Agriculture Act 1967 s 27(6). The most recent scheme was the Farm Structure (Payment to Outgoers) Scheme 1976, SI 1976/2126 (amended by SI 1981/1709; and extended by SI 1983/1882), which is now spent. Although the enabling provisions remain in force, no subsequent scheme had been made at the date at which this volume states the law.
3 As to the capital gains tax treatment of statutory compensation paid to an outgoing tenant under the agricultural holdings legislation see CAPITAL GAINS TAXATION vol 6 (2011) PARA 959.
4 Schemes may contain provision for treating a person as the occupier of land in respect of which he has granted to another person a licence or a tenancy for a term of less than from year to year: Agriculture Act 1967 s 27(5B) (added by the Agriculture (Miscellaneous Provisions) Act 1972 s 9(3)(b); and amended by the Agricultural Holdings Act 1986 Sch 14 para 38; and SI 1973/1402).
5 As to the meaning of 'uncommercial unit' see PARA 416 note 5.
6 As to the meaning of 'amalgamation' see PARA 416. As to approved amalgamations see PARAS 416, 417.

7   Ie arrangements approved by a Rural Development Board (see AGRICULTURAL LAND AND ALLOTMENTS vol 1 (2017) PARA 765). As to Rural Development Boards generally see AGRICULTURAL LAND AND ALLOTMENTS vol 1 (2017) PARAS 757–758.

8   Agriculture Act 1967 s 27(1) (amended by the Agriculture Act 1970 s 32(1), (3); and the Agriculture (Miscellaneous Provisions) Act 1972 s 9(3)(a)). As to powers of the Secretary of State, the Welsh Ministers and a Rural Development Board to promote amalgamations and boundary adjustments and the reshaping of agricultural units see the Agriculture Act 1967 ss 29, 48; PARA 420; and AGRICULTURAL LAND AND ALLOTMENTS vol 1 (2017) PARA 765.

9   Agriculture Act 1967 s 27(1)(d) (substituted by SI 1976/1771; and amended by SI 2011/1043).

10 Agriculture Act 1967 s 27(3), (4).

11 Agriculture Act 1967 s 27(2)(a), (b).

12 Agriculture Act 1967 s 27(2)(c) (amended SI 1973/1402).

13 Agriculture Act 1967 s 27(5A) (added by the Agriculture Act 1970 s 32(1), (3)).

14 Agriculture Act 1967 s 27(5).

419.   Loans for amalgamations and boundary adjustments.

The Secretary of State and the Welsh Ministers with the approval of the Treasury[1] may make or guarantee[2] loans to meet expenditure incurred in connection with an approved amalgamation[3] or boundary adjustment[4]. The expenditure must fall under one or more of the following heads:

(1)   survey and conveyancing costs[5];

(2)   compensation[6] for disturbance[7];

(3)   cost of carrying out works or facilities which the Secretary of State considers or the Welsh Ministers consider to be necessary or desirable as a consequence of an amalgamation, or to be necessary as a consequence of a boundary adjustment[8];

(4)   any part of the purchase price of land acquired or money given by way of equality of exchange[9].

Loans must be repayable within a period of 60 years[10] and may be made or guaranteed on such conditions as the Secretary of State deems or the Welsh Ministers deem fit[11]. A mortgage or charge securing such a loan may provide that it is redeemable only in the manner specified in it[12].

1   As to the Secretary of State and the Welsh Ministers see PARA 390. As to the Treasury see CONSTITUTIONAL AND ADMINISTRATIVE LAW vol 20 (2014) PARA 263 et seq.

2   The Secretary of State and the Welsh Ministers may guarantee loans made by such bodies as they may select: Agriculture Act 1967 s 28(3). Guarantees may relate to part of a loan, or to the interest payable on a loan, as well as to the whole of a loan: s 28(10).

3   As to the meaning of 'amalgamation' see PARA 416. As to approved amalgamations see PARAS 416–417.

4   Agriculture Act 1967 s 28(1) (amended by the Agriculture Act 1970 s 32(1), (4); and the Agriculture (Miscellaneous Provisions) Act 1972 s 9(1), (4)). As to the meaning of 'boundary adjustment' see PARA 416. Loans may be made through such agency as the Secretary of State or the Welsh Ministers may select and must be applied for in the manner which he directs or they direct and as a general rule within the period of duration of schemes under the Agriculture Act 1967 s 26 (see PARA 416): s 28(2).

5   Agriculture Act 1967 s 28(1)(a) (s 28(1)(a) substituted, and s 28(1)(aa) added, by the Agriculture (Miscellaneous Provisions) Act 1972 s 9(4); Agriculture Act 1967 s 28(1)(a) amended by the Agricultural Holdings Act 1986 Sch 14 para 39).

6   Ie under the Agricultural Holdings Act 1986 s 60(2)(a) (see AGRICULTURAL LAND AND ALLOTMENTS vol 1 (2017) PARA 545).

7   Agriculture Act 1967 s 28(1)(a) (as substituted and amended: see note 5).

8   Agriculture Act 1967 s 28(1)(aa) (as added: see note 5).

9   Agriculture Act 1967 s 28(1)(b).

10 Agriculture Act 1967 s 28(4).

11 Agriculture Act 1967 s 28(5). The conditions in Sch 3 (amended by the Agriculture (Miscellaneous Provisions) Act 1972 s 10(5); the Local Land Charges Act 1975 Schs 1, 2; the Agriculture Act 1970 s 33(1)(a), (c), (d); the Limitation Act 1980 Sch 3 para 7; and the Agricultural Holdings Act

1986 Sch 14 para 42) were applied by the Agriculture Act 1967 s 28(6), (7) to amalgamated units after loans or guarantees were given, but those provisions do not apply in relation to amalgamations or boundary adjustments approved under schemes made after the passing of the Agriculture (Miscellaneous Provisions) Act 1972 (ie after 8 August 1972) or treated by virtue of transitional provisions in such a scheme as approved thereunder: s 10(3). Conditions imposed under the Agriculture Act 1967 s 28(5) may now include requirements that the recipient or person whose indebtedness is guaranteed must make payments or repayments under specified circumstances: see the Agriculture (Miscellaneous Provisions) Act 1972 s 10(4).

12   Agriculture Act 1967 s 28(8).

420. Promotion of amalgamations and boundary adjustments by the Secretary of State and the Welsh Ministers.

The general powers of the Secretary of State and the Welsh Ministers[1] to acquire and manage land[2] include power to acquire, hold or dispose of land for the purpose of effecting amalgamations[3] of agricultural land[4] and reshaping of agricultural units[5], and for those purposes to enter into transactions involving loss[6]. A deed by which the Secretary of State conveys or the Welsh Ministers convey land may contain standard conditions[7], and the usual restrictions upon the operation of a notice to quit an agricultural holding[8] do not apply to a notice given by the Secretary of State or the Welsh Ministers and certified thereby to be given for the purpose of effecting an amalgamation or reshaping an agricultural unit, if the tenancy in question was granted under an instrument containing an acknowledgement by the tenant that it was subject to the relevant provisions[9].

1   As to the Secretary of State and the Welsh Ministers see PARA 390.
2   Ie the powers of the Secretary of State and the Welsh Ministers under the Agriculture Act 1947 ss 82, 90 (see AGRICULTURAL LAND AND ALLOTMENTS vol 1 (2017) PARA 742).
3   As to the meaning of 'amalgamation' see PARA 416.
4   As to the meaning of 'agricultural land' see PARA 10.
5   As to the meaning of 'agricultural unit' see PARA 10.
6   Agriculture Act 1967 s 29(1), (2).
7   Ie the conditions in the Agriculture Act 1967 Sch 3 (amended by the Agriculture (Miscellaneous Provisions) Act 1972 s 10(5); the Local Land Charges Act 1975 Schs 1, 2; the Agriculture Act 1970 s 33(1)(a), (c), (d); the Limitation Act 1980 Sch 3 para 7; and the Agricultural Holdings Act 1986 Sch 14 para 42). The conditions may be applied only with the concurrence of all interested parties: see the Agriculture Act 1967 s 29(3) (amended by the Agriculture Act 1970 s 33(2); and the Agricultural Holdings Act 1986 Sch 14 para 40). Power for limited owners to give the necessary consent is conferred by the Agriculture Act 1970 s 33(2) (amended by the Trusts of Land and Appointment of Trustees Act 1996 Sch 3 para 11).
8   Ie the restrictions in the Agricultural Holdings Act 1986 s 26(1) (see AGRICULTURAL LAND AND ALLOTMENTS vol 1 (2017) PARA 471).
9   See the Agricultural Holdings Act 1986 s 26(2); and AGRICULTURAL LAND AND ALLOTMENTS vol 1 (2017) PARA 471.

421. Recovery of grant; revocation of approval.

At any time after approving proposals for a grant for an amalgamation or boundary adjustment[1], or for an individual relinquishing occupation of an uncommercial unit[2], the Secretary of State and the Welsh Ministers may recover any such grant or part thereof and revoke the approval in whole or in part, if it appears to them:

(1)   that any condition imposed in giving approval has not been complied with[3];

(2)   in the case of proposals for the carrying out of work, that the work has been badly done, or is being unreasonably delayed, or is unlikely to be completed[4]; or

(3)   that in connection with the submission of proposals, the person submitting them gave information on any matter which was false or misleading in a material respect[5].

Before exercising their powers of recovery and revocation, the Secretary of State and the Welsh Ministers must notify the grantee in writing of the reasons for any action they propose to take, and accord the grantee an opportunity of appearing before, and being heard by, a person appointed for that purpose by the Secretary of State or the Welsh Ministers; and they must consider that person's report and supply a copy to the grantee[6].

1   As to such grants see PARA 416.
2   As to such grants see PARA 418. If the grant is a lump sum payable by instalments, or by way of annuity, the Secretary of State and the Welsh Ministers may, in cases within head (1) or head (3) in the text, direct that future instalments of the grant or annuity be not paid: Agriculture Act 1967 s 37(2). The Secretary of State and the Welsh Ministers have power to vary or revoke such a direction: s 75(6). As to the Secretary of State and the Welsh Ministers see PARA 390.
3   Agriculture Act 1967 s 37(1)(a) (s 37(1) amended by the Agriculture Act 1970 Sch 5 Pt I).
4   Agriculture Act 1967 s 37(1)(b) (as amended: see note 3).
5   Agriculture Act 1967 s 37(1)(c) (as amended: see note 3).
6   Agriculture Act 1967 s 37(4).

422. Offences.

Any person who knowingly or recklessly makes a false statement for the purpose of obtaining for himself or any other person a grant under the Agriculture Act 1967[1], or of inducing the Secretary of State, the Welsh Ministers[2] or a Rural Development Board[3] to make a loan or guarantee thereunder[4], is guilty of an offence[5]. Provision is made for the liability of directors and officers of a body corporate in respect of offences committed by the body corporate with their consent or connivance or through their neglect[6].

1   As to such grants see PARA 416 et seq.
2   As to the Secretary of State and the Welsh Ministers see PARA 390.
3   As to these boards and their power to make loans see AGRICULTURAL LAND AND ALLOTMENTS vol 1 (2017) PARA 757 et seq.
4   Ie under the Agriculture Act 1967 s 28 (see PARA 419) or s 47 (see AGRICULTURAL LAND AND ALLOTMENTS vol 1 (2017) PARA 757).
5   Agriculture Act 1967 s 69(1) (amended by the Agriculture Act 1970 Sch 5 Pt I; the Theft Act 1968 Sch 3 Pt I; and the Statute Law (Repeals) Act 1986). Until a day to be appointed the penalty on summary conviction is a fine not exceeding level 3 on the standard scale, imprisonment not exceeding three months, or both (Agriculture Act 1967 s 69(1) (amended by virtue of the Criminal Justice Act 1982 ss 38, 46)); as from that day the imprisonment option is no longer available (Agriculture Act 1967 s 69(1) (as so amended; prospectively amended by the Criminal Justice Act 2003 s 332, Sch 37 Pt 9)). At the date at which this volume states the law no such day had been appointed. As to the standard scale and the powers of magistrates' courts to issue fines on summary conviction see SENTENCING vol 92 (2015) PARA 176. As to fraud and related offences see CRIMINAL LAW vol 25 (2016) PARA 346 et seq.
6   See the Agriculture Act 1967 s 71.

(iv) Grants under the Agriculture Act 1970

423. Power to make grants.

Financial assistance may be given to farmers in accordance with the provisions of the Agriculture Act 1970[1], which authorise the making of schemes for the payment of grants towards capital expenditure incurred or to be incurred for the purposes of or in connection with the carrying on of an agricultural business[2]. While these provisions remain in force, those major schemes that have been implemented by statutory instrument under them have now mostly lapsed or been superseded by others introduced under the European Communities Act 1972[3]. The most recent scheme was made in 1989 and is now closed[4]. However, several discrete schemes remain in force under the Agriculture Act 1970 in relation to farm waste and restructuring grants in the pig industry[5].

1 See the Agriculture Act 1970 ss 28–30; the text and notes 2–5; and PARAS **424–427**. Before the enactment of this legislation capital grants for farm improvements were made under a number of statutes and statutory schemes, but a single scheme, the Farm Capital Grant Scheme 1970, SI 1970/1759 (lapsed) was introduced with effect from 1 January 1971 to consolidate grants for long term improvements to agricultural businesses. Subsequently, other schemes have been made under these provisions (although see note 3).

2 Agriculture Act 1970 s 29(1). For these purposes 'agricultural business' means a business consisting in, or such part of any business as consists in, the pursuit of agriculture and includes any other business of a kind for the time being specified by an order made by the Secretary of State or the Welsh Ministers which is carried on by a person also carrying on a business consisting in or partly in the pursuit of agriculture and is carried on the same or adjacent land: s 28(1) (amended by the Agriculture Act 1986 s 22). The amendment made by the Agriculture Act 1986 was necessitated by the extensification (or 'diversification') directives and regulations emanating from the European Community: see the Farm Business Specification Order 1987, SI 1987/1948; and the Farm Diversification Grant Scheme 1987, SI 1987/1949 (amended by SI 1988/1398). As to the meaning of 'agriculture' see PARA 10. As to the Secretary of State and the Welsh Ministers see PARA 390.

3 These schemes are:
    (1)   the Fruiting Plum Tree (Planting Grants) Scheme 1979, SI 1979/876 (lapsed);
    (2)   the Plum Material and Clearance Grants Scheme 1979, SI 1979/877 (lapsed);
    (3)   the Agriculture and Horticulture Grant Scheme 1980, SI 1980/1072 (this scheme is largely superseded by general grants for agricultural and horticultural businesses under the Agriculture Improvement Scheme 1985, SI 1985/1029, itself largely superseded by the Farm and Conservation Grant Scheme 1989, SI 1989/128 (lapsed)); and
    (4)   the Farm Diversification Grant Scheme 1987, SI 1987/1949 (lapsed).

4 See the Farm and Conservation Grant Scheme 1989, SI 1989/128; and note 3.

5 See the Farm Waste Grant (Nitrate Vulnerable Zones) (Wales) Scheme 2004, SI 2004/1606; the Pig Industry Restructuring (Capital Grant) Scheme 2001, SI 2001/251; and the Pig Industry Restructuring Grant (Wales) Scheme 2001, SI 2001/643.

424. Power to make schemes.

The Secretary of State and the Welsh Ministers[1] may, with the approval of the Treasury[2], provide by scheme[3] for the making of grants towards certain expenditure incurred or to be incurred for the purposes of, or in connection with, the carrying on or establishment of an agricultural business[4]. The expenditure is expenditure which satisfies all of the following conditions:

    (1)   it has been or is to be incurred in respect of matters specified in the scheme, or in respect of any work or facility certified[5] as necessary or desirable as a consequence of an amalgamation or boundary adjustment[6];

    (2)   it appears to the Secretary of State or the Welsh Ministers to be of a capital nature, or incurred in connection with expenditure of a capital nature[7]; and

    (3)   it is approved by the Secretary of State or the Welsh Ministers for the purposes of a grant under the scheme[8].

1 As to the Secretary of State and the Welsh Ministers see PARA **390**.

2 As to the Treasury see CONSTITUTIONAL AND ADMINISTRATIVE LAW vol 20 (2014) PARA 263 et seq.

3 Schemes are made by statutory instrument, may apply to England and Wales with or without other parts of the United Kingdom, may vary or revoke previous schemes with the same territorial extent, and have a maximum duration of seven years, which may be extended by further schemes: Agriculture Act 1970 s 29(2).

4 Agriculture Act 1970 s 29(1). As to the meaning of 'agricultural business' see PARA 423 note 2.
5 Ie under the Agriculture Act 1967 s 26(6) (see PARA 417).
6 Agriculture Act 1970 s 29(1)(a).
7 Agriculture Act 1970 s 29(1)(b).
8 Agriculture Act 1970 s 29(1)(c).

425. Payment and revocation of grants.

Grants under a scheme[1] are paid by the Secretary of State and the Welsh Ministers[2] at such time and in such instalments as they think fit[3]. The Secretary of State and the Welsh Ministers may, at any time after approving any expenditure for the purposes of a grant under a scheme, revoke the approval in whole or in part and, if any grant has been paid, recover an amount equal to the payment made, if it appears to them:

(1)   that any condition subject to which the approval was given or the grant has been made has not been complied with[4];

(2)   that any work in respect of expenditure on which the approval was given has been badly done, or has been or is being unreasonably delayed, or is unlikely to be completed[5]; or

(3)   that the applicant for the approval or payment gave information on any matter relevant to the giving of the approval or the making of the payment which was false or misleading in a material respect[6].

Before revoking an approval in whole or in part, the Secretary of State and the Welsh Ministers must give to the person to whom grant would be payable, or from whom payment would be recoverable, notice of the reasons for the revocation[7] and an opportunity of appearing before, and being heard by, a person appointed for that purpose by the Secretary of State or the Welsh Ministers[8]; and they must consider that person's report and supply a copy to the applicant[9]. Upon revocation of an approval, the Secretary of State and the Welsh Ministers may recover any payment already made, or a specified part of it[10].

1 For the power to make grants and schemes see PARAS 423–424.
2 As to the Secretary of State and the Welsh Ministers see PARA 390.
3 Agriculture Act 1970 s 29(3).
4 Agriculture Act 1970 s 29(4)(a).
5 Agriculture Act 1970 s 29(4)(b).
6 Agriculture Act 1970 s 29(4)(c) (s 29(4)(c) amended, and s 29(4)(c)(i)–(iii) substituted, by the Agriculture (Miscellaneous Provisions) Act 1976 s 15).
7 Agriculture Act 1970 s 29(4)(c)(i) (as substituted: see note 6).
8 Agriculture Act 1970 s 29(4)(c)(ii) (as substituted: see note 6).
9 Agriculture Act 1970 s 29(4)(c)(iii) (as substituted: see note 6).
10 Agriculture Act 1970 s 29(4) (as amended: see note 6).

426. Supplementary provisions as to capital grants.

Authorised improvements under the Settled Land Act 1925[1] may by regulation be extended to include matters in respect of which expenditure may be approved for grant under a farm capital grant scheme[2]. The powers of the Secretary of State and the Welsh Ministers to carry out improvements to livestock rearing land subject to rights of common of pasture[3], and to recover a proportion of the expenditure, may also be extended by regulations to include those matters[4]. Grants may be supplemented by an additional amount when made to a smallholdings authority[5].

1 See the Settled Land Act 1925 Pt IV (ss 83–89); and SETTLEMENTS vol 91 (2012) PARA 713 et seq.
2 Agriculture Act 1970 s 30(1) (amended by the Trusts of Land and Appointment of Trustees Act 1996 Sch 4). The regulations may provide in which part of the Settled Land Act 1925 Sch 3 (see

SETTLEMENTS vol 91 (2012) PARA 717) the additional matters are to be included: Agriculture Act 1970 s 30(1). At the date at which this volume states the law no regulations had been made in exercise of this power. Regulations are to be made by the Secretary of State or the Welsh Ministers with the approval of the Treasury: s 30(1). As to the Secretary of State and the Welsh Ministers see PARA 390. As to the Treasury see CONSTITUTIONAL AND ADMINISTRATIVE LAW vol 20 (2014) PARA 263 et seq.

3	Ie the powers of the Secretary of State and the Welsh Ministers under the Hill Farming Act 1946 s 12 (see PARA 414).

4	Agriculture Act 1970 s 30(3). At the date at which this volume states the law no such regulations had been made.

5	See the Agriculture Act 1970 s 51; and AGRICULTURAL LAND AND ALLOTMENTS vol 1 (2017) PARA 648.

427. Penalties for false statements to obtain grants.

Any person who, for the purpose of obtaining for himself or any other person any grant under a farm capital grant scheme[1], knowingly or recklessly makes a false statement, commits an offence[2].

Where a body corporate is guilty of an offence under the Agriculture Act 1970 or any order or scheme made thereunder and that offence is proved to have been committed with the consent or connivance of, or to be attributable to any neglect on the part of, any director, manager, secretary or other similar officer of the body corporate, or any person who was purporting to act in any such capacity, he, as well as the body corporate, is guilty of that offence and liable to be proceeded against and punished accordingly[3].

1	Ie any scheme made under the Agriculture Act 1970 s 29: see PARA 423 et seq.

2	Agriculture Act 1970 s 29(5). The offence is punishable on summary conviction by a fine not exceeding level 5 on the standard scale: s 29(5) (amended by virtue of the Criminal Justice Act 1982 ss 38, 46). As to the standard scale and the powers of magistrates' courts to issue fines on summary conviction see SENTENCING vol 92 (2015) PARA 176.

3	Agriculture Act 1970 s 110(1). Where the affairs of a body corporate are managed by its members, s 110(1) applies in relation to the acts and defaults of a member in connection with his functions of management as if he were a director of the body corporate: s 110(2).

(v) Grants under the Farm Land and Rural Development Act 1988

428. Grants in respect of farm businesses.

Schemes may provide for the payment of grants in connection with the establishment, expansion, promotion or marketing of farm businesses[1]. Such schemes may provide for the payment of grants towards certain expenditure[2] which has been or is to be incurred for the purposes of, in connection with, or in connection with any proposals for:

(1)	the establishment or expansion of a farm business[3] of such a description as may be specified in the scheme[4];

(2)	the establishment or expansion, for purposes connected with the establishment, expansion or carrying on of such a farm business, of any agricultural business[5];

(3)	the promotion of such a farm business[6]; or

(4)	the marketing of anything produced or supplied in the course of such a farm business[7].

Without prejudice to the generality of the above, a grant scheme made under these provisions may:

(a)	impose requirements to be complied with by persons applying for the grants[8];

(b)　　confer a discretion on the appropriate minister[9] as to the payment of the grants, as to the manner and timing of their payment, and as to their amounts[10];

(c)　　provide for the grants to be paid to persons on such terms as may be specified in or determined under the scheme and for the modification of any such terms in such manner as may be so specified or determined[11];

(d)　　provide for the terms on which the grants are paid to impose such requirements on the persons to whom they are paid, including requirements to be complied with after the payment of the grants and requirements as to the repayment of grants, as may be so specified or determined[12];

(e)　　provide for any discretion conferred by or under the scheme to be exercisable in such circumstances and by reference to such matters, and the opinion of such persons, as may be so specified or determined[13];

(f)　　contain such supplemental, consequential and transitional provision as the appropriate authority thinks fit[14]; and

(g)　　make different provision for different cases[15].

Pursuant to these provisions a number of schemes are in effect[16].

1　Farm Land and Rural Development Act 1988 s 1(1). Schemes under ss 1, 2 (see PARA 429) may be made, with the approval of the Treasury, by the 'appropriate authority', which in relation to any scheme means the 'appropriate minister' for the part of Great Britain to which the scheme extends or, if it extends to more than one part, the appropriate minister for each part to which it extends, acting jointly; the 'appropriate ministers' for England and Wales are the Secretary of State and the Welsh Ministers: ss 1(5), 2(6) (definition of 'appropriate minister' amended by SI 2002/794). As to the Secretary of State and the Welsh Ministers see PARA 390. As to the Treasury see CONSTITUTIONAL AND ADMINISTRATIVE LAW vol 20 (2014) PARA 263 et seq.

　　Functions conferred on the Secretary of State and the Welsh Ministers in connection with the Farm Land and Rural Development Act 1988 ss 1, 2 are to be treated as functions connected with agriculture for the purposes of the Agriculture Act 1986 s 17 (duty to balance interests when exercising functions connected with agriculture): Farm Land and Rural Development Act 1988 s 4(2).

2　Ie expenditure which appears to the Secretary of State or the Welsh Ministers to be neither expenditure of a capital nature nor expenditure which would fall to be treated for the purposes of the Agriculture Act 1970 s 29 (see PARAS 423–427) as incurred in connection with expenditure of a capital nature: Farm Land and Rural Development Act 1988 s 1(1)(b). Grants are paid out of money provided by Parliament: s 1(4).

3　'Farm business' means any business consisting in, or such part of any business as consists in, a business which is carried on by a person who also carries on an agricultural business at the same time and on the same or adjacent land and is not itself an agricultural business; and 'agricultural business' means a business consisting in, or such part of a business as consists in, the pursuit of agriculture: Farm Land and Rural Development Act 1988 s 1(5). As to the meaning of 'agriculture' see PARA 10.

4　Farm Land and Rural Development Act 1988 s 1(1)(a)(i).
5　Farm Land and Rural Development Act 1988 s 1(1)(a)(ii).
6　Farm Land and Rural Development Act 1988 s 1(1)(a)(iii).
7　Farm Land and Rural Development Act 1988 s 1(1)(a)(iv).
8　Farm Land and Rural Development Act 1988 s 1(2)(a).
9　See note 1.
10　Farm Land and Rural Development Act 1988 s 1(2)(b).
11　Farm Land and Rural Development Act 1988 s 1(2)(c).
12　Farm Land and Rural Development Act 1988 s 1(2)(d).
13　Farm Land and Rural Development Act 1988 s 1(2)(e).
14　Farm Land and Rural Development Act 1988 s 1(2)(f).
15　Farm Land and Rural Development Act 1988 s 1(2)(g).
16　See the Farm Business Non-Capital Grant Scheme 1988, SI 1988/1125; and the Pig Industry Restructuring Grant (Wales) Scheme 2001, SI 2001/643.

429.　Grants in respect of farm woodlands.

Schemes may provide for the payment of grants in connection with the conversion of land from agricultural use to woodlands, and the management of such land[1]. Such schemes may provide for the payment to the owners and lessees of land of:

(1)　grants towards expenditure which has been or is to be incurred for the purposes of, or in connection with, the conversion of land from agricultural use[2] to use for woodlands or the management of land that has been so converted[3];

(2)　grants for abating any financial loss which has been or will be suffered in consequence of the conversion of land from agricultural use to use for woodlands[4].

Without prejudice to the generality of these provisions, a scheme providing for the payment of grants may:

(a)　impose requirements to be complied with by persons applying for the grants[5];

(b)　confer a discretion on the appropriate minister[6] as to the payment of the grants, as to the manner and timing of their payment, and as to their amounts[7];

(c)　provide for the persons to whom the grants are payable to include persons who become owners or lessees of land after its conversion to use for woodlands[8];

(d)　provide for the grants to be paid to persons on such terms as may be specified in or determined under the scheme and for the modification of any such terms in such manner as may be so specified or determined[9];

(e)　provide for the terms on which the grants are paid to impose such requirements on the persons to whom they are paid, including requirements to be complied with after the payment of the grants and requirements as to the repayment of grants, as may be so specified or determined[10];

(f)　provide for any discretion conferred by or under the scheme to be exercisable in such circumstances and by reference to such matters, and the opinion of such persons, as may be so specified or determined[11];

(g)　contain such supplemental, consequential and transitional provision as the appropriate authority thinks fit[12]; and

(h)　make different provision for different cases[13].

Pursuant to these provisions a number of schemes are in effect[14].

1　Farm Land and Rural Development Act 1988 s 2(1). As to the meanings of 'agriculture' and 'agricultural' see PARA 10. As to the making of schemes see PARA 428 note 1. A grant paid by virtue of a scheme under these provisions is paid out of money provided by Parliament: s 2(5). Nothing in s 2 or in any scheme thereunder prejudices the power of the Forestry Commissioners to pay grants under the Forestry Act 1979 s 1 (see FORESTRY vol 52 (2014) PARA 43) or the power of the Natural Resources Body for Wales to pay grants under the Natural Resources Body for Wales (Establishment) Order 2012, SI 2012/1903, art 10B: Farm Land and Rural Development Act 1988 s 2(7) (amended by SI 2013/755).

2　As to references to 'the use of land for agriculture' see PARA 10 note 7.

3　Farm Land and Rural Development Act 1988 s 2(1)(a).

4　Farm Land and Rural Development Act 1988 s 2(1)(b).

5　Farm Land and Rural Development Act 1988 s 2(2)(a).

6　See PARA 428 note 1.

7　Farm Land and Rural Development Act 1988 s 2(2)(b). Where the Secretary of State carries out a review of the rates at which grants are payable under any schemes for the time being in force under these provisions, he may lay a report before Parliament stating whether, as a result of the review, he proposes that any modifications of those rates should be made and the modifications, if any, that are proposed; such a review had to be carried out, and such a report laid before Parliament, no later than 30 September 1991; and the Secretary of State must ensure that no more than five years elapse after the laying of such a report before another such review is carried out and another such report is so laid: s 2(3). As to the laying of documents before Parliament see the Laying of Documents before Parliament (Interpretation) Act 1948; and STATUTES AND LEGISLATIVE PROCESS vol 96 (2012) PARAS 1042, 1048. As respects Wales, the Welsh Ministers must lay a copy of the report before the National Assembly for Wales: see the Government of Wales Act 2006 s 162, Sch 11 para 36; and STATUTES AND LEGISLATIVE PROCESS vol 96 (2012) PARA 1035.

8   Farm Land and Rural Development Act 1988 s 2(2)(c).
9   Farm Land and Rural Development Act 1988 s 2(2)(d).
10   Farm Land and Rural Development Act 1988 s 2(2)(e).
11   Farm Land and Rural Development Act 1988 s 2(2)(f).
12   Farm Land and Rural Development Act 1988 s 2(2)(g).
13   Farm Land and Rural Development Act 1988 s 2(2)(h).
14   Three woodland grant schemes operated by the Department for Environment, Food and Rural Affairs within the England Rural Development Programme have been introduced under these provisions and remain in force:
     (1)   the Farm Woodland Scheme 1988, SI 1988/1291, which closed to new applications in 1992;
     (2)   the Farm Woodland Premium Scheme 1992, SI 1992/905, which closed to new applications in 1997; and
     (3)   the Farm Woodland Premium Scheme 1997, SI 1997/829, which closed to new applications in England in 2005 but applications may continue to be made by new occupiers of land, where that land is already subject to a conversion plan.

INDEX

Agricultural Production and Marketing

References are to paragraph numbers; superior figures refer to notes

References are to paragraph numbers; superior figures refer to notes

References are to paragraph numbers; superior figures refer to notes

References are to paragraph numbers; superior figures refer to notes

References are to paragraph numbers; superior figures refer to notes

References are to paragraph numbers; superior figures refer to notes

PLANT PROTECTION PRODUCTS
 adjuvants, marketing and sue of 133
 advertisement, prohibition on 136
 enforcement as to 137
 environmental regulations 372
 marketing and use of 132
 packaging and labelling
  requirements 135
 pesticide. *See* PESTICIDE
 power to control 130
 seeds treated with 134
PLANT VARIETY AND SEEDS
  TRIBUNAL
 meaning 285
 appeals to—
  attendance 290
  bringing appeals 287
  decisions 291
  enforcement 291
  further appeals 292
  hearing 289
  jurisdiction generally 286
  procedure 290
  withdrawing 288
 jurisdiction 286
PLANT VARIETY RIGHTS OFFICE
 continuation of 281
 Controller. *See* CONTROLLER OF
  PLANT VARIETY RIGHTS
 establishment of 281
RED MEAT INDUSTRY (WALES)
 levies—
  designated primary or secondary
   activity, imposition on persons
   carrying out 376
  entry powers 379
  estimates as to 377
  inspection powers 379
  powers of Welsh Ministers 374
  provision of information as to 378
  returns as to 377
  slaughterers or exporters,
   calculation of levy for 375
 objectives of 166
 Welsh Ministers—
  delegation of powers of 168
  functions of 167
  powers as to levies 374
ROYAL AGRICULTURAL SOCIETY
 establishment of 401
ROYAL HORTICULTURAL SOCIETY
 establishment of 402
RURAL DEVELOPMENT
 Common Agricultural Policy, under 9

RURAL DEVELOPMENT—*continued*
 Environmental Stewardship Scheme
  for England 8
SEED POTATOES
 marketing of 35
SEEDS
 cross-pollination, prevention of 128
 farm saved seed 241
 instituting proceedings as to 24
 plant protection products, treatment
  with 134
 Plant Variety and Seeds Tribunal. *See*
  PLANT VARIETY AND SEEDS
  TRIBUNAL
 powers of entry 18
 publication of notices 17
 regulations generally 15
 samples—
  powers of entry 18
  taking of 19
  tampering with 20
  testing of. *See* testing of samples
   below
  use of 19
 seed potatoes 35
 statutory statement: meaning 16
 taking of 19
 testing of samples—
  certification of results 22
  evidential value of test
   certificates 23
  procedure for 21
  testing of. *See* testing of samples
   below
 use of 19
SLUDGE
 agricultural land, use on—
  precautions after use 64
  records as to use and production 69
  regulations as to 372
  restrictions 63, 65
  soil, testing of 68
  supply of sludge, restrictions on 65
 disposal sites, restrictions on
  production and sale of crops
  grown on 66
 pollution 372
 records as to use and production
  of 69
 soil, testing of 68
 testing of 67
SOIL
 improvers, use of 99
 surface soil, restriction on removal
  from agricultural land of 14

References are to paragraph numbers; superior figures refer to notes